FOREWORD

When we decided to move from the dark fantasy of The Witcher to the dark future of Night City, we wanted to take what we've done in the past and expand on it in every way possible. With a new setting and a new perspective, we were ready to go further than ever before. The result: an open-world, story-driven RPG that not only has a mature, multi-layered narrative at its heart, but also blows the door wide open in terms of player choice in gameplay.

From the moment you begin your journey in Night City as V, an inexperienced but ambitious mercenary, it's up to you to shape who V is; what kind of cyberpunk you want to become. From your choices in quests and conversations to your actions in the heat of the moment, you're building the legend of V – your legend – with every step. In Cyberpunk 2077, freedom and experimentation are encouraged at every turn. Whether you're a hacker, a gunslinger, a nimble cyber-ninja or something else entirely – your build, and how that impacts your choices within this futuristic megalopolis, should feel like yours and yours alone.

With many different paths to take, there's really no wrong way to go about your business. It's this type of freedom that video games can capture like nothing else. With Cyberpunk 2077, we hope that your sense of discovery, and the feeling that you have just done something absolutely awesome, won't ever grow old – no matter how many times you play through.

You've got all the tools you need to take on the world of the dark future, so use this guide wisely and soon enough you'll become a Night City legend like no other.

Have fun!

Adam Badowski
Game Director, Cyberpunk 2077

CONTENTS

Index

If you prefer to play with a minimum of assistance, you can use the comprehensive index at the back of this book to search for a specific piece of information.

Update Notice

We have taken every step to ensure that the contents of this guide are correct at the time of going to press. Nevertheless, subsequent updates to the Cyberpunk 2077 game may contain adjustments, gameplay balancing, and even feature additions that could not have been included at press time. We will endeavor to provide online updates and information on any such significant changes once these have been notified to us by CD PROJEKT RED.

Interactive Map

This guide comes with a digital extension in the form of an interactive map. By visiting **maps.piggyback.com** and using the unique code printed on the flyer included in this book, you will have access to the premium version of our interactive map, completely free of charge. At some point in the future, we might need to cease supporting or offering the online interactive map. If and when this happens, then we will try to give as much notice as possible in advance, which could be by email or by a notice published on our website.

QUICKSTART

Cyberpunk 2077 is a vast, multilayered adventure with countless ways to play. During the many months that we worked with CD PROJEKT RED in creating this guide, one thing has been abundantly clear: a conventional walkthrough simply would not work. We also feel that it would be inexcusable to limit player agency in a game that exults in showering you with opportunities to personalize yourself, make decisions that matter, and leave your unique mark on Night City – for better or worse.

As we have no desire to prescribe an off-the-peg route through the main storyline and associated events, our approach instead focuses on ease of reference. We cannot possibly know how every reader might develop their version of V – and so our coverage of all potential endeavors features tried-and-tested paths that should work for all character builds and ability levels. Walkthroughs and accompanying annotated screenshots will usually show you multiple ways to beat each challenge. But how you actually go about things? That's up to you.

In this brief introductory section, we explain the purpose of each guide chapter and what you can expect to find there. For a first playthrough, though, arguably the most important section of all is the Completion Roadmap. This functions as the guide's central hub, a jumping-off point for all activities of note in Night City. It's here that we detail almost everything that you might hope to accomplish while playing Cyberpunk 2077, with page links to other sections of the guide that provide detailed guidance whenever required. Completionists will also be glad to hear that this section offers advance notice of missable opportunities and items.

1 GETTING STARTED ▶ OPENING CHAPTERS

This guide begins with two chapters designed to ease you into the game's opening hours.

The **NIGHT CITY** chapter (see page 6) serves as an introduction to the world as it stands in 2077. It includes explanations of era-specific technologies, terminology, and concepts, as well as notes on the distinct districts in the metropolis and brief bios of individuals of interest.

The **PRIMER** (see page 70) introduces all game concepts of significance with one essential objective in mind: getting you up to speed to start the adventure with confidence. It will prepare you for the game mechanics and systems that you will encounter during the game's Prologue.

2 GENERAL PLAYTHROUGH GUIDANCE ▶ COMPLETION ROADMAP

Our **COMPLETION ROADMAP** (see page 92) acts as a companion to the five subsequent walkthrough chapters.

The chapter is designed to serve as a reference hub, offering links to all activities of note in addition to the following essential tools:

- A comprehensive flowchart that provides an at-a-glance overview of the entire game structure and reveals how all jobs are unlocked.
- A guided tour through the main episodes of the core adventure, highlighting optional objectives that will be within your level range at critical junctures in the storyline.

If you ever feel a little overwhelmed by the sheer size and scope of the game, always refer to this chapter to see what you might expect to accomplish next.

3 INDIVIDUAL QUEST SOLUTIONS ▶ WALKTHROUGH CHAPTERS

To best reflect the open-ended nature of the game and cater for the needs of a wide range of gamers, this guide lays out individual quest walkthroughs without dictating the order in which you should tackle them. These appear in chapters dedicated to specific mission types:

- **MAIN JOBS** (see page 110)
- **SIDE JOBS** (see page 178)
- **CYBERPSYCHO SIGHTINGS** (see page 246)
- **GIGS** (see page 258)
- **NCPD SCANNER HUSTLES** (see page 300)

Whenever you have a question about a specific topic, you have access to a wealth of reference material in the final third of the guide.

You will also find a comprehensive index at the back of this book.

Map-related questions

The **ATLAS** (page 362) is a complete city map of the metropolis and its surrounding Badlands. You can use it to scour every inch of terrain and track the game's many points of interest and optional activities.

System-related questions

This guide's **REFERENCE & ANALYSIS** chapter (page 428) studies the many game systems that govern your prowess.

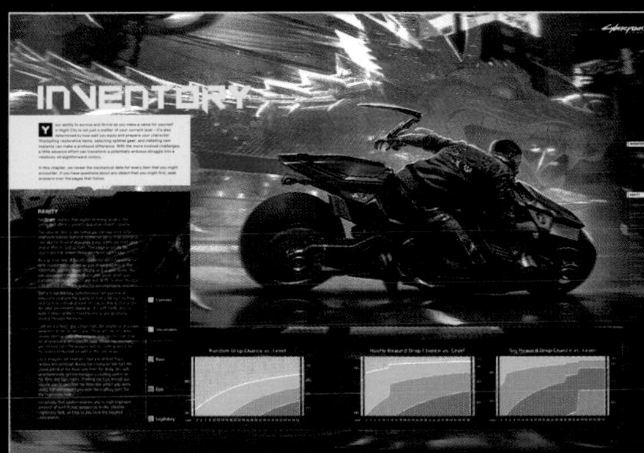

Item-related questions

The **INVENTORY** chapter (page 404) is home to a full appraisal of all items. If you aspire to use better weapons or cyberware, look no further.

Spoiler-sensitive questions

The **EXTRAS** chapter (page 454) covers highly sensitive topics such as game endings, romance possibilities, and Easter eggs. We strongly suggest you do not open these pages until after you've completed the adventure at least once.

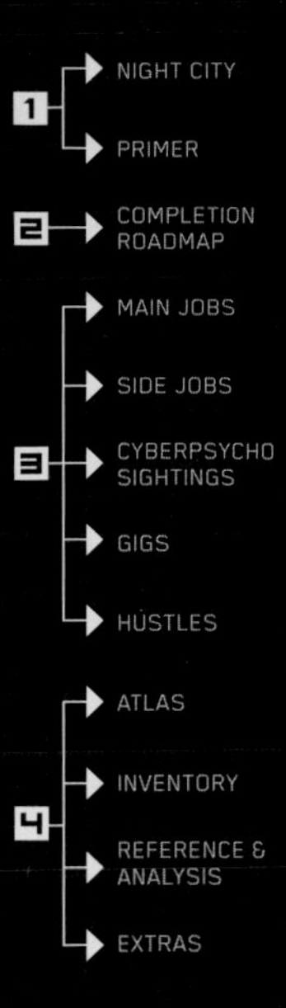

GAMEPLAY VARIATIONS

Cyberpunk 2077 is a game that fosters creativity and regularly presents small scenarios that are unique to each player.

The game as you experience it changes in real time in accordance with a multitude of factors:

- The entire adventure is nonlinear, with branching story paths leading to different outcomes and scenarios.
- Most collectibles you find in the game are randomized.
- Rewards, enemy levels, and mission difficulty all scale based on your own character progression.
- The movement patterns of each individual guard become unpredictable the moment they suspect your presence and they enter state of increased vigilance.
- Various parameters, particularly damage calculation, are subject to assorted modifiers.

These features mean that you might occasionally encounter gameplay variations in your playthrough. For example, a guard aware of your presence could end up in a completely different position than expected.

The point is: things might not always go exactly according to plan, in which case improvisation is the name of the game.

Throughout this guide, we do our utmost to prepare you for all sorts of situations and unforeseen events, not least by offering multiple methods to complete the most complex quests. If you struggle with one line of approach, there's undoubtedly another one that you can try: a door gated behind an attribute requirement, a quickhack that might remove a problematic guard from the equation, or a unique weapon or use of cyberware that could make short work of a tough opponent.

The game is replete with options and possibilities, and this book has been designed specifically to help you make the most of them. Just remember: whenever you adopt a strategy, always be prepared for moments of last-second creativity in your unique version of events.

NIGHT CITY

The world of Cyberpunk 2077 is vast and elaborate, with an absorbing and eventful backstory that charts the rise and fall – and rise anew – of the storied Night City. This opening chapter, carefully presented to avoid spoilers, both serves as an introduction to the world as it stands in 2077 (including explanations of era-specific technologies, terminology, and concepts) and as a guide to the remarkable metropolis that you will soon explore.

CAST

Cyberpunk 2077 has a large cast of characters, each with their particular agenda and a key role to play in the overarching story. In this brief, spoiler-free section, we introduce a selection of noteworthy figures that you will encounter in the adventure's opening hours.

V

The player character, V, can take whatever form your imagination and the in-game creation tools might align upon. Choosing the particulars and proclivities of your avatar is entirely up to you – both at the start, as you shape V to your desired spec, and throughout the game, as you further refine this unique individual through your choices and actions in the game world.

The one constant in the protagonist's profile is that V is an up-and-coming mercenary in Night City.

JOHNNY SILVERHAND

Singer and leading light of legendary band Samurai, Johnny is presumed long dead as Cyberpunk 2077's story begins. A rockerboy who started the group with close friend Kerry Eurodyne, he found fame at the turn of the century with all-time classics such as Blistering Love.

Johnny is notorious in certain circles for his reputed role as a member of the "Atlantis Group" – an organization that, if legend is to be believed, raided the Arasaka Tower in 2023 and detonated a nuclear device that devastated Night City.

JACKIE WELLES

A dependable "solo" (a mercenary who by preference works alone), Jackie is V's closest friend. As skilled with his fists as he is with his guns, Jackie has only operated in Night City's lower leagues. He dreams of exceeding his accomplishments by taking on high-risk, high-reward scores – and believes that teaming up with V might be exactly what will make this happen.

T-BUG

T-Bug is a skilled netrunner (akin to a hacker, but much more sophisticated – see page 67) who teams up with V and Jackie, assisting them as they pull their first jobs together. Though she typically doesn't get her hands dirty in direct confrontation, she plays an essential role in missions by manipulating systems to comply with the needs of the job – such as remotely opening doors and compromising security systems.

VIKTOR

Viktor is V's ripperdoc, patching up and upgrading the mercenary's cyberware as and when required. A virtuoso with his surgical exoglove, he has become something of a mentor for V as the story begins.

SURVIVE

ROGUE

An old-school cyberpunk, Rogue was in her prime as a mercenary at the beginning of the century, and a close friend of Johnny Silverhand. After withdrawing from direct action following Johnny's disappearance in 2023, she used her contacts and extensive experience to become a top-tier fixer. Now an octogenarian, though cosmetic engineering and rejuvenation treatments might suggest otherwise, Rogue runs the Afterlife – the club that V and Jackie visit as they prepare their first major heist with Dexter DeShawn.

DEXTER DESHAWN

Dex is a well-known fixer from the Afterlife who offers V a high-profile heist job during the Prologue. Unlike most fixers, he is known as a loner and is considered by some a risky partner. With V and Jackie aspiring to raise their profiles, Dex makes them an offer they can't refuse.

A TIMELINE OF RECENT HISTORY

1990-2020

TROUBLED YEARS & FOUNDING OF NIGHT CITY

Amid growing instability and ever-increasing collusion and complicity between elected politicians and major corporations, the world endures the first three Corporate Wars. In these, corporate establishments wielding more power than any government engage in both covert and overt conflicts, in a fight where the largest companies seek to assert global control.

The corporations monopolize critical global resources and exploit these without meaningful regulation or threat of sanctions. Coupled with the fallout (both literal and figurative) of two Central American wars and a thermonuclear conflict in the Middle East, the international community soon begins to suffer the effects of irreversible climate change, a global oil crisis, and a worldwide financial collapse of unprecedented scale.

No country is spared. In North America, the instability leads to a gradual secession of numerous US states, which declare themselves autonomous "Free States." This is how Night City – named after its founder, Richard Night – emerges in what was formerly California.

A relatively safe and prosperous haven in a ravaged world, Night City becomes one of the world's most desirable settings: an increasingly successful business hub, it acts as a significant magnet for capital and citizens from far and wide.

It is during this period that the Nomads emerge as a new societal phenomenon – an underclass of millions of Americans displaced by economic collapse who roam the nation in search of what little work, subsistence, and salvage they can find.

RICHARD NIGHT

Though Cyberpunk 2077 can be enjoyed with no prior knowledge, your journey takes place in a complex world supported by an astoundingly rich backstory. In this section, we offer a quick recap of key events that occurred in the century or so before you enter Night City in the game's Prologue.

2020-2023

FOURTH CORPORATE WAR

The Fourth Corporate War occurs between the two most prominent megacorporation rivals of the time: the Japanese behemoth Arasaka and the US-based Militech. Following a preliminary phase of covert ops and netrunning attacks, the two enterprises soon engage in open warfare. The intensity of the combat is such that it spreads globally and seriously disrupts global trade. The conflict culminates in the explosion of a nuclear device at Corporate Plaza at the heart of Night City. Tens of thousands of innocents die instantly, with many more perishing in the aftermath. The Arasaka Tower, Night City's most iconic skyscraper, collapses. The city is devastated.

Arasaka concedes defeat, although the victorious Militech is similarly diminished after securing what proves to be a pyrrhic victory.

Although the nuclear attack is later officially attributed to Arasaka, a popular underground conspiracy theory indicates that it in fact involved a mysterious band of mercenaries known as the "Atlantis Group." Its members, all regulars of the Atlantis bar, purportedly include legends such as Rogue and Johnny Silverhand. This rumor has never been substantiated, but the tale is still told to this day.

NETWATCH

ARASAKA

2023-2035

TRANSITION

By the end of the war, widespread discontent with unfettered corporate hegemony empowers governments to impose a major program of state regulation. In what remains of the United States of America, President Elizabeth Kress receives backing to nationalize Militech, while Arasaka is expelled and precluded from ever operating on the continent.

Scarred by severe poverty and economic recession, this period is beset by political turmoil and widespread civil unrest as governments struggle to reestablish the rule of law.

The net, heavily weaponized during the Corporate Wars, essentially experiences a similar demise, with governments seeking to regain control. NetWatch, an organization commissioned by the European Union to restore the internet to its former glory, tries – but fails – to retrieve all of the data lost in cyberspace. With innumerable hostile programs and rogue artificial intelligences operating in the dark depths of the net, a compromise is agreed: the formation of the Blackwall, a digital barrier that segregates all perilous AIs and deleterious code. This enables information to flow freely on the safe side of the Blackwall, although at the cost of abandoning enormous amounts of data to a cyber wilderness on the other side.

2035-2070

RECONSTRUCTION & REUNIFICATION

As the world experiences a spell of relative peace, the global economy enters a period of recovery as cities begin to rebuild – a process assisted both by governments and major corporations, the latter also working to restore reputations blighted by their erstwhile conduct.

This is broadly remembered as a period of strong economic growth, though Night City must compete to secure much-needed resources. With the US government keen to see the city collapse and major corporations considered *persona non grata*, it falls to the citizens of Night City to contribute most to the reconstruction effort – with assistance from Nomads and minor companies.

In 2069, freshly elected President Rosalind Myers declares it time for the former US to be reunified as the New United Stated of America (NUSA). Her government calls for all states that formerly seceded to submit to federal authority, which is met with fierce resistance and results in the Unification War, effectively a rematch of the Fourth Corporate War featuring the same protagonists. The federal government deploys the now-nationalized Militech to subdue the Free States, whose coalition is secretly financed and supported by a resurgent Arasaka corporation looking to re-establish its influence on the continent. The turning point in the conflict occurs in 2070, when an Arasaka supercarrier enters Coronado Bay, off the shore of Night City's Badlands.

With all parties, and particularly the NUSA, unwilling to commit to full-scale war, a peace treaty is soon agreed. The Free States remain autonomous, but they consent to extensive cooperation with the NUSA. Night City maintains full independence, although at a price: corporate interests are once again permitted to operate within its borders. Symbolizing this shift in the power structure, an Arasaka skyscraper is built on the exact location where the infamous Arasaka Tower stood before the 2023 nuclear disaster.

2070-2077

RECENT YEARS

The capital flows pumped in by corporations enable Night City to thrive once more – though increasingly, prosperity benefits the wealthy, leaving the poor to live in squalid conditions. Social polarization of such proportions has inevitable consequences, including an increase in crime, anger, and civil unrest, as well as a rising number of emerging issues relating to advanced technologies, such as addiction and cyberpsychosis.

On a global level, peace between states is to be welcomed – but any cheer is tempered by the catastrophic damage caused to the environment over the preceding decades. The climate crisis deteriorates yet further, with extreme meteorological events affecting all continents in addition to widespread pollution and scarce access to clean water.

NIGHT CITY

Night City is divided into six main **districts**, each with its unique ethnic groups, cultures, codes, and atmosphere. Though not an official district per se, the city's surrounding Badlands are inhabited, albeit sparsely, primarily by Nomads.

Each district features two or more **sub-districts**. Although neighboring sub-districts may share characteristics, each is unique in many ways – be that demographics, architecture, or the perils that visitors might face.

Wherever you go in the city, you can expect to encounter distinctive **factions** according to your location. These are well-defined groups that have unique characteristics and can often be distinguished by their dress codes, language and/or dialect, and cyberware.

Discovering each neighborhood and learning how best to interact successfully with its residents are significant features of the Cyberpunk 2077 experience.

Northern Oilfields

THE BADLANDS

WATSON

[Northside]

[Arasaka Waterfront]

[Kabuki]

[Little China]

[Japantown]

[North Oak]

WESTBROOK

CITY CENTER

[Downtown]

[Corporate Plaza]

[Charter Hill]

[Vista del Rey]

[Wellsprings]

HEYWOOD

[The Glen]

[Arroyo]

SANTO DOMINGO

[Coast View]

[Rancho Coronado]

PACIFICA

Eastern Wastelands

[West Wind Estate]

Southern Desert

[Northside]

[Arasaka Waterfront]

[Kabuki]

[Little China]

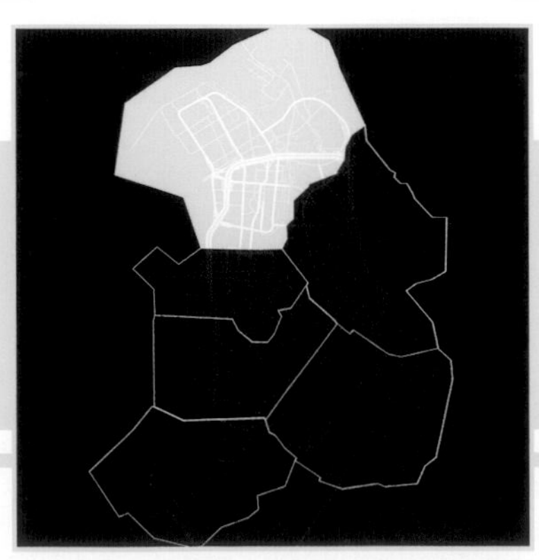

WATSON

Watson was once a prosperous district featuring various Japanese corporate offices, nightclubs, and all manner of amenities, as well as a flourishing industrial sub-district. The entire area is now a shadow of its former self. The decline began after the Unification War, when Arasaka took control and flushed out its Japanese competitors one by one. The primary seat of power and area of prosperity in Night City subsequently moved to the City Center, dooming the Watson denizens who remained – and those who would later join them – to unemployment and poverty.

WATSON | ARASAKA WATERFRONT

This entire sub-district is home to an enormous logistics and manufacturing facility. Arasaka fought hard to secure ownership of this valuable property in order to safeguard direct ocean access, thereby protecting daily shipments of raw materials that are either stored in vast warehouses or sent for processing to automated assembly lines.

The entire zone is heavily secured. Cameras, motion detectors, automated turrets, and well-trained guards ensure that no unauthorized personnel gain access.

WATSON ⋮ **NORTHSIDE**

Once a vibrant sub-district, Northside was a big center of employment where workers produced the tools and goods essential for Night City's continued development and prospering economy.

All that remains of the area's glorious past are abandoned factories and derelict buildings where those who lost their jobs live, or more precisely, try to survive.

MAELSTROM

Maelstrom, based in Northside, is a violent gang with a predilection for heavy use of cyberware. They run their illegal operations, such as improvised surgery rooms, unlicensed braindance recording studios, and storage for stolen goods, in the numerous abandoned buildings and warehouses.

Maelstrom members are legendary for their intensive use of implants. They worship cyberspace and the occult and have no reservations about disfiguring or dehumanizing themselves.

This heavy use of cybertechnologies is a means to transcend the weakness of their natural flesh and to attain purportedly superior altered states of consciousness. In the eyes of other Night City residents, however, they are naught but vicious and terrifying cyberpsychotics who should be avoided at all costs.

FEEL THE CHEMISTRY

WATSON ⋮ LITTLE CHINA

When the corporations based in the adjacent City Center district abandoned Watson's business centers, waves of (predominantly Chinese) immigrants took the opportunity to move in, repurposing the buildings for housing and small businesses.

The Little China neighborhood has a lot to offer, from cheap restaurants and shops to gambling dens, all with a distinct Oriental flavor. Many low-level corporate workers frequent this sub-district to enjoy its affordable food and entertainment.

V's apartment is located in this sub-district.

WATSON | **KABUKI**

Formerly controlled by Japanese medical corporations, later displaced by Arasaka after the Unification War, Kabuki is now a fairly deprived sub-district.

You can buy any junk imaginable in its maze of small alleyways – and virtually any black-market merchandise. Cyberware, illicit braindance recordings, drugs: you name it. Shady ripperdocs are also said to operate in black clinics, offering what they claim to be military-grade implants and other high-end augmentations. *Caveat emptor!*

the Mox

THE MOX

The Mox is a collective principally comprising sex workers operating in Kabuki. Distinguished by its lack of a conventional gang hierarchy, this group was founded after the death of Elizabeth "Lizzie" Borden, owner of the famous Kabuki-based brothel Lizzie's. Borden treated her staff well and sought to ensure that clients extended them the same courtesy. Her allegiance to her people was displayed when she had Tyger Claw gang members killed for the rape of one of her employees. In reprisal, the Tyger Claws murdered Lizzie and razed her club to the ground. The Mox rose from its ashes – a colorful group of dangerous prostitutes and punks with a mutual purpose of self-preservation.

[Japantown]

[North Oak]

[Charter Hill]

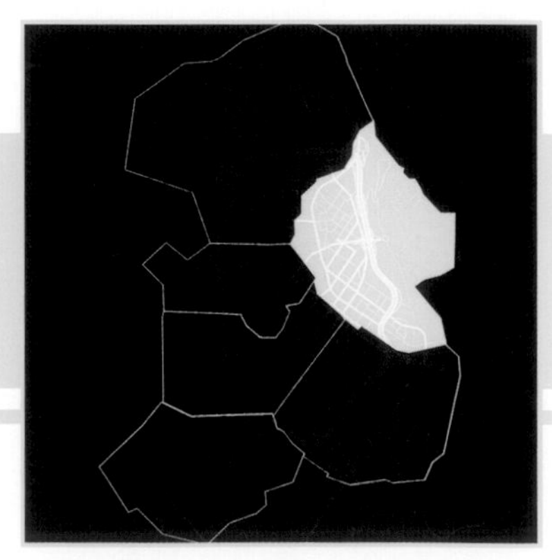

WESTBROOK

Undoubtedly Night City's most prestigious district, Westbrook is where the wealthiest congregate: both the one percent who can afford the opulent villas in North Oak and the corporate middle managers who aspire to join them, although mostly settling in the interim for Charter Hill. Locals and tourists alike mingle in Japantown, Night City's famous playground for the wealthy.

WESTBROOK | CHARTER HILL

Charter Hill is the North Oak antechamber and this is where those who aspire to join the super-wealthy choose to live. The typical Charter Hill resident is a mid-tier corporate employee who works long hours in the adjacent City Center, then blows off steam at night in nearby Japantown before getting a few hours' sleep in a modern apartment in this safe and tidy sub-district.

WESTBROOK | JAPANTOWN

In days gone by, Night City's Japanese community was broadly concentrated in Watson's Kabuki sub-district. Over the years, however, a demographic shift, combined with the gradual encroachment from nearby Little China, led Japanese families and businesses to relocate to Westbrook, across the bridge, giving birth to the Japantown sub-district.

The ultimate entertainment hub for the wealthy, and a famous tourist trap, Japantown bustles with fine restaurants, bars, high-end shops, and countless entertainment destinations. One of the safest places in Night City for hard-working corporate employees to party, Japantown is also renowned for its nightlife. Dozens of clubs, brothels, and casinos compete for business from corpo regulars and visitors alike – and are expertly run, ensuring the money flows all night long.

TYGER CLAWS

Members of this predominantly Japanese gang have three obsessions: melee weapons (usually sleek katanas), colorful Asian tattoos, and state-of-the-art motorcycles.

The Tyger Claws are heavily involved in Japantown's nightlife, particularly gambling houses, fighting arenas, brothels, and braindance clubs. Most of these establishments are perfectly legal and seemingly reputable, although they tend to front more sinister operations such as human trafficking and money laundering.

As a crime syndicate, Tyger Claws have a strict code of conduct, which low-ranking members and associates sometimes forget, especially when under the influence of abusive substances in a district that never really sleeps.

WESTBROOK | NORTH OAK

The exclusive dominion of elite CEOs, celebrities, and bankers, North Oak is home to the most palatial and luxurious villas in the city, as well as the most comprehensive security systems. Those who reside here are not just uber-rich; many exult in their station, flaunting their wealth and influence with indulgences such as jaw-dropping architecture and exotic menageries.

A prevailing aspiration for the hard-working inhabitants of Night City, North Oak is, in practice, almost unattainable. Only the most ambitious and career-oriented corporate employees will reside in this select residential sub-district – and even then, they will most likely never truly "own" their villa in the sense that their bank will.

[Downtown]

[Corporate Plaza]

CITY CENTER

City Center is a glass-and-steel landscape of skyscrapers, and it is the beating heart of corporate activity. A heavy police presence ensures that crime does not interrupt the productivity of the abundant workers based here; this is one of the safest areas in Night City.

CITY CENTER | DOWNTOWN

Downtown is a bustling, well-policed sub-district where legions of workers gather each day to keep Night City turning. That said, the business-like atmosphere doesn't mean that there's nothing to do – in fact, quite the opposite. Here you will find dozens of hotels, restaurants, bars, and high-end shops, as well as pleasure houses, in addition to countless other distractions. Things might not be as high-spirited as in Japantown, and this is by design: activities and distractions are tailored to enhance worker output. Many employees, having worked from dawn to dusk, choose to relax in the evening in a Downtown club, and spend the night in a nearby hotel, before conveniently walking a block or two to the office the next morning.

CITY CENTER | CORPORATE PLAZA

Corporate Plaza is the epitome of commercial power and extravagance, as well as being one of the world's quintessential networking hubs. This gigantic business center also feels like an embassy district, since many executives and agents enjoy benefits and privileges such as diplomatic immunity. With multiple international corporations based here, daily trade and continuous exchanges permeate the area with a sense of gravitas – a feeling enhanced by the heavy presence of elite security forces.

The painful memory of the 2023 nuclear blast that ravaged the entire neighborhood, leading to the collapse of Arasaka Tower, vividly endures. The Memorial Park roundabout that stands between the skyscrapers commemorates the victims of the attack. Both of the Fourth Corporate War belligerents, Arasaka and Militech, dominate the plaza – and are today more powerful than ever.

NCPD

You might well expect the Night City Police Department to protect civilians and to oppose gangs and organized crime; however, things are not that simple. Although ostensibly employed as law enforcement, the NCPD is more akin to a faction in Cyberpunk 2077. It's not unusual to see officers involved in illegal activities – or taking kickbacks to turn a blind eye to crimes committed by others.

More streetwise Night City citizens regard the NCPD with caution more befitting the city's gangs.

HEYWOOD

Heywood is primarily a residential district where a large contingent of Night City's middle class lives. Increased social segregation has resulted in greater income inequality, and, in many instances, poverty, for the local population; notwithstanding, Heywood remains a respected area in which the locals retain a strong sense of pride.

As a general rule, the closer you are to the City Center in the north, the safer you are in Heywood. Gang and criminal activity increases the further south you go.

HEYWOOD | WELLSPRINGS

Dense, colorful, loud, and relatively safe – Wellsprings most resembles the quintessential early-21st-century Californian beach town. The coastal strip close to Downtown is especially vibrant, with hordes of locals and tourists enjoying the large range of restaurants and shopping malls. There are few visitors here who do not wistfully imagine what it must be like as a celebrity on one of the yachts in the bay, or the owner of a luxury condo with a spectacular ocean view.

Leave the Waterfront and head south or east and the resort vibe gradually fades as you encounter more mid-tier buildings and a Latino population – and eventually this transitions into a shanty town as you near the Glen.

EL GUAPO
CAPTAIN
CALIENTE

HEYWOOD | THE GLEN

This is Night City's government sub-district which is distinguished by its celebrated City Hall. Although the building pales in comparison to the corporate towers in the City Center, it retains important symbolic meaning for the locals because this is where Lucius Rhyne, the man who would later become mayor, negotiated Night City's independence in 2070.

Much like Wellsprings, the northern part of the sub-district feels fairly safe and clean, with well-preserved buildings. As you head south, though, the transition is pronounced. You soon reach derelict blocks exposing urban decay and high instances of poverty, a visual manifestation of social polarization, where gangs reign as the real civil authorities.

VALENTINOS

The Valentinos operate primarily in the Glen, and sometimes also in sections of Heywood's two adjacent sub-districts. They can be identified by a variety of characteristics: gilded implants, guns, tattoos that fuse Catholic imagery with Mexican gang folklore, pimped-out hotrods, and, for men, a mustache.

The Valentinos are especially well-integrated and rooted in Heywood. A secret pact unites them with the local community, whereby the citizens remain loyal to the gang in exchange for protection. This hampers outside efforts against Valentinos, whether from the police or another group: with so many open doors available to its members, they rarely lack an alibi or a place to hide. Their status in these neighborhoods is such that Valentinos who die fighting against other factions are frequently immortalized (and sometimes almost sanctified) in music, song, and street art.

OPEN
NiCOLA™
THE
LOVE!

Insta Food
Insta Food
Insta Food
Insta Food

HEYWOOD | VISTA DEL REY

Located on the border of Valentinos and 6th Street Gang turf, Vista del Rey is Heywood's most deprived sub-district. Any resident with the wit and means to leave has already done so. Those that remain live in fear and abject poverty, sheltering in abandoned buildings or shacks. This decaying neighborhood is one of the most dangerous places in Night City.

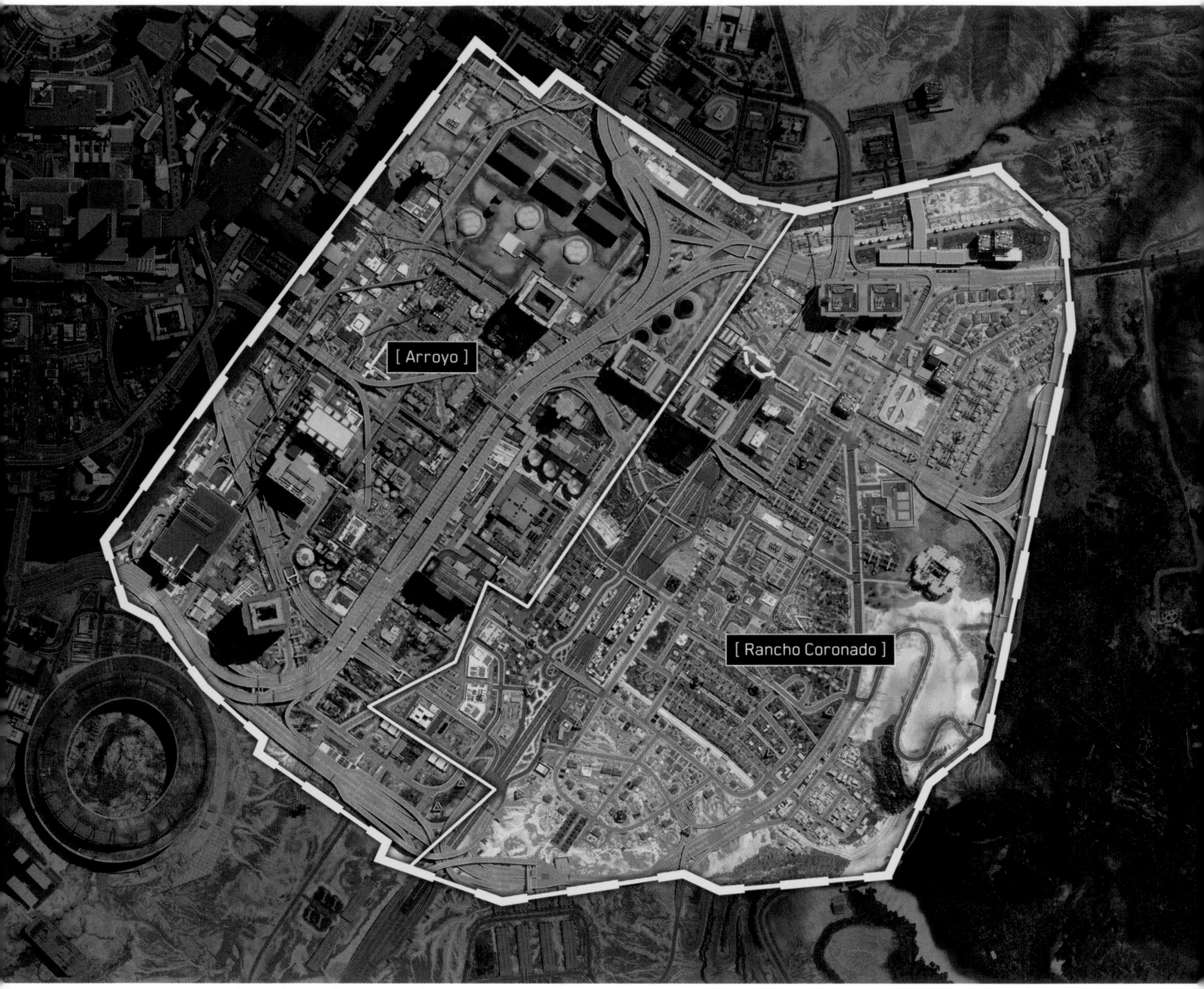

[Arroyo]

[Rancho Coronado]

SANTO DOMINGO

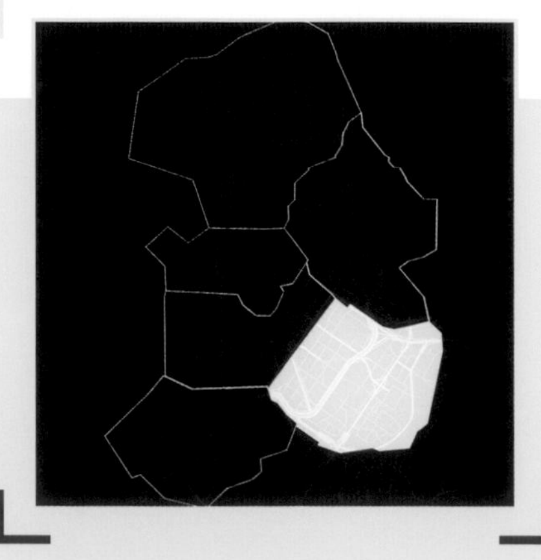

Although Santo Domingo is one of the districts least affected by the 2023 nuclear blast, it has become one of the poorest. Its initial design was based on functional suburban planning, with residential neighborhoods adjacent to factories where the locals would work. Long term, this did not come to pass, as the industrial facilities have been closed for many years and the majority of locals lost their jobs.

That said, Santo Domingo is currently the target of speculation by corporations hoping to benefit from the extremely low real estate prices. Regeneration through new developments and gradual gentrification might create some stimulus for this long-neglected district, although this will further exacerbate segregation, in that those who currently live here will never be able to afford the regenerated Santo Domingo.

SANTO DOMINGO | RANCHO CORONADO

Rancho Coronado was intended to be an ideal planned community within Night City: a suburban 20th-century postcard space, with cookie-cutter family houses located within minutes of shopping centers, parks, bars, entertainment, and, of course, factories and business where the residents would work. When full funding didn't materialize, those who had signed up for life in Rancho Coronado had to settle for an ill-conceived utopia.

Still, many locals – high-ranking factory employees for the most part – believe the area resembles the original vision, for all intents and purposes, and they enjoy a happy life without needing to subject themselves to the noise, fuss, and fury of Night City proper. However, others highlight the sub-district's general state of disrepair, and in particular, the elevated levels of toxicity resulting from close proximity to Night City's vast landfill site.

SANTO DOMINGO ⋮ **ARROYO**

Similar to Northside in Watson, Arroyo is a mass of factories – most now derelict since they closed, leaving legions of residents unemployed. These men and women are cooped up in vast mega buildings – some unfinished, most dilapidating. Certain industrial sites continue to operate, including power plants and a number of high-tech factories, although these cannot provide work for everyone. Corporations, having neglected the local economy, have provided little hope that things will improve for Arroyo's inhabitants.

6TH STREET

The 6th Street gang is built on patriotism, with heavy use of the stars and stripes from the US flag in its imagery. Its members, a selection of vigilantes and war veterans, evangelize self-defense and venerate their neighborhood: the larger part of Arroyo and a substantial area within Rancho Coronado.

The founders' original vision was to expel gangs and predatory, uncaring corporations from their turf. To do so, they armed and trained neighbors, evolving quickly into a powerful militia. Members do not regard themselves as a gang and are committed to their noble cause. All others, however, see just another gang of thugs who have resorted to violence, crime, and extortion to fuel their self-serving agenda.

PACIFICA

COAST VIEW & WEST WIND ESTATE

Pacifica was meant to be the ultimate coastal resort, treating tourists to an amusement park, boardwalk promenades, endless restaurants and boutiques, and non-stop entertainment – a vacation paradise within Night City's boundaries. The project started during the Reconstruction period, consuming billions upon billions of Eurodollars. It was initially intended to be constructed by thousands of Haitian refugees displaced by events on Hispaniola, but the advent of the Unification War prompted investors to withdraw their capital in fear of an invasion by the New United States of America.

Once finance had been pulled, the Haitian diaspora was left with nothing but broken promises: no jobs, unfinished buildings, and a tanking local economy. Worse still, Night City authorities – fearful that the area might quickly degenerate into a gang-dominated slum – resolved to raze the district to the ground. Its residents quickly united, working collectively to help their community, and fighting against agents at City Hall. This led to the formation of the Voodoo Boys gang. Given the fierce resistance, city government and law enforcement alike abandoned both Coast View and West Wind Estate.

Pacifica has been left to its own devices. NCPD officers do not answer calls originating here.

VOODOO BOYS

Forged in firefights ensuing from local members of the Haitian diaspora endeavoring to stop Night City from leveling the abandoned Pacifica project, the Voodoo Boys are one of the most mysterious gangs in Night City. They sport assorted signs of their Creole culture, from tattoos to dreadlocks, and often wear bone-made charms. Their distinctive trait, though, is their pursuit and knowledge of netrunning. They are believed to be on a quest to uncover the secrets of the Old Net, and they attempt to breach the Blackwall to make contact with the rogue AIs on the other side. Some are of the mind they are on a fool's errand, aiming for mystical goals such as boundless knowledge and eternal digital life. Their nemesis is the NetWatch corporation, whose very *raison d'etre* is to impede any such trespassing and illicit cyberactivity.

The Voodoo Boys bankroll their operation with a variety of criminal activities, including cyberhacking, freelance netrunning, and drug dealing.

ANIMALS

Members of this gang are unique in that they use custom, artisanal bio-augmentations rather than off-the-shelf components. This tailor-made approach enables them to maximize their musculature to the point where they appear more beast than being. Loaded with hormones and animal-procured supplements, they develop bulky, primal bodies and practice a variety of martial arts and combat techniques to become supreme fighters. They use their strength and skills not only for cage fighting, in which they habitually excel, but also for more standard jobs requiring physical prowess such as bouncers or bodyguards.

In contrast to other gangs, Animals do not converge in one particular area. They can be found – and hired – across the entire city, although they are most frequently encountered in and around south Pacifica's fighting arenas.

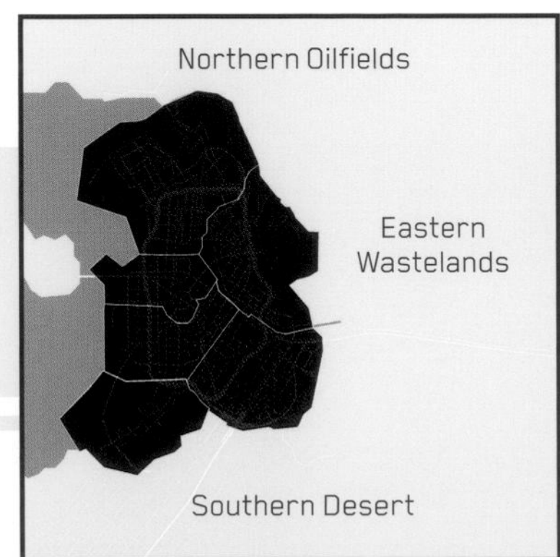

THE BADLANDS

Night City's Badlands have little to offer city dwellers. These are mostly arid and inhospitable terrains where only Nomads reside. In some areas, immense fields of highly toxic industries (particularly intensive farming and energy production) serve to feed and fuel the insatiable Night City.

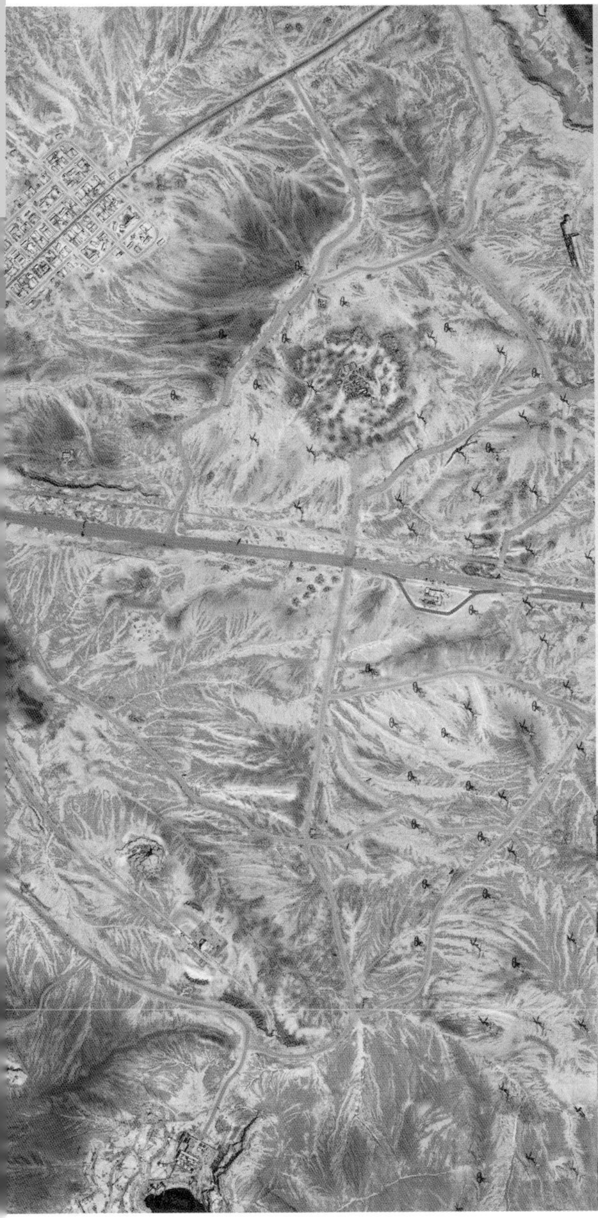

THE BADLANDS | NORTHERN OILFIELDS

Night City's economy never relied on oil, although the oil fields in the metropolis's Badlands contributed to its origins. Back in the 1990s, Coronado Bay was identified as a site by Richard Night because one of his principal joint-venture partners was Petrochem. The company extracted the oil (and naturally enjoyed a decidedly relaxed regulatory framework) while Richard Night built his first skyscrapers on the bay. The smoke-filled, highly toxic oilfields are often seen as an irreparable scar that justly disfigures the face of Night City – a mute, but telling, reminder of its shady beginnings.

ALDECALDOS

This Nomad faction operates in the west coast region, intermittently moving its caravans from one Free State to another. They are currently based in the Eastern Wastelands, in Night City's Badlands.

Some members are happy to work as farm laborers or at other temporary manual jobs they can find locally, whilst others prefer more illicit enterprises such as smuggling and transporting stolen cargo. Aldecaldos are generally reluctant to enter the metropolis, preferring to engage in more modest opportunities on the city's periphery.

THE BADLANDS

EASTERN WASTELANDS

The barren desert hellscape east of Night City is both testimony and legacy to the irreversible climate collapse that was triggered by the wars and the unfettered exploitation of natural resources during the Troubled Years (see page 16).

Little now remains in this area, with the exception of ghost towns and derelict structures prevailing from a distant past. Only Nomads and scavengers wander this wilderness – and even they struggle to find anything of use here.

THE BADLANDS

SOUTHERN DESERT

Contrary to what its name might suggest, Southern Desert is where a large measure of Night City's food requirements is produced. This is an agricultural powerhouse; the capital of greenhouse complexes, which are managed by corporations that have developed a vast and highly automated food industry. The remaining area is covered by solar panels and wind turbines that stretch as far as the eye can see and strive to meet the city's ever-growing energy requirements.

WRAITHS

A subgroup of the Raffen Shiv (see page 68), the Wraiths are Night City's rural gang. They prey on any target they can overpower, be that an unprotected farm or village or even a Nomad caravan. They have a reputation as unreliable mercenaries, little more than highway thugs who are rarely engaged by city clients.

CONCEPTS

In this section, we take a look at some features that are commonplace and unremarkable in the world of **Cyberpunk 2077**, but might not be immediately obvious when you start the game. The idea here is to offer select insights into the story's unique terminology, culture, and technologies before you engage with these in Night City.

AV

AVs are the aerial vehicles that zip around above Night City's wealthiest and busiest districts, and particularly the City Center. They are frequently used by high-level corporation employees to fly from one urgent meeting to the next, and by police, military forces, and freight companies.

BD / BRAINDANCE

Braindance is a cutting-edge neural technology, a high-octane virtual reality that enables users to play back and relive other people's real memories. In practical terms, BDs are digital recordings of someone's actual experiences – a slice of life, in a sense, though rarely featuring mundane events, and which is firstly edited by technicians, then streamed via a dedicated augmentation platform to the user's neural system.

This offers a powerful experience that largely surpasses all other media forms. BD viewers don't just spectate memories; they actually live them, feeling and perceiving whatever the recorder experienced and saw at that time. This includes everything from mood and emotions to physical sensations and thoughts. Even death itself can be experienced with terrifying accuracy.

Braindance was initially designed as a therapeutic tool for patients suffering from specific pathologies and as a method to rehabilitate convicts released from the penitentiary system – and such use persists to this very day. As the events of Cyberpunk 2077 unfold, BDs have long since supplanted classic mainstream entertainment such as movies and videogames. Consumed both at arcades and in the home, they are produced and published by large enterprises that specialize in the development of both authentic and artificial BDs – the former offering a faithful account, with the latter a resemblance by trained method actors.

The technology has given rise to a new generation of celebrities and influencers, who share actual or staged recordings of their lives, enabling fans to experience what it is like to be a millionaire living in a sumptuous villa and spending quality time with other superstars. An illegal market has also evolved, giving buyers access to "black" braindance (also called XBD): recordings of violent and sexual crimes, regarded by some as the ultimate fantasy.

Excessive or improper use of braindance is not without consequences. Unprepared or fragile users can be the subject of various side effects, ranging from addiction to dissociative identity disorder.

BLACKWALL

The Blackwall is a large-scale digital firewall that was built by NetWatch after the Corporate Wars.

With the net heavily contaminated and weaponized, NetWatch aimed to regain control over the legions of hostile programs and rogue artificial intelligences that had been unleashed to prowl its digital corridors. When it became clear that this was unfeasible, NetWatch had to compromise: the creation of the Blackwall, a barrier separating all dangerous AIs, but also surrendering oceans of valuable data.

The Blackwall has remained operational ever since, essentially restoring the net for corporations and standard users. Skilled netrunners regularly attempt to breach the wall and explore the mysteries of the cyberspace on the other side. Identifying and arresting these perpetrators is one of NetWatch's top priorities.

CORPO

"Corpos" is the common term for corporation employees. These number in the thousands in Night City, typically working endless hours in the City Center skyscrapers and then blowing off steam in the evening in the clubs of the Downtown or Japantown sub-districts.

There are clear sociological factors that make it easy to distinguish the different grades of corpo. Low-level employees are considered disposable, earning just enough money to afford a place to stay in the mostly safe neighborhoods, such as Little China. These members of the Night City precariat are the non-skilled workers that keep companies running, including drivers, janitors, couriers, and many others that remain somehow invisible. The majority compete in a rat race, working endlessly in the hope that a superior might one day notice them and promote them to a position of relative significance.

Mid-level corpos are wealthier, and can aspire to more upscale sub-districts, including Charter Hills, although they often choose to sleep in the City Center hotels to optimize their work-life balance, with work time overshadowing their waking hours.

High-level corpos are in a league of their own. Their social station exceeds that of leading civil servants and elected officials in world governments, enjoying diplomatic immunity and additional benefits that their corporation's power, wealth, and influence provide. Along with braindance celebrities and other superstars, they are among the happy few that can aspire to acquiring a villa in the North Oak hills.

CORPORATE WARS

Modern history has been defined by four Corporate Wars – conflicts between competing corporations so dominant and wealthy that they surpassed governments as the power-brokers in world politics.

The first three Corporate Wars occurred during the Troubled Years at the turn of the century, when preeminent establishments looking to expand their control attacked each other in an attempt to advance their hegemony.

The fourth Corporate War was the most devastating, and left an indelible mark on the memory of Night City. The two multinational hegemons at that time, Arasaka and Militech, locked horns, initially through covert ops and netrunning attacks, and then descending into full-scale military engagement. The conflict came to its climax on August 20, 2023, the day a nuclear device was detonated at the heart of Night City, killing tens of thousands and leveling the iconic Arasaka Tower. Arasaka was exiled from America, the victorious Militech severely diminished and subsequently nationalized.

CYBERDECK

Decks are cyberware – a form of modem directly implanted into the skull. Qualified users known as netrunners can explore cyberspace by connecting their decks to the net.

As with all implants, cyberdecks come in a broad quality range. The most basic enable users to physically plug into specific devices in order to override a barrier (for example, to open a locked door or to bypass or control security systems). The most advanced decks are implanted alongside built-in full-body cooling systems, irrigation support, and neural boosters, in addition to other enhancements, allowing for prolonged and supercharged netrunning raids.

CYBERWARE

Cyberware collectively refers to all implants, enhancements, and other digital devices that can be applied to modify the body – from minor enhancements to the transhuman fusion of bio-technology and flesh, in near-equal measures.

The most customary cyberware entails off-the-shelf implants, which users install themselves or have embedded with minor surgery in accredited clinics. Devices within this category can be both functional and hip – accessories by which people express their style and personality. One example, among many others not referenced at this point, is optics; these enable the wearer to zoom in on remote objects as well as to dynamically change the color of their eyes based on the ambient light.

More elaborate cyberware, such as advanced biological or cybernetic enhancements, must be installed by professionals: either at accredited medical centers or at black clinics, where ripperdocs of varying integrity, notwithstanding low respect for the Hippocratic oath, generally operate. If money is no object, you can replace or enhance practically any organ or limb – or indeed elect to have a full-body conversion. Relatively few people undergo this advanced surgery, but it does occur amongst individuals with particular profiles – such as corporate employees determined to get an edge over their rivals, or mercenaries and criminals looking to advance their dexterity, combat aptitudes, and resistance to pain.

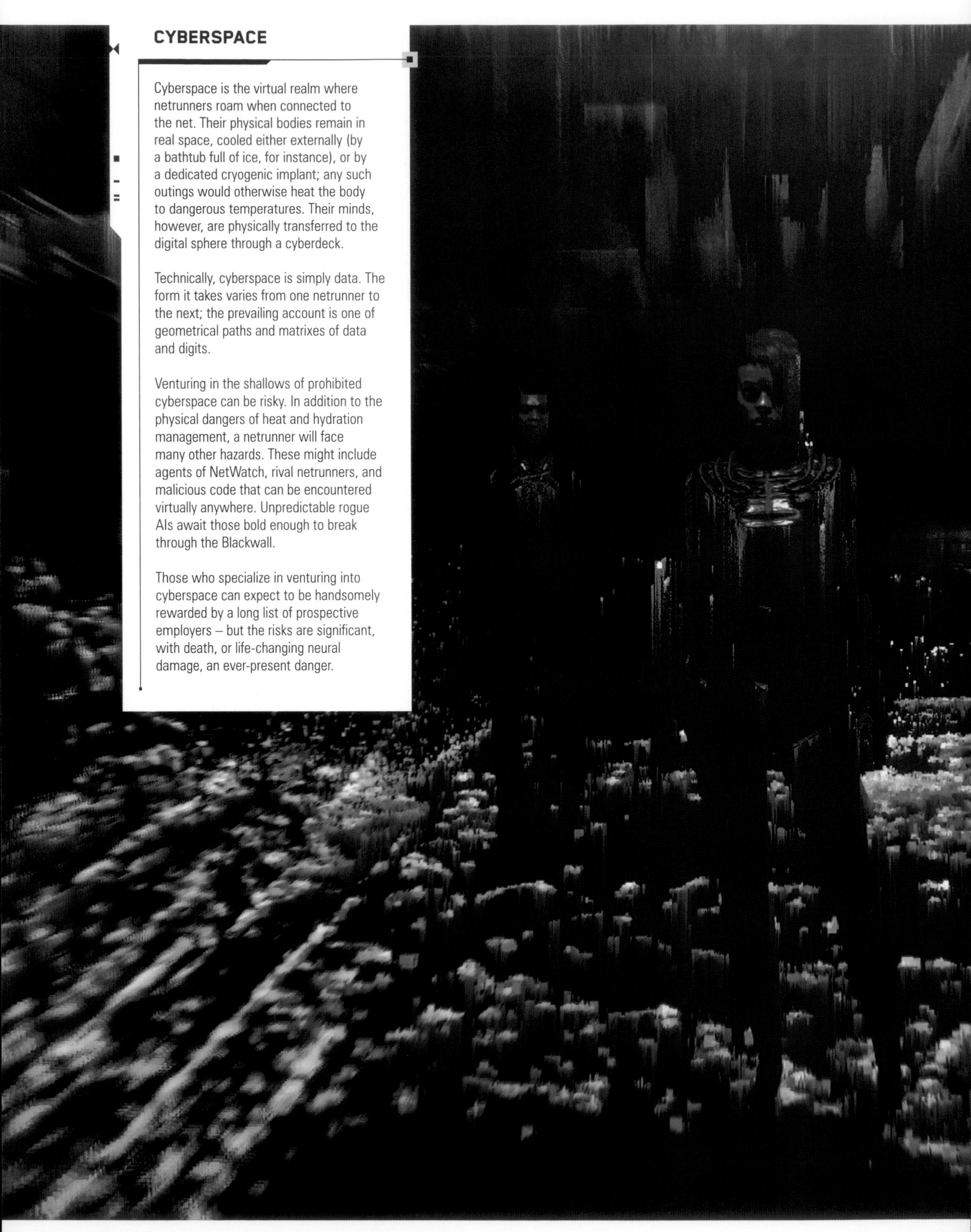

CYBERSPACE

Cyberspace is the virtual realm where netrunners roam when connected to the net. Their physical bodies remain in real space, cooled either externally (by a bathtub full of ice, for instance), or by a dedicated cryogenic implant; any such outings would otherwise heat the body to dangerous temperatures. Their minds, however, are physically transferred to the digital sphere through a cyberdeck.

Technically, cyberspace is simply data. The form it takes varies from one netrunner to the next; the prevailing account is one of geometrical paths and matrixes of data and digits.

Venturing in the shallows of prohibited cyberspace can be risky. In addition to the physical dangers of heat and hydration management, a netrunner will face many other hazards. These might include agents of NetWatch, rival netrunners, and malicious code that can be encountered virtually anywhere. Unpredictable rogue AIs await those bold enough to break through the Blackwall.

Those who specialize in venturing into cyberspace can expect to be handsomely rewarded by a long list of prospective employers – but the risks are significant, with death, or life-changing neural damage, an ever-present danger.

DOLL

Dolls are cyberware-enhanced prostitutes. The secret to their success is their behavioral chips, which enable them to change their personality instantaneously to satisfy each client's desires. Essentially, a doll adapts to every customer, catering to their particular fantasies: an intimate friend, a partner proficient in all sexual practices, a willing and talented actor in any elaborate fantasy... no labels required, they just perform.

If this sounds too good to be true, that's because it is. Many dolls experience significant damaging side effects over time.

Dolls are most frequently found in dedicated clubs referred to as "dollhouses."

€$

EDDIES

Dubbed after the Eurodollars symbol (usually presented as €$, "EDs," but still pronounced "Eddies"), this is the official currency of Night City.

FIXER

A fixer is an intermediary linking mercenaries with clients who offer a wide range of assignments: espionage, theft, sabotage, and contract killings. A good fixer will have a broad network of assets, and is always alive to the best opportunities in the district.

NET

The net is a blanket term that in fact refers to two distinct concepts.

- **The Old Net** (or Deep Net) is the network that used to connect all countries to one global communications platform. Then known as the "internet," this system was operational until the Fourth Corporate War. When a legendary netrunner named Rache Bartmoss was killed in this conflict, swarms of viruses and destructive AI programs were unleashed, flooding and damaging the entire system beyond repair. Technically, the Old Net does still exist in 2077, although now a digital warzone, a wild cyberspace where all but the very best netrunners become overwhelmed within seconds. With the backing of the European Union, the NetWatch corporation installed the Blackwall – a digital barrier that separates the infected areas of the Old Net.
- **The Shallow Net** is a fragmented net (in contrast to the global character of the Old Net) that corresponds to the remaining safe areas of the network – those within the limits of the Blackwall. Essentially, the Shallow Net comprises parceled areas, or hubs, that are predominantly separated. Night City is one such hub, a space shared by local corporations and public domains, enabling the free and (in principle) unfettered transfer of data within its limits.

A metaphor might help here. If the Old Net was an ocean of interconnected data, the post-war Shallow Net is a range of tiny volcanic islands dotted on the surface of the same vast expanse.

NETRUNNER

Netrunners are highly-specialized individuals equipped with a cyberdeck to plug in to the net and roam the depths of cyberspace. They do not just explore the net via a browser or even an advanced haptic interface; they actually feel the sensations as they live it themselves, physically experiencing and navigating the digital flows. This exposes them to a deluge of data, causing their bodies to dramatically heat up as their augmented neural systems process a torrent of information. Netrunners must take steps to regulate their body temperatures (such as ice baths or advanced full-body cooling components) in order to preserve body functions while they are in this "overclocked" state.

The intensity is such that most cannot comprehend it. Only the finest netrunners possess the required resilience, receptivity, and affinity to the digital realms to survive, let alone master, this prodigious experience. Those who thrive in this environment are a rare breed, highly sought-after by corporations and gangs alike – for they have the necessary talent to hack, steal, contaminate, and even destroy practically any program, and equally to ensnare rival netrunners.

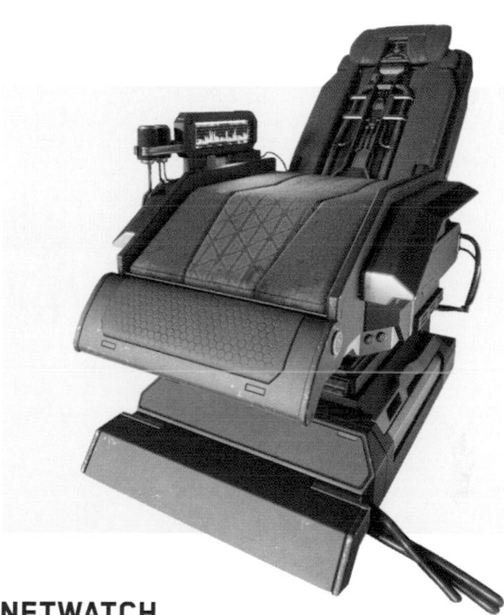

NETWATCH

NetWatch is an agency originally mandated to monitor the net as incidents of cybercrimes soared at the beginning of the 21st century. It now functions as the world's de facto law enforcement body for digital territories. The organization's primary challenges include monitoring and/or eliminating rogue AIs that emerged during the Corporate Wars, and the apprehension of netrunners who conduct unlawful activities in cyberspace.

NOMADS

The wars and global financial crisis of the Troubled Years (see page 16) left deep scars in North America, including the steady secession of multiple US states. In a matter of weeks, millions of Americans became jobless and homeless, leaving them with little but their cars and what few possessions they could carry. Rather than waiting idly, many families decided to venture out, looking for whatever opportunities they could find: farm work at harvest time, building work in major construction projects – and anything in between.

These domestic migrants emerged over the years to form seven structured Nomad nations - each featuring a hierarchy of sub-groups: tribes, clans, and finally, families. Each individual plays a particular role within this structure (such as a driver, homeschooling teacher, nurse, seasonal worker, cook), as all Nomads are expected to contribute to the collective.

Although Nomads specialize in their assigned trades, all – adults and children alike – have sufficient knowledge and skills to maintain and repair the bedrock of their nation's lifestyle: cars. Every Nomad is a proficient mechanic, with some working exclusively on maintaining the community's fleet in prime shape, enabling anyone to move on to their next destination.

RAFFEN SHIV

In addition to the seven Nomad nations, an infamous eighth exists: the Raffen Shiv. Their ranks are mostly made up of individuals exiled from traditional Nomad structures for crimes committed. A loose association of outcasts with no distinct hierarchy, Raffen Shiv are, in essence, gangs that prowl towns and cities, looking to rob, extort, or steal whatever loot they can from those ill-prepared to resist them.

REALSKINN

RealSkinn is the synthetic substance fitted as an overlay on most implants so that they resemble natural limbs.

RIPPERDOCS

Ripperdocs specialize in implanting and maintaining cyberware in people. They operate outside of the official medical establishment, usually running an unauthorized clinic where patients are referred by a ***sotto voce*** word-of-mouth.

Ripperdocs are as a rule less expensive than traditional practitioners, and the most skilled are true artisans, able to create and calibrate bespoke implants perfectly suited to their purchaser. Any decision on implants should not be taken lightly. Numerous shady ripperdocs operate in Night City's deprived districts in particular, and it's not uncommon for patients to suffer severe post-surgery complications or, worse, be lured into a remote basement where they are mugged and dismembered by scavengers.

SCAVENGERS

Scavengers are criminals who assault innocents to dispossess them of saleable organs, limbs, or implants, which they can then trade on the black market – primarily to gangs and corrupt ripperdocs.

Although they all pursue the same distasteful trade, scavengers usually operate in small groups with no official hierarchy to unite them.

STREET CRED

Street Cred is a transitory and subjective social "currency" that serves to gauge a mercenary's reputation. V can attain Street Cred by completing challenges in the game, particularly tasks bestowed by fixers.

PRIMER

With a game as vast, detailed and open-ended as Cyberpunk 2077, it's understandable that many players might feel daunted at the outset. This Primer chapter has been written to allay such anxieties with the perfect starting gift: just a **little** bit of information on a **lot** of subjects. We'll prepare you for concepts and game mechanics encountered during the opening hours of the adventure, but without ever touching upon story beats or spoiling any surprises.

ONSCREEN DISPLAY

The annotated screenshot below illustrates a typical gameplay screen.

01 **Health:** The red gauge in the upper-left represents V's physical integrity. Allowing your character's health meter to fully deplete will result in death – and the return to a prior save.

02 **Memory (RAM):** The segmented blue bar underneath the health meter corresponds to your cyberdeck memory. Every quickhack program that you trigger (remotely opening a door, for example) consumes RAM.

03 **Stamina:** When you utilize physically demanding actions (such as running, swimming, and performing melee attacks or dodges), a meter appears at the top of your screen. Each successive applicable action depletes the bar; it will regenerate once you cease such activities.

04 **Reticle:** A reticle appears when you have a weapon drawn, indicating the direction in which your projectiles will be fired if you press the trigger.

05 **Mini-map:** The mini-map at the upper-right of your screen shows your immediate surroundings, annotated with useful details such as mission objectives and assorted points of interactivity. See page 83 for details. The mini-map also indicates whether you are in a public (low-threat) or hostile (high-threat) area.

06 **Time:** The time of day is displayed just below the mini-map. Note that you can fast-forward using the main menu's Skip Time function – a convenient feature when you can only complete an objective at a specific juncture.

07 **Mission Status:** This details objectives for your current activity.

08 **Dynamic Information:** Onscreen notifications and context-sensitive prompts will appear in accordance with your actions and events in the world.

09 **Ammunition:** The first figure represents the number of shots remaining for your active weapon; the second details your total stock of the requisite ammo.

10 **Stance Indicator:** The icon in the bottom-right represents V's current stance. Crouching should be your default posture when stealth is desirable, enabling you to move quietly and maintain a low profile.

11 **Quick Access:** The icons in the lower-left corner of your screen represent the features and functions you can access instantly by pressing the corresponding buttons. The figure next to the phone icon shows how many unread messages you have. You can view these from the main menu. Certain jobs can become available contingent on your receiving a specific message, so make sure you consult them regularly.

ESSENTIAL COMMANDS

The opening hours of Cyberpunk 2077 are filled with opportunities to learn about and practice actions and abilities. The following recap of all essential button commands will prove useful should you forget a particular function, or miss a tutorial.

Note that some potential actions and interactions are activated via context-sensitive button presses. The relevant prompts will appear in the bottom-center of the screen as and when they are available.

NOTE FOR PC PLAYERS

To avoid confusion and convoluted lists of buttons and keys throughout this guide, we reference console button commands only. If you don't already own one, we can't overstate the difference that a good twin-stick pad will make. A PlayStation 4 or Xbox One controller will suffice; each pad can be configured for PC gaming with ease. Though Cyberpunk 2077 can certainly be played with mouse and keyboard if you prefer, it's worth noting that its creators recommend a gamepad for an optimal play experience.

BASIC MOVEMENT

L	**Walking**	Tilt L to move in any direction. The greater the gradient, the faster you walk.
L + L3/LS	**Running**	Running is the fastest movement speed. It gradually depletes your stamina gauge.
L + L3/LS + ◎/B	**Sliding**	If you press ◎/B while running, you will execute a slide and end it in a crouched stance. This can prove extremely useful when you need to reach cover in a firefight, or to get out of sight rapidly after running to avoid a hostile patrol.
⊗/A	**Jumping**	This can be employed to traverse gaps, hop onto elevated surfaces, and vault obstacles such as walls. Your jumping distance increases if you leap while running. Hold L forward while jumping and you will automatically pull yourself onto ledges within range.

STEALTH

◎/B	**Crouching**	An essential technique during infiltration situations, crouching greatly increases your ability to remain undetected. Tilt L and you will crouch-walk, enabling you to move steadily and silently. This is the best way to sneak up on an unaware enemy that you need to take down. As a general rule of thumb, whenever you enter a hostile area with substantial enemy forces, crouching should be your default stance if you wish to stay undetected.
▢/X	**Chokehold**	If you manage to stealthily approach an enemy from behind, this grappling technique offers a quiet way to remove them from the equation. Once you have grabbed your victim, you can choose between a lethal or non-lethal takedown. Both options are equally silent. Note that enemies far exceeding your current level (identified with a skull icon) are immune to takedowns.
L1/LB (hold)	**Scanning**	Hold L1/LB to activate your scanner. Scanning your environment reveals essential information with color-coded highlights: enemies (red), clues and job-related items (gold), devices (green) and interactive objects (blue). Improved optics will give you access to a zoom feature: while scanning, use D-pad to zoom in and out.
L1/LB (hold)	**Quickhack**	Whenever scanning a suitable target, your quickhack options, such as pacifying a device or blinding an enemy, will automatically be displayed. Navigate them with D-pad and confirm with ▢/X.
L1/LB (hold) + R3/RS	**Tagging**	Click R3/RS while scanning enemies to tag them. A tagged enemy will be highlighted by a glowing outline even after you turn off your scanner, making it far easier to track their movements. This is an invaluable tool in many stealth scenarios.

VEHICLES

▢/Ⓧ	**Get in/on**	To take control of a car or motorcycle, press ▢/Ⓧ. Note that you can also hijack a vehicle by holding the same button, though you will only succeed if you are stronger than the driver (which is determined by an attribute requirement – more on which later).
R2/RT (hold) + Ⓛ	**Drive**	Hold R2/RT to accelerate and steer with Ⓛ.
L2/LT (hold)	**Brake/Reverse**	To brake, hold L2/LT. From a stationary position, hold to reverse.
⊗/Ⓐ	**Handbrake**	Press ⊗/Ⓐ to activate your handbrake; high-speed applications of this to screech around corners are dangerous but endlessly entertaining.
△/Ⓨ	**Draw Weapon**	When on the passenger seat, you can ready your weapon with △/Ⓨ.
○/Ⓑ (hold)	**Get out/off**	Hold ○/Ⓑ when you want to leave a vehicle.

COMBAT

△/Ⓨ	**Draw / Change Weapon**	Pressing △/Ⓨ enables to you to draw, then cycle through, your available weapons.
R2/RT	**Attack / Shoot from the Hip**	Press R2/RT to use your currently selected weapon. This works for firearms, fists, and blades.
L2/LT (hold) + R2/RT	**Aim and Shoot**	To increase your accuracy with firearms, hold L2/LT to aim through your weapon's iron sights or scope.
▢/Ⓧ	**Reload**	V will reload automatically whenever a weapon runs out of ammunition, but this leaves you vulnerable for however long the process takes. We strongly advise that you get into the habit of manually reloading whenever an opportunity arises during shootouts, ideally from behind cover.
L2 R2 / LT RT	**Melee Combat**	During brawls, with fists or a melee weapon active, tap R2/RT for a light attack, or hold and release for a strong attack; block incoming blows by holding L2/LT.
○/Ⓑ (x2)	**Dodge**	Pressing ○/Ⓑ twice in rapid succession while moving in any direction causes V to dodge – a move that proves particularly helpful during melee encounters.

DAMAGE VARIATION

Whenever you deal damage, you will notice variations in the degree of injury inflicted. There are three main mechanics behind this:

- **Critical Hits:** Based on your attributes and gear, you have a Critical Chance stat. This determines the probability of each of your hits enjoying a damage multiplier. You also have a separate Critical Damage stat, which governs how large the multiplier is.
- **Modifiers:** Enemies can be more or less resistant or susceptible to various damage types: physical, thermal, electrical, and chemical.
- **Damage Deviation:** Every hit in the game is also subject to a random deviation from the expected result – so an attack that will on average deal 5 damage can occasionally inflict 4 or 6 instead.

COMMAND LIST

The following table details the controller commands that can be performed in Cyberpunk 2077 with the default settings.

L	Walk; steer vehicle
R	Adjust the camera angle
L3 / L	Press while walking to run; hold while driving to honk; simultaneously press both sticks to activate Photo Mode
R3 / R	Press while scanning to tag a target; with a firearm equipped, perform a melee attack; hold while driving to look behind you
✕ / A	Jump; while driving, use handbrake
□ / X	Interact (open door, confirm dialogue option, pick up collectible, grab enemy in a chokehold, get in a car, and so forth); reload weapon; hold for special interactions such as hijacking a vehicle
○ / B	Crouch; hold to leave a vehicle
△ / Y	Draw/Cycle weapon; double-tap to holster weapon; hold for specific interactions such as picking up a body; hold to display the weapon wheel; while driving, while on a vehicle's passenger seat, switch to combat mode
L1 / LB	Hold to scan
R1 / RB	Throw grenades or use gadgets; while in a vehicle, hold to select a radio station
L2 / LT	Aim using a firearm's iron sights or scope; in melee combat, hold to block; while driving, brake/reverse
R2 / RT	Use your weapon; in melee combat, tap to perform a light attack, hold for a strong attack; while driving, accelerate
←	Tap to open messages
→	Tap to call up your vehicle, hold to change vehicle; while in a vehicle, tap to switch the camera view
↑	Tap to use consumable item assigned to Quick Access slot
↓	Tap to answer incoming phone call; hold to make a phone call; tap to cycle through quest objectives
Touch pad / View	Display the pause menu
OPTIONS / Menu	Display the main menu

GAME STRUCTURE

Cyberpunk 2077 is a non-linear adventure set in a massive, diverse, and feature-packed game world.

The main storyline is experienced through a long sequence of primary missions, which are referred to as jobs. You can complete many of these in the order of your choosing, but you also have a huge map to explore – and it's positively teeming with side activities, points of interest, and miscellaneous opportunities.

Each district of Night City has its own distinctive layouts, atmosphere, and ambient events – not to mention dangers. To prepare for the latter, you can (and regularly should) work on upgrading and customizing your character, be that through gear, clothes, implants, or skills. How you decide to equip and develop V will have a direct impact on your efficiency and potential.

You've heard it before, but this is especially true and relevant in this game: *there is no right or wrong way to play*.

Some will choose to complete the main storyline as quickly as possible, while others will venture off the beaten path and lose themselves in the environment, secondary missions, and incidental events. Some will aim to wreak havoc whenever possible, while others will opt for stealth and devise clever solutions that enable them to avoid hazardous predicaments. There will be countless off-meta min-max character builds where people role-play their way through the game in unexpected and wonderful ways.

And all of these players can thrive. There is no *wrong* – just ***different***.

JOBS

Jobs in Cyberpunk 2077 are major assignments that serve to advance the core storyline.

Main jobs correspond to extensive missions that are often part of a quest line. For instance, one of your first goals after the Prologue will be to find a specific character, and it will take four sequential main jobs to achieve that objective. Unlike most other games, however, Cyberpunk 2077 often leaves you free to proceed in the order of your choice. Essentially, the plot is divided into branches, which you can approach how and when you see fit. What's more, you will be required to make all sorts of choices during the adventure: everything from "flavor" role-play dialog lines to critical decisions that might lead to significant repercussions for key protagonists – or even different game endings.

Side jobs are, in most cases, sizable assignments that feature key protagonists. If you are used to videogame side quests being small missions that seem like margin doodles when compared to main story activities in other games of this ilk, you will need to reconsider your expectations for Cyberpunk 2077. Several side jobs actually affect the game ending you will eventually reach, and can have a profound influence on potential relationships. In essence, many side jobs are just as significant as main jobs – the only difference being that you do not have to complete them to reach the conclusion of the central storyline (though we strongly recommend that you do).

This guide features dedicated Main Jobs and Side Jobs chapters (see pages 110 and 178) where you will find walkthrough coverage for every single mission in the game.

We also offer a special Completion Roadmap chapter (see page 92) where you will find a comprehensive overview of the game's structure. This includes an extensive flowchart revealing the exact unlock requirements for each installment of the story, and a suggested completion order for those looking for an optimized experience.

SAVING

Cyberpunk 2077 employs an autosave system that automatically records your progress whenever you hit discrete story milestones, such as reaching specific quest checkpoints or completing feats and challenges. There are multiple auto-save slots, which can be useful if you would like to experiment with dialogue variations – especially decisions that might seem as if they carry weight.

You can also manually record your progress and create additional save files via the Save Game option in the pause menu (/). In a game where you make frequent decisions, some with long-lasting consequences, this can enable you to restart from a previous point in the adventure if you're unhappy with your current state of affairs – or simply to go back later and see how events unfold with a different choice.

QUESTS UNLOCKED BY CALLS

Many jobs are activated by visiting a specific location or vendor marked on your map.

Some assignments, on the other hand, are initiated by an external condition – such as an incoming phone call. To ensure that these do not arrive in the midst of a battle or during a story-critical moment, the game uses a "token" system. This guarantees that missions are unlocked at an appropriate time.

The gist of the system is as follows: every time you complete a job of any kind, a token is spawned. The token is then consumed to unlock another queued, token-dependent quest – but only on the proviso that the following conditions are met:

- You are not in combat
- You are not in a hostile area
- You are not in a vehicle
- You are not in the middle of a conversation (face to face or by phone)
- You do not have a dialogue option displayed on the screen

As a rule, this system is pretty seamless – you'll find that new opportunities will arrive during downtime between missions, at sensible junctures that don't put you at risk, and you need not ever think about tokens. But should you ever find yourself waiting for a mission to become available, you now know the two important factors at play: keep completing objectives (of any kind: jobs, gigs, hustles, etc.), and avoid the activities listed above.

JOURNAL

The main menu's Journal gives you access to the list of all open quests. Whenever you want to pick one as your currently active job, select it and press ◎/⊗. Its waypoint and mission objective will then be displayed on your screen, with the path leading to it appearing as a dotted line on your mini-map.

FREE ROAMING

When not busy with jobs, you are free to roam Night City as you please – and you should, because the metropolis is packed with sights, activities, and collectibles.

- **Gigs** are assignments that you receive from local fixers in each of Night City's districts. Typically, a client asks you to do something for them – for instance, acting as an escort, performing a hitjob, or sabotaging a device. Do not underestimate these missions, though: they can be substantial, involving stealth sections or challenging hostile forces. Gigs are initially represented with a question mark on your map, then turn into a specific icon when you move closer.

- **NCPD Scanner Hustles** are bite-sized challenges encountered throughout Night City's various districts. They are smaller in scale than gigs, but more numerous in quantity. Hustles usually take place in a relatively confined area, such as a courtyard with a stash guarded by local thugs.

- **Hostile situations** are small events that occur randomly as you explore Night City. These depict typical scenes of violence that are part of daily life for the city's residents – from shootouts between gangs, to robberies, to attacks on innocent individuals. Whenever you come across such scenes, it's up to you to decide whether or not you wish to intervene. As a rule, you should not expect any particular reward other than the loot you might find on any neutralized foes. Given that the enemies encountered during hostile situations tend to be stronger than those from jobs, we suggest you do not take them lightly. Methodically scan them and identify their numbers before you open hostilities.

Both gigs and hustles may occasionally feature or refer to characters that appear in jobs. Many of them offer extra details or unexpected denouements to secondary narratives that you encounter during the main storyline.

REWARDS

All the assignments that you complete, as well as the enemies that you defeat, will typically grant you two types of rewards:

- **Experience Points (XP)** – Accruing XP enables you to gain levels, which in turn provide you with points to spend on your attributes and perks.

- **Street Cred** – A measure of your reputation in Night City, Street Cred gradually unlocks various rewards, including new items sold by vendors, shop discounts, and additional activities to partake in.

We'll come back to these topics, and character progression in general, a little later in this chapter (see page 84).

DIFFICULTY

When you start a new game, you have a choice between four difficulty settings. This is not a permanent decision, however: you can change it at any time from the Settings ➡ Gameplay ➡ Game Difficulty menu. The higher the level you go for, the more dangerous your enemies will be, in terms of both how much damage they can deal and take. If your goal is to enjoy the adventure without having to worry too much about combat, feel free to opt for the lowest setting – Story Mode.

The important thing to remember is that the game invites you to try new approaches and diversify your play style. In most missions, you have a wealth of options at your disposal: back doors or roof windows to sneak through, alternative dialogue resolutions, combat situations that you can avoid, and so forth. This means that, when you struggle with a specific situation, you often have other avenues that you can explore. This also means that no one will experience each job quite like you, and that any attempt to offer one perfect scenario for each challenge is an impossible task. Success in Cyberpunk 2077 is all about observation and creativity – which is why our walkthroughs focus less on prescriptive solutions for you to follow blindly, but more on options and intelligence designed to inform and improve decisions that are ultimately yours alone to make.

Should you wish to increase the difficulty of combat, consider tweaking **Aim Assist** on the pause menu's Settings screen: this enables you to adjust the level of assistance you require while aiming. By default, the game will automatically help your reticle to "snap" to the closest enemy in your direct field of view when you aim your weapon. Turning this off removes all targeting assistance – which will make combat harder.

RESOLVING SITUATIONS

One of the most laudable and enjoyable features of Cyberpunk 2077 is the freedom you are given to tackle many challenges in a manner of your choosing. This section offers an overview of different possible playstyles and solutions that you might employ on your travels.

NONVIOLENT METHODS

Strategic Decisions

Your personal story in Cyberpunk 2077 is defined by how you approach decisions as and when they arise. Most choices have short-term consequences, such as determining how you should proceed to complete an assignment, but others can have lasting repercussions that affect how critical events unfold.

As early as during the Prologue, for instance, a main job offers you multiple approaches, including – among several possibilities – meeting a corporate agent to cut a deal, or using your personal money to resolve a problem.

Dialogue Decisions

As you play quests, you will face countless instances where you are required to choose between a number of dialogue lines. In most cases, you can take all the time you want to make up your mind. Occasionally, however, you will see an animated timer, indicating that you must make your selection before the gauge is empty. If you fail to do so, the game will consider that you chose to be silent, potentially eliciting a different reaction than if you had opted for a specific line.

The majority of the dialogue decisions you make in the game are role-playing choices. Their primary purpose is to help build the style and identity of your version of V. At specific moments of the adventure, however, you will face dialogue choices that might lead to significant consequences, propelling V towards unique branching paths in the storyline. Our job walkthroughs highlight each and every instance of these major decisions, giving you a heads-up before you commit to any given option.

You will soon notice that dialogue options appear either in orange or blue. It's usually the case that orange entries correspond to critical lines that will advance the current quest, while text displayed in blue typically refers to optional conversational avenues – always a good source of background information.

Exclusive Interactions and Dialogues

From time to time you will encounter special interactions or dialogue lines that are marked with an icon. There are two kinds of these, and you can only select them if you meet specific conditions.

- **Backstory Lines:** These dialogue lines are exclusive to one of the three unique origins (Nomad, Street Kid, Corporate) that you can select at the beginning of the game, when you create and customize your character. If you are a Nomad, for example, you will have access to all Nomad-exclusive dialogue options in your playthrough.

- **Attribute Requirements:** You will also frequently run into attribute requirements. These correspond to actions or dialogue options that are available only if you have the required level in a given attribute. More often than not, having the proficiency required to unlock these can prove highly advantageous, enabling you to resolve situations in creative ways – for example, by hacking a device that a less adept V couldn't master, or talking your way out of a fight.

Whenever you run into one of these exclusive context-sensitive interactions, you can – as a rule of thumb – consider it to be an option worth exploring.

PUBLIC AREAS vs HOSTILE AREAS

When you explore the main urban zones of Night City, particularly large thoroughfares, you are usually in a public area – broadly civilized environments where you will generally be safe from harm (missions and events notwithstanding), and where you will be expected to refrain from drawing weapons or threatening behavior.

As you explore alleyways or complete objectives, however, you will frequently encounter hostile areas – an onscreen notification will appear when you enter one. Such locations feature potential hostiles, leaving it to you to find a way to complete necessary objectives, or simply make your way through to the other side. You are free to pull out a weapon in these areas, though resorting to brute force is rarely mandatory.

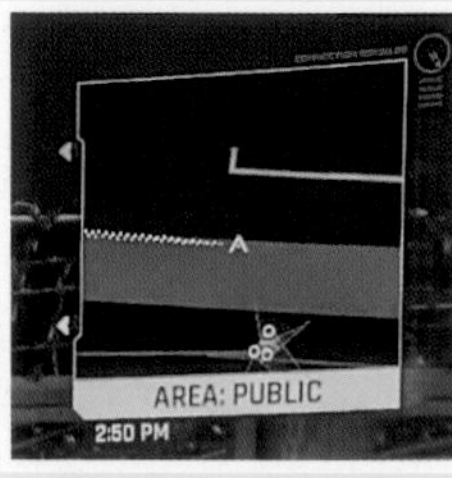

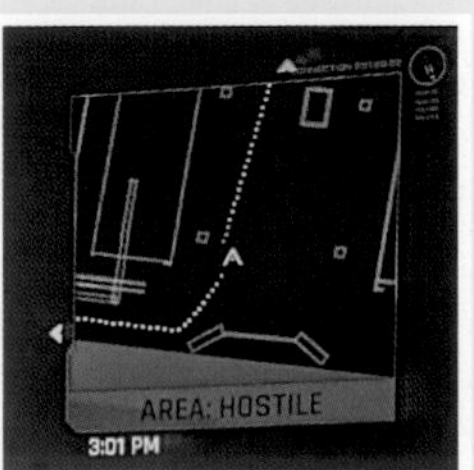

STEALTH

Generally offering the most profitable risk-to-reward ratio of all approaches, but demanding a greater investment of time and patience, a stealthy approach is often the most practical way to get through a potentially lethal situation.

Stealth Mechanics

There are two key factors that determine the success or failure of stealth:

Not being heard – First things first: crouch with ◎/Ⓑ. Moving with Ⓛ in this stance (known as "crouch-walking") causes far less noise. As long as you do not do anything reckless, such as firing a gun, staying crouched is the best way to ensure that enemies cannot hear you. (Note that surveillance cameras do not register noise.)

Not being seen – Remaining unseen requires you to stay out of the line of sight of potential hostiles and security devices. All hostiles have a defined cone of vision, which is represented as such on your mini-map. If you linger in the open within the cone, you will be detected; as long as you remain outside its confines, or behind suitable cover, you have nothing to fear.

Silent Takedowns

Whenever you manage to crouch-walk within reach of an unaware enemy, press ▢/Ⓧ to grapple them and secure a chokehold. You can then perform a takedown, either lethal or non-lethal. Note that enemies incapacitated by non-lethal takedowns will not regain consciousness, so the method performed is purely a moral choice.

There are many situations in the game where you can methodically dispatch all adversaries one by one with melee takedowns, without ever drawing a weapon or raising so much as a moment of fleeting suspicion – let alone an alarm.

In the opening hours of the adventure, you can successfully neutralize most foes with takedowns. You will soon need to learn to pay attention to who you're dealing with, though: enemies identified with a skull icon (who are five or more levels above your own level) will always foil grapple attempts.

If you run into one of these during an infiltration sequence, be aware that a silent takedown is not an option: you will have to either avoid them, or kill them with another method.

Hiding Bodies

After performing a takedown, always consider hiding the body if there is a danger it might be discovered – which is generally the case. You can pick it up by holding △/Ⓨ, then press ▢/Ⓧ when in a suitable position to discard it in an unguarded room or a nearby hiding place (such as a crate or car trunk).

As a rule, avoid leaving bodies in plain sight: more often than not, they will be found by other guards, causing them to enter an increased state of vigilance. You might be reluctant at first to take a few extra steps to move a body to another room, but you will soon realize how much this facilitates stealth infiltrations.

When you grapple enemies, note that you have several seconds before they can break free, so you do not need to take them down immediately. You can instead drag them in any direction, for example toward a nearby hiding place or around a corner, and only then neutralize them. In situations where you grab an opponent while within the cone of vision of another sentry, this technique might buy you enough time to get out of sight just before they detect you.

Tagging Enemies

To increase your chances of successfully sneaking through hostile environments, make a habit of scanning the environment and marking potential adversaries: hold L1/LB, then tag all visible foes with R3/R. Tagged targets are permanently surrounded by a colored outline, making it far easier to monitor their movements and the patrol routes they follow. The very process of scanning enemies dilates time significantly, which can give you some welcome breathing room during stealth infiltrations. Note that you should also tag surveillance cameras and turrets, as this reveals their detection radius – a great visual aid when you need to sneak past them.

When looking for targets to tag in your vicinity, pay attention to the mini-map in the upper-right corner of your screen. All individuals within the perimeter covered by the mini-map appear as gray dots, with a cone revealing their field of vision.

BREACH PROTOCOL

Breach Protocol is a method that you can use to hack enemy networks. As you explore hostile areas and enemy outposts, you will encounter two types of Breach Protocol targets, depending on whether your connection is physical or remote. Both connections require you to complete the same mini-game, but that's about all they have in common. The following table lists the features specific to each connection type.

BREACH PROTOCOL METHODS

Features	Physical Connection	Remote Connection
Hacking process	Triggered automatically	Triggered only if you cast the Breach Protocol quickhack
Hacked target	A specific device such as an access point, a computer, etc	Any enemy or generic device (such as a vending machine)
Cyberdeck requirement	None	A cyberdeck must be equipped
Mini-game objective/ reward	Procurement of datamining resources: primarily money and, if you unlocked the relevant Perks in the Breach Protocol skill tree, quickhack components or even quickhacks	Application of one or more daemons to the network, in accordance with the Perks that you have unlocked in the Breach Protocol skill tree; this can, for example, disable all surveillance cameras for three minutes
Effect on the network	None	All enemies or devices in the network are affected by the uploaded daemon(s)
Summary	**Useful to farm resources, particularly money and crafting components for quickhacks**	**Useful to weaken enemies or disable security devices such as cameras and turrets, greatly facilitating infiltrations in hostile areas**

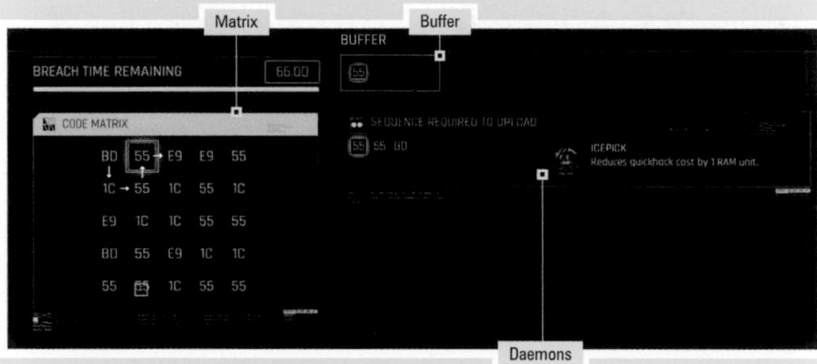

Irrespective of the connection type, Breach Protocol always requires you to complete a timed mini-game with the following rules:

- Your objective in these puzzles is to reproduce the sequence of numbers shown on the right of the display (each sequence corresponds to a daemon program you can upload).
- To do so, you can select the numbers (known as nodes) in the matrix on the left. This adds them to your buffer. If your buffer matches the sequence of a daemon, you receive the corresponding reward.
- You can only select a number from the currently active row or column, always starting from the top row. The first number you select determines which column is activated next.
- Follow this pattern of alternating between rows and columns to add the correct sequence to your buffer.
- Your buffer has limited capacity, so you need to plan your moves in advance to activate the correct sequence. You can increase the size of your buffer by developing your character.
- The higher your Intelligence, the lower the difficulty of the mini-game – and vice versa.
- If you struggle to identify a "path" through the matrix, it can sometimes prove helpful to begin from the end: look for the final number in the sequence, then work out the necessary route from there.

Quickhacks

Quickhacks are programs installed on cyberdecks that can be employed to manipulate devices in your immediate environment. All you need to do is scan a suitable target, then select the quickhack of your choice.

Every quickhack that you trigger has a memory (RAM) cost. If you are familiar with role-playing games, you can consider memory as your pool of magic points, and quickhacks as being equivalent to spells.

Quickhacks have all sorts of applications in the game world, but they can prove particularly helpful in stealth scenarios. You might remotely access a vending machine to distract a guard in your path, for example. Over time, as you secure improved cyberdecks, quickhacks, and perks (see page 85), you will be able to perform much more advanced tricks, such as crippling foes with more harmful effects, or even forcing them to commit suicide.

Combining hacking skills with traditional stealth maneuvers can prove extremely profitable. If you manage to disable two guards out of four in a room simply by crouch-walking to them from behind, but see no obvious way to safely approach the final pair, causing a distraction with a nearby device could be all you need to isolate one from the other. If you see no reason to employ non-lethal methods, you might alternatively lure them both to a single position – and then order one to detonate a grenade.

Cyberdecks can be purchased from (and installed by) ripperdocs. Quickhacks are sold by netrunners and can also be crafted, looted or datamined. Regularly updating them (along with the rest of your gear) is crucial to the progression of your character – a topic that we develop further on page 84.

Detection

Whenever you arouse the suspicion of potential hostiles, a distinctive icon will appear above their heads – or, if they are currently off-screen, on the edge of your display, with the icons indicating their approximate position. The icon is accompanied by a piercing sound. As explained earlier in this section, enemies can detect you for two reasons: either because you enter their field of vision (which can be avoided by hiding behind objects), or because you are making noise (easily prevented by crouch-walking).

Alert Indicators change based on your actions:

An empty Alert Indicator appears when you are positioned within an enemy's field of vision, or when you cause a noise that can be heard. The icon will fill quickly (with an increasingly loud sound emphasizing this process), unless you immediately (and quietly!) retreat out of view. If guards come to investigate, you will need to move elsewhere and avoid further indiscretions until their suspicion is allayed. If they find nothing at the identified position of interest, they will soon return to their posts or patrols.

If you quickly escape the gaze of a suspicious guard, the detection icon above his head will gradually deplete. Once the meter is empty, the individual forgets about you and returns to a standard behavior pattern.

If you fail to get out of a suspicious enemy's line of sight swiftly enough, the Alert Indicator will eventually fill up completely and turn red. At this point, you are identified – and all nearby antagonists will enter combat mode. You must then either defeat all active hostiles, or escape their attention until they revert to their normal behavior.

General Advice

Most hostiles you will encounter tend to stick to persistent patrol routes.

Here's a hypothetical scenario: one guard taking a clockwise stroll around a courtyard, while his nearby cohort patrols back and forth in front of an entrance, and a third inspects two devices in the room inside, lingering for several seconds in front of each.

Once you've taken the time to identify such patterns, you can choose your plan of action. Your instinct might be to neutralize each one in sequence, perhaps, or to wait for a specific moment to slip through the door and avoid all three entirely.

If you happen to be technically in view of a moving sentry, you don't necessarily need to panic. In our previous example, if you are within sight (but at suitable remove) of the guard taking the clockwise patrol in the courtyard, his Alert Indicator will begin to fill – but should his rightward progression see you leave his cone of vision before detection occurs, it will automatically drain. And so, in short: small measures of Alert Indicator growth are not to be feared if you know the exact moment when an enemy will turn away.

To increase your ability to remain undetected, here is a selection of simple but essential guidelines that you should try to adopt early on in your playthrough:

- The golden rule: stay crouched at all times if stealth is your goal. This will enable you to make no noise and to avoid prying eyes more easily.
- Preemptively tag as many guards and surveillance cameras as you can. This will give you a great edge as you plot a safe route to an objective or next destination.
- When on the move, try to stay close to solid objects such as crates, low walls, cars, furniture, and whatever else is found in your environment. When crouched behind a waist-high solid object, you will usually remain concealed even if a sentry directly on the other side looks in your direction.
- When you decide to cause a distraction to get a guard out of your way, consider the route they will take before you commit to the gambit. Take a second to visualize where their cone of vision will point, and be sure that there is a sufficient window of opportunity for you to make your move.
- If you leave bodies in the open, you will run the risk that other sentries might discover them – which will cause them to adopt an increased state of vigilance. You can avoid this by picking them up and concealing them in containers (such as fridges and crates) or unattended rooms. However, a well-placed body can also be employed as bait.
- In stealth scenarios, repeated usage of quickhacks on enemies will eventually cause you to be detected. One quickhack applied to a target will usually make them suspicious; cast a second one on the same foe and your position will be revealed after a short delay.
- Surveillance cameras are deaf, leaving you free to make noise in their vicinity. Though you will usually bypass them by moving past while they are at the opposite end of their rotation, you should note that there is a blind spot directly beneath their position. In addition, remember that not all surveillance cameras are active. Only the ones with a red scanning beam are hostile. If you spot cameras with green beams, feel free to ignore them altogether.

OPEN COMBAT

Once you have been fully detected by a hostile, you have a very brief window of opportunity to neutralize them before they trigger the alarm. Fail to do so and they – along with all their allies in the current area – will enter combat mode. Enemies will attack at will until you either fall to their assaults or escape their zone of influence.

Ranged Combat

- **Firing:** Press or hold R2/RT with a weapon equipped to "hip-fire" toward the center of your screen, using R to keep your targets in your sights as you move with L. Shooting in this manner is suitable for very quick close-quarters skirmishes, or when a target is at point-blank range.
- **Iron Sights/Scopes:** When a fight calls for a higher standard of marksmanship, hold L2/LT before you open fire. The viewing angle will switch from its default position to your weapon's iron sights or scope, facilitating improved aiming. The additional accuracy this offers will make it far easier to align shots on more distant targets, or to shoot at specific body parts.
- **Reloading:** V will reload automatically whenever an ammo clip is empty, but we suggest that you get into the habit of reloading manually by pressing ▢/X – ideally while in cover. As a general rule, you should always ensure that you have sufficient shots to take down at least one target whenever you emerge from concealment and take aim.
- **Cover:** When a fight is unavoidable, always position yourself so that you have easy access to cover. When V is located at the edge of a cover point, or is crouched behind a low barrier, hold L2/LT to quickly emerge and shoot with R2/RT as required, releasing L2/LT to immediately return to safety.
- **Movement:** Try to stay on the move as much as you can while facing multiple enemies, quickly alternating between different cover spots as you search for advantageous firing positions. This will prevent your opponents from camping in positions that suit them, and will also provide opportunities to take them down as they relocate. Note that many enemies will suspend fire while in motion, which is a tactical advantage you should exploit whenever possible.
- **Critical Hits:** You will notice that some of your shots deal increased damage. These are called *critical hits*. Both V and weapons have their own critical chance and critical damage stats: the former determines the percentage chance for certain bullets to bite harder, while the latter governs how much harder.

Ranged Combat (Continued)

- **Progression:** As you make progress in the story and explore Night City, you will secure more and more powerful weapons, each with their own specific features – such as homing or penetrating bullets. Multiple skills and perks can also give you an edge in shootouts, enhancing your proficiency with certain weapon types, or offering all sorts of additional boons.

Melee Combat

- **Attacking:** Use R2/RT to perform melee attacks – tap for a light attack, hold and release for a strong attack (which can break an enemy's guard). Multiple successive presses lead to combos.
- **Blocking:** Hold L2/LT to raise your guard. You will then automatically block all incoming attacks, reducing the damage that opponents can inflict. Note that fighting with your fists can be effective even against armed enemies, though this requires suitable preparation and character development to work optimally.
- **Stamina:** Attacking, blocking, and dodging all deplete your stamina bar, displayed at the top-center of the screen. Stamina regenerates over time, but sustained activity will empty it rapidly. Exhausting your stamina will reduce the efficiency of your stamina-dependent moves, so be sure to manage it well – look for opportunities to take a step back as it regenerates. Your overall stamina can be improved via cyberware and perks.
- **Perks:** You will gradually unlock new perks that will potentially improve your melee combat proficiency via bonuses and new capabilities. You might, for example, pick one that increases your chances to inflict a Bleeding status effect on enemies that you strike with blades, causing damage over time.

BRAINDANCE ANALYSIS

At various points in the storyline you will be required to explore the memories of other characters during braindance sessions. Your objective during these activities is to investigate and identify a number of key clues revealing crucial information.

Controls

All braindance commands are listed on your screen during the corresponding sequences. We summarize them in the following table.

Braindance Controls

L	Move around in editing mode
R	Adjust the camera angle in editing mode
□/X	Toggle between play and pause
△/Y	Hold to restart from the beginning
○/B	Exit the simulation
L1/LB	Toggle between editing mode and playback mode
R1/RB	Switch layer
L2/LT	Rewind
R2/RT	Fast-forward

Finding Clues

We suggest you always begin each braindance session by watching the whole recording once in playback mode, familiarizing yourself with the setting, the characters involved, and the events that occur. Once you have the gist of the scenario you can switch to editing mode (L1/LB) and start digging for information.

In editing mode you are completely free to move around (though within a defined radius of the person who recorded the braindance), and you can study the scene from any angle, pausing, fast-forwarding, or rewinding as you please. The session is represented by a timeline at the top of the screen. A typical recording will last a minute or two.

You will soon notice that there are actually three timelines, not just one. Each of these corresponds to a layer: visual, thermal, and audio. You can switch layers with R1/RB.

Your objective is to find clues, which are represented by a magnifying glass icon. The challenge is that these clues appear only at a specific space and time (for instance, an item on a desk at 00:32 in the recording), *and* on a particular layer. Colored segments on each timeline can indicate critical moments where you can expect to find evidence, but not all clues are highlighted in this manner.

To be thorough, you will need to observe the entire scene multiple times, from various angles, and alternating between layers. Once you've identified a clue, move close to it and focus on it to scan it. When you've collected all critical clues in a session, you can leave it with ○/B.

MAPS, MARKERS, & TRAVEL

Night City is a sprawling metropolis. To find your way from A to B, or to more profitably explore at your leisure, we recommend that you make regular use of Cyberpunk 2077's maps and fast travel functionality.

MAP

You can access the map at any time via the main menu (OPTIONS / ☰). Once on the map screen, your position is represented by a green triangle that points in the direction that V is facing.

The main ways to interact with the map are shown in the table on the right.

TRACKING

One powerful feature to take note of is the ability to track points of interest. If you need to reach a specific shop or quest location, for instance, select it with ⊗/Ⓐ and this will activate a route line on your mini-map. When you are not familiar with a specific sub-district, or struggle with the verticality of a tall building, tracking is a very welcome tool that makes it far easier to get where you need to be.

MINI-MAP

The mini-map shows a small portion of the main map that corresponds with your immediate surroundings. All icons that appear here are identical to those found on the main map. The mini-map can also display the route to a selected job objective or to a point of interest that you're tracking: this takes the form of a dotted line.

Active enemies are represented by gray dots on the mini-map; the dots turn red when they are suspicious of your presence or enter combat mode. Each individual's field of vision is also represented by a cone on the mini-map – a critical feature during stealth infiltrations. When an enemy has you in sight (causing their detection meter to start filling), their cone of vision turns red: this is your cue to swiftly retreat behind suitable cover.

Your mini-map features a compass (Ⓝ). The N icon always points north. Whenever you are following cardinal directions, bear in mind that the compass rotates in real time as you move the camera.

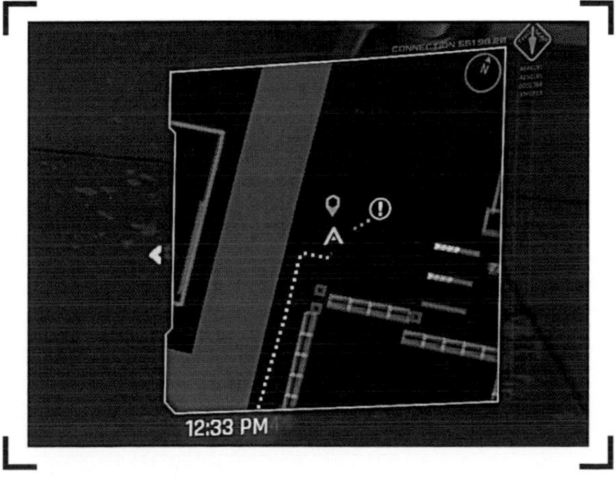

Commands

Ⓛ	Scroll
Ⓡ	If you free the camera: 3D rotation
L2/LT	Zoom out
R2/RT	Zoom in
⊗/Ⓐ	Track points of interest
△/Ⓨ	Jump back to V's position
✥	Display a complete legend
✥	Cycle through filters to only display icons within a given category
R3/RS	Toggle Free Camera mode

MAP & MINI-MAP LEGEND

Group	Icon	Icon
	V	Enemy (Unaware)
	Your Vehicle	Enemy (Suspicious/ Combat Mode)
	Main Job Waypoint	Client
	Side Job Waypoint	Fixer
	Cyberpsycho Sighting	Apartment
Gig Waypoints	Gun for Hire	Fast Travel
Gig Waypoints	Search and Recover	Drop Point
Gig Waypoints	Thievery	Clothing
Gig Waypoints	Agent Saboteur	Ripperdoc
Gig Waypoints	SOS: Merc Needed	Netrunner
Gig Waypoints	Special Delivery	Techie
NCPD Scanner Hustle Waypoints	Assault in Progress	Weapon Shop
NCPD Scanner Hustle Waypoints	Suspected Organized Crime Activity	Melee Weapon Vendor
NCPD Scanner Hustle Waypoints	Reported Crime	Medpoint
NCPD Scanner Hustle Waypoints	Hidden Gem	Food
	Tarot Card	Bar
	Ally	Joytoy

NAVIGATION

Whenever your current objective is marked by a waypoint, or you manually select a point of interest to track, the game automatically shows you a recommended path to follow in the form of a dynamic line on your map and mini-map. While this always defines a reliable route, it is not necessarily the most efficient or fastest option. If you study the map, and pay attention to your surroundings as you travel, you'll gradually acquire the ability to notice and take shortcuts. You're obviously not *supposed* to drive the wrong way along a one-way street – but if doing so will shave off a minute of travel, the temptation is hard to resist.

One important factor to consider is that your map is three-dimensional: it gives a clear sense of the elevation of buildings, freeway ramps, and so forth. You can use this to plan ahead and identify an optimal route.

As a rule, you will have to stick to roads while navigating Night City. Outside of the metropolis, however, the Badlands feature many flat plains. Here, you may decide to move in a straight line, heading directly for your objective, but such off-road excursions are at your own risk: be wary of obstacles, bumps, or gaps.

FAST TRAVEL

Every time you move close to a fast travel station, you unlock it automatically as a new possible destination. As the game features dozens of these terminals, they soon form a network that enables you to warp to virtually anywhere on the map. Fast travel positions include both dataterms found in the streets and NCART subway stations.

This proves particularly handy when carrying out optional objectives that might take you to the far reaches of Night City. Even main jobs regularly send you on substantial journeys. As long as you've already visited the location in question, fast travel positions allow you to move to the area of your choice, making the process of reaching any destination easy and near-instantaneous.

Note that fast travel is unavailable in certain circumstances, most notably during active combat and phone calls.

CHARACTER PROGRESSION

CHARACTER CREATION

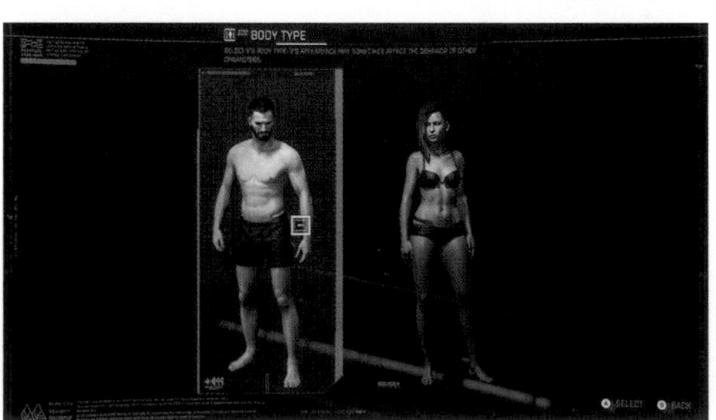

When you launch a new game, the first step you take is to create your character. Cosmetic options aside (of which there are a great many), you have three significant choices to make during this process:

- **Body Type & Voice Tone:** These parameters affect, as you can imagine, the appearance and the voice of your version of V. Your choice has an additional practical application: the romantic relationships you have access to depend on which combination of voice tone and body type you opt for. One romanceable character, for example, will only have a relationship with a V who has a male body type.
- **Backstory:** Your chosen backstory (Nomad, Street Kid, or Corporate) determines where your version of V comes from. In gameplay terms, your origins have significant consequences on your playthrough. First, each backstory has its own exclusive opening quest, along with another unique follow-up side job later on in the adventure. Furthermore, you will also be given certain options that are specific to your chosen backstory. When dealing with Nomads, for example, a Nomad V will have unique interactions available. This usually takes the form of special lines of dialogue: some offering additional narrative flavor or context, others with more practical applications (such as a bouncer letting you in for free, or a sympathetic individual revealing important information).
- **Attributes:** By default, V has a value of three points in all five attributes (more on these shortly). During the character creation process, you have seven additional points to spend as you please (within a maximum of three per attribute). Invest heavily in Body and Reflexes, for instance, and your fighting proficiency will increase… but your other aptitudes will be rather below-par as a consequence. If this is your first playthrough, we suggest a more balanced approach. Read the overview in the nearby "Attributes, Skills & Perks" section for more guidance.

After you create your character, it will not take long for V to level up. Character progression and development can take many forms, and will be an ongoing process as you explore Night City and play through the main storyline.

XP

Core progression is achieved by completing actions and jobs, which reward you with experience points (XP). You level up every time you hit specific milestones, which provides you with one point to spend on your attributes, and one on your perks. Higher levels, and by extension enhanced stats, will give you an edge over your opponents in all sorts of situations. The most palpable effect is that you will inflict greater harm on enemies while sustaining less damage in return, but there are many other areas where V's competency affects game difficulty.

As a general rule of thumb, levels – both V's level and that of enemies – give you a reliable indication of your chances should open conflict be triggered. Any foe a couple of levels above you will likely represent a significant challenge. The greater the difference in their favor, the higher the difficulty – and vice versa.

ATTRIBUTES, SKILLS, & PERKS

Attributes – Attributes are the cornerstone of character progression. There are five of them in total, as detailed in the Overview diagram overleaf. Each of these grants passive bonuses (permanent boons strengthening your character), and determines how much you can develop a subset of skills and perks. You receive one attribute point to allot to any of your attributes every time you level up. To spend points on an attribute, select it in the Character menu and hold □/ⓧ.

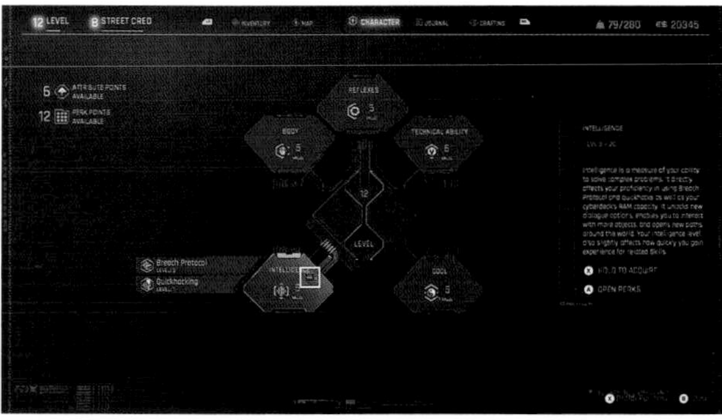

Skills – The game features 12 different skills, which all begin at level one. These are sorted in five subsets, each linked to a specific attribute. Both the Engineering and Crafting skills, for example, are governed by the Technical Ability attribute. All skills within an attribute subset are capped by the attribute in question – so if your Reflex stat is at three, for instance, you can only hope to develop the skills governed by Reflex up to rank three. You enhance skills ("skill up") by performing related actions in the game: for example, each successful silent takedown contributes to Stealth skill growth. Every time you skill up, you are granted a reward, such as a passive bonus or a Perk point.

Perks – Each skill in the game gives you access to a Perk tree. Perks are unique bonuses that enable you to specialize your character in specific fields, such as stealth, weapon mastery, and movement speed. Every time you level up, and occasionally when you skill up, you get a Perk point to spend. To allocate a point to a Perk, select it in the corresponding skill tree and hold □/ⓧ. While initial Perks are available by default, note that Perks further down each tree are locked by default, and require certain attribute levels to become available.

Though it's not something you need worry about in the opening hours of the game, you can find a comprehensive appraisal of all possible progression parameters in our Reference & Analysis chapter (see page 428). For now, the overview overleaf should provide enough information to inform your early choices.

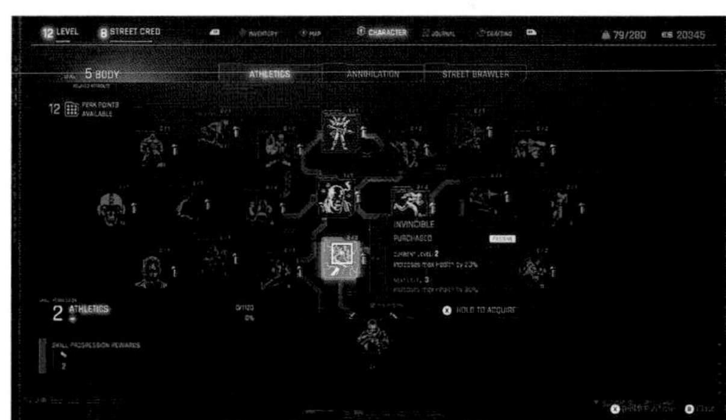

ATTRIBUTE REQUIREMENTS

As you explore Night City and complete jobs, you will often encounter attribute requirements. These are situations where an action can only be performed if one of your attributes is of a sufficient grade. For example, you might face a bouncer refusing entrance to a club, but you could potentially intimidate him (and therefore enter) if your Body attribute is at level 8 or above.

Such requirements typically occur in two sorts of situations: during dialogue with other characters, or when you encounter a secure device (a door, shutters, a computer, and so forth).

The importance of this system throughout the adventure can be quite significant. Many hostile situations can be resolved far more easily if you can pass a specific requirement, often enabling you to bypass entire enemy encounters or to enjoy massive shortcuts.

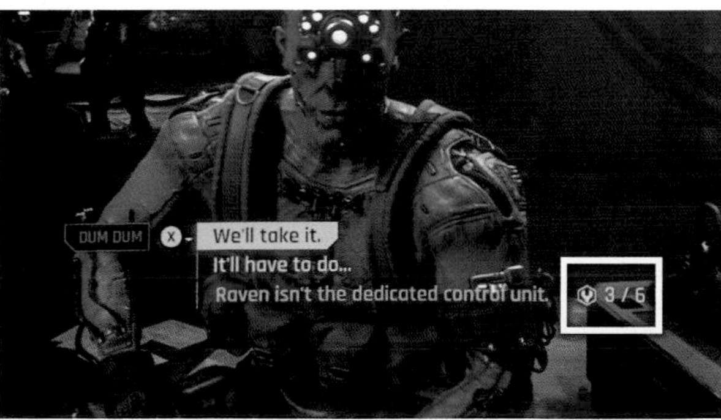

For instance, Body requirements will enable you to force-open certain doors, intimidate unfriendly characters, and carjack. Technical Ability requirements are used to open locked mechanical devices such as doors, shutters, and blinds. Intelligence requirements make it possible to breach door terminals and digital locks. And the list goes on and on.

ATTRIBUTES, SKILLS, & PERKS: OVERVIEW

ATTRIBUTES	PASSIVE BONUSES	SKILLS	INCREASED PROFICIENCY	PERKS
BODY	■ Increased blunt weapon damage, health, and stamina ■ Mastery of powerful weapons such as shotguns and machine guns	Annihilation	Shotguns and machine guns	18 Perks
		Athletics	Health and stamina	21 Perks
		Street Brawler	Bareknuckle fighting and blunt weapons	16 Perks
REFLEXES	■ Increased movement speed and attack speed ■ Improved chance to perform critical hits ■ Proficiency with rifles, handguns, and blades	Handguns	Revolvers and pistols	19 Perks
		Assault	Rifles and submachine guns	19 Perks
		Blades	Blades	16 Perks
TECHNICAL ABILITY	■ Increased Armor ■ Improved crafting ability ■ Proficiency with Tech weapons	Engineering	Grenades and Tech weapons	19 Perks
		Crafting	Crafting	17 Perks
INTELLIGENCE	■ Quickhacking proficiency ■ Increased cyberdeck's RAM ■ Reduced program upload duration and hacking mini-game difficulty	Breach Protocol	Hacking mini-game	19 Perks
		Quickhacking	Quickhacks, quickhack crafting, RAM	18 Perks
COOL	■ Increased critical damage ■ Improved damage resistances ■ Sneaking proficiency ■ Extended grapple time	Stealth	Stealth and sneak attacks	24 Perks
		Cold Blood	Stat boosts after defeating enemies	18 Perks

CYBERWARE & EQUIPMENT

Cyberware is a blanket term referring to implants that you can install by visiting ripperdocs. They can and will impact you in fundamental ways, greatly increasing your proficiency within certain fields, or adding entirely new skills to your arsenal of possibilities.

For example, you can install powerful Mantis Blades in your arms, which are boosted by any Blades Perks you may have activated. Other examples of cyberware abilities include double-jumps, faster health regeneration, stealth camo, and even the possibility to briefly alter the perceived flow of time to your advantage. The range and potency of these effects make implants especially valuable in terms of character development.

The same principles apply to equipment. Obtaining better weapons, clothing, and mods is key to constantly remaining on a par with or, even better, ahead of the game's difficulty curve. Overall, there's really little reason for sentimentality. A firearm, even one that you particularly enjoy, becomes effectively useless the moment you secure one with superior bite. You will find dozens and dozens of pieces of gear as you take jobs and explore Night City, and being suitably equipped for the task at hand should always be one of your top priorities.

STREET CRED

Street Cred is a "currency" measuring your reputation in Night City. You accrue Street Cred by completing all sorts of tasks, especially those encountered via exploration – such as Gigs and Hustles. Whenever you reach certain milestones, your Street Cred goes up a tier.

Obtaining Street Cred rewards you with various bonuses, including discounts and improved selections of items at shops, as well as access to more difficult Gigs.

PLAY STYLES & BUILDS

While the game does not feature a traditional class system, your play style – as well as how you decide to spend your attribute and perk points – will determine the areas in which your character excels.

The approach you take to developing your character is commonly referred to as a "build." You can combine all sorts of traits within a build, developing a stock of useful talents, or instead opt for ultra-specialization within one or two fields. There are pros and cons to all decisions you make, so feel free to experiment and find the ones that work best for you.

Examples of areas in which you may wish to invest include:

- Mastery of a specific weapon type (such as shotguns, rifles, or handguns) is an obvious choice if you plan to use brute force. If you then equip a weapon of that variety and acquire related perks, you can turn V into a killing machine – a type of mercenary known as a "solo" in the world of Cyberpunk 2077.
- A primary focus on physical prowess is another interesting build option. Points you spend in the Body attribute and Athletics perks will increase your carrying capacity, hand-to-hand combat damage, health, and health regeneration, as well as grant you various abilities while carrying bodies or grappling enemies. Points invested in Body will also enable you to pass attribute requirements to force-open doors (among other similar shortcuts), and therefore to bypass potentially tricky situations or entire confrontations.
- The Technical Ability attribute is the gateway to two complementary skills. Crafting makes you more proficient at collecting materials, creating new items, and upgrading existing equipment. A master crafter can eventually own a broad selection of gear to the highest Legendary tier. Engineering improves your proficiency with grenades and Tech weapons in particular. Specializing in this area will also enable you to pass attribute requirements to open doors or manipulate other mechanical devices, facilitating clever ways to complete objectives.
- Alternatively, you can invest in the Cool attribute and Stealth Perks to enhance a whole range of stealth-related parameters, such as crouch-walking faster, remaining silent even at full walking speed and when performing a takedown, or unlocking special aerial takedowns. Combine these with a few Quickhacking Perks and you could boost your memory, memory regeneration, and ability to cast quickhacks – making it even easier to infiltrate enemy territory without ever being detected.

Remember: these are mere suggestions to give you an idea of how you can develop your own version of V. All combinations are possible, and you can mix and match in myriad ways. A silent ninja who can deal punishing damage with shotguns if detected? An athletic netrunner who can deftly navigate arenas to wreak havoc among foes? The choice is yours. There is no right or wrong way to build your character – only a huge range of playstyles to choose from. You can find more details on possible character builds on page 438.

ENEMIES & THREATS

GANGS & FACTIONS

Virtually all enemies in the game belong to a gang or faction. These are well-defined groups where individuals share common traits, such as dress codes, cyberware, territories, and language or dialect. If you'd like a primer on what to expect in the many districts and sub-districts of Night City, see page 20.

Human adversaries often belong to an archetype, which determines the type of weapon they use and the abilities they have access to. You can find more information on this topic on page 446. You will also regularly run into mechanical opponents, in the form of drones and androids, who are particularly vulnerable to quickhacks. How you deal with each opponent will be heavily influenced by the choices you have made in developing your unique version of V.

POLICE

In addition to the enemies encountered during jobs and in hostile areas, the authorities may take an interest in your person should you perform illegal actions such as stealing, killing civilians, reckless driving, and other such infractions while in public areas. The more serious your offence, the greater the bounty on your head (as represented by stars near the mini-map).

The NCPD force sent to deal with you is proportionate to the current bounty, and can increase rapidly if the situation escalates – with reinforcements and turrets deployed. The best approach is always to escape a crime scene quickly, losing any police on your tail, and lay low for a while until the heat dies down.

DAMAGE RESISTANCE TYPES & ARMOR

All combatants in the game have three special damage resistance types:

- **Thermal** (heat and fire)
- **Chemical** (toxic substances)
- **Electrical** (shock damage)

In addition to elemental resistances, combatants may have **Armor** – a parameter that reduces the overall incoming damage, irrespective of its type.

Note that you can cause each type of elemental damage via assorted methods, but most commonly by using weapons of the corresponding variety. An example would be a rifle that deals a certain amount of base physical damage, but also offers an extra kick via supplementary thermal damage.

In the early game, foes that you encounter will often have a resistance of zero for all damage types. This means that they will take a standard amount of damage when you hit them.

As you progress in the story, however, you will regularly face hostiles with resistances and weaknesses, on a scale from 0 to 100%. These damage modifiers can be viewed by scanning your enemies (hold L1/LB).

- A resistance reduces the damage received by the target up to 100%, at which point the effect is negligible: the target is effectively immune.
- A weakness increases the damage received by the target. At 100%, damage is doubled – a situation that you should always seek to exploit.

Note that this principle also applies to V. Just like enemies, you have affinities to all three types of damage as well as armor, and you can alter these using skills, perks, equipment, and cyberware.

DAMAGE RESISTANCE SCALE

ENEMY ATTRIBUTES

Enemies have stats that influence their combat proficiency – such as a damage value which is based on their level and the properties of their weapon. They can have boosted or reduced health, or ability stats that grant them special behaviors such as grenade usage.

Observation is key to understanding what kind of threat you're dealing with. If in doubt, scan your foes to reveal their stat sheet, including essential parameters such as their level and resistances to the various damage types.

As a rule, their level is a reliable measure of the danger they might pose. When an opponent is of an equivalent or lower level, you should have little cause for concern; if their level is above yours, expect a more demanding encounter. The more the difference lies in their favor, the greater the challenge.

HACKING

Brute force is by no means the only way to get rid of enemies. Most of them are vulnerable to quickhacks, enabling you to impede them in all sorts of ways – if you have the required cyberdeck and quickhacks, that is.

During stealth scenarios, briefly blinding a sentry can be all it takes to give you an opportunity to sneak by. If a guard is in hot pursuit, you could cause his weapon or cyberware to malfunction, or you could render him unconscious with a non-lethal neural shock… we could go on and on.

The point here is that, while a solo V relying primarily on brute force can prove remarkably efficient, a netrunner V specializing in combat hacking maneuvers can be just as effective.

The cornerstone of netrunner strategies, quickhacks are the programs that you install on your cyberdeck and can then cast on your enemies. The beating heart of pure netrunner builds, but also hugely useful in other character setups, quickhacks are divided into four distinct categories:

- **Stealth Quickhacks** are used in infiltration scenarios to elude or escape the attention of enemies, for example by deafening them, or even by wiping their memory.
- **Combat Quickhacks** are the bread and butter of netrunners once enemies are aware of your presence. You can cast them to deal damage and exploit elemental weaknesses. They can be amazingly effective to destroy weak points, too.
- **Control Quickhacks** are also useful in combat situations, as they can greatly impede opponents. They can prove particularly decisive against bosses and mini-bosses when deployed to disable cyberware they rely on.
- **Ultimate Quickhacks** are the most powerful programs, but also the most costly in terms of RAM and upload time. Cast correctly, they can potentially eliminate targets instantly, or even turn them against each other.

RANDOM LOOT & UNIQUE COLLECTIBLES

Every time you take down enemies or locate generic item caches, you can loot them. The items you obtain are largely randomized, and scale based on your current level and overall progression. This means that, in most situations in the game, it is impossible to predict what pieces you will find. Your best bet to secure quality equipment, therefore, is to complete as many jobs and activities as you can: valuable items will inevitably pop out of the randomly generated loot.

There are, however, a few unique collectibles that appear when you meet specific conditions; for instance, when you defeat a given enemy or visit a particular room during a mission. Many of these can be missed and tend to be powerful items of the special Iconic type (see page 91), so acquiring them should be a priority. You can find an overview of these pieces in our Inventory chapter (see page 416), as well as reminders of when they are available during the course of a playthrough in our Completion Roadmap (see page 102).

ITEMS

Cyberpunk 2077 features a massive range of items, weapons, and equipment that you can use for all sorts of purposes. This short introduction presents all key concepts that you need to familiarize yourself with during the opening hours of the adventure. You can find much more comprehensive listings and descriptions in the Inventory chapter (see page 404).

WEAPONS & CLOTHING

You can equip weapons and clothing from the Inventory screen: simply select the appropriate item slots, then choose the required objects. To remove a piece, press △/Ⓨ while hovering over it in the same menu.

As simple as the system may seem, you will soon find that there is more to it than meets the eye, with multiple features enabling you to optimize your damage output and defensive capabilities.

Skill Proficiency

All weapons within a category are tied to a specific skill. The more proficient you are in a skill, the greater your potential damage output with its associated weapon type.

The adjacent table shows which skill governs your proficiency in each weapon category.

Weapon Types & Proficiency

Name	Related Attribute	Related Skill
Double-Barrel Shotgun	Body	Annihilation
HMG	Body	Annihilation
LMG	Body	Annihilation
Shotgun	Body	Annihilation
Fists	Body	Street Brawler
Blunt Weapons (All)	Body	Street Brawler
Gorilla Arms	Body	Street Brawler
Monowire	Body	Street Brawler
Blades (All)	Reflexes	Blades
Mantis Blades	Reflexes	Blades
Pistol	Reflexes	Handguns
Revolver	Reflexes	Handguns
Assault Rifle	Reflexes	Assault
Precision Rifle	Reflexes	Assault
SMG	Reflexes	Assault
Sniper Rifle	Reflexes	Assault

Firearm Classes

As you advance in the storyline, you will get the chance to put your hands on all sorts of advanced weapons. These can belong to three categories, each offering their own boons if you equip relevant cyberware:

- **Power** weapons pack a punch, dealing extra damage. Their projectiles have a chance to ricochet from solid surfaces, which can be used to hit enemies behind cover. A specific type of hands cyberware, called Ballistic Coprocessor, will increase your chance of triggering ricochet and the number of times it can occur with each bullet, while offering a visual representation of potential ricochet trajectory.
- **Smart** weapons fire projectiles that automatically home in on their targets if you install the Smart Link hands cyberware. This can prove extremely effective against foes hiding behind cover or moving at supernatural speed.
- **Tech** weapons have the ability to penetrate surfaces, including cover positions. Some can also be charged by holding the trigger, resulting in a more powerful attack upon release.

Note that certain perks will boost your proficiency with a given weapon type (such as certain Engineering perks with Tech weapons).

RARITY

Every weapon and piece of clothing in the game has a color-coded rarity rating. From least to most valuable:

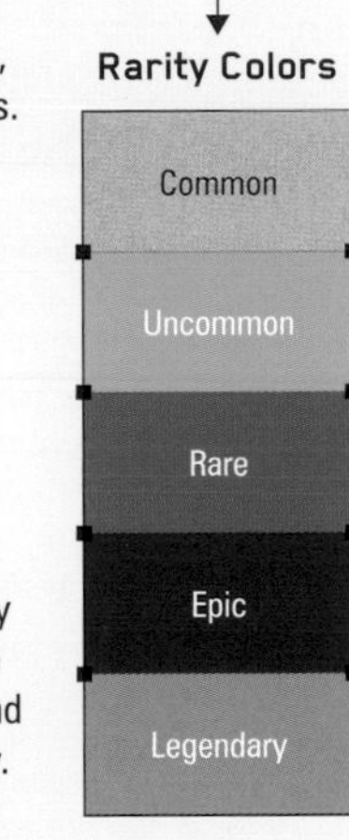

Rarer pieces tend to enjoy various bonuses, including superior stats and extra mod slots. This makes them highly desirable. High-end pieces, especially legendaries, can be obtained by defeating tough enemies, by completing quests, or – for those willing to invest heavily in their Technical Ability attribute – by crafting them.

Note that there is an additional, special category: **Iconic** items. These belong to a standard rarity rank (such as Epic), but they are one-of-a-kind pieces that typically have a distinct design, offer singular features, and can only be obtained in a very specific way. For instance, the Chaos gun switches to a new damage type every time you reload.

Modifications

All firearms and pieces of clothing can be equipped with modifications. Mod slots appear as small circles next to a piece's icon in your Inventory. As a rule, the greater the rarity level of an item, the more slots it offers for modification purposes.

Unadulterated weapons are naturally useful on their own, enabling you to deal damage based on the model you are currently wielding – but it should go without saying that mods can prove hugely beneficial. Being able to silence a firearm, to tailor the damage type inflicted to enemies, to install a scope, or to boost a parameter such as Crit Chance, are all obvious and desirable advantages.

The same general principle applies to clothing. Each piece of garment has an Armor value that grants you a defensive bonus. In addition, you can use any available mod slot to customize them with other boons – anything from resistance or immunity to status effects, to situational abilities such as making no noise as you land from a jump or fall.

Note that two items of the same clothing category, level, and rarity normally have identical data sheets. This system means that you can dress V exactly as you please, pushing the role-play factor to its maximum. You want your endgame solo V to wear a fancy limette dress and ballet pumps while gaining massive bonuses to your Crit Chance stat? With this system, everything is possible. You don't need to wrestle with choices between aesthetics and potency; you can have it *all*.

STASH

Every time you make a stop at your apartment, you can interact with your Stash – a small storage area by the living room. The same feature is also available by opening your car trunk, with your possessions pooled between the two.

You are free to transfer items from your Inventory to the Stash, and vice versa. Regularly filling your Stash with all sorts of weapons and ammo is a great way to ensure you can prepare quickly and efficiently before you head out on complex missions.

CRAFTING

Crafting is the act of creating new items (or to upgrade existing ones). To craft something in Cyberpunk 2077, you need two elements: specs (a recipe), and components (the ingredients). All of these can be gathered by exploring Night City and visiting vendors.

Once you have all the required items, select the item you wish to create at the main menu's Crafting section, and confirm your choice. It's as simple as that.

Perks in the Crafting skill tree play a crucial role when crafting. They will enable you, among other things, to accrue components more easily, to create more potent items, or even to have a chance to upgrade items for free. A master crafter can therefore potentially enjoy a superior range of high-quality weapons and gadgets. You can find a complete presentation of the crafting system on page 440.

WEIGHT

All items in your inventory have a weight attribute (). At first, you won't need to worry too much about it. As you accumulate gear, however, you will soon notice that the total weight of your items will approach your maximum carrying capacity, as displayed at the top of the Inventory menu. You can raise this cap by developing your Athletics skill but, even then, there's only so much you can keep in your backpack.

If you go beyond your maximum carrying capacity, V will endure a severe movement speed penalty. For this reason, it makes sense for you to engage in a spot of inventory management every now and then, divesting yourself of anything that serves no current or future purpose.

The most obvious way to get rid of unwanted items while making a profit is to sell them to a vendor. There's another method worth considering, though: dismantling. By holding △/Ⓨ while selecting an item, you can disassemble it – recycling it into crafting components that can then be used to craft other pieces.

COMPLETION ROADMAP

Offering a traditional linear strategy guide for Cyberpunk 2077 would be to do the game and those who play it a grave disservice. After all, a prescriptive approach to steering a player from prologue to epilogue would demand a standardized character build, which in turn would lead to a focus on one style of play, and deny the reader agency in favor of a so-called "optimal" path. This really wouldn't make for a good Cyberpunk 2077 playthrough, as we would strongly argue that the best route through the adventure is the one that **you** choose by virtue of every individual decision that you make.

This is why the vast majority of our mission walkthroughs for all main jobs and side jobs – plus a fair few minor secondary activities – reference multiple potential approaches, enabling you to devise a plan of action that suits your character build, moral compass, and preferred playstyle. The authors of this guide would like to serve as advisors on the journey you choose for your version of V – and not as taskmasters who lazily direct you to jump through the same sequence of hoops as everybody else.

In the absence of a straightforward A to B overarching walkthrough, then, this Completion Roadmap chapter has been designed as a hub for your first playthrough – and for those that will follow. No matter where you are in the story, you can always return here to make a decision on which new opportunity you might want to explore next.

Grab yourself a bookmark – you'll be returning to this chapter a lot.

NIGHT CITY
MEAT

INTRODUCTION

This Completion Roadmap chapter is designed to act as jumping-off point to the walkthroughs available in later pages, providing flowcharts and suggestions designed to assist your progression and overall play experience. The primary advantages of using it will be to discover when new missions become available, to obtain more generalized advice that may help your progression at key stages of the story, and to have the benefit of prior warning when you make choices that affect future events.

The chapter features five sections:

- This introductory section offers a quick overview of gameplay mechanics and features that you should ideally become familiar with early in the adventure.
- Next, you will find a flowchart that offers an at-a-glance overview that reveals how all jobs are unlocked (see page 98). If you plan on carving your own path through the game with a low level of assistance, this diagram offers a spoiler-free presentation of when you can begin major story episodes and side missions.
- To further prepare you to face the dangers of Night City, you will then find a diagram showing you the difficulty level range of each sub-district, giving a sense of which parts of the world are safe to explore based on your progression (see page 100).
- The difficulty diagram is followed by a directory of all jobs in the game (see page 101). As you may already have noticed, this guide uses abbreviations to refer to missions. For instance, the very first main job is labeled "MJ-01." This system is used consistently throughout the book, making it easy to track and identify quests.
- Last but definitely not least comes the completion roadmap itself (see page 102). This is where we offer a targeted overview for all main episodes of the core storyline, but also highlight optional objectives – within an appropriate level range – that you may want to complete along the way. Our guidance here will provide you with a general sense of what you might look to accomplish at any given time, with page references to detailed assistance in other chapters. We also include brief plot summaries of past events, and provide an overview of critical junctures where your decisions may affect future storyline events or mission availability.

PRIMER

The degree of freedom that Cyberpunk 2077 entrusts its players with can be a little surprising at first. For this reason, we strongly suggest that you take the time to read the Primer chapter (see page 70) to pick up advice and insights on subjects such as primary controls and features, the rhythm and structure of the game, and the many methods you can use to resolve situations.

If you do not wish to read the Primer yet and prefer to start playing right away, the following general advice will give you a brief rundown of essential points to consider as you begin.

CHARACTER SPECIALIZATION

During the character creation process at the beginning of the adventure, and every time you level up thereafter, you will receive points to spend on the five primary attributes: Body, Reflexes, Technical Ability, Intelligence, and Cool.

Your choices here are crucial. The attributes you develop will have positive ramifications on a whole subset of Skills, Perks, and abilities, enabling you, for instance, to become more resilient, more proficient with certain weapon types, or more adept at crafting items or hacking.

That said, you cannot excel in all areas, so you need to decide how you intend to specialize. Even opting to make your version of V a jack of all trades but a master of none is just another type of specialization: being moderately equipped for everything has its merits.

The developmental choices you make will affect your ability to use attribute requirements to your advantage. These correspond to actions or dialogue options that are only available if you have the required level in a given attribute. More often than not, having the proficiency necessary to unlock these can prove highly advantageous, enabling you to resolve situations in creative ways or bypass obstacles altogether – for example, by hacking a device or opening a door that a less adept V couldn't master.

Elect to become a genius techie and you will have access to all the doors and shutters that are gated behind Technical Ability requirements – while most of the other attribute requirements will

likely be closed to you. Conversely, split your points evenly across all attributes, and you will sometimes be able to pass multiple (low to medium) attribute requirements in one same area, and at other times fail to meet the requirements for any of them because they're too high. There is no right or wrong way to build your character – just choices with consequences. You can find a complete presentation of the system and ideas for prospective character builds on page 438.

STEALTH TACTICS

There are clear benefits to remaining undetected while you complete missions. This by no means implies that you should always try to infiltrate hostile areas with utmost care: if you have more fun riddling everything with bullets and causing as much chaos as possible, then you should not hesitate to do so. But if you favor stealth tactics, you can expect certain consistent advantages, including:

- The absence of enemy reinforcements (only sent if you are detected).
- Exclusive solutions to complete objectives (by triggering a conversation with a key individual, for example, which can sometimes lead to additional mission objectives).
- Occasional bonus rewards (awarded for completing optional objectives, many of which involve not raising the alarm).
- There are also certain conversations that can only occur if particular individuals live long enough to take part in them – moments that more trigger-happy players will often miss.

The following list of essential tips will help you to improve your proficiency at sneaking right under the nose of your opponents. For a more comprehensive presentation of the system, read our dedicated section on page 79.

- Crouching should be your default stance in all stealth scenarios. This makes you both silent and far less likely to be seen by hostile sentries.
- When on the move, stay as close as you can to solid objects such as crates and low walls. While crouched behind waist-high solid objects, you will usually remain concealed even if a guard directly on the other side looks in your direction.
- Preemptively tag as many guards (and surveillance cameras) as you can. Tagged targets are permanently surrounded by a colored outline, making it far easier to monitor their movements.
- Take the time to observe enemy patrol routes. Once you've identified their patterns, choosing your plan of action should pose little difficulty. For example, if you notice that an individual regularly stops for a few seconds in front of a computer, this is the perfect time to sneak past him.
- Avoid neutralizing foes when you could easily sneak past, but knock them out and hide the bodies when you can't. You will find various types of containers (such as crates and refrigerators) that will effectively remove bodies from the equation. This is important: when guards discover their unconscious allies, all troops in the area will subsequently enter an increased state of vigilance – which greatly complicates infiltrations.
- When you do need to incapacitate a foe, sneak up on them to perform a silent takedown. Most enemies are vulnerable to this staple technique. The exceptions are combatants who are multiple experience levels above you – they're always marked by a skull icon.
- Quickhacks offer a toolset almost tailor-made for stealth and pacifist playthroughs. You can experiment with functionality such as revealing all hostiles in the vicinity, taking control of surveillance cameras, remotely opening doors, making a target blind or deaf – and much more.

EQUIPMENT

There is a big range of items that you can acquire, whether from vendors, chest containers, or defeated enemies. Their importance can be profound, potentially enhancing your capabilities or providing much-needed health restoration while in the midst of a challenging battle.

Below, you will find a brief description of the principal item categories worth looking into:

- **Weapons** are the cornerstone of any strategy revolving around brute force – and indispensable emergency tools even for builds that focus on stealth. Each weapon has unique stats and properties, including possible special effects such as homing or piercing projectiles (for Smart and Tech weapons respectively). It often makes sense to specialize in a weapon type, as Skills and Perks that you gradually develop will make you more proficient with it.
- **Mods** can prove very potent too. These include things such as silencers that will enable you to pick off an awkward sentry with a clean headshot without alerting all the troops in the area.
- **Cyberware** also deserves your full attention. By visiting ripperdocs scattered around Night City, you can acquire all sorts of implants, each providing unique and often powerful boons: increased stats, resistance to status effects, health regeneration, or even brand-new abilities such as the double jump. Whenever you have money to spare, think cyberware.
- **Clothing** is not just a cosmetic choice, as all pieces also offer Armor. Furthermore, clothing can be improved via mods, adding further boons to their default stats, such as increased immunity to a given damage type, or even situational abilities such as making no noise as you land from a jump or fall.
- **Gadgets** are tools assigned to R1/RB. Press the button and they're activated. Grenades are included in this category.
- **Consumables** are items assigned to ✥, enabling you to activate them instantly while in the field. This is the most effective way to heal when things go awry.
- **Quickhacks** are the programs that you need to install on your cyberdeck to have access to the corresponding quickhacks. For instance, the Suicide quickhack will allow you to force an enemy to take their own life. Many such programs exist, enabling you to disable the cyberware of foes, cripple them with status effects, and so on.
- **Crafting** is the act of creating new items. As long as you have the required Perks, specs and components (the ingredients), you can craft virtually anything, including some of the most potent weapons in the game.

NAVIGATION & LEGEND

These simple tips will make you far more effective when navigating Night City:

- More often than not, it makes sense to fulfill optional objectives whenever you are passing through an area, particularly when you can arrange to start them and/or bring them to a conclusion *en route* to your next primary destination.
- Night City features dozens of fast travel terminals, as well as the NCART subway system. These enable you to move quickly to virtually anywhere on the map, expediting the process of traveling long distances.
- You have the ability to track points of interest, which will activate a route line on your mini-map. When you are not familiar with a specific sub-district, or struggle with the verticality of a tall building, this tool makes it far easier to get where you need to be.
- The mini-map shows a small portion of the main map that corresponds with your immediate surroundings. You will find the meaning of all key icons in the accompanying legend.
- Active enemies are represented by dots on the mini-map. Each individual's field of vision is also represented by a cone on the mini-map – a critical feature during stealth infiltrations. When an enemy has you in sight (causing their detection meter to start filling), their cone of vision increases in size and turns red: this is your cue to swiftly get behind suitable cover.
- Your mini-map features a compass. The N icon always points north. Whenever you are following cardinal directions, bear in mind that the compass rotates in real time as you move the camera.

Walkthrough Map Legend

Walkthrough Path	
Alternative Path	Padlock
Body Attribute Requirement Path	Body Attribute Requirement
Technical Ability Attribute Requirement Path	Technical Ability Attribute Requirement
Mission Objective	Boss
Surveillance Camera	Dialogue
Enemy	Clue
Turret	Elevator
Computer	Ladder

Map & Mini-Map Legend

V	Enemy (Unaware)
Your Vehicle	Enemy (Suspicious/ Combat Mode)
Main Job Waypoint	Client
Side Job Waypoint	Fixer
Cyberpsycho Sighting	Apartment
Gig Waypoints: Gun for Hire	Fast Travel
Search and Recover	Drop Point
Thievery	Clothing
Agent Saboteur	Ripperdoc
SOS: Merc Needed	Netrunner
Special Delivery	Techie
NCPD Scanner Hustle Waypoints: Assault in Progress	Weapon Shop
Suspected Organized Crime Activity	Melee Weapon Vendor
Reported Crime	Medpoint
Hidden Gem	Food
Tarot Card	Bar
Ally	Joytoy

GAMEPLAY VARIATIONS

One essential fact to acknowledge before you begin to use our Completion Roadmap (and the walkthroughs that follow it) is that the game as you experience it changes in realtime in accordance with a multitude of factors:

- Certain parameters can vary based on your current level. This includes, but is not limited to: whether an enemy can be grappled or not, the expected level of an attribute for a specific requirement, the amount of money required for a front payment in certain missions, the total damage you deal... and the list goes on and on.
- Almost all collectibles you can find in the game, including loot dropped by enemies and found in caches, are randomized. Likewise, rewards are either randomized or adjusted on the fly based on your current level.
- Enemy levels and mission difficulty scale based on your own character progression. As a consequence, what you experience in any given playthrough may differ radically from what others might encounter. One person's dread difficulty spike could be another person's cakewalk.
- The movement patterns of each individual guard become unpredictable the moment they suspect your presence and enter a state of increased vigilance. This happens most commonly when they find the body of one of your victims that you did not adequately conceal from sight.
- Missions that offer multiple possible resolutions can lead to completely different outcomes. For example: if you are sent to kill an individual but instead choose to let them live if they agree to leave Night City, you might find that their guards will not treat you as a hostile if you backtrack through the areas they occupy.

All of these features, and many other factors that we cannot hope to adequately detail here, mean that there is rarely a single best way to complete each mission. Instead, there are almost always multiple potential approaches – and each one could become redundant or require some additional measure of ingenuity to succeed after an unforeseen event.

This has influenced the format of our quest walkthroughs. Rather than attempting to insist on one best solution to follow blindly, we often offer possible scenarios and tactical advice gleaned from months of cumulative play time to help you to make your own informed decisions. Even if we tried to present standardized paths and foolproof methods, you would run the risk of constantly encountering variations or perceived errors. What if a guard we suggest to neutralize with a non-lethal takedown is immune to grapples in your playthrough because you're attempting to complete a mission while at a relatively low level? What if we recommend a specific quickhack as the ultimate way to defeat a boss, but you do not have it?

The very design of this game fosters creativity and regularly presents scenarios that are unique to each player. This is why we strongly recommend that you take the time to experiment. If you struggle with one line of approach, there's undoubtedly another one that you can try: a door that can be opened via an attribute requirement, a quickhack that can turn a problematic guard into a non-issue, or a unique weapon or cyberware type that can make short work of a tough opponent.

The game is a treasure trove of options and possibilities, and this book has been designed specifically to help you make the most of them. Whenever you explore a strategy, you should always be ready for some degree of improvisation should things not go exactly according to plan in your unique version of events.

GAME STRUCTURE FLOWCHART

This diagram shows the unlock order of all jobs in the game.

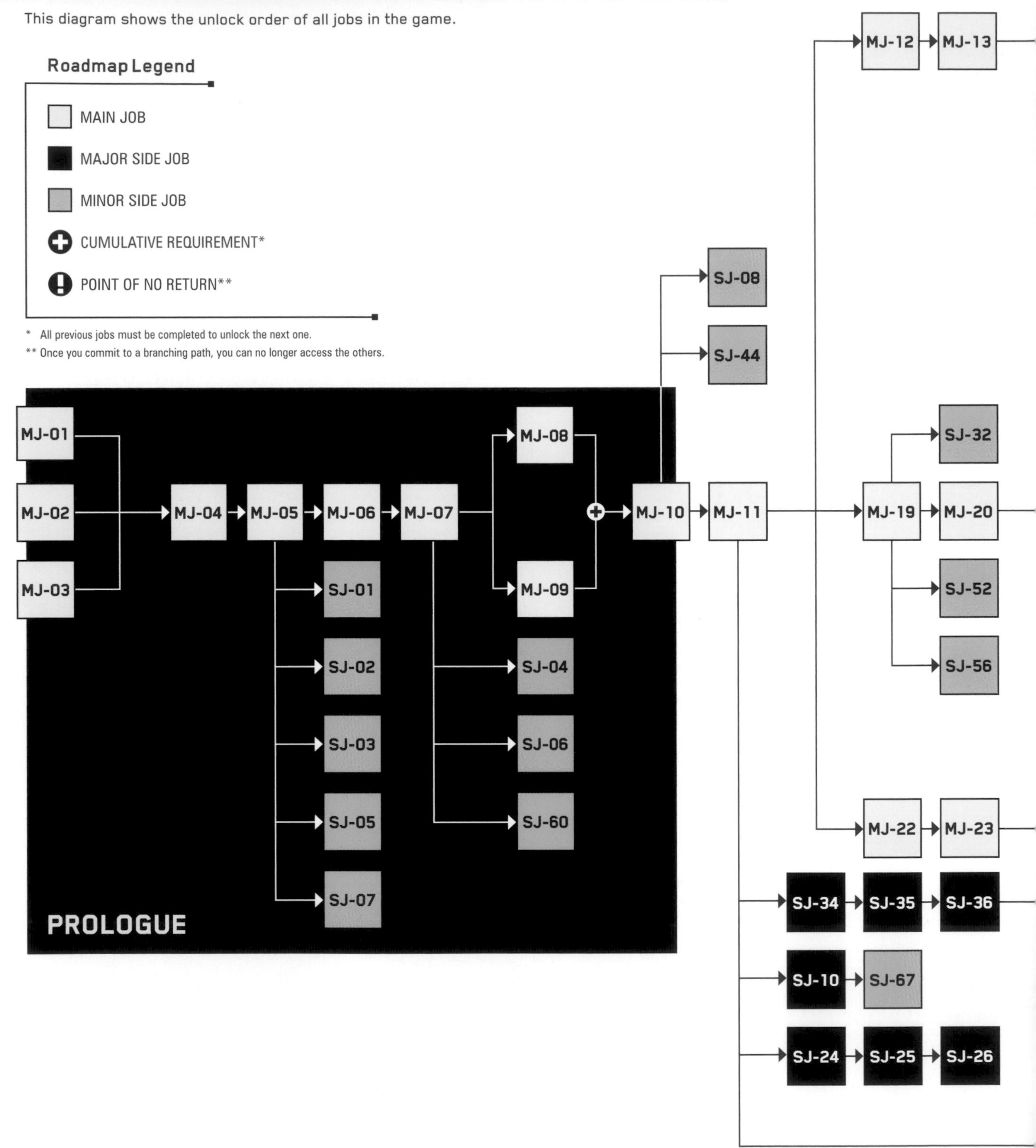

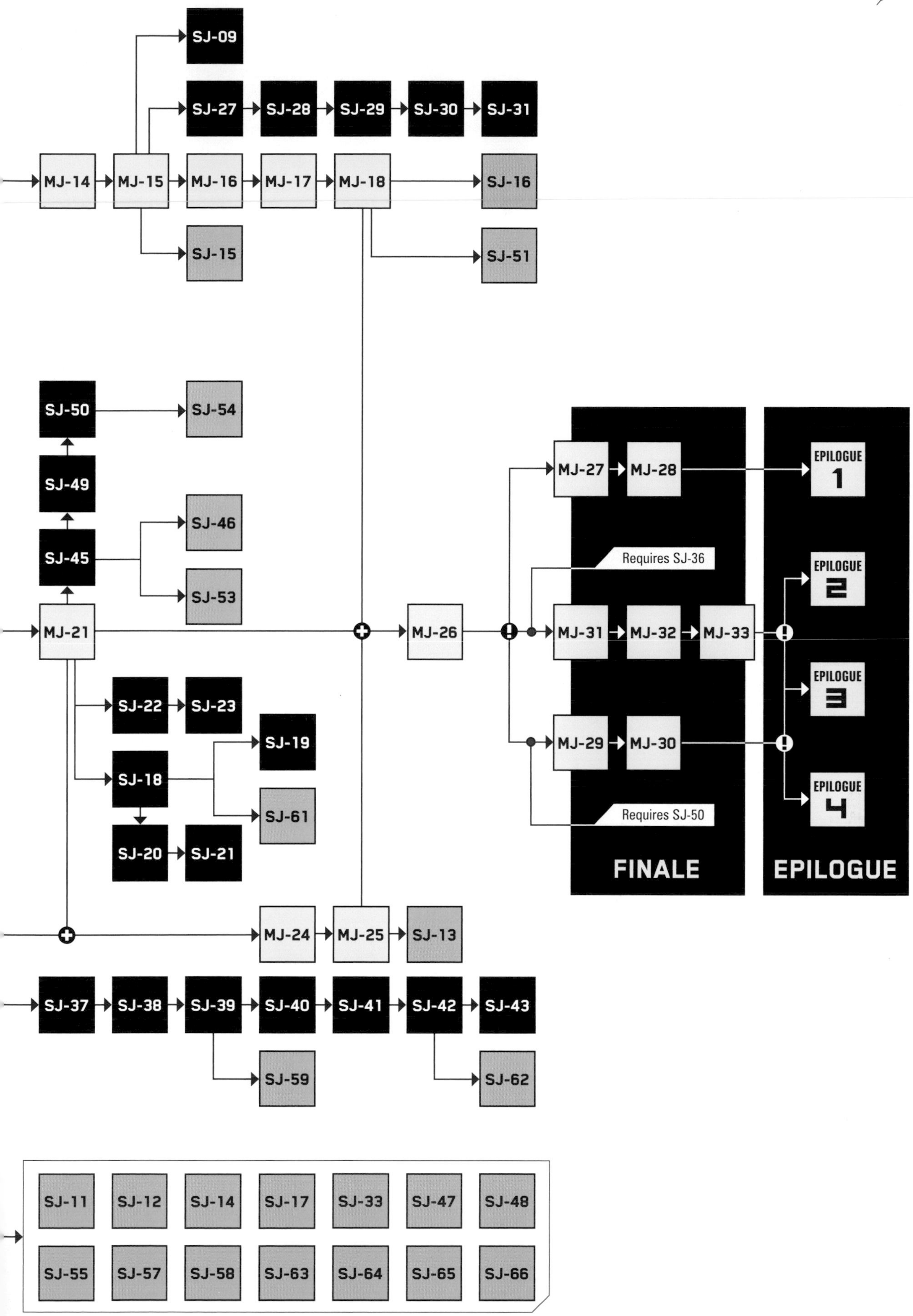

SJ-09
SJ-27 → SJ-28 → SJ-29 → SJ-30 → SJ-31
MJ-14 → MJ-15 → MJ-16 → MJ-17 → MJ-18 → SJ-16
SJ-15
SJ-51

SJ-50 → SJ-54
SJ-49
SJ-45
SJ-46
SJ-53
MJ-21 → MJ-26

MJ-27 → MJ-28 → EPILOGUE 1
Requires SJ-36
EPILOGUE 2
MJ-31 → MJ-32 → MJ-33
EPILOGUE 3
MJ-29 → MJ-30
EPILOGUE 4
Requires SJ-50

FINALE

EPILOGUE

SJ-22 → SJ-23
SJ-19
SJ-18
SJ-61
SJ-20 → SJ-21

MJ-24 → MJ-25 → SJ-13

SJ-37 → SJ-38 → SJ-39 → SJ-40 → SJ-41 → SJ-42 → SJ-43
SJ-59
SJ-62

SJ-11 SJ-12 SJ-14 SJ-17 SJ-33 SJ-47 SJ-48
SJ-55 SJ-57 SJ-58 SJ-63 SJ-64 SJ-65 SJ-66

OPEN WORLD DIFFICULTY

Districts and sub-districts each have a specific difficulty level range, which broadly corresponds to how challenging activities in the area tend to be. Though you are entirely free to explore and take in the sights of Night City after you complete the Prologue, it makes sense to take into account how tough enemy encounters might be before you begin stirring up trouble in a region.

This diagram shows you the difficulty level range of each location, which should enable you to better plan your journeys and activities to avoid difficulty spikes.

Difficulty Level Range Per District

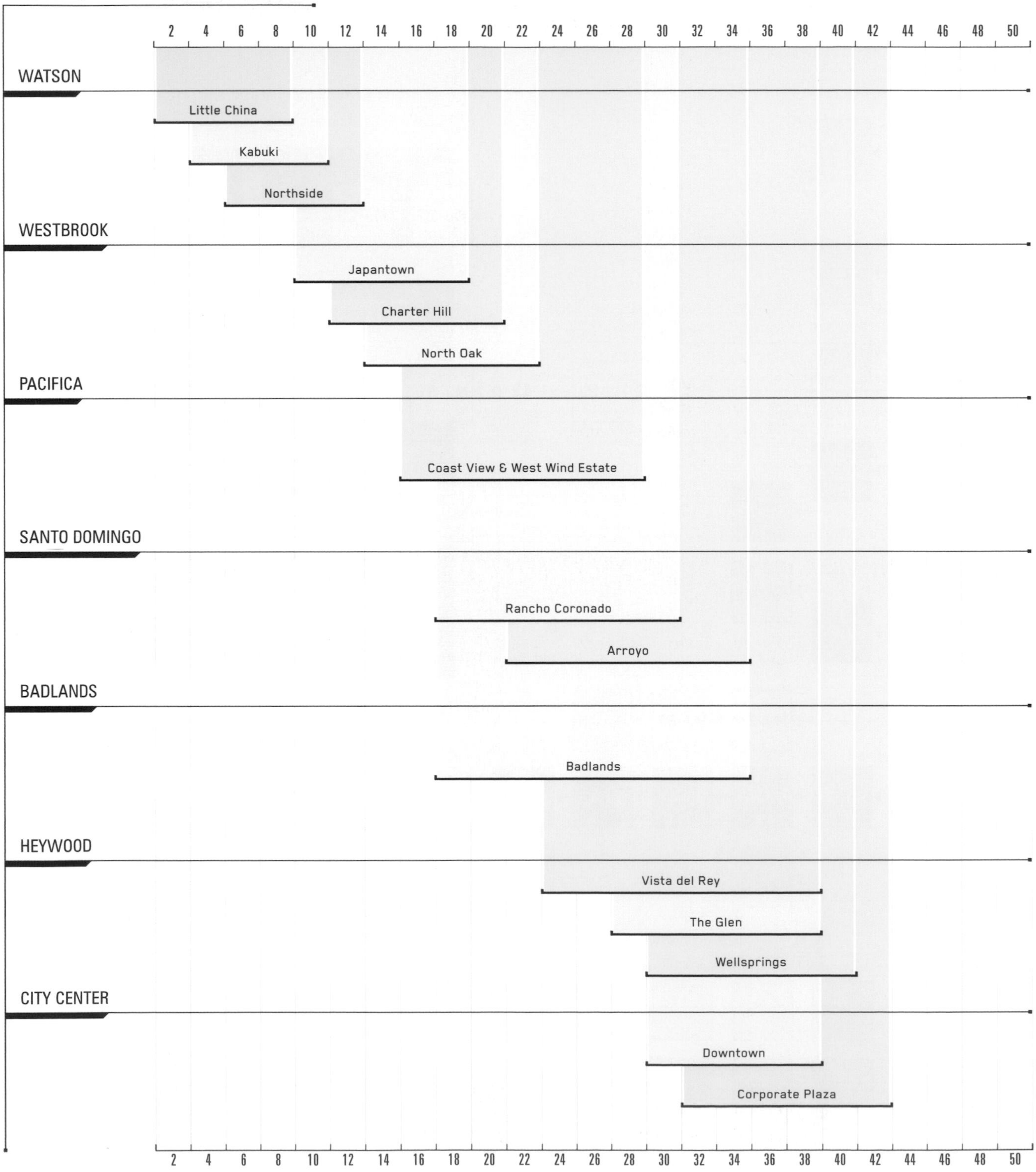

2 4 6 8 10 12 14 16 18 20 22 24 26 28 30 32 34 36 38 40 42 44 46 48 50

WATSON

Little China

Kabuki

Northside

WESTBROOK

Japantown

Charter Hill

North Oak

PACIFICA

Coast View & West Wind Estate

SANTO DOMINGO

Rancho Coronado

Arroyo

BADLANDS

Badlands

HEYWOOD

Vista del Rey

The Glen

Wellsprings

CITY CENTER

Downtown

Corporate Plaza

2 4 6 8 10 12 14 16 18 20 22 24 26 28 30 32 34 36 38 40 42 44 46 48 50

QUEST DIRECTORY

Main Job Directory

Name	#	Page
Automatic Love	MJ-12	134
Belly of the Beast	MJ-33	176
Disasterpiece	MJ-14	139
Double Life	MJ-15	142
Down on the Street	MJ-22	155
For Whom the Bell Tolls	MJ-29	172
Forward to Death	MJ-32	175
Ghost Town	MJ-19	149
Gimme Danger	MJ-23	156
I Walk the Line	MJ-17	144
Knockin' On Heaven's Door	MJ-30	172
Last Caress	MJ-27	166
Life During Wartime	MJ-21	152
Lightning Breaks	MJ-20	151
M'ap Tann Pèlen	MJ-16	143
Nocturne Op55N1	MJ-26	164
Play It Safe	MJ-24	158

Name	#	Page
Playing for Time	MJ-11	132
Practice Makes Perfect	MJ-04	115
Search and Destroy	MJ-25	162
The Corpo-Rat	MJ-03	115
The Heist	MJ-10	128
The Information	MJ-09	126
The Nomad	MJ-01	113
The Pickup	MJ-08	120
The Rescue	MJ-05	116
The Ride	MJ-07	119
The Ripperdoc	MJ-06	118
The Space in Between	MJ-13	138
The Street Kid	MJ-02	114
Totalimmortal	MJ-28	168
Transmission	MJ-18	148
We Gotta Live Together	MJ-31	174

Side Job Directory

Name	#	Page
A Day in the Life	SJ-47	230
A Like Supreme	SJ-39	222
Beat on the Brat	SJ-01	181
Big in Japan	SJ-08	187
Blistering Love	SJ-36	218
Boat Drinks	SJ-43	224
Both Sides, Now	SJ-27	209
Bullets	SJ-64	243
Burning Desire / Night Moves	SJ-04	184
Chippin' In	SJ-35	216
Coin Operated Boy	SJ-17	195
Don't Lose Your Mind	SJ-26	207
Dream On	SJ-19	198
Every Breath You Take	SJ-62	242
Ex-Factor	SJ-28	209
Ezekiel Saw the Wheel	SJ-55	236
Following the River	SJ-21	202
Fool on the Hill	SJ-44	225
Fortunate Son	SJ-54	236
Full Disclosure	SJ-15	193
Gun Music	SJ-46	230
Happy Together	SJ-12	191
Heroes	SJ-10	189

Name	#	Page
Holdin' on	SJ-37	219
Human Nature	SJ-24	205
I Don't Wanna Hear It	SJ-41	223
I Fought the Law	SJ-18	196
I'll Fly Away	SJ-53	235
Imagine	SJ-48	231
Killing in the Name	SJ-59	239
Kold Mirage	SJ-56	237
Losing my Religion/Sacrum Profanum	SJ-06	215
Love Rollercoaster	SJ-33	186
Machine Gun	SJ-63	242
Off the Leash	SJ-42	224
Only Pain	SJ-66	244
Pisces	SJ-30	211
Pyramid Song	SJ-31	212
Queen of the Highway	SJ-50	233
Raymond Chandler Evening	SJ-65	244
Rebel! Rebel!	SJ-40	222
Riders on the Storm	SJ-45	228
Second Conflict	SJ-38	220
Send in the Clowns	SJ-16	194
Shoot to Thrill	SJ-11	190
Sinnerman	SJ-22	203

Name	#	Page
Small Man, Big Mouth	SJ-67	245
Space Oddity	SJ-57	238
Spellbound	SJ-32	214
Stadium Love	SJ-58	238
Sweet Dreams	SJ-61	241
Talkin' 'Bout a Revolution	SJ-29	210
Tapeworm	SJ-34	215
The Ballad of Buck Ravers	SJ-14	193
The Beast in Me	SJ-09	188
The Gift	SJ-03	183
The Gig	SJ-07	186
The Gun	SJ-02	183
The Highwayman	SJ-60	240
The Hunt	SJ-20	200
The Prophet's Song	SJ-05	184
These Boots Are Made for Walkin'	SJ-52	235
They Won't Go When I Go	SJ-23	204
Tune Up & Epistrophy	SJ-25	205
Violence	SJ-13	192
War Pigs	SJ-51	234
With a Little Help from my Friends	SJ-49	232

COMPLETION ROADMAP

PROLOGUE

Recommended Level: 1-7

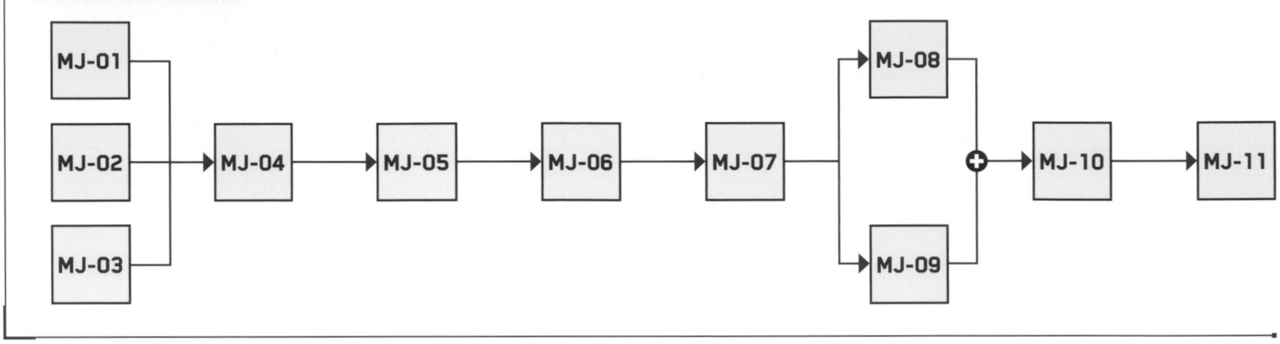

MJ-01, MJ-02, MJ-03 → MJ-04 → MJ-05 → MJ-06 → MJ-07 → MJ-08 / MJ-09 → MJ-10 → MJ-11

THE STORY SO FAR

After V and Jackie meet during your chosen origin story, they decide to team up, with the shared goal of becoming legendary mercenaries. Completing relatively minor gigs at first, they eventually draw the attention of a major fixer: Dexter DeShawn.

Dex offers them a high-risk, high-reward job, the opportunity of a lifetime: stealing the Relic, Arasaka's most prized and well-guarded piece of technology. This device is said to allow human minds to be copied as engrams onto shards that can be slotted into one's neural port, enabling a user to hear and see digitized personality constructs.

Some preparations are required for the heist: retrieving the Flathead (a military spiderbot prototype) from Maelstrom thugs, and meeting with Evelyn Parker (the client behind the whole operation) to scout the room where the Relic is concealed. This is achieved during a braindance session with the assistance of an expert BD editor by the name of Judy Alvarez.

OPTIONAL ACTIVITIES

#	Name	Page
SJ-01	Beat on the Brat – Champion of Kabuki	181
SJ-02	The Gun	183
SJ-03	The Gift	183
SJ-04	Burning Desire / Night Moves	184
SJ-05	The Prophet's Song	184
SJ-06	Losing my Religion / Sacrum Profanum	186
01	Playing for Keeps	262
02	Catch a Tyger's Toe	262
03	Bloodsport	263
05	Welcome to America, Comrade	264
06	Troublesome Neighbors	264
07	Woman of la Mancha	265
08	Shark in the Water	265
09	Monster Hunt	266
961	Cyberpsycho Sighting: Little China	249

MOMENTOUS DECISIONS

- **MJ-03 ("The Corpo-Rat" – see page 115)** – If you take the time to talk to Frank and explore all available conversation options, he will remember it, slightly altering his behavior in a future side job (SJ-51, "War Pigs" - see page 234).
- **MJ-08 ("The Pickup" – see page 120)** – How you choose to proceed to retrieve the Flathead will affect a later side job (SJ-38, "Second Conflict" – see page 123 for details).
- **MJ-10 ("The Heist" – see page 128)** – Just before you leave Delamain's cab after your escape from Konpeki Plaza, you need to decide what to do with the remains of the deceased. If you send them to his family or tell Delamain to wait until you return, you will unlock an exclusive side job (SJ-10, "Heroes"). If you send them to Viktor, you will instead have access to extra dialogue and scenes regarding the character in question in later main jobs.
- **MJ-11 ("Playing for Time" – see page 132)** – After your meeting with Takemura at Tom's Diner, you can subsequently access three distinct branches of the main storyline: finding Evelyn Parker, locating Anders Hellman, and (a little later) cooperating with Takemura.

UNIQUES & MISSABLES

- The Chaos pistol can be obtained during MJ-08 ("The Pickup" – see page 120) by looting Royce after neutralizing him either during the deal sequence or the boss fight. This powerful weapon's damage type is randomized every time you reload.
- The Kongou pistol can be found on the nightstand next to Yorinobu's bed in his penthouse during MJ-10 ("The Heist" – see page 128). This triggers ricochet effects without necessitating additional cyberware.
- After T-Bug opens the penthouse's balcony door during MJ-10 ("The Heist" – see page 128), climb up the stairs leading to the AV landing pad: the Satori katana lies inside the vehicle.
- Don't miss the Fenrir SMG on the table near the monk you need to rescue during SJ-06 ("Losing My Religion" – see page 186). This deals thermal damage, with increased odds to apply the Burn status effect.
- The O'Five can be collected during SJ-01 ("Beat on the Brat: Champion of Arroyo" – see page 181) after neutralizing Buck. This sniper rifle shoots explosive projectiles.

FINDING EVELYN PARKER

Recommended Level: 8-10

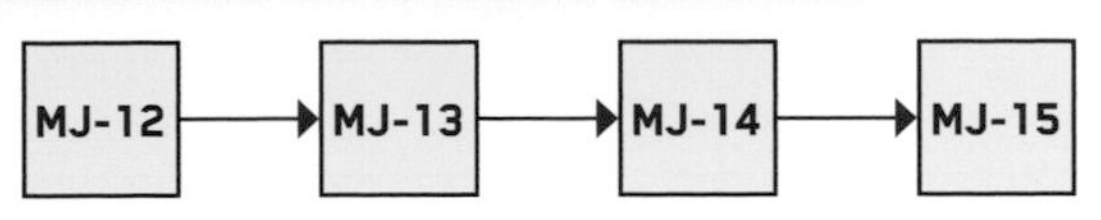

THE STORY SO FAR

Spoiler Warning: do not read any further until you have completed MJ-11 ("Playing for Time").

After the thwarted heist and your apparent demise, you find yourself resurrected thanks to the Relic, which you had to insert into your own neural port.

The good news is that you cheated death somehow. The bad news is that so too did your new brainpan bunkmate. Viktor makes a somber diagnostic: the personality of legendary musician (and alleged terrorist) Johnny Silverhand, who was stored on the Relic, has leaked from the shard. Silverhand now dwells within you, and slowly but surely spreads. It is only a matter of months before he asserts full control.

You now have a number one priority: finding a way to extract Silverhand from your body. One of your main leads is Evelyn Parker, the client who hired you for the heist. As she seems to have vanished into thin air, your best hope is to contact her associate, Judy Alvarez. Judy reveals that Evelyn used to be a doll and has since returned to the club where she was once an employee: Clouds. And so begins an investigation that sees you explore Night City at its ugliest.

OPTIONAL ACTIVITIES

#	Name	Page
SJ-07	The Gig	186
SJ-08	Big in Japan	187
SJ-09	The Beast in Me	188
SJ-10	Heroes	189
SJ-11	Shoot to Thrill	190
SJ-12	Happy Together	191
SJ-14	The Ballad of Buck Ravers	193
SJ-15	Full Disclosure	193
SJ-17	Coin Operated Boy	195
SJ-19	Dream On	198
SJ-20	The Hunt	200
SJ-21	Following the River	202
04	The Heisenberg Principle	263
10	Backs Against the Wall	267
11	Small Man, Big Evil	269
12	Last Login	268
14	Hippocratic Oath	270
15	Flight of the Cheetah	271
16	Dirty Biz	271
17	Many Ways to Skin a Cat	272
18	Rite of Passage	272
962	Cyberpsycho Sighting: Demons of War	249
963	Cyberpsycho Sighting: Help is on the Way	250

MOMENTOUS DECISIONS

- **MJ-12 ("Automatic Love" – see page 134)** – If you manage to avoid conflict in the Clouds club, and successfully interrogate Woodman, you will get a chance to run into him again during a later side job (SJ-28, "Ex-Factor" – see page 209).
- **SJ-09 ("The Beast in Me" – see page 188)** – When Sampson pulls off toward the end of the final race, the side job has three possible conclusions. You can ignore Claire's request and stay in the race, which will evoke her fury and cause her to be hostile when you later encounter her at Afterlife (though she is, it must be said, a character of no consequence after this story has concluded). If you opt to abandon the race and go after Sampson, an accident will occur: you can then either let Claire kill him to avenge her late husband or, if you attempted to talk Claire out of killing Sampson after the Santo Domingo race, you can convince her to let it go – and save Sampson's life.
- **SJ-12 ("Happy Together" – see page 191)** – If you fail to find out about the niche at the North Oak columbarium, things do not end well for Barry.
- **SJ-20 ("The Hunt" – see page 200)** – If you plan on making River your romantic partner, you must obtain the best outcome in this quest by heading straight to the correct farm. Should you guess wrong, this will permanently lock the next quest in line involving River, along with the possibility of ever having a more meaningful relationship with him. Additionally, in the final conversation after you find Randy alive, you should either try to convince River that vengeance will ultimately not make him feel any better, or tell him that you're happy to help him.
- **SJ-21 ("Following the River" – see page 202)** – If you want to enter a romantic relationship with River, choose the relevant dialogue options during the scene atop the water tower, and make sure you elect to kiss him in both instances where you are given the chance – and to confirm your interest the next morning. If you opt for any line where you say that you're not looking for a relationship, you will instead remain friends for the rest of the story.

UNIQUES & MISSABLES

- The Plan B pistol can be looted from Dex's body in the scrapyard after MJ-11 ("Playing for Time" – see page 132).
- The Cocktail Stick katana can be found in the make-up room of the Clouds club, upstairs, during MJ-12 ("Automatic Love" – see page 134).
- The Second Opinion pistol can be picked up in the office adjacent to Woodman's during MJ-12 ("Automatic Love" – see page 134).
- The Cottonmouth can be collected in Fingers' bedroom during MJ-13 ("The Space In Between" – see page 138).
- The Dying Night pistol is your reward if you manage to win the shooting contest during SJ-11 ("Shoot to Thrill" – see page 190).
- After you complete SJ-10 ("Heroes" – see page 189), you can find the La Chingona Dorada pistol on the table where all the offerings were displayed.
- The Tinker Bell blunt weapon is found under the tree closest to Peter Pan's house on the Edgewood farm during SJ-20 ("The Hunt" – see page 200).

MEETING THE VOODOO BOYS

Recommended Level: 11-12

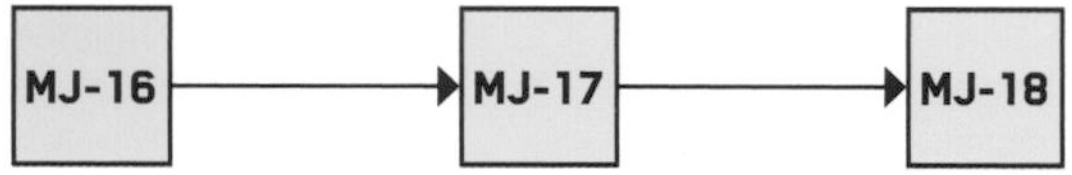

THE STORY SO FAR

Spoiler Warning: do not read any further until you have completed MJ-15 ("Double Life").

Your first lead to find a way to get rid of the Relic, Evelyn Parker, proved disappointing. Not only was Evelyn in no condition to assist you, having been hacked remotely by powerful netrunners while working at the Clouds club, but it also transpires she was naught but a single disposable piece in play on a crowded chess board.

The people who hired Parker are members of the Voodoo Boys – a gang of dangerous netrunners on a quest to uncover the secrets of cyberspace. They were clearly hoping that the Relic could somehow allow them to further their interests.

If the Voodoo Boys are so well informed about the Relic, surely they can help you to safely extract the shard from your body – along with the engram of Johnny Silverhand. The only way to find out is to meet them in their den, in Pacifica.

OPTIONAL ACTIVITIES

#	Name	Page
SJ-16	Send in the Clowns	194
SJ-23	They Won't Go When I Go	204
SJ-24	Human Nature	205
SJ-25	Tune Up & Epistrophy	205
SJ-26	Don't Lose Your Mind	207
13	Fixer, Merc, Soldier, Spy	269
19	Scrolls Before Swine	273
20	Occupational Hazard	273
21	Freedom of the Press	274
22	Lousy Kleppers	274
964	Cyberpsycho Sighting: Bloody Ritual	250
965	Cyberpsycho Sighting: Where the Bodies Hit the Floor	251
966	Cyberpsycho Sighting: Six Feet Under	251

MOMENTOUS DECISIONS

- **MJ-17 ("I Walk the Line" – see page 144)** – Once you meet the NetWatch agent inside the Grand Imperial Mall's cinema, you have an important decision to make. If you accept his deal, this will have grim consequences for Brigitte and her netrunners (thereafter causing the Voodoo Boys to regard you with hostility). Should you refuse, it's the agent who will suffer.

- **SJ-22 ("Sinnerman") & SJ-23 ("They Won't Go When I Go" – see page 203)** – The success of Joshua's braindance is determined by specific lines of dialogue that you can choose during your conversations with him. Broadly, encouragement is the way to go if you are determined to see this story through to its conclusion.

- **SJ-26 ("Don't Lose Your Mind" – see page 207)** – When you gain access to the core chamber, you have to choose between up to three options, which will determine Delamain's future. You can destroy the core to liberate the divergent Delamains, reset the core to restore the original Delamain, or hack the core to merge all of the Delamains. The Delamain installed on the vehicle (and, therefore, your conversations with him) will directly depend on the decision you make, and remain fixed for the rest of your playthrough.

UNIQUES & MISSABLES

- The Sir John Phallustiff can be obtained by completing the following steps: call Stout before you head to the All Foods warehouse during MJ-08 ("The Pickup" – see page 120), then accept her credchip and use it to buy the Flathead without cracking the chip or warning Royce. A few days later, Stout will message you and offer to meet at the No-Tell Motel: attend, and the weapon can be found as a collectible in the room after your liaison.

- The Mox shotgun is given to you by Judy if you share a romantic relationship with her, or after MJ-12 ("Automatic Love" – see page 134) if she decides to leave Night City. This enjoys a reduced reload speed and lowered spread while aiming.

FINDING ANDERS HELLMAN

Recommended Level: 13-16

MJ-19 → MJ-20 → MJ-21

THE STORY SO FAR

Spoiler Warning: do not read any further until you have completed MJ-18 ("Transmission").

After your encounter with the Voodoo Boys, you are back at square one. The Pacifica netrunners had neither the knowledge nor the technology to extract the Relic from your body. The only reason they were interested in the shard is that they hoped to be able to make contact with Alt Cunningham – Silverhand's ex-lover.

Cunningham, one of the best netrunners on the planet in the early years of the 21st century, is the woman who developed a revolutionary technology called Soulkiller. Her program could instantly eliminate any target connected to cyberspace and digitize their mind as an engram. She intended for it to be a weapon against powerful corporations such as Arasaka, keeping them in check in cyberspace – but with bitter irony, the corporation stole her work and repurposed it for their benefit.

Cunningham felt forced to use the program on herself, digitizing her persona (physically dying in the process) and escaping into cyberspace. Years of existing in uncharted cyberterritories, beyond the Blackwall, has severely altered Alt's consciousness. Today, she is much more rogue AI than human. The last link to her past life is Johnny Silverhand, and this is exactly why the Voodoo Boys were interested in the Relic in the first place: to convince Alt to let them join her past the Blackwall.

But if the Voodoo Boys turned out to be powerless, maybe Anders Hellman won't be. Hellman is Arasaka's leading bioengineer – an expert in neural networks, with a number of ground-breaking patents under his belt. Using Soukiller's source code, Hellman has created a piece of technology enabling much more than mere communication with engrams. The theoretical goal is to generate an enhanced personality construct capable of independent function and re-implantation into a new organic host-body – such is the truth behind the Relic project. This explains how Silverhand is slowing but surely taking over V's body.

At this point, you turn to the best fixer in town, and former dear friend of Johnny Silverhand: Rogue Amendiares. Rogue introduces you to a Nomad by the name of Panam and lays out the framework of a plan in which you could down a high-security AV from the sky to kidnap the VIP transported inside: Hellman.

OPTIONAL ACTIVITIES

#	Name	Page
SJ-18	I Fought The Law	196
SJ-22	Sinnerman	203
SJ-27	Both Sides, Now	209
SJ-28	Ex-Factor	209
SJ-29	Talkin' 'Bout a Revolution	210
SJ-30	Pisces	211
SJ-31	Pyramid Song	212
SJ-32	Spellbound	214
SJ-33	Love Rollercoaster	215
23	Olive Branch	275
24	We Have Your Wife	275
25	Greed Never Pays	276
27	Wakako's Favorite	277
29	Until Death Do Us Part	278
30	Tyger and Vulture	279

MOMENTOUS DECISIONS

- **MJ-19 ("Ghost Town" – see page 149)** – After you retrieve the Thorton, you have to choose between helping Panam to get her revenge on Nash, the former partner who betrayed her, or convincing her to stick to the original plan. If you agree to help, both of you head into the Raffen Shiv hideout in the nearby mines, where a major combat encounter will take place. If you instead refuse, you will skip the battle in question.
- **MJ-21 ("Life During Wartime" – see page 152)** – During the hostage situation, you can get the pilot to reveal where Hellman was taken. Achieving this means that you can go straight to the gas station, with limited enemy forces on site. Otherwise you will have to find Hellman's whereabouts on your own, leading to an increased enemy presence when you arrive.
- **SJ-28 ("Ex-Factor" – see page 209)** – How the conversation with Maiko unfolds depends on how you completed MJ-12 ("Automatic Love"). If you achieved a result where Woodman is still alive, and now avoid any potential forms of provocation during your discussion with Maiko, she will reveal that he is in the building, giving you a chance to kill him if you wish.
- **SJ-30 ("Pisces" – see page 211)** – When you reach Hiromi's office in the penthouse, Maiko confronts you with a choice. Whether or not you play along with her plan and accept her payment, or refuse it, are choices that will determine if Maiko becomes the new boss of Clouds. Your decisions will also affect access to the "Pyramid Song" side job and the possibility of romancing Judy.
- **SJ-31 ("Pyramid Song" – see page 212)** – If you meet the relevant criteria, this is the quest that can enable you to enter into a romantic relationship with Judy.

UNIQUES & MISSABLES

- The Widow Maker is a precision rifle that can be looted from Nash after defeating him during MJ-19 ("Ghost Town" – see page 149). It fires two projectiles per shot and deals chemical damage, with an increased chance to apply Poison and extra damage for charged shots.
- The Tsumetogi katana can be looted from the room where the meeting with Maiko and the Tyger Claw bosses take place during SJ-30 ("Pisces" – see page 211). It deals electrical damage with a chance to apply Shock, and also increases your electrical resistance.

COOPERATING WITH TAKEMURA

Recommended Level: 17-20

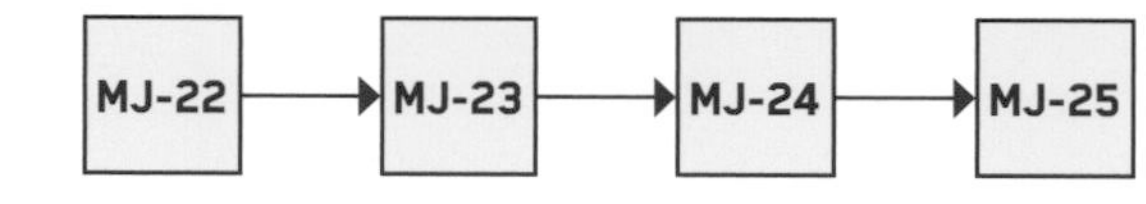

THE STORY SO FAR

Spoiler Warning: do not read any further until you have completed MJ-21 ("Life During Wartime").

Locating Anders Hellman proved a little more labor-intensive than anticipated. You first had to do Panam a favor by helping her to retrieve her vehicle from Raffen Shiv thugs. With her Thorton secured, she agreed to help you in return, drawing from her Nomad knowledge and experience to finalize the plan suggested by Rogue.

After successfully downing the AV transporting Hellman and extracting him from the gas station where he sought to hide, your hopes of finding a solution to remove the Relic from your body are soon dashed. According to Hellman, not only is the procedure something that could only be attempted by best-in-class specialists equipped with bleeding-edge prototype technology from Arasaka, it's also most likely impossible.

This leaves you with one final avenue to explore: cooperating with Takemura in an attempt to arrange a meeting with Hanako Arasaka, heiress to the corporate empire that bears her family's name.

OPTIONAL ACTIVITIES

#	Name	Page
SJ-13	Violence	192
SJ-35	Chippin' In	216
SJ-36	Blistering Love	218
SJ-37	Holdin' On	219
SJ-38	Second Conflict	220
SJ-39	A Like Supreme	222
SJ-40	Rebel! Rebel!	222
SJ-41	I Don't Wanna Hear It	223
SJ-42	Off the Leash	224
SJ-43	Boat Drinks	224
SJ-44	Fool on the Hill	225
SJ-45	Riders on the Storm	228
SJ-46	Gun Music	230
SJ-47	A Day In The Life	230
SJ-48	Imagine	231
SJ-49	With a Little Help from my Friends	232
SJ-50	Queen of the Highway	233
SJ-51	War Pigs	234
SJ-53	I'll Fly Away	235
26	A Shrine Defiled	276
28	Getting Warmer…	277
31	Family Heirloom	279
44	Flying Drugs	287

MOMENTOUS DECISIONS

- **MJ-23 ("Gimme Danger" – see page 156)** – After you visit the security room at the Japantown market, you can opt to join Takemura on a reconnaissance expedition at the Arasaka Industrial Park, or let him take care of it on his own. If you accompany him, Takemura will share important details regarding Jackie if you chose to send his body to Viktor rather than his family at the end of MJ-10 ("The Heist"). The reconnaissance scene also gives you an opportunity to cement a friendship with Takemura, which will alter various dialogue exchanges you have with him over the course of the story.

- **MJ-25 ("Search and Destroy" – see page 162)** – After your meeting with Hanako, there is an important optional objective that you may wish to attend to before you escape the building: rescuing Takemura. Choosing not to save him will mean that he takes no further part in the story. Conversely, rescuing him will give you a chance to go through important events with him during one of the game's possible finales.

- **SJ-35 ("Chippin' In" – see page 216)** – By retrieving the key from Grayson, you have an opportunity to acquire Johnny's old Porsche. Perhaps more importantly, during the scene near Johnny's grave in the oil fields, your dialogue choices will determine whether or not you become friends with Johnny. Your behavior here has important ramifications, in terms of both role-play (influencing future dialogue) and gameplay. Most pertinently, you must become friends with Johnny to gain access to the next side job in this quest line (SJ-36, "Blistering Love").

- **SJ-36 ("Blistering Love" – see page 218)** – By completing this quest, you unlock the game's optional finale that involves Rogue.

- **SJ-41 ("I Don't Wanna Hear It" – see page 223)** – If you resolve the situation with the Us Cracks with a positive outcome, they and Kerry will reach an agreement and release a song and video together in a later side job. You will also unlock a minor side job (SJ-62, "Every Breath You Take" – see page 242). If you react angrily and threaten the Us Cracks, on the other hand, these two events will not take place.

- **SJ-45 ("Riders on the Storm" – see page 228)** – This quest will end prematurely if you fail to meet Panam at the Raffen Shiv camp within 24 in-game hours. During your night at the Ingalls farm, make sure you flirt with Panam if you would like to make her your romantic partner.

- **SJ-53 ("I'll Fly Away" – see page 235)** – This quest is initially not represented by a waypoint, and it can be missed. You must complete it before you trigger SJ-50 ("Queen of the Highway"), otherwise it will become unavailable for the rest of your current playthrough.

- **SJ-49 ("With a Little Help from My Friends" – see page 232)** – If you choose to disclose Panam's plan to Saul, this storyline will end immediately, Panam will cut all ties (abruptly ending any possibility of a romantic relationship), and a potential game ending involving the Aldecaldos will be made unavailable in your current playthrough. Later, during your conversation with Panam at the junction, make sure you do *not* imply that you're helping her for the money if you aspire to have her become your romantic partner.

- **SJ-50 ("Queen of the Highway" – see page 233)** – After familiarizing yourself with the Basilisk controls and concluding the neural synchronization tests with Panam, you have an opportunity to formalize a romantic relationship with her when she asks you if you want to push the synchronization further. By completing this storyline, you also unlock one of the game's unique finales.

UNIQUES & MISSABLES

- Prototype Shingen: Mark V can be found in shipping container 667 in front of the warehouse during MJ-23 ("Gimme Danger" – see page 156). It fires explosive rounds, and its bullets can target up to three enemies when aiming.

- The Genjiroh pistol can be found behind a closed door on the way to the second sniper during MJ-24 ("Play it Safe" – see page 158). The door in question is located on your right when you walk out of the elevator, just before you reach the long ladder on floor 21. It's gated behind a Technical Ability requirement, but you can alternatively open it via the nearby terminal (the code is 2906). This handgun has multiple special properties.

- Don't forget to collect Oda's Jinchu-maru after you defeat him during MJ-24 ("Play it Safe" – see page 158). Its Crit Chance is increased to 100% while Kerenzikov is active, and its final combo attacks deal enormous amounts of damage.

- The Doom Doom revolver can be obtained during SJ-38 ("Second Conflict" – see page 220) by looting Dum Dum in the Totentantz club; note that this is only possible if you engineered a scenario in which Dum Dum did not die during MJ-08. It fires multiple rounds with increased power and fire rate, though this comes at the expense of increased recoil and bullet spread.

- The Gold-plated baseball bat is available at Denny's villa during SJ-38 ("Second Conflict" – see page 220). After the scene where Denny, Henry, and Kerry argue, Denny throws the bat into the pool, at which point you can retrieve it. It has a high chance to apply Bleeding, and a low chance to stun targets.

- The Apparition can be looted from Frank's body after SJ-51 ("War Pigs" – see page 234). This increases Critical Chance, fire rate, reload speed, and damage when your health is very low. Charged shots deal double damage.

- The Problem Solver is an SMG dropped by the large enemy guarding the Wraith camp's front entrance in SJ-45 ("Riders on the Storm" – see page 228). It boasts an increased ammo clip size and fire rate.

- While completing the Family Heirloom gig, don't miss the opportunity to collect Johnny's Shoes in the locker containing the bootleg you're after. This is part of a set required to earn a Trophy/Achievement.

FINALE

Recommended Level: 21-50

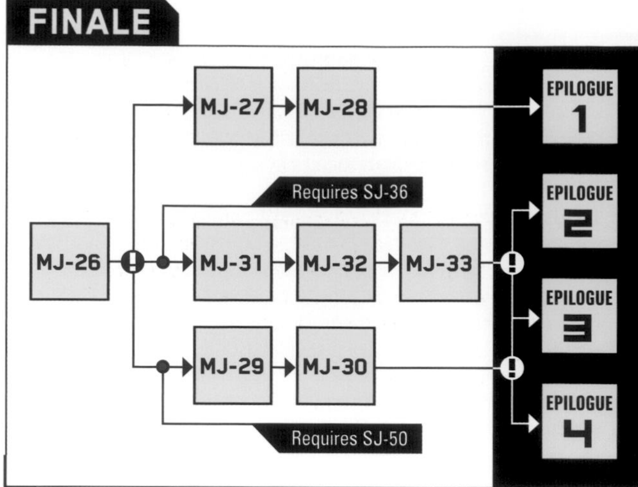

THE STORY SO FAR

Spoiler Warning: do not read any further until you have completed MJ-18 ("Transmission") and MJ-25 ("Search and Destroy").

Working with Takemura to arrange a meeting with Hanako Arasaka proved to be quite a challenge. After you hacked the parade float she was due to be on, Takemura managed to avoid her security and see her briefly on the float. Her unwillingness to cooperate forced Takemura to improvise and abduct her, finally giving you the opportunity to tell her what you witnessed at Konpeki Plaza: the murder of Saburo Arasaka by his own son, Yorinobu.

While reluctant to believe you at first, Hanako eventually reconsiders and later suggests you meet her at the Embers restaurant, where she makes an offer. If you will help her to convince Arasaka's board of directors of her brother's transgressions, she will have her best surgeons remove the Relic chip from your body.

However, after taking the time to reflect on your journey to date and discussing the situation with Johnny, it may be that you now have other avenues to explore...

POINT OF NO RETURN

Before you enter the elevator taking you to Embers, be well aware that you are reaching a point of no return: once on your way up to the restaurant, you will be locked out of all incomplete optional activities. If you have any unfinished business, such as side jobs and gigs (including those listed in the accompanying table), now is the time to take care of them. Once you press the elevator's button, it will be too late.

Key side jobs that can have repercussions on the game's Epilogue if you complete them include:

- **SJ-21 ("Following the River" – see page 202)** – Offers an opportunity to enter a romantic relationship with River if you meet the corresponding requirements (see page 456).
- **SJ-31 ("Pyramid Song" – see page 212)** – Offers an opportunity to enter a romantic relationship with Judy if you meet the corresponding requirements (see page 456).
- **SJ-36 ("Blistering Love" – see page 218)** – Unlocks a possible alternative ending (Rogue's path).
- **SJ-43 ("Boat Drinks" – see page 224)** – Offers an opportunity to enter a romantic relationship with Kerry if you meet the corresponding requirements (see page 456).
- **SJ-50 ("Queen of the Highway" – see page 233)** – Unlocks a possible alternative ending (Panam's path), as well as an opportunity to enter a romantic relationship with Panam if you meet the corresponding requirements (see page 456).

If in doubt about anything, consider creating a manual save file prior to entering the elevator, and keep it safe – just in case.

OPTIONAL ACTIVITIES (TO BE COMPLETED BEFORE THE POINT OF NO RETURN!)

#	Name	Page
SJ-52	These Boots are Made for Walking	235
SJ-54	Fortunate Son	236
SJ-55	Ezekiel Saw the Wheel	236
SJ-56	Kold Mirage	237
SJ-57	Space Oddity	238
SJ-58	Stadium Love	238
SJ-59	Killing in the Name	239
SJ-60	The Highwayman	240
SJ-61	Sweet Dreams	241
SJ-62	Every Breath You Take	242
SJ-63	Machine Gun	242
SJ-64	Bullets	243
SJ-65	Raymond Chandler Evening	244
SJ-66	Only Pain	244
SJ-67	Small Man, Big Mouth	245
32	Two Wrongs Makes Us Right	280

#	Name	Page
33	Error 404	280
34	Cuckoo's Nest	281
35	Family Matters	282
36	For My Son	282
37	Going-away Party	283
38	The Union Strikes Back	283
39	Serious Side Effects	284
40	Race to the Top	284
41	Breaking News	285
42	Hacking the Hacker	285
43	Severance Package	286
45	No Fixers	287
46	Big Pete's Got Big Problems	288
47	Trevor's Last Ride	288
48	Dancing on a Minefield	288
49	Sparring Partner	289

MOMENTOUS DECISIONS

- **MJ-26 ("Nocturne Op55N1" – see page 164)** – When you sit on the balcony with Misty after the scene in Viktor's clinic, you must make what is probably the most important decision in the entire story: choosing who you want to team up with to raid Arasaka Tower and complete the adventure. There are up to four primary options here, with a minimum of two, each leading to a unique finale.You can find a complete (**but spoiler-heavy**) presentation of all options in our Extras chapter (see page 457).

- During that same scene, you are also given an opportunity to call your romantic interest, should you have one. Doing so will cause additional interactions with the character in question to take place during the Epilogue. If you do not have a partner, or decide not to speak with them, they will play no part in the corresponding sequences.

- **MJ-28 (Epilogue)** – When asked if you will sign Arasaka's contract or not, be aware that your choice will influence the events that ensue.

- **MJ-30 & MJ33 (Epilogue)** – Inside Mikoshi, the decision you make during your conversation with Alt (between entering the well or crossing the bridge with her) is of the utmost importance, as it will determine the nature of the Epilogue that follows.

- **SJ-54 ("Fortunate Son" – see page 236)** – Leaving the clinic employee alive (or having sufficient netrunner skills to pass the relevant skillcheck) will enable you to find out about a virus installed on the implant. Knowing this will allow you to inform Bob when you return to the Aldecaldos camp, and ultimately to save Scooter's life (who will later potentially make an appearance in the game finale if you opt for Panam's path).

- **SJ-59 ("Killing in the Name" – see page 239)** – After deciding what to do with Swedenborg, you have a choice between telling Nancy the truth, or pretending that you have no new information. If you opt for the former, Nancy will send you further messages later on in the story. Additionally, the website you checked at the beginning of the quest will be updated, with people reacting differently depending on what you decided to do with Swedenborg.

- **SJ-62 ("Every Breath You Take" – see page 242)** – Failing this quest leads to the death of Blue Moon.

- **SJ-63 ("Machine Gun" – see page 242)** – Skippy will keep its personality if the Stone Cold Killer mode is active when you meet Regina – in other words, if you initially chose the Puppy-Loving Pacifist mode and did ***not*** tell Skippy that "killing is wrong." Otherwise, it will be reset to factory settings.

- **SJ-65 ("Raymond Chandler Evening" – see page 244)** – During the opening sequence, the quest will end prematurely and be locked off for this playthrough if you take too long to deal with the Valentinos, if you leave the bar without helping the corpo, or if you refuse to help Pepe. At the end of the quest, Pepe and his wife will remain together only if you let Cynthia explain her story to you – which will then enable you to tell Pepe that Cynthia was seeing a ripperdoc and emphasize that she truly loves him. In any other scenario, their relationship will end.

UNIQUES & MISSABLES

- The Prejudice assault rifle can be picked up from one of the tables behind the bar in the Afterlife at the beginning of MJ-29 ("For Whom the Bell Tolls" – see page 172).

- The Pride pistol can be collected close to where Adam Smasher kills your main ally during MJ-30 ("Knockin' on Heaven's Door" – see page 172).

- The Caretaker's Spade hammer can be found leaning against a tree near the conference table during MJ-30 ("Knockin' on Heaven's Door" – see page 172).

- While completing the Psychofan gig, don't miss the chance to pick up Johnny's Pants in a pink briefcase in the bedroom: this unique item is required to unlock a Trophy/Achievement.

- The Amnesty revolver can be earned by completing Cassidy's bottle-shooting challenge at the Nomad party during MJ-31 ("We Gotta Live Together" – see page 174).

- Divided We Stand is an assault rifle awarded for winning the shooting contest during SJ-58 ("Stadium Love"); it can also be looted from the sixers if you neutralize them.

#	Name	Page
50	MIA	289
51	Goodbye, Night City	289
52	Radar Love	289
53	Old Friends	290
54	Jeopardy	291
55	Bring Me the Head of Gustavo Orta	291
56	Sr. Ladrillo's Private Collection	292
57	Life's Work	293
58	Fifth Column	293
59	Psychofan	294
60	Eye for an Eye	294
61	Going Up or Down?	295
62	On a Tight Leash	295
63	The Lord Giveth and Taketh Away	296
64	Hot Merchandise	296
65	A Lack of Empathy	297

#	Name	Page
66	Serial Suicide	297
67	An Inconvenient Killer	298
68	The Frolics of Councilwoman Cole	299
69	Guinea Pigs	299
967	Cyberpsycho Sighting: A Dance with Death	252
968	Cyberpsycho Sighting: Lex Talionis	252
969	Cyberpsycho Sighting: The Wasteland	253
970	Cyberpsycho Sighting: Second Chances	253
971	Cyberpsycho Sighting: House on a Hill	254
972	Cyberpsycho Sighting: Discount Doc	255
973	Cyberpsycho Sighting: Too Little, Too Late	255
974	Cyberpsycho Sighting: On Deaf Ears	256
975	Cyberpsycho Sighting: Phantom of Night City	256
976	Cyberpsycho Sighting: Jealous Hearts	257
977	Cyberpsycho Sighting: Letter of the Law	257

MAIN JOBS

This chapter offers dedicated walkthroughs for every main job, sorted in ascending order of difficulty to help streamline your progression. If you are struggling with a particular mission, or suspect that you might be missing out on potential opportunities, you are in the right place.

The backbone of our coverage always takes the form of numbered steps, ensuring that you can easily follow the sequence of events in any given mission. As you will soon find out, however, many jobs in Cyberpunk 2077 are non-linear and offer an incredible degree of freedom. There are countless instances where a task can be accomplished in several different ways – and some of these might affect later opportunities, or future interactions with relevant characters.

To reflect the open-ended nature of the game, some sections of our walkthroughs are not prescriptive. Instead of trying to describe a single best way to complete an objective, we provide you with annotated maps and captions offering insights on possible paths and interesting features – with a strong emphasis on stealth and non-lethal tactics. In short: we draw your attention to profitable routes and possibilities, and you can then decide how you wish to proceed based on personal preferences and the proficiencies of your character.

Last but not least: if this is your first playthrough, we strongly encourage you to use the Completion Roadmap chapter (see page 92) as a companion to the walkthroughs you find here, as it provides flowcharts and suggestions designed to optimize your progression and overall play experience.

JOB DIRECTORY

Below you will find a directory of all main jobs, sorted both by difficulty and in alphabetical order. If you're looking for guidance on a specific part of the story, you can use this to jump to the relevant page instantly.

Just as a reminder, this guide uses abbreviations to refer to missions. For instance, the very first main job is labeled "MJ-01." This system is used consistently throughout the book, making it easy to track and identify quests, whether you are consulting our Completion Roadmap flowchart, looking for unlock conditions, or simply reading a walkthrough.

Main Job Directory (By Difficulty)

Main Job Directory (Alphabetical)

MJ-01

THE NOMAD

Unlock Condition:
Choose the Nomad background during the character creation process.

Notes:
The Prologue's opening job focuses on establishing V's background.

1

After talking to the mechanic, fix the engine and inspect the hotwire before getting in the car. Start the engine, then connect to the radio station. You can be on your way after you talk to the sheriff. Car controls are introduced in a short tutorial. The main commands you need to remember for now are R2/RT to accelerate, L2/LT to brake or reverse, and L to steer. Your destination is the telecom tower right ahead as you leave the auto shop. A suggested path is represented on your mini-map, though you are free to choose another route if you wish. Hold ◎/B to leave the car when you reach your destination.

2

Kick the fence gate open, then make your way up the tower by climbing the stairs and the ladder. Once at the top, open the control box and connect to the radio station to talk to Willie McCoy. Return to the car after the conversation.

3

Your next destination is an abandoned trailer to the east. Park outside the meeting place then head inside to meet Jackie Welles. After speaking to him, open the car trunk, then drive to the Night City border checkpoint.

4

After parking the car in the inspection area, you will be required to head to the border security building. Leave your weapon at the counter, then walk to room 2, just around the corner, where a border patrol officer is expecting you. Give him your bribe before heading back to the car; don't forget to retrieve your weapon at the front desk on the return journey. The final section of this mission has you fighting off pursuers as Jackie tries to lose them. Aim with R (simultaneously holding L2/LT if you wish), fire with R2/RT, and reload manually with ◻/X whenever you have a moment of respite. Head to the marked safe location when prompted to do so to complete the mission.

THE STREET KID

Unlock Condition:
Choose the Street Kid background during the character creation process.

Notes:
The Prologue's opening job focuses on establishing V's background.

1

Set your broken nose by looking at yourself in the mirror and pressing ⓐ/⊗. After your conversation with Pepe, head to Kirk on the second floor. Explore the various dialogue options with him as you see fit, then return downstairs once you have agreed on your task. Leave the bar via the door close to the arcade machines, then follow the waypoint until you run into Padre. Get in his car when the option becomes available.

2

After getting out of Padre's car, head straight to the marked elevator. Press the button inside to reach the underground parking level.

3

Walk to the end of the corridor to enter the parking area. You can talk to Rick in the booth on your right, but your objective is the car in the VIP sector. Disable the lock using Kirk's device, then get in the Rayfield. The mission outcome is the same no matter what dialogue line you opt for in the conversation that follows.

THE CORPO-RAT

Unlock Condition:
Choose the Corporate background during the character creation process.

Notes:
The Prologue's opening job focuses on establishing V's background.

1

Answer the incoming call by pressing ✪, then leave the toilet. Head to the designated elevator across the lobby to reach the Counter-Intelligence floor.

2

Take a left when you leave the elevator and follow the waypoint leading to Jenkins's office. Feel free to speak to Frank on the way. If you take the time to talk to him and explore all available conversation options, he will remember it, slightly altering his behavior in a future side job. You can optionally make a brief stop by Harry's desk if you wish. Once you arrive at Jenkins's office, sit on the chair and navigate the various options during the conversation as you see fit. Take the shard and the money that Jenkins offers you, then leave the room. Immediately as you exit the office, note that you can talk to Carter and read the report on the personal terminal at the nearby desk. If you sit, you can open the drawer, where you will find a cognitive booster and a trauma team card.

3

Once you're ready to proceed, head to the AV garage marked by the waypoint, then hop inside Jenkins's vehicle. After the AV has landed, walk to the bouncer and go downstairs, where you can sit with Jackie Welles to complete the mission.

MJ-04

PRACTICE MAKES PERFECT

Unlock Condition:
Complete MJ-01 ("The Nomad"), MJ-02 ("The Street Kid"), or MJ-03 ("The Corpo-Rat") in accordance with your chosen background.

Notes:
If you're keen to make the best start possible, we suggest that you read our extensive Primer chapter (see page 70), where you will find advice on all major game systems encountered during the adventure's opening hours.

This job, triggered automatically after you complete your origin story, introduces you to various key gameplay features and concepts at the core of the Cyberpunk 2077 experience. As tutorials guide you through the entire process, we do not duplicate the information here.

MJ-05

THE RESCUE

AREA MAP

Unlock Condition:
Complete MJ-01 ("The Nomad"), MJ-02 ("The Street Kid") or MJ-03 ("The Corpo-Rat") in accordance with your chosen background.

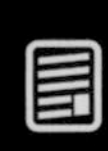

Notes:
This mission gives you an opportunity to put several concepts introduced during the tutorial into practice.

1

Follow Jackie into the elevator, then all the way to apartment 1237. Scan the door and select the remote activation quickhack. Once the door is open, head inside the apartment.

2

Follow Jackie and scan or inspect the woman's body in the second room. After you open the door to the next room, you have your first real opportunity to put your stealth skills to the test. Press ◎/Ⓑ to crouch, then move toward the scavenger. Once at close range, press ▢/Ⓧ to grapple your target, then perform a takedown – either fatal or non-lethal. Note how you can loot the body to collect valuable items such as consumables, weapons, or, occasionally, job items (including shards offering information on missions). Make a habit of looting virtually every opponent you neutralize: this will prove very beneficial in the long run.

3

Keep moving silently until you reach a doorway leading to a large room guarded by multiple scavengers. Stay crouched, make sure no one is looking your way, then join Jackie on the other side of the doorway and hide. Two scavengers will walk by, unaware of your presence. Wait until they stand still, then creep to them and quietly take down either of them in the same manner as before; Jackie will eliminate the other.

4

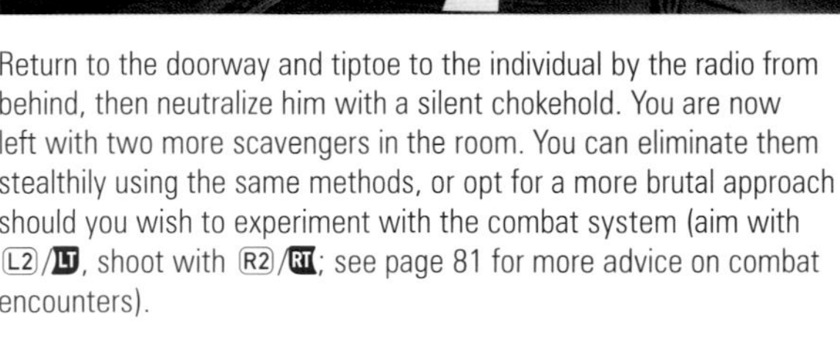

Return to the doorway and tiptoe to the individual by the radio from behind, then neutralize him with a silent chokehold. You are now left with two more scavengers in the room. You can eliminate them stealthily using the same methods, or opt for a more brutal approach should you wish to experiment with the combat system (aim with L2/LT, shoot with R2/RT; see page 81 for more advice on combat encounters).

5

The scavenger leader awaits in the next room, where your prior behavior will determine how things end. If you've been quiet so far, note that you can cause a suitable distraction for an easier finish by hacking the reflector close to him. If you've triggered open combat, try jumping through the window on your left and flank him by firing through the barred window; Jackie will use the diversion to take him down.

6

Once you make it to the room with the computer, open the door to your right and you will find Sandra Dorsett in the bathtub. Follow the onscreen instructions to save her, then carry her onto the balcony and set her down on the stretchers once Trauma Team arrives. You can now follow Jackie to the elevator, then to your car. You will need to call Wakako during the journey: hold ✪ and select her name in the list. Get into the passenger seat when you're ready to proceed.

7

You will be attacked by scavengers on the journey back to your apartment. Eliminate as many targets as you can in the first phase, then focus on the scavenger firing from the side door during the second. Once back home, rest in your bed to complete the job.

MJ-06

THE RIPPERDOC

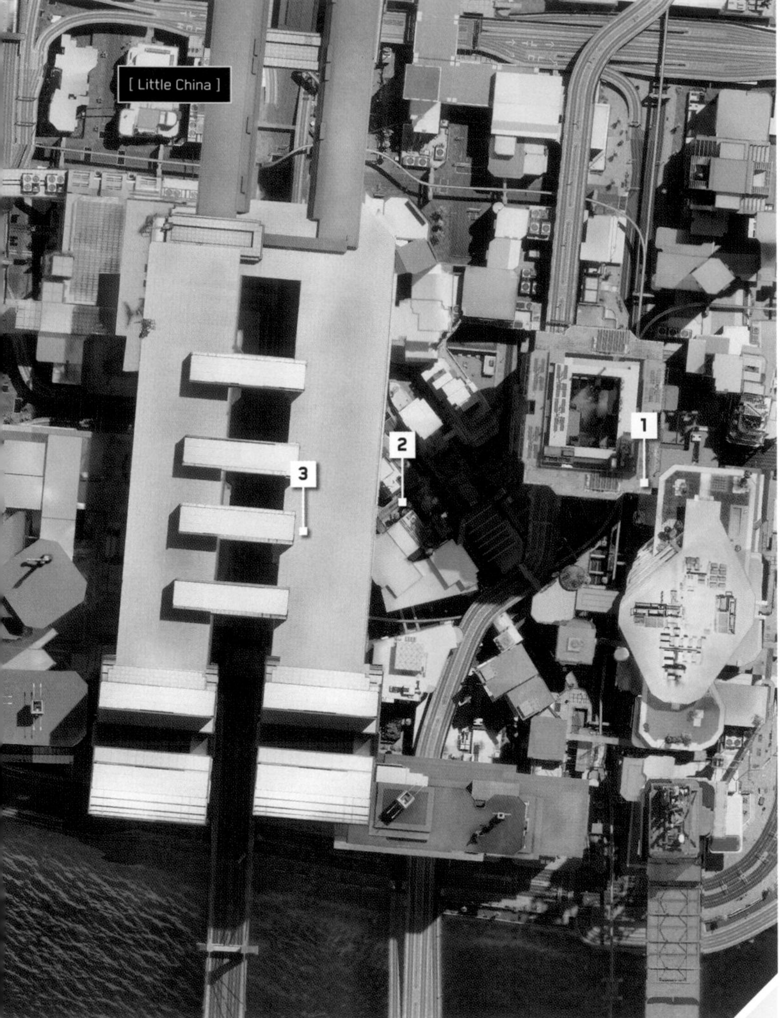

AREA MAP

Unlock Condition:
Complete MJ-05 ("The Rescue").

Notes:
When you reach the elevator at the beginning of this job, consider making a quick stop at the nearby 2nd Amendment shop: this is technically a side job, but it only takes a minute and will reward you with a gun, an M-10AF Lexington.

After you leave Viktor's clinic, a new side job (called "Paid in Full") will appear in your journal. This is a simple reminder that you will eventually need to pay the ripperdoc back – a task that you can complete much later in the adventure, whenever you have enough money to spare.

1

After getting out of bed, leave the apartment, go through the doorway ahead and proceed down the stairs. Your first goal is to reach the elevator across the atrium. Press the button inside to be taken to the building's entrance. Jackie awaits at a nearby food stall. Sit with him, call your car when prompted by pressing ⊕, then follow him and get in your car's driver's seat.

2

Your destination is the marked parking spot on a nearby street. The path suggested by your mini-map will suffice, though you should note that the actual route is up to you if you'd prefer a little sightseeing. Once your car is in position, follow Jackie by foot and enter Misty's Esoterica.

3

The door in the far back of Misty's shop will lead you to an alley. Head down the stairs right in front of you to meet Viktor, your ripperdoc. During the surgery, you will need to choose two implants to install: Kiroshi Optics in the Ocular System slot, and the Ballistic Coprocessor in the Hands slot. After the scene, head back outside by going through Misty's shop.

MJ-07

THE RIDE

AREA MAP

Unlock Condition:
Complete MJ-06 ("The Ripperdoc").

Notes:
When you are done with this mission, consider completing the side job called "The Gift." This takes place in the vicinity and introduces an essential hacking feature.

1

As soon as you leave Misty's shop, take a right and head toward the waypoint. You will find Dexter Deshawn's limo just a short stroll further down the street where you parked earlier. Get in his car when prompted to do so.

2

Lead the conversation with Dex however you see fit. The many optional lines of dialogue (displayed in blue) enable you to obtain extra details on the offer he's making you, so explore these as you wish. Afterwards, get out of his car to have a phone call with Jackie. At this point, you need to decide which of the next two jobs you intend to deal with first: retrieving the Flathead (MJ-08, see page 120), or paying a visit to the client, Evelyn Parker (MJ-09, see page 126).

THE PICKUP

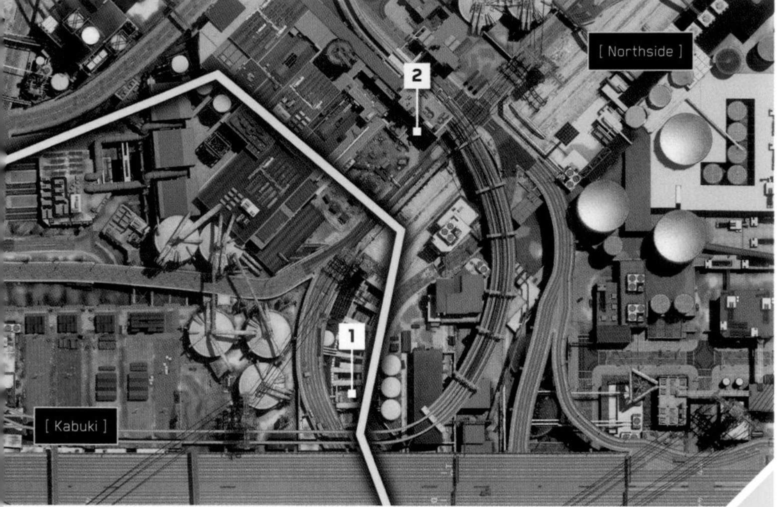

AREA MAP

Unlock Condition:
Complete MJ-07 ("The Ride").

Notes:
This is the first job in the main storyline that is defined by its non-linearity. Such freedom to complete objectives in a manner of your own choosing will now become more commonplace.

1

The first step is to decide if you would like to call and then meet with Meredith Stout in a storm drain in Northside. Meeting with her unlocks various possibilities for this mission, but is entirely optional.

2

Whether you've opted to meet with Stout or not, your core assignment is to head to the All Foods warehouse in Northside and retrieve the Flathead device from the Maelstrom thugs. There are many ways to achieve this objective.

EXCLUSIVE INTERACTIONS

This job features a few possible interactions that are exclusive to either a background or an attribute requirement:

- **Corporate:** As a corporate, you can tell Stout during your first meeting that you know the credchip she offers you is infected. This formally unlocks the objective to crack it in your Inventory menu (though you can do so irrespective of your background). You may then use the cleaned chip to buy the Flathead from Royce.
- **Nomad:** As a Nomad, you have an opportunity during the meeting with Stout to say that you've jumped convoys before, implying that you are happy to work for her. Next, whether you're a Nomad or not, you need to find the manifests revealing who the mole is at Militech (especially the message from Anthony Gilchrist called "Transports – LOA"): they are hidden on the computer in the small room in the west corner of the warehouse, on your left when you reach the large room after you go through the maintenance shaft. With these conditions met, if you engineer an outcome where Stout wins the Militech power struggle, you can sell the information to her on your way out of the warehouse: you will receive your reward as a package a little later in the story. If instead you reach an outcome where Gilchrist wins the power struggle, you can blackmail him as you leave the All Foods warehouse, saying you know he's the mole; he will also send you a package later on to buy your silence.
- **Technical Ability Requirement:** If your level of Technical Ability is sufficient, you have access to an exclusive line when talking to Jackie outside the All Foods warehouse, where V suggests to Jackie that he should tune his motorcycle. Doing so means that you will get to interact with the tuned version of the bike instead of the default setup in a later side job.
- **Street Kid:** If you mention the Black Lace drug when talking to Dum Dum, just before he shows you the Flathead, and if you opt for a peaceful resolution, Dum Dum will give you his inhaler as he walks you out of the warehouse.

RETRIEVING THE FLATHEAD

There are multiple ways to obtain the Flathead from Dum Dum and Royce, the leaders of the Maelstrom thugs based in the All Foods warehouse. These are documented in the accompanying flowchart. Take the time to read it carefully, as the decisions you make have direct consequences (as well as repercussions on a future side job – see page 222).

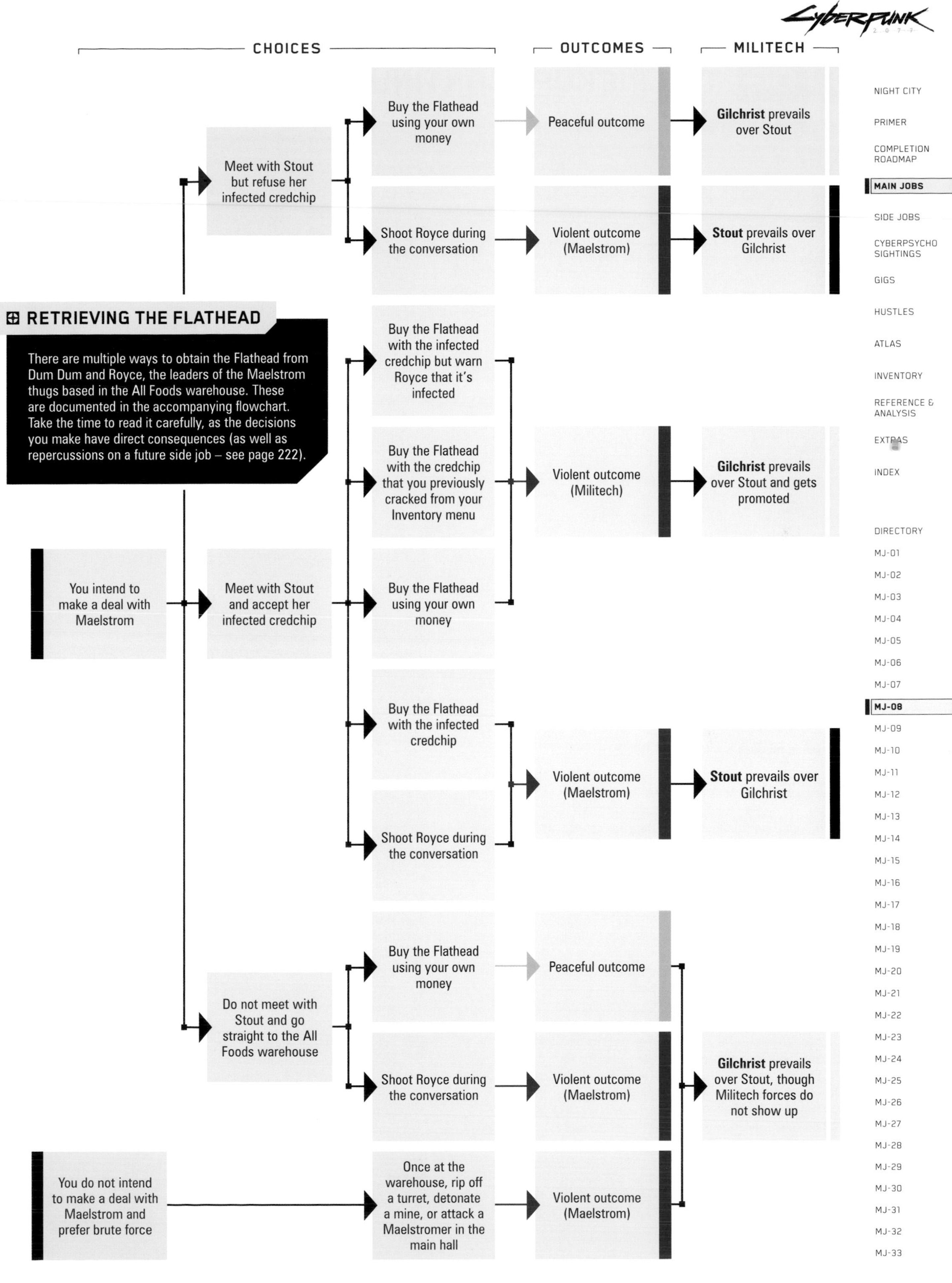

MJ-08 THE PICKUP (CONTINUED)

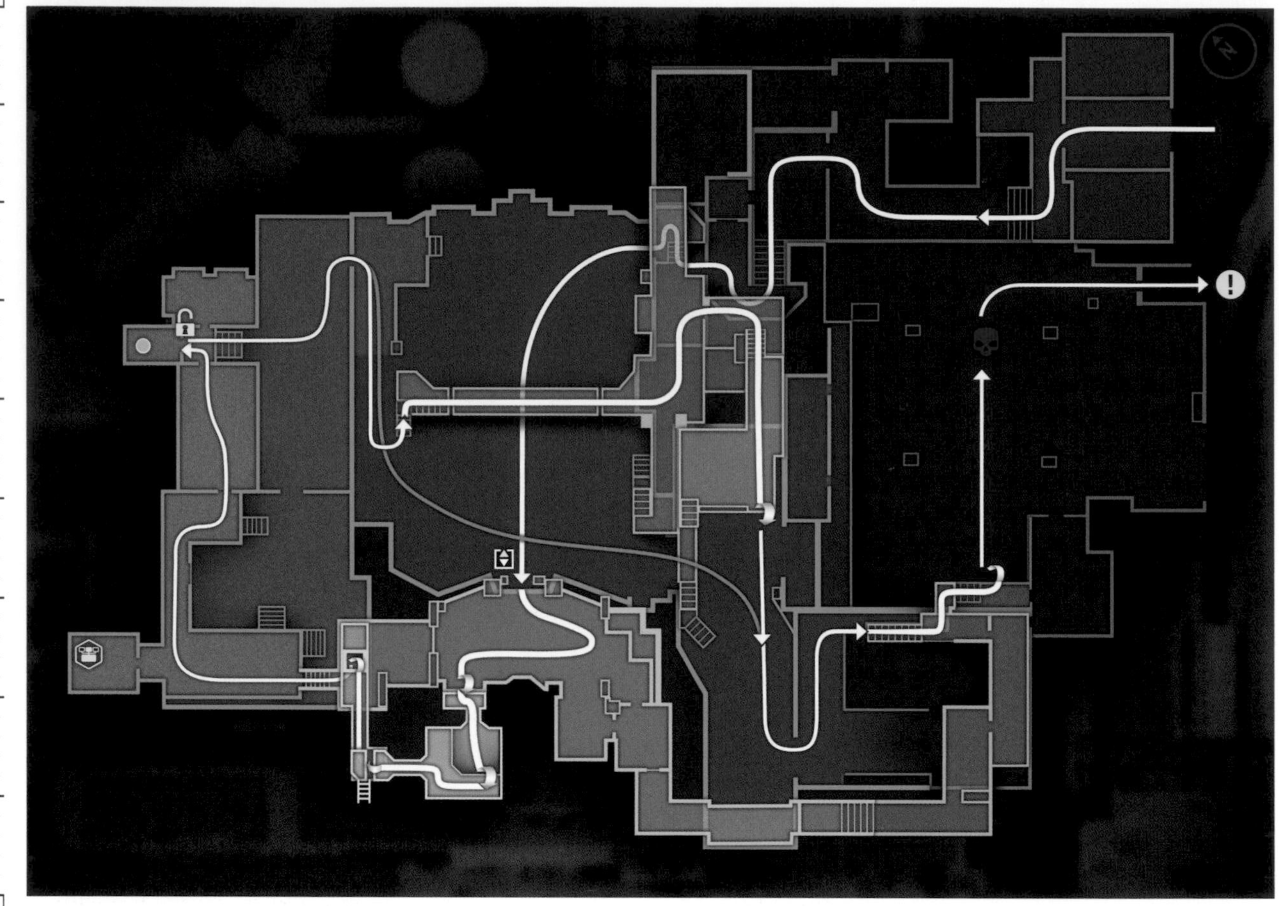

ALL FOODS WAREHOUSE

Your goal is to reach the warehouse's exit.

Maelstrom Conflict – If you triggered combat against Maelstrom, you will have to make your way out of the heavily guarded warehouse. Start by climbing up to the maintenance shaft via the ladder and crates. Activate the conveyor belt on the upper platform, then go through the narrow corridor and drop down twice. You will run into a first wave of enemies at this point, and you are free to deal with them as you please. If you want to rely on stealth, immediately crouch and proceed cautiously, tagging as many foes as you can (see page 79), and sneaking up on lone targets when no one is looking your way. If you prefer more aggressive tactics, try to always fight from a cover position that you can retreat to – for example, when you need to reload. The third room you go through – the production line – is large and heavily guarded. Turn right from the entrance to reach the stairs, then climb up and use the elevated walkway to go across. You'll find a door on your left on the other side. The rest of the path through the warehouse should pose little navigational difficulty. When you reach the final large room, be sure to heal and equip your best gear. It features either a boss battle against Royce, or a large group of Maelstromers.

Militech Conflict – If the warehouse is raided by Militech troops, you will also have a lot of enemies to face, but Maelstromers will fight on your side, providing valuable support. Not only will your allies shoot your mutual enemies, but they will also draw their fire, relieving some of the pressure on you. You can use this to quickly and efficiently take down many foes. When you reach the large room with the production line, note that you can take a shortcut: the Maelstromers will open the gate in the north corner, enabling you to bypass the entire section on the upper floor. Last but not least, the boss battle here will feature two Minotaurs instead of Royce – with Royce actually on your side.

In multiple scenarios, expect to face your first boss in the final room. This is a challenging encounter – see "Boss Battle" for guidance. Once you emerge victorious, you will find the warehouse's exit in the corner.

The convoy manifests are located on the computer in this small room, in the west corner of the warehouse. You can access it as you come out of the maintenance shaft. If you met with Stout before coming here, finding these messages will enable you to get an additional reward from either her or Gilchrist when you leave the warehouse.

Brick, the previous Maelstrom leader who was overthrown by Royce, is detained in a locked cell. How you behave here has repercussions on a later side job – see "The Maelstrom Power Struggle" for details.

Possible Scenarios: Overview

If you find the multitude of possibilities in the flowchart a little overwhelming, here is a breakdown of the main scenarios you can trigger:

- **Peaceful outcome:** To complete the mission without triggering combat, you need to purchase the Flathead with your own money during the deal sequence with Dum Dum and Royce. This can be achieved after either meeting with Stout by refusing her offer, or not meeting her at all.

- **Look for a deal with Maelstrom but trigger conflict against them:** This course of action happens if you say nothing when Jackie is asked to sit on the couch, shoot Royce during the deal sequence, or buy the Flathead with Stout's infected credchip. In any case, you end up having to escape via the maintenance shaft, then face the Maelstrom gang members on your way out. If you let Royce survive the deal sequence, you will face him as a boss in the warehouse's final room.

- **Attack Maelstrom preemptively:** This is triggered by attacking any thug, ripping off a turret, or blowing up a mine on your way to the All Foods warehouse's main room – preventing the deal sequence from ever happening. In this scenario, you will face multiple enemies on your way to the elevator, including Dum Dum, Lars, and Kurt. Next, you will have to eliminate the gang's netrunner in the room with the couches, then pick up the Flathead in its case in the small room to the south, behind a door. Finally, you will escape via the maintenance shaft, at which point you will be back on the standard path involving a conflict against Maelstrom.

- **Cut a deal with Maelstrom and trigger conflict against Militech:** This scenario can only happen if you first meet with Stout and accept her infected credchip. At this point, go to the All Foods warehouse and begin the deal sequence with the Maelstrom leaders. Now buy the Flathead with your own money, or with Stout's credchip (after warning Royce it's infected), or with Stout's credchip that you previously cracked (from your Inventory menu). In all three of these scenarios, the deal with Maelstrom will go smoothly. It is then Militech that will raid the warehouse, leading to a completely different combat encounter. In this variant, you can count on Maelstrom's support (unless you attack them, of course). They will fight Militech with you, and even support you during the boss encounter against the Minotaurs (both Royce, on a mech of his own, and Dum Dum if he's still alive).

The Maelstrom Power Struggle

Brick, the previous Maelstrom leader, was recently overthrown by Royce. He is now detained in a cell in the All Foods warehouse, as shown on the map overleaf. His fate is up to you.

- If you want to save him, open his cell door, either by hacking it if you have the relevant netrunner skills, or by using the four-digit code found on the computer in the adjacent room, in the Files category (9691). You also need to disarm the detonator near the door in the same room (or the laser mine itself in Brick's cell).

- If you want him to die, you can either kill him yourself (by setting off the explosive charge in the room adjacent to his cell, for example), or leave him imprisoned, which will lead to the same result.

Your choice here will affect a later side job (SJ-38, "Second Conflict," see page 220). Here is an overview of the possible outcomes:

- In the scenarios where Dum Dum and Royce live (in other words, if you do not trigger combat against Maelstrom), you get to meet them both again during SJ-38.

- In the scenarios where Dum Dum and Royce die, you obviously cannot encounter them again during SJ-38. They will instead be replaced by either Brick (if you save him) or Patricia (if you let Brick die). In the former instance, Brick will be grateful for your earlier act of mercy – allowing for a special peaceful outcome in that side job.

The Militech Power Struggle

Whatever path you elect to follow, your choice will inevitably have an impact on Militech's internal power struggle (between Stout and her rival Gilchrist). If you met with Stout prior to visiting the All Foods warehouse, you will encounter the victor of the struggle on your way out of the building. If you didn't meet with Stout, you will not see either her or Gilchrist, but their conflict will play out behind the scenes.

Who comes out on top depends on your approach – as documented in our flowchart – and has the following consequences:

- If Stout prevails, she gets promoted, which will be announced in the news on television. She will also contact you later on if you told her you were open to working for her again. This will unlock an opportunity to flirt with her, and even have a romantic liaison at the No-Tell Motel (more specifically in room 6 – where you will obtain a ***very special*** weapon). Gilchrist is killed, his corpse abandoned in the storm drain where you originally met with Stout.

- If Gilchrist prevails, the situation is largely reversed. He gets promoted (though only if you met with Stout), as announced on television news. Stout is killed with time-honored brutality: her feet secured in concrete, she is shaved and dropped in the bay, near the road leading toward the oilfields, to the north. (If you wait 48 in-game hours after completing the quest, you can actually see her by diving underwater.)

THE PICKUP (CONTINUED)

BOSS BATTLE

In any scenario where the warehouse is stormed by Militech, or you trigger a conflict against Maelstrom and do not neutralize Royce during the deal sequence, you have to face a boss just before you reach the warehouse's exit: Royce if you're fighting Maelstrom, or two Minotaurs if you're facing Militech. The latter scenario is rather straightforward: you can count on the assistance of Royce (and potentially Dum Dum) to defeat the two Minotaurs. Shoot from any suitable cover position while the mechs are distracted (if possible with Tech weapons or electric damage), and you should prevail in no time.

Royce, on the other hand, is a whole different ballgame, with multiple attack patterns and weaknesses that you can exploit.

Weaknesses

There are multiple factors that you can exploit to optimize your damage output against Royce.

- **Intelligent Shield:** Royce has a large shield that he uses to mitigate incoming attacks. However, you can deactivate it by destroying the battery at the rear of his exoskeleton. Scan and tag Royce and the battery will be permanently highlighted, making it easier to aim it. Note that Royce is weak to electric damage (and, conversely, resistant to chemical damage).

- **Frag Grenades:** These are highly recommended in this battle, not only because they deal significant damage, but also because their blast radius makes them effective at destroying Royce's battery unit.

- **Quickhacks:** Three types of quickhack can prove beneficial against Royce. ***Overheat*** causes damage over time. ***Weapon Malfunction*** briefly staggers the boss, which can be useful to prevent him from launching certain attacks or to have a window of opportunity to open fire without fear of reprisal. Finally, ***Short Circuit*** will instantly destroy the battery, leaving you free to deal damage to Royce from the get-go.

- **Tech Weapons:** If you have a Tech weapon at hand it can prove particularly useful here, as it will pierce through Royce's shield – enabling you to ignore the battery altogether.

- **Bladerunner Perk:** Spending points in the Bladerunner perk (Engineering skill) will grant you increased damage to mechanical enemies such as Royce.

- **Reload Stance:** Royce will regularly stop moving for a few seconds while he recharges his pulse weapon. This is your cue to get in as close as you need to and focus on raw damage, ideally targeting the battery if you have yet to destroy it.

Attack Patterns

Royce has numerous tricks up his sleeve. The following pictures will help you to know what to expect and how to react to each of his moves.

Pulse Shots: Royce's most frequent attack is an energy blast. You can either avoid it with a sideways dodge, or seek refuge behind suitable cover.

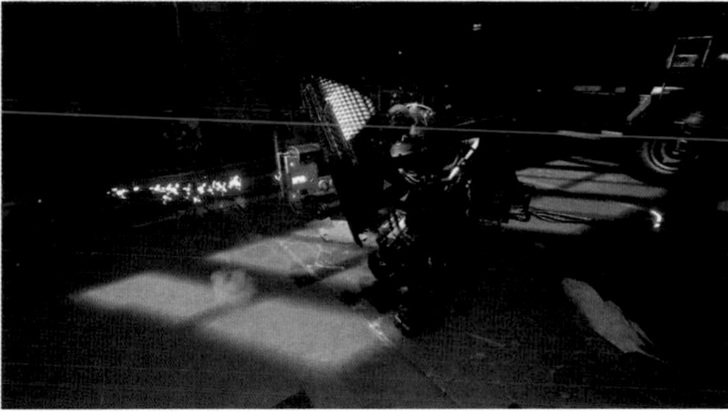

Laser Swipe: When Royce sweeps the room with a red beam, either crouch or hop over it.

Pulse Storm: When Royce kneels and starts charging this homing attack, swiftly move behind cover.

Pulse Impact: Whenever you espy telltale circular red dots beneath your feet, sprint away to safety.

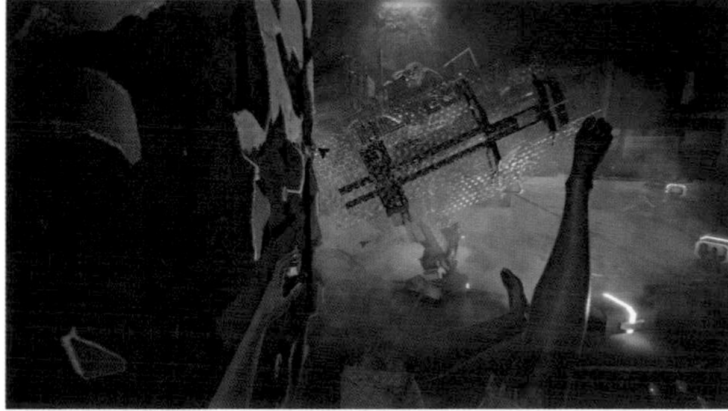

Floor Slam: If you get too close to Royce, he will slam the ground. You will be knocked down if this attack connects, leaving you dangerously exposed to follow-up assaults. This does not mean that melee specialists cannot compete against him, as a hit-and-run style is perfectly viable. If you bait this attack by dashing in and out of the trigger/effect radius, you can then sprint over and land meaningful blows to punish his every use of this gambit.

STEALTH TACTICS

Stealth tactics work very well against Royce, especially if you manage to get rid of his ally preemptively. To escape the boss's attention, you can simply hide until he forgets about you. The process is even easier if you blind him, either with the Reboot Optics quickhack or by hacking one of the reflectors in the arena.

Once Royce has lost track of you, you have two options:

- You can sneak up on him and perform a takedown to instantly destroy his battery. Repeat the maneuver and a second takedown will neutralize Royce for good.
- Alternatively, you could tiptoe across the arena to the exit and sneak out incognito, avoiding the battle altogether.

MJ-09

THE INFORMATION

AREA MAP

Unlock Condition:
Complete MJ-07 ("The Ride").

Notes:
This job acts as a two-step introduction to braindance investigations.

1

You will need to arrive at Lizzie's Bar in the evening to begin this mission. Note that you can use the main menu's Skip Time feature to fast-forward to the hour of your choosing if required. Once inside, head to the bar and sit on the designated stool. After you meet Evelyn Parker, follow her first to the VIP room, then to the braindance studio, where you will meet Judy Alvarez. Follow their instructions until you get to sit in the braindance editor chair. If you'd like to read a general introduction to this gameplay feature in advance, see page 82 of the Primer chapter.

2

After observing the recording's events once, you will revisit them – this time in editing mode. Controls are clearly detailed in the bottom-right corner of your screen, and Judy will require you to test all of them as part of this introductory session. Press □/X to play or pause; hold L2/LT to rewind to the beginning, then hold R2/RT to fast-forward to the 00:10 mark again; now hold △/Y to restart from the beginning of the recording. Once in editing mode (L1/LB), fast-forward to 00:22 then, using both sticks, adjust the camera so as to get a good view of the gun, which is highlighted in yellow. You can then align your reticle over the firearm to scan it.

BRAINDANCE CONTROLS

Control Overview

L	Move around (editing mode)
R	Adjust the camera angle (editing mode)
□/X	Toggle between play and pause
△/Y	Restart from the beginning
○/B	Exit the simulation
L1/LB	Toggle between editing mode and playback mode
R1/RB	Switch layer
L2/LT	Rewind
R2/RT	Fast-forward

3

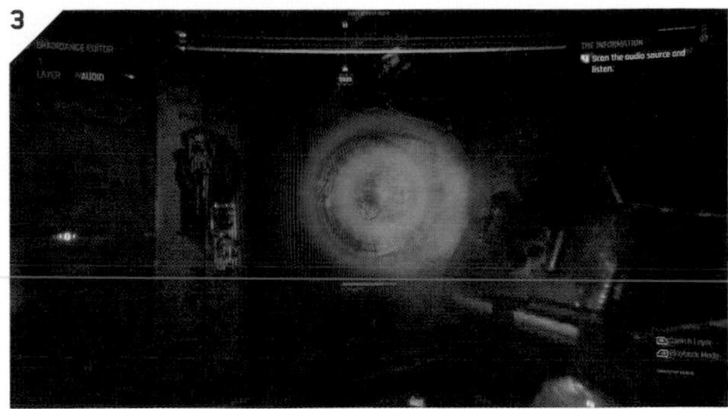

Judy now introduces you to a vital feature. By pressing R1/RB you can switch layer, in this case alternating between the visual and audio layers, though you will soon also have access to a third (thermal). Each layer is represented by a timeline at the top of your screen, with colored segments indicating critical moments where you need to find evidence. Switch to audio and you will see various sound sources nearby. Choose one – for instance, the fan directly behind the individual wielding the gun – and focus on it. Continue exploring the recording to familiarize yourself with what you've learned so far. When you change layer, Judy will ask you to scan the woman who gets knocked down at the 00:36 mark. Now scroll forward to 00:51 to witness the criminal's death, then roll back to 00:48 and scan the security monitor on the clerk's counter. At this point, you can exit the simulation by pressing ◎/B.

5

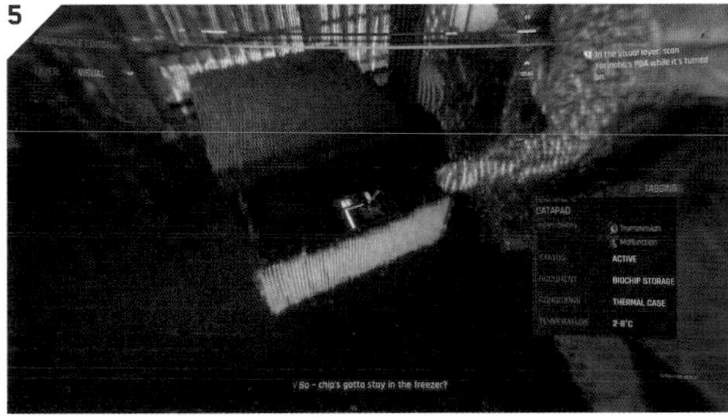

Once you've learned about the relic documentation, you need to find it. There are many points of interactivity to explore, including three devices linked to the security system (all three in the visual layer): the alarm system and the motion sensor camera near the entrance, as well as the automated turret mounted on the ceiling (02:08). Your primary objective, though, is the manual that Yorinobu stores in the nightstand at 02:45. Inspect this in the visual layer to proceed.

6

For the final step, you need to switch to the thermal layer, roll back to the 00:46 mark, and inspect the temperature source hidden under a floor panel, in the corner of the suite close to the counter where Evelyn pours drinks. Quit out of the editor with ◎/B. You are then just a couple of conversations away from completing the mission.

4

During the conversation that follows, you will need to call T-Bug so that she can assist you as you explore the next recording. When the sequence with Yorinobu begins, try to familiarize yourself with the layout of the suite in the default playback mode. After you trigger editing mode, visibility is somewhat reduced, which can make navigation and orientation in the room more difficult. Once you are ready, switch to the audio layer and scan the phone in Yorinobu's hand at the 00:34 mark.

MJ-10

THE HEIST

AREA MAP

Unlock Condition:
Complete both MJ-08 ("The Pickup") and MJ-09 ("The Information").

Notes:
This job begins in the Afterlife, a famous club at the south edge of Little China that you will visit multiple times throughout the adventure.

1

Head to the waypoint at the south end of Little China. Follow Jackie into the Afterlife and sit on the designated stool. Dex's bodyguard will soon lead you to a soundproof booth. Once inside, put the Flathead in its case, then sit on the leather chair. During the conversation that ensues, note that you can choose to tell Dex that Evelyn Parker offered you a deal to cut him loose. If you do so, Dex will increase your share to 40%. If not, you can still negotiate a better bargain with him – but he won't go above 35%. After you slot in Dex's shard and the meeting ends, you can either accept Jackie's offer to start the mission right away, or put it on hold if you have something else to attend to (in the latter case, don't forget to pick up the suit on the booth's table before you leave).

2

The next sequence takes place in the parking lot outside the Afterlife, where a Delamain cab awaits. Jack in to the socket and call Jackie when prompted to do so. Once at Konpeki Plaza, follow Jackie to the hotel's front desk and speak to the receptionist to check in. You have a few "flavor" role-play dialogue options here – but we'll leave it to you as to how you proceed to avoid spoiling anything. Ultimately, your goal is to take the elevator with Jackie and head to your suite on the 42nd floor. Once inside, scan the room to find an entry point for the Flathead: the tech shaft cover by the window.

3

Now take the control shard from Jackie. Once in control of the Flathead, you need to find a way forward into the vents. Scan the tech shaft cover on your right, just under the ceiling. Note that you can zoom in and out with ◌ to facilitate the process.

4

Repeat the maneuver once more in the next room, this time scanning the tech shaft cover by the window, just behind the room service maid. To get her out of the way, you will need to cause a distraction. Scan the terrarium AC unit on your right, by the entrance door, and lower its temperature. You can then send the Flathead through the aforementioned shaft, and through the grate in the corridor that follows.

5

In the next section, you have two targets to scan and activate successively: first the network node room door, then the CCTV access point. Next, switch the camera view with ◆.

6

In the dweller's room, scan the shaft grate on your left, then switch the camera view back to the other room using ◆.

7

Now scan the shaft grate and order the Flathead to use it. Switch the camera view back one last time to the dweller's room. Finally, instruct the Flathead to connect to the netrunner's chair. Once T-Bug is ready, head back to the elevator and take it to reach the Tavernier Suite.

8

The biochip is hidden in the safe built into the floor, which you discovered during MJ-09 ("The Information"). Scan the floor panel to reveal the location of the switch, on Yorinobu's nightstand. Use it, and don't forget to pick up the weapon on the other night stand; it might come in handy shortly. You may now jack in to the safe and retrieve the chip. Don't forget to pick up the weapon on the other night stand; it might come in handy shortly. When unwanted company arrives, hide inside the pillar behind the hologram.

9

After the cutscene, you need to escape. Go to the marked double door for T-Bug to unlock it. Before you head through, though, you have the option of heading up the stairs to the rooftop, where you will find two guards and a dead end. This brief detour has the merit of allowing you to obtain weapons, including a special katana in the AV. Observe the men's patrol routes from the steps, then approach them from behind to take them down silently. Irrespective of whether you went to the rooftop or not, you have the option of collecting a few items in the penthouse. Once you're ready to proceed, leave the penthouse through the door opened by T-Bug. Walk alongside the wall, then onto the ledge that leads to the ladder. You now have to make your way all the way down, back to Delamain's cab. This will require you to go through multiple floors – and they're all heavily guarded. See overleaf for details.

MJ·10 THE HEIST (CONTINUED)

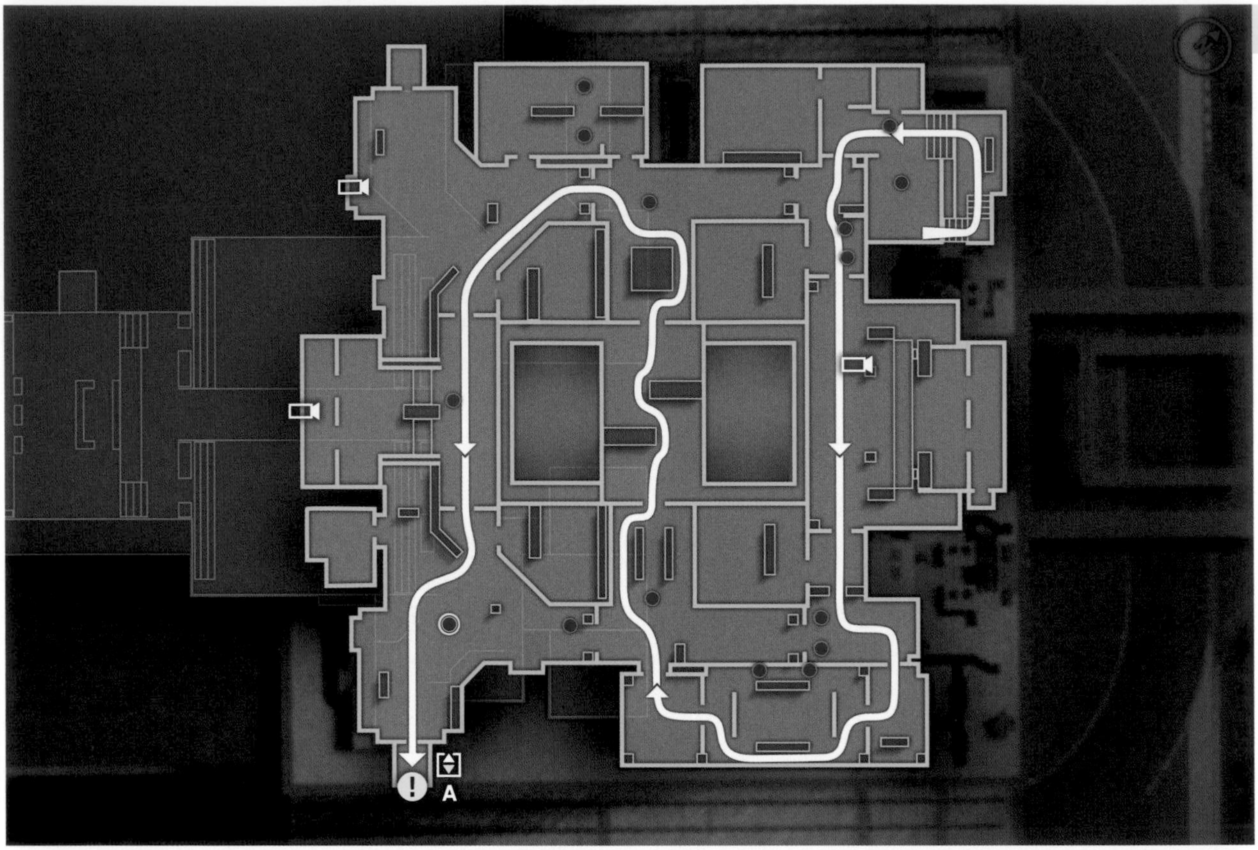

A

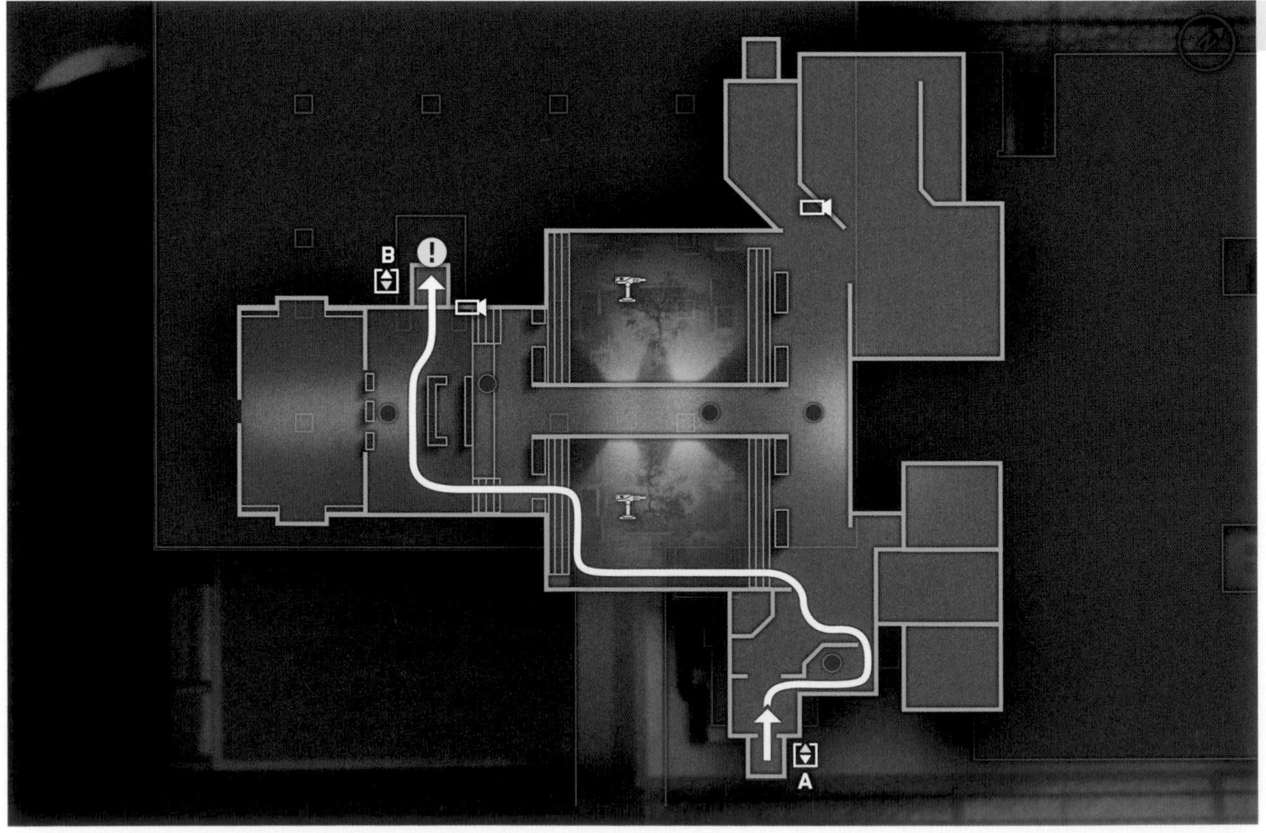

CONFERENCE ROOMS

We show one possible safe path through the conference rooms on the map. After you walk down the initial stairs, you will encounter two guards. Feel free to eliminate either while they look away (Jackie will take care of the other): doing so will enable you to pick up their weapons (including silencers), which will help should things go awry. When you reach the hallway, wait for the two security staff to finish their exchange, at which point they will part ways and each adopt their own patrol pattern. Disable all surveillance cameras (preferably with quickhacks), stay crouched at all times, and follow the path suggested on our map, advancing cautiously. Be sure to neutralize all guards on the way and hide their bodies behind solid walls if you don't want to take any chances.

Your objective is to take the elevator in the far corner. Before you can enter it, however, you will need to retrieve an access card from the nearby officer.

The officer carries the access card required to enter the elevator. Observe his patrol route and tiptoe behind him to perform a silent takedown, then search his body for the card.

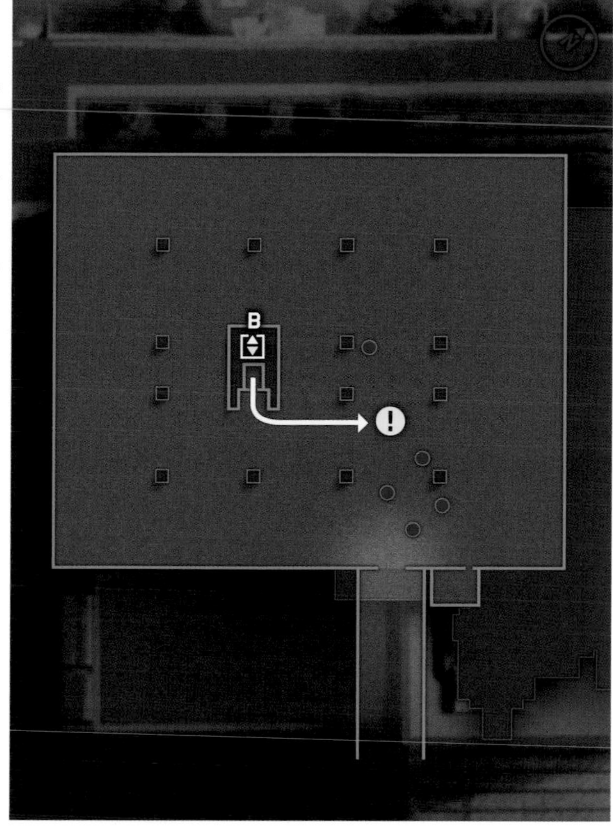

LOBBY

Your objective in the lobby (which you should recognize from earlier) is to take the elevator near the entrance down to the garage.

The presence of enemy forces makes this easier said than done. If you plan to use brute strength, try to take out your foes one by one and from solid cover – a fight in the open will expose you to intense enemy fire: turrets, guards and, once the latter are down, a Minotaur. If you prefer stealth tactics, be patient: by crouch-walking alongside the south wall and using the walls and planters as cover, you can quietly make your way to the elevator without touching an enemy. Just make sure you tag all foes, turrets, and surveillance cameras, and it's only a matter of making your move while they're all facing away from you. You can even sneak through the last section, by the reception desk, in this manner, as long as your timing is right. You can make your life much easier, though, by quickhacking the cameras, especially the one above the elevator, and by neutralizing the second guard.

There are two turrets, one on each side of the lobby. Based on how you have developed your character and the approach you take, you can either destroy them, ignore them, or quickhack them.

GARAGE

Your final goal is to make it into Delamain's cab.

The garage is under heavy surveillance, so there's little point in trying to sneak past enemies here. From the elevator, take a left and simply sprint to the cab to proceed.

FINAL STEPS

After you enter Delamain's cab, you have one more challenge to overcome – drones that give chase. Try to keep your aim steady and fire until they fall. If you struggle, consider casting the Short Circuit quickhack, which works wonders here.

You then have a decision to make.

- By choosing to send the remains of the deceased to his family (or telling Delamain to wait until you return), you will unlock an exclusive side job (see page 189).
- If you opt to send the remains to Viktor's clinic, you will instead have access to extra dialogue and scenes regarding the character in question in a later main job (see page 168).

After you leave the cab, head to the marked door right in front of you, climb up the stairs and knock twice on the door of room 204. The rest of the mission requires no further guidance.

PLAYING FOR TIME

Unlock Condition:
Complete MJ-10 ("The Heist").

Notes:
This is a mostly linear and plot-oriented gameplay section, so feel free to complete it on your own. If you need any help, this walkthrough focuses on the basics alone to avoid story spoilers.

1

Follow the only available path through the corridor, then head to the stage and grab the microphone. Head to the door and enter the helicopter outside. When prompted, man the turret and eliminate all hostile forces on the rooftop. Next, follow your allies inside the building and deal with the guards on your way as you head down the stairs. You will soon run into an elevator: deploy the bomb inside and arm it, then shoot the mechanism above the elevator. You can now speak to Rogue before heading through the nearby double door.

2

In the large room, pick off your enemies one by one. Note that you wield a powerful gun, so feel free to be aggressive. An effective strategy, for example, is to knock your targets down by shooting their legs, then finish them off with a few taps to the torso. Once the path is clear, use either staircase to reach the walkways upstairs and be ready to mow down a new wave of foes as they storm through the door. Head through it to face one last pocket of resistance.

3

You will find the access point you're looking for on the wall to your left. Jack in, then retrace your steps toward the rooftop. After the cutscene, sprint up the stairs and jump into the helicopter.

The following sequences (removing the debris, crawling forward, eliminating the motorcycles during the car chase) are story-oriented and best enjoyed with no additional guidance. Back at your apartment, feel free to eat something from the table, check your messages, and visit your Stash. As you exit the flat, you will be contacted by Takemura, who invites you to meet him at Tom's Diner, a short distance to the south of your current position. Take the elevator across the atrium then walk to your destination. Inside the restaurant, sit at Takemura's table. The job is completed after your conversation, leaving you free to explore the whole city and its countless activities as and when you see fit.

As far as the main story goes, you have two job opportunities available at this point, with a third one added to the list shortly thereafter: finding Evelyn Parker, who promised to help V get rid of the Relic (see page 126); locating Anders Hellman, one of the creators of the Relic (see page 152); and cooperating with Takemura to establish the truth about Saburo's death (see page 156).

MJ-12

AUTOMATIC LOVE

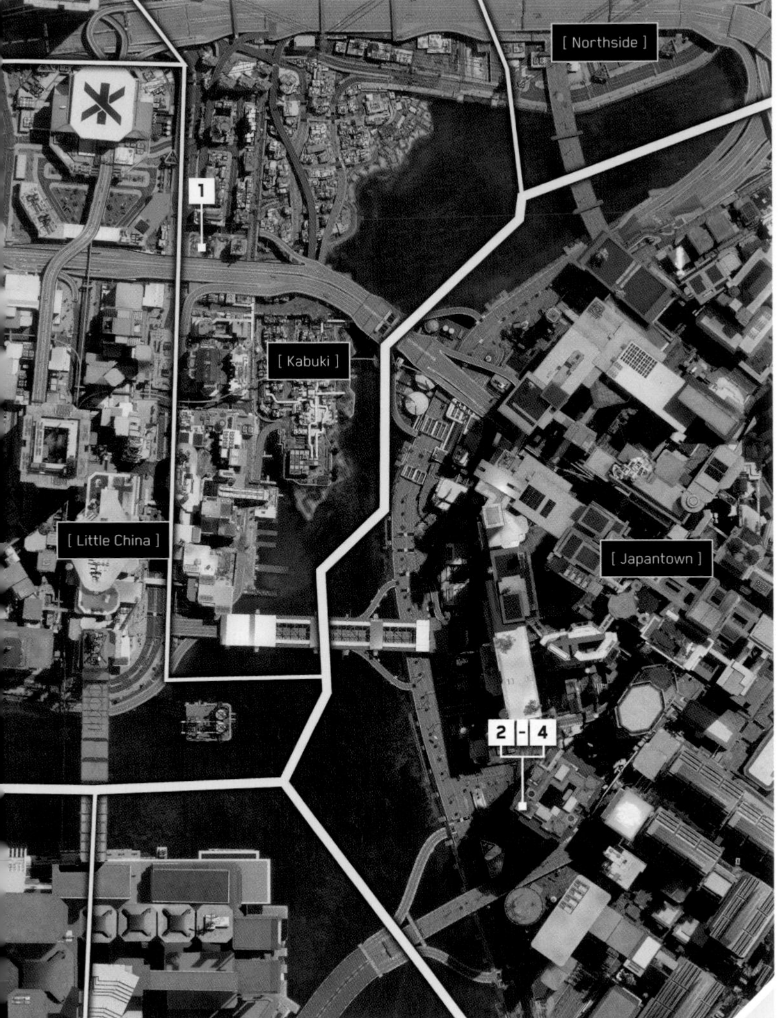

AREA MAP

Unlock Condition:
Complete MJ-11 ("Playing for Time").

Notes:
You will need to make a mandatory cash payment during this mission.

1

Head to Lizzie's Bar, speak to the Mox at the front door, then go downstairs to Judy's den (note that you can optionally call her on the way). During the conversation with Judy, you can choose to be honest with her (leaving you on good terms with her) or not to tell her anything (which will lead to a measure of reproach in future conversations). Pick up the cigarette case on her desk and speak to Johnny on the way out before heading to the H8 megabuilding. There happens to be a fast travel terminal right at its base, which can be handy if you've already unlocked it.

2

On arrival, head up the stairs and take the elevator to Clouds, which is up on the 12th floor. You will only be able to enter in the evening, so either use the main menu's Skip Time feature or sit on the designated bench to advance to 7 PM if required. Once you jack in to the terminal, the receptionist offers you two possible dolls: Angel or Skye. Your choice affects who you will talk to in the following scene, but is of no further consequence; you must pay the same amount to get in either way. Deposit your weapons in the designated security locker before you head to your chosen doll's booth. Your conversation with the doll can unlock unique opportunities, giving you access to critical information regarding Evelyn – see overleaf for details.

3

Next, follow the waypoint to reach the VIP area. You need to get in, but a bouncer will only permit holders of an access card to enter. If you try to force your way in, note that any acts of violence will be remembered and mentioned in future exchanges, both in this mission and in a later side job; you should also be mindful that you deposited your weapons in the locker earlier. The good news is that there are many alternative ways to get to the VIP area on the upper floor without raising the alarm – as detailed overleaf.

4

Once upstairs in the VIP area, you can speak to Tom in his booth, but your objective is to interrogate the owner, Woodman, in his office. Fighting your way through is of course a possibility (and unavoidable if you previously triggered conflict), though there are several ways to get to your target without bloodshed – once again, see overleaf for more details. Your conversation with Woodman has several possible outcomes, some of which end in his death (in which case you will find the clues you need by examining his computer). However, if you manage to convince him to tell you what he knows, he can survive this encounter. Should Woodman live, you will get a chance to run into him again during a later side job ("Ex-Factor" – see page 209). Finally, all that's left to do is leave Clouds. Don't forget to retrieve your weapons, and take the main elevator back down to ground level to complete the job.

SUCCESSFULLY INTERROGATING WOODMAN

If you manage to reach Woodman without raising the alarm, there are multiple possible scenarios where you can get him to give you the information you're looking for without killing him.

In any nonviolent outcome, note that Woodman will activate the nearby service elevator for you, providing a shortcut to the exit.

METHOD	PREREQUISITE	CORRECT DIALOGUE LINES
Cut a deal with Woodman	You have a high level of Intelligence and you either investigated booth 11 or read the files on the computer in the control room; note that, at the end of the conversation, you will need to honor your promise – failing to do so triggers open combat	1 "Looks like you've got a netrunner problem. I can help." 2 "Tit for tat – only if you help me."
	You have a corporate background	1 "You see only Tyger Claws. Got no idea who's behind them." 2 "Girl I'm lookin' for is linked to Arasaka."
Threaten Woodman	You completed the gig involving Jotaro Shobo ("Monster Hunt" – see page 266)	1 "Wanna end up like Jotaro Shobo?" 2 "Shobo had an unlucky meeting."
	You watched the holoprojection of Evelyn's episode in booth 11	1 "I'll tell the media everything." 2 "Gonna take this to the news."
	You've met River Ward by completing the "I Fought the Law" side job (see page 196)	1 "Could call NCPD vice right now." 2 "Maybe not, but then again..."
	You choose the following dialogue lines, having said nothing aggressive beforehand*	1 "Your bosses should know how you treat customers." 2 "You're higher-up than I thought."
	You choose the following dialogue lines, having said nothing aggressive beforehand*	1 "Let's not make this harder than it has to be." 2 "One way or another, I'll find out..."

* If you opt for aggressive or insulting behavior towards Woodman, or repeatedly ask about Evelyn, he will react negatively, potentially causing the threat strategy to fail.

MJ-12 AUTOMATIC LOVE (CONTINUED)

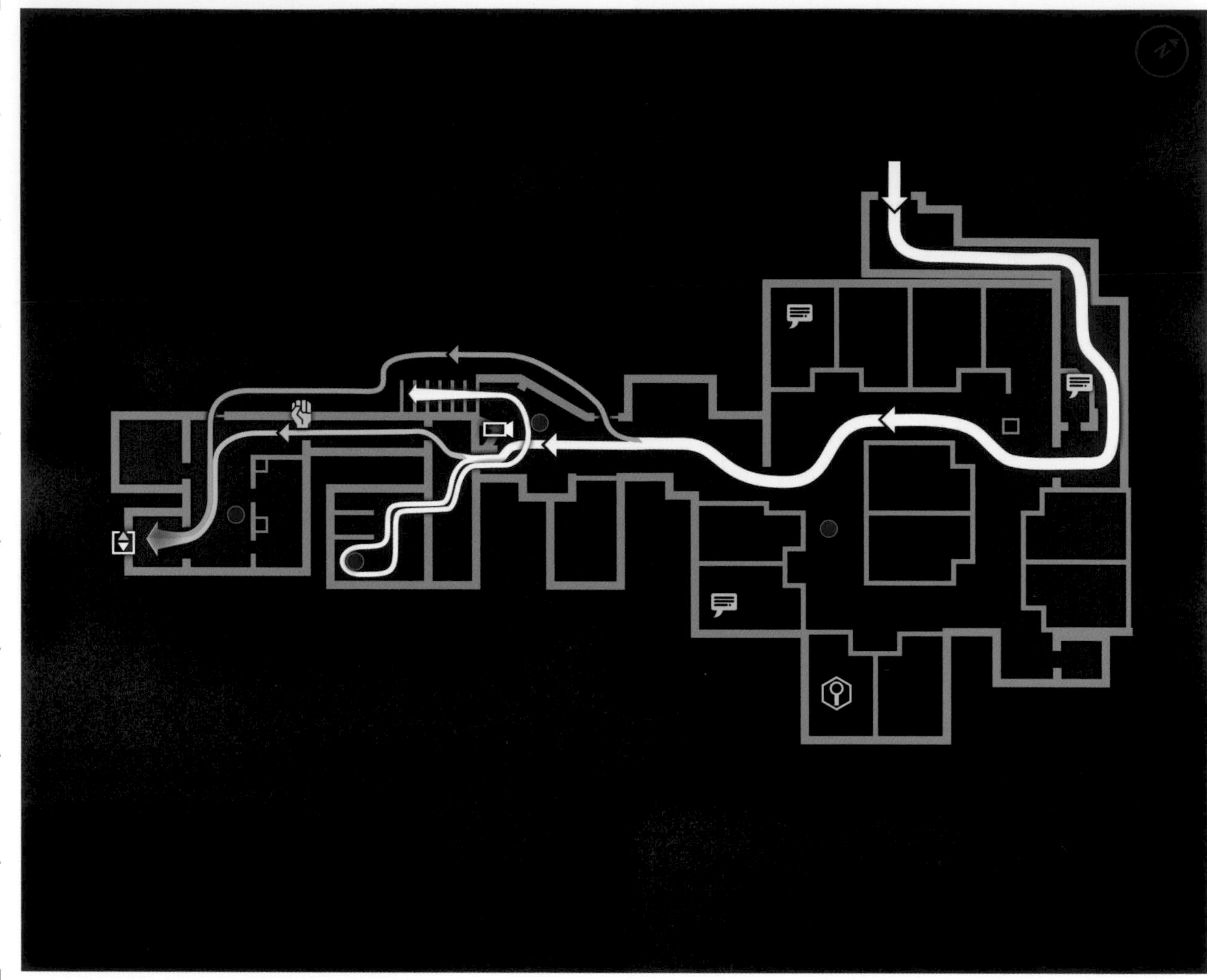

MAIN FLOOR INFILTRATION

You need to talk to Skye or Angel in either booth 6 or 9. During the conversation with the doll, ask about the incident involving Evelyn whenever given the opportunity, particularly about where the incident happened: the doll will reveal to you that Evelyn was attacked by a client in booth 11, and you can ask how to get into it. This will give you access to the booth.

If you unlocked it during your conversation with the doll (by asking where the incident happened), investigate booth 11. Scan and inspect both the blood stains, the wall-mounted port frame by the bed, and the holoview in the corner to visualize the scene via the security feeds. The information that you obtain this way can be profitably put to use in your imminent interrogation of Woodman.

After talking to your doll, your primary goal is to go through the door leading to the VIP area (it's both locked and guarded by a bouncer) – or circumvent it. One approach is to follow the Tyger Claw who briefly chats with the bouncer before heading into the restrooms. Take him down quietly from behind and steal his card (along with his weapon, which might come in handy in case things go awry). You can then walk right through the door and head up the stairs to the VIP area. Technically, you could obtain the card from any Tyger Claw in the club, but the one in the toilet is by far the most convenient.

An alternative solution to get to the VIP area, if you meet the Body requirement, is to force-open the door adjacent to the restrooms. This leads you to a backroom guarded by a Tyger Claw. Wait until he looks away then sneak to the elevator in the back, taking him down on the way if you wish. Note that you can collect a knife on a crate, which could be useful if the alarm is raised.

Yet another way to reach the VIP floor is to open the shutters right by the VIP area door. With both the camera and the bouncer's gaze directed elsewhere, hop through the window, then crouch and use the walkway outside to reach the backroom with the Tyger Claw and the elevator. Make sure you steer clear of the drone patrolling outside to avoid being detected.

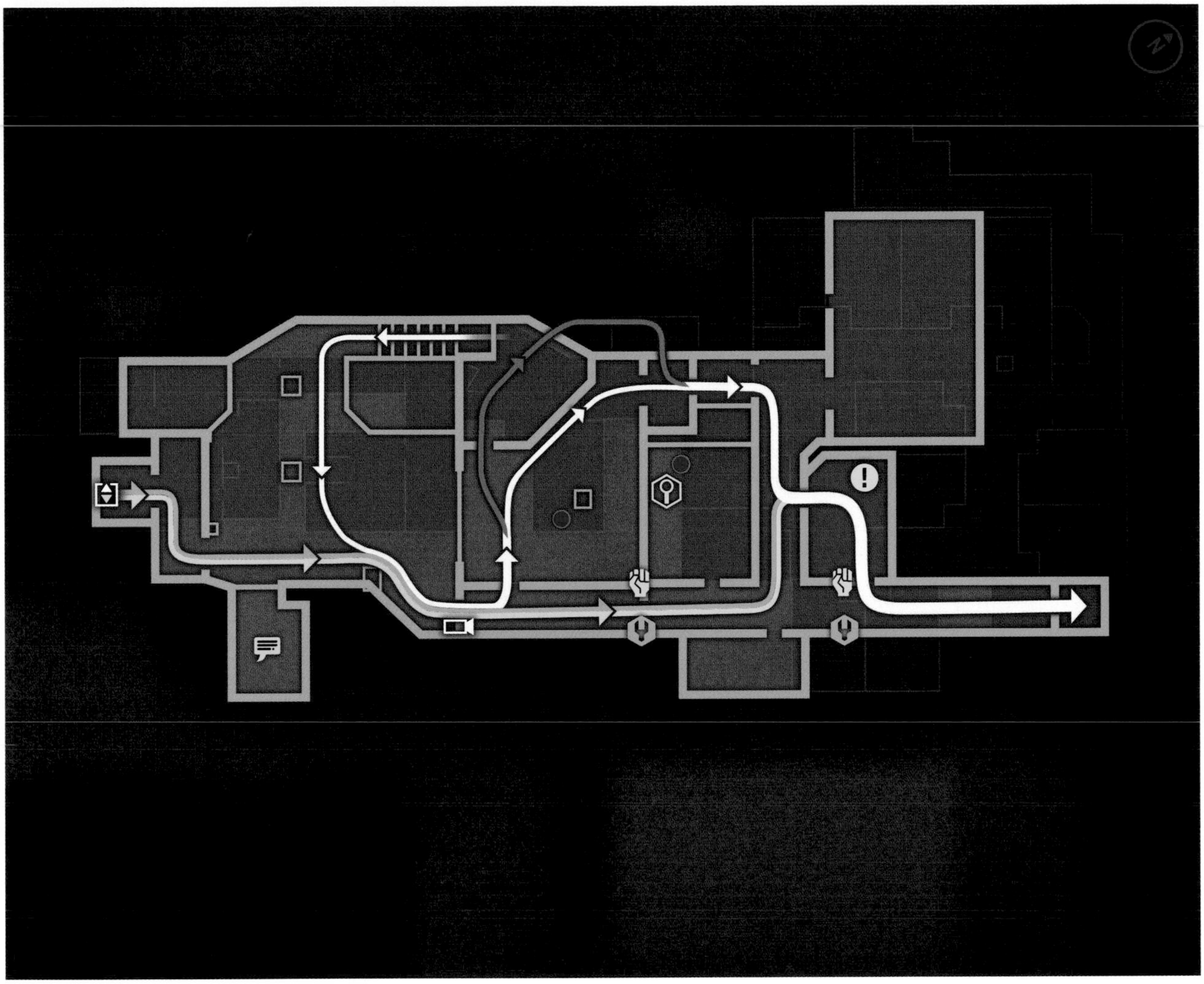

UPPER FLOOR INFILTRATION

Though you can head straight to Woodman if you wish, the normal way to reveal his position is by having a conversation with Tom in booth 2.

Your objective on this floor is to reach Woodman, currently situated in his office – but keep in mind that this is a hostile area. You have multiple nonviolent options here, as described in the entries that follow. For details on potential interactions with your target, refer to the "Successfully Interrogating Woodman" section on the previous double-page spread.

There's a camera that rotates above the door leading to the hostile area. Make sure you neutralize it first, or sneak through the door while it is facing away from you.

If your Technical Ability or Body attributes are high enough, you can open the locked door in the hostile area. You are then just a few steps away from Woodman's office.

Alternatively, you can enter the private lounge on the left and stealthily eliminate (or sneak by) the lone Tyger Claw guarding it. The nearby vending machine can be perfect to cause a distraction. Go through the door across the room and you will find Woodman's office beyond.

Another approach is to enter the private lounge and sneak through the door on your left. This leads you to a make-up room where you can open the shutters and bypass the Tyger Claw via a balcony. Note that Evelyn's jacket can be found in the make-up room.

Just opposite Woodman's office lies the club's control room. If you quietly take down the agent inside, you can then read multiple messages and files on the computer. This can be relevant to successfully interrogating Woodman. Note that you can also optionally retrieve some of Evelyn's belongings in the nearby locker room, as well as weapons which might come in handy if you trigger combat against Woodman.

MJ-13

THE SPACE IN BETWEEN

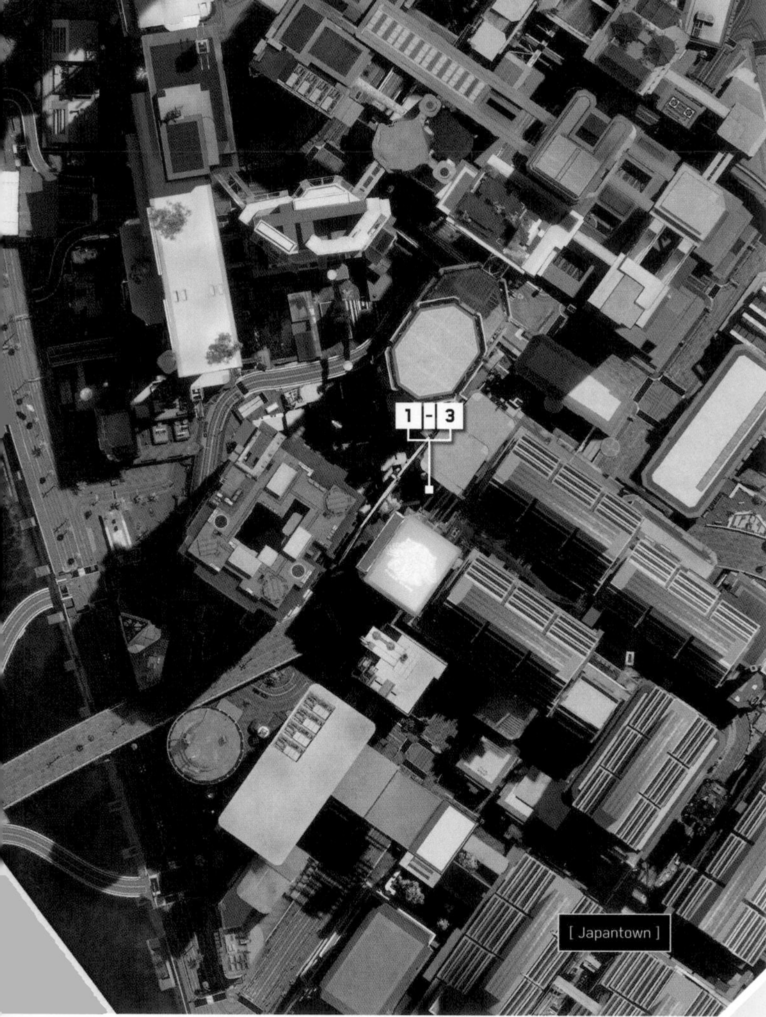

AREA MAP

Unlock Condition:
Complete MJ-12 ("Automatic Love").

Notes:
This job is triggered automatically after the previous one. Jig Jig Street is only a short stroll away so it makes sense to complete them back to back. You can call Judy on the way if you wish to keep her informed.

1

Fingers' clinic can be found in a small back alley at the far end of Jig Jig Street. You can use brute force to get rid of the thugs outside, or talk your way through. If you have the Street Kid backstory, the exclusive dialogue line available to you will resolve the situation instantly. If your Body attribute is high enough there is another unique option to intimidate your way inside. You could also force-open the side door or reach the window on the upper floor (via the nearby dumpster and the awning) to bypass the goons altogether. Failing all that, you can also simply say that you're looking for Fingers because you're an escort and you have a "busted implant."

2

Inside the clinic, several people are awaiting appointments with Fingers. You have multiple options here: enter the surgery room via the window in the waiting room, then the grate (gated behind a Technical Ability requirement); force-open the door leading to the surgery room (which is possible only if your Body attribute is high enough); speak with Judy until the surgery finishes; convince people in the waiting room to let you cut in line; hack the computer to secure the next appointment; or, if you're so inclined, simply wait your turn.

3

Once in the surgery room, your goal is to encourage Fingers to reveal where to find Evelyn. Feel free to proceed as you please, violently or otherwise, and with or without Judy's help. Note, however, that Fingers will not be available as a ripperdoc later on in the adventure if you harm him in any way. You will automatically transition to the next job at the end of the conversation.

MJ-14

DISASTERPIECE

AREA MAP

Unlock Condition:
Complete MJ-13 ("The Space in Between").

Notes:
This job is triggered automatically after the previous one ends.

1

To retrieve the Death's Head XBD you're looking for, the easiest option is to head straight to the dealer in the nearby underground passage and purchase it from him. If you don't find him by yourself, you can discover his whereabouts in one of three ways: by looking into the dark net with Judy (you will need to connect to one of the few terminals in Jig Jig Street, open the Pleasures of Night City website, breach into the Login page, then check out the Braindance section); by asking about XBDs in the local sex shop; or by speaking to Wakako on the phone or in her parlor to find out about that same sex shop.

2

Once you have retrieved the XBD, meet Judy by her van and enter the passenger seat. To best explore the braindance session, begin by watching the whole scene in playback mode to familiarize yourself with it. When you feel ready to proceed, switch to editing mode. Remember: your goal is to find out where the braindance was recorded. To achieve this, you need to scan the following three objects in the visual layer: the pizza on the countertop against the wall (around 00:15); the lab suit by the BD editor's desk (around 00:29), and the coffee cup on the BD editor's desk (around 00:45). Once V has deduced where the XBD was recorded, you can leave the simulation with ◎/Ⓑ.

3

Your next destination is an abandoned power station in Charter Hill. Unless you have other things to do in the meantime, you can accept Judy's offer to ride with her. Read the section that follows for a complete presentation of the power station's layout and how you can infiltrate it.

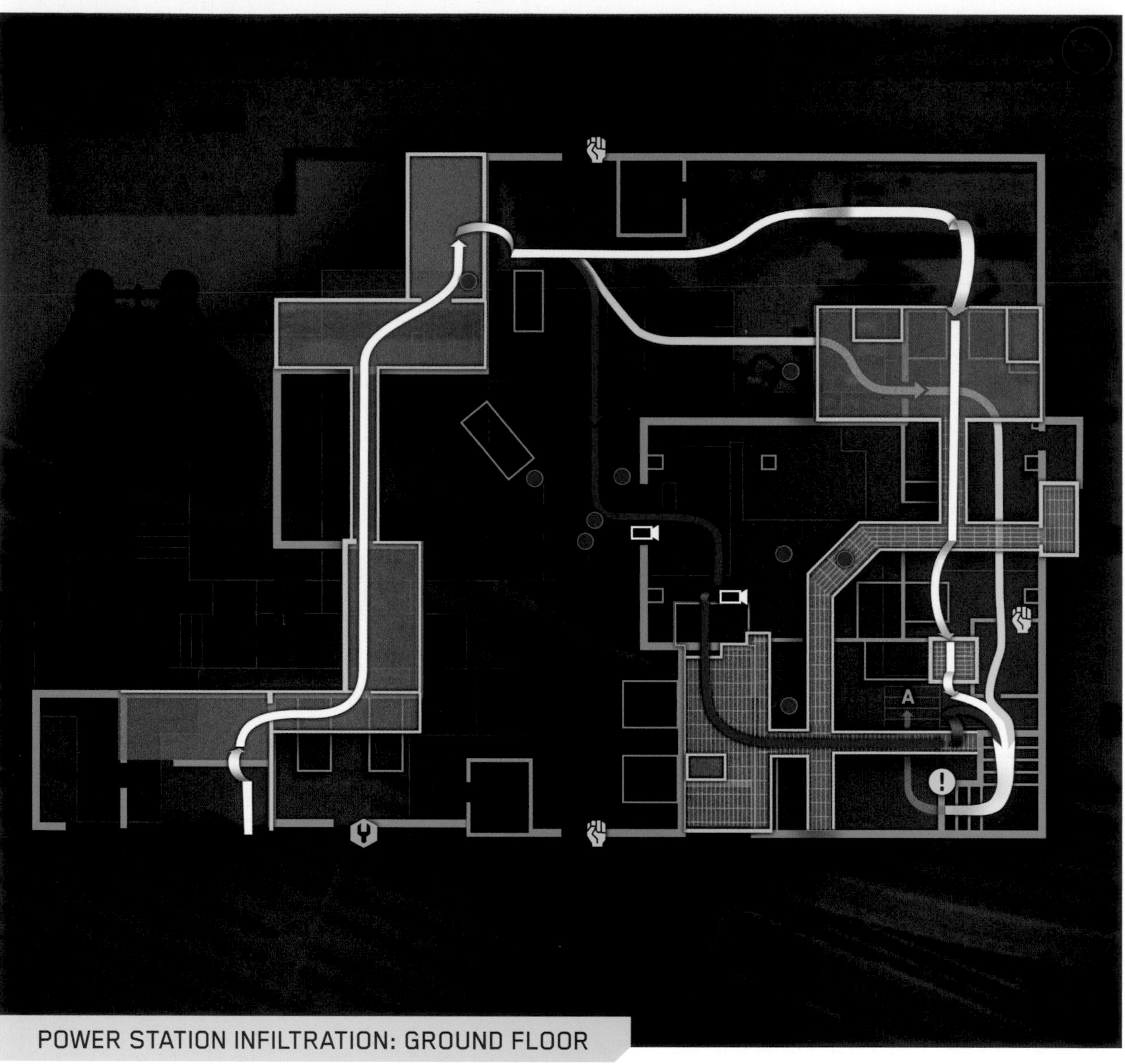

POWER STATION INFILTRATION: GROUND FLOOR

The stairs leading underground are your objective on the building's ground floor. They give you access to the basement (level -1).

Various doors lead into the power station's perimeter, though they are gated behind attribute requirements. A point of access with no such requirement is to climb onto the collapsed platform using the stacks of wood as a stepping stone. This option has the merit of getting you within easy reach of the computer in the small building opposite the warehouse, which you can use to turn off all the surveillance cameras in the local network. From here, a convenient stealth route into the compound involves climbing up to the elevated platform on the northeast side of the warehouse, which you can reach by hopping onto the stacks of pallets and the metal canopy. You will encounter a single guard on the way, but avoiding this sentry is easy. The door at the top gives you access to an elevated metal walkway. Sprint forward and jump across the gap, then drop down directly to the stairs when the guard who patrols beneath is elsewhere.

You can alternatively enter the warehouse via the door on the ground floor if you're prepared to deal with the local sentry. Once inside, you can force-open the door in front of you if your Body attribute is sufficient, arriving at the top of the basement stairs.

Getting through the front door unnoticed is eminently achievable, though you will encounter more guards on the way, and would be advised to preemptively deactivate the surveillance camera. Once inside, climb the stacks of pallets on your right to reach an elevated platform. Drop down on the other side when the guard patrolling the stairs area is away, then sneak to your objective.

POWER STATION INFILTRATION: LEVEL -1

Your goal is to reach the stairs leading down to level -2.

Shortly after reaching the first basement, you will find a room with two scavengers: one in front of a computer, and one on the other side. Both will be looking away from you most of the time, so it's easy to take them down silently and breach the computer if you wish. Further in, two more scavengers guard the main hallway. Their patrol routes regularly take them away from each other, so it's easy to judge a prime moment to deal with one silently before attending to the other. You will find two more scavengers standing guard in the final room. Judy will offer her help here, causing a distraction with smoke. Use this opportunity to stealthily eliminate your foes, then walk down the stairs leading to level -2.

If your Technical Ability is high enough, you have access to a shortcut, leading you close to the exit of the main hallway – though you will still need to avoid the gaze of both scavengers.

With a sufficient Body attribute, you can alternatively force-open the shutters in the room adjacent to the main hallway, avoiding the two sentries guarding it in the process.

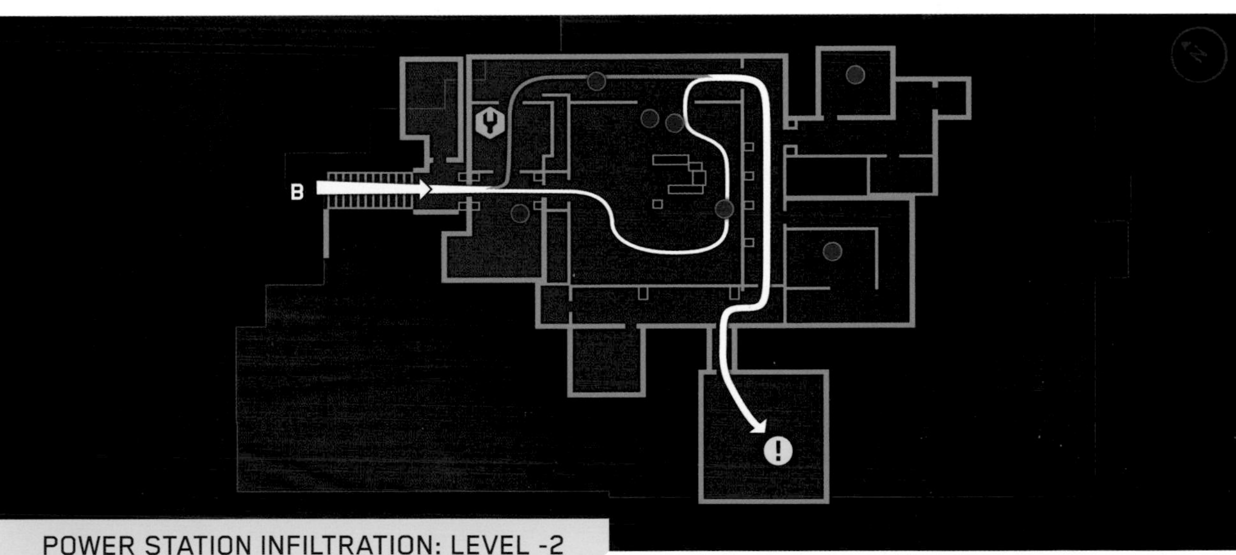

POWER STATION INFILTRATION: LEVEL -2

Evelyn, your objective, is found in this room. Once you have gripped the cable and pulled it, interact with Evelyn, then leave the room with her.

The first room features a single guard, easily incapacitated, and a computer that you can breach. The officer in the main room runs a circular patrol around the central structure. You can catch him off guard when he stops in the corner of the room opposite to the scavengers. Once he's down, use distractions to get rid of the others, before making your way to Evelyn.

If you meet the Technical Ability requirement, you can open the double door in the first room, offering a shortcut to bypass the main room. You have a single scavenger on your path here, who is thoughtfully facing away from you.

MJ-15

DOUBLE LIFE

AREA MAP

Unlock Condition:
Complete MJ-14 ("Disasterpiece").

Notes:
This job is triggered immediately after the previous one.

1

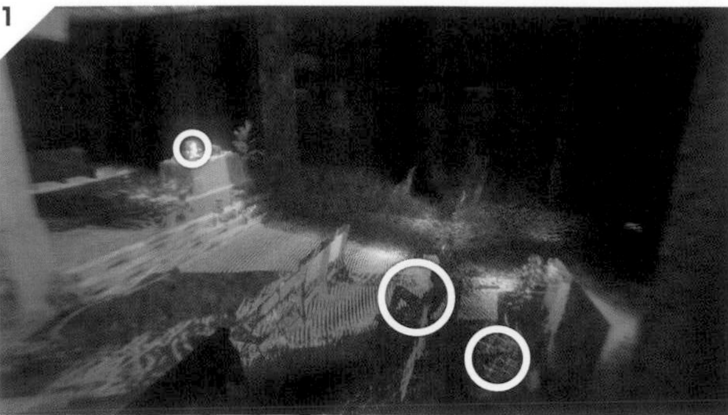

Talk to Johnny on the balcony, then enter Judy's apartment. After speaking with her you can optionally sit by Evelyn on the bed. Once you're ready, sit on the chair by Judy. During the first braindance session, you have three items in the visual layer to inspect: the Voodoo Boys hologram above the altar at 00:01; the unknown netrunner whenever she's highlighted (at 00:18, for example); and the flyers on the floor, between Evelyn and the netrunner, at 00:30. If you happen to have visited the chapel prior to viewing the braindance, note that V will recognize it immediately.

2

The second braindance session is initially difficult to understand. After uploading the language program, you can make sense of it. It features a single critical point of interest, this time in audio mode. Inspect the phone, then listen to the whole conversation again, from start to finish. After you leave the braindance, Judy enquires as to what Johnny Silverhand has to do with Evelyn and the failed heist. Your answer here will influence conversations in later side jobs that involve Judy. Talk to Johnny, then to her again, and leave the apartment to complete the job.

MJ-16

M'AP TANN PÈLEN

AREA MAP

Unlock Condition:
Complete MJ-15 ("Double Life").

Notes:
This job is triggered automatically after the previous one.

1

After your call with Mr. Hands, you will need to complete other jobs of any type before the next step is triggered. Mr. Hands will then call you again, this time with instructions to go to a chapel on Sloane in the Pacifica district. Make your way to the altar to meet with your contact.

2

Next, head to the butcher shop in the nearby shopping center and talk to the vendor. Look into the camera to be identified, then go through the door on your right to find Placide in the back of the shop. Follow him to his office in Batty's Hotel to transition to the next job.

MJ-17

I WALK THE LINE

AREA MAP

Unlock Condition:
Complete MJ-16 ("M'ap Tann Pèlen").

Notes:
This job is triggered automatically after the previous one.

1

Leave Batty's Hotel via the marked elevator, and head to the designated location to meet with Placide's people outside the Grand Imperial Mall (GIM). Two general scenarios are possible here. You can either follow Placide's instructions, connect to the access point on the van, fight Sasquatch and finally meet the NetWatch agent in the cinema – or you can bypass both the van and Sasquatch, making your way directly to the agent. Both approaches are covered overleaf.

2

Once you meet the NetWatch agent in the cinema's projection room, he will explain the situation and make you an offer. This is an important choice: if you accept his deal, this will have grim consequences for Brigitte and her netrunners (thereafter causing the Voodoo Boys to regard you with hostility). Should you refuse, it's the agent who will suffer. After backing your preferred horse in this race, follow the waypoint to leave the Grand Imperial Mall.

3

Your final goal is to return to Batty's Hotel. Placide's men outside the mall can take you there instantly if you wish – though you can get there on your own if you prefer. After a brief exchange with Placide, you will finally meet Brigitte. You must accept the offer she makes to complete the job and trigger the next one in line. If you refuse, you will need to return to her after a change of heart. If she is gone (which happens if you leave the hotel before you return), you will need to call her and meet her at the chapel.

BOSS BATTLE: SASQUATCH

Sasquatch is a heavy-duty Animal capable of dealing large amounts of damage if engaged at close quarters. Melee specialists might prefer to set aside their preferences and exploit her principal weakness: attacks from range.

Weaknesses

To tip the scales in your favor, feast on the following advice before you engage Sasquatch.

- **Juicer:** Sasquatch is artificially boosted by a Juicer installed on her back. This makes her immune to staggering, and significantly reduces any damage she takes. This also means that it's her primary weak spot: destroy the Juicer and Sasquatch will lose her resistances and immunities. It will also prevent her from using her hammer, greatly reducing her damage output.
- **Thermal Damage:** Sasquatch is weak to thermal damage because of her organic nature. The limited presence of cyberware on her body means that she is resistant to shock damage.
- **Limited Range:** You can turn the fact that Sasquatch fights primarily with melee attacks to your advantage. The most elementary approach is to confound her attempts to land blows by walking backwards as you open fire. This is especially effective after her Juicer has been destroyed.
- **Quickhacks:** Multiple forms of quickhack can prove effective against this opponent. *Short Circuit* will instantly destroy the Juicer, enabling you to deal substantial damage immediately. The memory cost required to cast this is significant, however, and even more so if Sasquatch has a higher level than you. *Overheat* causes damage over time, while exploiting the boss's elemental weakness. *Cripple Movement* hampers Sasquatch's ability to quickly move around the arena, drastically reducing the threat she represents. Along the same lines, *Cyberware Malfunction* disables Sasquatch's reflex boosters, limiting her ability to dodge. Finally, *System Reset* will instantly stagger the boss, which can be used to interrupt dangerous attack patterns or to create an opportunity to inflict severe damage. Though not a direct attack, note that you can also trigger a *Remote Activation* of the retractable advertising panels found in the arena: this can prove helpful if you want to clear the area of obstacles to focus on DPS after Sasquatch has been weakened.
- **Recovery Stance:** Whenever Sasquatch unleashes a full-power combo, she will stop moving for a few seconds to catch her breath. This is the perfect opportunity to deal withering damage, ideally targeting the Juicer if you have yet to destroy it.

Attack Patterns

Intelligent use of space and astute movement are essential in this fight. If Sasquatch catches you flat-footed, expect her to assail you with the following signature assaults.

Hammer Swings & Hammer Throw: Every time Sasquatch attacks you with her hammer, move backwards or dodge sideways. Her movements are relatively slow and predictable, so you don't need to be astonishingly fast – just sufficiently vigilant. When Sasquatch throws her hammer at you, try to find cover behind a solid obstacle – the weapon flies at high speed, making it hard to avoid. She will then run to the hammer to pick it up, which leaves her back completely exposed and enables you to easily target her Juicer. You could also decide to steal her hammer, but this is not a tactic we recommend: Sasquatch will then fight with her fists while moving at greater speed, making it harder to aim at her weak spot.

Breach Grab: If Sasquatch rushes forward and manages to grab you, she will breach your system. You need to hurry up and defeat the boss before the end of the countdown: when the time limit elapses, you die.

STEALTH TACTICS

If you manage not to get detected by Sasquatch, you can avoid the battle altogether and head straight for the cinema. You can do so by quietly moving from cover to cover whenever she looks away, and possibly by distracting her with the retractable advertising panels.

Once combat is initiated, you can escape this boss's attention by hiding for long enough, preferably after casting the Reboot Optics quickhack. Note that this works much more consistently if no other enemies are there to see you. When she loses track of you and returns to her standard patrolling behavior, you can then sneak up on Sasquatch and perform a stealth takedown to instantly destroy her juicer. Repeating the maneuver and executing a second takedown will permanently disable the Animal boss.

MJ-17 I WALK THE LINE (CONTINUED)

GRAND IMPERIAL MALL: GROUND FLOOR

The GIM's back entrance is a parking lot guarded by a few Animals. You can avoid them all if you keep a low profile and remain concealed behind the various containers and cars on the way. The first two sentries will mount motorcycles and ride away if you move close to them and wait. You can then head alongside the right-hand wall and enter the garage to give the other goons a wide berth. Use the crates as stepping stones to reach the elevated platform. Before you enter the corridor leading to the fitness center, note the presence of an access point behind a shelf that you can clear. As for the corridor itself, it features both a guard and a camera, which you can either sneak past (via the room on the left, for example) or quickhack. At the end of the corridor, stay crouched to avoid being detected by the two men having a conversation at the fitness center's entrance. Turn right, hop above the bar and keep moving alongside the right-hand wall until you reach the atrium. An Animal runs a short patrol route here, but he can't see you if you stay low.

If you arrive from the fitness center's ground floor, make your way to the left, and stick alongside the left-hand wall until you get close to the van. Move cautiously, tagging enemies on the way, and you should face little danger. Three hostiles are posted by the vehicle, but two of them will soon depart when you get close. Make your approach to the remaining one via the room on the left and you can quietly take him down from behind, then hide his body.

Once at the fitness center's entrance, you can opt to go left instead. Crouch-walk alongside the left-hand wall until you get to an Animal on a weight-training bench. At this point, turn right and head up the stairs to the upper floor **(B)**. You will find two more sentries at the top: hide behind the crates and wait until they split up and move away to slip through the opening and enter the atrium.

Another interesting option, if your Body or Technical Ability attributes allow for it, is to open either of the doors on your right in the corridor before the fitness center. This gives you access to a staircase leading straight to the atrium's upper floor – a shortcut without a single foe to worry about **(A)**.

The van you're looking for is found across the atrium. Once you reach it, connect to its access point. Remember, though: you can bypass this step if you wish and head straight for the cinema.

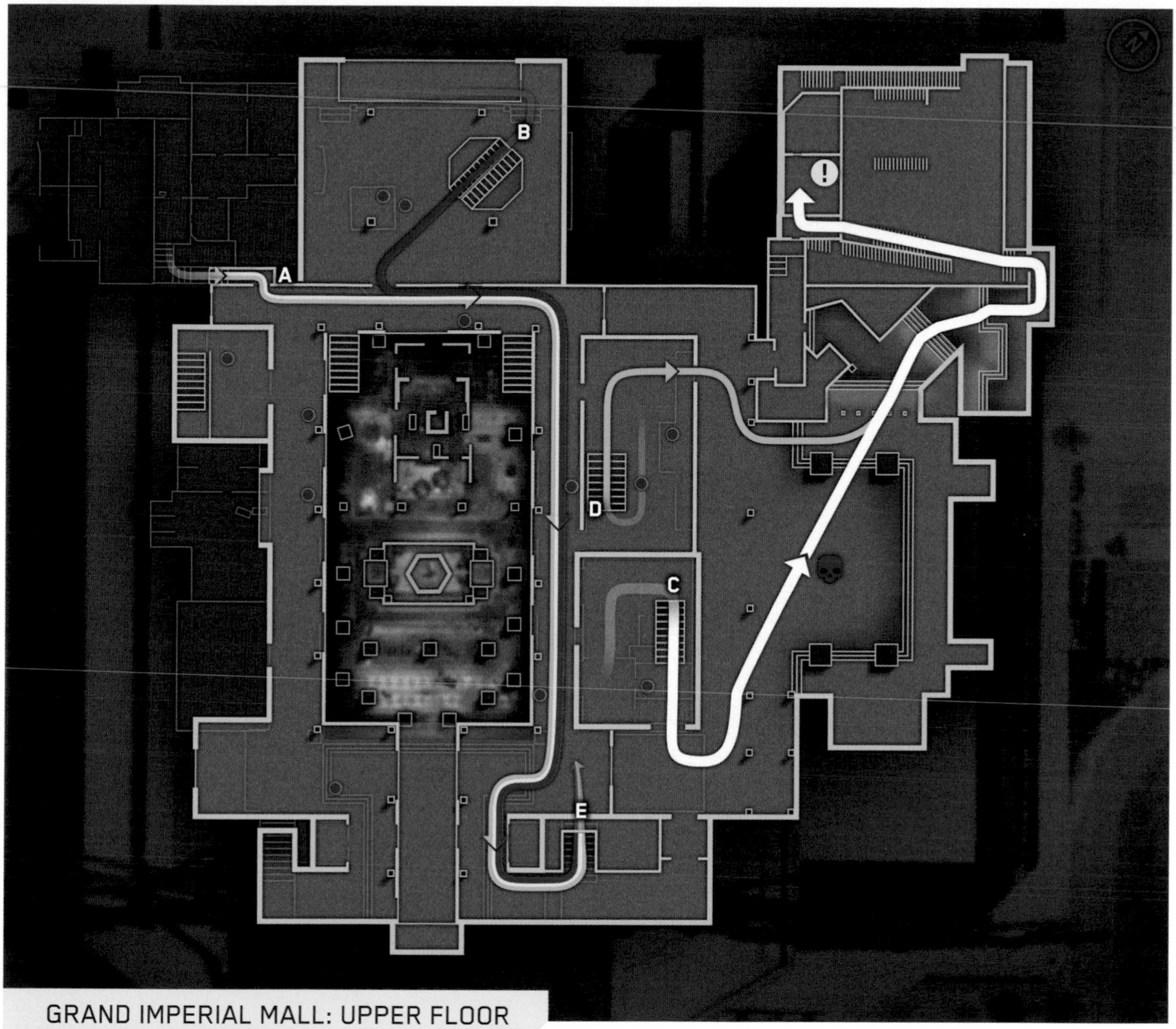

NIGHT CITY
PRIMER
COMPLETION ROADMAP
MAIN JOBS
SIDE JOBS
CYBERPSYCHO SIGHTINGS
GIGS
HUSTLES
ATLAS
INVENTORY
REFERENCE & ANALYSIS
EXTRAS
INDEX

DIRECTORY
MJ-01
MJ-02
MJ-03
MJ-04
MJ-05
MJ-06
MJ-07
MJ-08
MJ-09
MJ-10
MJ-11
MJ-12
MJ-13
MJ-14
MJ-15
MJ-16
MJ-17
MJ-18
MJ-19
MJ-20
MJ-21
MJ-22
MJ-23
MJ-24
MJ-25
MJ-26
MJ-27
MJ-28
MJ-29
MJ-30
MJ-31
MJ-32
MJ-33

GRAND IMPERIAL MALL: UPPER FLOOR

After connecting to the van, retrace your steps to that same room, where escalators offer a quick route to the cinema with only a few guards on your path (**C**).

Sasquatch patrols right outside the cinema where the NetWatch agent is found. You can find details on this boss battle on page 145. If you struggle, bear in mind that you can avoid the fight altogether by ignoring the van and sneaking into the cinema while Sasquatch is looking elsewhere.

The agent you need to meet is hidden inside the cinema– more precisely, in the projection room on the mall's upper floor.

If you arrive from the fitness center's upper floor or from the shortcut, the path to the van should be rather uneventful: take a left and go around the atrium in a clockwise direction, past the Kabayan Foods restaurant. You should have a single guard to worry about; quietly dispatch him, or avoid him, at your discretion. When you reach the far end of the atrium, go down the escalator on your left to arrive directly in front of the van (**E**). After connecting to it, you need to return upstairs to reach the cinema: you can do this either by retracing your steps (if you can force-open the gate shut by the NetWatch agent), or via the escalators in the room on the other side of the van.

Though a little unorthodox, you can skip a large section of gameplay here, both the detour by the van and the boss battle against Sasquatch. Get to the Kabayan Foods restaurant on the atrium's upper floor, and instead of continuing past it toward the van, head in and slip through the exit on the opposite side. You will emerge right next to the cinema (**D**). Hide behind the cover positions to remain unseen by Sasquatch, and sneak through the entrance when an opportunity arises. You can then meet with the NetWatch agent.

MJ-18

TRANSMISSION

AREA MAP

Unlock Condition:
Complete MJ-17 ("I Walk the Line").

Notes:
This job is triggered automatically after the previous one; it is intertwined with another interlude memory from Johnny.

1

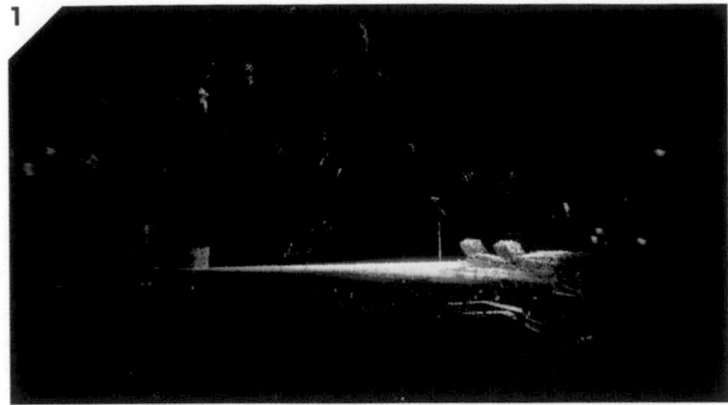

Follow Brigitte into the depths of the Voodoo Boys den, and get in the freezer to enter cyberspace. After exchanging a few more words with Brigitte, investigate the sound source: a microphone a short walk to your left.

2

During the sequence where you are looking for Rogue at the Atlantis, head upstairs and go through the door in the bar area. After your conversation with Rogue, a massive shootout ensues. Combat is unavoidable here, so use the various cover positions at your disposal to minimize the damage you take, focusing on taking down your enemies one after the other. Expect the same level of resistance on your way out of the Atlantis, during the escape in Johnny's Porsche, and inside Arasaka Tower. There are many foes to defeat on the path to the mainframe, including two turrets by the door which you need to blow with explosives. The interlude ends when you find Alt and disconnect her. The rest of the sequence in cyberspace is largely plot-oriented and best enjoyed without any form of guidance.

3

When you exit cyberspace, you are back in the hideout of the Voodoo Boys. The choice you made with the NetWatch agent determines how things unfold here: if you neutralized him and sided with the Voodoo Boys, you will be able to leave the chapel peacefully – unless you decide to provoke them, of course. If you accepted the NetWatch agent's deal and betrayed the Voodoo Boys, all the VDB netrunners will be dead and combat against their allies will be unavoidable – culminating in a duel against Placide in the chapel. Retrieve the key from his body to open the chapel door and leave.

MJ-19

GHOST TOWN

[Kabuki]
[Little China]
[Downtown]
[Japantown]
[North Oak]
[Corporate Plaza]
[Charter Hill]
[Vista del Rey]
[The Glen]
[Arroyo]
[Rancho Coronado]
Eastern Wastelands
1
2
3 - 5
6
7

AREA MAP

Unlock Condition:
Complete MJ-11 ("Playing for Time").

Notes:
You will need to make a payment during the opening sequence of this job.

1

To start this mission, head to the Afterlife and speak to Rogue. Agree to pay her when prompted to do so. Afterwards, go and sit on the designated stool while Rogue gets ready, then return to her booth and sit with her. When the conversation ends, call Panam to arrange a meeting.

2

Head to the marked location near the northern edge of Santo Domingo to meet with Panam. Get into the passenger seat when invited to do so. Follow Panam after your conversation with Mitch and Scorpion, take the toolbox in her tent, and put it in the car trunk before returning to the passenger seat.

3

Once at your destination, scan any three devices in your environment to find out that the power is down in the area. After reporting to Panam, scan the nearby transformer, then the fusebox on the adjacent rooftop. Return to Panam just below to discuss the plan and meet her at the power substation. Grab the jumper cables from the car's trunk, open the hood and connect them to the battery. Now return to the marked building and enter it (either by force-opening the door or by breaking the window) to restore power. With this achieved, you can get in position on the rooftop and wait for the Raffen Shiv to arrive.

MJ-19 GHOST TOWN (CONTINUED)

4

Turn on the power when Panam instructs you to do so. From your vantage point, you are in a perfect position to scan and tag all the Raffen Shiv patrolling the area, which will make this encounter less dangerous. Your goal is to retrieve Panam's vehicle, which will require you to steal the key from the guard holding it. He usually patrols right outside the bar's front door, but a direct approach is hardly compatible with stealth. If you want to remain incognito, consider instead entering the building from the west: quietly neutralize the foes you run into one by one, first outside, then inside the bar. You should find the key carrier near the entrance. Finish off the remaining Raffen Shiv if you wish, but your goal is to get to the Thorton. If you get in it and leave, you will need to meet Panam at the waypoint a short distance to the north. Alternatively, you can dispatch any survivors with Panam's support, and then be on your way together.

5

After you retrieve the Thorton, you have a choice to make. Panam wants to have her revenge on Nash, the former partner who betrayed her. If you agree to help, both of you head into the Raffen Shiv hideout in the nearby mines, where a major combat encounter will take place (see **6**), giving you a chance to loot Nash's unique (and powerful) weapon. If you instead refuse and convince her to stick to the original plan, you will skip the battle in question (see **7**), much to Panam's displeasure – but no actual long-lasting repercussions.

6

If you agreed to help Panam exact vengeance on Nash, brace yourself for an unavoidable battle in the mine. You face a large number of well-equipped Raffen Shiv, so tread carefully. There are enemies positioned both in the middle of the arena and on the elevated platforms surrounding it. If you have long-range weapons, this is a confrontation well-suited for patient marksmanship. Those who favor short-range engagements will need to dart from one cover position to the next, dispatching each opponent in turn. Nash, the leader, wields a powerful rifle, so proceed with caution. After the battle, loot your victims (particularly Nash) before you return to Panam's car and get in the passenger seat.

7

While Panam makes her deal with Boz at the Sunset Motel, all you have to do is stay in the car and wait patiently. Once the thugs are gone, join Panam in the nearby restaurant. She will suggest that you both spend the night here, at the motel (which you can refuse if you have other places to be). During the conversation, you can flirt with her and suggest that you share the same room – which she will consent to, though she will insist that you sleep in separate beds. If you don't agree to this (for the avoidance of all doubt, *very temporary*) compromise, you will end up in separate rooms.

LIGHTNING BREAKS

Unlock Condition: Complete MJ-19 ("Ghost Town").

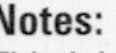

Notes: This job is triggered automatically after the previous one.

[Arroyo]
Eastern Wastelands
[Rancho Coronado]
Southern Desert

AREA MAP

1

This job's starting point is the gas station marked on your map, by the Sunset Motel. You can only meet Panam around midnight. After your initial conversation with Panam, take the passenger seat in her vehicle. During the journey, you will need to jack in and fire at designated targets to calibrate the turret.

2

Once at the satwave power plant, take out the security drones using the turret; note that the short circuit quickhack is an efficient alternative if you struggle with aiming. Next, run to the marked terminals inside the plant and interact with them to cause an overheat, then sprint back to the passenger seat. Panam will drive you to a hill overlooking the area. Take the detonator when she hands it to you, and activate it when prompted to do so. You then transition automatically to the next job.

MJ-21

LIFE DURING WARTIME

AREA MAP

Unlock Condition:
Complete MJ-20 ("Lightning Breaks").

Notes:
This job is triggered automatically after the previous one.

1

Focus your fire on the drones during the chase that ensues. You are then given an opportunity to do a little reconnaissance of the crash site. As usual, activate your scanner and examine all the targets beneath: the Kang Tao troops, the drones, the Aldecaldos, and so forth. Once you have a solid overview of the area, disconnect.

2

You can now head to the crash site, which is under the surveillance of multiple mechanical enemies, both androids and drones, as well as the powerful AV turret. Though brute force is a possibility if you have a sufficiently developed character, stealth may be preferable here. The accompanying picture shows you a suitable route to reach the AV Emergency Control powering the turret. Essentially, this means circling around the crash site counterclockwise and sneaking to the device while the droids are looking elsewhere. Once Panam storms the site in her vehicle, you need to defeat all Kang Tao operatives. Note that the Cyberpsychosis quickhack works wonders here, turning your foes against their own allies. Tech weapons are also warmly recommended.

3

With all enemies defeated, you can now open the AV's hatch and deal with a hostage situation. The hostage taker – the AV's pilot – will die no matter what you say. However, you can get him to tell you where Hellman was taken by choosing a very specific set of lines: see "AV Pilot Questioning" for details. If you succeed, you can go straight to the vantage point by the gas station in question (skip to **5**); if not, you will first need to track Hellman (**4**), and will face substantial reinforcements at the gas station.

4

If you failed to learn Hellman's location from the pilot, you need to identify the tire tracks of the vehicle that transported him. Activate your scanner, then hop on the designated motorcycle and follow the tracks until you reach the gas station. You will run into a few Kang Tao operatives on an airstrip on the way, including a sniper; feel free to engage or ride past them as you see fit. Your objective is the vantage point by the gas station.

5

The gas station where Hellman has sought refuge is protected by Kang Tao troops. Their numbers vary greatly in accordance with whether or not you obtained information from the pilot during the hostage situation. You can find a presentation of your options in the "Gas Station" section overleaf, which focuses on the scenario where reinforcements have arrived. In any case, take the time to tag as many enemies as you can from the vantage point: this will make it far easier to keep track of threats as you infiltrate the premises. When you reach Hellman, knock him out, then call Takemura. Next, pick Hellman up, take him outside through the garage gate, and lean him against the designated motorcycle. You can then conduct the interrogation however you please.

AV PILOT QUESTIONING

During the hostage situation, the default course of events is that either you or Panam will shoot the pilot before he reveals where Hellman was taken. There is only one way to get him to talk, and doing so proves very beneficial if you prefer to avoid firefights.

DIALOGUE LINES	INFORMATION REVEALED	CONSEQUENCES
"I just want Hellman" ▼ "I'm losing my patience"	Where Hellman was taken	You can go straight to the gas station, with limited enemy forces on site
Any other combination	None	You have to find Hellman's whereabouts on your own, with an increased enemy presence when you arrive

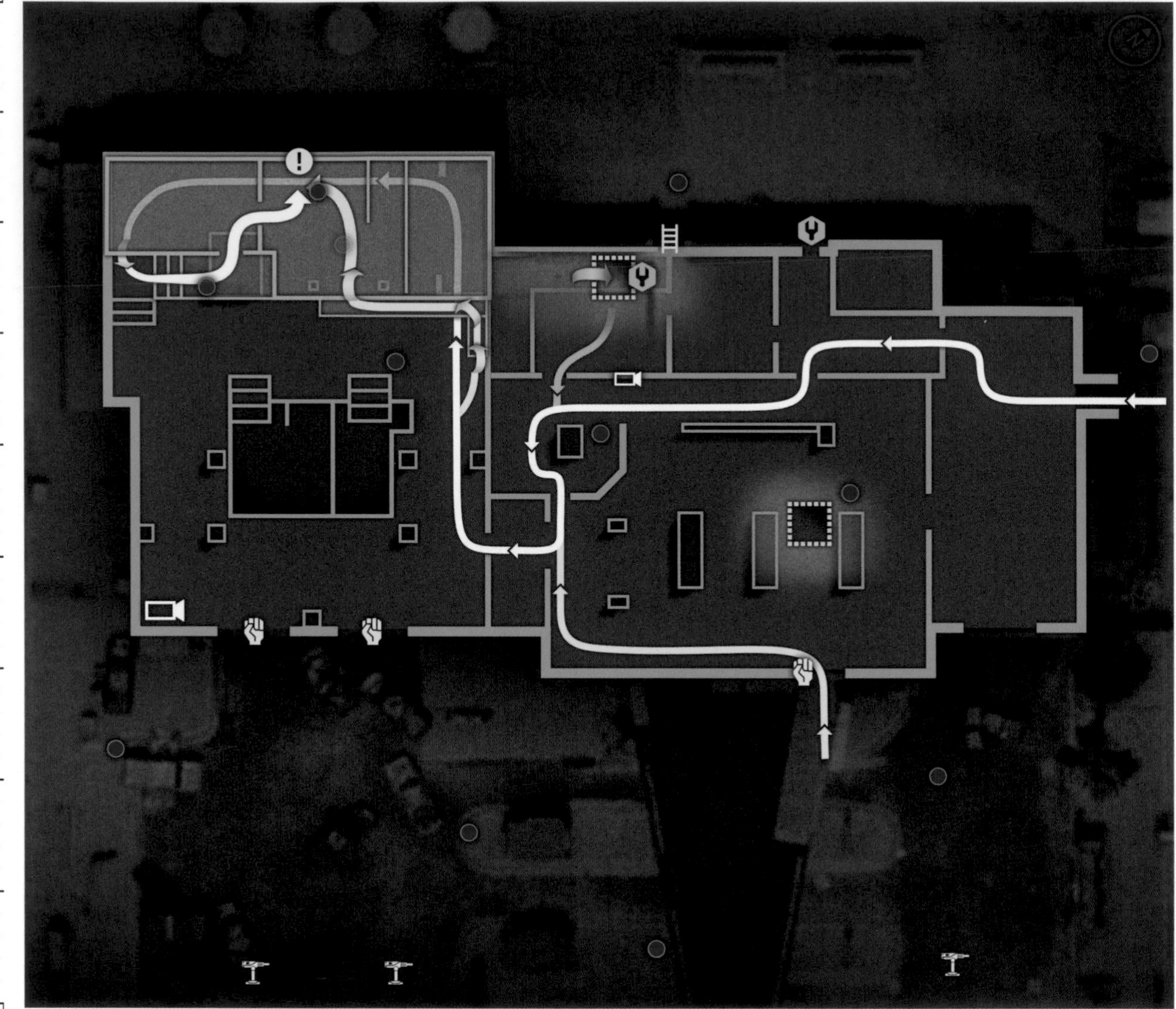

GAS STATION

Hellman, your objective, is situated upstairs, inside the gas station. The only way to get to him is via the stairs in the corner of the garage workshop.

Approach the gas station from the right, giving all troops out front a wide berth. Avoid the mines near the fence enclosure (reveal them with your scanner), then sneak to the door. In the storage room, go through the door on your right, then the next door on your left, to arrive behind a long counter. Quickhack the surveillance camera if you can, then follow the counter and stealth-kill the guard behind the bar. Now head to the garage workshop, where you'll find more potential assailants going about their business. The most annoying one is the soldier positioned on the stairs leading to Hellman. You can take him by surprise by making your approach from the storage area in the back, right underneath Hellman's location. You will find plenty of cover available to sneak past or eliminate the two guards on the way. Hellman awaits in the room at the top of the stairs.

If you have a high Technical Ability level, you could instead make your approach from the left side. Wait until the only enemy patrolling here moves away, then break the fence and climb up the steps. You will find a grate on the roof leading to a dropped ceiling; don't worry, it will hold your weight. Drop down and enter the adjacent room: it contains the station's owner, who will reveal Hellman's position, along with a computer that you can breach. Once you're ready to proceed, move to the main room and sneak past the man behind the bar before heading to the garage workshop.

The north garage gate can be force-opened, though this action will generally be in plain view of enemies here: to increase your chances, quickhack the nearby surveillance camera and drone. Once inside, keep left until you find the doorway leading to the garage workshop. You can then climb onto the shelving units next to the forklift to reach the air conditioning units above the storage area, and from here enter the office with Hellman via the open window.

MJ-22

DOWN ON THE STREET

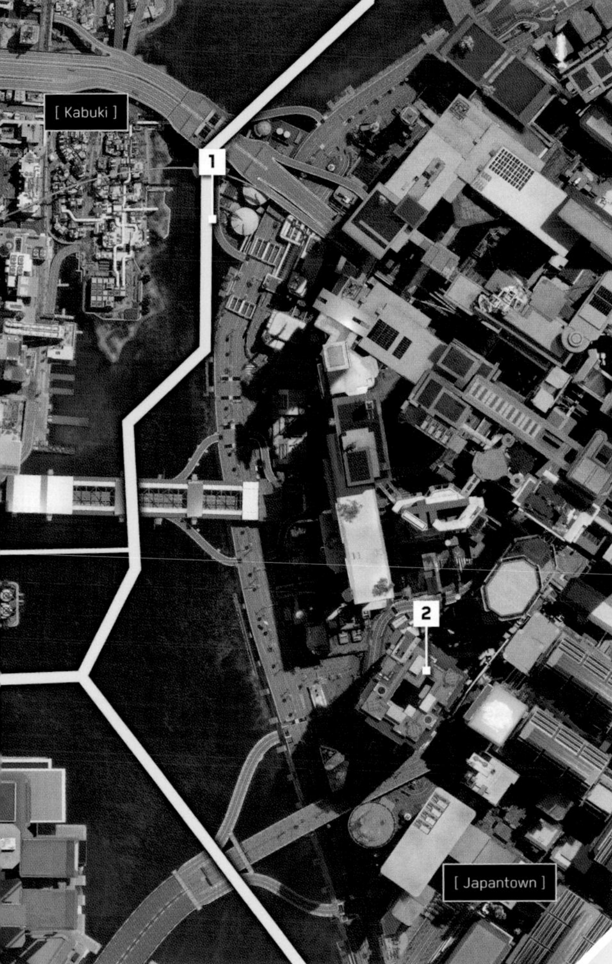

AREA MAP

Unlock Condition:
Complete MJ-11 ("Playing for Time").

Notes:
This job becomes available after you receive a call from Takemura.

1

Head to the Channel Street docks in Japantown and wait by the concrete failsafe parapet marked by a waypoint. After the meeting, Takemura suggests that you drive with him to Wakako's parlor; if you refuse, you'll need to make your own way there.

2

Head to Jig Jig Street and follow the waypoint to Wakako's shop, where Takemura awaits. After your conversation with Wakako, follow Takemura outside and talk with him. Your ally needs to gather more information, so you will need to wait 24 in-game hours (or skip time accordingly) before you can continue this story.

GIMME DANGER

Unlock Condition:
Complete MJ-22 ("Down on the Street") and wait 24 in-game hours.

Notes:
This job becomes available after you receive a call from Takemura.

AREA MAP

1

Head to Kanzaki Street in Japantown. The market area, where Takemura awaits, is found on an upper level and can only be accessed via a public elevator. After you follow Takemura and take the shard he offers you, he will ask you to break into a security room.

2

You can enter the security room either by force-opening the door (if your Body attribute is sufficient), or by going through the elevated grate on the left (with a second grate inside). Both options lead to the same room, where you can jack in to the access point on the terminal. Climb back up to the door via the ladder, talk to Takemura outside, then sit on the stool next to him. You are given a choice at the end of the conversation: join Takemura on a reconnaissance expedition at the industrial park, or let him take care of it on his own ("Ok, you handle that"). This is a more important decision than you might imagine (see "Befriending Takemura"), so think carefully before you answer. If you choose to accompany Takemura to Arasaka Industrial Park, you will be transported there immediately.

3

When you arrive at Arasaka Industrial Park, follow Takemura to the elevator and press the button to reach the roof. Once at the vantage point, agree to begin the reconnaissance. Your goal here is to scan the area down below, focusing on all the points of interest highlighted in yellow. Technically, you need to scan any four clues to complete this section, though more are available. Two special tactical options are worth noting here. First, there is a lone sentry on the far left, just outside the park's perimeter. If you have a Corporate background, you will hear him "freaking out" and expressing concerns about counterintel going through system logs, later giving you a chance to talk to him and convince him to open the gate for you. Second, if you look even further left, you will spot an Arasaka van on the road: exploring this lead will unlock the option to infiltrate the park by stealing the van and using it to drive into the compound. Once you're done with the reconnaissance, retrace your steps with Takemura all the way back to street level.

4

Read "Arasaka Industrial Park: Infiltration" for guidance on how to reach the parade float. After you hack the float in the warehouse, Takemura practically hands you the perfect exfiltration route on a silver platter. Wait until the coast is clear if you haven't eliminated all hostiles in the area, then climb up to the rooftop using the crates on the way as makeshift stairs. The mission ends when you leave the warehouse perimeter by dropping back down to street level.

BEFRIENDING TAKEMURA

Your decision to join Takemura or not on his reconnaissance expedition is important on multiple levels.

- First, it enables you to observe the layout of the compound you're about to infiltrate, giving you the opportunity to unlock two unique ways to enter the premises (either by van, or via an approach exclusive to the Corporate background).
- In addition, Takemura will share important details regarding Jackie if you chose to send his body to Viktor rather than his family at the end of MJ-10 ("The Heist").
- Finally, this scene with Takemura gives you an opportunity to befriend him, and amicably challenge his beliefs and convictions. Establishing a bond at this point will alter various dialogue exchanges you have with him over the course of the story, including during one of the game's finales.

ARASAKA INDUSTRIAL PARK: INFILTRATION

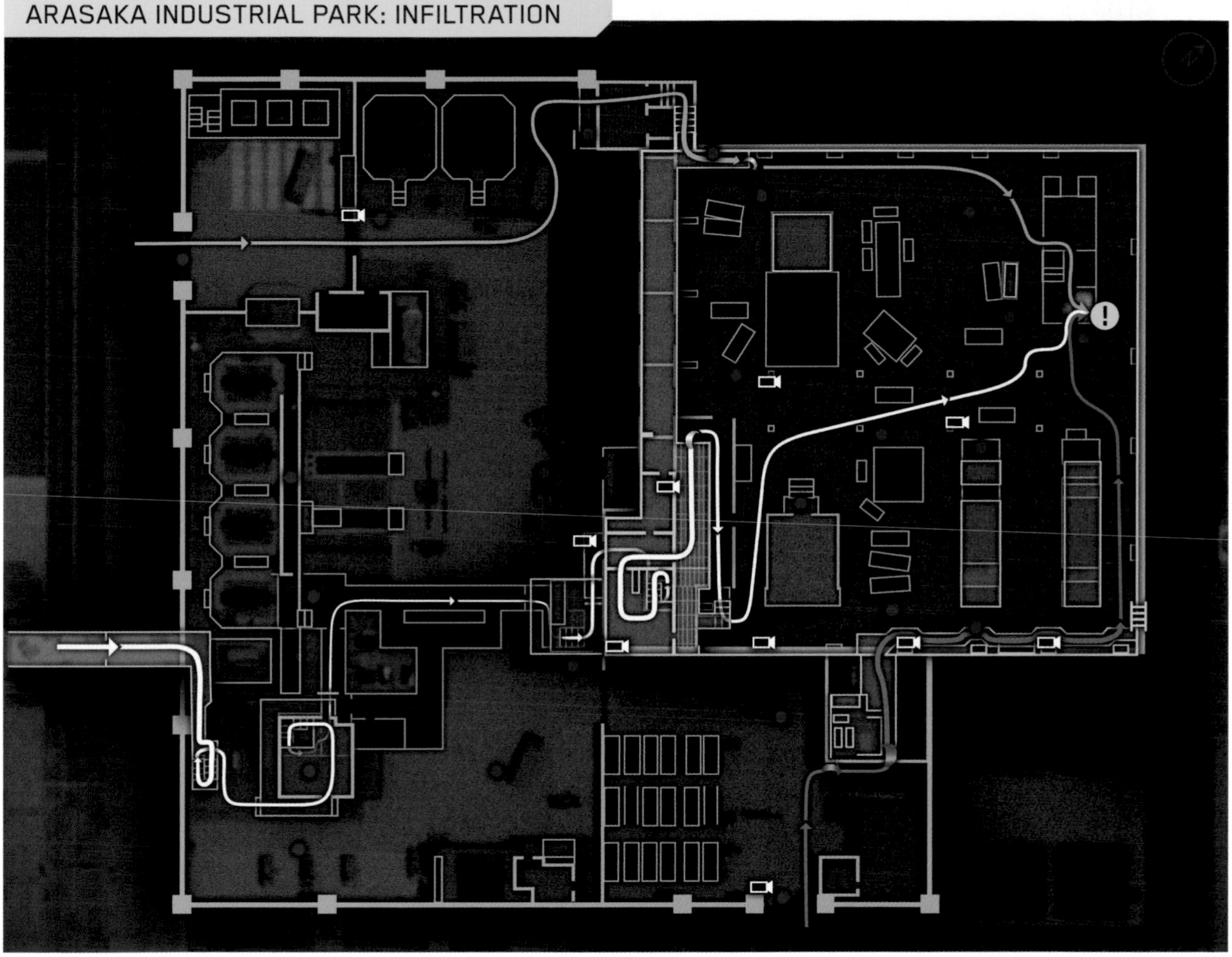

Using the footbridge as a point of ingress is a perfectly viable option; climb onto it via the crates in the work site where you did your reconnaissance. Neutralize or tiptoe past the two guards on the footbridge, then follow the path to the security building, crouch-walking at all times and sneaking past (or eliminating) any sentry you run into. Enter the security building via the door on the ground floor and neutralize the lone guard sitting in front of the screen. You will then need to walk down the stairs and navigate the service tunnel to reach the warehouse on the other side of the compound. Enter it by going through the double door, making sure the nearby surveillance camera doesn't detect you.

Another way to enter the compound is to go through the side entrance, a short walk past the facility's front door. This is also where you will arrive if you used the van to sneak into the premises. Distract the guard by the boom barrier using the surveillance camera above him, then crouch-walk to the pile of pallets just past the security booth. Now quickly hop successively onto the blue barrels, the gas tank, and the adjacent rooftop. This leaves you a few steps away from a door leading directly to the warehouse with the floats.

If you have a Corporate background and identified the lone guard by the gate, talk to him. Using the Corporate-exclusive dialogue line (about an "unscheduled inspection"), you can convince him to open the gate for you. Once inside, the sentries you run into will show no hostility toward you, enabling you to head to the double door leading into the warehouse building, or to walk alongside the wall to your left to reach the room in the corner. Head up the stairs to reach the warehouse with the floats. (Note that there's a powerful weapon to pick up on the way, inside shipping container 667 in the loading bay, though you will need to disarm the laser mine at the entrance.)

The float you need to infect is found in the large warehouse, across the industrial park relative to your starting position. The warehouse is guarded by an extensive security force (including soldiers, droids, and surveillance cameras), so it makes sense to tag as many enemies as possible from your elevated position on the walkway. You can then go down to ground level and cautiously crouch-walk to the waypoint. Use the many crates as cover to give all enemies a wide berth. Progress slowly and tag all foes one by one to be able to monitor their movements. Once near your destination, look out for the android patrolling nearby, then slip into the float and jack in to the terminal.

PLAY IT SAFE

Unlock Condition:
Complete both MJ-21 ("Life During Wartime") and MJ-23 ("Gimme Danger").

Notes:
This job becomes available after you receive a call from Takemura.

AREA MAP

1

After receiving Takemura's call, return to the Japantown market where you initially met with him. Take the shard he hands you to discover the specifics of the mission.

2

When the parade begins, cross the footbridge, then go up the long metal staircase. There are two ways to reach the first sniper. The most obvious is to follow the walkway and use the ladder at the end. The alternative is to go through the double door, climb up the ladder, then jump and pull yourself through the opening above. Both paths lead to the same place, a few steps away from the sniper, but the second route detailed has two noteworthy features: explosive devices (shoot or disarm them), and a computer that you can breach.

3

After neutralizing the first sniper, you have two ways to reach the second: a footbridge below your current position (described here), or another further above (see **4**). The lower one is only available if you have invested sufficient points in the Intelligence attribute. Drop from the first sniper's position and climb down the two ladders until you find a grate at the end of the path. A remote activation is all it takes to open that grate. Once on the other side of the footbridge, sneak up on the sentry leaning out of the window. Hop through that window and climb up the ladder directly on your left: this leads to an elevated platform. From your vantage point, tag the soldier on the other side and wait for him to lean his arms on the nearby railing before you neutralize him.

4

If you want to use the other route (the upper footbridge) after neutralizing the first sniper, make your way to the elevator, a short walk to the north. This will take you to floor 21. Now climb up the ladder at the end of the balcony and cross the street via the catwalk. Be cautious – one of the floor segments will fall right in front of you. Take a step back, then sprint and leap across the gap, either directly in front of you, or on the left side. At the end of the catwalk, you will find a grate. Go through it, then use the various walkways and ledges to descend in a counterclockwise spiral, avoiding – or, even better, quickhacking – the drones patrolling the area. At the bottom you will reach a door guarded by a lone soldier, with the second sniper just beyond. The soldier moves between two locations: one by the door, the other leaning his arms on the nearby railing. Neutralize him quietly when he's in the latter position.

5

As you enter the room leading to the second sniper, pay attention to the mine on the wall. Jump past its detection beam, or disarm it if you meet the corresponding Technical Ability requirement. If you have not been detected, you can now sneak to the second sniper and dispatch him quietly. After taking care of him, go through the double doors and be ready to jump over (or disarm) another mine. Now head up the staircase, paying attention to the two guards patrolling on separate floors: try to take them out while they're leaning out of windows. Follow the corridor at the top to emerge into the open air again, neutralizing any drones on the way, as well as the Arasaka soldier on the terrace while he's leaning on the railing.

6

Here, the route branches. One option (which involves a double jump or using the ladder inside the small building whose door is gated behind a Technical Ability requirement) is to climb up to the terrace above. This offers access to a service elevator that takes you to the foyer (see **7**). The other possibility is to leap onto the footbridge on the right while there are no floats passing by, leading to a climbing sequence (see **8**).

7

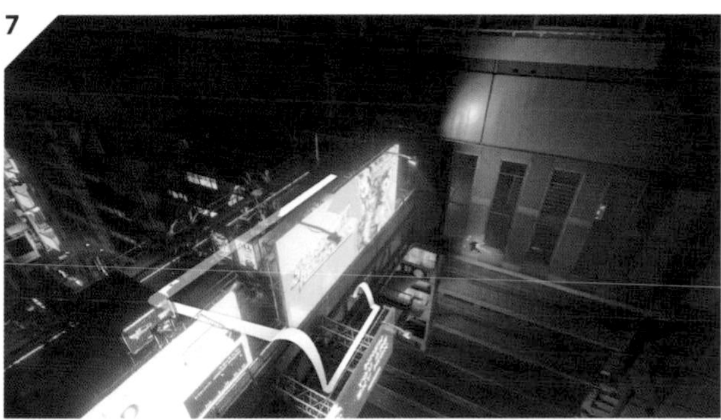

If you choose the terrace route, head directly to the elevator. You will come out on the foyer's upper floor. Go through the double doors in front of you to find yourself on the footbridge's roof. Neutralize any drone you see (the Short Circuit quickhack is perfect here) before you drop down onto the ledge on the left side, at the very end. Swiftly climb inside the footbridge through the window, a few steps behind the third sniper. Disarm the laser mines on the floor and finish him with a stealth takedown.

8

If you choose the footbridge route, make sure you cross between two floats to avoid taking any damage from their reactors. Once on the other side of the street, make your ascent as shown on the accompanying annotated screenshot, using the various stairs, crates, and ledges to reach the platform above. Sneak past the two guards just before you take the elevator to the upper construction area. Another soldier awaits at the top. Neutralize or creep past him, jump onto the metal walkway, then move to the end to find a ladder. Quietly get rid of any drone in the area (Short Circuit is the quickhack of choice for this) and climb the ladder. Do not linger here as you are exposed to enemy fire: swiftly slip through the window, disarm the laser mines on the floor, and quietly dispatch the third sniper.

9

After neutralizing the third sniper, head to the foyer. Two guards are posted on this floor, but they should be facing away from you; take them down or sneak directly to the right toward another elevator. This will deliver you to the balcony on floor 21. Follow the linear path to the Araska netrunner and jack her out. You are then attacked by a powerful foe: see "Boss Battle: Oda" for details on this epic fight. Once you defeat him, Oda's fate is in your hands – you can either let him live or finish him off. Showing mercy will result in his appearance in one of the game's possible finales, though no longer as an adversary. Whatever you decide, connect to the access point when you're ready to proceed.

10

After the cutscene, leave the room via the nearby double doors. Once outside, follow the walkway in a clockwise direction, then drop down and return to street level using the elevator at the end of the corridor.

MJ-24 PLAY IT SAFE (CONTINUED)

BOSS BATTLE: ODA

Oda is a fearsome cyberninja who can move at phenomenal speed – an asset both offensively and defensively.

Weaknesses

Oda can prove very hard to pin down, so it's important to make the most of his potential shortcomings to turn the battle in your favor.

- **Oni Mask & Smart Weapons:** Oda is equipped with a unique cybernetic mask that disrupts the bullets from your Smart weapons – the very firearms that can be the perfect counter to his remarkable agility. If you manage to destroy the mask, though, this will both stun Oda and disable the effect on your homing projectiles. You can then switch to a Smart weapon and inflict damage no matter how nimble your opponent might be.

- **Electric Damage:** Oda is weak to electrical damage, but resistant to thermal damage.

- **Tech Weapons:** Tech weapons pierce through objects. This means that, after tagging Oda, you can assail him with shots from behind cover positions, such as crates, while his attacks are rendered harmless when he fires in reply.

- **Grenades:** Accurate frag grenades can prove supremely effective. Any that inflict damage will not only hurt the boss, but also stun him – providing an opportunity to focus on pure damage output until he recovers his wits. EMP grenades are also highly recommended: when they connect, they temporarily cancel both Oda's Smart projectile disruption hardware, and the homing functionality of his own shots.

- **Quickhacks:** Many quickhacks can have a major impact during this battle. ***Weapon Glitch*** is ideal when Oda pulls out his SMG: this disrupts the homing capacity of his bullets, creating an opening for you to counterattack or move to close range. ***Cyberware Malfunction*** is one of the most potent options in this duel: it instantly destroys Oda's mask, enabling you to switch to Smart weapons; it also negates his high mobility for the duration of the effect. ***Detonate Grenade*** is perfect both to deal immediate damage and to knock down Oda for a brief window to focus on critical DPS. This technique only works once, though. Last but not least, you can employ ***Friendly Mode*** on the surveillance cameras around the arena: this will make the process of tracking your enemy much easier when he activates his stealth camouflage.

- **Limited Health:** As swift and disorientating as Oda may seem, do not lose hope: his health pool is actually relatively low. Once you gain the upper hand in this confrontation, it should not take long to defeat him.

Attack Patterns

Mobility: Oda is one of the fastest enemies you will encounter. He can dash and warp around the arena in the blink of an eye, both horizontally (either to dodge sideways or to rush toward you) and vertically (enabling him to reach elevated positions instantly). He also has the ability to dodge or block multiple shots in a row, his body moving at absurd speed. Rest assured that these abilities are only temporary: if you persevere, your shots will eventually connect.

Mantis Blades: Oda will often launch Mantis Blade combos. Your best course of action here is to backtrack and fire relentlessly. As long as you manage to maintain just enough distance between you and your foe, you can deal withering damage while remaining tantalizingly out of reach. Oda will need to catch his breath after performing these assaults, giving you an opportunity to riddle him with even more bullets.

Smart SMG: Whenever Oda draws his SMG, consider hiding behind any suitable solid cover: these homing shots can be devastating.

Optical Camo: After sustaining substantial amounts of damage, Oda will turn on his optical camo, becoming almost fully invisible, and run to a hiding place where he will begin to heal. If you do not react quickly, he can restore his entire health pool, so be swift: activate your scanner to reveal his footsteps and follow them until you locate him. You can then attack to interrupt the regeneration process and disable the optical camo.

STEALTH TACTICS

As with all other boss battles, it's possible to leave combat mode if you manage to escape Oda's attention and hide for long enough. The easiest way to achieve this is to either distract him with a surveillance camera, or cast the Reboot Optics quickhack on him.

Once Oda loses track of you, he will activate his optical camo and patrol the arena. If you manage to sneak up on him, you then have an opportunity to perform a stealth takedown, which will instantly destroy his Oni mask. The maneuver can be executed a second time, neutralizing Oda for good.

SEARCH AND DESTROY

Unlock Condition:
Complete MJ-24 ("Play It Safe").

Notes:
This job is triggered automatically after the previous one.

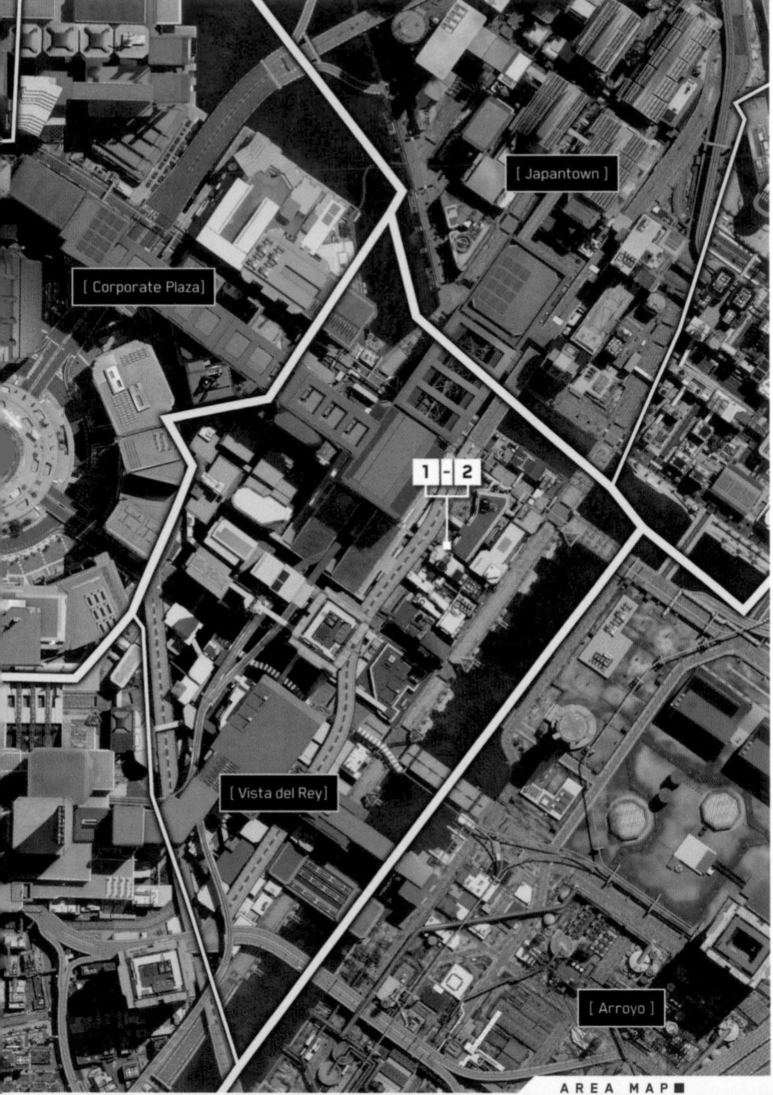

1

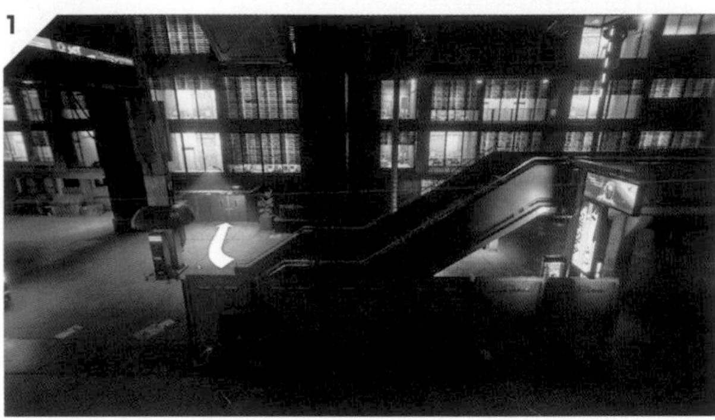

Head to Takemura's City Center safehouse. Enter the building via the double doors and go to unit 303 upstairs. Make sure you knock four times on the door: any other code will lead Takemura to open fire with fatal consequences. Once inside, impart what you know to Hanako, then go and check the hallway.

2

After the cutscene, you must escape the building, but there is an important optional objective that you may wish to attend to before you leave: rescuing Takemura. Choosing not to save him will mean that he will take no further part in the story. Refer to "Safehouse Escape" for details on how you can proceed.

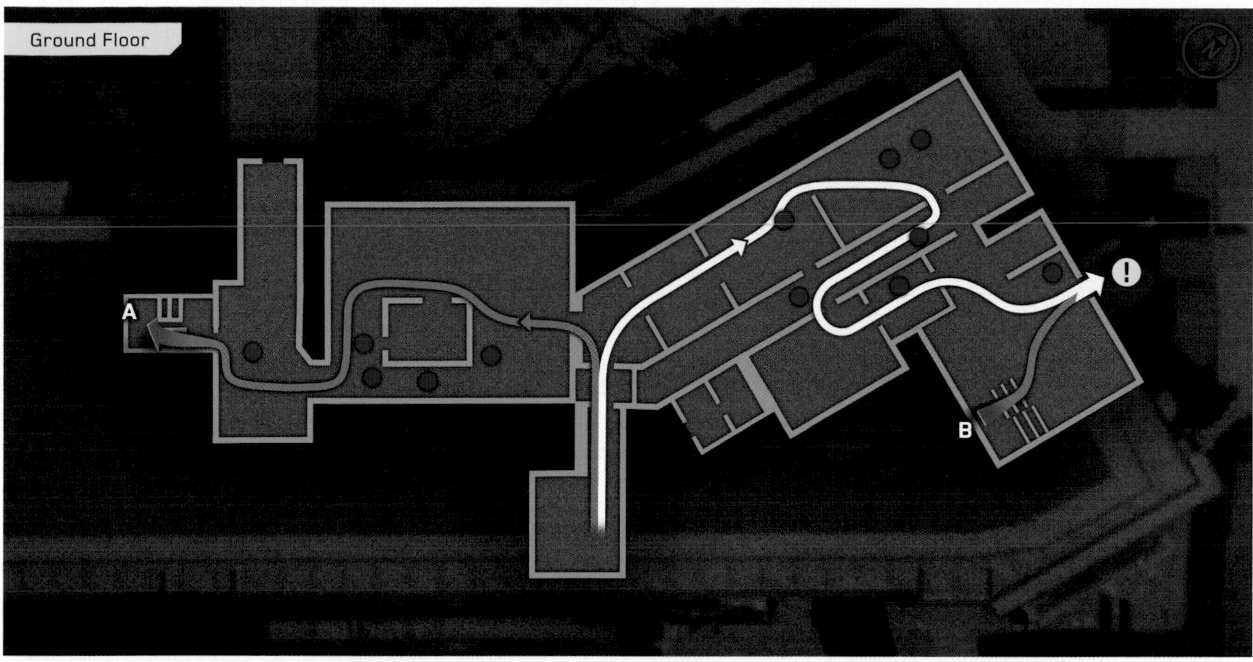

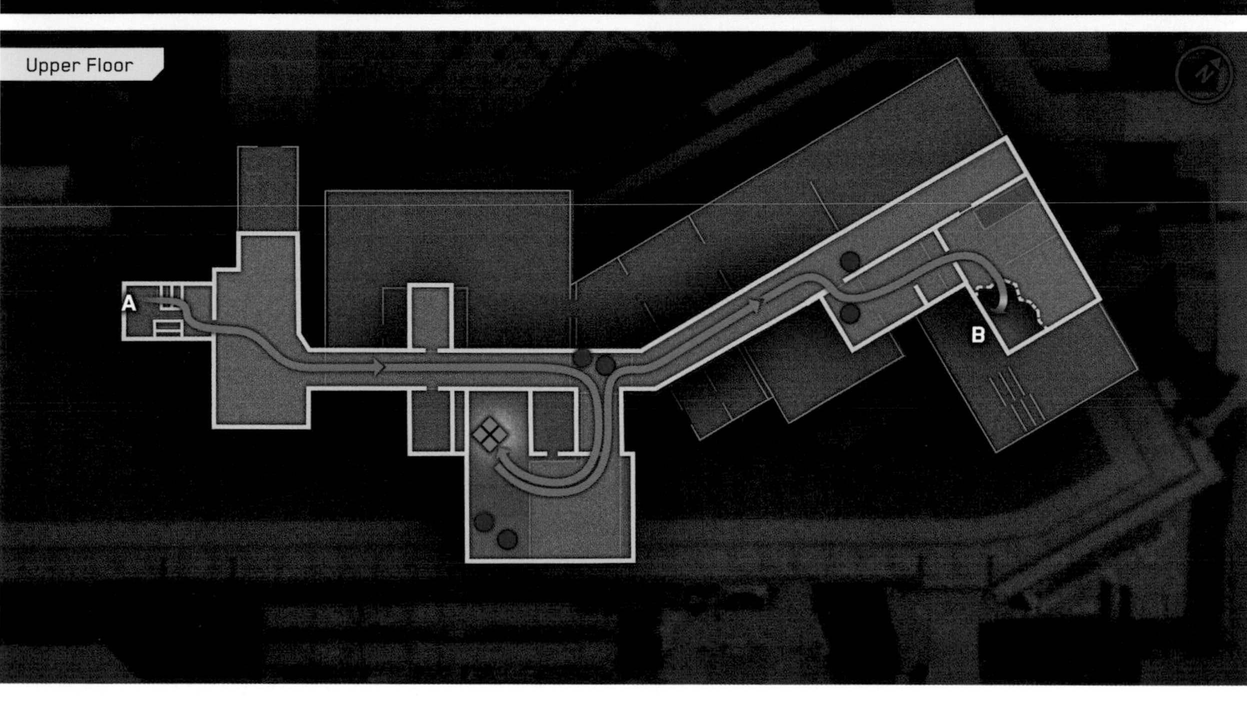

SAFEHOUSE ESCAPE

Your objective is to leave the building via the main entrance. To do so, you can head straight to this exit on your own, or make a detour to rescue Takemura. This act of kindness will not put you at a serious disadvantage: there is a shortcut close to his location that makes it trivially easy to escape afterwards.

If you wish to escape immediately, without saving Takemura, turn right when you reach the blue neon cross and follow the path to the exit. You will encounter several Arasaka soldiers *en route*, making it difficult to avoid open conflict. Move cautiously, crouch-walking at all times, and consider using distractions whenever required.

To save Takemura, you need to head to the left when you reach the blue neon cross. You can try to sneak past the troops, but they are aware of your presence and too numerous: combat is almost unavoidable. When you reach the stairs (**A**), climb up two floors (ideally taking a slight detour to collect a Tarot Graffiti collectible on the topmost floor – see page 225) and head into the long corridor. Take a right at the intersection and you will find Takemura in room 303. Now backtrack to the intersection, take a right again and brace for reinforcements. You will find an open door on your right a little farther along (room 307). Go through it, then drop down through the hole in the floor (**B**). This superb shortcut leaves you within immediate reach of the exit, with only a single, unaware foe standing guard.

NOCTURNE OP55N1

AREA MAP

Unlock Condition:
Complete MJ-18 ("Transmission") and MJ-25 ("Search and Destroy").

Notes:
Depending on the order in which you completed the two required jobs, this new job is available either immediately (if you completed MJ-25 last), or after you receive a call from Hanako.

POINT OF NO RETURN

Before you enter the elevator taking you to Embers, be well aware that you are reaching a point of no return: once in the restaurant, you will be locked out of all incomplete optional activities. If you have any unfinished business, such as side jobs and gigs – and in particular those that can have repercussions on the game's Epilogue (see page 108) – now is the time to take care of them. Once you press the elevator's button, it will be too late.

Whatever you decide, we suggest that you create a manual save file prior to entering the elevator, and keep it safe – just in case.

1

Head to Embers, the restaurant marked by a waypoint. Take the elevator up, then go and talk to Hanako by the piano. Leave via the same elevator after your conversation.

2

In Viktor's clinic, walk from the chair to the nearby table to collect the pills and your gun, then speak to Misty on your way out. Follow her to the elevator in the back alley and use it to get to the top floor. When you sit on the chair on the balcony, you have at least one critical decision to make, with long-term consequences – see "Finale Choices" for details. If you choose either Hanako's path or Panam's path, you will need to retrace your steps to the ground floor via the elevator to meet Misty, then follow her into her shop to complete the job.

FINALE CHOICES

During the scene that occurs on the balcony with Misty after your brief visit to Viktor's clinic, you have one or two important decisions to make, both of which will have a bearing on how your version of the Cyberpunk 2077 story will end.

Firstly, you are given an opportunity to call your romantic interest, should you have one. Doing so will cause the character in question to make an appearance during the Epilogue. If you don't, or would prefer not to involve them, you will be on your own in the corresponding scene.

Secondly, and most importantly, you need to choose who you want to team up with to raid Arasaka Tower and complete the adventure. Though the game features dozens of minor ending variations based on your actions, there are four primary paths here, irrespective of the background you chose during the character creation process:

- **Hanako's Path:** By default, your only option is accepting Hanako's offer and trusting Arasaka. This leads to a corporate-focused ending.
- **Rogue's Path:** If you have completed the "Blistering Love" side job (page 218), you will be given an additional option: asking for Rogue's help. This leads to an ending that heavily involves Johnny.
- **Panam's Path:** If you have completed the "Queen of the Highway" side job (page 233), you will be given yet another option: asking for Panam's help. This leads to a Nomad-centric ending.
- **Path of Least Resistance:** A fourth approach is possible – but exists purely as a roleplaying option (though it will almost certainly become a standard for "any%" speedruns). After selecting one of the three primary choices, opt to reconsider the situation. If you then look at either your hand holding the pills or your gun, a new possibility arises: committing suicide by crushing the pills ("Could also just put all this to rest"). This radical decision does enable you to reach the end credits immediately, and represents a genuine ending – but you will miss out on almost everything that follows. Unless you're simply curious to see how events unfold before reverting to a prior save, this is clearly not the option to pursue.

Remember: your choice here determines which ending you will reach. You can find a visual overview of all possibilities on our flowchart on page 98, along with links to corresponding mission walkthroughs.

Over the pages that follow, we first detail the scenario involving Hanako. The coverage of the path featuring Rogue begins on page 172, with the third storyline involving Panam found on page 174.

LAST CARESS

Unlock Condition:
Complete MJ-26 ("Nocturne Op55N1") and choose to team up with Hanako.

Notes:
This job is triggered automatically after the previous one.

AREA MAP

1

This job takes place in a single area, the residence where Hanako is held captive. After you neutralize the guard welcoming you, you have two primary objectives: first, eliminate four elite guards on the perimeter, then meet with Hanako in her bedroom and flee with her via an AV. As usual, there are many ways to achieve this. Read "Residence Infiltration" for an overview.

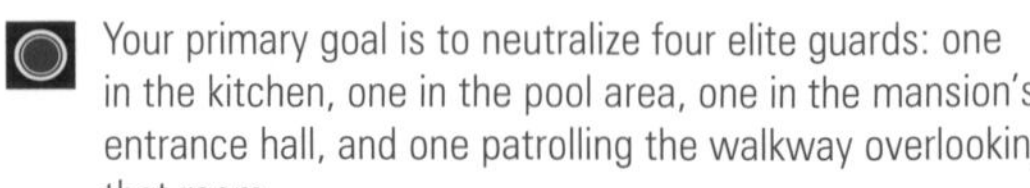

RESIDENCE INFILTRATION

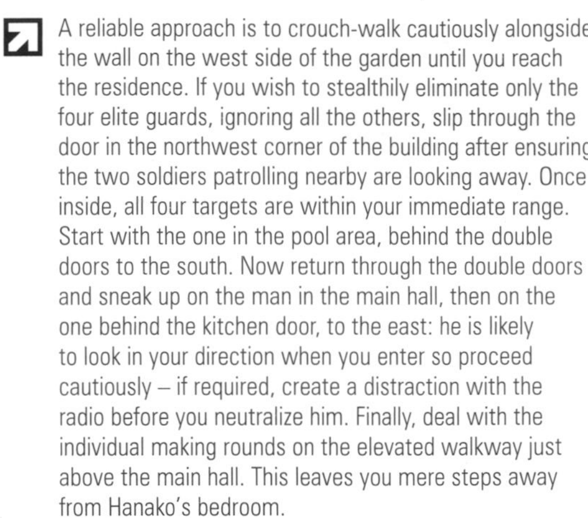

Your primary goal is to neutralize four elite guards: one in the kitchen, one in the pool area, one in the mansion's entrance hall, and one patrolling the walkway overlooking that room.

A reliable approach is to crouch-walk cautiously alongside the wall on the west side of the garden until you reach the residence. If you wish to stealthily eliminate only the four elite guards, ignoring all the others, slip through the door in the northwest corner of the building after ensuring the two soldiers patrolling nearby are looking away. Once inside, all four targets are within your immediate range. Start with the one in the pool area, behind the double doors to the south. Now return through the double doors and sneak up on the man in the main hall, then on the one behind the kitchen door, to the east: he is likely to look in your direction when you enter so proceed cautiously – if required, create a distraction with the radio before you neutralize him. Finally, deal with the individual making rounds on the elevated walkway just above the main hall. This leaves you mere steps away from Hanako's bedroom.

Once you have taken care of the four elite guards, you can make your way to Hanako's bedroom upstairs. Follow her to the AV to move on to Arasaka Tower, where the next mission in this job line takes place.

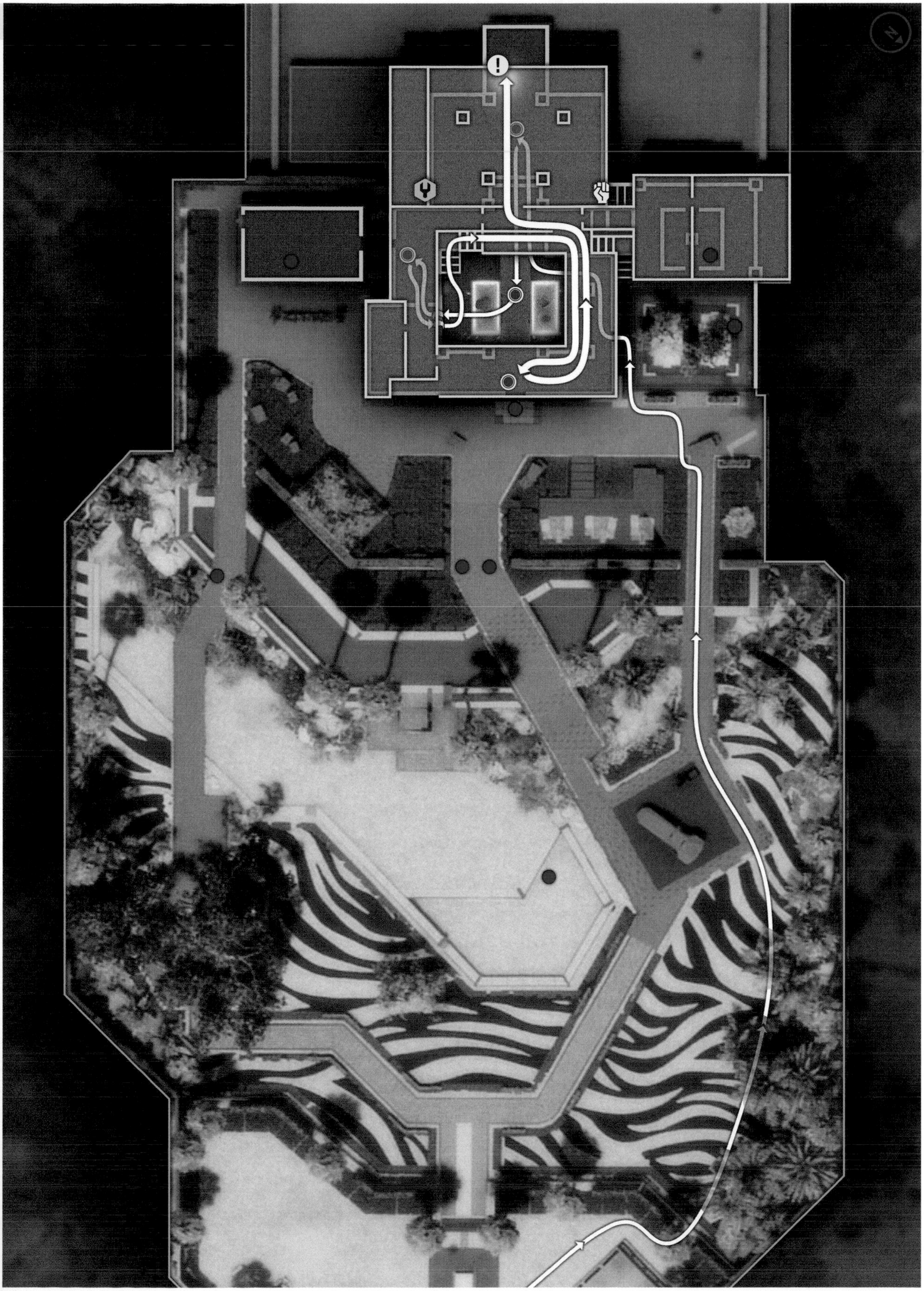

TOTALIMMORTAL

Unlock Condition:
Complete MJ-27 ("Last Caress").

Notes:
This job is triggered automatically after the previous one.

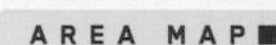

arasaka

1

In the opening section of this mission, all you have to do is follow Hanako and any onscreen instructions; to say any more here would be to offer entirely needless spoilers. It's during one of these scenes that you can get a special sequence involving Jackie if you chose to send his remains to Viktor at the end of MJ-10 ("The Heist"). After the board meeting, you will need to eliminate the Arasaka troops that storm the area. These are very powerful enemies, and count a mech among their numbers, so prepare in advance by selecting your favorite combat equipment. After the first wave of enemies, you can opt to go through the forest or follow the walkway straight to the elevator: you will run into troops on both paths. When you reach the waypoint, take the elevator to the upper atrium.

2

On arrival at the upper atrium, your goal is to reach another elevator two floors above. Navigation is easy, but you will encounter many hostiles on the way. Stealth tactics can be used here, but you will be given an additional option during the elevator ride if you saved Takemura during MJ-25 ("Search and Destroy"): he will offer his assistance (and supporting troops) to help clear the area. Whatever you decide, note that you can quickhack the drones to make things a little less intense if you have the required netrunner skills. Select the CEO Level on the elevator panel as your next destination, and resume your progression as before. You will then have to face a legendary rival; see "Boss Battle: Adam Smasher" overleaf for details. After you defeat Smasher, follow the waypoint to confront Yorinobu. Take the elevator down with Hellman when prompted to do so.

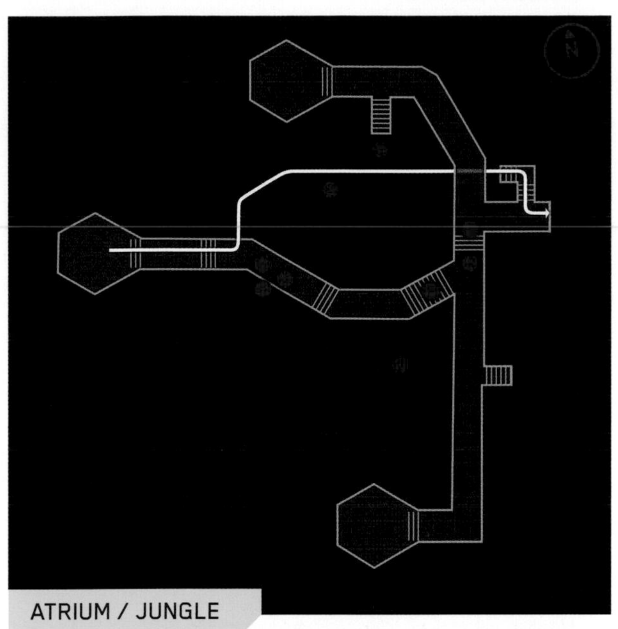

ATRIUM / JUNGLE

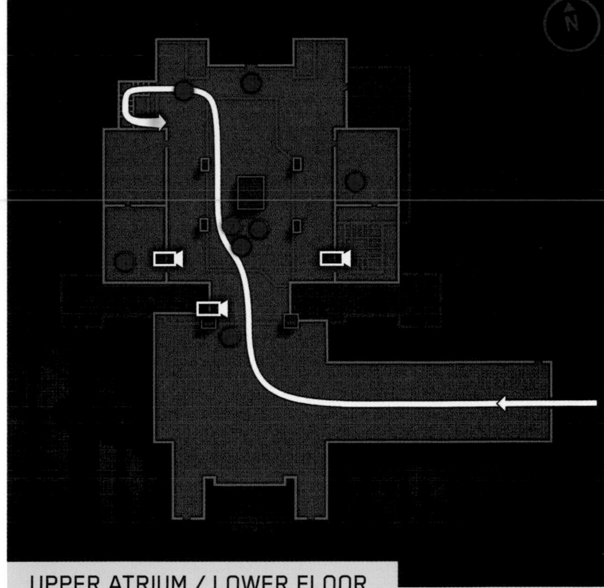

UPPER ATRIUM / LOWER FLOOR

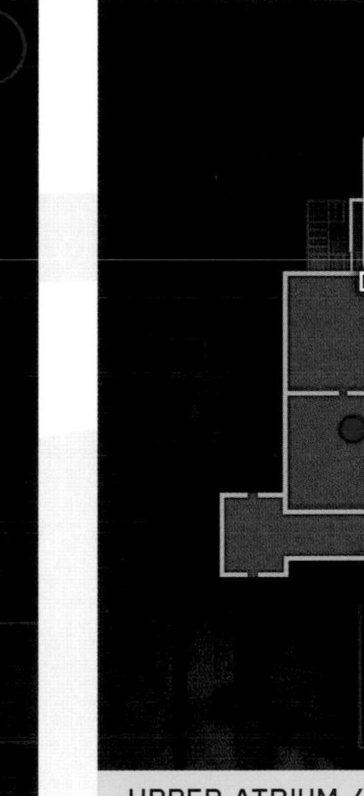

UPPER ATRIUM / UPPER FLOOR

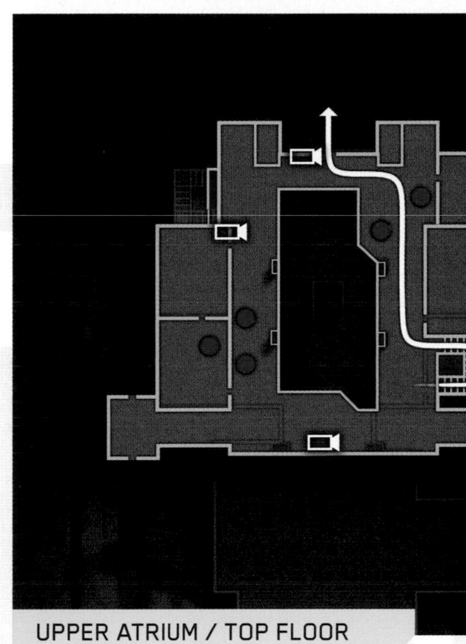

UPPER ATRIUM / TOP FLOOR

EPILOGUE

Unlock Condition:
Complete MJ-28 ("Totalimmortal").

This is an entirely story-oriented mission that is best enjoyed with no additional guidance. There are two important points worth mentioning, though:

- The choice you made during MJ-25 ("Search and Destroy") will determine who visits you during this Epilogue. If you saved Takemura back then, he's the one who will hand you the contract; if not, it will be Anders Hellman instead.

- When asked if you will sign Arasaka's contract or not, be aware that your choice will determine the nature of the ending that follows. We cover all endings in the spoiler-heavy Extras chapter (see page 457), but make sure you visit it only if you are not afraid of **major spoilers**.

MJ-28 TOTALIMMORTAL (CONTINUED)

BOSS BATTLE: ADAM SMASHER

The battle against Smasher consists of three distinct phases:

- **Phase 1:** Smasher, with his cyberware fully functional, focuses on short-range combat, using both melee assaults and projectiles.
- **Phase 2:** The boss has the right half of his body largely destroyed and switches to long-range tactics.
- **Phase 3:** Your opponent is severely diminished. Most of his combat functions are disabled, leaving him exposed to one last assault before you contemplate a final choice between mercy, or a *coup de grâce*.

Smasher's behavior changes in each phase, but his weaknesses remain broadly the same throughout.

Weaknesses

Smasher boasts overwhelming firepower, as well as physical attacks that can knock you off your feet. A very dangerous opponent, he is best neutralized with primarily aggressive tactics – the more swiftly you deal with him, the less exposed you will be to his assaults.

- **Cyber Heart:** Smasher is equipped with a cybernetic heart on the right side of his chest. This is his weak spot: any shot directed at the heart will deal severe damage. The catch is that the heart is initially protected by a front plate, which you will need to destroy before you uncover the vulnerability.
- **Chemical Damage:** Smasher is weak to chemical damage, but resistant to electrical damage.
- **Bladerunner Perk:** You can exploit the fact that Smasher is a mechanical combatant if you have invested points in the Bladerunner perk (Engineering skill).
- **Tech Weapons:** Tech weapons pierce through Smasher's front chest plate, enabling you to strike his heart weak point without having to destroy the armor beforehand. These weapons also prove very beneficial during the second phase, enabling you to shoot reinforcements through walls or solid cover positions; trigger the *Ping Personnel* quickhack to locate them instantly.
- **Frag Grenades:** Frag grenades are an excellent choice against this enemy, as they deal substantial damage both to him and his cyberware.
- **Quickhacks (Phase 1):** Four quickhacks are particularly noteworthy in this battle. *Weapon Malfunction* is outstanding in reducing the efficiency of the boss's bullet storm. With an especially resilient V, you could even consider staying in the open and focusing on damage-dealing over evasion. *Cyberware Malfunction* is the ultimate option for netrunner builds. This hack takes a long time to upload, but once it's complete, it deals enormous damage, destroys a large part of your foe's body, and moves you straight to the next phase of the battle. If you fight Smasher in Mikoshi, *Remote Activation* can be used to lower or raise retractable walls or servers, which might potentially offer you additional cover positions. You can also employ *Friendly Mode* on the turrets around the arena: these will deal gradual damage to your target, which can really add up over the course of the battle. A netrunner V with little in terms of firepower could even consider "kiting" Smasher, constantly retreating in a controlled manner to keep him within range of the turrets as he gives chase.
- **Quickhacks (Phase 2):** Once reinforcements join the fray, there are a few more quickhacks that you can put to use. *Ping* is the optimal solution to keep track of the whereabouts of both Smasher and the troops he summons. *Cyberpsychosis* is another brilliant choice when inflicted on powerful combatants such as Minotaurs, causing them to wreak havoc among their own ranks.
- **Mobility:** Smasher's melee assaults are hefty, but relatively easy to read. If you stay alert and on the move at all times, dodging them shouldn't be too taxing, leaving you with room to inflict counterattacks after each of his combos. Note that cyberware that increases your mobility (granting you the ability to double-jump, for instance) can work wonders here.
- **Rip Off Turrets:** If you fight Smasher while inside Mikoshi (during the MJ-30 and MJ-33 main jobs) and have a sufficiently high Body attribute, you can rip off the turrets in the arena. These provide enormous firepower, giving you a significant advantage in this battle.

Attack Patterns

Phase 1 – Melee Combos: Whenever Smasher performs melee assaults, try to evade his charge by dodging sideways. This will enable you to avoid not only the physical blows, but also the final potshot with which he concludes this combo.

Phase 1 – Jump Attack: When the boss leaps into the air, quickly sprint or dodge away from his landing position. If you are hit by the shockwave at the point of impact, you will be knocked down. Should you successfully escape the effect radius, you can attack without fear of reply while he is kneeling.

Phase 2 – Missile Rain: Whenever you notice telltale circular red dots beneath your feet, sprint away to safety. The explosion that ensues can be rather powerful.

Phase 3: Smasher is severely impaired during this final phase, almost to the point of representing no real danger. He does fire regularly with his heavy machine gun, but his rate of attack is too low to be a significant threat. Unless you are in a similar state of disrepair, consider facing him in the open and finish him off with your best weapon.

The subsequent decision to kill Smasher or let him live is a role-playing decision that is yours alone to make, and has no bearing on the events that follow.

Phase 1 – Bullet Storm: As soon as you identify that Smasher is about to rain bullets on you, swiftly move behind solid cover. Trying to tank or dodge these attacks will generally be too risky.

Phase 2 – Reinforcements: During the second phase, Smasher will call for reinforcements. Trying to deal with the boss and his lackeys simultaneously is a very risky strategy. We suggest that you prioritize the underlings, eliminating them in sequence before you resume your duel with Smasher. This is even more important if you wield melee weapons, as any time you spend in the open will potentially expose you to attacks from multiple angles.

Phase 2 – Fleeing Tactics: Smasher will regularly run away, or backtrack while shooting. Use these opportunities to inflict great damage, strafing as you fire to avoid his shots, if required.

STEALTH TACTICS

If your version of V is not specialized in combat, rest assured that you can eliminate Smasher exclusively with stealth tactics. The principle is the same as usual. First, you need to escape his attention by hiding until he forgets about you – a process that you can expedite by casting the Reboot Optics quickhack on the boss, or by causing distractions with the arena's multiple surveillance cameras and turrets.

Once Smasher loses track of you, all you have to do is sneak up on him and perform a stealth takedown. Each successful attempt will deal high damage and move the battle to the next phase.

MJ-29

FOR WHOM THE BELL TOLLS

Unlock Condition:
Complete MJ-26 ("Nocturne Op55N1") and SJ-36 ("Blistering Love"), and choose to team up with Rogue during MJ-26.

Notes:
This job is triggered automatically after MJ-26.

AREA MAP

1

Enter the Afterlife and head for Rogue's booth. After your conversation, follow Weyland and speak to Rogue again. You have an opportunity to gear up behind the bar, with all sorts of weapons and ammo available. Don't forget to collect the retrothrusters (which will enable you to double-jump), then pick up the shard next to where Rogue sits. Once your preparations are complete, proceed to the designated netrunner's room. Put on the netrunner suit before sitting on the chair. In cyberspace, head toward Alt to trigger a conversation. Upon your return to physical space, return to Rogue. The raid on Arasaka Tower will begin after you tell her that you are ready. Take the elevator with Rogue, choose the roof as your destination, then hop aboard the AV.

MJ-30

KNOCKIN' ON HEAVEN'S DOOR

Unlock Condition:
Complete MJ-29 ("For Whom the Bell Tolls").

Notes:
This job is triggered automatically after the previous one.

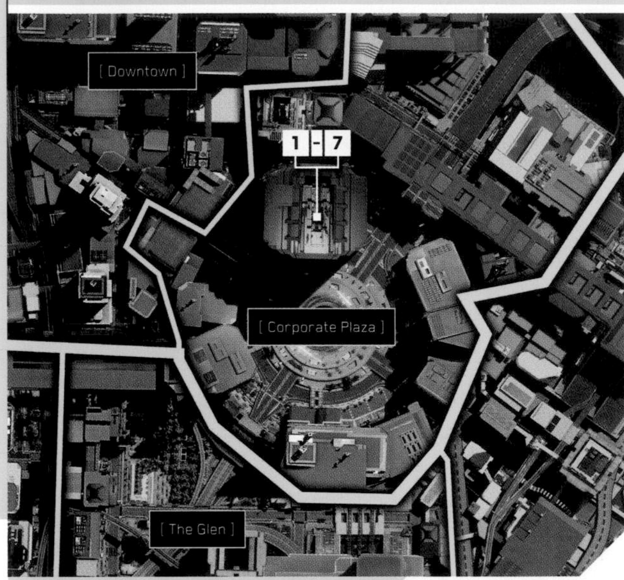

AREA MAP

1

The mission begins in the jungle within Arasaka Tower. Your primary goal is to locate a commanding officer, but you can optionally rescue Weyland first. This is an important choice: if you do not intervene, Weyland will play no further part in the mission. To save him, head toward the platform with the conference table, which is guarded by two Arasaka soldiers. Quietly take out the one patrolling on the other side of the table while he looks away; Rogue will neutralize his partner.

2

Next, follow Rogue to the waterfall area, where three guards are investigating the crash site. Two of them are stationary, while the third makes a short circular patrol: take one out and your allies will deal with the others.

3

Keep following Rogue and she will lead you straight to the commander – your main target. First, go up the nearby stairs and neutralize the man patrolling back and forth when he stops by the crate. You can then return to the hexagonal platform and sneak up on the commander. Search his body to retrieve the access token.

4

You can now head to the marked elevator. Dropping down from the walkway and going through the jungle will enable you to avoid the attention of the few remaining troops. Once through, head up the nearby stairs and call the elevator, then enter and press the Atrium button.

5

Once in the Atrium, follow Rogue and jump from the designated position to reach a platform down below: your retrothrusters will enable you to prevent the fall damage. Two guards will soon patrol the area, so stay low and behind cover if you wish to eliminate them stealthily. A quickhack is the best way to deal with drones whenever you run into them. You can now repeat this sequence twice: jump from the marked point to go down several floors and neutralize the troops there. Note the presence of grates on certain walls: these offer access to vertical shafts, which you can use as alternative routes for your descent.

6

Make one more downward jump and you will be within reach of the security room. Keep a low profile and sneak past the single patrol in the area. Consider quickhacking the surveillance camera above the door to avoid detection.

7

Inside the security room, sneak up on the lone guard and neutralize him, then examine the computer. Turn on the server room authorization in the Local Network tab, then enter the server room and connect Alt to the system. You should then make your way to the elevator one floor below. Use it to reach Arasaka Tower: Netrunner Operations. With nearby hostiles preemptively disabled by Alt, all you have to do is follow the waypoint to Mikoshi. Quickly head through the final door, making sure you are fully healed and equipped to face a fearsome opponent – see "Boss Battle: Adam Smasher" on page 170 for tips. After the fight, you have the option of talking to Weyland if you saved him in the jungle. When you're ready, proceed to the Mikoshi access point and connect to it.

EPILOGUE

Unlock Condition:
Complete MJ-30 ("Knockin' On Heaven's Door").

Inside Mikoshi, the decision you make during your conversation with Alt (between entering the well or crossing the bridge with her) is of the utmost importance, as it will determine the nature of the Epilogue that follows. Both versions are entirely story-oriented sequences that are best enjoyed with no additional guidance to avoid unnecessary spoilers. We cover all endings in the **incredibly spoiler-heavy** Extras chapter (see page 457).

MJ-31

WE GOTTA LIVE TOGETHER

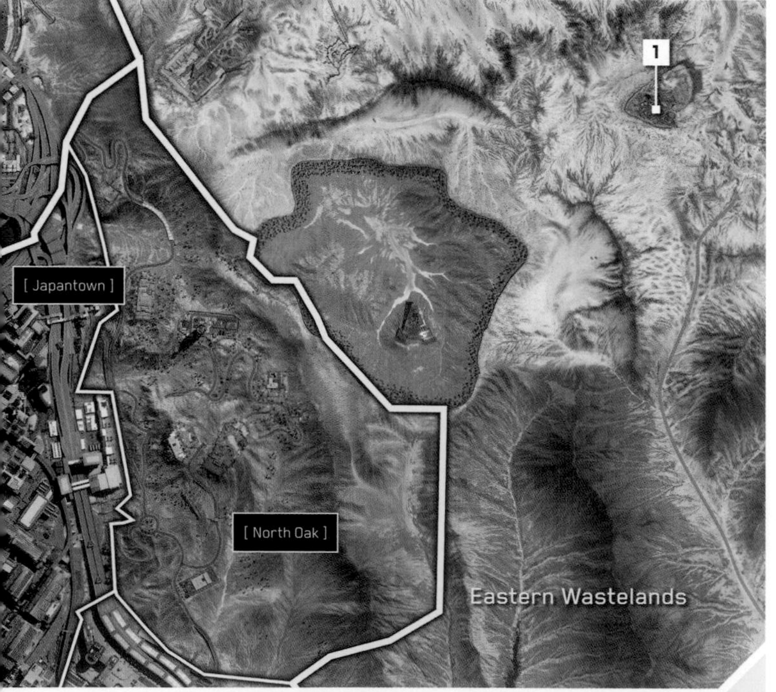

AREA MAP

Unlock Condition:
Complete MJ-26 ("Nocturne Op55N1") and SJ-50 ("Queen of the Highway"), and choose to team up with Panam during that mission.

Notes:
This job is triggered automatically after MJ-26.

1

This job is mostly plot-driven. Follow Mitch, then talk to Saul, Mitch, and Dakota. Get in the tub in Dakota's tent, then talk to Saul again after your foray into cyberspace. After the initiation, you can optionally collect some gear from Dakota and talk to Aldecaldos in the camp, including Mitch (who will give you access to a brief tutorial on how to control the panzer) and Cassidy (who will offer you to take part in a bottle-shooting challenge). When you're ready, join Panam between the solar panels and sit with her to complete the mission.

MJ-32

FORWARD TO DEATH

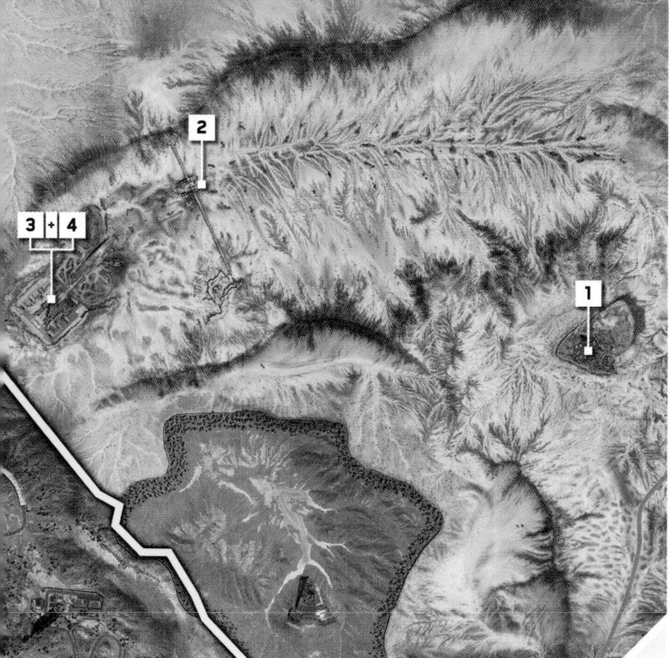

AREA MAP

Unlock Condition:
Complete MJ-31 ("We Gotta Live Together").

Notes:
This job is triggered automatically after the previous one.

1

Follow Panam to Saul's tent and slot in the shard he hands you. During the reconnaissance drone flight, carefully observe the site to familiarize yourself with its layout. If you have any last-minute preparations to make, be sure to take care of them before entering the panzer. This is a combat-heavy mission, so take your best gear with you – particularly weapons and ammo. The approach to the construction site is uneventful, until the panzer has a failure. During this sequence, methodically take down the multiple drones buzzing around with your sniper rifle. You cannot afford to miss too many shots, so aim carefully.

2

Next, you will need to unleash the full force of the panzer to ram into the barricades and crush your opponents. You have access to three functions: a standard forward cannon (R2/RT), a rain of missiles (L2/LT), and countermeasures (R1/RB). After you head through the gate, your tank will be disabled; your goal is to eliminate all enemies in the area. Panam's sniper rifle can do miracles here, as can quickhacks on the drones.

3

After the battle, escort Mitch and Carol up the metal staircase, then return to ground level to eliminate additional waves of enemies. Stay on the move, pick off the soldiers methodically one after the other, and remember that you can quickhack mechanical targets if your netrunner attributes allow for it. Grenades also prove remarkably effective against groups of foes – including when they're still aboard trucks.

4

The Militech strike team that arrives consists of heavy mechanical units, but you now have the panzer at your disposal again. Try to keep your enemies on one side to limit your exposure to incoming fire, and focus on a single opponent at a time, making the most of both main fire modes at your disposal. Once you have eradicated the whole squad, return to the tunnel.

BELLY OF THE BEAST

AREA MAP

Unlock Condition:
Complete MJ-32 ("Forward to Death").

Notes:
This job is triggered automatically after the previous one.

1

When you reach the end of the tunnel, exit the panzer and join Mitch and Saul. After the conversation, head to the control room with Panam and fire up the drill, then get inside the Arasaka building.

2

In the large room with the seismic dampers your goal is to climb up the ladder on the far left. Avoid the androids patrolling the area by moving alongside the lateral wall. Continue your ascent via the stairs and the next ladder, then slip through the grate.

3

The control room features two guards. Hide behind the nearby crate and wait for them to finish their conversation. When they both look away, take either one down stealthily; your allies will deal with the other. After talking to Saul you need to reach the security room, which can be achieved in a number of ways – see "Arasaka Manufacturing Level Infiltration." Once you have completed this step, Alt will clear the path, instantly dispatching all enemies standing between you and Mikoshi. You will, however, be on your own for the following boss battle against Adam Smasher. You can find tips and analysis for this epic fight on page 170. When the dust settles, go through the door and connect to the access point to trigger the Epilogue.

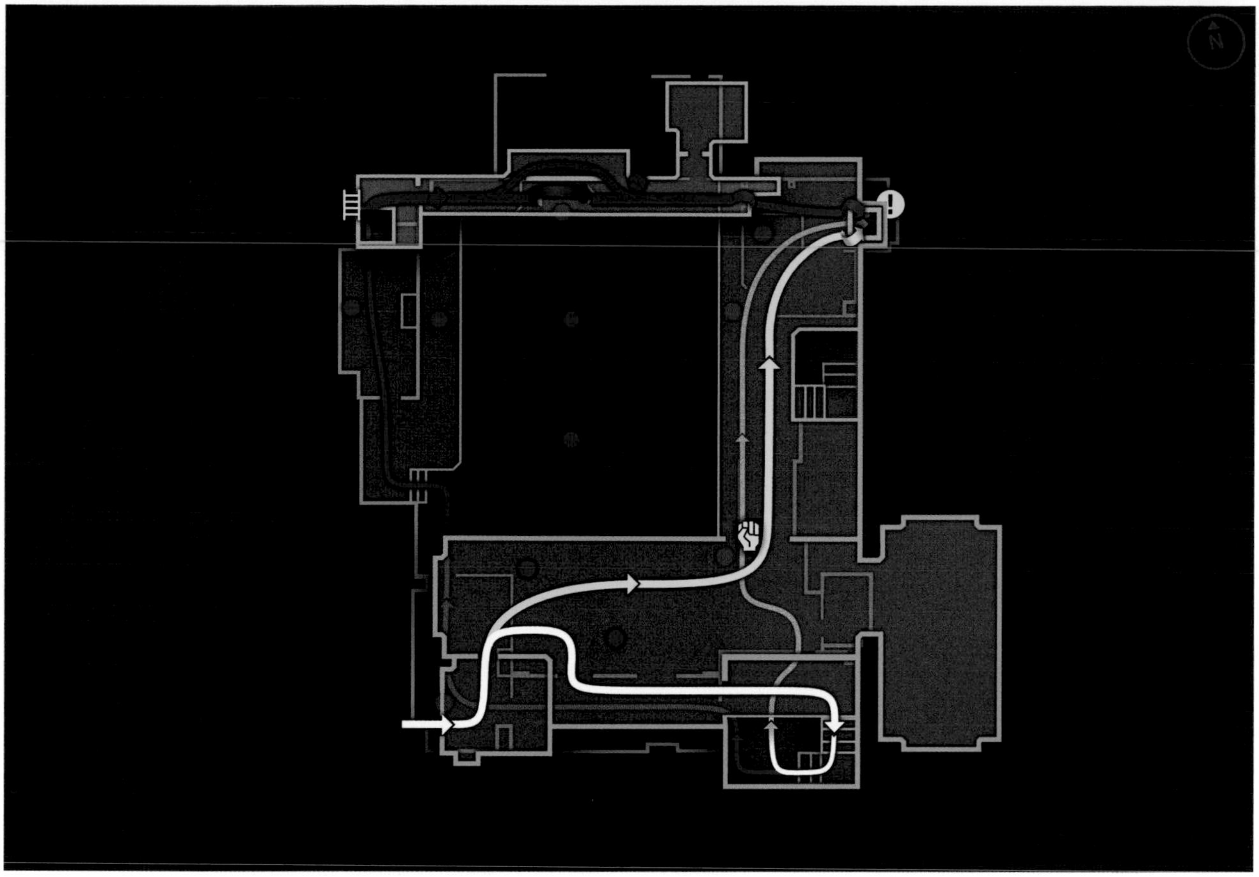

ARASAKA MANUFACTURING LEVEL INFILTRATION

Your objective is the security room, accessible either via a grate in the far corner of the upper floor, or a door on the lower floor. Before you can insert the shard into the access point, though, you will need to deal with the netrunner protecting it.

If you meet the related Body attribute requirement, you have the option of force-opening the gate in the control room. This offers a superb shortcut to the security room, with a single foe between you and the grate leading to it. Before dropping down, make sure the netrunner underneath is alone: a strong Arasaka soldier occasionally patrols the booth.

If physical strength isn't your forte, go down the stairs on the right of the starting room to access the lower floor. The central area with the assembly robots is guarded by a few troops, but equally, you have plenty of objects to hide behind. By watching carefully and crouch-walking from cover to cover, you can head straight to the room where the security room is found, neutralizing the two guards on your way. As always, tag all foes in advance as you progress to avoid unpleasant surprises. The netrunner in the security room is busy examining the access point and will pose no problem.

An alternative is to go downstairs and walk alongside the left-hand wall. The enemies you will encounter on this clockwise run are all on their own, and facing away from you – making for a sequence of elementary takedowns. When you reach a ladder, climb up to the walkway. Neutralize the guard here and you can drop down almost directly onto the grate leading to the security booth. You will notice a fourth hostile here, near the grate: dispatch him while he's facing the computer on the right, looking away from you. When the coast is clear, drop down into the security booth to arrive right behind the netrunner.

EPILOGUE

Unlock Condition:
Complete MJ-33 ("Belly of the Beast").

Inside Mikoshi, the decision you make during your conversation with Alt (between entering the well or crossing the bridge with her) is of the utmost importance: it will determine the nature of the Epilogue that follows. Both versions are entirely story-oriented sequences that are best enjoyed with no additional guidance to avoid unnecessary spoilers. All endings are covered in our spoiler-heavy Extras chapter (see page 457). Before you open those pages, though, be aware that they are full of **major story spoilers** for all other available conclusions.

SIDE JOBS

This chapter features dedicated walkthroughs for every side job, sorted in ascending order of difficulty to reflect the approximate order of progression you'll encounter during a typical playthrough.

Whether this is your first journey through Cyberpunk 2077 or not, we advise that you use the walkthroughs found here in conjunction with the Completion Roadmap chapter (see page 92). This will enable you to plot a personal yet optimal route through the story, and avoid instances where you might miss important unlocks, events, or other moments of note.

As with the Main Jobs chapter, our coverage here features numbered steps that detail a broad path from start to finish for each side job, including advice on critical decisions and actions that may have immediate or lasting repercussions. Whenever there are multiple potential approaches to complete objectives, we offer annotated maps and a selection of feasible strategies – leaving it up to you to decide how you wish to proceed, based on your personal preferences, role-playing inclinations, and character build.

Side jobs is a blanket term that refers to all sorts of assignments in Cyberpunk 2077. Some can be relatively short and uncomplicated, self-contained scenarios where you can act as you please – while others can rival main jobs in terms of scope and significance, with major storylines played out over the course of several sequential side jobs.

To enable you to pick the right kind of side job for any given play session, we have categorized them as follows:

- **Major Side Jobs** are assignments that feature key protagonists. Much like main jobs, they can be sizable: with some, you will need to complete all missions in a given series. There are alternative main story endings that can only be unlocked via major side jobs, and your choices can potentially have a profound effect on your relationships with principal characters – including romances.
- **Minor Side Jobs** generally offer stories and situations that can be easily resolved in a single sitting, and usually feature new faces. Many of them show different aspects of life in Night City, and are less intense than the situations encountered elsewhere. Side jobs can also occasionally tie up loose ends from separate storylines, or allow you to get to know more about characters that you have encountered in other jobs.

Many side jobs are unlocked by accepting an offer made in a phone call. As a general rule of thumb, **you should never decline job offers unless you are certain that you do not want to be involved.** A single refusal can sometimes close off an entire side-story for the rest of your playthrough. The good news, however, is that you do not typically need to complete them immediately, and can usually agree to get right on it – but actually carry on with what you're doing, and later head to the mission start point at your leisure.

On a similar note, be wary of dialogue options where V might express a desire to curtail his or her involvement in a given side job – as these, too, can sometimes bring a storyline to a premature end. We highlight instances where this is the case in our walkthroughs where appropriate.

Lastly, should you ever find yourself waiting for a call to unlock a specific mission, note that Cyberpunk 2077 employs a "token" system to manage the flow of its missions. The gist of it is that you need to complete jobs and tasks of any kind to unlock further jobs, and that new opportunities can only arise if you are not actively involved in combat, conversation, or any ongoing activity (including driving and swimming). We offer a more detailed overview of this system on page 76.

JOB DIRECTORY

Below you will find a directory of all side jobs, sorted in alphabetical order. If you're looking for guidance on a specific part of the story, you can use this to jump to the relevant page instantly.

Just as a reminder, this guide uses abbreviations to refer to missions. For instance, the very first side job is labeled "SJ-01." This system is used consistently throughout the book, making it easy to track and identify quests, whether you are consulting our Completion Roadmap flowchart, looking for unlock conditions, or simply reading a walkthrough.

SJ-01

BEAT ON THE BRAT

Unlock Condition:
Complete MJ-05 ("The Rescue").

Notes:
Minor side job.

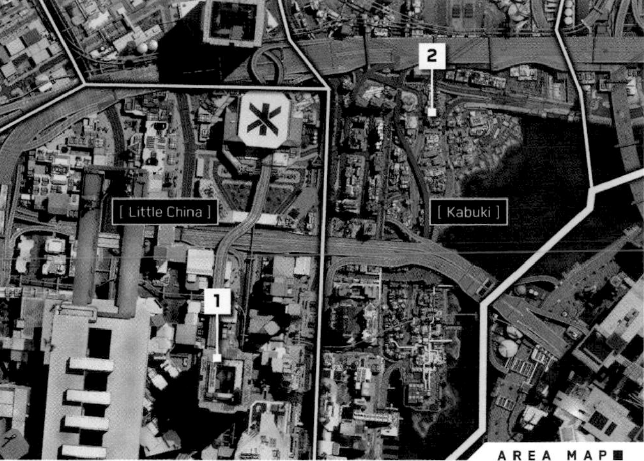

1

As you exit your apartment for the first time after completing MJ-05 ("The Rescue") and head toward the elevator, coach Fred challenges you to a fistfight. This serves as an introduction to bare-knuckle combat (see "Combat Tips" for details). After defeating your android sparring partner, speak to coach Fred. This initiates a storyline in which you can defeat multiple opponents across Night City to test your mettle. In some of those fights, you wager a certain amount of money. If you win, the pot is yours; if you lose, it's gone – though you can then try again until you emerge victorious. The only exception to this is the finale, which can only be fought once – win or lose.

2

Champion of Kabuki (lv. 5): Here, you face not just one opponent, but twins. If you feel confident, you can take the opportunity to raise the stakes. The key to winning this fight is to stay on the move, avoiding a situation where you face both men simultaneously. Instead, try to maneuver carefully so that one twin impedes the other, deal some damage, then retreat and repeat.

3

Champion of Arroyo (lv. 22): Buck, a war veteran, is your opponent in this duel. If you are sufficiently prepared, you can ask him to sweeten the pot by adding his sniper rifle to the wager – but there's a catch. If you win the fist fight with the weapon in the pot, Buck will renege on the deal and refuse to hand it over. Worse still, he will tell his fellow thugs to attack you. Draw your weapon and neutralize them all quickly. Don't forget to collect the rifle once the dust settles. If the sniper rifle was not part of the deal, on the other hand, you can leave the arena peacefully – though you can still choose to antagonize Buck and deliberately trigger a battle to then put your hands on the sniper rifle.

4

Champion of the Glen (lv. 28): At the Glen arena, your opponent – César – puts his car forward as a stake. After you defeat him, you can choose between various options: keep the car and the money, allow your opponent to take one of the two, or even to walk away empty-handed. Note that this decision will have a minor knock-on effect later on in this storyline: if you allow César to keep either his car or the money, he will make an appearance as a spectator in the finale (and, even later, send you a picture of his newborn baby).

5

Champion of the Animals (lv. 30): This fight takes place in an arena in Rancho Coronado that is also the stage of a gig ("For My Son," see page 282). In most scenarios (if you haven't completed the gig yet, or if you did so stealthily), you will find a bouncer by the gate. To enter, you either need to pay him, or intimidate him (if you meet the corresponding Body attribute requirement). Alternatively, you can avoid him altogether by entering via the shutters on the northeast side of the building: jump onto the red containers and slip through. Once inside, talk to Rhino to proceed. There is no wager for this bout. Note that if you completed the "For My Son" gig in a violent way and shot everybody inside the arena, including Rhino, coach Fred will contact you and give you a free win for lack of an opponent.

6

Ticking Time Bomb (lv. 28): This Pacifica fight is actually an optional bonus encounter that doesn't count toward the tally of four required to unlock the finale. You can even complete it after the finale if you wish. To unlock it, you need to first complete SJ-16 ("Send in the Clowns" – see page 194) and wait for a couple of in-game days to pass.

Feel free to double the stakes before hostilities begin if you wish. Ozob's attacks are slow but powerful, so stay light on your toes as you circle him and wear him down with quick flurries. After you land a few clean punches to his head, the grenade on his nose will detonate – so be sure to back away quickly after you land blows in that general area.

COMBAT TIPS

- You can block by holding L2/LT. As long as you have stamina left, blocking prevents any damage.
- Press R2/RT for light attacks, tapping repeatedly to perform combos. Your opponents in bareknuckle fights can break your combos after the second or third hit: when this happens, look for another opportunity to strike.
- Hold then release R2/RT for strong attacks. This is the best method to break the guard of a rival when they are on the defensive.
- If you block at the last second, within the final frames before an incoming attack connects, you will automatically deflect and perform a powerful counter that stuns the target. With practice, you can make this an instinctive reaction that serves as the best defense *and* offense. Learning enemy attack patterns and deflecting consistently is the most surefire way to victory.
- You consume stamina both when you attack (every single punch depletes your gauge), and when you defend (each blow you block or dodge drains the meter). The best way to manage your stamina is to stay on the move, circling your rival and dodging as much as you can (with a rapid double-tap of ◎/B), then attack only when you see clear openings.
- Recommended preparations for this quest include the Gorilla Arms cyberware, a well-developed Body attribute for health and stamina, and the following Perks:
  - **Athetics:** Invincible, True Grit
  - **Street Brawler:** Flurry, Crushing Blows, Efficient Blows, Rush, Relentless, Dazed

7

Finale (lv. 35): This climactic battle is unlocked only after you complete the first four "Champion" quests described above, in addition to the MJ-18 main job ("Transmission" – see page 148). To trigger this final fight, head to Pacifica's Grand Imperial Mall and wait on the designated bench, then walk to the fitness center inside the mall when prompted. César (from "Champion of the Glen") will come to watch your fight if you let him keep either the car or the money after your earlier fight. Similarly, if you took out Logan without raising the alarm during the "For My Son" gig (see page 282), or if you skipped that gig altogether, Rhino will also be among the spectators. The twins from the Kabuki bout are also always present. When you're ready, talk to coach Fred by the ring. If you're interested, you can listen to his proposition: he suggests you throw the fight to double your money. Accepting this offer and losing the fight on purpose will reward you with additional cash, but less Street Cred. In any case, expect Razor to put up a tough fight when you enter the ring. As with other bouts, focusing on deflecting and wearing him down with fast jabs and short combos when openings appear is the safest strategy, particularly if you manage to hit your rival in the abs – his weak spot.

SJ-02

THE GUN

Unlock Condition:
Complete MJ-05 ("The Rescue").

Notes:
Minor side job.

AREA MAP

1

This short assignment requires you to talk to Wilson, the owner of the 2nd Amendment weapon shop, across the atrium relative to V's apartment. It can be completed during the Prologue when you leave your apartment for the first time, and offers the reward of a free weapon.

SJ-03

THE GIFT

Unlock Condition:
Complete MJ-05 ("The Rescue").

Notes:
Minor side job.

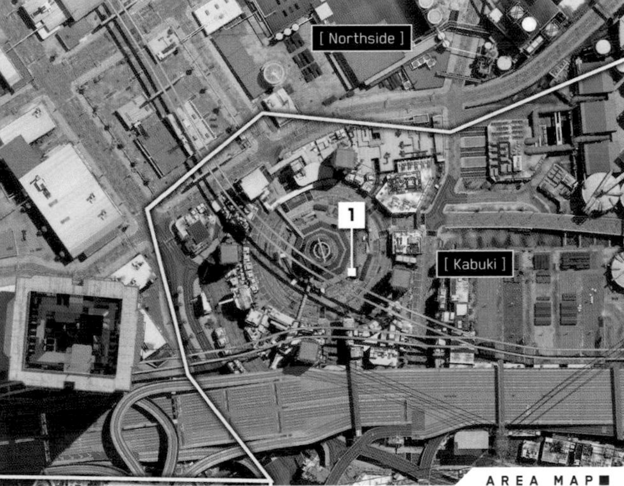

AREA MAP

1

This job becomes available just before you reach your apartment for the first time during the Prologue. The next morning, you can head to the highlighted netrunner shop. Dex will drop you off close to it at the end of MJ-07 ("The Ride"). Yoko, the vendor, will give you a netrunner program that T-Bug left for you. Take it from her inventory, equip it in your cyberdeck from the Inventory menu, then cast Ping on the surveillance camera, before you hack the training access point at the end of the counter. This job essentially serves as a tutorial for quickhacks and breaching – two staple netrunner tactics.

BURNING DESIRE / NIGHT MOVES

Unlock Condition:
Complete MJ-07 ("The Ride").

Notes:
Minor side job.

AREA MAP

1

2

This quest is triggered by approaching the man running outside the entrance to a residential building in Little China. Note that the job name differs depending on whether you play it during or after the Prologue (as quests triggered after the Prologue are named by Johnny).

Agree to help, then drive him to the designated ripperdoc to the north, wasting no time: should you take too long, the man will eventually leave the car and die, causing the quest to fail. The job will formally end after the flaming crotch man calls you at a later date – usually after you have completed a handful of other jobs.

THE PROPHET'S SONG

Unlock Condition:
Complete MJ-05 ("The Rescue").

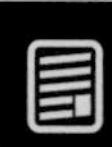

Notes:
Minor side job.

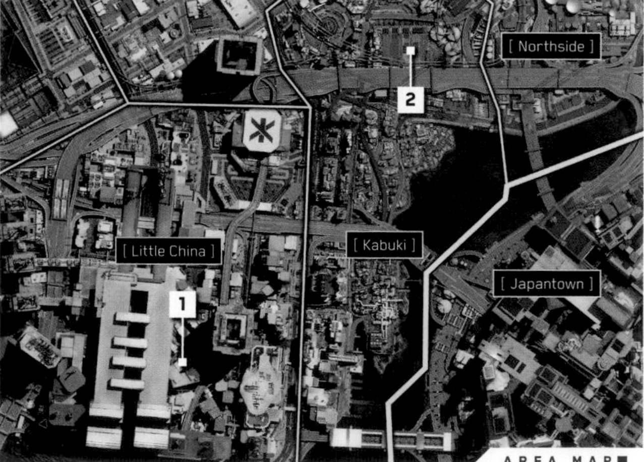

AREA MAP

1

A strange man called Garry the Prophet rants about assorted conspiracy theories right outside Misty's Esoterica. The following principles govern this quest:

- Garry is available at any time outside of his sleeping hours (usually 5-10 AM). If you come in the morning and skip time, note that you will need to walk away and come back to find him awake again.
- Every time you encounter him, Garry randomly talks about one of five subjects.
- You need to have listened to all five conspiracy theories, and conversed with Garry each time, to trigger the next phase of this side job.

- After you discuss a topic with Garry, it will never be brought up again.
- The vampire conspiracy becomes available only after you complete MJ-11 ("Playing for Time"), so this side job can only be completed then, at the earliest.
- To trigger two conspiracy theories in a row, you need to walk far enough from Garry in between each one. A side job marker will appear on your map to reflect the availability of a new step.
- By default, you have a choice between two dialogue lines for each subject. A third, bonus line can be unlocked for each conversation, as detailed in the accompanying table. This is entirely optional, though: the quest will advance no matter which line you choose.
- During the fifth speech, which is always about Nomads, Garry will be attacked by Nomads. You need to assist him if you want to trigger the final phase of this quest, which only formally begins at this point. It's possible to save him in one of three ways: by neutralizing the Nomads; by selecting the Nomad-exclusive dialogue line (only available if you chose the corresponding background); or by calling on your association with the Nomads (only available if you've already completed SJ-50 ("Queen of the Highway" – see page 233).

To sum up: drop by to visit Garry on multiple occasions, preferably after you completed the Prologue, to witness all five of his speeches (each time taking part in the conversation), and rescue him during the fifth one when he's attacked by Nomads.

2

Bonus Dialogue Line Availability

Conspiracy Theory	Unlock Condition	Topic Referred To
Cyberspace	Complete MJ-18 ("Transmission")	Alt Cunningham
Reptilians	Complete SJ-18 ("I Fought the Law")	President Meyers
Vampires	Complete MJ-25 ("Search and Destroy")	Hanako Arasaka
Eye Implants	From the beginning of the game	Kiroshi Optics
Nomads	Complete MJ-19 ("Ghost Town")	V's encounter with Nomads

Once Garry puts you on the track of a mysterious meeting, head to Kabuki and talk to Johnny outside the marked old factory, before heading to the designated hiding place. If you wait and watch, you will observe Maelstromers handing over a mysterious chip to corpos. To complete the quest, you need to claim the chip – either by attacking the gang members before the exchange, or mugging the corpos afterwards. If you leave or wait for too long, enabling the corpos to leave with the chip, the mission ends prematurely. All enemies tend to be close to each other at first: tossing a few grenades can work miracles here.

After acquiring the mysterious chip, note that you can crack it from your Inventory menu to reveal a cryptic message. The chip can be sold, but keeping it will allow you to question Garry's disciple about it when you return to the usual spot, by Misty's Esoterica, to complete the job. Note that the disciple will only answer you if you have previously made generous donations to Garry, or if you make a donation to her.

LOSING MY RELIGION/ SACRUM PROFANUM

Unlock Condition:
Complete MJ-07 ("The Ride").

Notes:
Minor side job.

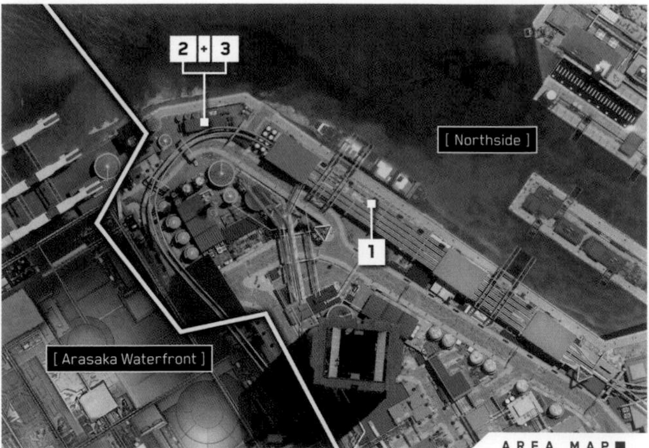

1

Talk to the Buddhist monk meditating close to the Northside docks. To save his brother, head to the Maelstrom hideout to the northwest. The monk asks you to accomplish this without bloodshed. Whether you succeed or not will be reflected in the quest's closing conversations.

2

The brother is held captive inside a small warehouse. Before you can save him, you first need to neutralize all Maelstromers inside. To get the best possible entry point for a strategy that involves no kills, go around the building to find an elevated opening at the rear. Climb up to it using the containers as stepping stones. This puts you in a great position to methodically deal with the thugs in sequence.

3

From the rear entrance, drop down and quietly take out the first Maelstromer. You can then crouch-walk toward the front, stealthily eliminating the other rank-and-file goons as you reach them, finishing with the guard posted outside, at the front entrance. You can then free the prisoner (don't forget to collect the unique submachine gun close to him) and return to the first monk to share the good news.

Note that you can run into this individual later for an optional conversation in Japantown. Look directly in front of the Cherry Blossom Market fast travel terminal, at the foot of the giant Buddha statue.

THE GIG

Unlock Condition:
Complete MJ-05 ("The Rescue").

Notes:
Minor side job.

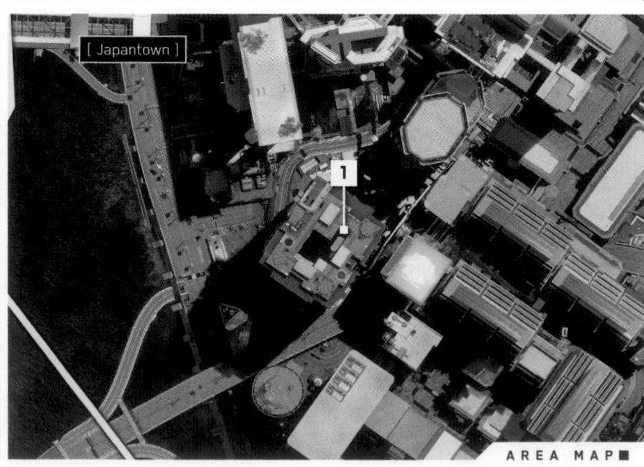

1

This quest is actually the conclusion of the MJ-05 ("The Rescue") main job, which you started during the Prologue but could not quite complete due to the Watson district lockdown. It simply requires you to collect your reward from Wakako. Meet her in her parlor on Jig Jig Street and remind her about the job you completed when you saved Sandra Dorsett.

During the conversation, Wakako also mentions a personal link that you can retrieve from Cassius Ryder – a ripperdoc based in Watson. Pay him a visit, open his inventory and you can collect the item and a tattoo for free.

BIG IN JAPAN

Unlock Condition:
Complete MJ-10 ("The Heist").

Notes:
Minor side job.

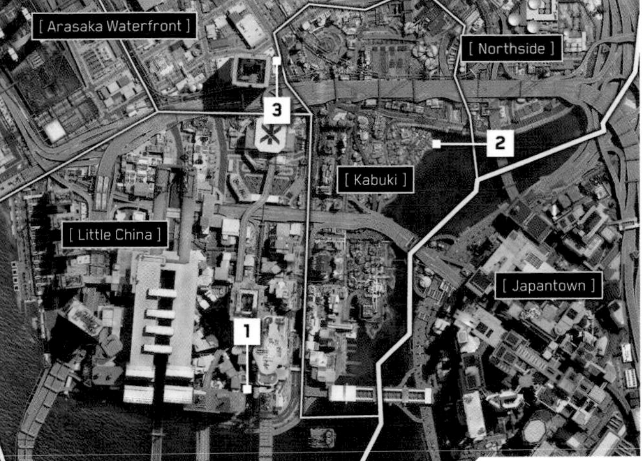

AREA MAP

1

Speak to Dennis in the Afterlife and accept his offer.

2

You now need to find a "container" in the favelas on the Kabuki waterfront. The object in question is actually a refrigerator that can be found in the hut closest to the water. After opening it, call Dennis, collect the "package," then leave the waterfront area, ideally without being detected by Tyger Claws. One viable route involves following the walkway that runs parallel to the north wall, up multiple sets of steps. You will run into four Tyger Claws on your way: the first one regularly moves to the left, leaving you free to sneak past; the second one can be drawn to your position by causing a distraction with one of the vending machines; the last two are more annoying as they keep an eye on each other, so a quickhack is your best bet to deal with them here. If you opt for combat, be sure to hide the "package" you're carrying in a safe spot before you open hostilities, then eliminate all foes in the area. Once the dust settles, walk all the way up to the top of the steps.

Note that an alternative route involves crouch-walking alongside the edge of the beach, with your feet in the shallow part of the water – just keep heading south. When you get to the end of the beach, you will find steps leading back to the street, and you can then walk straight to the designated car and place the "package" in the trunk.

3

Finally, drive to the delivery point at the foot of Megabuilding H11 and talk to Dennis to complete the assignment.

THE BEAST IN ME

Unlock Condition:
Complete MJ-15 ("Double Life").

Notes:
Major side job.

AREA MAP

RACING TIPS

If you are not an adept driver, it might be prudent to practice high-speed driving before you begin. The following tips will also help:

- During the races, the direction you need to follow is clearly marked by a luminous path, so navigation should never be a problem. Your primary goal is to go through the holographic gates that serve as checkpoints.
- The most appropriate racing style is a sensible compromise between speed and safety. If you drive the car as if riding a cannonball, flying in straight lines and crashing at each corner, your chances of winning will be close to zero. Instead, treat each turn with respect, either releasing the accelerator in advance or braking before you begin to steer. If you're an adept driver, you can experiment with applying the handbrake briefly to drift into an optimal racing line.
- If your car begins to lose traction, instantly release the accelerator: this will help you to regain control of the vehicle.

1

After you receive a call from Claire, visit her garage shop in Arroyo during daylight hours; if required, use the main menu's Skip Time feature and fast-forward to noon. Note that you can also meet her at night at the Afterlife. Accept her offer if you wish to begin this quest line. You will then need to perform well in three separate qualifying races to make it into the finals. These don't take place immediately, however: you'll need to head to the designated meeting point in each district and call Claire after you receive a message from her.

In the opening section of this side-story, you will need to choose between racing in your own car (make sure you select the one you want as your active vehicle before answering the call), or using Claire's vehicle: The Beast. Claire's ride offers a solid balance of speed and traction, so feel free to opt for it.

2

City Center: This race is all about sharp turns and speed. As your rivals ride high-end corporate vehicles, you will need to strike the right balance between maintaining a good pace and slowing down appropriately in anticipation of each bend. There is also a little traffic to contend with, so it's best to minimize risks and make steady progress.

3

Badlands: This race features hardly any traffic, but you have to deal with uneven terrain and frequent obstacles, as well as your car skidding on the dirt. Release the accelerator whenever the vehicle loses traction, and always keep an eye on the next gate in the distance to optimize your racing line.

4

Santo Domingo: This is a technical race, combining 90-degree turns in busy streets, straights where you can put your foot down, and challenging hairpins as you ascend the North Oak hills.

After the race, Claire will ask you to meet at the dam. You then have three options: agree to help her kill Sampson, talk her out of it by saying that you will keep driving but only to win ("My priority's winning"), or refuse to play any further part. If you opt for the latter response, the side-story will end immediately.

5

The Big Race: This final race starts normally, but you will eventually face a dilemma when Sampson's car pulls out of the race due to damage. You can either work with Claire by going after Sampson, or ignore her request and focus on winning the race. See "Possible Outcomes" for details.

POSSIBLE OUTCOMES

When Sampson pulls off toward the end of the final race, the quest has three possible conclusions:

- If you decide to ignore Claire's request and stay in the race, you have the opportunity to win it and claim the prize money. However, this means that Claire will be furious with you, affecting your relationship when you later encounter her in her capacity as a bartender at the Afterlife.
- If you opt to abandon the race and go after Sampson, an accident will occur. The default course of events is that Claire will then kill him to avenge her late husband.
- There is a third possible scenario: if you attempted to talk Claire out of killing Sampson after the Santo Domingo race, you can intervene before she executes him. Approach them and tell Claire that you want to hear Sampson out as he explains that he is not responsible for Dean's death. Maintain this position every time a line of dialogue is offered, and you can convince Claire to let it go, and save Sampson's life.

In both scenarios where you go after Sampson, Claire will gift you her vehicle, the Beast. If you finish the race instead, you will not get this reward. Additionally, if you convince Claire not to kill Sampson, he will also gift you his car to thank you for saving his life.

SJ-10 HEROES

Unlock Condition:
Choose to send Jackie's body to his family (or tell Delamain to wait until you return) at the end of MJ-10 ("The Heist") and complete MJ-11 ("Playing for Time"). If you chose to send Jackie's body to Viktor instead, note that you do not have access to this quest, though you will still receive two messages from Mama Welles (the second one three days after the first), giving you access to Jackie's bike.

Notes:
Major side job.

AREA MAP

1

When Mama Welles sends you a message asking you to call her back, do so at your earliest convenience. The side job formally begins when you make your way to El Coyote Cojo in Heywood to meet with her. Take the key she gives you, then head to Jackie's garage in the nearby back alley.

2

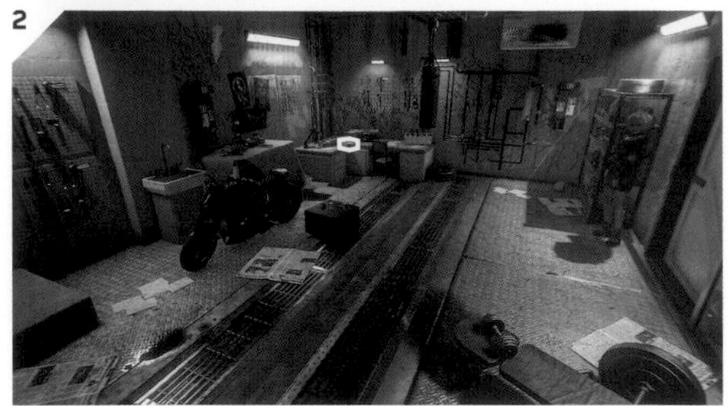

As you approach the garage, you will notice Misty sitting by the door. Once inside, there are multiple items that you can scan and examine. After inspecting the locked door, pick up the key on the desk. This gives you access to Jackie's room, where yet more items await, including a computer that you can jack into. In total, there are four possible offerings that you can get for the *ofrenda*: the book on the workbench, the basketball on the floor, the leather belt on the desk, and the tequila bottle on the coffee table. You can take them all for now, though you will only need to select one for the *ofrenda*, with your choice leading to different lines of dialogue.

When you leave the garage to return to El Coyote, Misty says that she would prefer to stay behind. Here you can either convince her to come with you to the event, or say that you understand why she doesn't want to. Again, your decision will influence dialogue at the *ofrenda*. Back at El Coyote, talk to Mama Welles and sit on the couch, next to Viktor. How the rest of the quest unfolds is up to you.

At the end of the ceremony, Mama Welles will offer you Jackie's bike – in its tuned version if you selected the corresponding dialogue line during the conversation with Jackie, just before entering the All Foods warehouse during MJ-08 ("The Pickup" – see page 120).

SJ·11

SHOOT TO THRILL

Unlock Condition:
Complete MJ-11 ("Playing for Time").

Notes:
Minor side job.

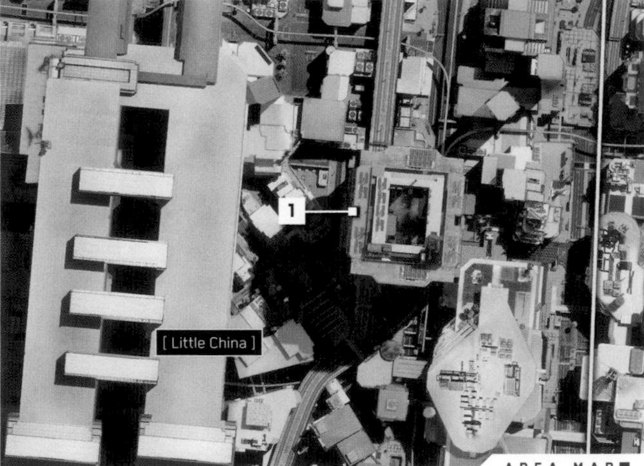

AREA MAP

1

When Wilson contacts you about the competition at his shooting range, accept his offer to take part, then head to his weapon shop – just across the atrium relative to V's apartment. When the contest is about to begin, get into booth 4 and ready your weapon (which must be a low-caliber). Good options here include the Unity or Lexington handguns, as they have a high fire rate and large ammo clips. Your goal is to shoot as many targets as possible – any targets, not just the ones in your lane. Try to be quick and efficient, hitting targets before your rivals and reloading at strategic intervals when no targets are in sight.

The mission is completed no matter what ranking you get, but you obtain improved rewards for finishing second (extra Street Cred) or, even better, first (a custom Lexington with unique stats).

SJ-12

HAPPY TOGETHER

Unlock Condition:
Finish the holocall with Takemura in your apartment at the end of MJ-11 ("Playing for Time").

Notes:
Minor side job.

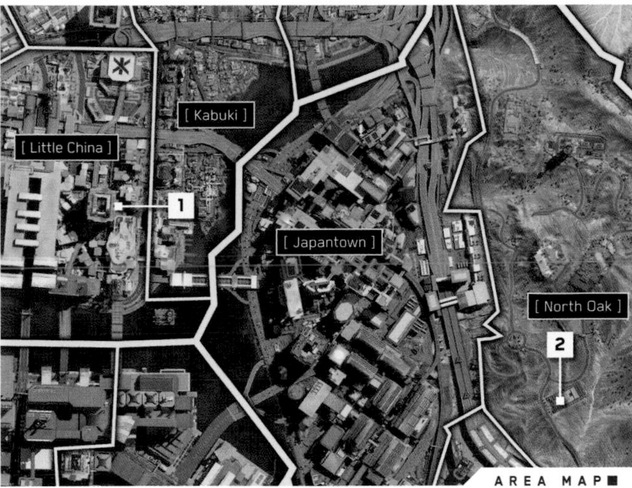

AREA MAP

1

This quest starts close to V's apartment, on the level just below. Speak to the NCPD officers – Petrova and Mendez – knocking on Barry's door (condo #0613). After they've gone, knock on the door yourself. You will have no luck either – but come back three in-game hours later after moving sufficiently far away and Barry will answer the door if you knock again. Once he invites you inside, the conversation you have with him is important.

- In the default course of events, you listen to Barry and try to cheer him up, then report your conversation to Petrova and Mendez. In this scenario, things do not end well for Barry.
- You reach a happier outcome, however, by selecting the optional dialogue lines (those appearing in blue on your screen) and showing your interest in his story. Specifically, you should inquire how Andrew died, and if he was like a grandpa to Barry. By asking these questions, you will unlock an alternative path with additional scenes.

2

If you found out about the niche at the North Oak columbarium, head there now and inspect the niche to discover the true nature of Barry's friend. You can then return to Petrova and Mendez and reveal your findings to them. This will cause Mendez to react differently, radically change the outcome for Barry, and improve your final reward.

VIOLENCE

Unlock Condition:
Complete MJ-25 ("Search and Destroy").

Notes:
Minor side job.

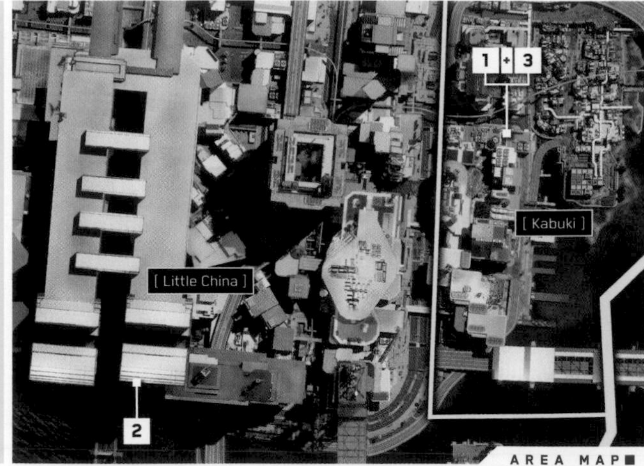

AREA MAP

1

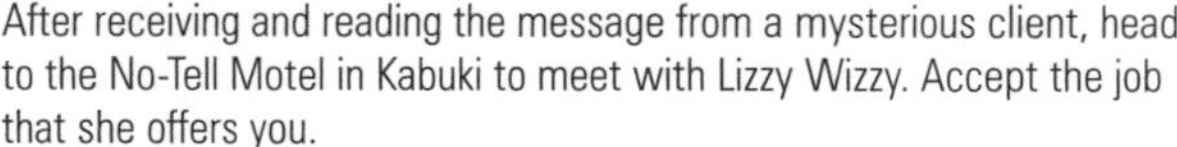

After receiving and reading the message from a mysterious client, head to the No-Tell Motel in Kabuki to meet with Lizzy Wizzy. Accept the job that she offers you.

2

Aim to arrive at the Riot club between 6 PM and 6 AM, or skip time accordingly. The bouncer at the front door will let you in, and you can even get him to give you access to Liam if you have a Street Kid background. Alternatively, you can bribe or intimidate the barman inside – or head straight to the VIP lounge if you prefer. From the bar, the VIP zone can be reached by taking two elevators: the one backstage, then the adjacent elevator in the secondary lobby. With a sufficient Intelligence level, you can also hack the door terminal leading into the secondary lobby directly from the garage area. When you get to the VIP lounge, stay behind the double glass door and listen to Liam as he talks to a woman by the name of Asa Risu. You could also follow the conversation remotely by taking control of the nearby surveillance camera. After their conversation is over, return downstairs and steal the surveillance data from the security computer in the secondary lobby. Note that it's also possible to interrupt the conversation between Liam and Asa Risu and convince Liam to pay you for your silence, though you will risk triggering combat if you linger or if Liam feels threatened.

3

You can now call Lizzy, but you have a decision to make. If you lie to her ("You were right, an affair..."), the quest ends here. If you tell her the truth ("It's worse..."), Lizzy will call you back later and the quest will continue. She will ask you to come back to her room in the No-Tell Motel. Feel free to question her, but you will eventually need to decide whether you agree to help with her final request. Refusal ends the story here; accepting leads to an improved cash reward. To complete the final part of this job, take the object to be disposed of to the garbage chute in the hotel's lobby. Alternatively, you could exit the room via the balcony and discard it in one of the dumpsters or car wrecks.

SJ-14

THE BALLAD OF BUCK RAVERS

Unlock Condition:
Complete MJ-11 ("Playing for Time").

Notes:
Minor side job.

AREA MAP

1

2

You will trigger this quest by discussing the musical ability of a street performer with Johnny in the market area close to Jig Jig Street.

Once the quest is active, head to the designated noodle restaurant and speak to the cook behind the bar. Next, head to the marked stall keeper, Karim, a few steps from the restaurant. After convincing him that you're a real fan, you will get a chance to purchase the Samurai concert recording from him – and complete the quest in the process of doing so.

SJ-15

FULL DISCLOSURE

Unlock Condition:
Complete MJ-15 ("Double Life").

Notes:
Minor side job; note that this job takes place in the same location as the "Last Login" gig (see page 268), so it makes sense to complete both objectives simultaneously.

[Northside]
1 + 2
[Kabuki]

AREA MAP

1

This job is triggered when you receive a message from Sandra Dorsett, someone you should recall from the MJ-05 Prologue job. Once you have the coordinates of the databank, head to the site marked on your map in Kabuki. There are three ways to enter the premises:

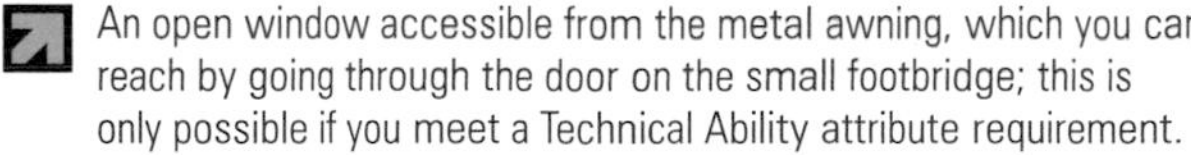

- The door in the middle via a Body attribute requirement.
- An open window accessible from the metal awning, which you can reach by going through the door on the small footbridge; this is only possible if you meet a Technical Ability attribute requirement.
- The door or the garage gate on the left.

SJ-15 FULL DISCLOSURE (CONTINUED)

Once inside, your goal is to make it to the room on the east side, where you will find the databank on a crate, between a jukebox and an armchair.

- If you arrive from the force-opened door, neutralize the scavenger seated on the couch. The room with the databank is then right in front of you, but you should make your approach from either side to avoid the gaze of the scavenger on the armchair.
- If you entered via the upper-floor window, you can go down the set of stairs on your right – at which point this route merges with the previous one.
- Coming from the left side, sneak up on the lone scavenger in the garage, then take the door to your right to end up in the room with the databank.

To get rid of the scavenger on the armchair, consider causing a distraction with the vending machine in the adjacent room, to the south. You can now safely retrieve the databank from the crate and leave – unless you want to deal with the "Last Login" gig to kill two birds with one stone (see page 268).

POSSIBLE OUTCOMES

After securing the databank, you need to call Dorsett. She will send you the coordinates of her apartment in Little China. Before you return the databank to her, you need to decide whether you wish to crack it (from your Inventory) and read it beforehand. Your decision, and how you approach the conversation with Dorsett, will determine the nature of the outcome.

Action	Consequence
You return the databank without reading it, or you read the databank and admit you did, then say you don't care and will do nothing.	Default reward
You read the databank but pretend you didn't.	Lower reward
You read the databank and admit you did, then congratulate Dorsett.	Higher reward
You read the databank and admit you did, then congratulate Dorsett and discuss daemons with her (only possible with high Intelligence).	Best reward
You read the databank and admit you did, then try to blackmail Dorsett.	Dorsett and her turret attack you

SJ-16

SEND IN THE CLOWNS

Unlock Condition:
Complete MJ-18 ("Transmission").

Notes:
Minor side job.

1-2

After you have received and read Ozob's message, give him a call and accept his offer. He essentially hires you as a driver, with the following steps to complete:

1 First, drive to Japantown, park your car at the indicated spot at the Japantown market entrance and honk (hold L3/).

2 With Ozob in the car, drive to the indicated parking spot in Little China, close to Misty's Esoterica. When he comes out of the restaurant where he made a brief stop, you will be attacked by Tyger Claws. Get out of the car and give him a hand to defeat the enemies. Note that you can retreat to the adjacent streets and alleyways to fight them on your own terms.

SJ-17

COIN OPERATED BOY

Unlock Condition:
Complete MJ-11 ("Playing for Time").

Notes:
Minor side job.

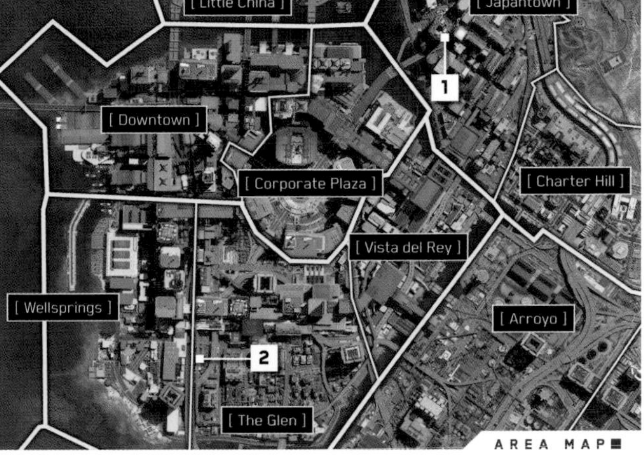

AREA MAP

1

This quest is triggered when you interact with a strange, talking vending machine that calls itself Brendan. It is located at the base of Megabuilding H8, right next to the steps and the local fast-travel station (Megabuilding H8).

The quest has multiple stages, requiring you to visit Brendan as and when you see fit between other assignments. They are as follows:

- You can first catch a glimpse of Brendan as a technician is working on the vending machine. There are no possible interactions here.
- A little later, you will find Brendan behind a dumpster. He will call out to you, introduce himself, and ask you to move the dumpster that blocks his view. Note that this can only be achieved if you meet a (minor) Body attribute requirement.
- You then get to witness a conversation between Brendan and Theo, a girl who complains about her boyfriend.
- After some time passes, you witness a thug in the process of defacing Brendan. You can get rid of him in three ways: through brute force (if you select the corresponding timed dialogue option); by remaining silent when faced with that same timed dialogue option; or by using the dialogue line exclusive to the Street Kid background.

2

The final step in this quest takes place when you find Brendan missing, with Theo telling you he was taken away. Head to the service point marked on your map, in the Glen to the southwest, and talk to the clerk. To reach Brendan peacefully, you can either bribe the clerk or convince him by choosing the dialogue line gated behind a Technical Ability attribute requirement. If you force-open the door, hack the door's lock, or threaten the clerk, you will need to destroy a ceiling-mounted security turret. Once Brendan has been updated, return to Theo to tell her what happened and complete the assignment.

I FOUGHT THE LAW

Unlock Condition:
Complete MJ-21 ("Life During Wartime") and have reached the second Street Cred tier in Westbrook, Heywood, or City Center (see page 258 for details).

Notes:
Major side job.

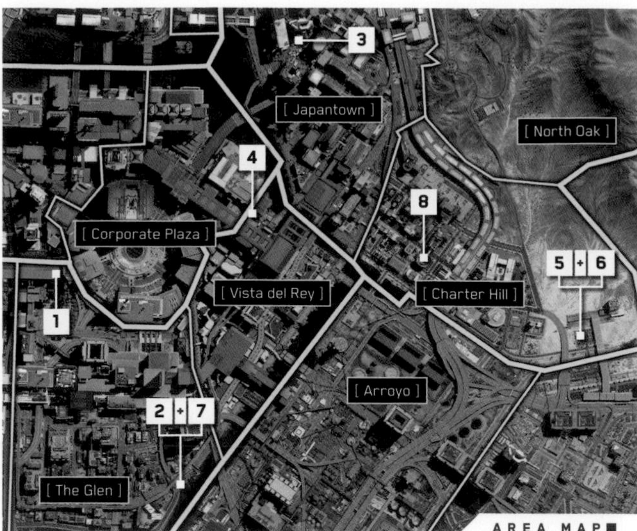

AREA MAP

1

After you receive Elizabeth Peralez's call, make your way to the marker. Get into her car to meet her and her husband, then accept their offer to explore the braindance recording they have. We suggest you first watch the entire sequence to familiarize yourself with the events that take place before you enter editing mode. There are three critical clues that you need to inspect to proceed: the mayor's conversation with his deputy (audio layer, starting at 00:15), particularly the mention of the Red Queen's Race; the assassin as he passes the security gate (visual layer at around 01:00); and finally, the CCTV screen by the gate, which suffers a security glitch (visual layer, 01:02). Once you've gone through all three, you can exit the braindance and talk to Jefferson in front of his AV. After their departure, call detective River Ward.

2

Next, head to Chubby Buffalo's and sit at River's table, then ride shotgun in his car. He suggests two possible leads: one mandatory (meeting with River's CI), and one optional (meeting the murderer's boss). We'll start with the latter here, but feel free to proceed as you please.

3

Head to the opposite end of the Japantown market to find Christine Markov at her stall. As you return to River's car, you will find two Tyger Claws waiting for him. If you want to avoid a fight, all you have to do is stay back a few steps and let River deal with them. If you get involved, the situation is likely to escalate – unless you have a Street Kid background and choose the corresponding dialogue line. Either way, River will invite you to go and talk to his CI next. You can agree to ride with him, or make your own way there.

4

River's CI awaits in a sex shop in Vista Del Rey. Talk to Neil, the clerk at the counter, then give chase when he runs away – either follow him (force-open the door or smash the glass panel and hop through it), or head back outside and catch up with him in the nearby alleyway. After the interrogation, River will propose that you go to the Red Queen's Race together. Unless you have more pressing things to do, feel free to ride with him.

5

The entrance to the Red Queen's Race is hidden inside a warehouse under heavy Animal guard. The club can be accessed via a door in the large shipping container in the middle of the building. For a complete presentation of the area, please refer to the section titled "Red Queen's Race: Warehouse."

6

Inside the Red Queen's Race, your objective is to check the computer in the office at the far end of the club, on the upper floor (you can also find an optional clue in the adjacent room). There are only two prospective foes guarding the main room: one Animal patrolling on the ground floor (who regularly takes a rest in the private rooms on the right side), and another who walks up to the upper walkway when you arrive. Try to tag them both in advance, and follow the latter on his way upstairs, then neutralize him there. Now sneak through either door on the east side and you will be mere steps away from the office with the computer – it's the one behind glass double doors. If you want to incapacitate the Animal boss, you will find him right underneath your position, running a short patrol route on the lower floor. Interrogating him will reveal additional information on the case, but make sure you stay quiet as there are guards sleeping in the area. When you're ready, examine the computer in the office to find some compromising footage in the "Files" section. You can then leave immediately by accepting River's offer.

7

Back in the Chubby Buffalo's parking lot, confront Detective Han with River. After the conversation, call Elizabeth Peralez. She will invite you to visit her at her apartment in Charter Hill.

8

Use the intercom, then take the elevator to the penthouse and sit on the couch in the living room to discuss the case. After what then transpires, leave the apartment to complete the job.

RED QUEEN'S RACE: WAREHOUSE

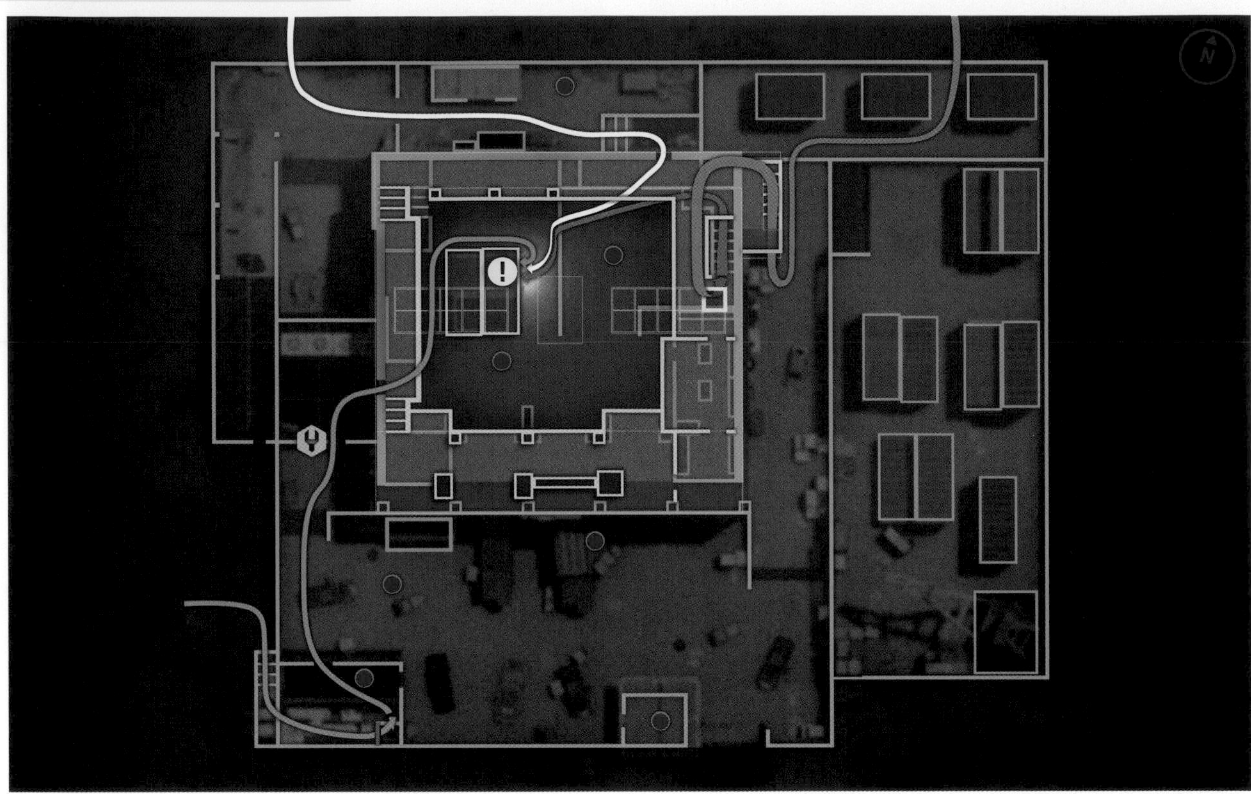

- Your objective is the door in the large shipping container in the middle of the warehouse. Opening it reveals stairs that give you access to an elevator, and in turn to the Red Queen's Race club.
- You can enter the warehouse in a variety of ways. A convenient route is to go through the missing fence section at the rear of the perimeter. You end up directly in front of an open door, with no patrols in the area. Once inside, hide behind the crate right in front of you, and wait for an opening (or create a distraction) to sneak to the container leading into the club.
- An alternative path is to enter the hostile area via the other broken fence section. Use the ladders and metal staircase to climb to the rooftop, then drop down onto the walkway overlooking the warehouse. Tag all enemies, then pick the right time to make your approach to the container leading into the subterranean club.
- Another feasible route if you have invested a few points in your Technical Ability is the small opening, accessible via steps to the left of the main gate. From here, enter the crawlspace underneath a small storage room, with a grate offering access to the room itself. Tag the two Animals patrolling the area just outside, and once both move away, crouch-walk alongside the wall to your left. Meeting a Technical Ability attribute requirement will enable you to break a fence here. You will find a door just beyond leading into the warehouse. Go around the central container clockwise, paying attention to sentries in the area, until you reach the club's door.

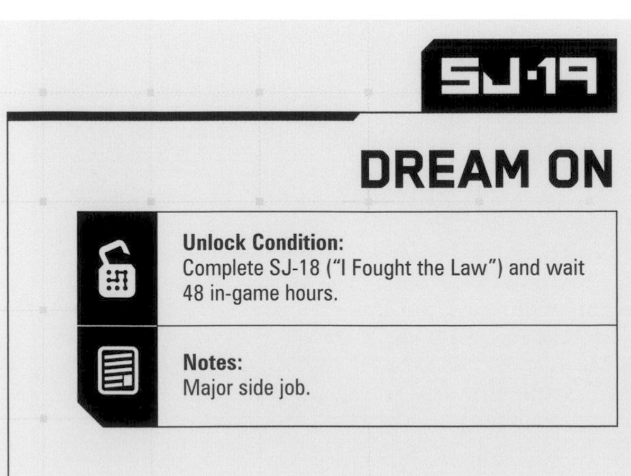

SJ-19

DREAM ON

Unlock Condition:
Complete SJ-18 ("I Fought the Law") and wait 48 in-game hours.

Notes:
Major side job.

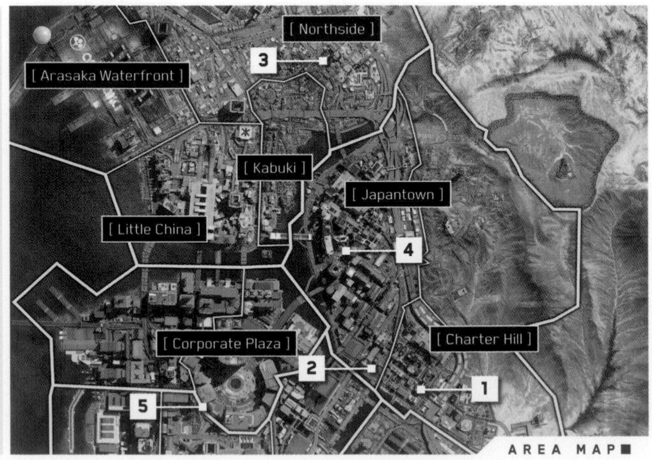

1

After receiving Jefferson's call, head to his apartment in Charter Hill. Sit on the couch in the living room to be briefed. After the conversation, Elizabeth will offer to show you around the penthouse. As per usual in these cases, your tool of choice is your scanner. Activate it and focus on any object highlighted in yellow to examine it. There are many points of interest around the house, and various ways to solve the mystery behind the break-in. This is a very enjoyable investigation, so we suggest you first attempt to complete it on your own. Should you require assistance, the following tips will help:

- Examine the traces of blood on the floor in the upper-floor hallway, by the bedroom. Stay in scan mode and follow the blood trail until you end up in the media room, where you can move a piece of furniture and scan to detect the presence of a hidden door. If your Body attribute is high enough, you can force-open that door to reveal a hidden room.

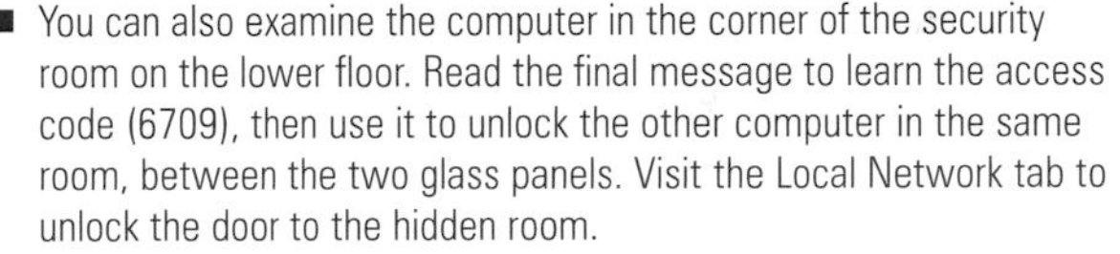

- You can also examine the computer in the corner of the security room on the lower floor. Read the final message to learn the access code (6709), then use it to unlock the other computer in the same room, between the two glass panels. Visit the Local Network tab to unlock the door to the hidden room.
- In the hidden room, scan the strange computer on the wall and pay attention to the cables. Use the ladder and the grate to reach the roof, where the cables will lead you to an old signal transceiver. After examining this, scan your surroundings and focus on the transmission source – an antenna visible in the distance to the west. You can then report your findings to Elizabeth.

2

With the transmission source identified, leave the apartment and get in your car and drive to the area where the surveillance van is parked, by the antenna. The vehicle will begin to pull away as you approach, so be prepared to sprint back to your car and tail it until it reaches its destination in Northside. If you allow it to get too far ahead you will eventually lose it, causing this entire storyline to end prematurely. Should this happen, load your most recent save and try again.

3

Once you reach the Maelstrom hideout in Northside, be on your guard: this is a hostile area. Your objective is the access point on the van. There are many ways to approach it – see "Maelstrom Hideout" overleaf for guidance. After you have jacked in, call the Peralez to tell them what you found. Elizabeth will ask you to meet her in person at a ramen shop.

SJ·19 DREAM ON (CONTINUED)

4

Head to the ramen shop suggested by Elizabeth, at the Japantown market, and sit on the designated stool next to her.

5

Finally, go and meet Jefferson at City Center's Reconciliation Park. When you sit on the bench with him, you have a decision to make: either you tell him the truth about the brainwashing he's been subjected to, or you follow Elizabeth's instructions and do not add anything to her version of the story. This is a pure role-playing choice: take whatever approach feels right to you.

MAELSTROM HIDEOUT

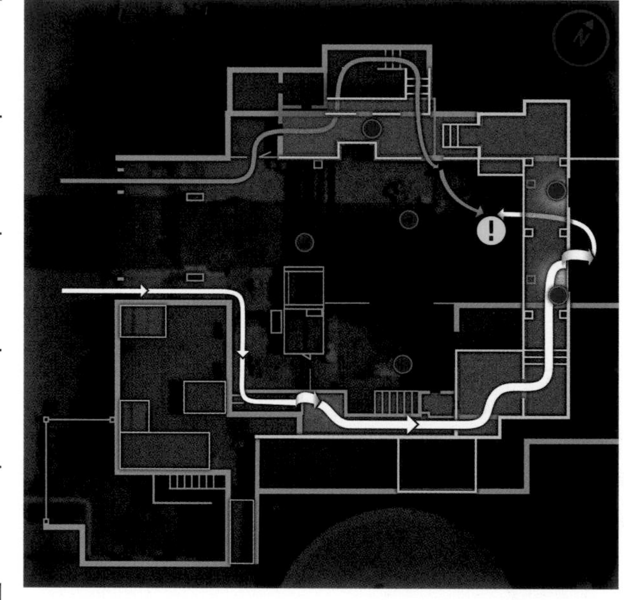

Your objective is the access point on the van, at the far end of the hideout.

Crouch-walk alongside the right-hand wall at all times, using the crates as stepping stones to reach the upper platform. Inside the building that extends out above the van's position you will encounter two potential foes as well as a surveillance camera. Quickhack the latter and simply wait for an opening to hop through the nearest window on your right (after opening the corresponding shutters): you will land just a few steps from the van.

Infiltrating the compound via the left side is a practical alternative. Move alongside the wall until you reach a fenced enclosure, then enter the building either by using the door on the left, or by opening the shutters and hopping through the window. Neutralize the Maelstromer patrolling inside before making your way upstairs. Now go through the double doors, take out the guard, and, after making sure the path is clear, drop down to reach the van.

SJ·20

THE HUNT

Unlock Condition:
Complete SJ-18 ("I Fought the Law") and wait 24 in-game hours.

Notes:
Major side job.

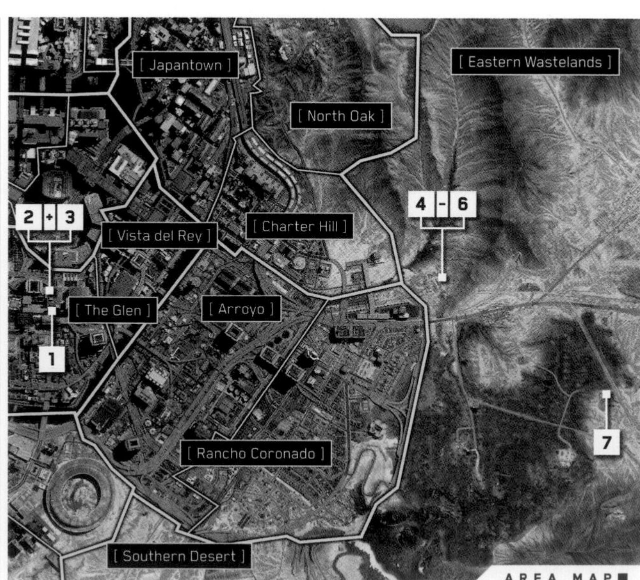

AREA MAP

1

After receiving River's call, read the message he sends you to find out about your meeting point on Pacific Boulevard and Market Street. Note that the meeting can only take place in the evening, from 7 PM – sit and wait at the designated location to fast-forward to the correct time. Head to River's car when he arrives and enter the passenger seat. After he explains the situation, leave the car and follow him across the road.

Your goal is now to break into the NCPD lab. If your Tech Ability attribute is high enough, you can open the door in the alleyway to your left when facing the main entrance. If not, you can instead climb up onto the wall enclosing the back yard using the piles of tires and crates as stepping stones, or force-open a gate on the main street if your Body skill allows for it. From the yard, head up the metal staircase to find an open window. Both paths (the door and the window) lead to the same corridor. Once inside, you do not need to be stealthy as the building is empty for the day.

2

The evidence room is the large central room. It features two side rooms: enter the right-hand one, then scan and search the drawers in the filing cabinet. After Yawen's sudden arrival, follow her into the adjacent room, before returning to River's car via the front entrance.

3

Once at your destination, follow River – first into the house to talk to Joss, then into the trailer outside. You goal here is to find clues. As usual, turn on your scanner and look for objects highlighted with the characteristic yellow glow. There are several clues in the trailer (including the nightstand's locked drawer, which you can open with the key found in the kitchen), but the most critical one is in Randy's bedroom – the laptop under the bed. After you scan it and River turns it on, you need to find a way to unlock it, either by meeting the Intelligence attribute requirement, or by typing the correct password (which you can guess by examining the clues in the area). If you struggle, the password is revealed by turning on the record player on the shelves opposite the bathroom: "Liberum Arbitrium."

4

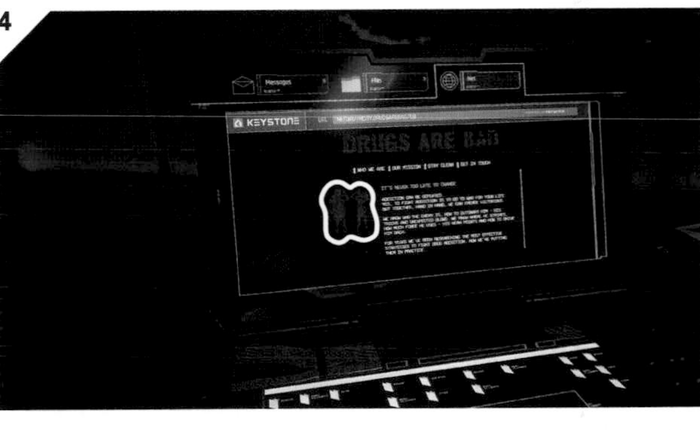

Now sit with River and explore the computer. After reading all the entries in the Messages and Files tabs, visit the site in the Net tab and click the strange picture on the left. This will open a hidden link, giving you access to new sections: Join Us and Files. Click the Files section, then return to the Files tab on the computer to find out that the "ATT_CART_VIDEO" cartoon matches the name of the missing file on the website. When you're done investigating the website, note that you can even get Harris's IP address by breaching the computer (if you meet the Intelligence attribute requirement). Either way, return to the house and speak to Joss again. Agree to spend the night in the trailer and go to sleep when you're ready.

5

When River wakes you up, he will ask you to explore a series of three braindances, featuring Tony as a child at his school, Tony as a child at his father's barn in Texas, and finally, an adult Tony at another barn in Night City. As ever, it's best to first relive each braindance in its entirety before you switch to editing mode and start the investigation. We encourage you to look for all the clues to best enjoy the sequence. Important evidence to scan is represented by colored segments on the timelines. Two critical clues in the third braindance are particularly relevant if you wish to secure the best outcome for this job:

- The solar panel at 00:27, in the room adjacent to the one with the computer.
- The farm model number at 01:00, on the wall between the two farm gates.

SJ-20 THE HUNT (CONTINUED)

6

When you're done exploring the third braindance, there are two possibilities: either you have found one of the two critical clues and River will drive you straight to the correct farm; or you haven't found either of the critical clues and will need to guess the correct farm name.

ROMANCE REQUIREMENT: RIVER

If you plan on making River your romantic partner (an option available only to a V with a female body type), be aware that you must obtain the best outcome in this quest by heading straight to the correct farm. Should you make an incorrect guess (or leave the farm prematurely without helping River, causing him to die), this will permanently lock the next quest in line involving River, along with the possibility of ever having a romantic relationship with him.

Furthermore, in the final conversation after you find Randy alive, you need to show some interest. Do not leave him to pursue his chosen course of action on his own ("count me out"), as doing so will also prevent the possibility of a romance. Instead, you should either try to convince River that vengeance will ultimately not make him feel any better ("Don't do it, River"), or tell him that you're happy to help him ("We both will").

In the latter instance, the correct answer is "Edgewood." If you guess incorrectly, you will first go to the wrong farm – where you can expect a violent encounter. When you eventually reach the Edgewood farm, you will encounter hostile turrets and mines. You can deactivate the farm's security system if you wish. To do so, enter the house on your right when you arrive, either via the shutters on the closest wall, or the front door (with a surveillance camera above) on the opposite side. Go up the stairs and enter the bedroom. You will find a secret door to the right of the computer, which you can open with a switch hidden under the desk: it reveals two computers, with Local Network tabs enabling you to power off both the turrets and the cameras. You then have only the mines to worry about, which can either be avoided or disarmed.

7

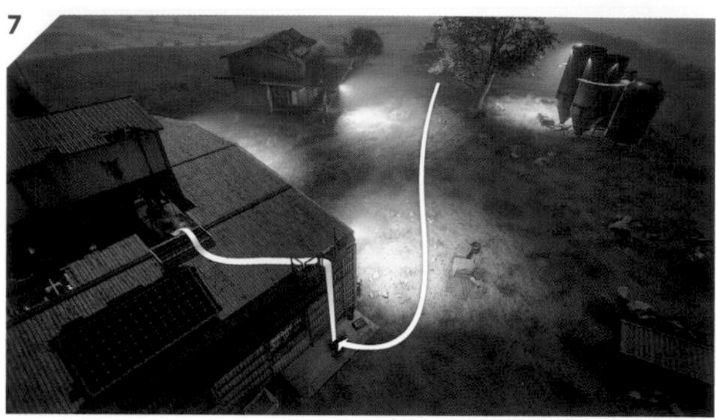

As the barn gate is closed, you need to climb up to the roof via the ladder on the left side, then drop down via a roof window. Run to the computer in the central room to switch off the braindance systems. You can now go and rescue all the victims. Randy is the abductee closest to the central room. After the cutscene, you get to discuss the whole case with River. Your choices here can have a significant impact on your relationship with River – see "Romance Requirement: River" for details.

SJ-21

FOLLOWING THE RIVER

Unlock Condition:
Complete SJ-20 ("The Hunt") and wait 24 in-game hours.

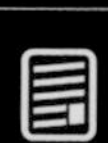

Notes:
Major side job.

AREA MAP

1

When River calls you, be sure to accept his invitation if you want to undertake this quest – even more so if you want River to be your romantic partner. Now head to Joss's house and wait for River at the designated waypoint. The entire mission is plot-driven and requires no real guidance. (You can let the children win during the augmented-reality game by weakening, but not finishing off, targets, and you can find a way to jump above the water tower fence on your own if you don't want River to give you a boost, but these are details.)

The most important choices take place toward the end if you would like to kindle a romance with the ex-cop. See "Romance: River" for details.

ROMANCE: RIVER

There are three main conditions for a romance with River to occur:

- First, your V needs to have a female body type.
- Second, you need to have successfully saved Randy during "The Hunt."
- Third, you must have selected dialogue lines where you indicated your interest in River during the final conversation of "The Hunt."

If you meet these conditions, the romance formally begins during the scene atop the water tower. The relevant dialogue options are pretty obvious (as, for that matter, are the ones where you turn River down). Make sure you elect to kiss him in both instances where you are given the chance, and to confirm your interest the next morning when he asks you where this is going ("I feel good around you"), and the romance will be assured.

If you opt for any line where you say that you're not looking for a relationship, you will instead remain friends for the rest of the story.

SJ-22

SINNERMAN

Incorporating "There is a Light That Never Goes Out"

Unlock Condition:
Complete MJ-21 ("Life During Wartime").

Notes:
Major side job.

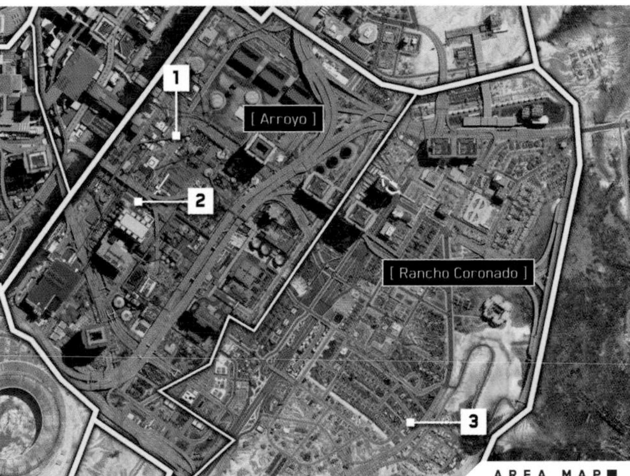

AREA MAP

1

This job is unlocked when you receive a call from Wakako. Head to the specified position outside the Dewdrop Inn in Arroyo, then sit on the bench. Speak to Bill when he arrives and take the wheel.

Important: There are multiple instances, including dialogue options, where you can choose to abandon this quest as you play it. Should you select these, this story will end immediately.

2

Once the NCPD armored car transporting Joshua passes by, give chase. If you lose them, the quest will fail, so do not linger. The car will eventually be stopped by a truck in the middle of the road. Jump out and head toward the armored vehicle, but remain unarmed: if you threaten either Joshua or the police officer, the quest will end prematurely. You can still technically complete it by killing Joshua (earning you a reward from Wakako), but you will then miss out on all the subsequent steps.

If you want this quest line to continue, approach Joshua and accept his offer; as before, if you refuse it and opt to leave, the mission ends here for good. After agreeing to work with Joshua, hop in the armored car – which causes the mission to formally transition to "There is a Light That Never Goes Out." From this point on, your behavior toward Joshua will determine the fate of the braindance he intends to record. The principle is simple: if you make encouraging or validating comments when Joshua discusses his faith, the braindance will be a success; if you mock him or choose cynical lines, it will be a failure. See "Undermining Joshua" for details.

SJ-22 THERE IS A LIGHT THAT NEVER GOES OUT

3

You will make regular stops during this storyline: first at Zuleikha's house, then at the PieZ restaurant, and finally at a braindance studio (though the latter sequence is actually part of the follow-up side job, "They Won't Go When I Go"). From a gameplay perspective, this should require no guidance whatsoever. Just enjoy the story developments, and pay attention to the lines of dialogue you select if you want to engineer a specific outcome for Joshua's braindance. In the parking lot outside the restaurant, Rachel will attempt to bribe you as she fears you might be instilling doubt in Joshua's mind. If you have a corporate background, you can negotiate an even better deal. If you take her improved offer, though, note that this will end the mission and storyline prematurely.

UNDERMINING JOSHUA

The success of Joshua's braindance is determined by six specific lines of dialogue that you can choose during your conversations with him. Whenever you select one of these comments, points are added to a hidden tally. If your score is at least four (out of a maximum of six) by the end of "They Won't Go When I Go," the second part of this questline, the braindance will be deemed a failure.

Comment Values

Setting	Dialogue Line	Value
Zuleikha's house	"Yeeeep, still not buyin' it."	1
Zuleikha's house	"Whoa. Insane, that's what this is."	1
Car ride to the restaurant	"Where we gonna eat?"	1
Restaurant	"Can we please stop talking about faith?"	1
Braindance studio*	"Got pure intentions, but this isn't the way to act on them." Or, "This is crazy, don't do it."	2

* Note that the sequence in the braindance studio is part of the next quest.

THEY WON'T GO WHEN I GO

Unlock Condition:
Complete SJ-22 ("Sinnerman") and wait 12 in-game hours.

Notes:
Major side job.

AREA MAP

1

After you receive Rachel's call and agree to help her, head to Japantown. Talk to Vasquez at the security gate, then to Rachel and Joshua inside the braindance studio.

2

Joshua will ask you to take an active part in the braindance recording. Here, you can choose to accept, to refuse but instead just sit and watch the scene, or to not take part at all (in which case this story ends here). After the recording is finished, speak to Rachel to complete the quest. She will call you back a few days later to discuss your compensation: the reward will depend on the success or failure of the braindance.

SJ-24

HUMAN NATURE

Unlock Condition:
Complete MJ-11 ("Playing for Time").

Notes:
Major side job.

AREA MAP

1

After you receive a message informing you that your car is waiting for you, head to the designated parking lot; you'll find the vehicle on the upper floor. Following the incident that occurs as you leave the parking lot, you will receive a message from Delamain inviting you to visit his headquarters: this triggers the "Tune up" quest.

TUNE UP & EPISTROPHY

Unlock Condition:
Complete SJ-24 ("Human Nature") and read the message from Delamain.

Notes:
Major side job.

1

Head to the Delamain HQ, in Vista Del Rey, and talk to the receptionist. Agree to speak to Delamain and he will send a drone that you can follow to navigate the building. You then transition automatically to the "Epistrophy" quest. Once in the control room, take Delamain's special scanner, then leave the premises.

AREA MAP

Your goal is now to find seven wayward Delamain cabs and return them to the fold, each one offering a different scenario. Once you get close to a vehicle, the scanner that Delamain gave you will be activated: you then need to stay within range (as indicated by the signal strength meter on your screen) until the connection with the divergent cab is established. At this point, a conversation will begin and you can do whatever it takes to send the cab back to headquarter. If you have any problems, refer to the accompanying map and our guidance for each vehicle.

Once you have dealt with all the missing cabs, return to Delamain HQ to complete the assignment. One final word of caution: make sure you do not damage the cabs too much: destroying any of them would cause the job to fail.

2

In **Wellsprings**, you will find the wayward cab on the road by the shore, near the Parque Del Mar fast travel station. You will need to disable it by dealing sufficient damage to it. You can do so either by ramming into it or using weapons (either press △/Ⓨ while driving, then open fire with R1/RB; or leave your car and shoot the cab while running around it).

3

In **North Oak**, your target awaits on the large roundabout at the foot of the hill. Enter the cab when it stops and drive it back – *slowly* – to Delamain's garage.

4

The divergent cab in the **Badlands**, in the middle of the landfill, simply requires you to sit in it.

5

The cab in the **Glen** is found on the road that runs alongside the river. All you need to do here is speak to the driver. Note that there is an alternative (though cruel) solution: you can also push the vehicle into the river.

6

The insubordinate cab in **Northside** is hidden, meaning that you do not have a marker guiding you to its exact position. You will find it in the yard shown here, across the road from the "Longshore North" fast travel station. As you approach, it will drive away. Give chase until it crashes.

7

In **Coastview**, the cab can be found near the Drop Point directly west of the stadium. It will require you to give chase again, but its real plan is to draw you into a trap, where goons will ambush you under a bridge. You will need to take them all down before you can proceed, so make sure you prepare accordingly.

8

Rancho Coronado's cab lies in a residential area, near the base of an antenna tower. When you come close, it will start driving erratically, making the process of following it to stay within scanner range awkward. Once the connection is established, you will need to destroy a number of flamingo statuettes in the area, all marked with waypoints, to return the vehicle.

SJ-26

DON'T LOSE YOUR MIND

Unlock Condition:
Complete SJ-25 ("Epistrophy") and wait 48 in-game hours.

Notes:
Major side job.

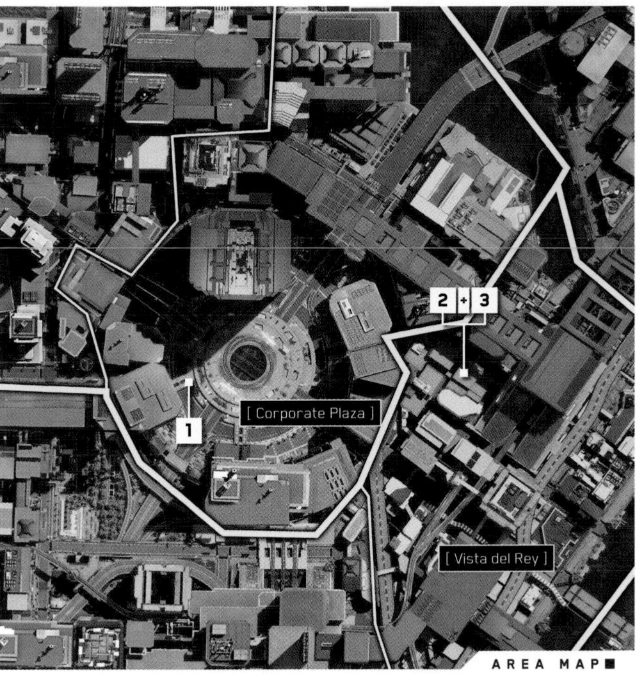

1

This episode is triggered when you run into a traffic accident at Corporate Plaza, at which point you will be invited to call Delamain. Alternatively, if you do not run into the accident for a period of 48 in-game hours, Delamain will call you. After your conversation, return to Delamain HQ.

2

The door inside the building is malfunctioning, so you have to find another way in. You have two potential points of ingress, both to the right of the main entrance: a door that requires you to meet a Technical Ability attribute requirement in the garage area, and a grate on the roof that you can reach by climbing over the crates in the alleyway beyond. Both lead to the same location. See "Delamain HQ Infiltration" for details on how to proceed once inside.

3

When you get to the control room, hear out the complaints of the divergent Delamains. At this point, you gain access to the core chamber and have a choice to make, which will determine Delamain's future. You have two primary options here, and potentially an additional one:

- You can destroy the core to liberate the divergent Delamains: shoot it with a weapon from a safe distance to avoid the explosion that ensues.
- You can reset the core to restore the original Delamain, but be aware that this will not quite bring back the Delamain you once knew.
- If you have a sufficiently high level of Intelligence, you can also hack the core to merge all of the Delamains.

After you make your decision, you can leave the chamber via the side exit and take the designated car (which is now yours) in the garage to leave the building. The Delamain installed on the vehicle (and, therefore, your conversations with him) will directly depend on the choice you made, and remain so for the rest of your playthrough.

SJ-26 DON'T LOSE YOUR MIND (CONTINUED)

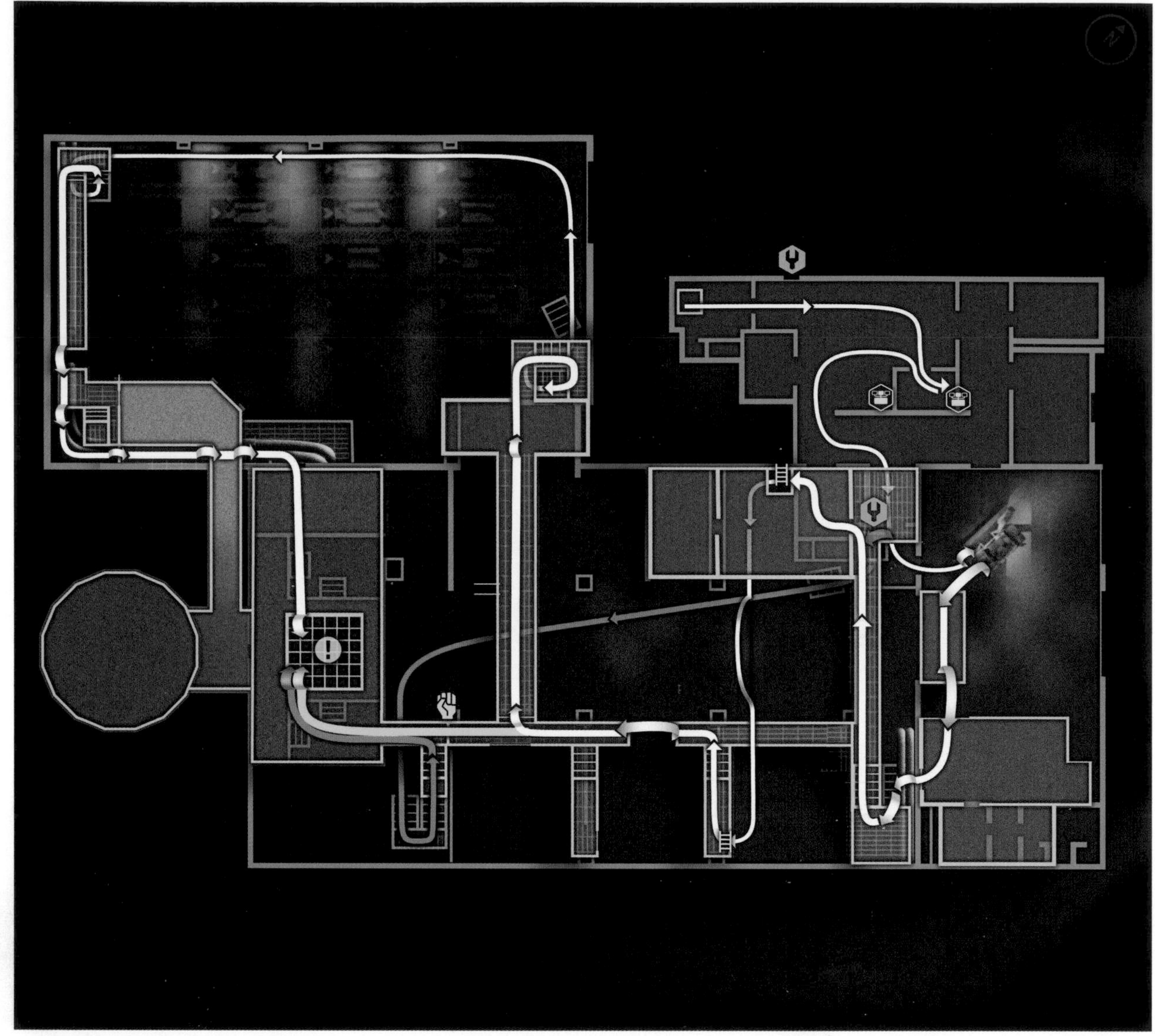

DELAMAIN HQ INFILTRATION

Your objective is to reach the control room, at the opposite end of the building.

Once inside the building, head to the small office with a computer. You can either breach it, or type in the code found in one of the emails on another nearby station (1234). Unlock the gate via the Local Network tab, then proceed through it. Follow the hallway and enter the workshop, where rogue drones roam. The floor in the workshop is electrified, so you will need to avoid it. Take the door on your left to reach a room with a car lift. Jump onto the car lift, then from here to the ledge above the garage door and to the elevated platform. An open window on the southwest side of the room, by two large pipes, will give you access to the stairs on the other side. Follow the elevated walkway until you reach a small room with a floor grate: drop down and push the car at the bottom. Now hop on it and leap across the room toward the waypoint. Use the ladder in the back, between the two repair booths, to reach the catwalk above. Cross the room one more time via the perpendicular section of the catwalk to enter the garage. Multiple vehicles are driving erratically and ramming into each other here, so try to give them a wide berth. To reach the exit, you will need to go through the room counterclockwise: going up the stairs in the southwest corner, jumping past the missing floor panel in the metal walkway, using the pipes to climb over the small room on the east wall, and finally dropping down onto the pipes on the other side. Go through the opening in the east wall and you will end up atop the control room: drop down through the hole to enter it.

As you follow the previous route, you will notice a door that can be force-opened on your left when you reach the catwalk in the workshop. If you can meet the corresponding Body attribute requirement, this gives you immediate access to the control room via the opening in its ceiling.

If you have a sufficiently high Technical Ability, you can make your life much easier in this mission. As soon as you pass the double door at the workshop's entrance, look to your right: you will find a grate in the floor, revealing an underground section with a switch: turning this off shuts down the electricity, enabling you to walk straight to the control room.

SJ-27

BOTH SIDES, NOW

Unlock Condition:
Complete MJ-15 ("Double Life") and wait 24 in-game hours.

Notes:
Major side job.

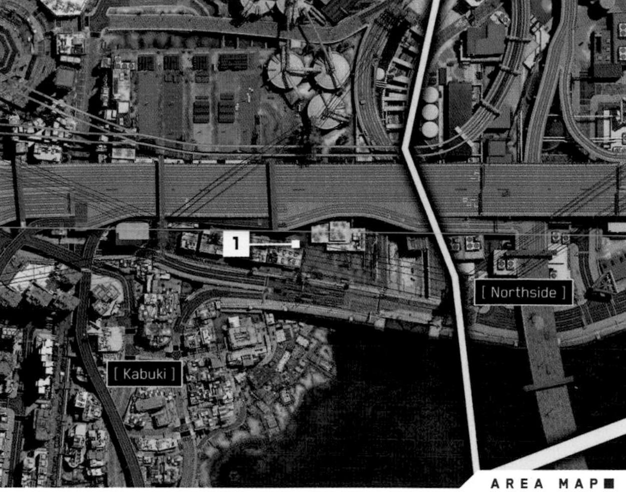

AREA MAP

1

After receiving Judy's call, go to her apartment. Interact with the intercom to have her open the door, then head into the bathroom to talk to Judy. Take Evelyn's body to the bedroom and set her down on the bed. Talk to Judy again after she hangs up, then leave the bedroom and close the door behind you. The quest ends after the conversation on the rooftop terrace.

SJ-28

EX-FACTOR

Unlock Condition:
Complete SJ-27 ("Both Sides, Now") and wait 12 in-game hours to receive a message from Judy, then wait another six in-game hours and be sure to stay sufficiently far away from Judy's apartment.

Notes:
Major side job.

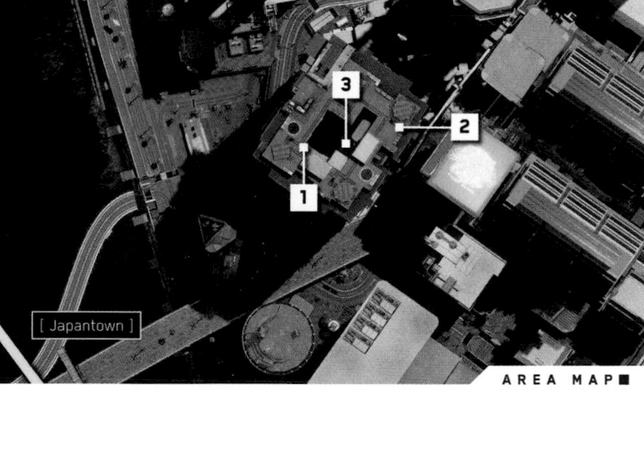

AREA MAP

1

When Judy calls you, she will ask for your help. Be aware that **if you refuse, the entire quest line will end here** – and you will also forgo any possibility of a romantic relationship with her. If you refuse by mistake, however, note that you can call her back to get a second chance. If you offer assistance, head back to the H8 Megabuilding between 5 AM and 8 AM. Take the elevator to floor 12, then go left when you exit it. Head up the stairs and make your way counterclockwise around the atrium (don't miss the ladder against the wall to your right towards the end) until you find Judy on the balcony above Clouds. Talk to her, then follow her inside to meet Maiko.

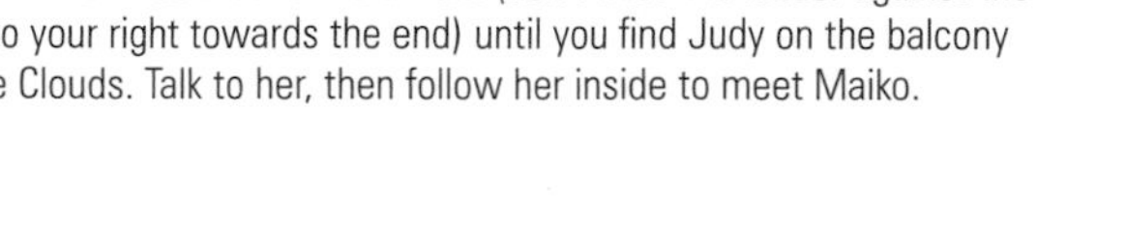

SJ-28 EX-FACTOR (CONTINUED)

2

How the conversation with Maiko unfolds depends on how you completed MJ-12 (see page 134), and more specifically in accordance with your actions with Woodman. If you achieved a result where Woodman is still alive, and you now remain calm during your discussion with Maiko, avoiding any potential forms of provocation, she will reveal that he is in the building – on the maintenance floor – as you leave. In all other instances, the quest will end after you return to the ground floor with Judy and finish your conversation with her.

3

If Maiko revealed to you that Woodman is in the building, Judy will discuss him on the way back, and suggest that you kill him. Should you agree to her request (you can also convince her to give up and leave), enter the elevator and press the button for the Maintenance floor. The conversation with Woodman will always end badly, so you may wish to arrive fully prepared and to make a preemptive attack. You have ample room to maneuver and all sorts of cover positions, so it's not an especially demanding fight. Once he falls, leave the building via the elevator and speak to Judy to complete the mission.

SJ-29 TALKIN' 'BOUT A REVOLUTION

Unlock Condition:
Complete SJ-28 ("Ex-Factor") and wait six in-game hours to receive a message from Judy, then wait another six in-game hours.

Notes:
Major side job.

AREA MAP

1

After Judy's call, you need to pay a visit to her apartment in the evening, between 5 PM and midnight. Sit on the designated stool in the kitchen. At the end of the scene, you need to tell the others if you will join them or not. Be aware that **choosing to let them down will permanently lock off the rest of this quest line**, including the option to romance Judy. You have the possibility to change your mind later on, though, by giving Judy a call and saying that you agree to help her.

Following V's dizzy spell, Judy will invite you to get some rest and sleep on her couch. There are no major repercussions for doing so. She will also offer to pay you for your services: accepting this will earn you an additional money reward.

SJ-30

PISCES

Unlock Condition:
Complete SJ-29 ("Talkin' 'Bout a Revolution") and wait six in-game hours to receive a message from Judy, then wait another six in-game hours.

Notes:
Major side job.

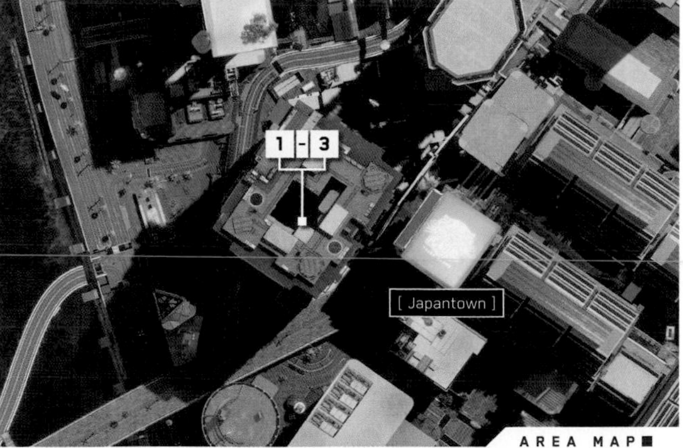

AREA MAP

1

After Judy's call, head to the H8 Megabuilding during the afternoon; 4 PM should be a good time to arrive. Meet with her and the others, then take the elevator to the maintenance floor, which is guarded by three goons; deal with them as you see fit. A stealth approach shouldn't prove too taxing if you hide behind the pillar immediately to your left as you leave the elevator. One of the hostiles will move close and then obligingly turn their back to you, an invitation that it would be churlish to refuse; it should be simple to incapacitate the other two afterwards. When the coast is clear, talk to Judy then use the service elevator close to her to reach the roof.

3

Two more Tyger Claws guard the penthouse's main floor. The first one can be ignored, with the other patrolling around the bar. Coming from the balcony, hop over the railing to your left and sneak behind the bar to eliminate the guard there – or pay him a wide berth if you prefer. Go through the adjacent doorway (this is where you arrive if you opened the shutters), and walk up the stairs. You will find one more sentry upstairs: wait until he turns his back to you to strike silently, then get into Hiromi's office and talk to Maiko. The meeting can be resolved in a number of ways – see "Pisces: Conclusion" for details. Once it's over, leave the apartment via the door on the lower floor and return to street level using the marked elevator. The quest will end after your conversation with Judy.

2

Jump onto the rooftop directly on your left as you leave the elevator, and climb down the ladder on the other side. From here, you can either enter the penthouse directly via the nearby shutters, thus bypassing all guards on the way to the office upstairs, or, alternatively, use the door on the balcony (guarded by a sentry). Note that it might be sensible to make time to neutralize all hostiles in the area – this way, you will have less to worry about if an imminent decision leads to an open combat scenario.

PISCES: CONCLUSION

When you reach Hiromi's office in the penthouse, Maiko doesn't follow the plan that was agreed on. She confronts you with a (timed) choice, which will have significant consequences. Here is an overview of the possible scenarios.

Scenario	Consequences
You play along with Maiko's plan (*"Hiromi has to go,"* then *"Maiko'll run things as she does now"*), and accept her payment.	• Peaceful resolution with the Tyger Claws • Maiko becomes the new boss of Clouds. • Judy is furious at you. Both the "Pyramid Song" quest and the possibility to romance Judy are permanently locked off.
You play along with Maiko's plan (*"Hiromi has to go,"* then *"Maiko'll run things as she does now"*), but refuse her payment.	• Peaceful resolution with the Tyger Claws • Maiko becomes the new boss of Clouds. • Judy admits this was all for the best. The "Pyramid Song" quest and the possibility to romance Judy are open to you.
You do not play along with Maiko's plan. Instead, you declare the dolls' independence, or attack the Tyger Claws.	• Hostile resolution: you have to kill all Tyger Claws, including Hiromi. • Maiko does not become the new boss of Clouds. After the meeting, you can choose to kill her or not. • Judy is happy with your choice, though shocked if you killed Maiko. The "Pyramid Song" quest and the possibility to romance Judy are open to you.

PYRAMID SONG

Unlock Condition:
Complete SJ-30 ("Pisces") without playing along with Maiko's plan or accepting her money, and wait 24 in-game hours.

Notes:
Major side job.

AREA MAP

1

After Judy's call, meet her at dawn (around 6:30 PM) at the bungalow by the Laguna Bend lake. After you talk to her and agree to dive with her, take the wetsuit she prepared for you and follow the onscreen instructions. Note that if you refuse, you can still call her back later on to say that you have changed your mind.

When you reach the diner, there are four items that you can scan and inspect, exactly as you would during a braindance analysis session: the diner's sign on the ground, a picture frame, an old camera, and a hockey stick. The camera can even be collected and offered as a gift to Judy. All four items are on the left side of the street, in front of the diner and Judy's old house next door. When you're done, tell Judy that you're ready to go.

2

The next three optional clues are across the street, by the gas station: an old car, a doll, and an umbrella. Once again, tell Judy when you're ready to proceed.

3

To enter the church, look for the opening on the right side when facing the front entrance, where the collapsed water tower hit the wall. The rest of the quest is for you to enjoy.

ROMANCE: JUDY

There are two main conditions for a romance with Judy to occur:

- First, your V needs to have a feminine body type and voice tone.
- Second, you need to have refused to go along with Maiko's plan during "Pisces," or otherwise to have turned down Maiko's payment.

If you meet these criteria, make sure you accept this quest, along with all of Judy's invitations: first to dive with her, and then to spend the night in the bungalow. Declining her suggestion to stay the night will preclude further romantic possibilities, so consider your response carefully.

After you turn on the generator, key decisions await if you would like to make Judy your long-term partner. First, make sure you kiss her when given the opportunity in the bathroom (or hug her if you missed your chance). Then, the next morning, join her on the pier outside and tell her your night together was "the beginning of something amazing." If you fulfill these two conditions, Judy and V will enter a relationship, and Judy can then (potentially) make an appearance during the game's epilogue. You will also gain the use of her apartment, with an access point to your personal stash.

If, on the other hand, you lean away instead of kissing her, or tell her that your time together was just "a pleasant distraction," the romantic path will end for this playthrough and Judy will leave Night City. Leaning away will still give you access to her apartment, though, while the latter option will not.

SPELLBOUND

Unlock Condition:
Complete MJ-19 ("Ghost Town").

Notes:
Minor side job.

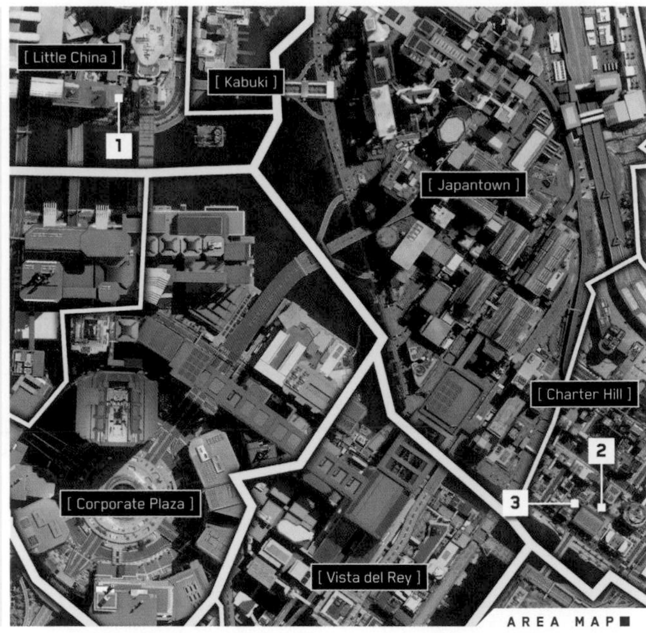

AREA MAP

1

To start this quest, talk to Nix in the netrunner room behind the bar at the Afterlife; note that you can alternatively trigger it by visiting the Smuggler's Cache website to obtain R3n0's number. Accept Nix's offer, then call R3n0.

2

Go to the meeting point – a bar on a footbridge in Charter Hill – to meet with R3n0. Nix instructed you to buy the book of spells. You can do so at full price, or with a 50% discount if you use the dialogue line exclusive to the corporate background. If you don't care to part with the cash, you can alternatively incapacitate R3n0, though you will then need to breach her computer to obtain the coordinates of the cache – which requires that you fulfill an Intelligence attribute requirement.

3

Whatever you decide, collect the book from the stash, a suitcase on a small plaza a short walk to the west. Feel free to inspect and decrypt it from the Shards menu if you can, before returning it to Nix. He will initially make you a fairly low offer. You can say that you're not selling at that price, and he will double his offer – at which point you can ask him to triple it, and he'll accept. You can also choose to keep the item for yourself, if you prefer.

LOVE ROLLERCOASTER

Unlock Condition:
Complete MJ-11 ("Playing for Time").

Notes:
Minor side job.

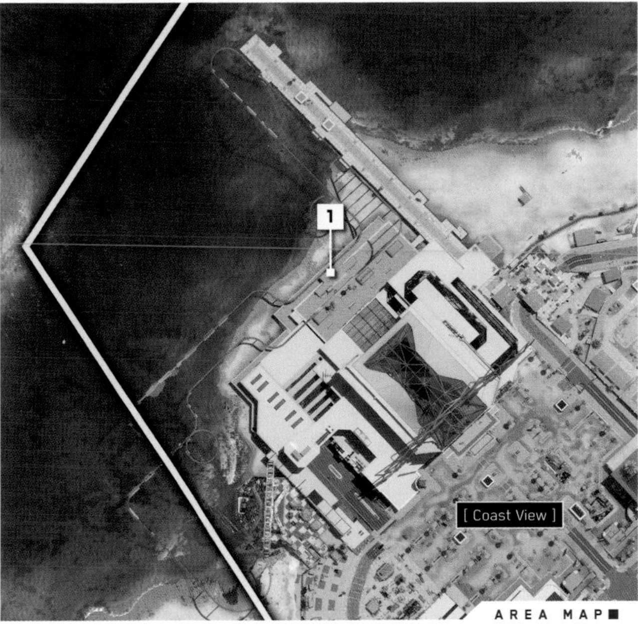

AREA MAP

1

Head to the quest marker by the rollercoaster in Pacifica. Offer your help to the man trying to repair the car, then scan it to discover a control panel behind the nearby railing. After rewiring it, return to Jean. The mission is completed after either you or Jean ride the rollercoaster.

TAPEWORM

This side job is a little unusual in how it plays out. It consists solely of four dialogue sequences with Johnny, which occur at very specific junctures after four main jobs at the heart of the storyline:

- When you leave the Clouds club at the end of MJ-12 ("Automatic Love").
- On your way out of the chapel after you speak to Alt at the end of MJ-18 ("Transmission").
- After your conversation with Anders Hellman at the end of MJ-21 ("Life During Wartime").
- After you talk to Hanako Arasaka at the end of MJ-25 ("Search and Destroy").

At this point in the story, you can technically complete the game's finale. However, you also unlock a substantial chain of side jobs that concern Johnny and his past. We cover these quests over the pages that follow.

CHIPPIN' IN

Incorporating "A Cool Metal Fire"

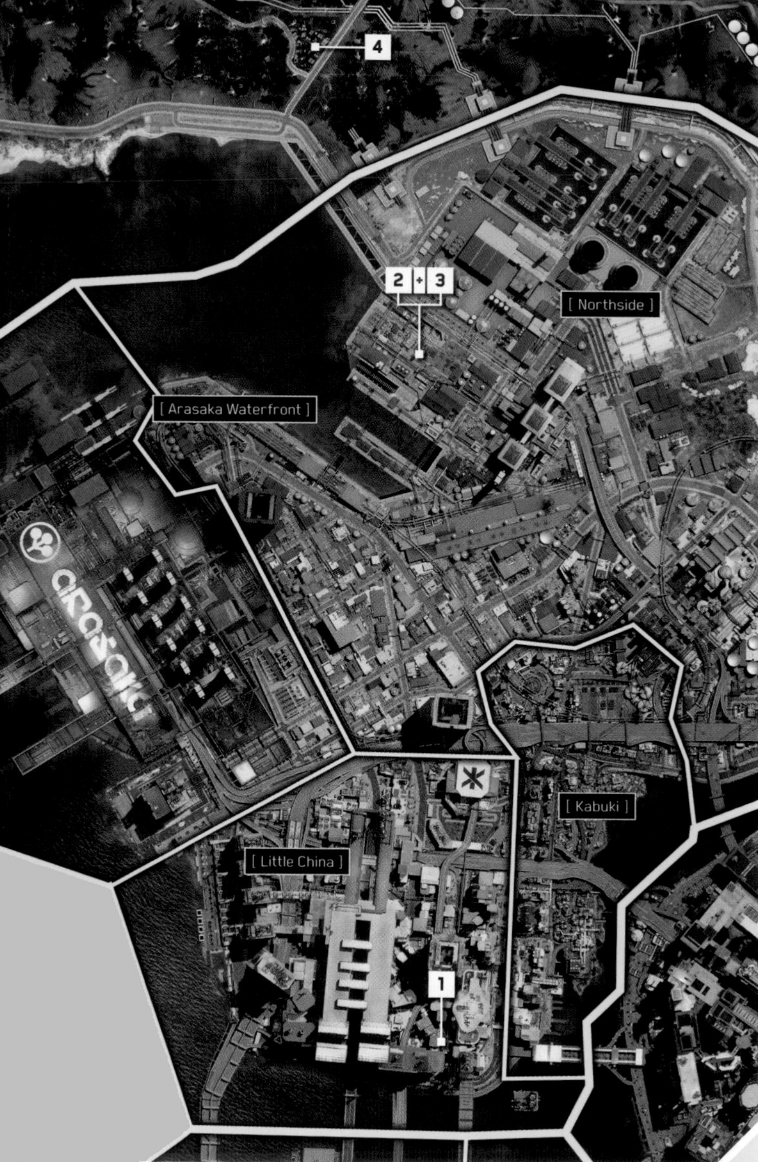

AREA MAP

Unlock Condition:
Complete SJ-34 ("Tapeworm").

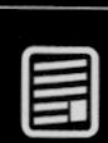

Notes:
Major side job.

1

Head to the Afterlife and speak to Johnny at the club's entrance. After the scenes with Johnny and Rogue end, you will find yourself in a hotel room in Northside. At this point, you will need to wait for Rogue to call you, so complete other jobs until she does.

After Rogue's call, meet her and Weyland at the Afterlife to discuss your plan.

2

You can now head to the shipyard at the northern edge of Northside, where your goal is to find a computer in the middle of a Maelstrom hideout. This section can be approached in various ways – see "Maelstrom Camp" for details.

3

After examining the computer and reading the message regarding the Ebunike, make your way to the long metal staircase leading to the ship's deck; note that you will have to deal with two guards in the railyard, as well as a few more foes on the ship's deck itself. An inevitable battle is triggered when you reach the far end of the ship. To defeat Grayson, stay on the move and take cover behind the many crates in the area. When Grayson falls, his fate is up to you. Letting him live ("Got lucky today") has one major benefit: he will offer you a key giving you access to a special reward. To obtain it, lower the large container hanging from the crane by pressing the control panel button at the top of the nearby ladder. Now head to the container and open it to find Johnny's old ride inside. This is your one and only chance to get this Porsche, so it's not one that you should pass up.

4

Use the Porsche (or your own vehicle if you prefer) to reach your next destination: Johnny's grave in a landfill in the oil fields. Note that your dialogue choices in this sequence will determine whether you become friends with Johnny or not. The lines leading to a friendly or unfriendly relationship are all rather self-explanatory: when discussing a possible epitaph for Johnny, for example, you can choose between "The Guy Who Saved My Life" and "Terrorist and Raging Asshole" – which should leave little room for interpretation.

Your behavior here has important ramifications, in terms of both role-play (influencing future dialogue) and gameplay. To be specific, you must become friends with Johnny to gain access to the next side job in this quest line ("Blistering Love"), which in turn must be completed to unlock one of the possible game endings. **To sum up: if you do not want to miss out on any opportunity, make sure you opt for the scenario where V and Johnny become friends.**

MAELSTROM CAMP

Follow Rogue in the camp's outskirts and she will guide you over a pile of containers (beware of the two thugs patrolling nearby). After you open the container's doors, you will arrive inside the hideout. If you cautiously crouch-walk clockwise alongside the left-hand wall, you will only run into two sentries on your way to the building with the dataterm: one before the small building in the corner, and another right after it. Both are isolated and easy to neutralize or avoid. You'll have to deal with one more Maelstromer when you enter the building with the dataterm via the ground floor door, but you have plenty of crates to hide behind. The computer awaits on the other side of the glass panel door.

From your starting position with Rogue at the hideout's entrance, you can take a more direct path to the dataterm if you've invested sufficient points in your Technical Ability attribute. Walk alongside the right-hand wall, wait for the nearby thug to move away, then break the fence and head through. Sneak past the enemy a few steps further in, and keep following the wall to your right: you will soon reach a door, which requires you to meet another Technical Ability attribute requirement. The dataterm lies just behind it.

The dataterm is hidden in a small room inside the building by the rail yard. Examine it and read the files it contains. You now need to make your way to the Ebunike, just across the nearby railyard.

SJ-36

BLISTERING LOVE

AREA MAP

Unlock Condition:
Complete SJ-35 ("Chippin' In") and become friends with Johnny during the scene in the oil fields, then call Rogue.

Notes:
Major side job.

1

After calling Rogue, head to the Afterlife in the evening (from 5 PM to 2 AM) and pick her up; you can use Johnny's car if you have it for additional flavor dialogue. Take her to the Silver Pixel Cloud drive-in at the location marked on your map in North Oak.

2

When you get to the drive-in, exit the car and enter the small building. Examine the computer and read the files to obtain a code: 0000. Type that code on the terminal to open the door.

3

Once in the parking lot, walk up the metal staircase and head into the room at the top. Activate the projector panel before you return to Rogue on the parking lot. During the scene that follows, note that you can have an opportunity to kiss and make out with Rogue if you select dialogue lines that indicate your interest in her.

ALTERNATIVE GAME ENDING: ROGUE

By completing this quest, you unlock one of the game's unique finales – in this case, a conclusion involving Rogue. To avoid spoilers, we'll notify you on the next step to take when the time arrives later in the main storyline. This is clearly flagged in-game (and, naturally, in our coverage) as a "point of no return," so rest assured that you won't accidentally miss it.

SJ-37

HOLDIN' ON

AREA MAP

Unlock Condition:
If you became friends with Johnny, complete SJ-36 ("Blistering Love"); if you didn't become friends with Johnny, complete SJ-35 ("Chippin' In").

Notes:
Major side job.

1

This quest begins when Johnny asks you for a talk after you have completed Blistering Love. To get things started, meet him by the pond at the foot of the North Oak sign. After your conversation, head to Kerry's villa.

2

Kerry won't open up if you use the intercom but you can jump over the property wall via the rock outcrop to the right of the gate. Your goal is to go through the mansion's front door, with a few (unique-looking) androids patrolling the area. Take the time to tag them, then sneak past if you'd prefer to avoid a battle. Advancing alongside the left-hand wall will enable you to stay clear of four of them. You can then wait for the fifth, walking back and forth right outside the house, to move past the door – then slip through once it is facing away from you.

3

Inside the villa, you can trigger a few short dialogue sequences with Johnny by examining various points of interest, such as the guitar collection, the dining room table, the bed, the car in the pool, and so forth. To proceed, check out the double doors by the guitar collection, and agree to take the pills. Follow Kerry upstairs, then call Nancy after the cutscene to transition to the next mission.

SECOND CONFLICT

Unlock Condition:
Complete SJ-37 ("Holdin' On").

Notes:
Major side job.

AREA MAP

1

Head to the Totentanz in the northern part of Watson and walk up the stairs. Enter the elevator and press the button to get to the third floor. The gang members you run into here will vary in accordance with decisions you made during the MJ-08 prologue quest (see page 121).

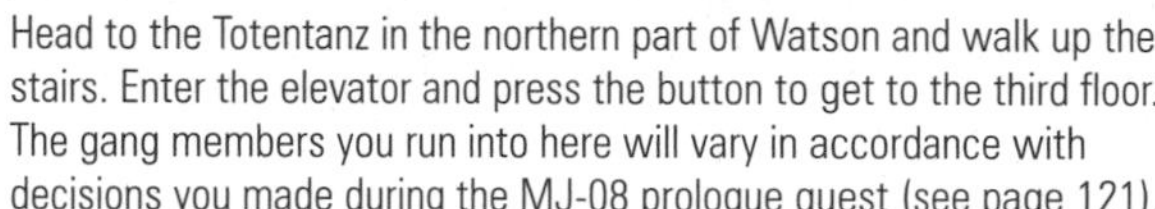

- If you opted for a scenario in which Royce and Dum Dum survived, they will be here again.
- If you killed Royce and Dum Dum and saved Brick, Brick will be your host.
- If you killed Royce and Dum Dum but did not save Brick, you will have to deal with Patricia.

2

Follow your guide inside the club until you meet the leader, then talk to Nancy. If you're welcomed by Brick, he will express his gratitude, allowing for a completely peaceful resolution. If you're facing Patricia, she will take you to a back room, and armed conflict is then unavoidable. After you rescue Nancy, simply follow her to the exit, killing all Maelstromers you run into on the way (you may then skip to step **3**). In the scenario where you are dealing with Royce and Dum Dum, you have the option of sneaking Nancy's data out of the Totentanz. However: from the moment you carry the data, all Maelstromers will treat you like a hostile, so keep a low profile. See "Totentanz Escape" for details on how to quietly leave the club. Note that successfully extracting the data from the Totentanz will allow Nancy to publish a prize-winning article, which she will tell you about by text message.

3

Once back outside, follow Nancy to her car and ride with her to N54 News, then make your way to Denny's mansion in North Oak. Your goal is to find Denny and Henry. Using the intercom doesn't help much, but following the tire tracks that go off-road in front of the entrance will lead you to an interesting scene at the back of the property. At this point, you need to choose between Denny and Henry, as they refuse to play together. Your decision will determine which of the two appears at the concert, and will affect corresponding dialogue.

TOTENTANZ ESCAPE

Your goal is to reach the elevator on either floor. Remember: if you are facing Patricia, combat is inevitable, and if you are dealing with Brick, you automatically get a peaceful outcome. The following advice only applies to the scenario where you meet Dum Dum and Royce.

After receiving the data from Nancy, walk down the stairs and immediately take a right. Enter the men's toilet and slip through the window. Circle back via the metal ledge and crouch before you reach the next open window. You will notice guards here. Wait until they all look away to hop inside. Stay behind cover and sneak up on them to take them down silently, one after the other. When they're all neutralized, head to the corridor on the far left. Here, slip through the door to the right: it leads to a series of rooms with three sentries that are fairly easy to approach from behind, and ultimately leads to the elevator.

If you have invested enough points in the Technical Ability attribute, you can take a slightly different path. Go down the stairs, turn right, then open the double doors on your left. Proceed through the room with the three guards, quietly dispatching them one by one. When you reach the corridor on the far left, use the door to the left, then the next one immediately in front of you. Quickhack the camera at the top of the stairs, and you can then reach the elevator on the upper floor.

A LIKE SUPREME

Unlock Condition:
Complete SJ-38 ("Second Conflict") and wait 24 in-game hours.

Notes:
Major side job.

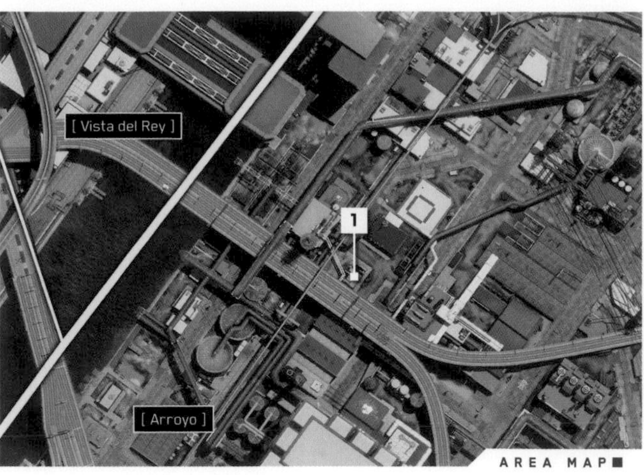

AREA MAP

1

After receiving Nancy's call, head to the Red Dirt club in Arroyo in the evening. In this largely story-driven job, all you have to do is talk to the members of the Samurai band and follow the onscreen instructions. There are many possible scene variations and optional lines of dialogue to explore depending on whether you chose to invite Denny or Henry to play. All of these have no long-term consequences, though, and only matter from a role-play perspective.

REBEL! REBEL!

Unlock Condition:
Complete SJ-39 ("A Like Supreme") and wait 12 in-game hours while outside Kerry's villa.

Notes:
Major side job.

AREA MAP

1

After receiving Kerry's call, go to the Foodscape joint in Rancho Coronado, at the corner of Gray and Mallagra, between 12:30 and 3:30 AM. Wait for him, then enter the passenger seat in his car when he arrives.

2

When you reach your destination, take the gear from the trunk and set up the stinger at the spot that Kerry shows you, then hide with him under the bus shelter. Once the van stops and its passengers are out, make them lie on the ground, grab the keys and open the back of the van. Kerry will then ask you to throw a grenade at the van. When NCPD cars arrive, step on the gas until you lose them. Kerry will then invite you to stop and have a coffee with him at his favorite joint: a Capitan Caliente restaurant.

SJ-41

I DON'T WANNA HEAR IT

Unlock Condition:
Complete SJ-40 ("Rebel! Rebel!").

Notes:
Major side job.

AREA MAP

1

After Kerry calls you, head to the food stall outside the Riot club and wait for him at around 7 PM. He will ask you to find a way into the club. You have a few options here.

- You can buy tickets from the man just off the back of the line in front of the club. If you have a Street Kid background, you can even get a discount on the price. It's also possible to enter via the fire escape door, in the alleyway to the left of the front entrance. To reach it, either jump from the opposite rooftop (accessible from the bridge above), or drop the fire escape ladder by shooting it. This route takes you into the club's storage room. Another approach consists of stealing the tickets from the two fans in that same alleyway – all you have to do is scan them both.
- Alternatively, you could also sneak through the garage area on the right, where two doors can be opened if you meet attribute requirements (Body for one, Intelligence for the other's terminal). Both options give you immediate access to the backstage area, where the Us Cracks await.

2

Once inside the club, make your way to the dressing room backstage. If you used the garage door with a Body attribute requirement, this is immediately to your right as you arrive. If you used the door with an Intelligence requirement, you will need to take the staff elevator. Arriving from the other paths, you have to go through the door watched by a security guard in the bar area. There are three ways to achieve this: by convincing the security guard to let you in (which requires you to meet a Technical Ability requirement); by talking to Kerry and distracting the roadie at the bar to steal his pass; or by retrieving an employee badge from the storage room, near the bar (your entry point if you entered via the fire escape door).

3

You will find the Us Cracks to your right as you enter the dressing room. You can resolve the situation in one of two ways: with diplomacy, agreeing that Kerry's manager is at fault (the upper lines of dialogue), or by reacting angrily and threatening them (the lower dialogue options). Your choice will impact the next job involving Kerry. If you resolve the situation with a positive outcome, Kerry and the Us Cracks will reach an agreement and release a song and video together. If not, there will be no such event – though this will not unduly affect the potential for a romantic relationship with Kerry. Note that Kerry and the Us Cracks reaching an agreement is a requirement for a later minor side job (SJ-62, see page 242).

OFF THE LEASH

Unlock Condition:
Complete SJ-41 ("I Don't Wanna Hear It") and wait 12 in-game hours.

Notes:
Major side job.

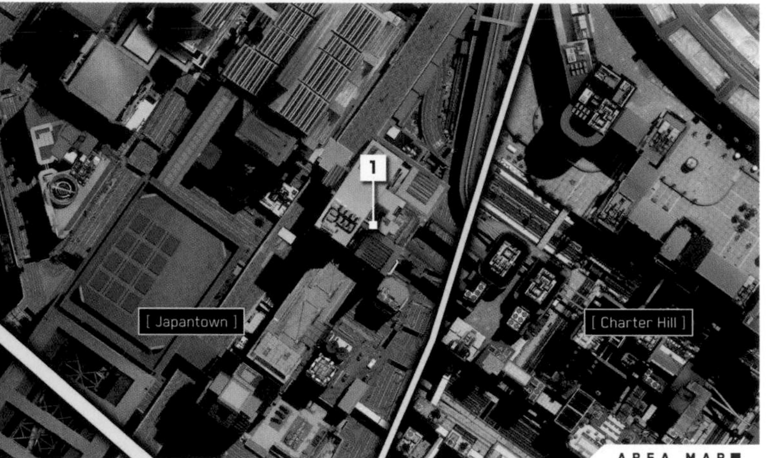

This quest plays out differently in accordance with the outcome of the previous part of the story, "I Don't Wanna Hear It." If Kerry entered into an arrangement with the Us Cracks, you will be invited to a party and concert; if not, Kerry will still invite you, but there will be no party. Either way, head to the address you receive after Kerry's call, the Dark Matter in Japantown, and tell the bouncer you're there to meet Kerry. Take the elevator to the lounge. Once upstairs, talk to Kerry and follow him onto the terrace.

FLIRTING WITH KERRY

No matter the outcome with Kerry and the Us Cracks, a V with a masculine body type and voice tone has the opportunity to flirt with Kerry during the scene on the rooftop terrace. All you have to do to achieve this is to be understanding (avoiding all lines implying that you have better things to do, or that he doesn't need you). You then have the option of kissing him during your conversation. Note, however, that doing so is *not* a requirement to enter a romantic relationship with the rockerboy.

BOAT DRINKS

Unlock Condition:
Complete SJ-42 ("Off the Leash") and wait 24 in-game hours.

Notes:
Major side job.

After you receive Kerry's call, head to the yacht at the Night City Marina at around 7 PM. Once on the deck, accept his offer to go for a cruise around the bay. If you refuse, this will end the quest abruptly – along with any aspirations you might have had to romance Kerry. The rest of this sequence is largely story-oriented, so you can enjoy it without any further assistance.

ROMANCE: KERRY

Once the yacht is in the middle of the bay during "Boat Drinks," Kerry will ask you to vandalize it with him. You are free to accept or refuse, as the choice has no lasting consequences – other than for the yacht, of course.

If you intend to make Kerry your romantic partner, now is your chance to make your move. Note that this is only possible if your version of V has a masculine body type and voice tone, though. There are two steps that you need to complete: first, when Kerry asks for your help inside the yacht, make sure you kiss him; then, after the scene on the beach, you need to select the dialogue line confirming you want to be with Kerry. Doing so will cause Kerry and V to enter a relationship; Kerry can then potentially make an appearance during the game's epilogue.

SJ-44

FOOL ON THE HILL

Unlock Condition:
Complete MJ-10 ("The Heist").

Notes:
Minor side job; this job is triggered when you scan your first tarot card graffiti. It requires you to find 20 pieces of graffiti around Night City (all marked with the icon). You can find screenshots showing each graffiti location overleaf.

SJ-44 FOOL ON THE HILL (CONTINUED)

301 The Fool

On the outside wall of V's apartment.

302 The Chariot

On a wall adjacent to Tom's Diner.

303 The Sun

On the wall by the tunnel.

304 The Magician

On the pillar supporting the elevated highway, facing Lizzie's.

305 The Empress

At the bottom of the staircase that leads to the Afterlife's entrance.

306 The Emperor

On a wall next to Konpeki Plaza's main entrance.

307 The Hierophant

At the beginning of an underground section, a few steps away from where you meet Oda with Takemura during the "Down on the Street" main job.

308 The Hermit

On the side of the church that leads into the Voodoo Boys crypt.

309 Strength

On the side of the small building where you first meet with Panam.

310 Wheel of Fortune

Under the sign of the Sunset hotel.

On the cistern opposite the Electric Corporation power plant.

At the base of the antenna tower, in the middle of the solar farm.

On the outside wall of Hanako's residence.

Behind the screen of the Silver Pixel Cloud drive-in.

In an underground passage at the base of Arasaka Tower.

On a water tower in the oilfields, not far from where a body of significance was discarded.

On one of the walls in the North Oak columbarium.

On the side of the building where the Embers restaurant is found.

On the topmost floor of the building where Takemura has his safehouse (see page 162).

On the balcony where you chat with Misty during MJ-26 ("Nocturne Op55N1" – see page 164), though you can reach it beforehand via the elevator in the alleyway between Misty's Esoterica and Viktor's clinic.

RIDERS ON THE STORM

Unlock Condition:
Complete MJ-21 ("Life During Wartime"), then wait 12 in-game hours.

Notes:
Major side job.

AREA MAP

1

This quest is triggered when you receive a call from Panam. Head to the Aldecaldos camp in the Badlands, where you can talk to her and her veterans, then accept Mitch's offer to observe the camp via his drone. During this brief reconnaissance session, keep your scanner on at all times (you will need to inspect both the tire tracks and the truck), and try to memorize the layout of the perimeter. Before you take the van's wheel and move on to the next step, accept the Spiked Superjet offered by Mitch. Note that you can make your way to the Raffen Shiv camp on your own if you prefer, but doing so means that you will miss a conversation with Panam (unless you catch up with her). Also, be aware that if you happen to have visited the Raffen Shiv camp prior to this mission, any enemies that you eliminated then will not be present during this job, making it significantly easier.

2

Once at the Raffen Shiv camp your goal is to rescue Saul, who is detained in the cellar of the main building. You can storm the main entrance and fight your way in if you're confident in your equipment and combat skills (one of the guards at the entrance wields an iconic weapon that you can collect) – but if you'd rather play safe, there are viable routes for stealth infiltrations. Not raising the alarm has many advantages, not least in that it prevents reinforcements from ever joining the fray. For more details on the layout of the camp and its many points of interest, see "Raffen Shiv Camp: Infiltration."

QUEST FAILURE CONDITIONS

You can fail this mission before it even properly begins if you complete one of the following actions:

- You choose to go to the Raffen Shiv camp by your own means, and do not join Panam there within 24 in-game hours.
- You choose to ride with Panam but you drive to another destination, and after she throws you out of the vehicle, you do not join her at the rendezvous point within 24 in-game hours.

In either of these scenarios, you will receive a message from Panam and the mission will be locked off for this playthrough, with multiple long-term consequences: you will never see Panam again (preventing a possible romance with her), the Aldecaldos will leave the Badlands, and you will lose the possibility to trigger the game ending involving the Nomads. Consider your actions carefully, then.

3

After rescuing Saul and getting in Panam's van, you will need to eliminate your pursuers if you were spotted during the infiltration. When you reach the Ingalls farm, follow Saul inside. You have two minor tasks to complete: turn on the power via the electric panel in the small bedroom, then adjust the fuse on the external panel. When morning comes, follow Panam to the motorcycles outside to receive your compensation for this mission: Panam's very own sniper rifle.

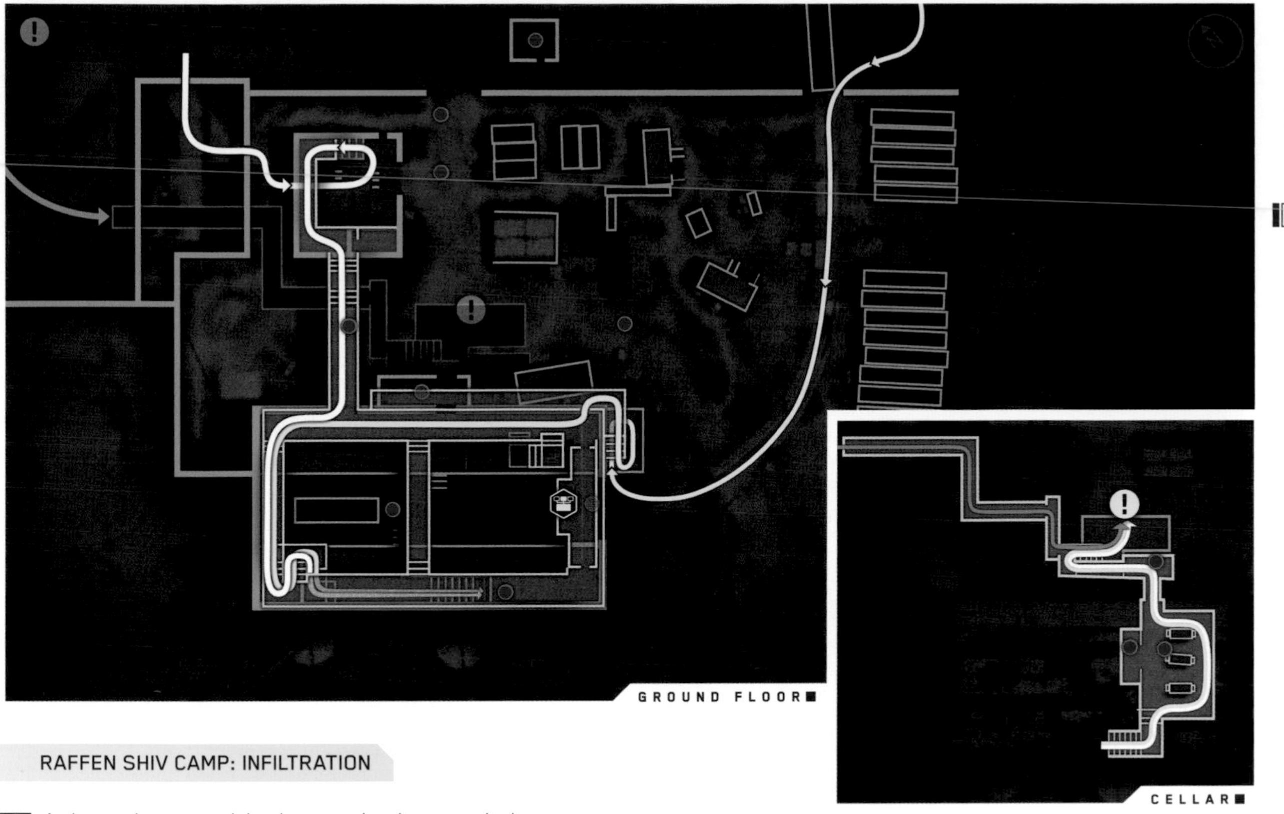

RAFFEN SHIV CAMP: INFILTRATION

An interesting approach involves entering the camp via the electrical substation on your right when you face the main entrance. This route has the added benefit of not exposing you to the snipers posted on the warehouse's rooftop. Break or jump over the fence gate, stealthily eliminate the lone guard inside the enclosure, then knock down the next gate and hop through the open window on your right. Inside the garage, make your way up the stairs and you will find a single guard on your path, on the footbridge. Once inside the main building, turn right and crouch-walk alongside the wall to your right, traveling counterclockwise; you will soon find stairs leading to the ground floor, with another set of stairs nearby providing access to the cellar. Neutralize the three guards in the cellar as you please before you free Saul. Retrace your steps all the way back to where you entered the camp and get in the back of Panam's van.

Another valid plan is to enter the camp via the green container, on your left when facing the main entrance – though be warned that a guard roams in this area. Once inside the perimeter, head for the main building while avoiding the attention of the three potential hostiles in the area – or take them out them if you prefer to err on the side of caution. Their patrol routes keep them mostly separate, and you have plenty of cover available – though you should pay attention to the snipers on the rooftop. When you reach the corner of the main building, head up the steps to find a door at the top. You enter the building right in front of the security room, and on the same walkway as in the previous path, which you can follow counterclockwise to reach the cellar (read from the sentence "Once inside…").

If you have invested sufficient points in your Technical Ability attribute, you have access to the ultimate shortcut for this mission. From the main entrance, head to the right of the compound and you will find a ventilation system: open it to find a tunnel that will lead you directly to the cellar where Saul is being detained. Free him and retrace your steps to complete the objective without running into a single foe.

This is the room where you can optionally check the security feed to discover Saul's whereabouts. Alternatively, you could also find out where Saul is detained by overhearing guards discussing his position (either the pair chatting in the middle of the main building's ground floor, or the duo almost directly underneath the footbridge).

Saul is held captive in the cellar, accessible either via the stairs on the main building's ground floor, or the ventilation system that can only be reached via a Technical Ability attribute requirement. Note the presence of a Nomad who has been eviscerated in the room just before the cellar: inspecting her body will trigger a brief exchange between V and Panam, and Saul will also mention her when you rescue him.

If you manage to remain undetected, Panam will pick you up outside the Raffen Shiv camp, near the ventilation system access point. If you are spotted, she may instead storm the compound and wait for you in front of the main building's large gate. If there's a danger that you might be overwhelmed by local forces, it might be prudent to make a dash for her position.

ROMANCE REQUIREMENT: PANAM

During your night at the Ingalls farm, you will have the opportunity to flirt with Panam. If you intend to make her your romantic partner, make sure you fulfill the following two conditions: first, invite her to make herself more comfortable and take her shoes off, then follow up by saying you have "a few ideas." Missing this chance will preclude any possibility of a relationship with Panam for the rest of your playthrough.

SJ-46

GUN MUSIC

Unlock Condition:
Complete SJ-45 ("Riders on the Storm").

Notes:
Minor side job.

AREA MAP

1

Speak to the Aldecaldo at the entrance to the industrial site, then join Carol and Cassidy in their tense meeting with scavengers. This can end in one of three ways:

- You talk to them, but they eventually attack you after recognizing you from the MJ-05 ("The Rescue") main job.
- Intuitively understanding that conflict is inevitable, you make a preemptive attack (but cause Carol to react angrily after the battle).
- If you have a sufficient Body level, you can intimidate the scavengers and get them to pay your friends without a fight.

In the first two (hostile) scenarios, you need to eliminate all enemies in front of you, including a sniper who can deal large amounts of damage. Note that you can open hostilities with a bang, *literally*, by shooting the propane tank right next to the scavengers.

SJ-47

A DAY IN THE LIFE

Unlock Condition:
Complete MJ-11 ("Playing for Time").

Notes:
Minor side job.

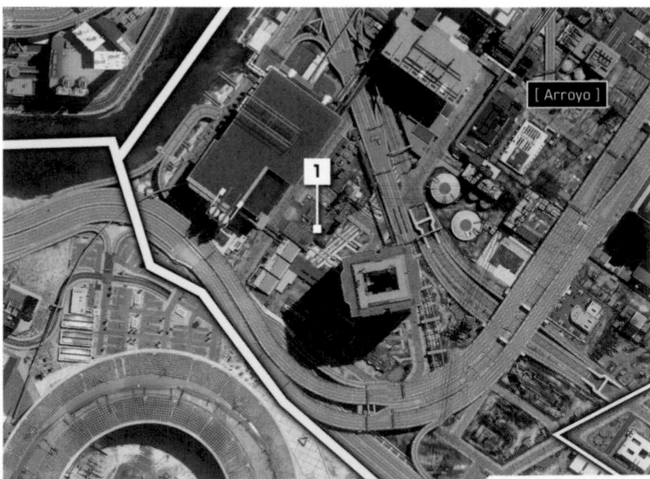

AREA MAP

1

To trigger this quest, you first need to go and chat to Darrell, a stall keeper in Arroyo. Now leave, and pay him another visit once the side job waypoint icon appears on your map. Agree to help him, then go talk to the thugs who are trying to steal his motorcycle. Prepare yourself first, as a battle is inevitable here – unless you have reached the second tier of Street Cred in Santo Domingo (see page 258), in which case the thugs will recognize you and flee after you threaten to deal with them.

If you choose not to help Darrell, the thugs will kill him. If you assist him, however, he will offer a discount at his shop.

SJ-48

IMAGINE

Incorporating "Stairway To Heaven," "Poem Of The Atoms," and "Meetings Along The Edge"

Unlock Condition:
Complete MJ-11 ("Playing for Time").

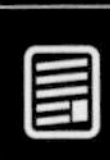

Notes:
Minor side job.

AREA MAP

1-4

In this quest, a Zen master invites you to sit with him; whether you pay him or not is at your discretion. He will guide you through a meditation braindance – and then vanish afterwards. This process happens four times in total (with a different job name each time, but all in the same quest line), and takes place in the following locations:

1 **Earth Meditation ("Imagine"):** On a bench close to a small pagoda just southwest of Corporate Plaza.

2 **Water Meditation ("Stairway To Heaven"):** In front of a pagoda in the southeast of Japantown.

3 **Fire Meditation ("Poem Of The Atoms"):** In the middle of a roundabout in North Oak.

4 **Air Meditation ("Meetings Along The Edge"):** On a tourist viewpoint with a coin-operated viewer just south of Rancho Coronado, on a clifftop overlooking solar farms.

After the fourth and final meeting, you will find a collectible on the ground right next to you, which you can use to decorate your apartment.

SJ-49

WITH A LITTLE HELP FROM MY FRIENDS

Unlock Condition:
Complete SJ-45 ("Riders on the Storm"), then wait 12 in-game hours.

Notes:
Major side job.

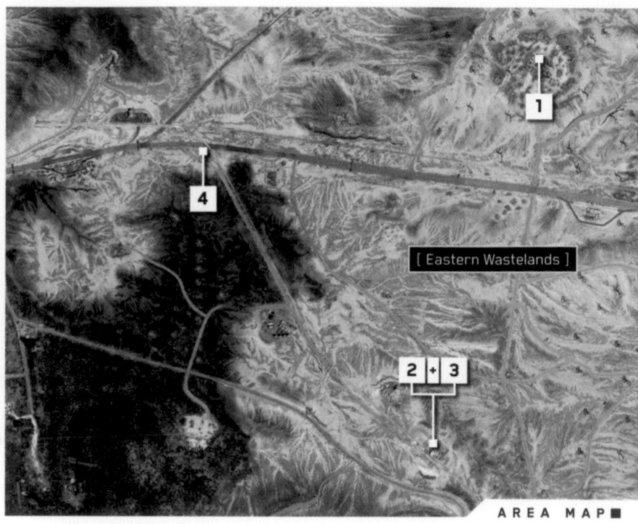

AREA MAP

1

After receiving Panam's call, head to the Aldecaldos camp. Panam and her Nomad friends are in the midst of a heated discussion. Follow them until they ask if you intend to help them. **This is a critical moment.** If you choose to disclose Panam's plan to Saul, there will be serious consequences: this storyline will end immediately, Panam will cut all ties (abruptly ending any possibility of a romantic relationship), and a potential game ending involving the Aldecaldos will be made unavailable in your current playthrough. If you do agree to help Panam, all of these options will remain open.

Assuming that you agree to help them, your friends will ask if you intend to ride with them, or to meet them at the rendezvous point.

2

At the junction, talk to Panam – and the other Aldecaldos if you wish. If you speak to Mitch, he will ask you to scan the generator for him, then fix it. There are three ways into the control tower: the front door (with a Technical Ability attribute requirement); the back door (gated behind a Body requirement, leading to a grate); and the balcony above the back door, which you can reach via the adjacent high voltage equipment.

3

At the top of the control tower, your goal is to find a punch card. Look inside a drawer lying directly on the floor, in the storage room, then return to Panam. Now head to the adjacent room and insert the card in the reader. Speak to Panam one more time before rejoining the others outside. Sit with them by the campfire. After the cutscene, take the passenger seat in Panam's vehicle.

4

During the train chase, try to shoot at the coupler. If you succeed, the train will ram into one of the Militech vehicles, thinning the enemy ranks in the scene that follows. Either way, the train will soon stop, and you will face off against Militech troops. Consider flanking them to take them by surprise. Once the dust settles, return to your vehicle and escort the trucks back to the Aldecaldos camp. After Saul's warm welcome, speak to Panam to complete the quest.

ROMANCE REQUIREMENT: PANAM

During your conversation with Panam at the junction, she will at some point ask you why you are helping her. If you intend to make her your romantic partner, make sure you do *not* imply that you're doing it for the money ("Not doing it for free"), as this would preclude any possibility of a relationship with Panam for the rest of your playthrough. Any other of the possible answers are fine, on the other hand.

SJ-50

QUEEN OF THE HIGHWAY

Unlock Condition:
Complete SJ-49 ("With a Little Help From My Friends") and wait 24 in-game hours.

Notes:
Major side job.

AREA MAP

ROMANCE: PANAM

There are four main conditions for a romance with Panam to occur:

- First, your V needs to have a male body type.
- Second, you must have flirted with Panam at the end of SJ-45 ("Riders on the Storm").
- Third, you must *not* have disclosed Panam's plan to Saul at the beginning of SJ-49 ("With a Little Help from my Friends").
- Fourth, during your conversation with Panam at the junction, you must *not* have implied that you're helping her for the money.

After familiarizing yourself with the Basilisk controls and experiencing neural synchronization with Panam, you have an opportunity to formalize a romantic relationship with her when she asks you if you want to push the synchronization further ("Would you like to try it out?"). If you refuse her offer ("Nice, but I've had enough, thanks."), this will end your relationship. If you accept ("Oh yeah. Let's go."), she will become your romantic partner for the rest of the game (and potentially make an appearance during the epilogue).

ALTERNATIVE GAME ENDING: NOMADS

By completing this storyline, you unlock one of the game's unique finales. When the time is right, we'll let you know how to trigger it.

1

After receiving Panam's call, accept her invitation and head to the Aldecaldos camp. Talk to Panam, then hop aboard the Basilisk and jack in. This panzer's controls should be natural to you: move around with L, adjust the camera with R, and open fire with R2/RT.

2

Simply follow Panam's instructions to familiarize yourself with the process of operating the tank. When the Raffen Shiv attack the camp, you can then put your new skills into practice. Head to the combat area and eliminate all enemies – which shouldn't prove too taxing with the firepower at your disposal. After the battle, speak to Saul and follow Panam. The rest of the mission is story-oriented, requiring no gameplay guidance.

NIGHT CITY
PRIMER
COMPLETION ROADMAP
MAIN JOBS
SIDE JOBS
CYBERPSYCHO SIGHTINGS
GIGS
HUSTLES
ATLAS
INVENTORY
REFERENCE & ANALYSIS
EXTRAS
INDEX

DIRECTORY
SJ-01 - SJ-03
SJ-04 - SJ-06
SJ-07 - SJ-09
SJ-10 - SJ-12
SJ-13 - SJ-15
SJ-16 - SJ-18
SJ-19 - SJ-21
SJ-22 - SJ-24
SJ-25 - SJ-27
SJ-28 - SJ-30
SJ-31 - SJ-33
SJ-34 - SJ-36
SJ-37 - SJ-39
SJ-40 - SJ-42
SJ-43 - SJ-45
SJ-46 - SJ-48
SJ-49 - SJ-51
SJ-52 - SJ-54
SJ-55 - SJ-57
SJ-58 - SJ-61
SJ-62 - SJ-64
SJ-65 - SJ-67

SJ-51

WAR PIGS

Unlock Condition:
Complete MJ-18 ("Transmission") and have a Corporate background.

Notes:
Minor side job.

AREA MAP

1

After receiving a call from Frank, go to the designated location in Kabuki. Move the dumpster and open the briefcase that it reveals. During the conversation that ensues, there's a strong chance that you will not convince Frank to change his mind – in which case he will attack you. (Note that you are free to attack him first if you're itching for a fight.)

It is possible, however, to resolve the situation without drawing a weapon. This can be achieved by selecting specific dialogue lines, chosen in accordance with how you behaved with Frank during the Prologue. Your reward is the same no matter how you proceed here.

Unique Outcomes

Behavior during the Prologue	First dialogue choice	Second dialogue choice	Outcome
You explored all dialogue options with Frank	"You're pathetic"	"Want you to open your eyes"	You convince Frank to start a new life
You did not explore all dialogue options with Frank	"I'm nobody to Abernathy"	"Gotta start over"	You convince Frank to start a new life
You did not explore all dialogue options with Frank	"I'm nobody to Abernathy"	"Not my problem"	Frank makes a drastic decision

SJ-52

THESE BOOTS ARE MADE FOR WALKIN'

Unlock Condition:
Complete MJ-19 ("Ghost Town") and have a Nomad background.

Notes:
Minor side job.

1

This quest is triggered when you receive a message saying that the GPS of your old Nomad car has been activated. Go to the indicated location and scan your old car. Next, open the hood and examine the engine. When the stranger – the car's new owner – arrives, it's up to you to decide if you let her have the car, or reassert ownership.

SJ-53

I'LL FLY AWAY

Unlock Condition:
Complete SJ-45 ("Riders on the Storm").

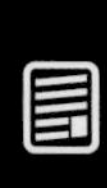

Notes:
Minor side job; this quest is initially not represented by a waypoint. It is triggered when you approach Mitch on the hill just outside the Aldecaldos camp. You must complete it before triggering SJ-50, otherwise it will no longer be available for the rest of your playthrough.

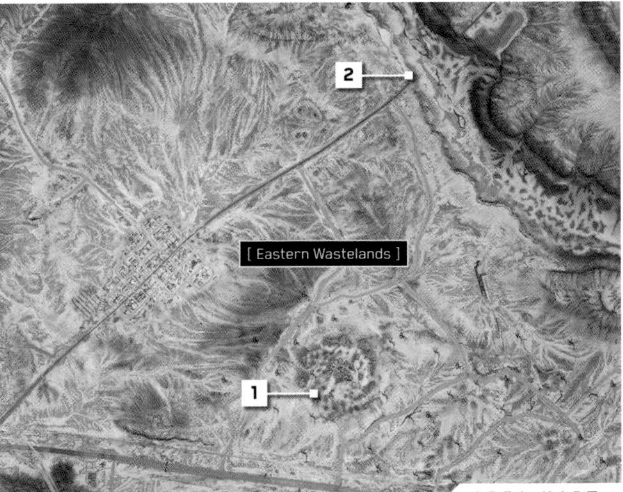

1

Join Mitch on the hill with the burial site, just southwest of the Aldecaldos camp, and agree to help him. Get in his car after the conversation and follow him.

2

Talk to Mitch again at the collapsed bridge, and follow his instructions: pick up the gas canister, put it on the passenger seat, and light the rag on fire.

FORTUNATE SON

Unlock Condition:
Complete SJ-50 ("Queen of the Highway").

Notes:
Minor side job.

1 Visit Bob and Emily's tent at the Aldecaldos camp and agree to help them, before heading to the hospital in Little China.

2 The employee you have to meet is found by a van in a loading area at the hospital. Be aware that NCPD forces will attack the moment you pick up the briefcase, so prepare accordingly. Your enemies will park their vehicles by the gate, which makes for a natural bottleneck. If you rush here and toss a couple of grenades as they arrive, you can wipe out most of them instantly. When the battle is over, confront the man and decide if you want to punish him or let him go. Leaving him alive (or having sufficient Intelligence to meet the relevant attribute requirement) will enable you to find out about a virus installed on the implant. Knowing this will enable you to inform Bob when you return to the Aldecaldos camp, and ultimately to save Scooter's life (who will potentially make an appearance in the game finale if you opt for Panam's path). The quest will end after the surgery is complete – which will happen after eight hours, at which point you will receive a message from Bob inviting you to visit him at the Aldecaldos camp.

EZEKIEL SAW THE WHEEL

Unlock Condition:
Complete MJ-11 ("Playing for Time").

Notes:
Minor side job.

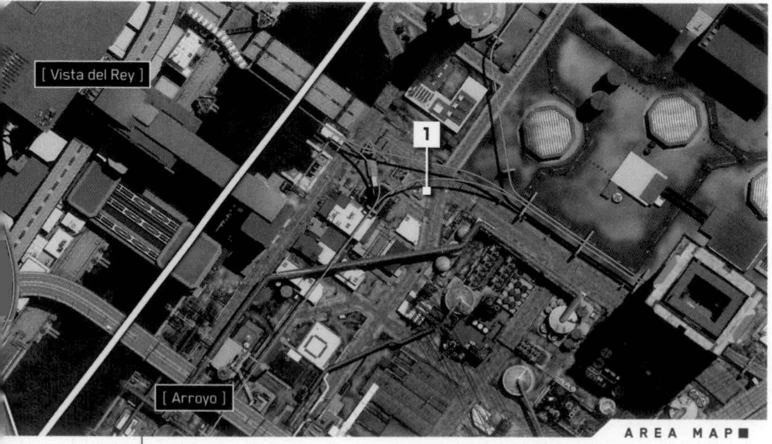

1 This quest takes place inside a small diner in Arroyo. As soon as you sit on the stool and place your order, thugs will barge in and attempt to rob the customers. Though an instinctive reaction will be to draw a weapon and confront the goons, note that the owner will be extremely displeased with the violence that follows.

There are three potential peaceful resolutions: pay the thugs to make them leave, intimidate them if you meet the corresponding Body attribute requirement, or scare them because they're on 6th Street territory (available only if you have a Street Kid background). Any one of these nonviolent outcomes will earn you a free drink and the gratitude of the owner.

KOLD MIRAGE

Unlock Condition:
Complete MJ-19 ("Ghost Town").

Notes:
Minor side job.

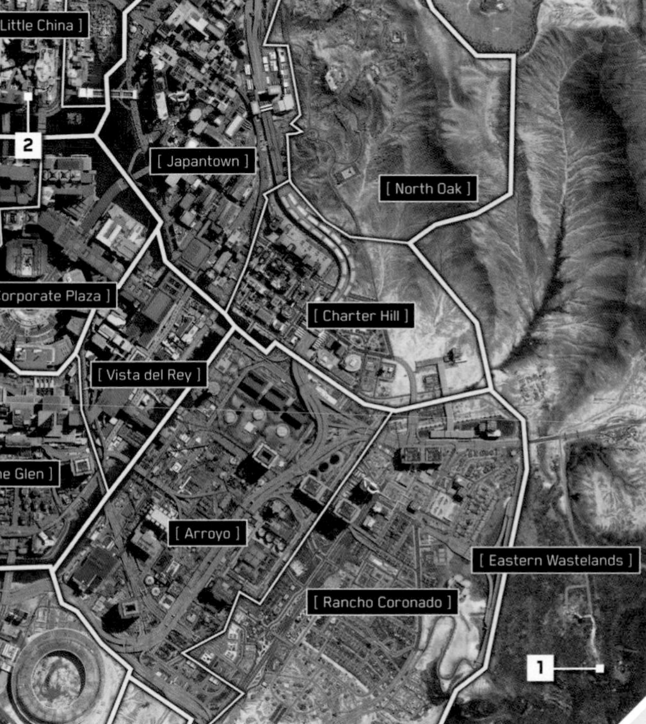

AREA MAP

1

Approach the refrigerator abandoned in the landfill east of the city, then scan the contents of the fridge and pick up the cyberdeck.

2

Next, head to the Afterlife, talk to Nix in the netrunner room behind the bar, then set down the deck on the desk. When Nix is in danger, you can save him in one of two ways:

- By overriding the electric box to the right of the door. This will cause the data on the cyberdeck to be lost, though you will still get the reward from Nix.
- By breaching the computer adjacent to the netrunner chair and successfully completing the hacking mini-game. This preserves the data on the cyberdeck.

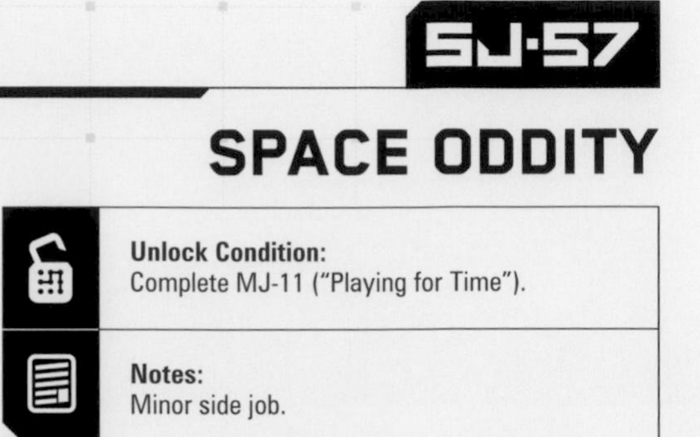

SPACE ODDITY

Unlock Condition:
Complete MJ-11 ("Playing for Time").

Notes:
Minor side job.

1 Talk to the homeless men by the building near the gas station in Rancho Coronado. The suitcase they found is actually a military briefcase, which you can either buy from them, or claim without recompense by intimidating them (if you meet the Body attribute requirement) or by selecting the Street Kid exclusive dialogue option. Once you have it, go around the building and examine the corpse by the dumpster to obtain a shard that provides access to the suitcase; you can alternatively hack it if your Intelligence level is sufficient (which will result in lighter enemy presence in the next step). Either way, you are now free to browse the files on the computer, where you will find messages offering background information and, more importantly, a "launch.exe" program in the Files tab that reveals the coordinates of a drop point.

Your objective is protected by a Militech interception squad: six men deployed in a circle around a seventh. Neutralizing them without causing a commotion is not easy, though approaching from the southeast helps: crouch-walk to reach a position between the parallel pipelines, then cautiously take down each foe one by one, clockwise. Once they're all down, open the drop pod to complete the job.

STADIUM LOVE

Unlock Condition:
Complete MJ-11 ("Playing for Time").

Notes:
Minor side job.

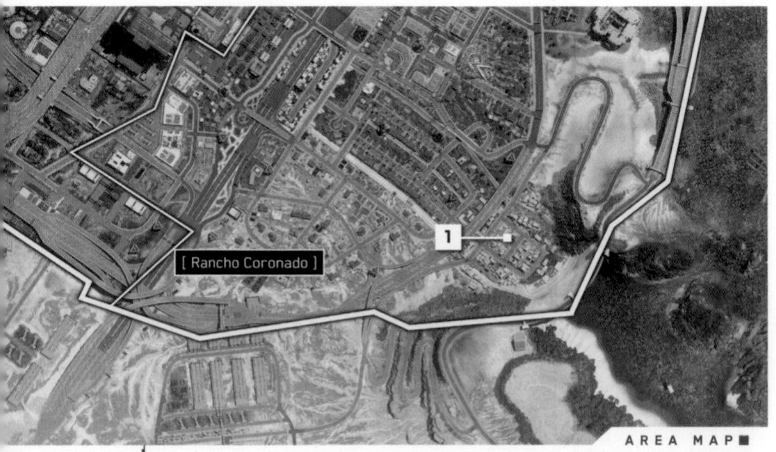

This quest begins when you approach the source of commotion in Rancho Coronado – a 6th Street party on the roof of a building by the elevated highway. Note in advance that it will inevitably end in combat if you have previously triggered combat against 6th Street gang members during the "Life's Work" gig (see page 293). Speak to the leaders by the couch, making sure you avoid any form of obvious or indirect provocation. Say you just want to "have some fun," then that you would like to participate in the shooting competition. Take and equip the gun on the nearby table, then move to the first station.

The challenge requires that you score 44 points by shooting targets at four successive stations, while imbibing drinks that increasingly complicate the aiming process. To improve your chances of success, manually reload ahead of each session, and collect the ammunition placed next to each glass. Be aware, though, that this is a very difficult feat to achieve, requiring lightning-fast shooting skills. If you succeed, you will obtain an iconic weapon as a reward; if not, you can also obtain the item by looting it from its owner if you're prepared to cause a bloodbath.

SJ-59

KILLING IN THE NAME

Unlock Condition:
Complete SJ-39 ("A Like Supreme").

Notes:
Minor side job; you will need to have invested at least a few points in your Intelligence attribute to be able to progress in this mission.

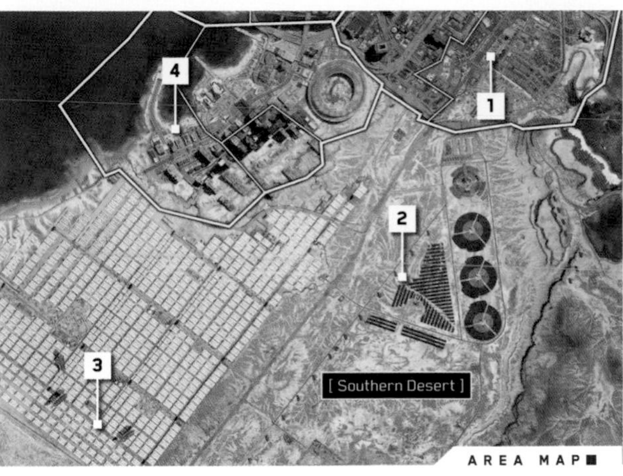

To trigger this quest, you will need to receive specific messages from a mysterious man called Swedenborg-Riviera. The final message you receive will contain a link to a website, formally unlocking the mission. Using any computer, for example, the one in your apartment, check out the domain in question ("timetowakeup.web"). You can then call the journalist investigating Swedenborg, Bes Isis, a.k.a. Nancy, who you met during the "Second Conflict" side job (see page 220). If you haven't completed that quest yet, you need to do so first.

After obtaining the coordinates of the last signal from Nancy, head to the designated location in Rancho Coronado and scan the area for clues, particularly the fuse box on the right. You can also follow the sound emitted by the device you're looking for. Head up the metal staircase to discover a pirate router on the penultimate floor. Hack it to reveal a new signal source in the Badlands.

1

2

Just as before, scan this new area to reveal power cables despite the sandstorm. A few Wraiths guard the perimeter (as part of an NCPD Scanner Hustle – see page 341), but you can use the reduced visibility to sneak past them unnoticed. The power cables lead to the roof of a nearby trailer, where another router awaits. Examine it to reveal a third signal source.

3

When you make it to the designated site in the Biotechnica farm, look up and scan the broken railing. Use the ladders to climb all the way to the top of the structure, where you will find yet another router.

4

The next step in a job that increasingly seems to be a wild goose chase takes you to Pacifica's amusement park. Head to the fortuneteller bot in the designated area to have a conversation with Johnny, during which you can optionally have your fortune told by the machine. When instructed to do so, examine the router mounted on the fortuneteller bot. After talking to Johnny, you need to decide what to do with Swedenborg. You have up to three options:

- You can leave it as it is so that it continues to spam the net with the same anticapitalist aphorisms – to Johnny's great pleasure.
- You can disconnect it from the net using the router.
- Finally, you have a third option if you have the required Intelligence level: modifying it so that it generates even more nonsense.

Your decision made, call Nancy to complete the quest. You have a choice between telling her the truth about Swedenborg, or pretending that you have no new information. If you opt for the former, Nancy will send you more messages later on in the story. Additionally, the website you checked at the beginning of the quest will be updated, with people reacting differently depending on what you decided to do with Swedenborg.

THE HIGHWAYMAN

Unlock Condition:
Complete MJ-07 ("The Ride").

Notes:
Minor side job.

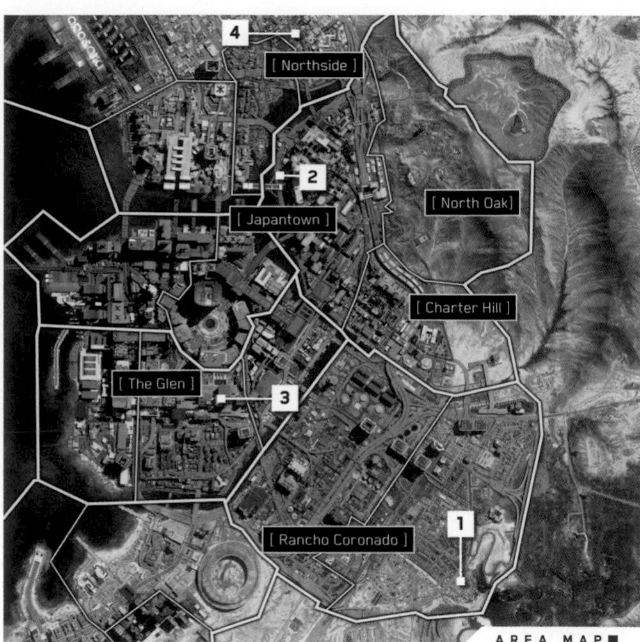

AREA MAP

1

Head to Josie's garage, at the foot of the dam in Rancho Coronado, and open the door. Inside, you can scan and search the wrecked motorcycle. The clue you're looking for, however, is on the desk. Read the message on the laptop and take a look at the picture of Josie and her lover, James.

2

Make your way to Japantown and speak to James – he's the Tyger Claw on a bench, a short distance to the north of the bridge leading to south Kabuki. Make a note of the date daubed on the bench in question, as it's a pertinent detail.

3

Your next stop is the metro station just south of Memorial Park, right by the Glen North fast travel position. Activate your scanner to reveal spots of human blood on the ground. Follow them to the nearby alleyway and you will find Josie's body behind a dumpster, along with an unsent message to James.

4

Finally, make your way to Northside to visit Josie's secret garage – right across the road from the All Foods warehouse where you retrieved the Flathead during the Prologue. The door is locked, but you should already have the code if you paid attention to the date on the bench where James was seated: 0214. Type it and you will finally discover the stolen bike, which you can claim if you are so inclined. Return to James, still on the same bench in Japantown, to bring this story to a close.

SJ-61

SWEET DREAMS

Unlock Condition:
Start SJ-18 ("I Fought the Law") and advance the investigation until you leave the Japantown market (or choose to skip that section altogether).

Notes:
Minor side job; you will need to make a significant cash payment to Stephan at the beginning of this quest.

AREA MAP

1

This job is triggered when you pass by Stefan, a man who sells braindance recordings just outside the Japantown market. Agree to pay for his virtu and editor, then follow him into the nearby room.

2

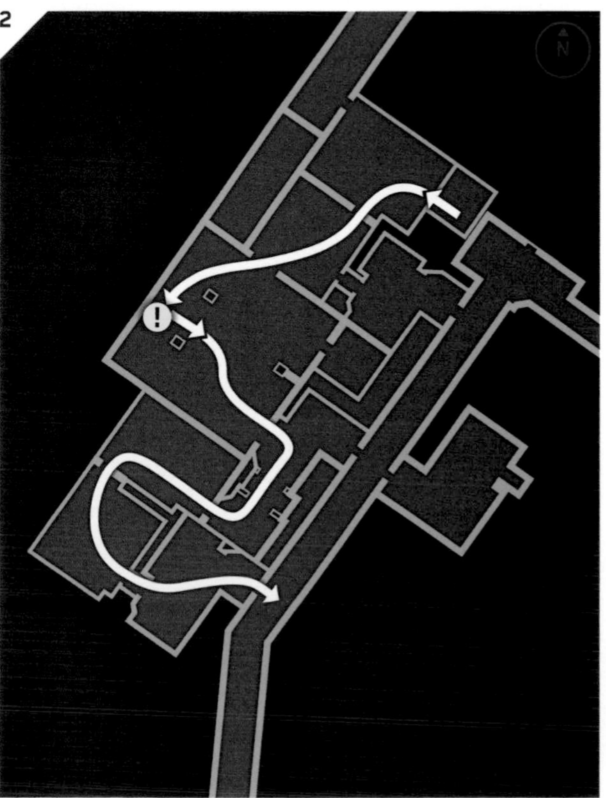

After using Stefan's BD player, you wake up in a familiar scavenger hideout – in the very bath tub where you found Sandra Dorsett during the Prologue. The layout should be very familiar to you. As you come out of the first room, neutralize the scavenger repairing the wall and hide his body near the bath tub – don't forget to collect his weapon. Now head to the main room, where you can find your equipment in a locker on the right-hand side (west wall). The room is heavily guarded, though, so you will need to proceed cautiously if you wish to remain undetected.

- Tag as many enemies as you can see, then start by neutralizing the goon who is patrolling nearby and stops by the closest pillar.
- Next, feel free to sneak to the locker with your equipment, on your right. The pillar should conceal you from the sentries having a conversation. Once you have your full arsenal back, dealing with the remaining scavengers should be a formality.
- Finally, take the elevator back to street level and return to where you met Stefan to confront him. You can choose to let him go, banish him from Night City, or execute him. The final reward you receive is identical in all outcomes.

EVERY BREATH YOU TAKE

Unlock Condition:
Complete SJ-42 ("Off the Leash"), and make sure Kerry and the Us Cracks come to an agreement at the end of SJ-41 ("I Don't Wanna hear it").

Notes:
Minor side job.

AREA MAP

1

2

Warning: if you would prefer to solve the puzzle central to this job for yourself, stop reading now!

After you receive a call from Blue Moon, go to the meeting spot at Kabuki Roundabout and sit on the designated bench. Your goal is to identify the stalker who is threatening to kill Blue Moon. There will be a number of false alarms as events unfold, but the solution is right in front of you from the very beginning, literally a few steps away from the bench: the stalker is not a he but a she – it's the girl with a ponytail who asks Blue Moon if she can take a picture with her. Consider tagging her immediately: this will make the process of monitoring her movements much easier.

The key to the tailing sequence is to remain calm, and stay at a safe distance. Should you reveal yourself to the stalker, she will run away, requiring you to sprint after her. We suggest that you patiently follow the stalker from the moment you get up from the bench. Stay right behind her until you reach the footbridge, where you can quietly grab her from behind before she shoots. Blue Moon will leave it up to you to decide what to do with the stalker. You can kill her yourself, if extrajudicial executions are your style, or tell Blue Moon that the NCPD should take care of her.

Note that you can fail this quest if you perform certain actions:

- If you do anything to perturb Blue Moon, she will call it a day – and be killed by the stalker. Red Menace will then be furious and confront you.
- Walking away from the quest area will also result in failure.
- Finally, you can trigger a unique scenario by neutralizing the wrong person and calling Blue Moon to tell her that you dealt with the stalker. In this case, the job will be considered as complete; however you will receive a text message a few days later informing you that Blue Moon was murdered.

MACHINE GUN

Unlock Condition:
Complete MJ-11 ("Playing for Time").

Notes:
Minor side job.

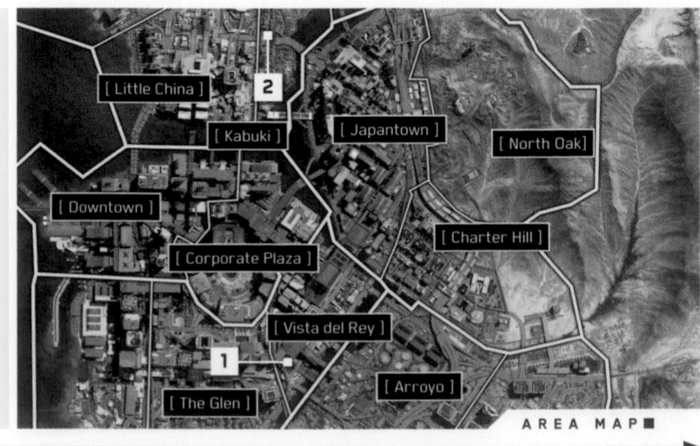

AREA MAP

1

This quest is triggered when you pick up a gun next to a body in an alleyway marked by a waypoint in Vista Del Rey. This Smart gun has an autonomous AI named Skippy that asks you to choose between two firing modes, both with a homing feature: Stone Cold Killer, which targets all bullets at the head, or Puppy-Loving Pacifist, which aims at the legs instead. This seems like the end of the quest but there's actually more to it – and your choice of firing mode will influence the final outcome. After you neutralize 50 enemies, Skippy will initiate another conversation, and automatically switch to the firing mode you had not selected (except in one scenario: if you initially chose the Puppy-Loving Pacifist mode and tell Skippy that "killing is wrong," you will then stay in this mode).

2

After two in-game days, Skippy will call out to you again, this time telling you that it has discovered the name of its previous owner: Regina Jones. If you want to complete the quest, you will need to return the gun to her at the apartment marked by a waypoint in Kabuki. You can keep Skippy for yourself, but the quest will remain uncompleted until you visit Regina, who offers a payment for its return. When you're ready to take it home, use the intercom, then take the elevator to floor 2. Note that Skippy will keep its personality if the Stone Cold Killer mode is active when you meet Regina – in other words, if you initially chose the Puppy-Loving Pacifist mode and did *not* tell Skippy that "killing is wrong." Otherwise, it will be reset to factory settings.

SJ-64

BULLETS

Unlock Condition:
Complete MJ-11 ("Playing for Time").

Notes:
Minor side job.

AREA MAP

1

To start this quest, you first need to talk to Zane inside the Jinguji shop Downtown. What you actually say to him is irrelevant. You can then leave, walk a couple of blocks away, let one in-game day pass (or skip time accordingly), and return once the side job marker has appeared on your map.

After you have a second conversation with Zane, the shop will be attacked by a powerful cyberpsycho. The room's close confines leave you with little space to maneuver, but there are enough cover positions to allow for standard firefight tactics. Focus on thermal damage if you can. You could also cast the Overheat quickhack, or even more powerful programs such as System Reset if you own them. Once the man's health meter falls significantly, MaxTac reinforcements will come in and lend you a hand.

When the battle ends, you will be required to sit on the couch next to Zane to give your statement. The job ends after the conversation, but if you move a few blocks away, wait for two in-game days and come back, you will find that the Jinguji shop has reopened, and Zane will offer you a discount on his clothes.

RAYMOND CHANDLER EVENING

Unlock Condition:
Complete MJ-11 ("Playing for Time").

Notes:
Minor side job.

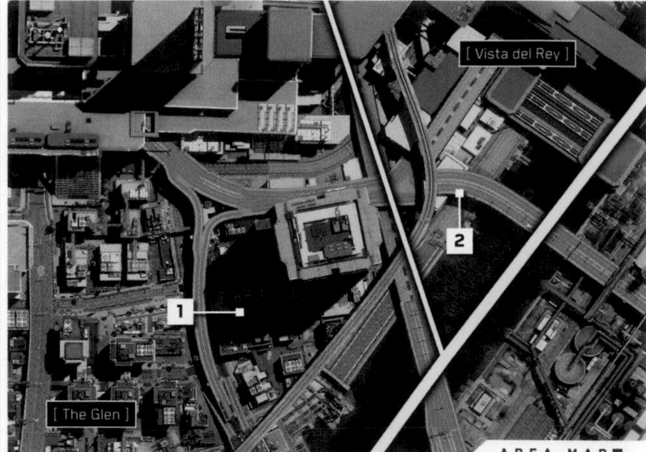

AREA MAP

1

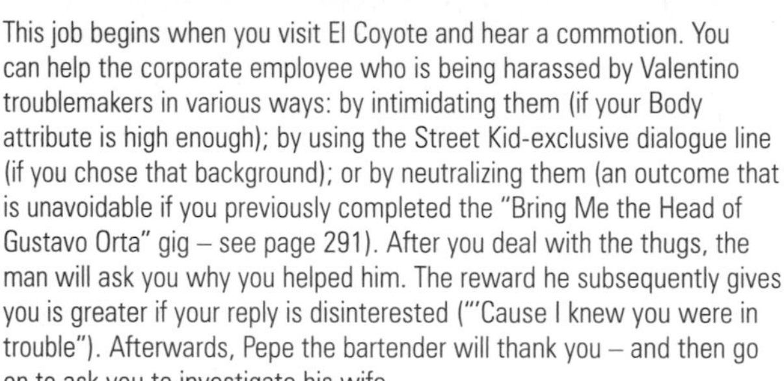

2

This job begins when you visit El Coyote and hear a commotion. You can help the corporate employee who is being harassed by Valentino troublemakers in various ways: by intimidating them (if your Body attribute is high enough); by using the Street Kid-exclusive dialogue line (if you chose that background); or by neutralizing them (an outcome that is unavoidable if you previously completed the "Bring Me the Head of Gustavo Orta" gig – see page 291). After you deal with the thugs, the man will ask you why you helped him. The reward he subsequently gives you is greater if your reply is disinterested ("'Cause I knew you were in trouble"). Afterwards, Pepe the bartender will thank you – and then go on to ask you to investigate his wife.

Important note: Your actions during this opening sequence can cause the quest to end prematurely and be locked off for this playthrough. This will happen if you take too long (over three in-game hours) to deal with the Valentinos, if you leave the bar without helping the corpo, or if you refuse to help Pepe.

Head to the workplace of Pepe's wife between 8 AM and 6 PM, on the road that runs alongside the river in Vista del Rey. You can sit to skip time if required. Standing on the opposite sidewalk, scan Cynthia – she's easy to recognize due to her pink jacket. Follow her as she starts walking, maintaining a sensible distance to remain unnoticed (coming within five meters of her will cause the mission to fail). When she enters a building a little further down the road, follow her inside, then head into the apartment on the upper floor and talk to her.

There are different possible outcomes to the quest depending on your choices here. In short, Pepe and his wife will remain together (and you will get an extra reward from Cynthia during a follow-up call) if you let Cynthia explain her story to you (*"Go on – let's hear it"*), and then if you explain to Pepe that Cynthia was seeing a ripperdoc (*"She was at a ripper's, getting a scan"*), and state that she truly loves him (*"She loves you, you gonk"*). In any other scenario – should you leave prematurely, or if you don't tell Pepe the full truth – their relationship will end.

ONLY PAIN

Unlock Condition:
Complete MJ-11 ("Playing for Time").

Notes:
Minor side job.

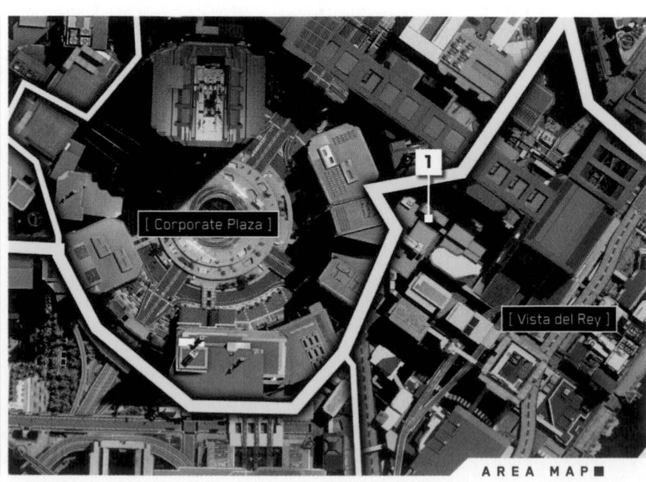

AREA MAP

1

This quest takes place in an alleyway directly east of Memorial Plaza, where NCPD officers have beaten up a corporate employee by the name of Nigel Hamilton. If you approach them, they will order you to "move along." You have three options here:

- If you choose not to get involved and leave, the quest will end prematurely, and remain unavailable in your current playthrough.
- If you approach the officers and start questioning them, the situation will soon escalate – leading to a brutal close-quarters fight. You only face three enemies, but you have little room to maneuver. Use powerful weapons and try to take them down quickly one after the other. Note that you can choose to strike first and dispatch one of them preemptively to initiate the fight. Tossing a couple of grenades can also work wonders.
- A peaceful resolution is only possible if you have a Street Kid background. Should you qualify, select the two dialogue lines exclusive to your origin story and you can convince the officers to leave without further incident.

Once the NCPD officers are no longer an issue, wake up Nigel. If you can meet a Cool attribute requirement, you can ask for a payment; you then have the option to extort double the amount if your Body attribute is sufficient.

SJ-67

SMALL MAN, BIG MOUTH

Unlock Condition:
Complete SJ-10 ("Heroes") and have a Street Kid background.

Notes:
Minor side job.

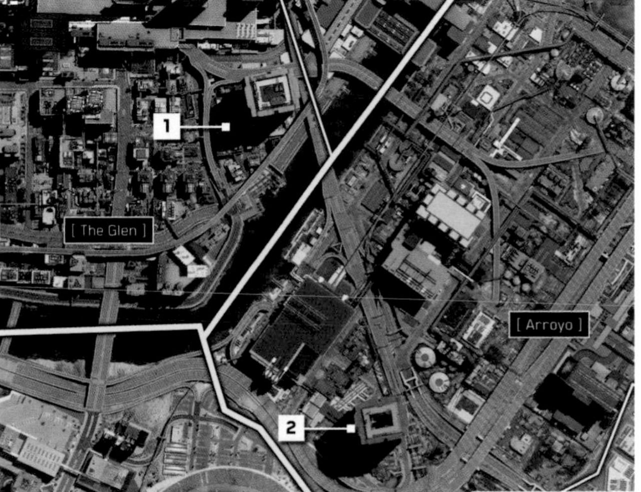

1

After receiving a call from Kirk and agreeing to meet him, pay him a visit at El Coyote Cojo and accept his offer.

2

Next, meet Kirk at the foot of Megabuilding H4 in Arroyo. Your goal is to retrieve goods from a van in a nearby garage, with multiple Valentinos standing guard, both inside and outside. You can enter the premises either from the parking lot, using the crates to cover your approach, or by hopping over the fence to the south and going around the building clockwise. Move to the right of the entrance and you will be in a position to quietly eliminate the lone enemy to the right of the van. From here, take down the other two guards as you please – distractions or other quickhacks can really help here. Once all enemies are down, collect the goods from the rear of the van and confront the Valentinos who attacked Kirk. You can avoid a fight by allowing them to humiliate you – otherwise a (brutal) battle will ensue. Tossing a grenade to open hostilities while your foes are close to each other can be a great start. Swiftly take cover, focus your fire on one target at a time, and don't hesitate to retreat a little if you feel overwhelmed.

CYBERPSYCHO SIGHTINGS

There are 17 cyberpsychos that you can encounter in Night City. Whenever you move close to their approximate locations, expect to receive a brief from Regina Jones – a fixer and ex-reporter who is concerned about the so-called "epidemic" of cyberpsychosis incidents in the metropolis.

Your goal in this quest line is to neutralize all 17 targets by whatever methods you deem necessary or appropriate, including nonlethal takedowns. You should note, however, that these are no standard enemies: they are more akin to mini-bosses, and you can expect them to pack a punch. They all have weaknesses that you can exploit, though, which we reveal in the walkthroughs that follow.

Taking down the cyberpsycho at each site is not your only objective, as there is always at least one shard or email on a computer that you can find in the area which will shed light on events that took place prior to your involvement. Once you acquire and read all information pertinent to each individual case, you will need to send the data to Regina via your message application. Only then will the job be considered as complete.

There are a few general points of interest that apply to all cyberpsycho encounters:

- Quickhacks that cause the target to lose track of your precise whereabouts can be very helpful if you favor stealth tactics. Quickhacks such as Reboot Optics and Memory Wipe prove particularly effective. After you cast them, seek cover behind a solid obstacle and wait for the right opportunity to sneak up on your opponent. System Reset is also incredibly potent: it takes a while to upload but, once activated, instantly disables the target in a non-lethal way.
- Most cyberpsychos do not carry grenades, so the Detonate Grenade quickhack is rarely of use – but this also means that a solid cover position will always continue to be just that unless your foe moves in to flush you out personally.
- Melee combat can lead to short and brutal encounters against cyberpsychos. If you're suitably equipped, proficient at dodging and blocking, and astute at exploiting openings, this combat style might enable you to defeat some targets within seconds. Equally, though, you can expect to be overwhelmed and fall just as rapidly. Melee specialists are therefore advised to have a backup plan should a toe-to-toe fight appear unwinnable.
- Last but not least, many firearms can prove remarkably efficient in these encounters. The homing projectiles of Smart weapons work wonders against enemies who make frequent use of cover positions. The ricochet feature of Power weapons can be invaluable in confined areas. As for Tech weapons, they can pierce through solid surfaces and, potentially, kill targets with a single shot when fully charged.

This chapter covers all cyberpsycho investigations sorted in ascending order of difficulty. While you should feel free to complete them gradually as you progress in the adventure, it's worth noting that they can be rather less challenging once you have high-end equipment and Perks at your disposal later in the story.

OVERVIEW MAP

This map reveals the whereabouts of all 17 cyberpsychos. You will find short walkthroughs for each of these over the following pages, with numbered icons enabling you to instantly match each map location with the corresponding entry.

WATSON

LITTLE CHINA

 961

Unlock Condition: Complete MJ-05 ("The Rescue").

Approach & Clue: You will find this cyberpsycho in the waterside storage facility accessible from the promenade that runs alongside the river. He carries a shard, with a second available on the body of a victim inside the open garage. The latter shard is encrypted, so you will need to crack it from the main menu and solve a hacking minigame to make sense of its contents.

Combat: Alec Johnson's combat behavior depends on how close you are to him. He uses a heavy machine gun at long range, and switches to Gorilla Arms if you move close. After he loses 50% of his health meter, he will focus exclusively on melee combat. One important consideration is that the arena you fight in is filled with cover positions. You can use this to your advantage by popping in and out of cover to take potshots at your opponent while he wields his HMG.

Once he switches to melee, however, he becomes much more dangerous if you stick to firearms, as it is difficult to kite your foe in this area. Have a powerful quickhack or a shotgun at the ready, even if these are not your specific areas of expertise. Cyberware that gives you access to the Sandevistan time-dilation feature can make a world of difference here, making it far easier to evade his close-range assaults.

Even if your specialty is melee combat, we suggest that you refrain from moving in to engage this opponent while he stands on the elevated platform. His machine-gun fire will likely cause heavy damage during the approach, and he'll doubtlessly greet you with a powerful punch before you can start a swing of your own. It's better to bide your time.

Noteworthy Quickhacks

NAME	NOTES
Overheat, Suicide	Causes damage
Weapon Malfunction	Useful when Johnson uses his heavy machine gun
Cyberware Malfunction	Useful when Johnson uses his Gorilla Arms
System Reset	Instantly neutralizes the target

DEMONS OF WAR

 962

Unlock Condition: Complete MJ-05 ("The Rescue").

Approach & Clue: This job takes place on an unfinished section of elevated highway that was intended to connect Kabuki to Japantown. Important information that sheds light on this story can be found on the body of a victim near the end of the road, and in three messages found on the laptop inside the blue shipping container.

Combat: Matt Liaw is equipped with long-range firearms – including a sniper rifle. Walking alongside the parapet on the left (east) side of the road, you can carefully move to within point-blank range if you would prefer to avoid a sniper duel. Make sure you tag Liaw on first sighting, and hide until he loses track of you if you are detected. You can then sneak up on him for a stealth takedown or align a clean headshot with your most powerful weapon at close range. The Weapon Malfunction quickhack can be valuable here, as it will cause Liaw to drop his current weapon. If you initiate a duel at close range, be wary of Liaw's sub-machine gun: this can cause massive damage if he catches you off-guard.

Noteworthy Quickhacks

NAME	NOTES
Overheat, Suicide	Causes damage
Weapon Malfunction	Makes Liaw drop his sniper rifle, greatly reducing his firepower
System Reset	Instantly neutralizes the target

HELP IS ON THE WAY

 963

Unlock Condition: Complete MJ-05 ("The Rescue").

Approach & Clue: Head to the residential building by the river on Allen Street to find multiple Militech vehicles locking down the area. You will find a shard on the body at the top of the stairs leading to the atrium of the designated building, where Mower awaits, then a second one on the target after you defeat her.

Combat: There are no cover positions in the atrium, and Mower utilizes stealth camo and fast movement implants, so consider camping at the edge of the corridor from which you arrive. Make sure you tag her, then retreat if you get detected; wait there until her concentration wavers. You can then return to the atrium and take her by surprise – by sneaking up on her, by aligning a clean headshot with your best weapon, or by casting quickhacks. If she should gain the upper hand any point, sprint back to the corridor to catch your breath.

Note that Mower's stealth camouflage can be disabled with EMP grenades; it will also break after she sustains heavy damage. If you can, equip gear providing resistance to electrical damage, as this will reduce the risk of electrocution via the surface water when her systems malfunction.

Noteworthy Quickhacks

NAME	NOTES
Overheat	Causes damage
Cyberware Malfunction	Disrupts Mower's stealth camouflage and ability to warp around
System Reset	Instantly neutralizes the target

BLOODY RITUAL

 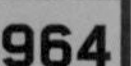

Unlock Condition: Complete MJ-11 ("Playing For Time") and visit the area at night (after 8 PM).

Approach & Clue: You will find this disturbing ritual scene in Northside, deep in Maelstrom territory. Search the corpse of the gang member who dies in front of you to find a first (encrypted) shard. Crack it from the main menu (which will require you to solve a hacking minigame), then examine the other clues in the area with your scanner until Zaria Hughes makes her presence known.

Combat: Zaria Hughes is a very dangerous foe who uses both Mantis Blades and firearms to attack you. She also has the ability to briefly disrupt your optics, seemingly vanishing at will and then appearing out of nowhere. Sniping tactics are not viable here, as Hughes will disappear if you leave the arena, so you will instead need to circle your enemy and attack until she falls.

Two tricks can help you to win this battle. First, try to equip gear granting resistance to thermal damage. Second, try to impede your opponent's movement and kite her so that she draws her pistol: she is far less dangerous with this firearm than when she uses her Mantis Blades.

Noteworthy Quickhacks

NAME	NOTES
Overheat, Short Circuit	Causes damage
Cyberware Malfunction	Disrupts Zaria's Mantis Blades and ability to warp around
Cripple Movement	Useful to slow down your opponent
System Reset	Instantly neutralizes the target

WHERE THE BODIES HIT THE FLOOR

965

Unlock Condition: Complete MJ-05 ("The Rescue").

Approach & Clue: This job takes place in a side alley near the Totentanz club, close to the Pershing Street fast travel terminal. You will find Ellis Carter in a dead end, with his back turned, meaning that you can sneak up on him and commence hostilities with a decisive blow. There are three shards in the area: one held by Carter, another in the dead end where you initially encounter him, and a third next to the body of the victim by the dumpster.

Combat: If you are sufficiently powerful, you can sneak up on Ellis Carter when you first arrive (or after escaping his attention following an initial altercation) and take him down with a single attack. A stealth takedown is also a possibility.

Carter is equipped with cyberware that enables him to move rapidly and to dodge bullets, so a frontal assault can be tricky – unless you can neutralize his implants with quickhacks, that is. He will try to home in on you and unleash a flurry of machete blows, so you should endeavour to constantly circle around him while keeping him just out of range. The best choice of weapon here is either a powerful shotgun or a weapon with a high rate of fire and a large magazine: these remain effective despite the target's Kerenzikov-induced evasive movement. This strategy is, of course, much easier if you can slow him down with the Cripple Movement quickhack.

Noteworthy Quickhacks

NAME	NOTES
Overheat	Causes damage
Cyberware Malfunction	Disrupts Carter's ability to warp around and dodge bullets
Cripple Movement	Useful to slow down your opponent to a crawl, making him a sitting duck
System Reset	Instantly neutralizes the target

SIX FEET UNDER

966

Unlock Condition: Complete MJ-05 ("The Rescue").

Approach & Clue: You will reach the location where this assignment takes place by following the train tracks that run alongside the highway. You have a single shard with pertinent information to find here, and it's carried by the cyberpsycho himself.

Combat: Lely Hein lurks at the end of the tracks. Tag him immediately, then play hide and seek until he loses track of you. You can then move close to his position to perform a stealth takedown, align a clean headshot, or apply quickhacks.

Hein tends to make smart use of cover, which could lead to a protracted sniper duel if you engage him on his terms. If you do opt for a ranged engagement, consider using grenades to displace him from cover.

Noteworthy Quickhacks

NAME	NOTES
Overheat, Suicide	Causes damage
Weapon Malfunction	Temporarily reduces Hein's firepower
System Reset	Instantly neutralizes the target

NIGHT CITY
PRIMER
COMPLETION ROADMAP
MAIN JOBS
SIDE JOBS
CYBERPSYCHO SIGHTINGS
GIGS
HUSTLES
ATLAS
INVENTORY
REFERENCE & ANALYSIS
EXTRAS
INDEX
OVERVIEW MAP
WATSON
PACIFICA
BADLANDS
SANTO DOMINGO
CITY CENTER
HEYWOOD

PACIFICA

A DANCE WITH DEATH

 967

Unlock Condition: Complete MJ-05 ("The Rescue").

Approach & Clue: Diego Ramirez is found at the very end of the long pier, but you are advised to inspect the van parked directly underneath it before you engage him – what you find there changes the complexion of this story. You can find a shard on Ramirez himself once he falls, and another on the body of the leader of the group that attacked him.

Combat: Diego Ramirez wields a shotgun and can warp around the pier at lightning speed, making him a dangerous foe – and so taking steps to make a decisive opening to this battle is strongly recommended. The System Reset quickhack can obviously provide you with an instant victory, but a headshot with a powerful weapon works just as well. You can also opt for a stealth takedown. Should things go awry, consider applying the Weapon Malfunction quickhack to reduce Ramirez's firepower, then be swift to finish him off.

If you find yourself in a firefight, keep a solid cover position close to you at all times, as Ramirez's shotgun can inflict major pain.

Noteworthy Quickhacks

NAME	NOTES
Overheat, Suicide	Causes major damage
Cripple Movement	Useful to slow Ramirez down
Cyberware Malfunction	Disrupts Ramirez's ability to warp around
Weapon Malfunction	Ideal to reduce Ramirez's firepower
System Reset	Instantly neutralizes the target

LEX TALIONIS

 968

Unlock Condition: Complete MJ-18 ("Transmission").

Approach & Clue: To trigger this side job you will need to open the garage door a few steps to the north of the Grand Imperial Mall. This gives you access to a high-security netrunner den, so make sure you come prepared. After taking down the target, read the messages on the computer at the back of the den.

Combat: The challenge in this encounter is that you do not face a lone foe. SpaceBoy can count on the support of multiple surveillance cameras, drones, and droids. Unless you are supremely strong, it makes sense to destroy or quickhack them one by one, advancing slowly but surely. If you have developed your netrunner skills, this is definitely a good time to put them to use. Casting Cyberpsychosis on the androids, for instance, can make a significant difference. If you prefer to go in with all guns blazing, EMP grenades and weapons that deal electrical damage are highly effective. Once the security measures have been dealt with, you can finally take care of SpaceBoy himself.

Noteworthy Quickhacks

NAME	NOTES
Cyberpsychosis	Ideal against the drones and droids
Short Circuit, Overheat, Suicide	Causes damage
Weapon Malfunction	Enables you to attack without fear of reply for a few seconds
System Reset	Instantly neutralizes the target

BADLANDS

THE WASTELAND

Unlock Condition: Complete MJ-05 ("The Rescue").

Approach & Clue: Move to the designated location and you will find a shard on the body by the crashed vehicle, along with a cyberware case to scan in the adjacent shipping container. If you activate your scanner, you can then follow a blood trail to the northeast. Euralio Alma is found in the camp by the elevated railway, and carries a second shard that you can collect once he falls.

Combat: Euralio Alma is equipped with an exoskeleton similar to the one used by Royce (see page 124). Just like him, Alma has a weak point in the form of a battery on his back. Your priority is therefore to destroy this by shooting it, by targeting it with the Short Circuit quickhack, or by successfully performing a stealth takedown (possible if you approach from the north). Once this has been taken care of, you can deal damage normally, darting in and out of cover as required. Other tools that you might employ to further simplify the battle include frag grenades, the Weapon Malfunction quickhack, Tech weapons, and electrical damage.

Noteworthy Quickhacks

NAME	NOTES
Short Circuit	Causes major damage and instantly destroys the exoskeleton's battery
Weapon Malfunction	Briefly staggers your opponent, enabling you to unleash a powerful assault
System Reset	Instantly neutralizes the target

SECOND CHANCES

Unlock Condition: Complete MJ-05 ("The Rescue").

Approach & Clue: After examining the body at the marked position, scan the nearby tracks. These will point you toward another Raffen Shiv car to the east. There's a body with a shard (and a sniper rifle) just a few steps to the southwest, but you will immediately find yourself under enemy fire. The cyberpsycho, Zion Wylde, is posted on an elevated platform directly to the south. He also carries a shard.

Combat: If you're an adept marksman, consider taking cover behind one of the nearby rocks and engage in a sniper duel. Alternatively, you can use the rocks to conceal your approach and stay out of Wylde's sight as you close the distance between you. Once he has lost track of you, creep underneath the platform. The most obvious way to reach his position is to climb up the ladder – though this entails disarming the laser mines around the platform, and two more as you reach the top of the ladder, ideally via quickhacks. Note that you can take control of the surveillance camera for remote deactivations. If you have cyberware enabling you to double-jump, you could alternatively attempt a leap from the rock to the east.

Once you get to the platform, try to be decisive: your goal should be to inflict overwhelming damage immediately and end this confrontation here and now. If you do not swiftly disable Wylde, he will try to drop down and escape to find cover in the desert – drawing you once again in a sniper duel, though this time you will occupy the better vantage point.

Noteworthy Quickhacks

NAME	NOTES
Overheat, Suicide	Causes major damage
Weapon Malfunction	Useful to disrupt Wylde's ability to fire, making it easier to move in closer or attack
System Reset	Instantly neutralizes the target

HOUSE ON A HILL

Noteworthy Quickhacks

NAME	NOTES
Overheat, Suicide	Causes damage
Weapon Malfunction	Useful to temporarily interrupt Milton's assaults, giving you a chance to counterattack
System Reset	Instantly neutralizes the target

Unlock Condition: Complete MJ-05 ("The Rescue").

Approach & Clue: The farm where this job takes place is highly secure, with a fence surrounding the property, laser mines near the front entrance, drones patrolling inside the perimeter, and turrets on the rooftop – a scenario worthy of respect and careful planning for most, but a playground for a talented netrunner. Go through the missing fence section on the west side and deal with the mechanical devices first, ideally by casting Cyberpsychosis. Sam Milton, the cyberpsycho, is found inside the garage and will attack you when you move close. You can find a shard in Milton's possession once you have dealt with him one way or another. A second can be collected from the body of Natasha Greene, found close to the car park outside the garage.

Combat: Milton wields a powerful shotgun and moves swiftly, so don't linger in the open unless you have disabled his weapon with a quickhack. If you can disappear from sight, it's possible to approach him from behind to align a perfect headshot or perform a stealth takedown.

In the event of a firefight, stay clear of the car in front of the garage: Milton's shotgun can easily make it explode. Naturally, this hazard works both ways: causing the vehicle or gas tanks in the area to explode when your target is in close proximity can be an efficient way to wrap up the battle quickly.

SANTO DOMINGO

DISCOUNT DOC

 972

Unlock Condition: Complete MJ-05 ("The Rescue").

Approach & Clue: This side job takes place in the yard of a shady ripperdoc clinic in Rancho Coronado. When you arrive, you will find a security guard fighting your target: Chase Coley. Wait a while and the former will be defeated, enabling you to focus on the cyberpsycho. Pick up the shard on his body when he falls and read the emails on the laptop inside to make sense of the chain of events that led to this situation.

Combat: This battle has similarities with your fight against Royce (see page 124). Effective weapons include frag grenades, the Short Circuit quickhack, Tech weapons, and electric damage. If you're looking for a non-lethal outcome, you could also opt for EMP grenades and stealth takedowns.

Noteworthy Quickhacks

NAME	NOTES
Short Circuit	Causes major damage and instantly destroys the exoskeleton's battery
Weapon Malfunction	Briefly staggers your opponent, enabling you to unleash a powerful assault
System Reset	Instantly neutralizes the target

TOO LITTLE, TOO LATE

 973

Unlock Condition: Complete MJ-05 ("The Rescue").

Approach & Clue: This assignment takes place in a homeless camp in the underpass of the elevated highway, to the south of Megabuilding H4. You can find a shard behind a plastic curtain, to the right of the camp's entrance, and a second on a body at the opposite (north) end of the camp. Tamara Cosby will appear near the entrance when you move close to the latter.

Combat: Cosby is a netrunner, so expect her to cast quickhacks such as Overheat on you. The good news is: you can interrupt the uploading process by inflicting sufficient damage to her. She will also instruct two turrets to fire at you, so it might be advisable to disable these beforehand. The time she needs to upload programs leaves her exposed to concerted assaults, including grenades when she takes cover behind solid objects. Precise headshots aligned from a distance are also a great option. However, sprinting to Cosby's position and assailing her with close-quarters combos might be the best strategy of all – Cosby does not excel in terms of mobility, and her quickhacks can do little to mitigate the effects of melee blows.

Noteworthy Quickhacks

NAME	NOTES
Short Circuit, Overheat, Suicide	Causes major damage
Weapon Malfunction	Useful to prevent Cosby from firing at you, giving you a free hand to attack her.
System Reset	Instantly neutralizes the target

CITY CENTER

ON DEAF EARS

974

Unlock Condition: Complete MJ-05 ("The Rescue").

Approach & Clue: Cedric Muller is located on the ground floor of a parking lot that can be accessed via the elevated highway. There are two shards available in the area – one on the body between the two reflectors, and another in the chest container near the wall.

Combat: Muller wields a shotgun, making him particularly dangerous. One way to avoid a difficult confrontation can be to tag him from a safe distance and make a clean headshot with a powerful sniper rifle. If you engage him at close range, try to break line of sight and wait until he loses you, then sneak up on him and unleash a devastating barrage of attacks (including quickhacks) for maximum effect.

One thing to keep in mind is that Muller has the ability to heal once. If he does so after you've inflicted heavy damage, it pretty much resets the battle – which can be very unfortunate. If you're not confident in your ability to take him down in one assault, consider dealing just enough injury to bait him into using his single-use restoration trick: once he has done so, you are clear to go all-out to end the fight.

Noteworthy Quickhacks

NAME	NOTES
Overheat, Suicide	Causes major damage
Weapon Malfunction	Briefly stuns Muller, enabling you to attack without fear of reprisal
System Reset	Instantly neutralizes the target

PHANTOM OF NIGHT CITY

975

Unlock Condition: Complete MJ-05 ("The Rescue").

Approach & Clue: Norio Akuhara can be found in an alleyway with multiple Tyger Claw motorbikes, close to the Night City Center for Behavioral Health building. There are two shards in the area: one in the chest container by the wall, and a second held by Akuhara himself. An important thing to note about this battle is that Akuhara will vanish after you deplete half of his health meter. You can then find him a short distance to the west: follow the alleyway until you end up on a plaza, where you will find Akuhara... and a group of Tyger Claws ready to back him up.

Combat: Tag Akuhara from outside the hostile area, just before you pass the fence gate. This will enable you to keep track of your foe whenever he moves at pace. In the first half of the confrontation Akuhara wields a blade, which you can use to your advantage: fire from a safe distance, backtracking as your foe attempts to close the gap. You should be able to empty multiple clips before he gets a chance to hit you. In the second half of the fight, he switches to a firearm. It's prudent to remain in the alleyway to avoid taking fire from multiple opponents at once. Be methodical at this point, eliminating one target at a time until they are all down.

Note that quickhacks work particularly well against distance. Furthermore, if you manage to escape his attention (if necessary with the help of a quickhack such as Memory Wipe), it's possible to sneak up on him to perform a stealth takedown.

Noteworthy Quickhacks

NAME	NOTES
Overheat, Suicide	Causes major damage
Cripple Movement	Useful when Akuhara wields his katana
Weapon Malfunction	Useful when Akuhara uses a firearm
System Reset	Instantly neutralizes the target

HEYWOOD

JEALOUS HEARTS

976

Unlock Condition: Complete MJ-05 ("The Rescue").

Approach & Clue: Head to the designated promenade in Wellsprings to find Dao Hyunh experiencing a cyberpsychotic episode on the terrace of a seaside restaurant. You can collect two shards here: one from Hyunh, and the other from her sister.

Combat: Dao Hyunh wields a handgun. You enjoy the element of surprise here, so make your first move count: consider aligning a headshot with your best weapon or applying a lethal quickhack from your vantage point on the promenade. It's important to end the battle before it even begins if you can, ideally in a single assault while Hyunh is still on the restaurant's terrace, unaware of your presence. Fail to do so, and she will climb up onto the promenade – where she is much more dangerous, and you will have few cover positions to make use of.

Noteworthy Quickhacks

NAME	NOTES
Short Circuit, Overheat, Detonate Grenade, Suicide	Causes damage
Weapon Malfunction	Gives you a window of opportunity to attack without fear of damage in return
System Reset	Instantly neutralizes the target

LETTER OF THE LAW

977

Unlock Condition: Complete MJ-05 ("The Rescue").

Approach & Clue: Enter the fenced area via the open door, but be prepared to deal with a large number of mines once you step into the premises – you can easily identify them thanks to their telltale red laser beam. The entire location is booby-trapped so advance slowly and cautiously, disarming all explosives if you meet the corresponding attribute requirements. Gaston Philips is found at the rear of the hostile area. Try to get rid of as many explosives as possible before you engage him – ideally all of them – to make the encounter more manageable. You will find this story's shards on Gaston himself, with further information available on the computer.

Combat: Gaston Philips moves fast and hits hard. Taking him down quickly is key here. A powerful quickhack such as Suicide is optimal, though you can also sneak up to him and open hostilities with a stealth attack, powerful blow, or headshot. There are many crates and cover positions available, and you can even leave the perimeter to catch your breath if you feel overwhelmed – with another possibility to perform a stealth takedown when you return.

Noteworthy Quickhacks

NAME	NOTES
Detonate Grenade, Overheat, Suicide	Causes damage, especially if you trigger a chain reaction
Short Circ Cyberware & Cripple Movement	Limits your opponent's ability to warp around the arena
Weapon Malfunction	Gives you a window of opportunity to attack
System Reset	Instantly neutralizes the target

GIGS

This chapter offers a walkthrough for every gig in Cyberpunk 2077, sorted for each sub-district in ascending order of difficulty.

Gigs are assignments that you receive from fixers. They are initially represented by distinct icons ([?]) on your map. When you move close to their positions, the question mark is replaced with an icon that reveals the category of the gig activity in question:

Gig Categories

 SOS: Merc Needed

 Search and Recover

Thievery

 Gun for Hire

Agent Saboteur

 Special Delivery

Whenever you move within range of a gig, you will receive a call and/or a text message from the local fixer that provides details of your task. You can also consult the Journal menu if you want to read a full brief. While you're there, don't forget that you can manually select the gig in question in your Journal: this will activate waypoints for the quest, as well as a route line on your mini-map. When you are unfamiliar with a specific area or the layout of a complex building, this tool will make it much easier to navigate.

There are always computers and shards that you can encounter during gigs. These provide you with additional information on key events and conversations, and shed light on the motives of the various characters involved in each of these side-stories.

As ever in Cyberpunk 2077, you can employ all sorts of methods to achieve your goals, including brute force. You should note, however, that a non-violent, stealthy approach yields practical advantages. Granted, this demands a greater investment of time and patience in some instances, if only in terms of observing enemy patrols – but the benefits can be noteworthy, especially as detection can often lead to reinforcements joining the fray.

With practice and advance knowledge of the layout of each area of operation, it's possible to ghost straight to your objective, darting from cover to cover in accordance with enemy movements, and later retracing your (silent) steps without incident. Remaining undetected will often please the client, leading to congratulations from the fixer and – in cases where you complete an optional mission objective such as not raising the alarm – a bonus reward.

Gigs are unlocked in district-specific Street Cred tiers, from 1 to 4. The first tier in each district is available from the beginning of the adventure. You will then gain access to the other three tiers gradually as you obtain Street Cred, as shown in the accompanying table.

District	Street Cred Level Required			
	Tier 1	Tier 2	Tier 3	Tier 4
Watson	1	4	8	15
Westbrook	1	10	20	35
Pacifica	1	12	32	42
Santo Domingo	1	21	38	50
Badlands	1	5	11	18
Heywood	1	13	22	30
City Center	1	9	18	32

Many gigs will require you to visit a Drop Point as a final step, usually to deposit an item or to collect a bonus payment whenever you complete an optional objective. These are clearly marked on your map ( ), and you will generally find one within a short distance of your current locale.

In all gigs where your goal concerns a person of interest who can either be killed on site or rendered unconscious and delivered back to the client, you need to weigh up the value of either approach.

- As a rule, opting for a non-lethal takedown means that you will need to carry the target back to a vehicle sent by the fixer, which can complicate matters – as you'll often need to neutralize assorted guards and goons to facilitate your departure.

- Conversely, if you kill the target, you will be free to leave by the fastest route available, with nothing slowing your progress or hindering your movements.

Finally, an important point to remember is that many gigs can be completed in different ways. If your objective is to kill an individual, deciding instead to spare them should they agree to leave Night City is a perfectly fine outcome too. Cyberpunk 2077 is, on many levels, a non-linear game, so feel free to be creative and explore various approaches.

GIG DIRECTORY

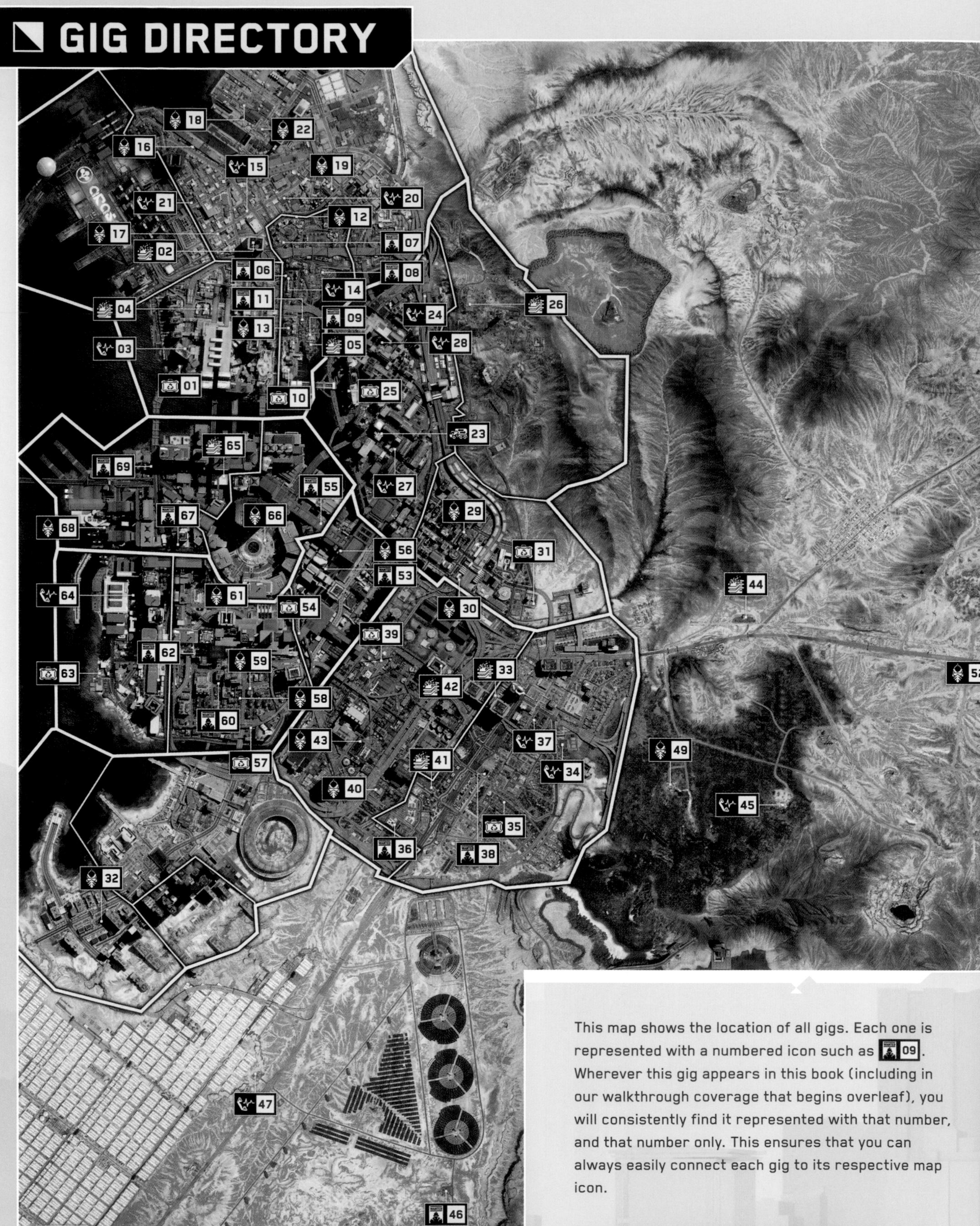

This map shows the location of all gigs. Each one is represented with a numbered icon such as 09. Wherever this gig appears in this book (including in our walkthrough coverage that begins overleaf), you will consistently find it represented with that number, and that number only. This ensures that you can always easily connect each gig to its respective map icon.

This table lists all gigs in alphabetical order for ease of reference. The walkthroughs in this chapter are grouped in accordance with the area of Night City that they take place in.

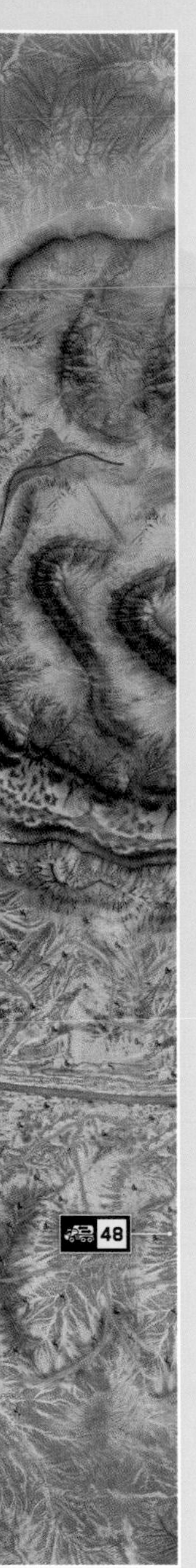

Name	Icon	Area	Page
A Lack of Empathy	65	Downtown	297
A Shrine Defiled	26	Japantown	276
An Inconvenient Killer	67	Downtown	298
Backs Against the Wall	10	Kabuki	267
Big Pete's Got Big Problems	46	Badlands	288
Bloodsport	03	Little China	263
Breaking News	41	Arroyo	285
Bring Me the Head of Gustavo Orta	55	Vista Del Rey	291
Catch a Tyger's Toe	02	Little China	262
Cuckoo's Nest	34	Rancho Coronado	281
Dancing on a Minefield	48	Badlands	288
Dirty Biz	16	Northside	271
Error 404	33	Rancho Coronado	280
Eye for an Eye	60	The Glen	294
Family Heirloom	31	Charter Hill	279
Family Matters	35	Rancho Coronado	282
Fifth Column	58	The Glen	293
Fixer, Merc, Soldier, Spy	13	Kabuki	269
Flight of the Cheetah	15	Northside	271
Flying Drugs	44	Badlands	287
For My Son	36	Rancho Coronado	282
Freedom of the Press	21	Northside	274
Getting Warmer...	28	Japantown	277
Going Up or Down?	61	The Glen	295
Going-away Party	37	Rancho Coronado	283
Goodbye, Night City	51	Badlands	289
Greed Never Pays	25	Japantown	276
Guinea Pigs	69	Downtown	299
Hacking the Hacker	42	Arroyo	285
Hippocratic Oath	14	Northside	270
Hot Merchandise	64	Wellsprings	296
Jeopardy	54	Vista Del Rey	291
Last Login	12	Kabuki	268
Life's Work	57	The Glen	293
Lousy Kleppers	22	Northside	274

Name	Icon	Area	Page
Many Ways to Skin a Cat	17	Northside	272
MIA	50	Badlands	289
Monster Hunt	09	Kabuki	266
No Fixers	45	Badlands	287
Occupational Hazard	20	Northside	273
Old Friends	53	Vista Del Rey	290
Olive Branch	23	Japantown	275
On a Tight Leash	62	Wellsprings	295
Playing for Keeps	01	Little China	262
Psychofan	59	The Glen	294
Race to the Top	40	Arroyo	284
Radar Love	52	Badlands	289
Rite of Passage	18	Northside	272
Scrolls Before Swine	19	Northside	273
Serial Suicide	66	Corporate Plaza	297
Serious Side Effects	39	Arroyo	284
Severance Package	43	Arroyo	286
Shark in the Water	08	Kabuki	265
Small Man, Big Evil	11	Kabuki	267
Sparring Partner	49	Badlands	289
Sr. Ladrillo's Private Collection	56	Vista Del Rey	292
The Frolics of Councilwoman Cole	68	Downtown	299
The Heisenberg Principle	04	Little China	263
The Lord Giveth and Taketh Away	63	Wellsprings	296
The Union Strikes Back	38	Rancho Coronado	283
Trevor's Last Ride	47	Badlands	288
Troublesome Neighbors	06	Kabuki	264
Two Wrongs Makes us Right	32	Coastview	280
Tyger and Vulture	30	Charter Hill	279
Until Death Do Us Part	29	Charter Hill	278
Wakako's Favorite	27	Japantown	277
We Have Your Wife	24	Japantown	275
Welcome to America, Comrade	05	Kabuki	264
Woman of la Mancha	07	Kabuki	265

LITTLE CHINA

PLAYING FOR KEEPS

01

■ **Unlock Condition** – Street Cred Tier 1 ■ **Type** – Search and Recover

1

To begin this gig, head to Kashuu Hanten. Your goal is to steal Jacob's eye implant from the storage room at the back of the joint, which you can reach by going through the alleyway on the side instead. You have a single Tyger Claw to neutralize outside (and a vending machine conveniently positioned to distract him), and one more inside.

2

You end up right in front of the storage room, but the door is locked. You have a few options here:

- You can force-open the door if your Body stat allows for it. The implant is on the shelves to your left as you enter.
- Another possibility is to take the key from the bartender, though this will require you to at least knock him out – leading to a fight.
- There is a third and entirely more cunning way to resolve the situation. When you enter the joint from the alleyway, read the messages on the computer near the storage room to discover that the Tyger Claws run an underground poker room. Retrace your steps to the front entrance and use this piece of information to confront the barman. Be patient, and he will bring you the implant.

Once you have the implant, head to a nearby Drop Point to obtain your reward.

CATCH A TYGER'S TOE

02

■ **Unlock Condition** – Street Cred Tier 1 ■ **Type** – Agent Saboteur

1

Head to Megabuilding H11 and use the elevator marked on your map to reach the underground server room.

2

Coming out of the elevator, the paths to both the left and right lead you to the server room. Disable all surveillance cameras, then take the time to tag the four guards. You will soon notice that they have short patrol routes that leave them exposed for several seconds at a time, so the safest option is clearly to neutralize them sequentially. You can then take the door on the far right side (or the one on the left if you meet a Technical Ability attribute requirement) to access the main computer. When you're ready, upload B@d's malware to either computer, then leave the area via the elevator.

BLOODSPORT

■ **Unlock Condition** – Street Cred Tier 2 ■ **Type** – SOS: Merc Needed

1

Head to the Tyger Claw dojo in the southwest of Little China. The first challenge is to infiltrate the building and reach the basement.

- If your Body level is high enough you will find a convenient shortcut in the nearby alleyway, in the form of a door that can be force-opened.
- You can also climb to the rooftop, where there are two ways to get inside the building. The first is a roof window that can be opened via a Technical Ability attribute requirement, just above the side entrance, leading directly to the basement stairs.
- If you can't meet the Technical Ability requirement on the roof, the alternative is another roof window above the front entrance – but be mindful of the guard patrolling underneath. After neutralizing him (for instance with an aerial takedown when his phone call ends), you are free to access the computer in the adjacent office, enabling you to turn off two surveillance cameras – though you will have more to disable on your way. Now crouch-walk around the dojo counterclockwise, darting from cover to cover to sneak past the fighters training there. Take a right when you reach the workout room (with one more Tyger Claw) and you will find the basement stairs behind the door.

2

The basement features two paths: you can either go through the corridor on your left and face a camera (a non-issue if you deactivated it from the office upstairs, or if you pacify it with a quickhack), or head into the room directly in front of you, with another camera and a Tyger Claw on the way. Roh is being detained in the far room, with a guard watching over him. Neutralize the latter before you rescue the coach. Retrace your steps to the ground floor and leave the building via the door immediately up the stairs: it can be opened from the inside without needing to meet an attribute requirement. Walk Roh back to the front gate and escort him to the fixer's transport.

THE HEISENBERG PRINCIPLE

■ **Unlock Condition** – Street Cred Tier 3 ■ **Type** – Agent Saboteur

1

Your goal in this gig is to find a drug lab in a large basement. The front of the building is initially guarded by three Tyger Claws. The two just inside will split after they're done talking, clearing the way for you. Stay close to the wall and you can crouch-walk past the one that remains at the entrance. You can reach the basement via two routes:

- By dropping down the elevator shaft on the right (which offers a nice shortcut, but requires a sufficient Body attribute level). Neutralize the nearby guard before you proceed.
- Using the door in the far left corner, which leads to stairs. Consider disabling the surveillance camera to be safe.

2

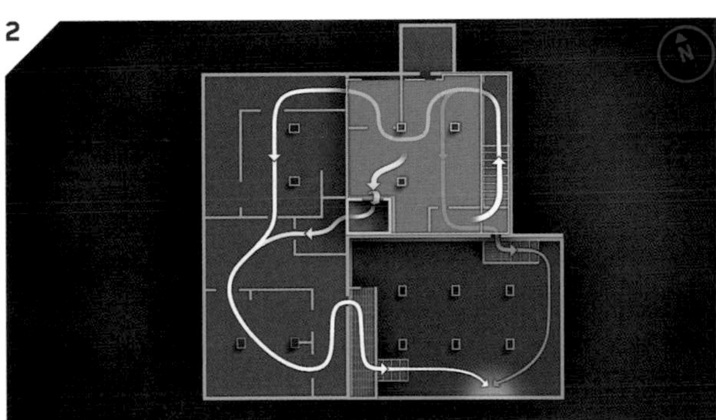

Once you make it to the basement, multiple paths are available, in accordance with your starting point. All of them feature surveillance cameras, which you would do well to quickhack preemptively if you want to avoid detection.

- If you arrive via the elevator shaft, you can crouch-walk to the lab by going through the basement counterclockwise, with a single foe on the way.
- If you took the stairs, there are two options here. If your Technical Ability level is high enough, you can open the door on your left – a massive shortcut leading straight to the lab.
- Otherwise, you will need to navigate the entire basement section counterclockwise, neutralizing or sneaking past a few enemies on the way. Advance slowly and wait for enemies to turn away from you before you make your move.

Once you make it to the lab, take the time to tag the three Tyger Claws guarding it, then neutralize them quietly in sequence. With the path clear, destroy the drugs however you please (shooting will suffice, though installing malware on the nearby laptop is more silent), then retrace your steps back to street level.

KABUKI

WELCOME TO AMERICA, COMRADE

05

■ **Unlock Condition** – Street Cred Tier 1 ■ **Type** – Agent Saboteur

1

Head to the docks on the east side of Kabuki. Your objective is to plant a GPS transmitter on a car stored inside a shipping container. The area features multiple guards, but there are two routes that should enable you to sneak to your objective without incident.

- The first option is to climb up on the front entrance's control booth, then drop down on the other side and crouch-walk alongside the fence. The guards by the boom barrier will be oblivious to your presence as long as you don't linger, but do pay attention to the surveillance camera on the main building and the robot patrolling in front of it. Now follow the embankment until you get to the car, using the various cover positions on the way to hide from the surveillance camera and the android.
- The second option is to use the side fence door, found to the east relative to the main gate (though breaking it requires a high Technical Ability attribute level). Neutralize the surveillance camera on your left, then quickly sneak to the embankment, ignoring the guards. The embankment will take you directly to the car, with the containers providing generous cover.

2

When you reach the car inside the container, plant the transmitter, then leave the docks to complete the assignment.

TROUBLESOME NEIGHBORS

06

■ **Unlock Condition** – Street Cred Tier 1 ■ **Type** – Gun For Hire

1

Head to the residential block at Cortes and Kennedy. Your target in this gig is a Tyger Claw by the name of Taki Kenmochi, who runs a pachinko parlor. After you enter the block by the alleyway directly under a freeway ramp, turn right, then left, and you will reach the mission's hostile area.

2

If you're looking for a quiet resolution, distract the first guard (at the north end of the alleyway) using one of the vending machines on your left and neutralize him while he's busy examining the device. Next, use a similar ruse with the second Tyger Claw, this time quickhacking the generator on the other side of the fence: swiftly crouch-walk up to him and take him down before carrying his body back to the alleyway, out of sight. You can now sneak up on Kenmochi inside the pachinko parlor, ignoring the bouncer by the door on the other side. Pick her up if you're opting for a non-lethal extraction, then retrace your steps to carry her to the fixer's transport. Place her in the car trunk to complete the assignment.

WOMAN OF LA MANCHA 07

■ **Unlock Condition** – Street Cred Tier 1 ■ **Type** – Gun For Hire

1

Head to the Kabuki market, where you need to discover where Anna Hamill lives. You can achieve this in many ways, some of which are only available if you meet or exceed attribute or Street Cred thresholds. In no particular order, you could try asking Robert, the local ripperdoc; offering a payment to a prostitute in a dingy corner; threatening or paying Imad, a man sitting on a chair (unless you're a Nomad yourself, in which case he will be happy to help you); or, last, but by no means least, breaching the computer inside the hotel, in the small storage room next to the entrance (which requires you to rent a room, remotely activate the front door's terminal, or open the side door via a test of your Technical Ability attribute).

2

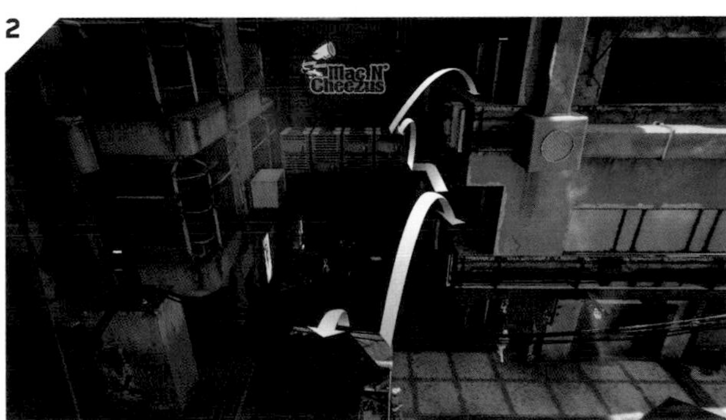

There are two staircases that can take you to room 303, both on the west side of the market. The first is freely accessible but involves jumping to Hamill's balcony via air conditioning units (these will electrocute you, though the damage is limited if you're fast); the second can be reached by opening the side door (gated behind a Technical Ability requirement) or the front door (either by renting a room or hacking its terminal). Alternatively, you can just make your way up to Anna's balcony by jumping onto it via the stalls, balconies, and air conditioning units, as shown above (once again, do not linger here). When you confront Anna, be sure to freeze completely. The conversation can go one of three ways:

- She attacks you (the default scenario).
- You tell Anna that it was her superiors who put a bounty on her head. This can be achieved by choosing the following dialogue lines: "Here to warn you" ➡ "Just wanna help you" ➡ "Your buddies at the NCPD." This will cause her to drop the case, but it will later be revealed on the radio that she eventually eliminated her superiors and was killed in the ensuing shootout.
- Note that if your V has the Nomad background, you can optionally continue the conversation until you reach lines specific to that origin story. In this outcome, Anna will leave town and remain alive.

SHARK IN THE WATER 08

■ **Unlock Condition** – Street Cred Tier 1 ■ **Type** – Gun For Hire

1

Your target in this gig is Blake Croyle. He is found inside a pharmaceuticals shop on the east side of Kabuki, with multiple Animals guarding the perimeter and two more inside the shop. We recommend a stealthy approach, as any form of alarm being raised will lead to a potentially lengthy battle against extensive reinforcements.

You can enter the building in various ways: the front door (leading to a room guarded by an enemy), the garage gate, the back door (which puts you in an ideal position close to Blake but requires a high Technical Ability level), and finally, a ladder on the side of the building (which will get you to the roof, with a grate giving you access to an elevated walkway inside the building). No matter your preference, we suggest you take the time to quietly neutralize the Animals patrolling outside if you intend to extract Croyle from the premises. They generally stay away from each other, so this should pose little difficulty.

2

Inside the shop, you will find Croyle sitting in front of a computer in a corner. Unless you're treating this as a crude gangland-style killing and are actively spoiling for a fight against reinforcements, it's prudent to pacify the two nearby Animals before you deal with your target. You can then pick up the unconscious Croyle and carry him to the fixer's car.

MONSTER HUNT

■ **Unlock Condition** – Street Cred Tier 1 ■ **Type** – Gun For Hire

1

Make your way to the Ho-Oh casino, on Kabuki's east side. This is one of the most complicated gigs, so make sure you come well prepared. If you are planning to extract the target from the site, note that it's advisable to incapacitate all potential hostiles on your chosen path to make your escape much easier. There are multiple ways to approach this mission, but we've narrowed things down here to our two favorite strategies.

- The most obvious approach is to go through the front entrance. All you have to do here is distract the bouncer blocking access to the hostile area (by quickhacking the nearby arcade machines, for example), and slip through while he's looking elsewhere. You will end up at the foot of the stairs leading to the upper floor.

ALTERNATIVE PATH

There is a completely different approach to completing this mission where you only briefly set foot inside the casino. It's available only if you meet a Technical Ability attribute requirement. First, break the door in the fence section close to the front entrance. Once this is open, climb up the ladder, go up one floor via the fire escape, then head inside the apartment. Walk to the opposite end, clockwise, until you reach a balcony; crouch to avoid the gaze of the Tyger Claw.

Hop onto the nearby air conditioning unit and crouch-walk on the ledge that leads to the casino's balcony. Quickhack the surveillance camera, quietly take down the sentry, and you can then deal with Jotaro, who stands on the other side of the opening in the wall. You could also kill him with a silenced sniper rifle from the ledge, without technically setting foot in the casino.

When Jotaro is neutralized, go back to the balcony (with or without his body depending on whether your approach was nonlethal or fatal) and drop down via the awning to arrive back at the front entrance.

- Another option is to crouch-walk through the garage gate. You can ignore the two guards and sneak through the door to the right to reach a small storage room. You could also force-open the shutters by the vending machine to get here. Hop through the open window, then take the door on your right and the double doors that follow to reach the stairs leading to the upper floor.

2

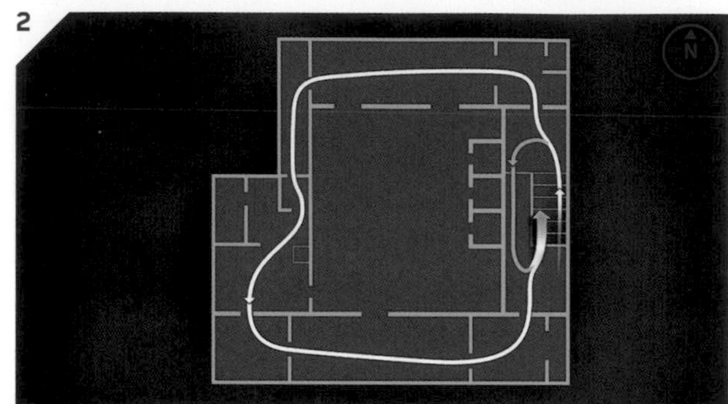

- Here, you can bypass the entire floor if you have sufficient Technical Ability: open the fence gate and head straight to the uppermost floor.
- Otherwise, you will need to go through multiple rooms, paying attention to numerous sentries and surveillance cameras. If you move counterclockwise, closely hugging the apartment's outer wall at all times, you can avoid all of them and reach the staircase unnoticed.

3

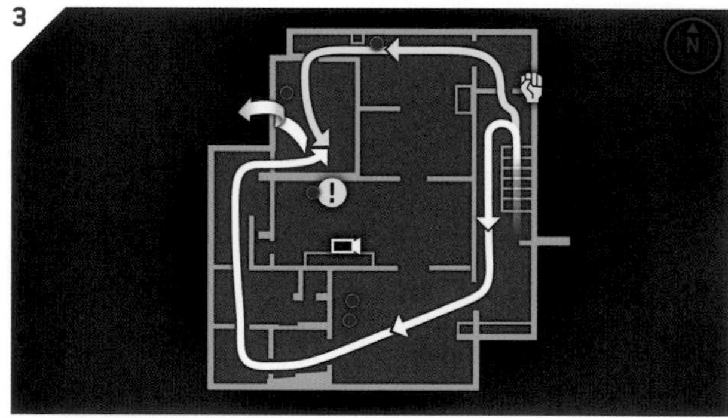

- Once on the uppermost floor, consider force-opening the door right in front of you if your Body attribute allows for it. From here, move counterclockwise, neutralizing the Tyger Claw by the braindance chair, and then the one on the balcony, after quickhacking the surveillance camera. From this position, quietly neutralize Jotaro Shobo through the opening in the wall when his patrol route takes him there, for example with a headshot using a silenced weapon, or with a fatal quickhack. You could also wait until Jotaro leans out of the window in the small room by the balcony.
- Alternatively, go through the staircase's double doors. You arrive in a large room, with two Tyger Claws who will soon look away from you. Take them down in turn, then move clockwise and deal with Jotaro Shobo incognito either through the opening in the wall or in the small room by the balcony.

After neutralizing Jotaro, drop from the nearby balcony to the awning below, then drop again to reach the street.

BACKS AGAINST THE WALL

10

■ **Unlock Condition** – Street Cred Tier 1 ■ **Type** – Search and Recover

1

Head to the designated housing block on Columbus Street and climb up the stairs. To get into the marked apartment, you can either force-open the entrance door, or hop through the window and use the fire escape stairs. Once inside, you need to head to the upper floor via the collapsed floor section that forms a ramp. The highly agitated individual in possession of the stolen medicine has shut himself away in what used to be the flat's bathroom. He will initiate a conversation when you open the door: freeze and *do not move* for the rest of the scene, or you will trigger a fight. For a peaceful resolution, you need to convince him that his actions would only serve to strengthen the Establishment's stranglehold on society and benefit the very politicians he opposes. (If you're unsure, just select the topmost dialogue lines.)

William will eventually calm down, giving you the opportunity to retrieve the stolen medicine from a yellow wall-mounted container. Stow the merchandise at the nearby Drop Point to end the gig.

SMALL MAN, BIG EVIL

■ **Unlock Condition** – Street Cred Tier 2 and complete the "Monster Hunt" gig ■ **Type** – Gun For Hire

1

Head to the rooftop slums near Allen Street, close to the docks on the east side of Kabuki. You can reach them via the fire escape steps in the alleyway perpendicular to Allen Street.

2

Your target, a man by the name of Jae-Hyun, is located at the far end of the hostile area. We suggest two possible approaches.

- If you're comfortable taking a few simple jumps, climb to the rooftops via the air conditioning units adjacent to the top of the staircase. The single sentry posted here will turn away from you after a few moments; quietly neutralize her, then look down when you reach the ladder. Disable the surveillance camera, tag the closest guard and Hyun himself, then sneak up on both.
- If you prefer to go through the slum maze, you will need to avoid the two sentries at the hostile area's entrance by going through the room on the right. You can then use the many walls as cover as you quietly sneak past or incapacitate enemies one by one. Move with great caution, as it's easy to be taken by surprise.

If you opt to kill Hyun, you can retrace your steps; a ladder on the left enables you to get back to the rooftops. If you prefer a non-lethal takedown, you will need to convey his body to the car sent by the fixer.

LAST LOGIN

12

■ **Unlock Condition** – Street Cred Tier 2 ■ **Type** – Thievery

1

Head to the housing block on Eisenhower Ave, as marked on your map. There are multiple ways to enter the premises.

- The door in the middle via a Body attribute requirement.
- An open window accessible from the metal awning, which you can reach by going through the door on the small footbridge; this requires a Technical Ability attribute requirement.
- The door or the garage gate on the left.

2

Your goal inside is to make it to the stairs that go down to the basement. These are found in the main room, which is guarded by two scavengers that you can easily sneak past (or neutralize) after tagging them.

- If you arrive from the force-opened door, you are within immediate reach of the basement stairs (a few steps forward, then to your right), with only one of the two scavengers in your path.
- If you entered via the upper-floor window, you can go down the set of stairs on your right – at which point this route merges with the previous one.
- Coming from the left side, you will first need to go through the garage. Hide in the storage room directly on the left until one of the two guards leans on the nearby railing. You can then neutralize him and dump his body in the crate. Repeat this with the second guard before you head up the stairs. Use the metal walkway to get to the upper-floor path, then go down the stairs on the other side of the building – where all routes merge.

3

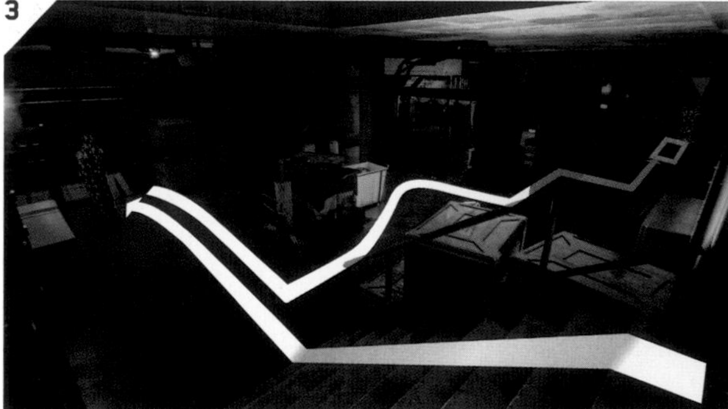

Once you make it to the basement, stay low and close to the foot of the stairs. Try to tag the two scavengers in the surgery room: when one of them comes your way and stops by the crates, take him out – then deal with his colleague in the surgery room. You can now safely retrieve the laptop on the desk right by the ripperdoc chair, then head for the nearest Drop Point.

RIPPERDOC DISCOUNT

While in the basement, read the file on the computer in the surgery room to discover that Charles, the ripperdoc neighbor, has a secret deal with the scavengers. If you then pay him a visit via the nearby door, you can tell Charles that you know how he gets his parts and don't believe his excuses. He will then offer you a discount on his wares in exchange for your silence.

FIXER, MERC, SOLDIER, SPY 13

■ **Unlock Condition** – Street Cred Tier 4 and complete the "Welcome to America, Comrade" gig ■ **Type** – Thievery

1

Head to Hotel Raito on Adams Street. You will need to pay, distract, or disable the receptionist to be granted access to the elevator.

- There's a key on the counter, right in front of his chair – but he will attack you if you take it. You could try to distract him by commenting that the show on TV looks interesting, but it's a risky maneuver.
- A straightforward approach is to pay for a room on the floor below your target. If you have a Street Kid background, you can persuade the receptionist to reduce the cost by 50% – just don't let him call Akulov!
- You can slip through a door gated behind a Technical Ability attribute requirement, and sneak up on the receptionist.

However you elect to proceed, take the elevator when you're ready.

2

When you leave the elevator, use the staircase to reach the floor above. You can enter the penthouse in one of three ways:

- Open the door on your left if your Technical Ability is high enough.
- Break the large glass panel in front of you to get to a balcony. Here, you will find a door that you can force-open with a sufficient Body level.
- The final option is to break the glass panel and jump from the balcony to the penthouse's terrace via the wooden lattice panel – just beware of the surveillance camera on the far wall.

3

All three approaches ultimately lead to the living room, where the shard is found in a bag just below the TV. There are only two hostiles in the area: tag them both and wait. When the man (Akulov) goes out onto the terrace on the north side for a smoke, this is your cue to sneak in: crouch-walk straight to the bag, collect the shard and leave. Unless you are fully confident in your ability to take them down instantly with sneak attacks, we suggest you steer clear of both foes as triggering open combat would lead to the arrival of reinforcements.

Once you make it back to street level, call Regina and deliver the briefcase to the client at the marked position, a short distance to the southwest. Your choices during the conversation have no lasting repercussions, so speak freely.

HIPPOCRATIC OATH

14

■ **Unlock Condition** – Street Cred Tier 1 ■ **Type** – SOS: Merc Needed

Your goal is to exfiltrate a woman, Lucy Thackery, who is being detained in a Clean Cut ripperdoc clinic that has been taken over by Maelstromers.

1

Clinic Infiltration

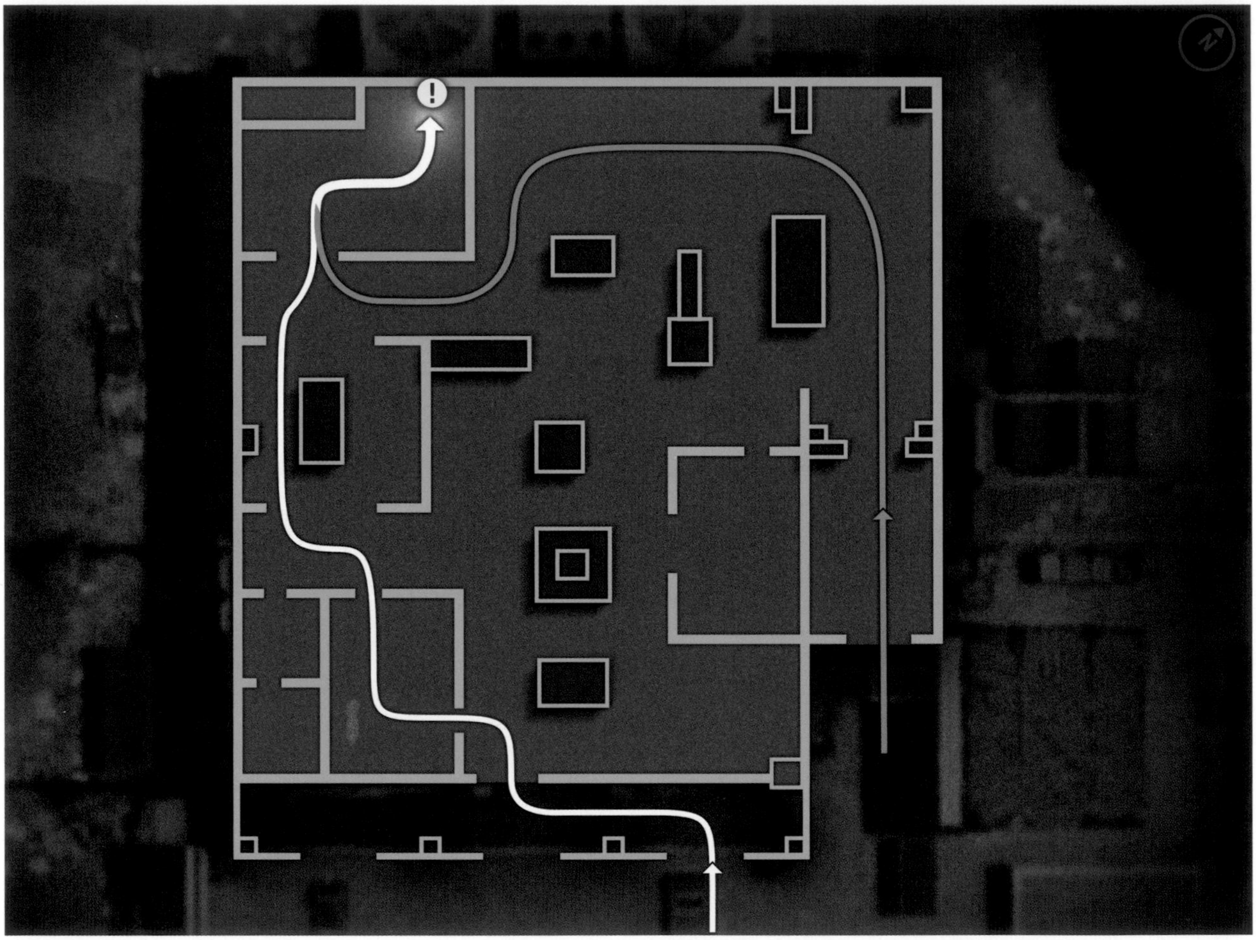

If you plan on entering via the front door, wait until the closest Maelstromer comes out of the building, then go through the office behind the reception desk on your left, making sure both the surveillance camera and the goon inside are facing away. The double door a little further in is where you need to go to find Lucy; sneak past the Maelstromer on the way. Once you're familiar with the layout of the clinic, this is a rather easy path: you can simply head straight to Lucy from the entrance, only briefly waiting for the second Maelstromer to look away if required. Getting in and out with reasonably careful timing alone also means that you do not need to worry about hiding bodies.

The side door can only be opened by meeting a Technical Ability attribute requirement, but offers a relatively straightforward path. Crouch-walk counterclockwise alongside the right-hand wall, and you will face a surveillance camera as well as a couple of guards on the way – all prime targets for silent takedowns while they look away.

Your objective is Lucy Thackery, situated in the west corner of the building. Once you reach her, Lucy will ask you to help her save a wounded patient before leaving. You should obviously stay low if you haven't neutralized the Maelstromers in the area. You can either cooperate (follow her instructions: scan then treat the victim), or simply do nothing. Either way, you then need to get Lucy out of the clinic. Retrace your steps and you will find the fixer's car parked outside.

FLIGHT OF THE CHEETAH 15

■ **Unlock Condition** – Street Cred Tier 1 ■ **Type** – SOS: Merc Needed

1

This mission requires you to escort a man by the name of Hwangbo to safety. He's hiding in room 1237 of a motel in Northside. After meeting with him, you have three options.

- If you've invested points in your Body attribute, take a right when you leave the room: you will find a staircase at the end of the walkway, leading to double doors that you can force-open to leave the compound.
- Otherwise, head left as you leave room 1237, go down the steps on the north side of the motel, then climb up the steps leading to the other building. This will enable you to avoid most of the Tyger Claws patrolling the area. Drop down through the broken section of the railing to end up behind a container. If you neutralize the nearby sentry, you can optionally steal a car before speeding through the main entrance. If you would prefer to get to Hwangbo's vehicle, you will need to go through the main entrance on foot. Tag all foes in the area, watch them carefully, and proceed when no one is looking your way. Quickhacks such as Reboot Optics can help here.
- If your Technical Ability attribute is sufficient, you can alternatively use the double door in the southwest corner to leave the premises without encountering a single Tyger Claw.

2

Once you have a vehicle, drive to the waypoint marked on your map, at the freeway underpass close to the large Biotechnica plant.

DIRTY BIZ 16

■ **Unlock Condition** – Street Cred Tier 1 ■ **Type** – Thievery

1

This gig requires you to find Gottfried and Fredrik's BD recording studio, which is hidden in a Maelstrom-controlled compound near the Northside docks. Among many possible approaches, the following two stand out:

- If you go through the front entrance, walk up to the boom barrier just outside of the hostile area. While you wait for the two Maelstromers to stop talking, neutralize the two surveillance cameras with quickhacks: one on the nearby security building, and one mounted on the pillar above the steps. Once the guards split up, sneak up on both guards in turn – they're both close to a hiding place where you can dump their bodies. Now walk up the steps and tag the two men talking at the top. They will soon go their separate ways. Distract the one who stays outside to smoke using the nearby air conditioner, then quietly take him down (another crate is conveniently located near the corner). You can then head up the steps to the northwest. Wait until the Maelstromer on the roof looks away before you hop through the open window to reach the studio.
- If you meet the Technical Ability attribute requirement, there's a door in the fence on the northeast side of the perimeter that you can break. This enables you to avoid the front entrance, but you will still need to pacify the camera above the steps, at which point the route merges with the previous one.

2

Once inside the studio, enter the editing room and pick up BD_9430 from a small shelf in the far wall. You can also wake the duo from their braindance session (they carry shards), or explore the adjacent room (gated behind a Technical Ability attribute requirement), but these steps are entirely optional. When you're ready, leave either by retracing your steps, or by going through the nearby room with the collapsed staircase. Take the recording to the nearest Drop Point to complete the mission.

MANY WAYS TO SKIN A CAT 17

■ **Unlock Condition** – Street Cred Tier 1 ■ **Type** – Thievery

In this mission, your objective is to steal a van from an RCS warehouse, but you first need to gain access to it via a specific computer. Among the various possible approaches, there are two standout choices:

- Hop through the missing fence section in the south corner of the compound, then head straight to the door on your right, steering clear of the sentry in the courtyard and the surveillance camera above the door. Go up the stairs to reach an elevated walkway.
- Alternatively, if you invested a few points in your Technical Ability attribute, enter via the door in the fence on the north side when the guard moves away. Disable the two surveillance cameras, then immediately turn right and crouch-walk toward the vending machine. Use it to climb up to the building's rooftop. From here, you can drop down through a roof window to reach the elevated walkway where both routes merge. Before you begin your ascension, note that you can find a shard with a Notice of Expiration on the desk in the nearby ground floor office (which is guarded by two sentries) – just go through the door right by the vending machine. The shard is a reference to SJ-56 ("Kold Mirage").

Immediately quickhack the surveillance camera above the nearby glass door, then go through the latter and quietly neutralize the guard on the other side. Interact with the computer to gain access to the van (and, optionally, to switch off the surveillance cameras in the network), then return to the walkway and follow it in a counterclockwise direction. Pay attention to the Tyger Claws patrolling the rooms on your right: tag them or observe their movements on the mini-map, and sneak past or take them down when the time is right. At the end of the walkway, stairs will lead you directly to the van. Sneak to it, then take the wheel: the garage entrance will open automatically, as will the fence gate on the left. You can now drive to the indicated location: the Tyger Claws will not give chase even if you are seen driving away.

RITE OF PASSAGE

18

■ **Unlock Condition** – Street Cred Tier 2 ■ **Type** – Thievery

To get into the Maelstrom hideout inside the Meaty Fish building, go through the large garage door and deal with both the surveillance camera and the lone Maelstromer there. Once you reach the main corridor inside the clinic, take a right and go up the stairs. There are multiple thugs in the adjacent rooms, but they won't have the time to notice you as long as you remain crouched and do not dawdle at any point.

Upstairs, your goal is the computer in the large server room behind the double doors. If you can meet a Body attribute requirement, it's accessible directly from the top of the stairs. If not, you will have to go through the neighboring rooms, dealing with a handful of guards on the way. As long as you're cautious and take the time to tag them all and disable the surveillance cameras (especially the one in the server room), this should pose no real challenge. After retrieving the data, you either need to retrace your steps to the garage or, if your Technical Ability attribute is high enough, take the door leading to a long corridor on the south side of the building. In the small room at the end, open the shutters and drop down to the street outside.

SCROLLS BEFORE SWINE 19

■ **Unlock Condition** – Street Cred Tier 2 and complete MJ-11 ("Playing for Time") ■ **Type** – Thievery

1

The footage you need is found on a computer in a small storage room inside the DTR warehouse. There are, as always, many possible avenues of approach. One that proves particularly effective is to climb to the rooftop via the crates and the long awning on the south of the compound, as shown above. Briefly pause at the beginning of the awning and tag the sentries in the area. Once their patrol routes take them away, resume your advance. A roof window enables you to drop down directly into the unguarded room with the computer and steal the data. Note that you can watch the footage by examining the computer, which unlocks an additional potential outcome when you report to Aaron.

2

Retrace your steps and return the footage to Aaron at the designated waypoint – a residential building a short distance to the northeast. Take the stairs to the upper floor and use the intercom by his door. During the conversation, you can simply give the footage back to Aaron to obtain the agreed payment. If you took the time to view the footage earlier, however, you might be inclined to mention this: Aaron will double your reward. Taking him down, on the other hand, would yield no reward.

OCCUPATIONAL HAZARD 20

■ **Unlock Condition** – Street Cred Tier 1 ■ **Type** – SOS: Merc Needed

1

Your task for this gig is to rescue Hal Cantos from an Autowerks warehouse in Northside. If you meet the related Technical Ability attribute requirement, feel free to enter via the main entrance (the double doors). Otherwise, climb to the rooftop via the dumpster, open the shutters, and hop through the window.

2

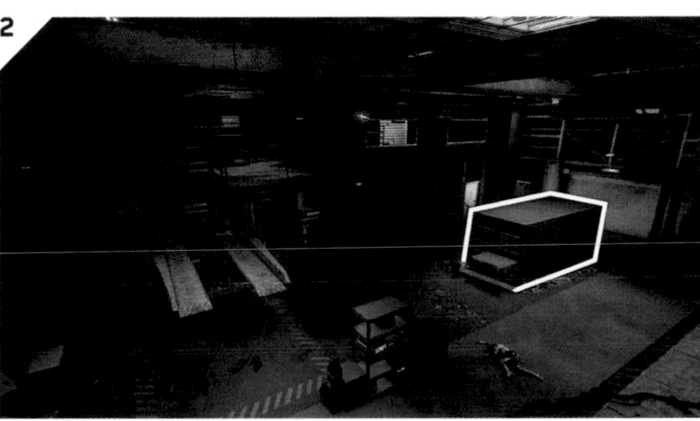

Once inside you will need to choose how to deal with Anna, a Mox experiencing a cyberpsychotic episode in the warehouse. The most obvious approach is to eliminate her, then free Hal. There is, however, a more creative solution. The room in the west corner of the building, on the upper floor (your arrival point if you entered via the shutters), contains a Mox who will tell you that you can link to Bex, whose body lies nearby, to hack Anna, weakening her in the process. You can then tag her and sneak up on her for a more peaceful outcome.

Once you have dealt with the situation, head to the container on the west side of the warehouse to free Hal. Note that if you leave without saving Hal and do not return within 24 in-game hours, you will fail the gig. Also, talking to Hal before neutralizing Anna and lying to him (by pretending that you dealt with the threat) will technically complete the quest, but leads to a reduced reward.

FREEDOM OF THE PRESS

■ **Unlock Condition** – Street Cred Tier 3 ■ **Type** – SOS: Merc Needed

1

Head to the old WNS News building marked on your map. To enter it, you can either open the door by meeting a Technical Ability attribute requirement, or climb up to the roof via the dumpster and break the glass panel – and then drop through the new opening. Once inside, your task is to reach the office overlooking the shooting stage, but the path is littered with traps. Advance cautiously with your scanner on, disarming or shooting the many mines on the way, and quickhacking or destroying the turrets.

2

When you find Max, freeze and be ready to answer the first question he asks you ("You a corpo?") quickly. If you move toward him or say nothing before the dialogue timer is depleted, he will commit suicide, causing the mission to fail. Throughout the rest of the conversation, reason with him until he agrees to follow you (or neutralize him while his back is turned), then leave via the exit at the end of the nearby corridor. The walkway at the back of the building leads directly to the fixer's transport. You can then collect your reward at the nearest Drop Point to complete the assignment.

LOUSY KLEPPERS

■ **Unlock Condition** – Street Cred Tier 3 ■ **Type** – Thievery

1

In this gig, Maelstromers have taken control of a Wicked Tires warehouse. Your goal is to retrieve a shard hidden inside.

- Among the various points of ingress, one safe option is to approach from the south, via the narrow alleyway, then jump over the fence and slip through the door.
- Alternatively, you could go through the broken wall section to the north of the warehouse, wait for the two nearby guards to split, climb to the roof (beware of the surveillance camera and the sentry there), and drop down via the second (furthermost) of the two roof windows.
- A third option also takes you through the broken wall section, but you then enter the small room at the north end of the warehouse, and force-open the door inside to get in.

2

Once inside, you can find the databank right next to the van, conveniently positioned on the other side of the vehicle relative to the Maelstromers. Make sure you immediately disable the surveillance camera above it to avoid complications.

- If you arrive via the front entrance, quickly sneak to the right, sticking to the right-hand wall, and you will find your objective just a short distance away.
- If you dropped from the roof, jump down from the shelves directly next to the databank.
- If you force-opened the door to enter the premises, move counterclockwise alongside the outer wall until you reach the van.

Once you have secured the databank, feel free to sneak out via the front entrance, turning left to avoid the sentries and surveillance camera above. At this point, you can either go through the front gate, or jump from the top of the blue container to get over the tall fence section. Deliver the databank to the nearest Drop Point to complete the assignment.

JAPANTOWN

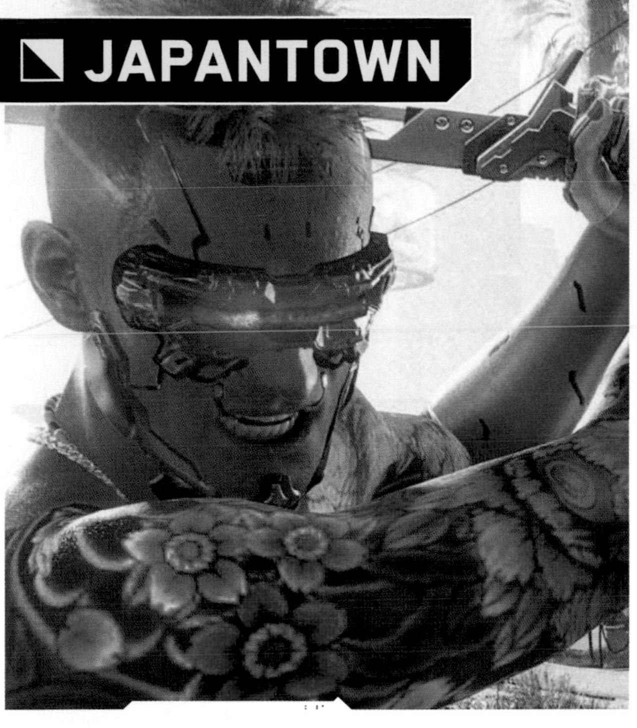

OLIVE BRANCH

23

■ **Unlock Condition** – Street Cred Tier 1 ■ **Type** – Special Delivery

1

Meet with Sergei Karasinsky in an alleyway near Silk Road, at the heart of Japantown. After your conversation, go through the door next to him and get in the car. You now need to drive the vehicle to a Tyger Claw restaurant to the north of your position. During the ride, however, you will hear calls for help from the car's trunk. If you stop and open it, you will discover a man inside. You are then free to either keep him there or let him go. This is a moral choice that will only affect dialogue sequences – your reward will be unchanged.

2

Park the vehicle at the back of the designated diner. After a brief conversation, leave the area to complete the mission.

WE HAVE YOUR WIFE

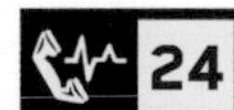

24

■ **Unlock Condition** – Street Cred Tier 1 ■ **Type** – SOS: Merc Needed

1

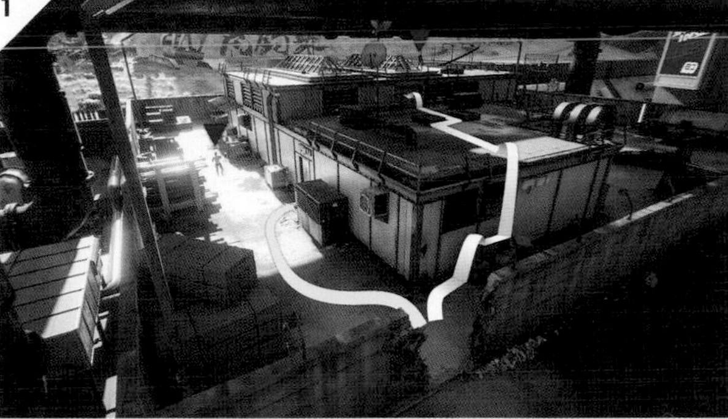

Head to the marked position, a building by Raymond Street near the northern edge of Japantown. You enter a hostile area the moment you go through the broken wall section, a few steps to the north of the front gate. Among the multiple ways to get into the building, we would recommend the following two: either the back door (yellow arrow) on the north side of the building if you have sufficient strength to force-open it, or the shutters on the rooftop (white arrow), accessible via crates by the west wall. In both cases, pay attention to the many surveillance cameras in the area, both outside and inside. Once in the garage, the door leading to the basement where Lauren is detained is in the northeast corner. We suggest you take down the Tyger Claw that patrols near that door by, for example, causing a distraction with the floodlight above him: this will remove a potential complication for the return journey. There's a crate in which you can hide the body right by the door.

2

When you reach the basement, you can hop onto the elevated walkway to bypass all the guards and reach the room right next to Lauren's cell – on the opposite (west) side relative to you. Drop down from the walkway once in the room with the computer, and quietly neutralize the guard who talks to Lauren, then speak to her. She will follow you as you make your way back outside. Move alongside the north wall and up the stairs, crouch-walking at all times to reduce the possibility of detection. Exit the building exactly as you entered it, via the back door or the roof window (the latter can be reached by route of the crate and shelving unit opposite the door). Once outside, escort Lauren to the fixer's vehicle, parked nearby.

GREED NEVER PAYS

 25

■ **Unlock Condition** – Street Cred Tier 1 ■ **Type** – Search and Recovery

1

Your first objective in this gig is to enter Leah Gladen's apartment, in a residential building on the west side of Japantown. This can be achieved in various ways:

- By quickhacking the elevator terminal to open the door.
- By taking the stairs and opening the maintenance door via a Technical Ability attribute requirement.
- By causing a distraction (with the nearby TV, for example) and stealing the elevator's access token while the receptionist is looking away.
- Or by climbing up the scaffolding outside and hopping through the apartment's open window.

In the first three scenarios, type the code 2137 to unlock the apartment's door (it's included in your mission brief), or open it via a Technical Ability attribute requirement if you prefer.

2

Once inside, scan the vending machine to your right from the entrance and Johnny will notice that it conceals a secret door. To unlock it, press the button next to the small kitchen table. You can now enter the hidden room, where you will find two important messages on the computer on the desk.

3

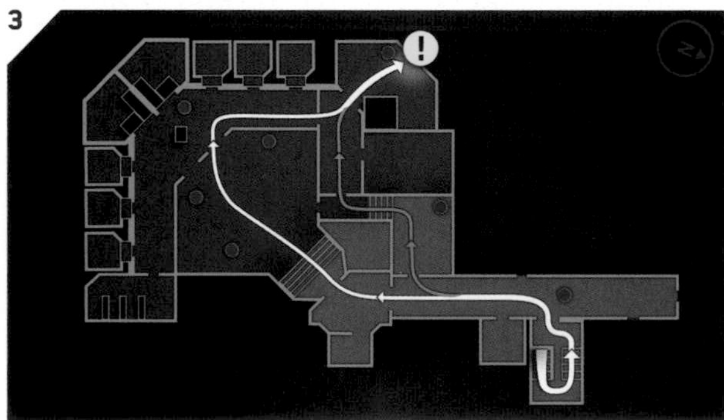

Head southeast to get to the Wired Head, as marked on your map. Whether you take the stairs or the elevator, you end up in the same corridor. Neutralize the Tyger Claws at the top of the stairs and at the front entrance (distractions can greatly help). From here, you have two possibilities.

- The side door is gated behind a Technical Ability attribute requirement. If you can open it, sneak past the unaware guard and you will find a further door on your right leading directly to the back office, where your objective awaits.
- Alternatively, go through the front door to reach the club's main lounge. Most enemies keep looking away from you. The only problematic one is guarding the final door. Use the adjacent refrigerator to cause a distraction and sneak up on him. Note that you could also go through the door by the bar to bypass him, though this requires you to meet a minor Technical Ability attribute requirement. Either way, head to the back office, where a lone foe can be pacified with a stealth takedown.

After you retrieve the lockbreaker from the suitcase by the computer in the back office, retrace your steps outside; you can actually use the service corridor to leave without any attribute requirement. Deposit the item at the nearest Drop Point to complete the mission.

A SHRINE DEFILED

 26

■ **Unlock Condition** – Street Cred Tier 3 ■ **Type** – Agent Saboteur

1

Head to the Shinto shrine at Milagro Terrace. Most of the area is open to the public, with the exception of the security building in the north (where you can deactivate surveillance cameras if you wish), and the main temple area that you need to go through. While the front door is heavily guarded, the two small side alleys each offer alternative points of entry. The one on the left features shutters that are not locked, but guarded by a sentry (who can be easily distracted with the forklift and taken down quietly). The one on the right is unguarded, but the shutters leading inside can only be force-opened.

Crouch-walk once inside the main temple, and use the walls to avoid the gaze of Tyger Claws. Make sure you disable the surveillance cameras on both sides of the doorway leading to the backyard. Enter the honden via the double doors, then make your way to the computer inside to install the virus. Retrace your steps to leave the shrine complex, then collect your reward at a Drop Point to complete the assignment.

WAKAKO'S FAVORITE

27

■ **Unlock Condition** – Street Cred Tier 2 ■ **Type** – SOS: Merc Needed

1

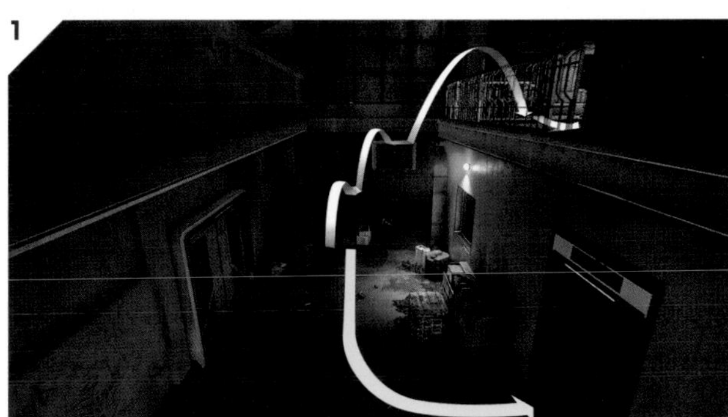

Chang Hoon Nam's hideout can be found in a residential building in the heart of Japantown. There are two possible entrances. The first, on the ground floor, is accessible in the alleyway behind the Chinese restaurant but requires you to have invested a few points in your Body attribute. The second can be reached via the walkway above, which you can climb to by using the nearby dumpster and air conditioning unit as stepping stones.

2

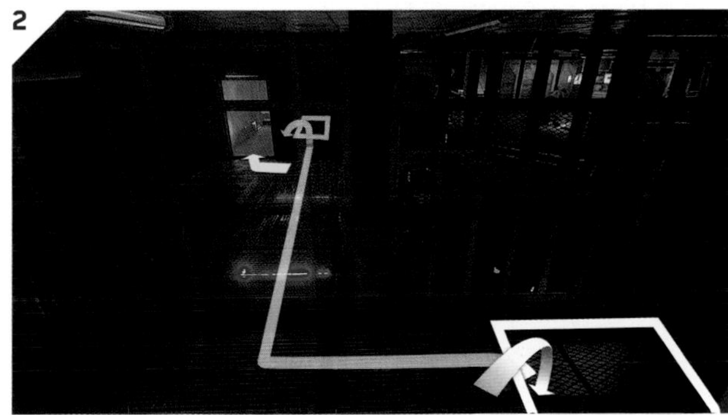

Once inside, note that the stairs leading to the basement are booby-trapped: make sure you disarm (or destroy) the mines on the walls. After examining Chang Hoon Nam's body on the netrunner chair and checking the emails on the adjacent computer, your goal is to retrieve a shard hidden in the nearby storage room, in a container on a shelving unit. You can reach it either by force-opening the glass door, or via the underground passageway accessible by opening a grate in the fenced area – but be warned that this route features laser mines that you must deal with. Return to Chang Hoon Nam and slot in the shard to wake him up.

GETTING WARMER...

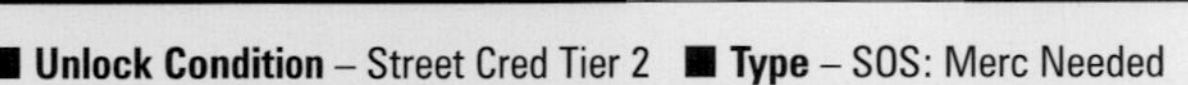

28

■ **Unlock Condition** – Street Cred Tier 2 ■ **Type** – SOS: Merc Needed

1

Your task in this gig is to rescue a woman by the name of 8ug8ear, who is trapped in her apartment in a residential building in Japantown. You can reach her in various ways:

- One option is to enter the building via the main door, and head up the stairs to the top floor. Wait until the guards turn away from you (or distract them with a quickhack) before taking them down, then enter the apartment.
- There's a fire escape on the northeast side of the building (gated behind a Technical Ability attribute requirement) that leads to the other end of the same corridor (or to the rooftop).
- Alternatively, you can use either staircase to reach the rooftop, where you can neutralize both the patrol and the man on the phone on the balcony just below (on the east side) before entering the flat.

Either way, take the coolant on the bathroom sink and use it to lower 8ug8ear's body temperature before disconnecting her using the computer on the wall. Now pick her up and either retrace your steps via the stairs, or drop down directly from the balcony back to street level; you will both survive the fall. Put her in the trunk of the fixer's car to end the assignment.

UNTIL DEATH DO US PART

29

■ **Unlock Condition** – Street Cred Tier 1 ■ **Type** – Thievery

1

Your objective is to retrieve Mr. Gutierrez's shard in his penthouse on 28 Runstreet, which you can reach by using the elevator in the building's main lobby. You then have to deal with the apartment's heavy security measures, including patrolling drones, surveillance cameras, and motion detectors on the doorways connecting the apartment with the terrace. Accomplished netrunners might prefer to attempt this mission without assistance, as it's a fun playground in which to put your skills to the test.

2

From the elevator, there are multiple ways to enter the penthouse.

- The most obvious solution is to open the door to your left as you leave the elevator (which requires a high Technical Ability level).
- A completely different approach is to break the window opposite the elevator. Once outside, climb to the rooftop via the planter on the upper-floor terrace, and you can force-open a grate to drop into a fitness room.
- If you do not meet either of the attribute requirements, break the window opposite the elevator, then hop onto the penthouse's terrace, where you will find broken blinds to the right of the steps; this entrance takes you into the dining room. Quickhack the drone in the area if you don't want to take unnecessary risks.

3

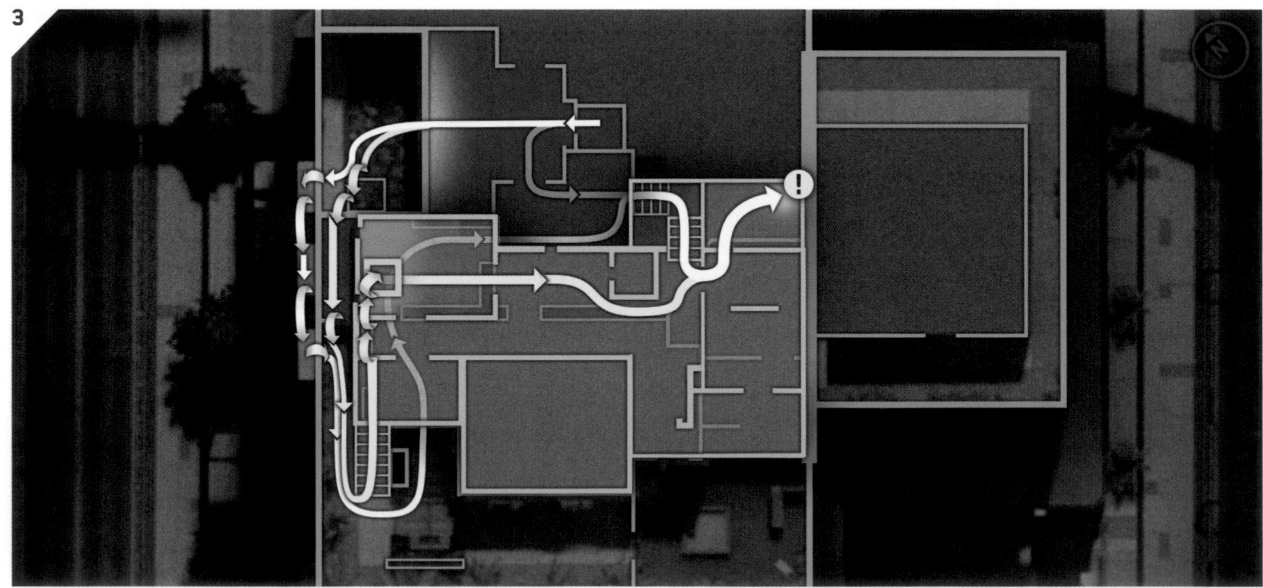

- If you opened the double door by the elevator, you are now in the entrance hall. Pay attention to the surveillance camera on your left: quickhack it if you can, or tag it otherwise. When the coast is clear, head up the stairs on your left and you will find the office at the top, directly on your left.
- If you arrive from the fitness room, follow the corridor to the bedroom and the office will be on your left.
- Coming from the dining room, head straight through the adjacent kitchen and you will reach the entrance hall. Quickhack or avoid the surveillance camera, then go up the stairs: the office is at the top, on your left.

Collect Mr. Gutierrez's shard on the desk, then use the computer to activate an emergency reset of the penthouse security. This will shut down all drones and turrets, facilitating an easy departure. Take the elevator and deposit the shard in the Drop Point opposite the building to complete the assignment.

TYGER AND VULTURE 30

■ **Unlock Condition** – Street Cred Tier 1 ■ **Type** – Thievery

1

Head to the marked sewer tunnel entrance in Charter Hill. Follow the path until you reach the casino entrance (white arrow), where a Tyger Claw asks for a payment before you can enter. If you do not wish to resort to violence, you have two options here: accepting his offer, or quickhacking the TV behind the man to cause a distraction and quickly sneaking inside behind his back.

Note that you can bypass most of this mission if your Technical Ability level is sufficiently high: a door gated behind an attribute requirement can be found by the next sewer entrance to the southeast (blue arrow). This leads directly to the room with the shard you're looking for, with two guards who should remain oblivious to your presence unless you announce your arrival: one on the elevated walkway, and another looking at a computer in the room with a netrunner.

2

If you used the front door, enter the casino itself, where your goal is to find a netrunner. You can locate him by breaching a computer – for example, the one in the storage room beyond the bar (stay low and immediately disable the surveillance camera on the other side when you open the door). A message on the computer here will reveal that the netrunner is situated on the upper floor. You can conveniently access it through a hole in the ceiling in the adjacent room, thereby avoiding the Tyger Claw guarding the stairs. The alternative is to use the main stairs, though you will first need to distract the sentry guarding it with the nearby arcade machine.

Once upstairs, deal with the surveillance camera, neutralize or sneak past the sentry running a clockwise patrol on the walkway, then head to room #6 and quietly take down the Tyger Claw by the computer. The individual on the netrunner chair is in cyberspace, and will remain unaware of your presence unless you are detected. You will find Vortex's shard on the desk by the netrunner chair. Leave the area by going through the door next to the computer, then deliver the credchip to the Drop Point just above your position, at street level.

FAMILY HEIRLOOM 31

■ **Unlock Condition** – Street Cred Tier 4 and complete MJ-19 ("Ghost Town") ■ **Type** – Search and Recover

1

Your goal in this mission is to retrieve a bootleg Samurai recording from a parking lot on Crockett Street. There are multiple ways to enter the premises: a door with a Technical Ability attribute requirement (blue arrow); a door by the garage gates (white arrow, both on the east side); and a door that can be force-opened on the west side (yellow arrow).

2

Whichever entrance you use to get to the parking lot, crouch-walk counterclockwise alongside the right-hand wall, disabling surveillance cameras, tagging all enemies you can see, and using the many cars, crates, and low walls to remain undetected. Your primary target is the bootleg hidden in a red locker in the room by the garage workshop – consider neutralizing the lone enemy here to err on the side of caution.

With the recording secured, the final step is to decide if you also wish to take the car in the adjacent workshop. This is probably worthwhile: there's a single foe to deal with. You can then just hit the gas to leave the area. Deliver the bootleg (and the car if you retrieved it) to Dan at the designated location to complete the assignment.

COASTVIEW

TWO WRONGS MAKES US RIGHT

32

■ **Unlock Condition** – Street Cred Tier 3 ■ **Type** – Thievery

1

Make your way to the unfinished metro station in Pacifica. The van you need to steal can be found at the bottom of the construction site. You will need to sneak past an Animal as you crouch-walk down the stairs, ideally while she's busy consulting the computer. Continue your downward journey until you reach the floor with motorbikes and cars.

2

When the two men part ways after their conversation, sneak past the closer one, then hide between the pillar and dumpster behind him. From here you can see the van, with an Animal patrolling the area, and another one inspecting the wheels. Tag them, then tiptoe to the vehicle while they're looking elsewhere. You can now get in the van and escape at full speed via the tunnel. Park the van at the lot by the market to end the mission.

RANCHO CORONADO

ERROR 404

33

■ **Unlock Condition** – Street Cred Tier 1 ■ **Type** – Agent Saboteur

1

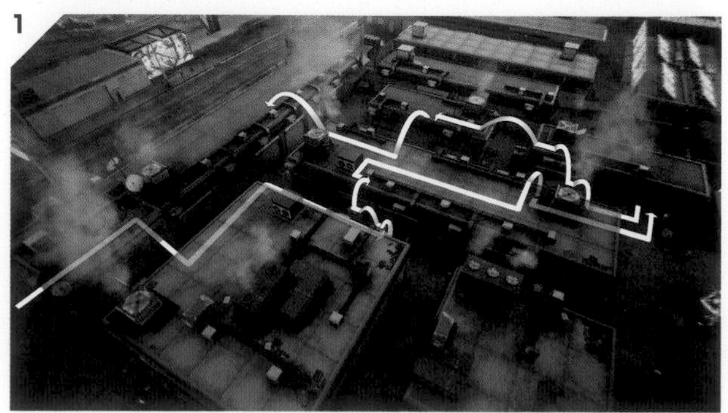

Head to the garage area near Megabuilding H07. The security building by the boom barrier at the entrance is worth a quick stop: after eliminating the thug inside, you can breach the computer to switch off all surveillance cameras and read an email revealing the position of your objective: garage 66. There are numerous ways to reach it, though the most efficient approach is to take to the rooftops via the crates in the first alley on your right (close to a camera), as this enables you to reach the garage directly, avoiding all intervening guards at ground level. On arrival, hide behind the crate close to garage 66 to avoid the gaze of the sniper on the opposite roof, and neutralize the turret to simplify the infiltration if you can; failing that, you will need to time your movements with rather more care. You should also tag the sixers patrolling the area for added safety. When you're ready, quickly sneak to the computer and upload the virus to the servers, then immediately return to the rooftops via the blue shipping container. Jump while sprinting to leap from one building to the next, and you'll enjoy a swift and uneventful return journey.

CUCKOO'S NEST

34

■ **Unlock Condition** – Street Cred Tier 2 ■ **Type** – SOS: Merc Needed

1

Head to the psychiatric hospital where you need to rescue Jasmine Dixon, located in room 7 on the upper floor. There are two ways to enter the building:

- The front entrance is open to the public. Once inside, it gives you access to two routes.
- A few steps to the south of the front entrance, you can leap to scaffolding, which will in turn give you access to the hospital's roof. This is a tricky jump, barely within your reach, but it's possible to make it by persisting. Having access to charged jumps or double jump via legs cyberware helps a lot here. Use the crates to the south as stepping stones to reach the next roof in line and you will find double doors that can be force-opened if you have a suitable Body level. This offers a brilliant shortcut that leads almost directly to your target.

2

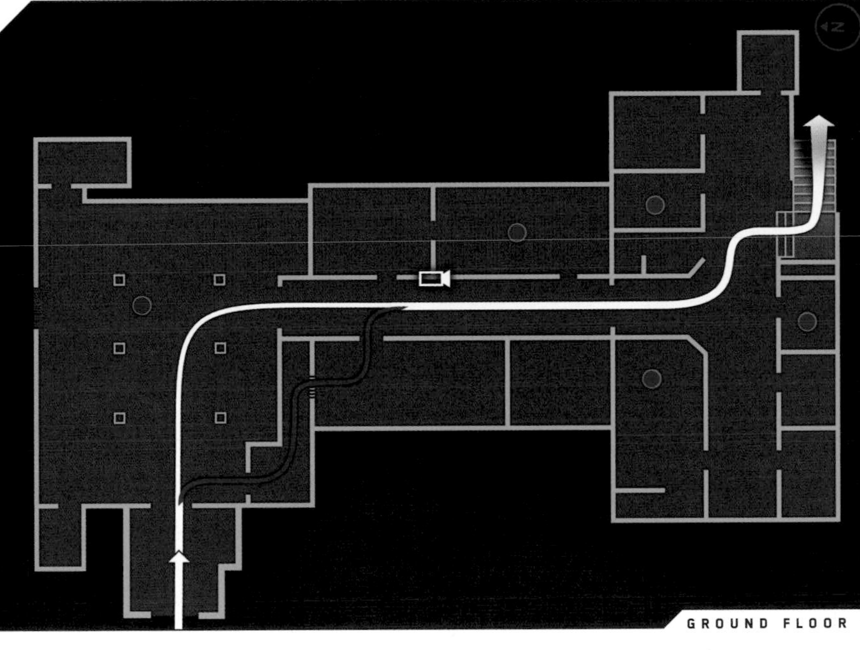

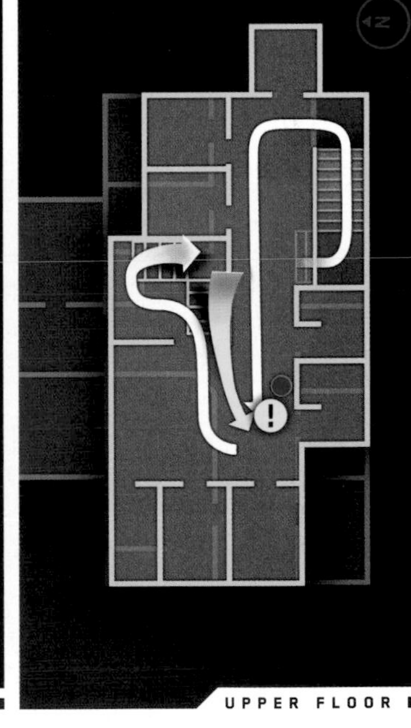

- The front entrance gives you access to the main hall. You can, optionally, steal a shard that will reveal Dixon's exact location – it's in the office in the corner, gated behind a Technical Ability attribute requirement. Either way, you will need to go through the double doors on the south wall. Open them, but do not enter the hostile area yet. Instead, observe the corridor. If you cannot quickhack the camera, wait until it rotates away, then swiftly move to its blind spot, directly beneath the device. When it sweeps back to the opposite side, move to the other end of the corridor, beyond the double doors, and hide behind the crate. You will see the stairs on your left: creep to them to reach the upper floor. Sneak up on the guard stationed in front of room 7 and take him down, then search him to find a key. You can then open the door to free Jasmine Dixon.
- Just as a point of interest, there is an alternative path you can take from the hospital's main hall. Open the door in the southwest corner, then the grate in the next small room, and you will arrive in a room adjacent to the corridor with the surveillance camera – at which point this route merges with the previous one.
- If you arrive from the rooftop, simply go down the stairs to arrive close to room 7. Neutralize the guard, collect the key, then set your target free.

After you rescue Dixon, escort her through the nearby double doors to reach the rooftop, then make your way back to ground level. Head to the fixer's transport, a short distance to the north, to complete the assignment. Note that Dixon will eventually go to the car on her own (and you will receive a different closing message from the displeased fixer) if you deliberately move away from the vehicle.

FAMILY MATTERS  35

■ **Unlock Condition** – Street Cred Tier 2 ■ **Type** – Search and Recover

1

Your first task in this gig is to enter Juliet's house in Rancho Coronado. If you meet the relevant attribute requirements, you can do so via the front or back door. Alternatively, you can climb to the rooftop by jumping from the low wall in the back yard – this gives you access to an open window on the upper floor.

2

Once inside, there are clues that you can examine with your scanner, including in the bedroom upstairs. Your real objective, however, is the shard hidden in a safe in the office on the ground floor. To open the safe, you will first need to obtain a key found in the basement. The catch, though, is that the cyberpsychotic Rose is lurking in the area. Identify her on your mini-map and try to neutralize her with a powerful sneak attack or the System Reset quickhack to avoid a protracted battle. Once she's neutralized, you can inspect Rose's body and that of her sister to retrieve shards and the key that will open the safe in the office. Messages on the nearby computer, and additional shards in the house, will reveal more about this particular story. After you have retrieved the datachip from the safe, head to the nearest Drop Point to complete the assignment.

FOR MY SON  36

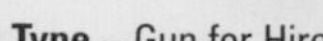

■ **Unlock Condition** – Street Cred Tier 3 ■ **Type** – Gun for Hire

1

Head to the marked fighting arena.

- The Animal guarding the main gate asks for an entrance fee. You can pay him, or try intimidation if your Body stat is high enough. Note that you will not be required to pay if you previously won the duel against Rhino as part of the "Beat on the Brat" side job (see page 181).
- A clever way to avoid him altogether is to enter via the shutters on the northeast side of the building: jump onto the red containers and slip through.

2

- If you arrived via the front entrance, you will need to sneak through the (guarded) VIP zone and walk up the stairs to your right. Neutralize both Logan and the Animal in the adjacent room, then pick up Logan.
- Arriving from the shutters, you will find a large yellow pipe on your right, which you can use to climb to the elevated walkway above – make sure no sentry is patrolling there, though. Logan is in the room that overlooks the arena. If your Technical Ability level allows for it, you can open a door leading straight to him (there's a guard here, but you can distract him with the vending machine). If not, you will first need to use the ladder to reach the door on the other side, then take down both Logan and the Animal in the adjacent room.

You can then follow the waypoint to leave the warehouse via the staircase in the corner, which leads to an emergency exit that opens from the inside. Once outside, put Logan's body in the trunk of the car sent by the fixer to complete the mission – or just depart if you left him cooling inside.

Note: If you remain fully undetected and choose to keep Logan alive during this gig, he will later appear as a spectator in a future side job ("Beat on the Brat" – see page 181).

GOING-AWAY PARTY

37

■ **Unlock Condition** – Street Cred Tier 2 ■ **Type** – SOS: Merc Needed

1

Flavio, the man you have been commissioned to rescue, is located on the upper floor of a house in Rancho Coronado. The obvious points of entry at the front and back of the building are well guarded, but there's a safer option: an opening on the right side of the front porch. This gives you access to the crawlspace under the house, then to the house itself via a hole in the floor. Conveniently, this hole is right next to the stairs that lead to the upper floor. Wait for the two nearby sixers to finish their conversation (one of them will head upstairs so stay low and close to the railing) before you head on up.

2

Move cautiously to the top of the stairs. Tag the sixer at the back of the corridor, then sneak up on him when he turns away from you. Once the coast is clear, you can enter the nearby bedroom to find Flavio. Scan and revive him, then exchange a few words. Once he's ready to follow you, retrace your steps downstairs. Instead of dropping down through the hole in the flooring, enter the adjacent garage and use the car to transport Flavio to the designated meeting point with a Nomad smuggler.

THE UNION STRIKES BACK

38

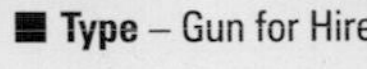

■ **Unlock Condition** – Street Cred Tier 4 ■ **Type** – Gun for Hire

1

Your target, a man by the name of Vic Vega, can be found in an office on the upper floor of the designated building in Rancho Coronado. To enter the premises, you have multiple options:

- Using the garage door or gate (requiring a high Technical Ability or Body level, respectively).
- Going through the small room by the front desk after neutralizing the security guard.
- Slipping through the small restroom window on the north side of the building.
- Distracting the receptionist (using the TV behind her) and stealing a keycard on her desk to go through the main double doors.

The latter approach will require you to navigate the main room on the ground floor. Move counterclockwise in a crouched stance and you shouldn't have any problems in remaining unseen. If you enter via the garage, you have a single foe to worry about: the man in the security room, who can be avoided by crouching and moving alongside the counter.

2

Climb up to the intermediate landing and wait until the two men at the top stop talking and return to their patrols. Now take a right and go through the conference room: stay on the near side of the table and you can sneak past the guard patrolling on the other side. Vega is found in the next office in line, on the floor's west corner. Slip in and neutralize Vega quietly. Simply hop through the window to make your escape, with or without the body, depending on whether you used non-lethal or fatal tactics. In the former case, you will need to dump the body in the trunk of the car sent by the fixer, a short stroll to the southeast. The mission is completed after you collect your reward at the nearest Drop Point.

ARROYO

SERIOUS SIDE EFFECTS

■ **Unlock Condition** – Street Cred Tier 1 ■ **Type** – Search and Recover

1

This gig takes place at the Dewdrop Inn, in Arroyo. There are multiple ways to get inside without triggering conflict: renting a room at the front desk, force-opening the shutters in the side alley to the north, performing the same feat at the door at the top of the fire escape, opening the back door via a Technical Ability attribute requirement, or opening the shutters on the west side of the hotel. Once you're in, you have an optional objective: finding Booker Updike. He (or, rather, what remains of him) can be encountered in room 103, on the ground floor. You can open the door either through a Technical Ability attribute requirement, or by bribing or intimidating the techie working in the corridor; if you came in via the window on the west side of the building, you will arrive in this very room. Scan Updike's body on the bed, then turn your attention to the ventilation system and a duct above the windows to find out where the acid is stored: in room 203. You can also discover this information by checking out the computer in the room close to the reception lobby or in the office on the upper floor (the latter being gated behind a Technical Ability attribute requirement).

2

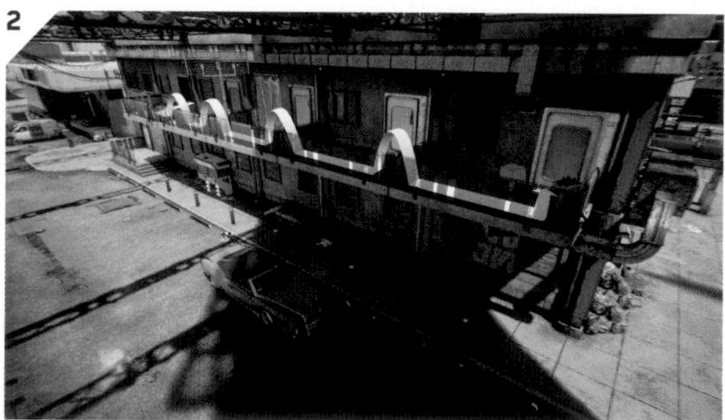

The acid container is found in room 203. To enter, you will need to either force-open the door, or go through room 200 and, once outside, hop over the railings until you reach the final balcony in line, giving you access to room 203's back door. The room has been turned into a lab and is guarded by a few sixers; neutralize or ignore them as you please. After securing the acid hidden in the small chemical chest, head back outside (dropping down from the balcony to the street will suffice) and deposit the hazardous cargo at the nearest Drop Point to end the mission.

RACE TO THE TOP

■ **Unlock Condition** – Street Cred Tier 1 ■ **Type** – Thievery

1

In this gig, you need to infiltrate the Kendachi factory on El Camino Rd. As the front entrance is heavily guarded, we suggest one of the three following approaches:

- If your Technical Ability allows for it, you can open a fence gate on the northeast side of the compound. Head left (making sure you disable both surveillance cameras on the way) and you will soon find a long ladder: this leads to a metal walkway that offers access to the factory interior, mere steps away from Matheus's office.
- Alternatively, you could climb onto the scaffolding at the west corner of the perimeter and hop over the fence. Crouch-walk clockwise alongside the outside wall and, just before reaching the front gate, make a quick stop to ensure the path toward the open garage gate is clear. Sentries might get a glimpse of you on the way, but not long enough to fully detect you. Slip in when the man guarding the garage gate looks away. Once inside, crouch-walk alongside the left-hand wall. You will soon reach an underground passage that will lead you mere steps away from a ladder.
- A third option, if you have a very high Body attribute, is to use the scaffolding and force-open the gate near the south corner of the building.

2

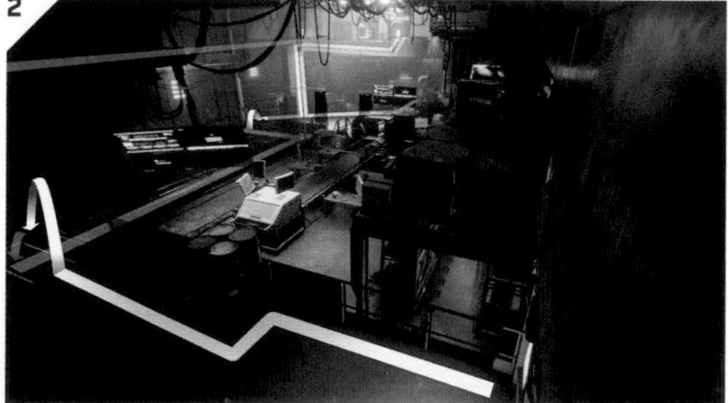

- If you arrive from the ladder on the east corner of the factory, simply follow the metal walkway, which will lead you straight to the office. There's a guard patrolling the area, but he should be facing away from you at all times.
- At the end of the underground passage, hop up and look around for sentries. As soon as the coast is clear, climb up the ladder to reach the elevated metal walkway. Take a right to reach the office.
- If you entered by force-opening the gate near the south corner of the building, climb up the ladder on your right to reach the walkway, then turn right at the top to get to the office.

Steal the incriminating data from the computer, then return outside via the door to the northeast, at the end of the metal walkway. Go down the ladder and you can exit the perimeter by going through the fence gate (if your Technical Ability is high enough), or by climbing to the top of the pile of crates and boxes in the east corner and leaping over the fence.

BREAKING NEWS

41

■ **Unlock Condition** – Street Cred Tier 2 ■ **Type** – Agent Saboteur

1

Get into Ted Fox's car in Arroyo, then head to the factory's parking lot across the road. The van on which you need to install a tracker is behind the closed garage door. This can be force-opened – though you will then be in plain sight, visible to the two surveillance cameras (one above the garage gate, one on the security building).

- Our favored stealth approach is to jump to the billboard's metal structure in the east corner. From here, hop onto the adjacent building, then drop down inside the perimeter and crouch-walk alongside the east fence toward the building. Open the shutters at the end of the path, and you can quietly neutralize both men inside – one in the office, and another in the garage. After planting the tracker, calmly retrace your steps outside, and use the small section of scaffolding to clear the fence before returning to the parking lot where you met Ted. Collect your reward at the nearby Drop Point to end the mission.

- An alternative route is to climb onto the roof via the dumpster on the west side, with a roof window offering direct access to the garage. This route leaves you rather more exposed to detection, however, so make sure you deactivate the surveillance cameras preemptively.

HACKING THE HACKER

42

■ **Unlock Condition** – Street Cred Tier 2 ■ **Type** – Agent Saboteur

1

Head to Megabuilding H06 and use the marked elevator to get to the residential floor at the top of the atrium. You can bypass the first two guards by going through the room on the right after opening the industrial shutters. The 6th Street hideout itself features multiple possible entrance points. One of the smoothest approaches, though, is to sprint and jump from the top of the stairs to the other side of the collapsed walkway, as illustrated in the accompanying screenshot (make sure you disable the nearby surveillance camera first, of course). You will easily clear the yellow railing with a sufficient run-up. Follow the only available path behind the fence to enter the hideout. You could also go through the apartment on the right if you're not comfortable with long jumps.

2

This route gives you a direct access to the room with the netrunner's computer. After dealing with the surveillance camera, stealthily kill the nearby guard, Lucius Thoran (ending his life is required to complete the optional objective and obtain the corresponding bonus reward), then upload the virus and retrace your steps back to the elevator. Collect your reward at the Drop Point once you have returned to street level to complete the assignment.

SEVERANCE PACKAGE

43

■ **Unlock Condition** – Street Cred Tier 2 ■ **Type** – Thievery

1

Your target in this gig is a computer on the upper floor of the Cytech factory. To avoid the main entrance, which is well guarded, you have the option of hopping over the fence from the pipe structure on the east side of the perimeter. You can reach it via a gas tank a few steps to the east. To be safe, tag the civilian working by the crates and the security agent patrolling alongside the fence before you drop down from the pipe structure. To get inside the factory itself, you have several options. The following two generally work very well:

- Advancing cautiously alongside the east fence, disable the surveillance camera, then sneak past or neutralize the guard. You will find a back door around the corner, with another camera and another sentry posted nearby, either busy on the phone or patrolling just inside. We suggest you neutralize him before you proceed, as he can otherwise prove problematic.
- Alternatively, you can simply head to the large open gate, a few steps away. Peek inside to observe the local camera: wait until it rotates away from you before you enter.

2

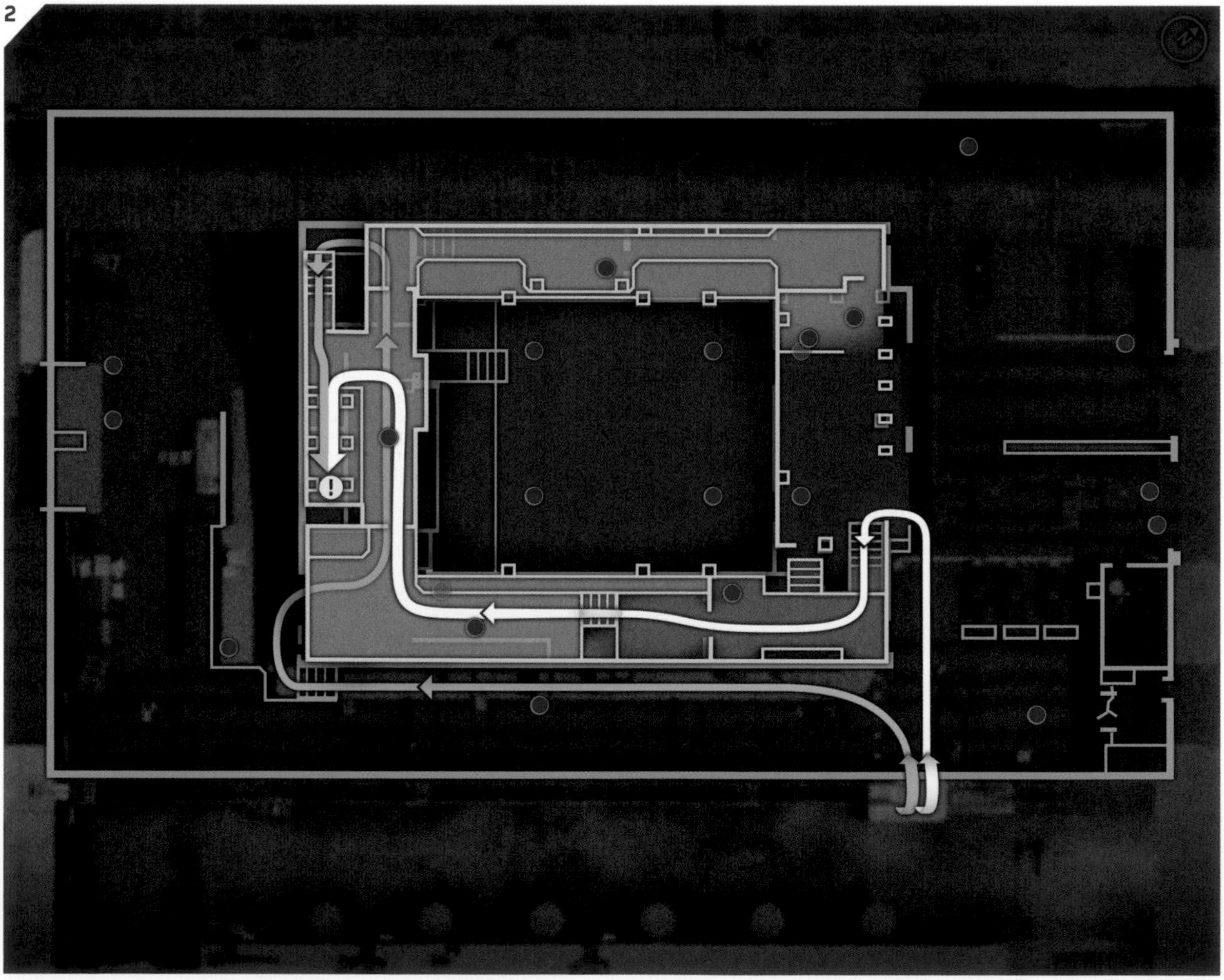

- Arriving from the back door, you need to go through the security room, where both a guard and a surveillance camera await. You can then turn left and go up the stairs to reach the server room where the target computer is located – with a lone sentry facing away from you.
- If you arrived through the front gate, you will find stairs immediately on your left. Make your way to the other side of the building: you will find a civilian, a guard and a surveillance camera in your path, but they're easy to sneak past. You will also need to deal with the man and the camera in the server room.

Once you get to the computer, steal the data before retracing your steps back outside, where you can exit via the front entrance by sneaking alongside the truck by the boom barriers.

BADLANDS

FLYING DRUGS

44

■ **Unlock Condition** – Street Cred Tier 1 ■ **Type** – Agent Saboteur

1

The Wraiths have taken control of a building with a communications antenna in the Eastern Wastelands. It has three possible points of entry – but we recommend the back door, as it is lightly guarded. Neutralize the enemy just inside, then go up the stairs counterclockwise. You will encounter two additional Wraiths as you ascend, but both are facing away from you.

2

Beware of the Wraith patrolling the roof. Once you have dealt with him, head up the steps and you will find a transmitter at the base of the antenna. Turn off the power if you meet the corresponding Technical Ability attribute requirement, or simply destroy it, either with a weapon or a quickhack. When your deed is done, retrace your steps outside of the outpost to receive a call from Dakota. Collect your reward from a Drop Point to complete the assignment.

NO FIXERS

45

■ **Unlock Condition** – Street Cred Tier 1 ■ **Type** – SOS: Merc Needed

1

The beneficiary of your talents in this gig, Iris Tanner, is held captive by Wraiths in the Eastern Wastelands. You will find her in a building at the rear of the outpost – the one with a metal door. There are multiple potential approaches, though crossing the perimeter via the empty container northwest of the hostile area has the major advantage of keeping you away from most enemies. Remotely disable the turret and quietly neutralize the Wraith outside the garage, then head straight south to the building where Iris is being held captive – the two thugs outside are looking the other way, so you can ignore them. Incapacitate the man in the small room, then repeat this with the one guarding Iris (a distraction can help here). You are then free to escort her to safety. To complete the optional objective, you must also reclaim her vehicle – but this is easy, as you actually passed the van on your way to Iris. Retrace your steps to the garage, get in the van, and drive Iris to Dakota's hideout. The mission ends after you speak to the fixer in her office.

BIG PETE'S GOT BIG PROBLEMS

WANTED 46

■ **Unlock Condition** – Street Cred Tier 2 ■ **Type** – Gun for Hire

1

2

Your objective in this gig is to find Big Pete, who is located in the basement of an autoshop in the Southern Desert. There are many possible points of entry, but we'll focus on one that proves especially reliable – on the west side of the building, where you only have to worry about two men busy shooting at a car wreck. You can either neutralize them quietly or give them a wide berth. Your goal is to use the small piece of furniture to jump to the platform, where a door offers access to the elevated walkway inside.

Before you proceed, observe the Wraiths patrolling the ground floor, as they can potentially see you through the walkway. As soon as they look away, move to the right, hop over the railing, and sneak to the basement.

Once in the underground den, you will find Big Pete alone and with his back turned to you. To complete the gig, feel free to either kill him and retrace your steps outside, or talk to him and decide to let him go.

TREVOR'S LAST RIDE

47

■ **Unlock Condition** – Street Cred Tier 2 ■ **Type** – SOS: Merc Needed

1

Your mission objective, Trevor's body, is located inside a Wraith outpost – an abandoned hotel in the Southern Desert. On arrival, make your way to the south corner of the perimeter, then climb onto the wrecked cars. From here, follow the narrow path between the back of the hotel and the cliff, until you reach the building's northwest corner. You should then walk up the stairs, enter the second room on your right, and drop down through the hole in the floor. At this point, two men will have a short conversation outside. When they're done, one of them will depart, while the other will enter the room where you are waiting. Stay out of sight until he turns away from you, then take him down. You are now free to collect Trevor's body from a freezer and retrace your steps via the narrow path alongside the cliff. To err on the side of caution, you should consider neutralizing the Wraith posted close to the front entrance before you leave the area. Drop Trevor's body in the trunk of the car sent by the fixer, parked a short distance to the south, to complete the mission.

DANCING ON A MINEFIELD

48

■ **Unlock Condition** – Street Cred Tier 1 ■ **Type** – Special Delivery

1

This gig has you travel to the edge of the Eastern Wastelands, where you must search for a vehicle in the middle of a minefield. There are two principal hazards here: mines, *of course*, but also patrolling Militech drones that you can sneak past, destroy, or quickhack.

The car is located at the foot of a functional wind turbine, so it's not too hard to find. Scan the body by the vehicle to complete the optional objective, identify a clear path, then get in and drive *very cautiously* to leave the area; your destination is Dakota's garage. Collect your reward at the nearest Drop Point to complete the mission.

SPARRING PARTNER 49

■ **Unlock Condition** – Street Cred Tier 3 ■ **Type** – Thievery

1

This gig takes place in the waste facility in the Eastern Wastelands. Your objective is to retrieve a shard from a broken bot. You could buy the bot from the man at the front desk to get it delivered directly to you, outside the building. If you are not prepared to pay, you can circumvent most of the hostile area by making your approach from the south, just outside the perimeter. Sneak in via the rooftop next to the old satellite dish and you need only make a short foray into hostile territory to retrieve the shard from the robot in the back of the old van. With that done, leave the hostile area and deliver the chip to the Drop Point a short distance to the north.

MIA  50

■ **Unlock Condition** – Street Cred Tier 3 ■ **Type** – SOS: Merc Needed

1

The abandoned farmhouse from which you must rescue Ben is situated in the Southern Desert. There are numerous possible approaches, but a solid strategy is to sneak into the garage from the east. Once inside, use the stairs to get down to the basement. The door here is locked: you can either force-open it, or fetch the key close to the computer, on the desk. After talking to Ben, retrace your steps and use the car in the garage to escort him to a driver to the east who is awaiting his arrival.

GOODBYE, NIGHT CITY  51

■ **Unlock Condition** – Street Cred Tier 3 ■ **Type** – SOS: Merc Needed

1

Bruce Welby, the man you have been hired to rescue, is detained in a Militech compound near the edge of the Southern Desert. There are many ways to get to your target, but we've identified two that are particularly reliable:

- The first one is only available if you have a sufficiently high Technical Ability level. If so, enter the compound from the east and go around the central building counterclockwise. Two doors will lead you directly to Bruce – and then straight back out.
- If you can't take the first route, consider approaching from the south instead. You will find a Militech employee close to the gate: neutralize him, then go clockwise around the building in front of you until you reach and enter the security room. Once inside, go up the stairs to your right. Be aware that a few guards are patrolling around the structure, with another one inside the security room, but you can ignore them if you crouch-walk at all times.

When you get to the detention room, immediately disable the surveillance camera and the turret. You will find Bruce unguarded. Tell him to come with you and guide him cautiously as you retrace your steps to exit the compound. You could even decide to steal the truck parked nearby and leave via the main gate, which will open automatically for a Militech vehicle. Back outside the hostile area, head to the meeting point with Archie to the southwest. You can then collect your reward from a Drop Point to conclude the mission.

RADAR LOVE  52

■ **Unlock Condition** – Street Cred Tier 3 ■ **Type** – Thievery

1

The radar you are commissioned to appropriate is located in a Militech base at the Lone Star Motel, in the middle of the Eastern Wastelands. With a number of cameras, turrets, and guards stationed on the perimeter, your initial assumption might be that a stealth infiltration will be prohibitively difficult. There is, however, a route that enables you to bypass the security setup with ease. If you approach the outpost from the southwest, there's a gray container that you can get inside, just outside the corner of the base. Jump up from the crate inside to reach the top of the container, then hop over the fence. You can now leap onto the canopies, then – after making sure the coast is clear – go swiftly through the garage's front entrance, hop in the vehicle with the radar, and hit the gas – don't let up until you are clear of the area. Park inside Dakota's garage to complete the gig.

VISTA DEL REY

OLD FRIENDS

 53

■ **Unlock Condition** – Street Cred Tier 1 ■ **Type** – Gun for Hire

1

Head to the dive bar on the corner of Congress and Pigeon Street. Your target, Karubo Bairei, can be found in the kitchen behind the bar. The most straightforward way to reach him is to go through the door at the back of the building, though this requires a moderate level of Technical Ability. If you excel in this skill, you'll obtain direct access to your target, with no other foes on the way.

2

There is no other stealth approach so you might as well just use the front door if Technical Ability isn't your forte. If you intend to get to Karubo undetected, you will have to sneak through the door behind the bar. The bartender regularly leaves his position, so you only need to be patient. Quietly neutralize Karubo from behind, pick up his body, then wait and watch for an opportunity when you cannot be seen through the opening in the wall. Now quickly slip through the rear door and leave the building (depositing the body in the car sent by the fixer if you used non-lethal tactics, and collecting your reward at the nearest Drop Point immediately afterwards).

Note that a completely different approach is possible if you have a powerful (and, preferably, silenced) rifle. Climb up to the roof and look through the roof window. When Karubo moves close to the opening in the wall by the bar, you should have a clean shot to pick him off without being noticed.

JEOPARDY

54

■ **Unlock Condition** – Street Cred Tier 1 ■ **Type** – Search and Recover

1

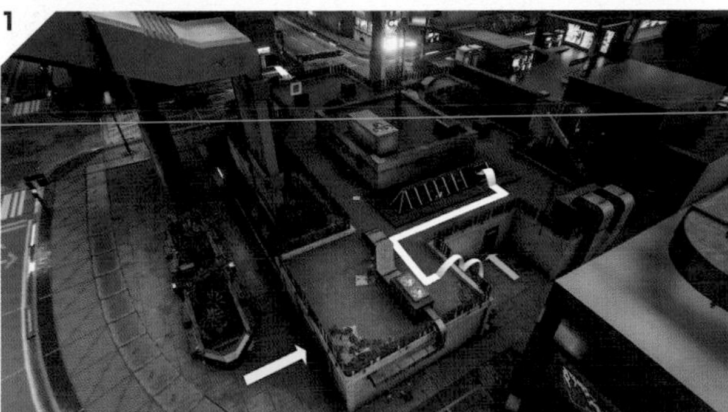

Head to La Cartina, a funeral house. Your objective is to reach a body in the morgue, so you first need to make your way to the basement. The door at the rear of the building and the garage gate can be opened by meeting Technical Ability and Body attribute requirements respectively. You could also go through an open roof window. All three options give you immediate access to a corridor guarded by a single sentry, where you can also find an elevator and stairs leading to the basement. You could alternatively go through the front entrance. Distract the Valentino in the lobby, then slip through the door he was guarding, marked "Private." Turn right, and you will find the stairs at the other end of the corridor.

2

The basement features two rooms, with one Valentino in each. Take them both down quietly before you retrieve the shard from Jim Greyer's body, which is laid out on the morgue table with the surgical lights. Retrace your steps outside and deposit the item at the nearest Drop Point to complete the assignment.

BRING ME THE HEAD OF GUSTAVO ORTA

55

■ **Unlock Condition** – Street Cred Tier 1 ■ **Type** – Gun for Hire

1

Head to the apartment complex where Gustavo Orta resides, in Vista Del Rey, and take the elevator to the 32nd floor.

2

There are a few ways to get to Orta:

- The easiest, only available to you if you have a Street Kid background, is to ring the intercom at the entrance, and casually walk upstairs.
- You can also force-open the front door, wait for the Valentino on the phone to finish his conversation, then sneak to the stairs directly on your right once the coast is clear.
- A third option involves opening the shutters in the hallway and leaping from the narrow ledge to the nearby balcony. Crouch-walk to the doorway then head inside and immediately turn right, moving alongside the wall with the windows. Disable the surveillance cameras and you can optionally neutralize the Valentino by the pool table before you proceed up the stairs, where a single sentry stands between you and Orta.
- If you have the double-jump ability, note that you can leap directly from the narrow ledge to the upper-floor balcony to reach Gustavo's office.

You are free to kill or incapacitate Orta – but you would be wise to first listen to his explanation. If you choose to believe him, he will leave Night City and you won't need to worry about his men on your way out. Opting for a non-lethal extraction entails a lot of extra work here – though you can go to all the trouble if you wish. The mission will be considered as complete when you collect your reward at the nearby Drop Point.

Valentinos

SR. LADRILLO'S PRIVATE COLLECTION

■ **Unlock Condition** – Street Cred Tier 2 ■ **Type** – Thievery

1

Make your way to Dicky Twister, a club at the corner of Congress and Pajaro Street. You are tasked to retrieve a shard with compromising materials, found on a desk upstairs.

- If you have a very high Body level, the easiest solution by far is to use the dumpster at the building's north corner to get to a terrace, where you can force-open a double door leading almost directly to the desk on which the shard is found. If not, there are still multiple options – though they will require a little more work:
- A door that can be force-opened on the north side.
- Another door with a Technical Ability attribute requirement on the east side.
- The front entrance – where a Technical Ability attribute requirement may enable you to pretend that you are there to fix a sound problem. Failing that, you can also simply pay for admittance.

2

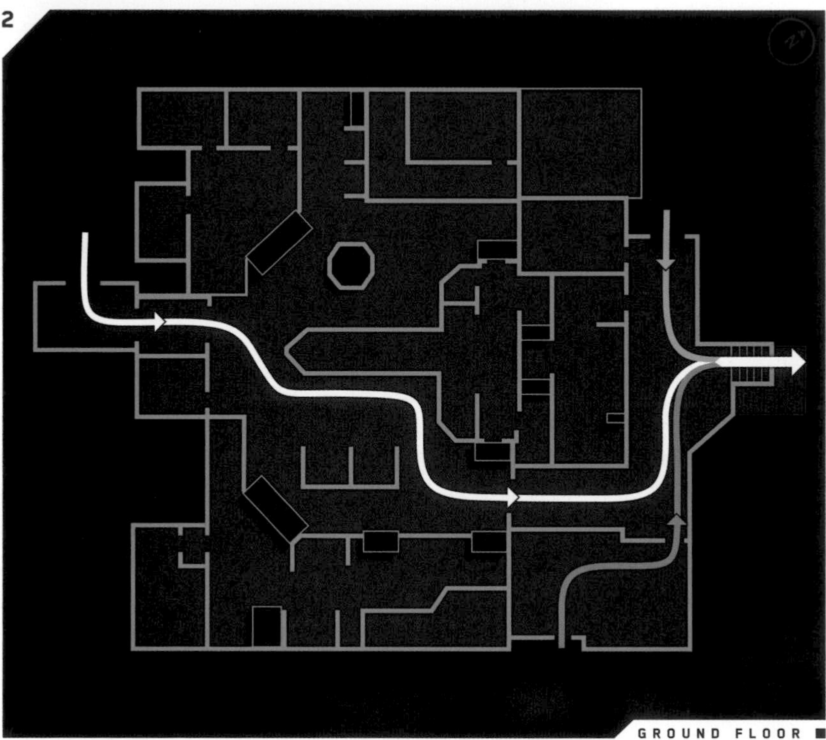

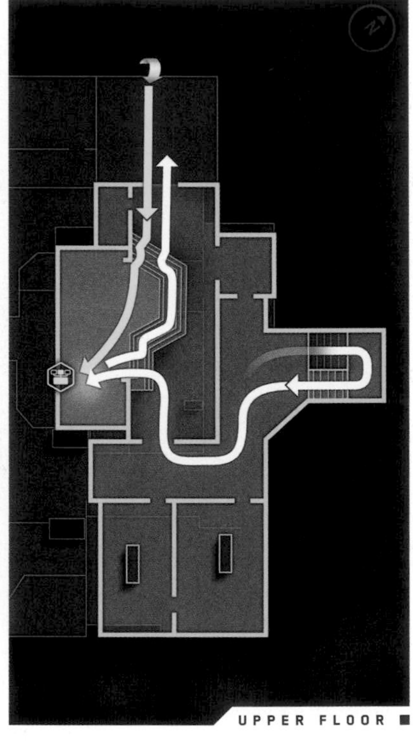

Once inside, your goal is to get to the upper floor, where the shard is found – as shown on this map. All suggested paths (except for the first, which goes directly to the upper floor) lead to the same hallway: directly if you used a door gated behind an attribute requirement, or after going through the double doors on the other side of the club if you arrive via the front entrance (distract the guard using the nearby speaker). The hallway features a single sentry who runs a short patrol route between the stairs and a pile of cardboard boxes. It should pose no real challenge to sneak past, though you can distract and neutralize her if you prefer – there's a vending machine positioned nearby. The surveillance cameras can prove a little more problematic: either quickhack them, or bypass them while they're at the opposite end of their rotation.

3

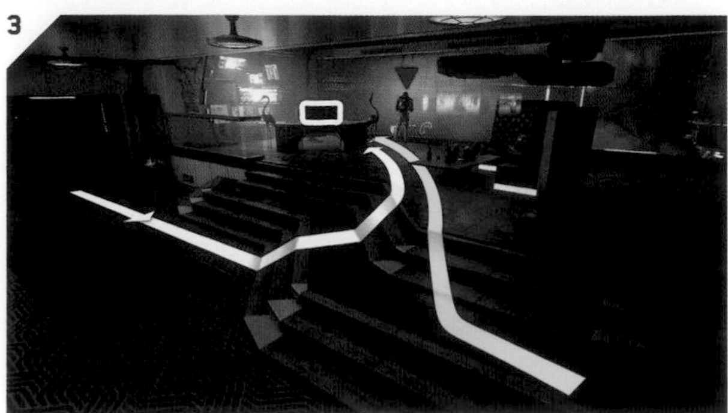

When you get upstairs from the hallway, the desk with the shard can be found behind the long glass panel directly in front of you. You can access it via the corridor to the left, where you will encounter a surveillance camera and a Valentino facing away from you. Neutralize the second camera and the final sentry patrolling near the desk, steal the data from the computer, then head through the double doors to the northwest to arrive on a balcony (your point of ingress if you entered via the first possible route). Jump down to street level and walk to the Drop Point to deliver the shard.

THE GLEN

LIFE'S WORK

57

■ **Unlock Condition** – Street Cred Tier 1 ■ **Type** – Search and Recover

1

This gig requires you to retrieve a car from an autoshop controlled by 6th Street thugs. You can force-open the second garage gate (marked "2") if you invested sufficient points in your Body attribute. But other entrances work just as well: the front door, the open garage gate, or the back door.

2

A few sixers patrol inside the autoshop. If you are about to be detected, note that you can drop into the vehicle maintenance pit to disappear. To reduce the difficulty of a stealth approach, we suggest you tag as many targets as you can from the doorstep, then crouch and head straight for the storage area, where you can safely hide behind the two shelving units that form a right angle. From here, you're in a great position to quietly take down the two guards on your path: one at the bottom of the stairs, the other at the top. You can then safely enter the office and upload the virus to the computer. With that accomplished, go back outside, get into Jake's car, and head to the location marked on your map. Drive with care to complete the optional objective of not damaging the vehicle, then talk to Jake at the destination to complete the mission.

FIFTH COLUMN

58

■ **Unlock Condition** – Street Cred Tier 1 ■ **Type** – Thievery

1

Your objective in this gig is to steal incriminating data from the office on the upper floor of the El Pinche Pollo restaurant. To reach it without causing a commotion, you have two options. The first one is to go through the door to the left of the bar, which is gated behind a Technical Ability attribute requirement. If you choose this path, you will first need to distract the nearby guard using the surveillance camera above him before you quietly neutralize him. The alternative solution is available only if you have completed SJ-10 ("Heroes" – see page 189). Should you meet this condition, ask the Valentino guarding the stairs if he's Jackie's friend, and he'll let you go right through.

2

Once in the office upstairs, you have two threats to worry about: a guard on the phone by the window, and a surveillance camera on the other side of the room. Make sure you disable both silently, then steal the data from the computer. You can then leave via the open window and collect your reward at the local Drop Point to complete the mission.

SEX ON WHEELS

Three in-game days after you complete the Life's Work gig, head to Rancho Coronado and you will receive a message triggering the minor Sex on Wheels side job, which has two possible scenarios:

- If you completed Life's Work by delivering the car to Jake, Jake will contact you and give you the coordinates of a "free" vehicle. All you have to do is go to the designated position, get in the driver seat and leave to add the Quadra Turbo-R to your collection.
- If, on the other hand, you failed to deliver the car to Jake during Life's Work, you will instead get a message from El Capitan informing you about suspicious activity in the same garage. Your objective here is also to steal the Quadra, though you will first need to deal with a number of thugs. Either eliminate them using brute force, or deploy quickhacks to get them out of the way and sneak to the vehicle.

PSYCHOFAN

■ **Unlock Condition** – Street Cred Tier 1 ■ **Type** – Thievery

1

Head to the marked residential building and take the elevator to the 17th floor. If you can pass a Technical Ability check, you can go direct to apartment 1702 and open the door. Otherwise, head up the stairs to the right, and drop down onto the apartment's balcony from the rooftop.

2

Kerry Eurodyne's guitar is hidden in a locked shrine room on the apartment's upper floor. The safest way to open the door is to scan the still of Kerry and Slayton on the nightstand and then enter the code (2065) at the door terminal. Once you have the guitar, leave the flat via the front door, take the elevator back to street level, then deliver the item to the nearby Drop Point to complete the mission.

You could also force-open the shrine room (if your Body stat is high enough) or hack the computer in the adjacent bedroom (if your Intelligence allows for it), but using the first method or failing the mini-game in the second would trigger the alarm, causing security to be sent after you. You could then opt to take the elevator to the basement to avoid some of the enemies.

EYE FOR AN EYE

■ **Unlock Condition** – Street Cred Tier 1 ■ **Type** – Gun for Hire

1

Your target, Tucker Albach, lives in a condo on the corner of Scoffield Sinkyone Street. Security agents guard the area, both inside and out. To get in, you can opt for the door at the rear of the building if you excel in Technical Ability, or instead head for the guarded front door on the south side. To eliminate the security agent, consider causing a distraction with the generator a few steps to the east; the nearby dumpster will enable you to hide his body after you take him down.

2

Once inside, security is only a real issue on the ground floor. As long as you crouch-walk cautiously, though, you should have plenty of time to sneak past prospective foes – or neutralize them if you prefer. Go through the plastic curtains to find the staircase and head straight up to the top floor. Quickhack the nearby refrigerator to cause a distraction and lure away the guard posted in front of Albach's door, and you can then sneak up on him once he falls for this staple trick. When you meet Albach in her office, a conversation begins. You can choose to kill her, or hear her out and accept her offer of a better payment if you let her live. Take the money from the safe in the corner if you wish, then retrace your steps downstairs and exit the building.

GOING UP OR DOWN?

61

■ **Unlock Condition** – Street Cred Tier 3 ■ **Type** – Thievery

1

Go the Glen's Megabuilding H01 and head to the underground hostile area via the marked door, which is to your right after you go up the entrance stairs. You have a single target to worry about in this area: El Gallo, who runs a clockwise patrol route in front of the elevator, making frequent stops to inspect devices.

2

You can deal with this situation in a number of ways. The most obvious is to kill or neutralize El Gallo; you can also feasibly sneak over to the toolbox inside the jammed elevator to obtain the scandium rods, then leave without disturbing him. If you wish, you can even speak to El Gallo and convince him to give you the rods, either by avoiding threatening him ("You have scandium rods, right?" ➡ "You won't get anything fixed in that state" ➡ "Nope, none at all"), or by choosing a dialogue line gated behind a demanding Technical Ability attribute requirement. However you choose to proceed, deliver the scandium rods to the Drop Point by the building's entrance to complete the mission.

WELLSPRINGS

ON A TIGHT LEASH

62

■ **Unlock Condition** – Street Cred Tier 1 ■ **Type** – Gun for Hire

1

Head to the bus depot near Megabuilding H02 in Wellsprings. Your target, Jose, can be found upstairs in the building's main room. There are many possible approaches, but two are particularly noteworthy:

- Enter the perimeter from the left (west) by climbing over the fence section at the end of the dead end, and use the ladder to reach the rooftop. Neutralize or sneak past the single guard there, and you can then go through the door gated behind a Technical Ability attribute requirement, then get in the room to the right and take Jose down from behind.
- An alternative solution is to go through the hole in the outer wall to the right (east) of the main entrance. Disable the surveillance camera and crouch-walk alongside the east wall, quietly eliminating the female thug on your way while she's looking away; you can then hide her in the nearby crate. Next, slip through the door and you will end up in a storage area, where two Valentinos are having a conversation. Sneak up on the closest one when they're done talking, then deal with the other while he's busy examining the shelving unit on the other side of the double doors. Finally, make your way up the stairs in the northeast corner of the hostile area, which takes you to Jose's room.

After you deal with Jose, who will be too busy having a phone conversation to notice you, feel free to read the messages on his computer if you want to fulfill the optional objective and understand who was behind the operation. You now need to leave the depot by retracing your steps – with or without Jose, depending on whether you have chosen to spare his life or kill him. The mission is completed after you call Padre and collect your reward at the nearest Drop Point.

THE LORD GIVETH AND TAKETH AWAY

 63

■ **Unlock Condition** – Street Cred Tier 2 ■ **Type** – Search and Recover

1

Go to the Valentinos autoshop at the western edge of Wellsprings. Your goal is to steal an SUV found inside. Among the many possible ways to reach it, there are three noteworthy approaches:

- If you have a high Body stat, climb over the fence on the west side of the property (making sure you disable the surveillance camera preemptively) and force-open the garage door: you will then see the SUV right in front of you.
- Hopping over the same fence, another approach is to use the dumpster or the ladder around the corner to get to the rooftop. Drop down through the hatch gated behind a Technical Ability attribute requirement, and a door will lead you to the same position, a few steps away from the vehicle.
- Alternatively, an effective option is to climb over the outer east wall. Wait until the female Valentino turns away from you after her phone call, then crouch-walk to her and quietly take her down; hide her body in the nearby car trunk. Next, drop down into the hole in the floor behind the car. Follow the underground passageway to reach the SUV.

2

All three suggested paths lead you to the same position. Crouch and hide behind the SUV. From here, you are in the perfect position to quietly take down the two Valentinos in the area, starting with the woman. Once both are down, you will be free to get into the SUV and deliver the vehicle to the Nomad at the marked position.

HOT MERCHANDISE

 64

■ **Unlock Condition** – Street Cred Tier 4 ■ **Type** – SOS: Merc Needed

1

Your first objective is to get inside the marked electronics store in Wellsprings. The front door is unsuited for stealth approaches, as the Animal behind the counter will spot you immediately. The good news is that, with sufficient Technical Ability or Body attributes, you can use a door (blue arrow) or a garage gate (yellow arrow) on the west side: both lead to a (guarded) storage area. Alternatively, you can open the shutters on the south side (white arrow): these give you access to an office, where you need to neutralize an Animal. From here, move carefully toward the counter in the main room to trigger a conversation between two thugs, then immediately return to the office. Wait until one of the thugs leaves the building: only then is it safe for you to head to the storage area, crouch-walking behind the counter to avoid being seen by the Animals in the main room. Neutralize or sneak past the guards in the storage area as you head to the stairs to the south.

2

You'll encounter a single hostile in the basement. Tag the Animal, then sneak up and neutralize him when he's looking away. You are then free to deal with Rebecca, the netrunner. As with many of these gigs, a simple execution and swift departure will suffice – but if you would prefer a non-lethal resolution, knock Rebecca out, then pick her up and carry her outside via the exit on the south side of the room. Place her in the trunk of the car sent by the fixer to complete the assignment.

ANIMALS

CITY CENTER

A LACK OF EMPATHY

65

■ **Unlock Condition** – Street Cred Tier 1 ■ **Type** – Agent Saboteur

1

The Empathy club can be found just north of Memorial Plaza. You can either go to the public entrance on the left (where you will need to deposit your weapons in a locker before you can gain entry), or to the service door on the right. Note that if you have the ability to double-jump and a high Body attribute, you can actually leap straight to a metal platform at the rear of the club and force-open a door leading directly to the mission's objective. In any case, should you manage to complete the optional objective of uploading the virus without raising the alarm, you will receive a bonus reward.

2

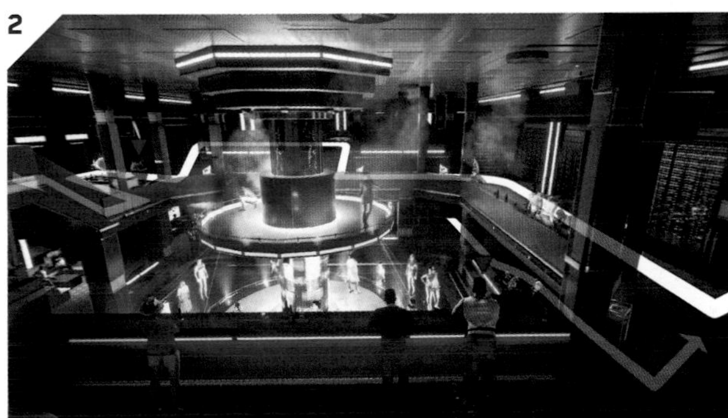

From the public entrance, an effective stealth approach is to go to the stairs in the far left (southwest) corner, then go around the upper floor counterclockwise and sneak past the guard by the fish hologram, as shown on the above picture. Head up the stairs to enter the server room (marked "Private"). If you used the service door, walk to the south end of the building, where you will find a staircase with a single (unaware) enemy. Sneak behind him and go up two floors to end up in front of the server room. Once inside, neutralize the Animal, infect the computer with the virus, then leave the club via the door leading directly outside. Retrieve your weapons from the front entrance before you make your way to a Drop Point to complete the assignment.

SERIAL SUICIDE

66

■ **Unlock Condition** – Street Cred Tier 2 ■ **Type** – Thievery

1

This gig has you steal data from a computer at the bottom of the security center inside Memorial Plaza's metro station. Avoiding conflict is recommended here as it will avoid the arrival of reinforcements.

There are a few ways in: a door on the west side that can only be opened via a Technical Ability attribute requirement (leading to a storage room), or the security room itself, which has two doors (the west one exposing you to less unwanted attention) and a grate on the roof. Wait until the two Militech guards finish talking, when one of them will leave; this is your cue to make your move and go through the glass door.

2

You then reach a corridor (where you can optionally save a civilian being beaten up by a guard): take a left here and you will arrive in the storage room (where both paths merge if you took the other door earlier). Dispatch the sole sentry, then go down the staircase at the back of the room, making sure you avoid or disable the surveillance camera at the top. Once in the basement, take out the man near the computer, disable the surveillance camera on your left, then steal the data and retrace your steps upstairs. You can leave the area by going through the storage room door – there is no Technical Ability attribute requirement from this side.

AN INCONVENIENT KILLER

■ **Unlock Condition** – Street Cred Tier 2 ■ **Type** – Gun for Hire

1

Your target, Jack Mausser, is located inside the 7th Hell Club, Downtown, directly west of Memorial Plaza. To get in via the front door, you will either need to pay the bouncer outside, or select a dialogue line exclusive to the Street Kid background. You could also opt to use the service elevator located a few steps to the east, though opening it will require you to meet a Technical Ability attribute requirement, and you would then have to deal with guards in the storage area before you reach the club's main room.

Note that there is a computer in the security room at the entrance that you can use to turn off all surveillance cameras in the club, but it's guarded by an enemy and gated behind a Technical Ability attribute requirement.

2

Mausser can be found in the VIP area upstairs, but the two direct approaches are guarded by Animals. If you are prudently opting to avoid direct conflict, enter the main room with the dance floor and use the stairs on your right (south side) to get to the upper floor. Turn around once at the top and go through the door just above the stairs, at which point you will enter a hostile area. The worker inside will soon move to inspect a device, so you can sneak past him to reach a ladder.

3

The ladder leads to a small walkway overlooking the stage. Go through the window on the other side and drop via the opening in the floor to land in a restroom adjacent to Mausser's office. He will speak to you immediately when you enter his room. At this point, you have three choices. The first option is to tell him that you are there to talk, and suggest that he should leave town. This actually works, and is the optimal outcome: you can then retrace your steps to leave the premises and claim the full reward at the Drop Point. The second option is to execute Mausser in cold blood, but there's clearly no benefit in doing so. The third approach is to knock him out and then attempt to extract him from the premises – which will obviously mean a lot of blood, sweat, and tears. Unless you're up for a challenge, it's better to just take the man at his word.

THE FROLICS OF COUNCILWOMAN COLE

68

■ **Unlock Condition** – Street Cred Tier 3 ■ **Type** – Thievery

1

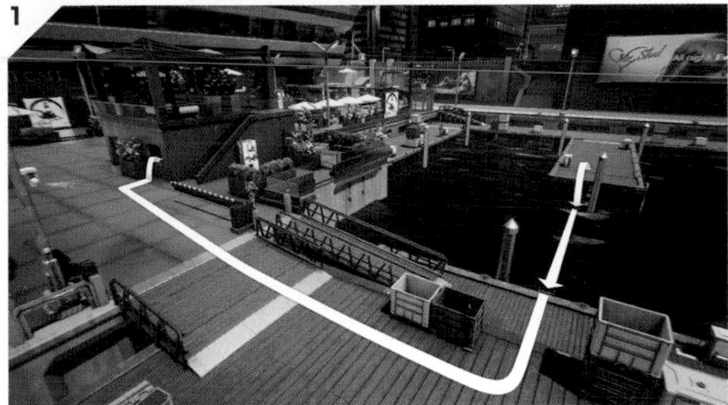

Your task is to infiltrate the marina on Gold Beach Street, with an optional objective requiring you to do so without being detected. The docks are under heavy surveillance, but the good news is that you can bypass the vast majority of threats by taking to the water. Swim toward the pier directly south of the docks and climb up the ladder. Sneak past the sentry who is busy making a call (making sure you disable the camera behind him), then swiftly hop through the security room's open window to avoid the gaze of the next guard in line. Download the incriminating recordings from the computer, then retrace your steps and jump back into the water. Use any of the ladders to get back up to the docks to the south and leave the hostile area. Collect your reward from the nearest Drop Point to complete the mission.

GUINEA PIGS

69

■ **Unlock Condition** – Street Cred Tier 3 ■ **Type** – Gun for Hire

1

The target for this gig is a corpo by the name of Joanne Koch, who can be found in the Biotechnica hotel. With the front entrance heavily guarded, you have a few other options to explore. Two of them require you to meet a Technical Ability attribute requirement – a door on the west side of the building, and a door on the left side of the lobby, both of which offer a clear path to the elevator. Alternatively, you can also use the path to the right of the bar while no one is looking. Immediately adopt a crouched stance and make your way through the corridor behind the bar. This leads to a security room: either sneak past the guards, or neutralize them if you want to explore the computer and deactivate all turrets and surveillance cameras in the hotel. The elevator is just behind the room's north door.

2

Once on the 19th floor, avoid or neutralize the guards in the hallway and make your way to penthouse 243. If your Technical Ability level allows for it, you can unlock the door. Otherwise, you will need to go up the staircase (behind the door to the left), and drop down into the apartment via a roof window a few steps to the west. Your method of entry has no real bearing, as Koch is too immersed in a braindance to hear you.

3

If your goal is to complete the mission with the fewest possible complications, it might be prudent to coldly shoot or strangle Koch, then retrace your steps and leave the hotel. If you instead choose to interrupt her session, Koch will ask for the opportunity to back up her data, but this is a ruse. Refuse, and she makes a break for it to call for help; accept, and she will walk to her computer and calmly use it to call security – which is why taking the initiative makes sense here. If you opt to deliver an unconscious Koch to the client, you will need to take her body to the roof, eliminate two sentries there, and then place her in an AV.

HUSTLES

NCPD Scanner Hustles are bite-sized scenarios that you can encounter throughout Night City and its immediate surroundings. Though usually smaller in scope than most gigs and jobs, they are far more numerous and can prove quite challenging.

This chapter contains detailed information for all hustles in the game, with sub-districts sorted in ascending order of difficulty. Note that it is meant to be used in conjunction with the Atlas (see page 364), where you will find annotated maps revealing the exact position of each hustle.

INTRODUCTION

NCPD Scanner Hustles are unique undertakings that can offer all sorts of challenges. You can expect stealthy infiltrations, open combat, exploration, and navigational puzzles – and many combinations thereof. Most of them (with the exception of one category: Hidden Gems) are represented with a specific icon on your in-game maps. You will also find *all* hustle locations marked on the maps included with this guide.

These activities are best described as one-off set-piece events that generally take place in a relatively small area – such as a back alley, or parking lot. As you complete your objective, you will usually have access to documents or clues that will shed light on the scenario in question. In fact, shards and computer messages you can find during hustles occasionally provide additional context, backstory, or even closure for some of the subplots you will encounter elsewhere in jobs and gigs.

The short stories told in hustles are often expressed in an indirect, sometimes cryptic, way: you are given a few pieces of the puzzle, but it is up to you to make sense of what transpired prior to your arrival. As the game itself does not offer a brief or mission summary for hustles, our coverage includes a concise story outline for every entry.

MINOR ACTIVITY TYPES

Icon	Type	Description
	Assault in Progress	A crime is underway (a settling of scores between gang members, for instance), so expect to find hostiles on the premises.
	Reported Crime	A person has been killed, with clues on their body leading you to a stash that you can loot – sometimes nearby, sometimes in a totally different district. If you select this type of hustle as your active quest in the journal after you find the clue, a waypoint will lead you to the stash.
	Suspected Organized Crime Activity	A group of thugs have taken control of a hideout. Your mission is to put them all out of commission, then loot their stash, designated by the mission's icon.
	Hidden Gem	Someone has been killed while trespassing or taking excessive risks. Activities in this category do not appear on the in-game map, but we do reveal their position in this guide.

Before you embark on a hunt for hustles, take note of the following tips:

- **Difficulty:** Each hustle has a (hidden) recommended experience level. The Danger Level you can see in the game is calculated by comparing your experience level with the one recommended for the assignment in question. If you try to complete it while under-leveled, you will likely find enemies will be far too strong for you. There are workarounds, of course – especially pure stealth approaches, or making use of high-tier equipment that levels the playing field. As a rule, though, you should generally take this rating under advisement and leave high-level hustles until later. All activities in this chapter are sorted by sub-districts, which themselves appear in increasing order of difficulty. In other words, the further you go in this chapter, the harder the hustles will be.

- **Location:** If you struggle to plot a course to the exact location of a hustle, don't forget to track it on the map: the game will automatically show you a recommended path to follow in the form of a dynamic line on your mini-map. With a little experience, you will also learn to recognize telltale signs that indicate the close proximity of a potential hustle even without advance notice. These cues can be subtle – a gang vehicle parked at the entrance to an alleyway, armed guards in an incongruous location, a chance sighting of what appears to be the scene of a recent accident or incident – but you will soon find that it will usually pay to pursue a hunch.

- **Hiding Bodies:** A stealthy approach is generally the best strategy for hustles, but make a habit of concealing the bodies of foes that you neutralize. You will rarely have proper hiding places at your disposal, but there is usually room to improvise. As a rule, try to conceal your victims carefully out of sight – even if that might mean taking the time to carry them outside the hostile area. Fail to do so, and someone might espy a prone notice of your handiwork, causing all remaining enemies to enter an increased state of vigilance.

- **Distractions:** Employing quickhacks to cause distractions can prove beneficial, but remember that enemies are often tightly spaced during hustles, which can lead to unexpected results. As a rule, try to begin by sneaking up on isolated targets and neutralizing them quietly. Once you have thinned the enemy ranks, distractions are used to deal with those in more challenging positions.

- **Key Items:** Most hustles require you to obtain a specific collectible for the assignment to be considered as complete – more often than not a shard with an archived conversation. The object that you need to loot it from (such as a body or container) always shines with a golden hue. In hustles where the collection of an item is the sole objective, tangling with enemies in the area is purely optional.

LITTLE CHINA

OPPOSITES ATTRACT

601

ATLAS P. 377

Objective: Eliminate all enemies and loot the chest container by the landing pad.

Story: Scavengers have an agreement with a Trauma Team crew. Once a week, the crew stops on one of the rooftops in Little China and sells implants and waste material from work.

Strategy: Get to the rooftop via the large yellow pipe and the ladder to the southeast of the hostile area. Advance cautiously toward the north, quietly taking down isolated sentries, especially the sniper on the rooftop, and disabling surveillance cameras. Go up the stairs and eliminate the scavengers in the landing pad area, then the final ones on the platform above. Note that you can also reach the hostile area via a ladder connected to the elevated freeway to the northeast: in this scenario, you would have to work your way downward.

ASSAULT IN PROGRESS

602

ATLAS P. 377

Objective: Loot the chest container behind the van.

Story: Maelstromers were sent by Gottfrid and Fredrik (encountered in the "Dirty Biz" gig) to steal servers from a warehouse packed with high-end electronics. They left no survivors.

Strategy: Wait until the first two Maelstromers go on separate patrols, then sneak up on them one by one.

WORLDLY POSSESSION

603

ATLAS P. 377

Objective: Search Griffin's body, then loot the bag at the columbarium.

Story: R.J. Griffin was a wealthy North Oak resident burdened with debts. Rather than paying them off, he decided to sell everything he had, hide the money, and start a new life. His principal creditor located him and killed him before he could change his identity.

Strategy: Griffin's body lies among trash bags, right by the river. You can actually avoid all guards on the platform above by jumping in the water, for example from the spot where a railing section is missing, a few steps to the west of the hostile area. Swim to the body and retrace your steps when you're done. You can now head to the North Oak Columbarium, where a marker will take you to the location of the urn. Sneak up on the two thugs from the northeast for easy silent takedowns before you loot the bag on the ground.

ASSAULT IN PROGRESS

604

ATLAS P. 377

Objective: Loot the chest container on the ground outside the shop.

Story: Blake, a loan shark who also appears in the "Shark in the Water" gig, has sent Animals to vandalize a shop owned by a man who refuses to pay his debts.

Strategy: Use the nearby vending machines to draw the closest Animal to your position for a silent takedown, then deal with the other two.

ASSAULT IN PROGRESS

606

ATLAS P. 377

Objective: Loot the container by the van.

Story: Maelstromer Mike Kowalsky identified a warehouse to raid. He and his crew had a device that would give them the ability to delay the alarm by 30 minutes if they respected a very specific procedure. They didn't, and the police arrived – leading to a shootout.

Strategy: If you don't want to get caught in the shootout, wait until it ends. You can then use the car and blue barrels as cover to sneak up on your foes.

PARANOIA

605

ATLAS P. 378

Objective: Loot the shard by Dirty Fred's body, then the stash.

Story: Dirty Fred is a homeless man receptive to conspiracy theories, particularly those of Garry the Prophet (encountered in the "Prophet's Song" side job).

Strategy: Sneak up on the two scavengers then collect the shard by Dirty Fred's body, under steps by the road. It contains directions to his stash, which is located on the ledge above a Turbo shop, in the north of Little China.

TYGERS BY THE TAIL

607

ATLAS P. 377

Objective: Defeat all enemies and loot the chest container on the bench.

Story: Vendors from a Little China market decided to stand up to the Tyger Claws extorting them, leading to a bloodbath.

Strategy: You can sneak up on at least a few Tyger Claws but a battle is almost inevitable.

ASSAULT IN PROGRESS

608

ATLAS P. 377

Objective: Loot Hunter Hyland's body.

Story: Ex-soldier Hunter Hyland, more recently the owner of a newspaper kiosk in Little China, was recently contacted by a journalist named Max Jones. Hyland's former corporate employer had him killed to prevent him from talking.

Strategy: Quickhack the vending machine to distract the first Tyger Claw and stealth-kill him. You can then approach the other two from behind.

ASSAULT IN PROGRESS

609

ATLAS P. 377

Objective: Loot the chest container by the computer.

Story: A group of Tyger Claws have secured a rooftop with an antenna, and are using a device to track police activity in the area.

Strategy: Climb the ladder to get to the rooftop and sneak up on the Tyger Claw patrolling on the west side. You can then deal with the ones near the computer – shooting the gas tank close to them is a viable option.

ASSAULT IN PROGRESS

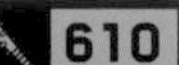

610

ATLAS P. 378

Objective: Loot the bag on the ground.

Story: Kyle, a medical center employee, had an arrangement with Maelstromers where he would "write off" medical supplies, then sell them to the gang. After realizing that his actions were arousing suspicion, Kyle decided to end his dealings with Maelstrom – who, in turn, decided to end Kyle.

Strategy: You can enter the hostile area from the south or north. Either way, move alongside the east wall and eliminate the Maelstromer when his patrol route leads him here. Deal with the one at the top of the steps next. You can then finish off the remaining two.

ASSAULT IN PROGRESS

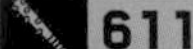

611

ATLAS P. 377

Objective: Loot the bag inside the ripperdoc clinic.

Story: Leif Wyke, a ripperdoc, had an arrangement to treat injured Tyger Claws. He recently decided to supplement this income with a new sideline: when he couldn't save a Tyger Claw, he would secretly extract their implants and sell them to scavengers. The Tyger Claws found out and murdered Leif.

Strategy: Sneak up on the sentries outside when they're away from each other, then deal with the two Tyger Claws inside the clinic.

UNDERAGED DEALERS

612

ATLAS P. 378

Objective: Loot the backpack on the basketball court.

Story: Gakuto and Choki were two brothers stealing drugs from the Tyger Claws and then dealing them on the gang's turf. The Tyger Claws sent a squad to slaughter them.

Strategy: Arriving from the north, sneak up on the Tyger Claw on the steps. From here, wait until the others are isolated before you strike.

DANGEROUS CURRENTS

613

ATLAS P. 377

Objective: Loot the chest container by the wrecked car, then the one on the seabed.

Story: Mike was supposed to retrieve a package smuggled in by boat. The cargo had to be dropped in a dangerous area with strong currents due to bad weather conditions.

Strategy: If you approach from the southeast, via the narrow passage between the wall and the ventilation block, you can creep up to eliminate the first thug. Hide the body, then repeat with the hostiles by the car. After looting the chest, head to the marked location on the shore: you will find another container to loot on the seabed.

HIDDEN GEM

614

ATLAS P. 377

Objective: Loot Shiva's body inside her den.

Story: Shiva was a netrunner who aspired to join the Voodoo Boys. The gang offered her a chance to prove her worth by hacking the servers at the Russian embassy (a reference to the "Fixer, Merc, Soldier, Spy" gig – see page 269). The test was beyond her skills, and she was killed by the embassy's firewall.

Strategy: There are two turrets between you and the garage Shiva operated from. If they're active, you can either destroy or quickhack them.

HIDDEN GEM

615

ATLAS P. 378

Objective: Loot the body inside the Dime a Duzz shop.

Story: A braindance dealer was found dead, presumably killed by Bryce Stone, the televangelist whose son's murder was recorded in a braindance.

HIDDEN GEM

616

ATLAS P. 377

Objective: Loot the body next to the wrecked car in the tunnel.

Story: Laszlo Nagy was a habitual drunk-driving thug who died in a car accident on his way back home.

HIDDEN GEM

617

ATLAS P. 377

Objective: Loot the body in the fenced area; disable the two drones to take no chances.

Story: Clippy was a techie trying to jailbreak some stolen prototype drones. He was killed by them after failing to deactivate their security locks.

HIDDEN GEM

618

ATLAS P. 377

Objective: Loot the body in the alleyway.

Story: Sergey Kirk was an NCPD officer investigating the Tyger Claws. He was killed during a fake meeting with a witness, which was actually set up by the Tyger Claws themselves.

HIDDEN GEM

619

ATLAS P. 377

Objective: Loot the shard inside the shipping container, which is gated behind a Body attribute requirement.

Story: A wholesaler delivered expired synthetic meat to two brothers, who had no idea they were being ripped off.

HIDDEN GEM

620

ATLAS P. 377

Objective: Loot the metal box inside the garage; you will need to meet a Body attribute requirement to open the gate.

Story: Tyger Claws had a stash where they stored weapons and mods under the supervision of one of their senior members, Suzu Ikeda.

HIDDEN GEM

621

ATLAS P. 378

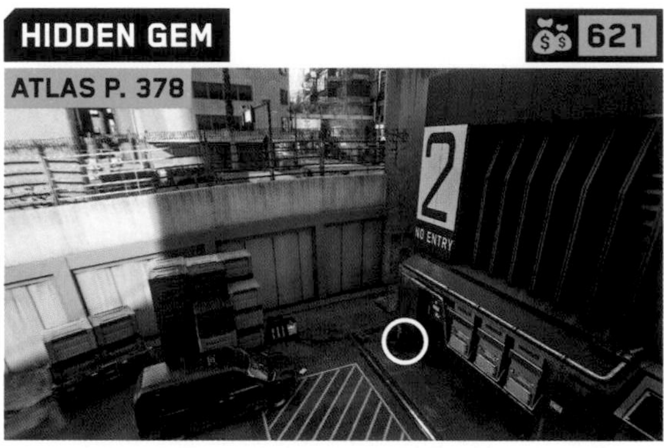

Objective: Loot the body in the storage area.

Story: Lady Space was an independent netrunner hired by the Tyger Claws to eliminate a key witness in a coma in a hospital. She managed to hack the patient's infusion pump to deliver an overwhelming dose of anesthetics, but was killed by the hospital's security system before she could escape.

HIDDEN GEM

622

ATLAS P. 384

Objective: Loot the container on the topmost platform.

Story: Some employees were sent to investigate a power drain at a wastewater plant. Not knowing that the system had been hacked by BeePass, a netrunner, they were killed by the reprogrammed defense systems.

Strategy: You can access the plant via ladders on either side, at river level. The area is guarded by a couple of turrets, which you can destroy or quickhack. Climb up the ladders by the large water tank to reach the uppermost platform.

ASSAULT IN PROGRESS

623

ATLAS P. 378

Objective: Loot the chest container inside the garage.

Story: While investigating an illegal implant market in Kabuki, an NCPD officer (Anna Hamill, encountered during the "Woman of La Mancha" gig) managed to get Evan Flakes, a local market vendor, to talk. When he did not receive the protection promised by the police, Flakes decided to run away, storing all his goods in a small garage, and planning to later move everything onto his sister's boat.

Strategy: Enter the premises via the small opening in the fence on the north side. From here, you can sneak up on all foes in sequence.

ASSAULT IN PROGRESS

624

ATLAS P. 378

Objective: Loot the container by the forklift.

Story: Tyger Claws raided a small warehouse to steal shipments of chemicals that they use to produce Glitter.

Strategy: Sneak up on the isolated Tyger Claws (one leaning against an old car, one close to a container), then draw the remaining few away from their allies for quiet takedowns.

PROTECT AND SERVE

 625

ATLAS P. 378

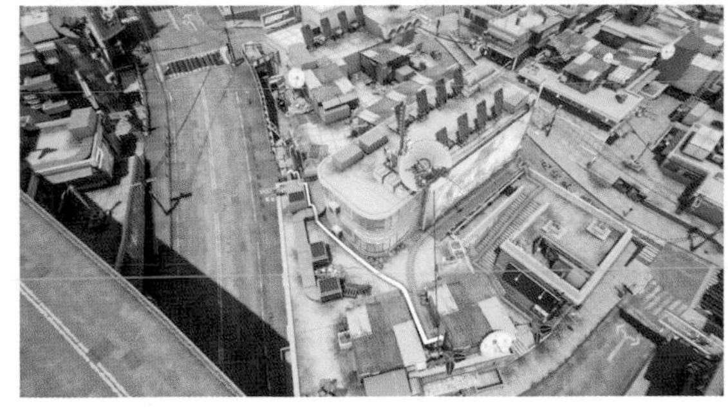

Objective: Read the message on the computer at the rooftop slums, then loot the police stash.

Story: Tyger Claws use rooftop slums to store Glitter. Their boss, Michiko Ogata, pays NCPD officer Eddie Pulaski to turn a blind eye to their business.

Strategy: Climb the steps to the south of the hostile area to reach the slums. You can neutralize all the isolated Tyger Claws with stealth takedowns, ignoring the two sitting on couches. Once you have examined the computer, head to the police stash to the northwest. You can climb up via the dumpster at the north corner of the building, or via the steps and the billboard on the other side.

ASSAULT IN PROGRESS

 626

ATLAS P. 378

Objective: Loot the bag on the crate between the containers; you can also optionally check the body of Tracy Owens, found inside the shipping container closest to Upmann.

Story: Peter Upmann is a human trafficker smuggling abductees into the city via shipping containers, then selling them to Tyger Claws who force them into prostitution.

Strategy: Note that this hustle is unavailable during the "Every Breath You Take" side job. Sneak up on the multiple sentries at the edge of the hostile area. You can then either crouch-walk to the bag on the crate and leave, or eliminate all remaining foes in any manner you please.

ASSAULT IN PROGRESS

 627

ATLAS P. 378

Objective: Loot the chest container on the uppermost rooftop.

Story: Tyger Claws based in rooftop slums are in charge of the distribution of Glitter, their most successful drug (a fact introduced by the "Heisenberg Principle" gig).

Strategy: Use the steps to the south to get to the rooftop slums. Proceed slowly and take out all foes silently, one at a time. When you encounter pairs, just wait – they will soon end their conversation and part ways.

ASSAULT IN PROGRESS

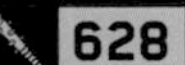 628

ATLAS P. 378

Objective: Loot the container by the garage door.

Story: Goons raided a medical center with a list of items to look for provided by Charles, the ripperdoc encountered during the "Last Login" gig. The operation was a success, but there were casualties. The gangsters are lying low with their van in an underground parking lot until the dust settles.

Strategy: Crouch-walk to the east side of the van and quietly eliminate the thug patrolling near the entrance when he moves close to the pillar. Next, deal with the one by the garage door when he moves to the east side of the van. This leaves only two targets to deal with.

ASSAULT IN PROGRESS

629

ATLAS P. 378

Objective: Loot Keiko's body, on the west side of the footbridge.

Story: Keiko was a Mox who wanted to abandon her life as a prostitute and escape her Tyger Claw pimp, Jotaro Shobo. With the help of her lover, Jake, she had her locator implant removed from her body – but the Tyger Claws found out and murdered them both.

Strategy: Get up to the footbridge via the stairs on the east side of the street. From here, it should be easy to sneak up on the three Tyger Claws.

NIGHT CITY
PRIMER
COMPLETION ROADMAP
MAIN JOBS
SIDE JOBS
CYBERPSYCHO SIGHTINGS
GIGS
HUSTLES
ATLAS
INVENTORY
REFERENCE & ANALYSIS
EXTRAS
INDEX

INTRODUCTION
LITTLE CHINA
KABUKI
NORTHSIDE
JAPANTOWN
CHARTER HILL
NORTH OAK
WEST WIND ESTATE
COASTVIEW
RANCHO CORONADO
ARROYO
BADLANDS
VISTA DEL REY
THE GLEN
WELLSPRINGS
DOWNTOWN
CORPORATE PLAZA

ASSAULT IN PROGRESS 630

ATLAS P. 378

Objective: Loot the chest container inside the hut closest to the water.

Story: Tyger Claws planned to celebrate the birthday of one of their members in the slums by the river.

Strategy: This area is under heavy surveillance, but you can sneak to the chest container without attacking any guard. Make your approach via the rooftops, starting from the north, and move cautiously. Check that the coast is clear before you drop down in front of the door, then quickly loot the chest container inside and leave the premises.

HIDDEN GEM 631

ATLAS P. 378

Objective: Loot Watcher's body.

Story: Watcher, also known as Dominic Avery, was a low-level netrunner. He was asked by the legendary B@d to jack in a program that would jailbreak the system in Kabuki. Watcher struggled with the system's defenses but, despite B@d's instructions, chose to persist instead of calling for a more experienced hacker. He died during the operation.

Strategy: The challenge here is purely navigational. To reach the top of the antenna structure, go up the steps to the northwest, then follow the path via the rooftops and the ladders – as illustrated in the accompanying picture.

HIDDEN GEM 632

ATLAS P. 378

Unlock Condition: Complete 623

Objective: Loot the body in the shelter under the bridge.

Story: Some young Tyger Claws smuggling netrunner equipment were caught red-handed by NCPD forces.

HIDDEN GEM 633

ATLAS P. 378

Objective: Loot the body on a couch.

Story: Two brothers purchased synthetic meat to resell it. The shipment was expired so the brothers could not pay the wholesaler, who had them killed.

HIDDEN GEM 634

ATLAS P. 378

Objective: Loot the body in a homeless camp under the highway.

Story: Jerry Young was a dealer who used children to sell drugs. He was killed by one of them who challenged his authority.

HIDDEN GEM  635

ATLAS P. 378

Objective: Loot the body in a shack on a roof.

Story: Jaida Archer was a black braindance editor who wanted to record the agony of a specific individual of a muscular nature. The man in question had connections and Archer ended up dead before she knew it.

HIDDEN GEM 636

ATLAS P. 378

Objective: Loot the body on the footbridge.

Story: David Glenn was a wannabe rockerboy who harassed the wrong waitress in a karaoke bar. She had powerful connections who killed Glenn after he threatened her.

HIDDEN GEM 637

ATLAS P. 378

Objective: Loot the safe hidden between air conditioning units.

Story: Tyger Claws had a stash where they regularly left cash to bribe local NCPD officers.

HIDDEN GEM 638

ATLAS P. 378

Objective: Loot the body at the foot of scaffolding, then climb up to the suitcase near the top of the structure.

Story: Lynn Salazar was a journalist who published an article on a poisoning scandal by a Biotechnica employee. She was found dead soon thereafter.

HIDDEN GEM  639

ATLAS P. 378

Unlock Condition: Complete the "Woman of la Mancha" gig (see page 265)

Objective: Loot the body in the dumpster behind a food booth on the topmost floor of Kabuki Market, close to the elevator.

Story: Ken Maki was a Tyger Claw sent to extort protection money from a strong shop owner. The encounter did not go well for the gang members.

HIDDEN GEM 640

ATLAS P. 378

Unlock Condition: Complete the "Woman of la Mancha" gig (see page 265), making sure you learn about Anna Hamill's location by paying or threatening Imad, then wait 48 in-game hours

Objective: Loot the body close to Kabuki Market's drop point.

Story: Anna Hamill (assuming you let her live during the "Woman of la Mancha" gig, but didn't convince her to leave Night City) went after the officers who tried to have her killed. She managed to eliminate Bill Adams.

HIDDEN GEM  641

ATLAS P. 378

Objective: Loot Philip's body.

Story: Philip was a gambler who had a nigh-perfect evening at the Ho-Oh casino. After winning a substantial sum of money and a cat – a prize of incredible value in a world where most animals are extinct – he got drunk to celebrate. Philip's hot streak abruptly ended during his drive home.

Strategy: Jump in the water and look for Philip's body on the bed of the canal.

HIDDEN GEM 642

ATLAS P. 378

Objective: Loot Oleg Orlov's body.

Story: Oleg Orlov was a man who bought a drone to protect his savings. When the drone started malfunctioning, Oleg contacted Hal Cantos (encountered during the "Occupational Hazard" gig), not knowing that Hal wasn't qualified for such a job. The "repaired" drone later experienced a system failure and killed Oleg.

Strategy: The challenge here is to reach the rooftop where Orlov's home is found. There's a fire escape staircase to the south: use this to climb to the topmost floor, go through the hut a few steps to the west, then follow the long balcony toward the north. You have a single drone to neutralize here. To enter the house, either open the fence gate (if you meet the Technical Ability attribute requirement), or drop through a hole in the roof.

VICE CONTROL

643

ATLAS P. 372

Objective: Defeat all enemies and loot the designated chest container near the small pagoda structure.

Story: The police want to get rid of homeless people who have established an unauthorized squat, but have failed to secure the mayor's approval for the eviction. They have instead commissioned scavengers to deal with the squatters.

Strategy: Use the southwest entrance to enter the slums. By walking alongside the right-hand wall, you can make a stealthy approach and gradually take down all scavengers in the area. Don't forget to deal with the snipers on the scaffolding and the men at both entrances to complete the assignment.

JUST SAY NO

644

ATLAS P. 372

Unlock Condition: Complete the "Vice Control" hustle

Objective: Eliminate all Maelstromers and loot the designated chest container at the southeast end of the area.

Story: Maelstromers have seized a large open-air factory and turned it into a drug manufacturing facility. They are using it to produce low-end pain editors and cyberpsychosis inhibitors that help their members cope with the aggressive augmentation of their bodies.

Strategy: If you approach from the northwest you can cautiously move southeastward, quietly eliminating your enemies one by one and disabling the surveillance camera. Note that you will also run into androids, which are immune to stealth takedowns – but not to quickhacks. If you are detected, a netrunner will try to hack you. He is posted at the top of the large spherical tank just east of the main entrance. If you struggle to find the last few foes in the area, check the outline of your mini-map and note that a few snipers are stationed on the steps around the spherical tanks.

ASSAULT IN PROGRESS

645

ATLAS P. 377

Objective: Loot Martin Lorenz's body.

Story: Martin Lorenz was a technician working in a Megabuilding. Every time he saw Tyger Claws poised to raid the premises, he warned the residents in advance so that they could lock themselves up inside. When the Tyger Claws found out, they murdered Martin.

Strategy: Approaching from either the south or the ladder on the west side, you can avoid the Tyger Claws in the lower area with the containers, leaving you with only a couple of foes to neutralize.

NO LICENCE, NO PROBLEM

646

ATLAS P. 373

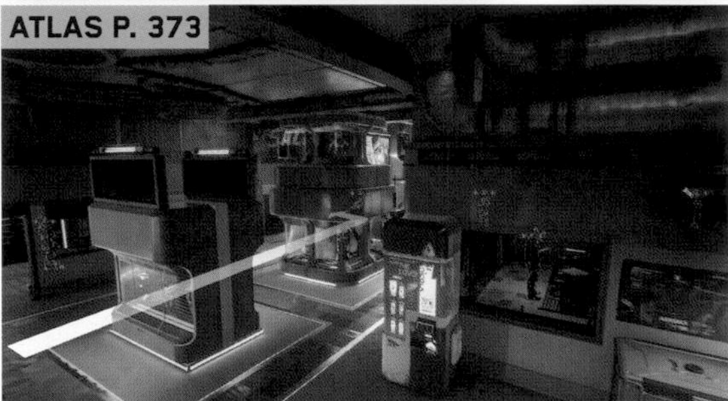

Unlock Condition: Complete the "Hippocratic Oath" gig (see page 270) and wait 24 in-game hours.

Objective: Eliminate all enemies and loot the bag in the surgery room.

Story: After Lucy Thackery was rescued, Maelstromers looked for a new ripperdoc. They recruited a man by the name of Kaiser, not knowing that he was unqualified for the job. As a result, multiple surgeries went wrong, leaving a number of Maelstromers with life-changing injuries – or worse.

Strategy: It's a good idea to complete this hustle directly after the gig that unlocks it. Move a few blocks away, skip time, then return to the clinic. You will be familiar with the layout and can swiftly eliminate all enemies.

ASSAULT IN PROGRESS

647

ATLAS P. 373

Objective: Loot the yellow equipment case near the back of the van.

Story: Maelstromers have found high-end netrunner gear hidden in an abandoned train. They have set up a deal with the Voodoo Boys to exchange the gear in return for information.

Strategy: Arriving from the north, lurk behind the freight cars and wait for opportunities to sneak up on isolated targets and hide their bodies. Proceed cautiously, using distractions if required, and you can take down the whole group without raising the alarm.

ASSAULT IN PROGRESS

648

ATLAS P. 373

Objective: Loot Alvin's body.

Story: Alvin Simmons, a Maelstromer, embarked on a solo raid against the Tyger Claws, killing many of them. His actions were not sanctioned by his bosses, so they decided to offer him up to the Tyger Claws to avoid a full-blown gang war.

Strategy: Make your approach from the south to take out the lone sentry first, by the car. The ones that are close to each other can be a little more annoying to sneak up on. Keep your weapon at the ready in case you are spotted.

DREDGED UP

649

ATLAS P. 373

Objective: Loot the briefcase in the garage area, then the chest container next to Kenton's body in the sewers. Note that this hustle becomes available only after you've complete the Prologue.

Story: Kenton was a Maelstromer overseeing the storage of suppressants in garages. After B@D, a netrunner hired by Wraiths, found out about these garages, the rival gang launched a surprise attack and killed all Maelstromers. Kenton was the last to fall as he attempted to hide in the nearby sewers.

Strategy: After looting the briefcase in the garage area, use the staircase a short distance to the south to reach the storm drain, where you will find Kenton's body and the stash in front of a door.

NEEDLE IN A HAYSTACK

650

ATLAS P. 372

Objective: Loot Soga's body, then search the suitcase in the container to the west.

Story: Soga was a Tyger Claw sent to mark a container stored in Northside. The scavengers who ambushed him were over-eager and killed the Tyger Claw too quickly, leaving them unable to identify the container in question.

Strategy: Stealth-kill the scavenger trying to open a shipping container, then deal with the other two by Soga's body. After looting the body, open the designated shipping container to reach the suitcase inside.

ASSAULT IN PROGRESS

651

ATLAS P. 372

Objective: Loot the chest container near the van.

Story: Maelstromers have ordered a special drug for a party at the Totentanz club (a location visited during the "Second Conflict" side job).

Strategy: Arriving from the north, sneak up on the sentry patrolling back and forth in the alley. You can then try to eliminate all remaining targets near the van with a grenade.

ASSAULT IN PROGRESS

652

ATLAS P. 373

Objective: Loot the body of the NCPD officer.

Story: Reggie, a principled NCPD officer, was betrayed by his boss, commissioner Fawlter, and deliberately sent into a Maelstrom ambush.

Strategy: Approaching from the east, you can crouch-walk straight to the police car, loot the body of the officer, and retrace your steps. You will be seen but you can sprint away immediately.

ASSAULT IN PROGRESS

653

ATLAS P. 378

Objective: Loot the bag on the crate close to the Maelstromers.

Story: A group of Maelstromers have set up a deal to purchase cars from the Aldecaldos to smuggle goods through the Badlands. The last time they hired a Nomad to do this for them, he disappeared with their goods – a reference to the "Dancing on a Minefield" gig. It transpires that this new arrangement was a ruse: when the Aldecaldos arrived in the parking lot, the Maelstromers slaughtered them to exact revenge.

Strategy: Stealth is not an easy option here. The Maelstromers are in a tight group, so a grenade can cause significant damage.

ASSAULT IN PROGRESS

654

ATLAS P. 374

Objective: Loot the bag close to the second vehicle.

Story: Esteban Ramirez, a homeless veteran of the corporate wars, contacted journalist Max Jones to talk about his mistreatment by his former employers. The comms line he used was not encrypted, however, and Militech sent troops to eliminate him.

Strategy: Make your approach from the east and you can sneak straight to the bag, timing your moves to avoid nearby sentries, then retrace your steps.

ASSAULT IN PROGRESS

655

ATLAS P. 372

Objective: Loot the bag by the picnic table.

Story: A truck driver working for a medical manufacturer had a sideline of providing Maelstromers with supplies for their ripperdoc clinics. After he invoked their ire by hiking his prices on multiple occasions, the thugs decided to make one last large order – and then kill the driver.

Strategy: Sneak up on the two Maelstromers by the van when they move away from each other, then deal with the remaining two at the picnic table.

ONE THING LED TO ANOTHER

656

ATLAS P. 373

Objective: Examine the computer under the elevated freeway, then loot the chest container at the foot of the antenna.

Story: Tyger Claws are in the process of installing high-end technology allowing for radio-hacking of police frequencies.

Strategy: The Tyger Claws are fairly easy to sneak up on, but you also have to deal with a drone. Quickhacks work best here, though brute force is also an option. After reading the messages on the computer, head to the top of the nearby silo where, after dealing with one more Tyger Claw on the way, you will find the container at the foot of the antenna.

DON'T FORGET THE PARKING BRAKE!

657

ATLAS P. 370

Objective: Loot the shard behind the computer, under a blue sunshade; then investigate the van lying at the bottom of the nearby storage pool.

Story: Scavengers who had stolen a van full of merchandise forgot to use the parking brake.

Strategy: Sneak up on the lone scavengers first, then deal with the ones sitting around a table.

ASSAULT IN PROGRESS

658

ATLAS P. 372

Objective: Loot the suitcase at the rear of the hostile area.

Story: Mercenaries were sent to steal a suitcase with corporate documents, including a valuable patent, but the operation didn't go smoothly. They are expecting back-up to extract one of their men, Nils, who was shot during the operation.

Strategy: Use the dumpsters and crates to sneak up on the mercenaries one by one.

HIDDEN GEM

659

ATLAS P. 373

Objective: Loot the chest container by the far wall.

Story: A warehouse containing valuable components is defended by Militech security equipment.

Strategy: You have to deal with drones and a turret here. An advanced netrunner can pacify them all in mere seconds. If you resort to brute force, make use of the gas tanks in the warehouse to easily annihilate the drones.

HIDDEN GEM

660

ATLAS P. 373

Objective: Loot Drudge's body.

Story: Drudge was a Wraith techie who was looking for a powerful compressor in Northside, but died during the attempted theft.

Strategy: The challenge here is to reach the body on the rooftop. To do so, follow the path shown in the accompanying image, jumping from one container to the next.

HIDDEN GEM 661

ATLAS P. 378

Objective: Loot Izaiah's body.

Story: Izaiah was a homeless man scavenging parts in Northside. When he found an abandoned Max Tac Turret, he decided that he would restore it to make a profit. Unfortunately, he received incomplete instructions on how to bypass the turret's safeguards, and was killed when it was activated.

Strategy: All you need to do here is either destroy or quickhack the turret before you loot Izaiah's body.

HIDDEN GEM 662

ATLAS P. 372

Objective: Loot Hax's body.

Story: Hax was a netrunner who tried to get to Fredrik and Gottfrid (two Maelstromers encountered during the "Dirty Biz" gig) while in cyberspace. He failed to break their defenses and died in his den.

Strategy: The area is guarded by two turrets. Destroy or quickhack them if they're active, then open the garage door to find Hax.

HIDDEN GEM 663

ATLAS P. 378

Objective: Loot the body of the Maelstromer on the elevated platform.

Story: Maelstromers got their hands on a shipment of Malorian drones. One of the gang members decided to try starting them up before anyone had taken the time to jailbreak them. Their deaths were, at very least, mercifully swift.

Strategy: A netrunner can make short work of the drones here. Otherwise, you will need to destroy them. Once they're down, go up the stairs on the left to reach the body on the elevated platform.

HIDDEN GEM 664

ATLAS P. 372

Objective: Loot the body in the dead end, not far from Megabuilding H11.

Story: Jack Fisher, an NCPD officer selling confidential information to Maelstromwas killed while he was accepting one final bribe.

HIDDEN GEM 665

ATLAS P. 372

Objective: Loot the body at the top of the spherical tank.

Story: Vessel was a netrunner who jacked in to the network of Megabuilding H12 looking for the data of a man in the building growing poppies for drug-dealing purposes. He was caught by the system's defenses and died on the spot.

HIDDEN GEM 666

ATLAS P. 373

Objective: Loot the body atop containers in the storage area.

Story: A Maelstromer in the process of tagging graffiti of the gang on a building fell and died.

HIDDEN GEM

667

ATLAS P. 373

Objective: Read the email on the laptop inside the truck container with a door gated behind a minor Body attribute requirement.

Story: Thugs stole goods from a DTR warehouse and left a van behind when they swapped vehicles during their escape.

HIDDEN GEM

668

ATLAS P. 372

Objective: Loot the body at the bottom of the steps.

Story: Oscar Walsh, the son of the owner of a company, tried to foment a coup against his own father. Unwilling to face the consequences of his actions after the coup failed, he decided to commit suicide.

HIDDEN GEM

669

ATLAS P. 370

Objective: Loot the body outside the Barely Illegal building.

Story: Thugs running a brothel with sex slaves were tracked by the father of one of the abducted girls detained there.

HIDDEN GEM

670

ATLAS P. 369

Objective: Loot the body next to the car.

Story: Nathan Goodwin was a solo working for a corporation. He was killed while recording a meeting between a corrupt politician and Maelstromers. The meeting didn't go well – the politician was rescued by Trauma Team, while Goodwin's insurance had recently been cancelled.

HIDDEN GEM

671

ATLAS P. 373

Objective: Loot the body next to the crashed AV.

Story: Tobias Hart was a corporate employee trying to get contracted by Arasaka. His AV was hacked as he was on his way to a meeting with Arasaka. He was killed shortly after the emergency landing.

HIDDEN GEM

672

ATLAS P. 378

Objective: Loot the body next to the burning car.

Story: Thugs delivering Arasaka gear from Northside to Pacifica were chased by a truck and died while trying to escape.

HIDDEN GEM

673

ATLAS P. 379

Objective: Loot the open shipping container in the underpass.

Story: Billy Bell, a homeless man, found a cyberdeck in a junkyard and died while trying to explore cyberspace.

ASSAULT IN PROGRESS

674

ATLAS P. 385

Objective: Loot the suitcase on the ground, next to the van.

Story: A store owner refused to pay Tyger Claws for their protection, so the gang arranged a demonstration of *exactly* the kind of misfortune that their *eminently affordable* services would have insured against.

Strategy: Coming from the south, you can sneak up on the Tyger Claws with relative ease if you cause distractions with the nearby vending machines.

ASSAULT IN PROGRESS

675

ATLAS P. 385

Objective: Loot the bag on the ground, between the two garage ramps.

Story: Tyger Claws intercepted a truck transporting top-shelf braindance equipment, killing the driver in the process.

Strategy: Use the scaffolding on the right side of the front entrance to jump over the wall. Sneak up on the Tyger Claw guarding the gate, then neutralize the others when they're similarly isolated.

LOST AND FOUND

676

ATLAS P. 384

Objective: Loot the body in the back alley, then attend to the stash.

Story: Jacob Ostapchuk was a drug dealer who was killed by junkies.

Strategy: Approaching from the west, you can silently neutralize all scavengers in the alley by proceeding counterclockwise. After you loot Jacob's body, head to the designated drug lab, hidden in a garage in the northeast of Japantown. Multiple Tyger Claws guard this small area, so stealth is unrealistic. You can, however, open hostilities with a bang by detonating the gas tank close to your enemies, but you will still have to face a few survivors after the explosion. Once the coast is clear, search the stash – particularly the locker in the corner.

ASSAULT IN PROGRESS

677

ATLAS P. 384

Objective: Loot the bag by Anderson's body.

Story: Laurie Anderson was a regular customer at the Ho-Oh casino (visited during the "Monster Hunt" gig). One day, she installed illegal software on a slot machine to cheat and win the grand prize, a feat that initially went unnoticed... but it didn't take the Tyger Claws very long to catch on.

Strategy: Use the vending machines to isolate each Tyger Claw in turn and neutralize them easily. There's even a dumpster nearby to hide their bodies.

ANOTHER CIRCLE OF HELL

678

ATLAS P. 384

Objective: Loot Dante's body, then the chest container in the stash.

Story: A netrunner by the name of Dante was hired to steal compromising data from the cousin of Weldon Holt, a politician campaigning to become the mayor of Night City. Dante was killed by a defense program during the botched operation.

Strategy: Use the scaffolding to the south to reach the building's rooftop, and from there jump to the ledge leading to the yellow structure where the body rests (beware the drone hiding there). After looting it, head to the man's den, a garage a short distance to the north, where you will find equipment to acquire and a computer to examine.

ASSAULT IN PROGRESS — 679

ATLAS P. 384

Objective: Loot Max Smith's body.

Story: Max Smith was an NCPD officer sent to Redwood Street to lower the crime rate in the area. Tyger Claws decided to make an example of him to remind the police that this was *their* turf.

Strategy: You face multiple Tyger Claws here. Hide behind a nearby van and then, taking the patrol route of the one in the middle into account, take all targets down when they are isolated.

ASSAULT IN PROGRESS —  680

ATLAS P. 384

Objective: Loot the body in the car's trunk.

Story: Toru Inagaki, a Tyger Claw, was knocked out by a mercenary and trapped in the trunk of a car. He managed to contact his fellow gang members from there. The Tyger Claws came to his rescue, leading to a deadly chase in which both the driver and Inagaki died.

Strategy: Arriving from the alley to the northwest, disable the surveillance camera and distract the nearest guard with a vending machine. Once he's down, cause another distraction to make the Tyger Claw sitting on the steps look away, then quickly neutralize the one by the trunk. You can then either loot the body in the trunk or eliminate the third enemy.

ASSAULT IN PROGRESS —  681

ATLAS P. 384

Objective: Loot the bag on the bar counter.

Story: Maelstromers recently visited this bar, got drunk, and ended up having a party. The owner was terrified, so neglected to call the Tyger Claws who run the area. The Claws found out about the incident and decided to punish the bartender.

Strategy: Approaching from the east, crouch-walk alongside the wall to your right and you can sneak up on all Tyger Claws one by one.

ASSAULT IN PROGRESS —  682

ATLAS P. 384

Objective: Loot the bag near the body of O'Brien.

Story: A Tyger Claw convict who snitched to get his sentence reduced is under the protection of a man called O'Brien. The Tyger Claws have found out about O'Brien and have sent men to kill him, so that they can later get to the prisoner who betrayed them.

Strategy: Approaching from the northwest, use the market stalls to sneak up on the sentry isolated from the others. If you then take out the one close to the motorbike, this leaves you with only two Tyger Claws to deal with.

ASSAULT IN PROGRESS — 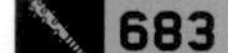 683

ATLAS P. 378

Objective: Loot the backpack on the ground near the thugs.

Story: Gavin Kaczynski, son of a rich corpo, was attracted to the Japantown dealer who used to sell him his drugs. After she refused his advances, he sent his corporate security to beat her to death.

Strategy: Coming from the southeast, you can eliminate the closest guard stealthily, then deal with the others.

MODERN LABOR MARKET —  684

ATLAS P. 384

Objective: Eliminate all enemies and loot the box on the ground, by the couches.

Story: Tyger Claws are compelling the poor and vulnerable to perform forced labor, selling their services to corporations looking for a cheap and disposable workforce.

Strategy: Approaching from the south, you can use stealth tactics to neutralize all enemies in the market area. With that accomplished, go around the staircase structure counterclockwise to sneak up on the three men near the couches. Finally, go upstairs to deal with the remaining thugs on the upper floor.

HIDDEN GEM 685

ATLAS P. 384

Objective: Loot the bag by Matt Maksymowiz's body.

Story: Matt Maksymowiz was an inveterate gambler who was constantly indebted and late paying his rent. His landlord, Natalie Brooks, locked him out of his apartment and threw his belongings down a garbage chute. Matt slipped while trying to retrieve his goods, and didn't survive the fall.

Strategy: To begin this traversal puzzle, drop down on the metal awning to reach a ladder. From here, go down counterclockwise, using the platforms and ledges to reach the bottom of the shaft.

HIDDEN GEM 686

ATLAS P. 379

Objective: Loot the body on a landing pad.

Story: A high-level corpo from Orbital Air staged his own abduction, leaving his bodyguards dead, to hide the fact he was recruited by a competitor.

HIDDEN GEM 687

ATLAS P. 378

Objective: Loot the body on the shore.

Story: Nina Gutierrez was pushed from the Japantown bridge by her husband (a reference to the "Until Death Do Us Part" gig.

HIDDEN GEM 688

ATLAS P. 379

Objective: Loot the body in the side alley.

Story: Bart Longer was a corporate engineer who tried to switch companies. Instead of exfiltrating him with an AV, his prospective employer abandoned him at the last minute, causing him to be eliminated by his corporation's security.

HIDDEN GEM 689

ATLAS P. 378

Objective: Loot the body on the antenna relay above the street.

Story: Z3D was a netrunner who disguised himself as a technician as he connected to the Tyger Claws' network from a rooftop. His goal was to retrieve Kiroshi merchandise hidden by his fellow netrunner 8ug8ear (encountered during the "Getting Warmer..." gig). Z3D was caught red-handed and killed on the spot.

HIDDEN GEM 690

ATLAS P. 384

Objective: Loot the body inside the shack on the rooftop, above Jig Jig Street's entrance.

Story: Norris Stones was a thug filming sex workers from Jig Jig Street and selling the recordings on the black market. He was told to stop by the Mox, then killed with a baseball bat after refusing to comply.

HIDDEN GEM

691

ATLAS P. 385

Objective: Loot the safe above the gym.

Story: Animals used a stash to store boosters. Some of them did not respect the rules and took too much, causing them to overdose or go berserk.

HIDDEN GEM

692

ATLAS P. 384

Objective: Loot the body on the walkway, close to the tree.

Story: Petr Soboti was a renowned drug dealer. He was killed for his greed by an unknown individual who pretended to have a new product to put on the streets.

HIDDEN GEM

693

ATLAS P. 384

Objective: Loot the bag next to the chair.

Story: Philippo Bergamo was a journalist who tried to blackmail a corrupt NCPD officer. He was killed shortly after making his demands.

HIDDEN GEM

694

ATLAS P. 384

Objective: Loot the body in the van, a short walk from the Crescent & Broad fast travel position.

Story: Max Corvin was a crook who tried to sell a van full of rubber chickens to a company selling organic meat.

HIDDEN GEM

695

ATLAS P. 384

Objective: Loot the body in the alleyway.

Story: Samuel Singleton was an ambitious employee climbing the ranks of corporations. He was killed for his excessive pride by a mysterious individual.

HIDDEN GEM

696

ATLAS P. 378

Objective: Loot Oriana's body.

Story: Oriana was a mercenary working for Wakako. During a mission where she was commissioned to steal a briefcase, she was terminally wounded and died while trying to hide from her pursuers.

Strategy: Oriana's body is found on a fire escape staircase. You can reach it by climbing up via the adjacent dumpster and air conditioning unit.

ASSAULT IN PROGRESS

 697

ATLAS P. 389

Objective: Loot the backpack on a crate, next to a computer.

Story: Factory workers who were not paid their full salary decided to organize a strike. Their boss hired Militech to put an end to the action. The Militech team failed to convince the irate laborers to return to work, and were granted authorization to simply shoot them instead.

Strategy: This site is heavily guarded. If you enter the perimeter from the south through the missing fence section, you can move alongside the warehouse's east wall, where you only need to avoid (or quickhack) a guard and a drone. When you reach the building's northeast corner, your objective is on the other side of the van. You can either make a run for it, quickly loot the backpack and sprint away, or methodically neutralize all sentries in the area.

ASSAULT IN PROGRESS

 698

ATLAS P. 385

Objective: Loot the bag lying on an old mattress.

Story: Satoko Ito, a high-level corpo, wanted her son Hideo to follow in her footsteps. Rejecting this, he left home and joined a band of thugs. Shamed by her son's behavior, Satoko eventually ordered a corporation hit squad to eliminate the entire group – including Hideo.

Strategy: Coming from the southwest, neutralize the sentries on the concrete platform, then methodically sneak up on all the remaining foes. Using bodies as bait to draw individuals into ambushes can prove very effective here.

ASSAULT IN PROGRESS

 699

ATLAS P. 385

Objective: Loot the suitcase on the ground.

Story: Rick Morales was a NightCorp employee working in the tunnel construction department. When the corporation found out that he had sold the blueprints for a maglev tunnel (quick aside: it's actually the one you go through during MJ-32), they ordered his immediate elimination.

Strategy: Sneak up on the two sentries on the sides, then on the ones in the middle – you have plenty of vending machines to cause distractions if required.

ASSAULT IN PROGRESS

700

ATLAS P. 385

Objective: Loot the backpack on the ground.

Story: Tania used to deal drugs for Maelstrom in Charter Hill. After she decided to ply her trade for the Tyger Claws instead, Maelstromers were sent to eliminate her.

Strategy: If you approach from the south, you can sneak up on two oblivious Maelstromers, with vending machines making it easy to distract them. Sneak up on the other two to clear the area.

YOU PLAY WITH FIRE...

 701

ATLAS P. 389

Objective: Loot Zeitgeist's body, then the stash.

Story: Zeitgeist was a netrunner hired to steal data from Kiroshi. He infiltrated their compound and managed to connect to an access point in the park, but couldn't survive the subnet's defense programs. His body is still there, and is due to be picked up by NetWatch. His stash reveals that he also used to pull data from private computers to blackmail victims.

Strategy: Sneak through the front entrance to the south and move counterclockwise alongside the electric fence. A netrunner can wreak havoc by casting Cyberpsychosis on the android. Otherwise, observe enemy patrol routes and strike when guards are isolated. Once you obtain the coordinates of Zeitgeist's den, a short distance to the south, visit it to complete the task.

ASSAULT IN PROGRESS

 702

ATLAS P. 390

Objective: Loot Takeshi's body.

Story: A band of mercenaries supported by a netrunner by the name of Takeshi Ono pulled a job against Arasaka. One of them was caught and started talking. This enabled Arasaka to track down Takeshi, who was hiding in a homeless camp under a freeway.

Strategy: Approaching from the south, go around the hostile area counterclockwise, quietly neutralizing all targets on the way.

HIDDEN GEM 703

ATLAS P. 389

Objective: Loot Pushkin's body in the storm drain.

Story: Alex Pushkin, a senior quality control assistant at Biotechnica, was abducted, but his corporation's security failed to intervene.

HIDDEN GEM 704

ATLAS P. 389

Objective: Loot the body on the food vendor's rooftop.

Story: A merc by the name of Ryan Saylor was sent to kill a target, but he was overwhelmed by security forces.

HIDDEN GEM 705

ATLAS P. 389

Objective: Loot the body on the billboard's metal platform; you can reach it by shooting the ladder to make it drop.

Story: Elizabeth Murphy was a netrunner who witnessed a secret meeting involving an important man. She was identified by security forces and killed.

HIDDEN GEM 706

ATLAS P. 389

Unlock Condition: Complete SJ-18 ("I Fought the Law" – see page 196)

Objective: Loot the Militech corporal's body next to the van.

Story: A Militech operation to abduct a VIP ended up with all protagonists dead after an attack by another faction.

HIDDEN GEM 707

ATLAS P. 389

Unlock Condition: Complete 697 (see page 319).

Objective: Loot the body in the shipping container. The area can be entered via a missing fence section, either on the east or north side.

Story: Zhang Qiao, a bio-engineer who developed revolutionary genetically modified tomato seeds, was killed by Biotechnica, who deemed it easier to steal the seeds rather than buy them.

HIDDEN GEM 708

ATLAS P. 389

Objective: Loot the body between the air conditioning units.

Story: Gerard Novak and Noah Johnson met up to sort out a debt between them once and for all.

HIDDEN GEM 709

ATLAS P. 389

Objective: Loot the body near the Trauma Team crate.

Story: Charlie Brown was a junkie who stole a bag full of meds abandoned in a hurry by a Trauma Team unit. He died from an overdose after consuming some of the substances in the bag.

HIDDEN GEM

710

ATLAS P. 389

Objective: Loot the body in the underground control room.

Story: M0ng was a netrunner who attempted to hack the Kiroshi network, but was fried by the defense systems before he had a chance to steal any data.

CRASH TEST

711

ATLAS P. 385

Objective: Loot Frank Hover's body, then find his stash.

Story: Frank Hover was a drug dealer in North Oak. That is no longer the case.

Strategy: Loot the body of the deceased dealer on the side of the road, then head to the designated alleyway to the west, in Japantown. Four Tyger Claws guard the area: sneak up on the first one, on the metal walkway and neutralize the next one with a distraction before you finish off the other two. Loot the small box by the computer inside the stash to complete the assignment.

TABLE SCRAPS

712

ATLAS P. 379

Objective: Loot Joe's body on the sidewalk, then attend to the computer and container in his stash.

Story: Jalapeño Joe was a homeless man who took notes on the habits of North Oak residents – until his amateur investigations were curtailed by a corporate enforcement unit.

Strategy: Coming from the west side, walk alongside the wall and you will have a brief opportunity to grapple one of the soldiers before the others react. After looting the body, you can head to Joe's stash, in the underpass of the freeway between Japantown and North Oak. Be careful: it's booby-trapped! Read the messages on the computer and open the container to complete the hustle.

ASSAULT IN PROGRESS

713

ATLAS P. 380

Objective: Loot Diana's body, near the crashed car.

Story: Diana Cuno was a Biotechnica employee. An embarrassing leak in the company caused her bosses to make her a scapegoat. Security forces were sent to liquidate her.

Strategy: If you approach from the north, via the hill overlooking the tunnel, you can drop down behind the Arasaka troops. Stealthily dispatch the netrunner, followed by the bodyguards, and you are then clear to inspect the body of Diana.

PRIVACY POLICY VIOLATION

714

ATLAS P. 379

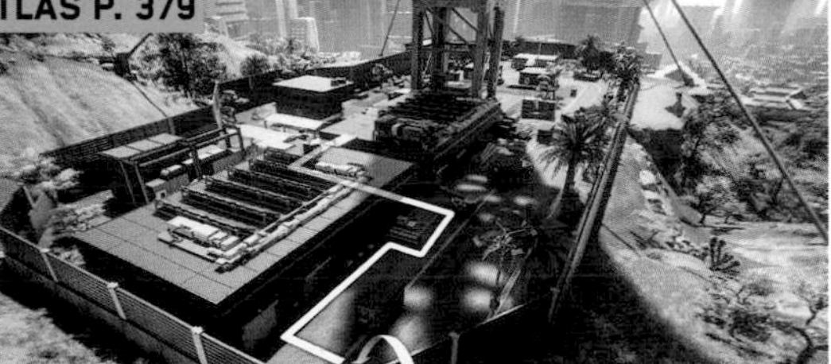

Objective: Defeat all enemies and loot the military briefcase in the storage area in the south of the compound.

Story: Impala Automatics have lost their right to occupy a compound.

Strategy: If you want to avoid a direct confrontation with every foe in the area, you can actually jump over the fence from the perimeter's northeast corner, where a steep slope gives you just enough height. Once inside, perform stealth takedowns on all the enemies you run into (and quickhacks on all the mech units), methodically covering the area from east to west.

WEST WIND ESTATE

HIDDEN GEM

715

ATLAS P. 385

Objective: Loot the delivery drone.

Story: Dealers selling drugs to the rich in North Oak bought a drone to deliver their product. During a delivery to Kerry Eurodyne that exceeded the maximum load weight, the drone crashed.

Strategy: The drone wreck lies inside the "O" of the North Oak sign. To reach it, drop the fire escape ladder at the southeast end of the structure by shooting it. You can then get to the long walkway that runs alongside the giant letters, taking care to hop over the missing floor panels. Use the ladder midway along the walkway to get down to the drone's location.

ASSAULT IN PROGRESS

716

ATLAS P. 397

Objective: Loot Monica Steiner's body.

Story: Monica Steiner was the woman who paid for the assassination of Logan, an Animal leader (as seen during the "For My Son" gig). Fearing for her life, she contacted a smuggler to help her leave Night City, but was caught by Animals during her escape.

Strategy: Sneak up on the two Animals guarding each end of the underpass (the concrete benches will hide you as you navigate from one to the other), then repeat this with the two in the middle, starting with the one standing.

SUSPECTED ORGANIZED CRIME ACTIVITY

717

ATLAS P. 397

Objective: Eliminate all scavengers and loot the chest container under the metal canopy.

Story: Scavengers have taken over an old Pawn Shop, where they store the cyberware they have scavenged from the district. They trade with Nomads looking for cheap replacements of their own implants.

Strategy: The area is well guarded, so a pure stealth strategy is unlikely to work. You can definitely sneak up on the few sentries on the perimeter and try some distractions, but the sheer number of enemies and the presence of a sniper on a vantage point make direct action unavoidable. Equip a powerful weapon, and make the most of the gas tanks to engulf your foes in explosions whenever possible.

ASSAULT IN PROGRESS

718

ATLAS P. 391

Objective: Loot the chest in front of the shipping container.

Story: Scavengers have found a container that dropped onto the beach from a flying transport.

Strategy: Approaching from the south, sneak up on the scavengers one by one when they're isolated.

ASSAULT IN PROGRESS

719

ATLAS P. 397

Objective: Loot the bag on the ground.

Story: A group of Wraiths have found an old, sealed-up Militech bunker. They are looking to open it to steal the gear inside.

Strategy: Making your approach from the south, you will find almost all enemies facing away from you, ripe for quick stealth takedowns. Pay attention to the only sentry that goes on a short patrol route from time to time.

HIDDEN GEM

720

ATLAS P. 397

Objective: Loot Fara's body.

Story: Fara, a member of the Voodoo Boys, was sent by Placide to kill scavengers who had found high-end netrunner components. The Voodoo Boys underestimated the scavengers and were all killed – including Fara, who was thrown from a window.

Strategy: Use the ladder a short distance to the west of the recent defenestration to reach the rooftop where Fara landed.

HIDDEN GEM

721

ATLAS P. 397

Objective: Loot the suitcase by the two bodies.

Story: Amelia Herbert, heir to a great fortune, was in love with a rockerboy called Sid. After realizing that his daughter wouldn't change her mind, her father had them both killed.

Strategy: Head up to the rooftop via any of the staircases in the corners of the building. You have to deal with only three enemies, all gathered around the bodies of Amelia and Sid, making stealth tactics tricky. An explosion is all it takes to mow them down all at once; contagion quickhacks also work great.

HIDDEN GEM

722

ATLAS P. 397

Objective: Loot Viper's body in the work site inside the fenced enclosure; you can drop down from above to avoid the nearby guards and turret.

Story: Lee Viper was an Animal who consumed narcotics. He died from an overdose while sexting after he both inhaled and injected himself with turbo-amphetmines.

HIDDEN GEM

723

ATLAS P. 397

Objective: Loot Miz's body by the Delamain.

Story: Phea Miz was a thug who stole from scavengers. Escaping in a Delamain, she chose to fire back at her pursuers and was shot through the cab's open window.

HIDDEN GEM

724

ATLAS P. 397

Objective: Loot the body on the film set, near the shipping containers.

Story: Fred Kudo was a TV producer filming a scene with actors dressed like Voodoo Boys. The real gang discovered them and massacred the entire crew.

HIDDEN GEM

725

ATLAS P. 397

Objective: Loot Smith's body near the crashed car.

Story: Two thugs named Tadita Smith and Naserian Lott dared each other to race on an unfinished road and jump out of their car last. The one who won the challenge couldn't make it out of the vehicle on time and died when her car crashed.

HIDDEN GEM

726

ATLAS P. 391

Objective: Loot Oblonsky's body at the foot of the rollercoaster, in front of the sewer pipes.

Story: Yelena Oblonsky was a scavenger who attempted to climb the rollercoaster while drunk – and fell to her death.

HIDDEN GEM 727

ATLAS P. 391

Unlock Condition: Complete MJ-18 ("Transmission" – see page 148)

Objective: Loot the body above the highway's tunnel entrance.

Story: Silans, a subordinate of Aveg's, planned to get rid of Placide by delivering in person a shard with Placide's details to NetWatch agents. The Voodoo Boys took them by surprise during the transaction and killed all those involved.

ASSAULT IN PROGRESS 728

ATLAS P. 392

Objective: Loot the chest container by the speakers.

Story: Animals needed generators to power up one of their buildings in Pacifica, so they decided to buy some from the Valentinos. The trade was arranged, but the Animals (wrongly) thought they were being handed inferior pre-owned units. They started shooting, killing all Valentinos in the process.

Strategy: The area is crawling with Animals, but you can actually avoid almost all of them if you arrive from the south. Neutralize the one patrolling on his own, then sneak up on the guard right next to your objective. If you time your moves carefully, you can be in and out in a few seconds, completely incognito. Another strategy is to turn the local turret to friendly mode.

ASSAULT IN PROGRESS 729

ATLAS P. 392

Objective: Loot the backpack on the ground, near Susan's body.

Story: Susan Santoro was an NCPD officer working in the braindance department. Having spent so long absorbed in violent scenes, she started feeling jaded and sought greater stimulation in black braindance. One of the thugs delivering XBD materials to her noticed her badge and panicked, killing her in the process.

Strategy: Make your approach from the south, alongside the long wall. From here you can sneak up on the lone scavenger, then stealthily kill the other two by the car.

ASSAULT IN PROGRESS 730

ATLAS P. 392

Objective: Loot the chest container on the planter, by the radio.

Story: Ellen Verde used to be a mercenary. Tired of executing targets, she decided to quit, but her former fixer refused to let her go and had her assassinated instead. Scavengers who heard the commotion arrived in the hope of looting something valuable.

Strategy: Quietly neutralizing all scavengers can be tricky here, given how packed they are. You could opt for open conflict, but there's another possibility: arriving from the ramp to the northwest of the hostile area, hide behind the crate in the corner and disable the turret. From here, you can crouch-walk straight to the chest: there's just enough time to retreat immediately without being detected. If you do trigger the alarm, simply make a run for it.

ROADSIDE PICNIC 731

ATLAS P. 392

Objective: Loot Nina's body, then the container in her hideout.

Story: Nina Chelo tried to make a living by smuggling goods in from the combat zone outside the city – but then her luck turned, and she took a bullet. She holed up in the Pacifica slums, but died before her friend Lucy Thackery (encountered during the "Hippocratic Oath" gig) could find and help her.

Strategy: Examine Nina's body in the Pacifica slums, then visit her hideout – a garage in front of the Grand Imperial Mall's front entrance. You will need to climb onto the scaffolding to reach it. Don't forget to disarm or remotely deactivate the laser mines by the garage gate.

ASSAULT IN PROGRESS  732

ATLAS P. 393

Unlock Condition: Complete hustle 728 and main job MJ-18 ("Transmission").

Objective: Loot the chest container by a dumpster.

Story: Animals are regrouping on the stadium's parking lot, and are watching for the Voodoo Boys tracking them after the Grand Imperial Mall job.

Strategy: There are too many enemies to opt for pure stealth tactics here. A netrunner, however, can wreak havoc among them by quickhacking the turret and by casting cyberpsychosis on one of the stronger foes.

WIPE THE GONK, TAKE THE IMPLANTS 733

ATLAS P. 391

Objective: Eliminate all enemies and loot the chest container on the roof at the far end of the amusement park.

Story: The old amusement park has become a scavenger base where they store stolen implants.

Strategy: Coming from the main entrance, make extensive use of your scanner and mini-map to track and neutralize all scavengers in the area. Setting cameras to friendly mode can help here. Their loose spacing makes it relatively easy to take them down one by one. Advance slowly, stay low at all times, and pay special attention to the sentry posted on a roof by the Ferris wheel.

HONEY, WHERE ARE YOU?  734

ATLAS P. 392

Objective: Loot Marvin's bag (by his body), then the backpack by the car.

Story: Marvin Hilton was one of Zetatech's most trusted engineers. He wanted to leave his wife and start a new life in Venezuela with someone else, so he hired a smuggler to prepare his transfer. His wife, who suspected something was afoot, hired a mercenary to investigate. The mercenary came to realize just how wealthy Marvin was – and decided to rob and kill him.

Strategy: Marvin's body lies on the terrace of an abandoned restaurant. Sneak up on the foe whose patrol route isolates him for a telling moment, then eliminate the mercenary who remains stationary. After inspecting Marvin's body, head south to his car. Loot the backpack on the ground, near the car, to complete the mission.

HIDDEN GEM  735

ATLAS P. 392

Objective: Loot the bag by Theo Faron's body.

Story: Theo Faron worked with a group called The Human Project to save a child and her mother from Arasaka, extracting them on a speedboat. Though Theo completed his mission, he did so at the cost of his own life.

Strategy: Head to the beach and collect the contents of the bag by the boat.

HIDDEN GEM  736

ATLAS P. 392

Objective: Loot the suitcase by the netrunner chair.

Story: Spectral Kid was a netrunner who wanted to infiltrate the Voodoo Boys' private network. Having underestimated their defenses, he was killed during the operation.

Strategy: Spectral Kid's den can be accessed via the alleyway adjacent to the concrete steps. You have a turret to neutralize before you can open the garage door.

HIDDEN GEM  737

ATLAS P. 391

Unlock Condition: Complete the "Race to the Top" gig (see page 284)

Objective: Loot the body on the old mattress.

Story: Matheus Stove was a former Kendachi employee who lost his job. Chased by the Valentinos, he was desperately trying to get a face change from a ripperdoc but could not pay him because his bank accounts had been frozen.

HIDDEN GEM 738

ATLAS P. 392

Objective: Loot the body on the rooftop, which you can reach by hopping from the nearby street, then the nearby safe hidden under construction equipment.

Story: Tom Norton was a homeless man hiding corporate materials in his hideout. After drinking too much, he talked about his stash to others, leading to his death and the stash being broken into.

HIDDEN GEM 739

ATLAS P. 391

Objective: Loot the body on the shore, a few steps from the roller coaster.

Story: Eddy Gale tried to record a braindance of himself riding a bike on the rollercoaster. He fell to his death in the process.

HIDDEN GEM 740

ATLAS P. 392

Objective: Loot the body close to the beach, at the foot of Hotel Merquiss.

Story: John Aronson aspired to be a real-life superhero called Butt-Kicker. He was killed attacking criminals.

HIDDEN GEM 741

ATLAS P. 392

Objective: Loot the body on a Hotel Merquiss terrace.

Story: Bart von Ochman was part of a band aspiring for a breakthrough. The band owed the Animals money and couldn't pay them back. They were killed while recording a clip of their latest song.

HIDDEN GEM 742

ATLAS P. 392

Objective: Loot the body on the chapel's roof.

Story: Lauren Murphy was a thug looking to blow up a bomb on the roof of the Pacifica chapel to decimate the ranks of the Voodoo Boys. He failed to install the device properly and only killed himself.

HIDDEN GEM 743

ATLAS P. 392

Objective: Loot the shard on the small table with many bottles.

Story: Odrin Johnson was a drunkard collecting alcohol bottles.

HIDDEN GEM 744

ATLAS P. 391

Objective: Loot the container in the submerged car's trunk.

Story: Larissa Almeida was a cage fighter who refused an offer from Valentinos to intentionally throw a fight for a bribe. The thugs who murdered her took the time to make her death look like an accident.

Strategy: Go to the end of the pier adjacent to the rollercoaster and jump into the water to find Larissa's car on the seabed.

ASSAULT IN PROGRESS

 745

ATLAS P. 394

Objective: Loot the briefcase by the car.

Story: Ivan Vassiliev was the president of a workers union in Rancho Coronado. Campaigning for Jefferson Peralez and rallying many colleagues to join him, he was perceived as a problem by political rival Weldon Holt. Julia Bonet, a mercenary paid to deal with Vassiliev, initiated contact by pretending to be a journalist, then murdered him during their meeting.

Strategy: Approaching from the southeast, hide behind the crates and you can quietly take down all guards one after the other.

ASSAULT IN PROGRESS

746

ATLAS P. 394

Objective: Loot the bag on the ground.

Story: Diego Ferro was a bartender whose venue was often patronized by drunk Sixers. One night he lost his temper, and attempted to throw the Sixers out. One of the thugs, Luke Anderson, punched Diego – who then hit his head as he fell, and died where he lay. Luke called a friend, Mike, to help him get rid of the body.

Strategy: Make your approach from the northwest and you'll have plenty of cover available to sneak up on the two men, without even paying attention to the two sentries near the main entrance.

ASSAULT IN PROGRESS

 747

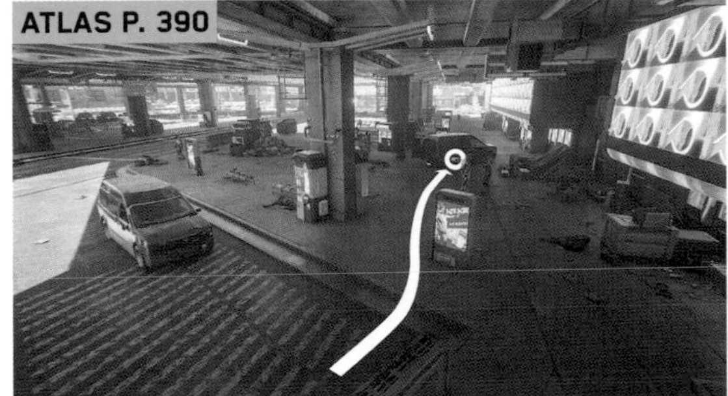

ATLAS P. 390

Objective: Loot the bag next to the van.

Story: A patient escaped a secure hospital and sought refuge at an abandoned bus station. The institution's security team was dispatched to bring him back but, after failing to identify him, was ordered to round up all the homeless in the area.

Strategy: Approaching the bus station from the south, move northward alongside the main building. You can sneak behind Bradley Burrows, loot the bag by the van, and immediately be on your way. If you prefer to eliminate all enemies, use the many devices in the area to isolate them and take them down one at a time.

ASSAULT IN PROGRESS

 748

ATLAS P. 390

Objective: Loot the chest container close to the pickup truck.

Story: Elis Hauk, a security agent, was sent by his boss Vic Vega to convince a business owner to pay protection money – an offer he rebuffed. Hauk and his men were ordered to return and behave in a manner that might adequately illustrate the value of the proffered arrangement.

Strategy: If you arrive from the small alleyway in the southeast corner of the area, you can crouch-walk alongside the wall to reach the pickup truck – sentries will be aware of your presence, but not long enough to detect you if you hide quickly. From here, you can snatch the contents of the briefcase and flee.

ASSAULT IN PROGRESS

 749

ATLAS P. 389

Objective: Loot the body of Darius Marks.

Story: The Tyger Claws received a tip about a 6th Street hideout and attacked, knowing that the Sixer presence would be reduced following the death of their previous leader (see the "Going-Away Party" gig).

Strategy: A shootout begins when you arrive, making stealth tactics rather awkward. Consider instead throwing a few grenades in the middle of the fray. If you aim well, almost all enemies will fall, leaving you in an ideal position to finish off the few survivors.

ASSAULT IN PROGRESS

 750

ATLAS P. 394

Objective: Loot the bag on the crates.

Story: Militech paid Sixers to intimidate the workers on a construction site that the corporation wanted to purchase.

Strategy: Making your approach from the southeast, hide behind the forklift and wait for openings to neutralize the nearby Sixers when they're isolated. Use distractions to sneak up on the remaining ones for a conflict-free resolution, or mow them down with a grenade when they're close to each other.

NIGHT CITY
PRIMER
COMPLETION ROADMAP
MAIN JOBS
SIDE JOBS
CYBERPSYCHO SIGHTINGS
GIGS
HUSTLES
ATLAS
INVENTORY
REFERENCE & ANALYSIS
EXTRAS
INDEX

INTRODUCTION
LITTLE CHINA
KABUKI
NORTHSIDE
JAPANTOWN
CHARTER HILL
NORTH OAK
WEST WIND ESTATE
COASTVIEW
RANCHO CORONADO
ARROYO
BADLANDS
VISTA DEL REY
THE GLEN
WELLSPRINGS
DOWNTOWN
CORPORATE PLAZA

ASSAULT IN PROGRESS

 751

ATLAS P. 394

Objective: Loot Pablo Silva's body.

Story: Pablo Silva was a Sixer faithful to the old 6th Street leader. After the coup, he was sentenced to death by the new management.

Strategy: Use quickhacks on devices such as the forklift and reflector on the north side of the hostile area to isolate the nearby Sixers and neutralize them. You can repeat this with the radio on the crate to deal with the final foes.

SUSPECTED ORGANIZED CRIME ACTIVITY

 752

ATLAS P. 394

Objective: Eliminate all enemies and loot the bag on the couch.

Story: After a new boss took over 6th Street, the gang has been going through a purge.

Strategy: Make your approach from the north to quietly neutralize the Sixers in the front yard, making sure you disable the surveillance cameras on the way. Next, sneak up on the foes on the edge of the back yard. You can neutralize most of them if you're patient; eliminate the remaining few however you see fit. Don't forget to visit the bunker before you leave.

ASSAULT IN PROGRESS

 753

ATLAS P. 390

Objective: Loot the backpack on the table in the living room.

Story: Priscilla O'Connor was a friend of Juliet Horrigan, a mercenary who recently killed a Sixer. Priscilla was captured and tortured by Sixers, who try to force her to reveal what she knows about Juliet.

Strategy: Ignore the two Sixers on the porch and sneak into the garage, quickly neutralizing the sentry inside. You can now enter the house corridor, tag all three enemies inside, and take them down one at a time when they turn away from you.

WELCOME TO NIGHT CITY

 754

ATLAS P. 395

Objective: Loot the dealer's body, then his stash.

Story: A Wraith by the name of Jake was sent by his boss to deal drugs in Rancho Coronado, on 6th Street turf. Despite his attempts to be discreet, Sixers located him and killed him.

Strategy: Loot Jake's body inside his house, then head to his stash at the foot of the dam. Sneak up on the Sixer on the left, then deal with the two inside the garage. You can then loot the chest container on the floor.

A STROKE OF LUCK

 755

ATLAS P. 394

Objective: Loot Robert's body, then plunder the container on the back porch of his nearby house.

Story: Robert Czmerkowski was a junkie who falsified his grandmother's will to be the sole inheritor of her estate. To celebrate, he called his dealer, who brought a sizeable quantity of product. Robert died of an overdose shortly afterwards.

Strategy: Loot Robert's body in the drainage tunnel, then head to his house – just a short walk to the south. There are three Sixers in the backyard, but you don't need to eliminate them: simply hop up on the gas tank and from here to the ledge with the chest, just above.

JUSTICE BEHIND BARS

756

ATLAS P. 394

Objective: Read the message on the computer, then loot the bag on the house porch.

Story: James Benben is a prison guard who was bribed by Sixers to smuggle weapons inside his prison. Their plan is to have inmates kill imprisoned sixers who are loyal to the gang's previous boss.

Strategy: The computer is guarded by a Sixer, with two additional ones just a few steps away. You can distract the latter with the microwave close to them, then sneak up on the former and quickly read the message on the laptop. This reveals a new waypoint to the south, leading you to Benben's house. When you get there, try causing a distraction with the nearby speaker to thin the enemy ranks before neutralizing the men by the door. You will find the bag you need to loot on the porch steps.

ASSAULT IN PROGRESS

757

ATLAS P. 394

Objective: Loot the bag on the ground, in front of the car.

Story: Ben, a mechanic working for the Sixers, used to replace parts from their cars with cheaper alternatives, then sell the more expensive components on the side. When the Sixers found out about this scheme, they decided to punish him.

Strategy: Approaching from the alleyway to the east, sneak up on the Sixers by the car, before dealing with the remaining ones. An explosion can also work well to mow down the three gangsters close to the target in a single hit.

ASSAULT IN PROGRESS

758

ATLAS P. 394

Objective: Loot the container by the pool.

Story: Forest Ealy and Kayla Brown were thugs who trapped people in cyberspace and demanded ransoms to free them. A wealthy father of one of their victims tracked the thugs down by tracing a money transfer, and then had them killed.

Strategy: Make your approach from the east and quietly take down the lone sentry. From here, crouch-walk around the pool clockwise, stealthily neutralizing all enemies – unless you prefer to just loot the chest container and make a quick departure.

DESPERATE SONS-OF-BITCHES

759

ATLAS P. 395

Objective: Eliminate all Wraiths and loot the chest container in the middle of the area.

Story: Wraiths have set up a hideout at the foot of an abandoned Megabuilding construction site. They use it as a base from which they smuggle people on the run out of Night City.

Strategy: Enter the perimeter from the missing fence section in the south corner. From here, you can gradually and quietly neutralize all the Wraiths you run into, going clockwise. Observe their patrol routes carefully, stay behind cover, and strike when no one is looking. Quickhack the androids if you can and pay attention to the snipers on the elevated platforms.

HIDDEN GEM

760

ATLAS P. 394

Objective: Loot the body on the rooftop, accessible via the nearby ladder.

Story: Lucas McClintock was a corrupt police officer stealing drugs from his precinct to sell them to 6th Street. He and his partner were killed by the gang after they failed to deliver the amount they had promised.

HIDDEN GEM 761

ATLAS P. 394

Objective: Loot the body on the house porch.

Story: Prince Boehner, a drug wholesaler, was killed by one of his clients after she confirmed he was cutting his product with filler.

HIDDEN GEM 762

ATLAS P. 394

Objective: Loot the body in the underpass.

Story: Aurelie Moore was a rockergirl just out of rehab. She died from an overdose after spending the evening celebrating with her band.

HIDDEN GEM 763

ATLAS P. 394

Objective: Loot the body next to the Ferris wheel cabin.

Story: Kendric Feller and Octavius Brown, two gang leaders, met to discuss an ongoing dispute. They failed to reach an agreement and the meeting ended up in a bloodbath.

HIDDEN GEM 764

ATLAS P. 395

Objective: Loot the body on the balcony.

Story: Vincent Vack was a thug sent to kill Butch, a boxer who won a match that he was supposed to lose.

HIDDEN GEM 765

ATLAS P. 390

Objective: Loot the shard inside the shipping container.

Story: Lopez was a netrunner who got traced by NetWatch. He stored his belongings in a stash before attempting to leave the city.

HIDDEN GEM 766

ATLAS P. 395

Objective: Loot the shard next to the body, close to the truck.

Story: Brenton Ernest was a thug trying to smuggle goods. He was arrested by rivals disguised as police officers and killed on the spot.

HIDDEN GEM 767

ATLAS P. 394

Objective: Loot the body close to the police cars.

Story: Seth Miller, a 6th Street criminal, was freed by fellow gang members as he was transferred to a courthouse.

HIDDEN GEM 768

ATLAS P. 394

Objective: Loot the body inside an open shipping container in the storage facility; you will need to disable the android guarding the entrance.

Story: Arthur Narvy was a techie resetting stolen androids to have them refurbished on the black market. He was killed by one such device that proved dysfunctional and violent.

NIGHT CITY
PRIMER
COMPLETION ROADMAP
MAIN JOBS
SIDE JOBS
CYBERPSYCHO SIGHTINGS
GIGS
HUSTLES
ATLAS
INVENTORY
REFERENCE & ANALYSIS
EXTRAS
INDEX

INTRODUCTION
LITTLE CHINA
KABUKI
NORTHSIDE
JAPANTOWN
CHARTER HILL
NORTH OAK
WEST WIND ESTATE
COASTVIEW
RANCHO CORONADO
ARROYO
BADLANDS
VISTA DEL REY
THE GLEN
WELLSPRINGS
DOWNTOWN
CORPORATE PLAZA

Objective: Loot the chest in the central alley between the shipping containers.

Story: Sixers were expecting to receive a container at the docks, but it was sent to a warehouse in Rancho Coronado instead. They are now searching for it.

Strategy: Go around the compound clockwise, using the barrels and crates as cover to remain unseen. This will enable you to reach your objective incognito, with a single, unaware Sixer to deal with in front of the chest.

HIDDEN GEM

 769

ATLAS P. 390

Objective: Loot Dean's body.

Story: Dean Simons, a factory logistics coordinator, regularly provided 6th Street with advance notice of incoming transports – until his employers figured out he was behind the leaks. They then set a trap, including heavy security in a transport that was supposed to be a simple walk-in, walk-out job. All the Sixers in attendance were killed, so the gang went after Dean to exact vengeance.

Strategy: Make your approach from the back alley to the north and wait for a sentry to move close to the corner. Distract him with the nearby reflector then neutralize him. This will leave you with three Sixers facing away from you, and close to each other. An explosion is all it takes to eliminate them all simultaneously. Stealth takedowns are also possible if you're careful.

ASSAULT IN PROGRESS

770

ATLAS P. 388

ASSAULT IN PROGRESS

771

ATLAS P. 388

Objective: Loot the bag leaning against the crate.

Story: Matheus Stove, a Kendachi employee, used to inform Valentinos about weapon shipments that they could hijack. When he realized he was under surveillance, Matheus asked his contact with the Valentinos to move all the gear in his stash.

Strategy: Position yourself on the east side of the hostile area. Using the containers and crates as cover, you can methodically neutralize all Valentinos with silent takedowns. Be patient: wait until they are alone, then hide their bodies afterwards.

SUSPECTED ORGANIZED CRIME ACTIVITY

772

ATLAS P. 388

Objective: Eliminate all enemies and loot the bag on the crate.

Story: Sixers have set up a large open-air lab where they produce the drugs they sell.

Strategy: Starting from the south entrance, you just need to be methodical to catch all of the Sixers you run into when they are vulnerable, and stealthily work your way through the premises. Once you reach the one on the phone by the van, wait until the sentry at the west entrance turns around, then cautiously neutralize both. This leaves you with a final enemy on the stairs to deal with.

ASSAULT IN PROGRESS

773

ATLAS P. 393

Objective: Loot Frank Kaufmann's body.

Story: Frank Kaufmann owned an auto shop and took care of 6th Street cars. After being approached by Tyger Claws, he agreed to install GPS trackers that would enable Tyger Claws to monitor Sixer movements. When the Sixers were later ambushed by Tyger Claws, they soon figured out what had happened – and killed Frank.

Strategy: Coming from the east entrance, move alongside the north wall until you reach the far wall of the dead end. From here, you can methodically neutralize each enemy in turn, waiting until the man patrolling back and forth looks away if required.

DISLOYAL EMPLOYEE

774

ATLAS P. 393

Objective: Loot the backpack right next to Thomas's body, then his stash.

Story: Thomas Red was a communications technician at the Caroll factory who occasionally sold confidential information to journalists to pay for his wife's medical treatments. As soon as his company found out about his leaks, they had him killed by 6th Street enforcers.

Strategy: Coming from the south, hide behind the stacks of pallets to observe the Sixers. When you notice an opening to sneak up on the one on the left, neutralize him. Take down the others around the corner, then finish with the one examining Thomas's body. After looting it, head to his stash, on the other side of the building.

ASSAULT IN PROGRESS

775

ATLAS P. 393

Objective: Loot Tony Falcetti's body.

Story: Tony Falcetti used to be a 6th Street leader. Released from prison after a ten-year stretch, he hardly recognized his old gang, which now freely cooperated with corporations. As he represented a threat to the new management, they unsentimentally sanctioned his murder.

Strategy: Approach the area from the north and you will find two lone Sixers, ripe for a quick takedown. Now head toward the pile of pallets in the middle and you can deal with the remaining enemies in the same fashion.

ASSAULT IN PROGRESS

776

ATLAS P. 388

Objective: Loot Jimmy Kreutz's body.

Story: Jimmy Kreutz was a race driver who hired a trusted Sixer mechanic by the name of Hilary McKenna. After Jimmy didn't leave enough time for Hilary to properly modify his car, Jimmy lost a race due to engine failure. Jimmy threatened Hilary and paid her a visit to punish her – but was instead killed by Sixers.

Strategy: Use the alleyway to approach the hostile area from the west, where you can quietly take down all sentries from behind, one after the other, finishing with the one inside the garage.

ASSAULT IN PROGRESS

777

ATLAS P. 393

Objective: Loot the bag in the trunk of the partly-buried car.

Story: Seamus Horgan was a Sixer who accidentally killed David Benny, one of his boss's accountants. He attempted to hide the evidence by sinking the accountant's body and car in concrete on a construction site.

Strategy: Sneak up on the isolated Sixers first, before eliminating the ones close to each other.

ASSAULT IN PROGRESS

778

ATLAS P. 393

Objective: Loot the body of the leader.

Story: The Creators, a group of young environmentalists, organized a protest against the construction of a new corporate-financed building in Arroyo. A security officer accidentally killed a protester, leading his friends to attack – which caused the security personnel to open fire in unison, leaving all Creators dead.

Strategy: Enter the premises from the east and stealthily eliminate the sentries between you and the body.

ASSAULT IN PROGRESS

779

ATLAS P. 389

Objective: Loot the bag on the ground, by the officer's body.

Story: Billy Jackson, a rockerboy, mowed down several people while drunk-driving, but bribed the NCPD to bury the case. When a new officer decided to investigate, Jackson sent some thugs to the junkyard where his car was kept for them to destroy any remaining evidence. The deeply unfortunate NCPD officer ran into the thugs at the junkyard and was killed.

Strategy: Arriving from the south, quietly neutralize the lone thug. Repeat this with the other ones on the edge of the hostile area, and finish with the ones near the officer's body.

SUPPLY MANAGEMENT

780

ATLAS P. 389

Objective: Loot the backpack against the crate, then the body on the nearby rooftop.

Story: Richard Ribisi was a Petrochem employee engaged in undercutting the company by selling stolen boosters to other employees. When the corporation found out, they sent their security to dispatch him.

Strategy: From the main gate, quickly crouch-walk to the main building to your right. From here, you can sneak up on all enemies in the area one after the other. After looting the backpack, use the nearby steps to get to the rooftop, then hide behind the ventilation units on your left (northeast side of the building) to avoid the gaze of the troops on the other side. You will find Richard's body at the end of the rooftop, with all foes in your path looking away from you.

HIDDEN GEM

781

ATLA P. 388

Objective: Loot the body on the topmost platform of the scaffolding.

Story: A mercenary was hired to eliminate Councilman John McLean. He tried to do so from an elevated vantage point, but was identified by the politician's security drones.

Strategy: Climb to the top of the scaffolding, either via the scaffolding itself, or the adjacent shipping containers and rooftop.

HIDDEN GEM

782

ATLAS P. 389

Objective: Loot the body on the vantage point, which you can reach by climbing up the metal staircase and ladder.

Story: Oscar Jones was a sniper hitman. After shooting a target, he had to confirm the victim's death, but was surprised by the arrival of Trauma Team, leaving him with an impossible choice: being killed by Trauma Team, or by his employer for failing the contract.

HIDDEN GEM

783

ATLAS P. 388

Objective: Loot the shard inside garage number 3.

Story: A van full of drugs was intended to reach a wealthy client by the name of Bartolomeo Mordelini.

HIDDEN GEM

784

ATLAS P. 394

Objective: Loot the body in the storm drain.

Story: Arnold Blake was sent to save a boy by the name of Jimmy O'Connor who was about to be killed by a cyborg hitman. Overwhelmed by the fire power and resistance of the enemy, Blake and the boy were killed.

HIDDEN GEM

785

ATLAS P. 388

Objective: Loot the body between the shipping containers.

Story: Two thugs looking to open a container filled with cyberware were killed by the explosion of the welder they were using to break into the stash.

HIDDEN GEM

786

ATLAS P. 393

Objective: Loot the body at the rear of the facility adjacent to the Cytech factory.

Story: A boxer nicknamed Popeye challenged a former commando who joined the Sixers into a fight and was slaughtered.

HIDDEN GEM

787

ATLAS P. 393

Objective: Loot the body in the basketball hoop; you'll need to jump from the barrels underneath to reach it.

Story: Alex Stephens was a shop owner under the protection of the Valentinos. Harassed by Animals, he asked his Valentino contact to get rid of them, which ended up in a bloodbath.

HIDDEN GEM — 788

ATLAS P. 389

Objective: Loot the shard close to the body in the underpass.

Story: An exchange of spies between Arasaka and Militech did not go as smoothly and quietly as anticipated.

HIDDEN GEM — 789

ATLAS P. 393

Objective: Loot the body in the shipping container storage facility.

Story: Danny Rossi was a mercenary hired to abduct a bride. Caught by security forces giving chase, she was killed in his car with the bride in his trunk.

HIDDEN GEM — 790

ATLAS P. 393

Objective: Loot the bodies inside the shipping container (whose door is gated behind a minor Technical Ability attribute requirement).

Story: Susan Martin, a woman involved in an illegal operation, was wounded and abducted by an ex-police officer firmly intent on eliminating the group that attacked her.

HIDDEN GEM — 791

ATLAS P. 388

Objective: Loot Tom Morris's body on the scaffolding.

Story: Tom Morris was hired by Ted Fox (encountered during the "Breaking News" gig) to take pictures of a secret deal between 6th Street and Kendachi. To accomplish this, he needed to climb to a vantage point on nearby scaffolding. Unfortunately, his leg calibrations were incomplete, and he slipped and died from the resultant fall.

Strategy: Your goal here is to reach the body near the top of the scaffolding via multiple ladders. On the third level, you will need to use a ventilation unit as a stepping stone to reach the level above.

ASSAULT IN PROGRESS — 792

ATLAS P. 390

Objective: Loot the chest container outside the warehouse.

Story: A band of scavengers heard about an imminent rave at a warehouse by Lawler Tunnel. They then raided the site to extract implants from the wealthy ravers.

Strategy: Make your approach from the south and slowly move northward, stealthily neutralizing all scavengers when they turn away from you, and finishing with the ones inside the warehouse.

COMRADE RED — 793

ATLAS P. 390

Objective: Loot the body on the trailer roof, then the body inside the bunker.

Story: Valentin Krylov and Shelma were two Soviet agents based in the Badlands. During a netrunning operation, Shelma was trapped in the net. To keep her body temperature down, Valentin tried to push the air conditioning to the maximum, but ended up causing a power surge that killed him – and Shelma shortly afterwards.

Strategy: Loot Valentin's body on the roof (taking care to destroy or quickhack the turret beforehand), then open the bunker door and loot the body on the netrunner chair inside.

BLOOD IN THE AIR —  794

ATLAS P. 381

Objective: Loot Harry's body, then search the chest container.

Story: Harry "the Handyman" Sullivan was a Wraith eavesdropping on Nomads and Militech. He was shot by Militech when they found him fixing a device on a wind turbine, and died of blood loss while trying to escape.

Strategy: Inspect Harry's body, then go to the wind turbine to the northeast. You can sneak up on the first soldier when his patrol route takes him to the north, then quietly deal with the other two. Open the chest container by the van to complete the assignment.

ASSAULT IN PROGRESS

795

ATLAS P. 381

Objective: Loot the chest container by the car.

Story: Tyger Claws murdered Wraith captain Steve "Razor" Kovalsky and made it look like he had been killed by Sixers. Their goal was to start a war between the Wraiths and 6th Street.

Strategy: Make your approach from the north to be concealed by the rocky outcrop, then quietly neutralize all foes, moving in a counterclockwise progression.

ASSAULT IN PROGRESS

796

ATLAS P. 381

Objective: Loot the chest container at the foot of the tree.

Story: Militech are trying to push the Wraiths further from the city to secure the border. In this particular skirmish, they have just raided a Wraith listening post.

Strategy: Approach from the west and quietly eliminate the guards patrolling on the outer edge, leaving the one in the middle until last.

EXTREMELY LOUD AND INCREDIBLY CLOSE

797

ATLAS P. 395

Objective: Loot Darnell's body, then the chest inside the Biotechnica container.

Story: Darnell Moore was a metal scrapper at the dump. One day he found a Biotechnica container and tried to connect it to a generator. This triggered a sonic shockwave that killed him.

Strategy: Sneak up on the two guards, examine Darnell's body in his shelter, then head to the nearby shipping container and open the chest inside.

ASSAULT IN PROGRESS

798

ATLAS P. 381

Objective: Loot the suitcase by Colleen's body.

Story: Colleen Dodd was the partner of a smuggler called George Johanson (a reference to the "Dancing on a Minefield" gig). George wanted to complete one last job before leaving the city with Colleen, but she was killed by Militech troops who mapped the location of the smuggler's den.

Strategy: Sneak up on the two guards posted outside George's den and quickhack the drone if it's on your way. This leaves you with a number of troops inside the den. An explosion can work well to take them all down at once, especially as gas tanks are scattered in the area.

ASSAULT IN PROGRESS

799

ATLAS P. 381

Objective: Loot the backpack by the tent.

Story: Brandon Murphy was a corporate employee who had to flee Night City after talking to a journalist (Mendoza, mentioned in another hustle). Brandon was caught by Wraiths in the Badlands.

Strategy: Approach from the east and you should have little difficulty in sneaking up on all enemies. Be patient if they look toward each other: their patrol routes will eventually isolate them.

ASSAULT IN PROGRESS

800

ATLAS P. 381

Objective: Loot the chest container inside the gas station.

Story: Multiple Wraith car engines failed in little more than a month. After looking into the situation, the Wraiths found out that the owner of a gas station they often used for refueling had been watering down the gas. The Wraiths decided to extract recompense from both the owner *and* his customers.

Strategy: First sneak up on the Wraiths stationed outside the gas station, then deal with the ones inside the building.

ASSAULT IN PROGRESS

801

ATLAS P. 381

Objective: Loot the container in the middle of the camp.

Story: A group of Wraiths heard that the Aldecaldos were up to something at the nearby train station (a reference to the "With a Little Help from my Friends" side job), so they decided to set up a camp on a hill overlooking it.

Strategy: Sneak up on the three Wraiths on the perimeter, then deal with the one in the middle.

ASSAULT IN PROGRESS

802

ATLAS P. 395

Objective: Loot the chest container by the car wreck.

Story: Nasim Perlman was hired by Tucker Albach (encountered during the "Eye for an Eye" gig) to dispose of her car.

Strategy: Arriving from the east side of the parking lot, you can sneak up on each enemy in turn.

ASSAULT IN PROGRESS

 803

ATLAS P. 395

Objective: Loot the bag on the ground by the tent.

Story: Two civilians, Jack and Dennis, were meeting at a small camp in the wilderness. They were killed by Militech troops hunting for smugglers.

Strategy: Make your approach from the east, as you will be concealed by the wind turbine. Eliminate the closest soldier when no one is looking your way. You can then move around the camp counterclockwise, dealing with each foe in turn, saving the soldier by the tent until last.

SUSPECTED ORGANIZED CRIME ACTIVITY

  804

ATLAS P. 381

Objective: Eliminate all enemies and loot the stash.

Story: Wraiths set up a small camp that they use as a staging area when ambushing corporate trucks. Their most recent acquisition was a tank full of chemical waste, which they intended to weaponize.

Strategy: Approaching from the east, you can take down at least two lone Wraiths while no one is looking your way. Try to repeat this with other enemies on the edge of the area. If open conflict is triggered, don't be shy to make use of the many gas tanks in the locale.

I DON'T LIKE SAND

 805

ATLAS P. 381

Objective: Loot Madison's body, then search her car.

Story: Madison Wilson was a mercenary working for Dakota, the fixer. During her last, and most fateful, operation, she was chased by Militech and tried to ride through a sandstorm to escape them. When her car stalled, she decided to continue on foot.

Strategy: Make your approach from the north to quietly eliminate the lone soldier on that side. You can then go around the area counterclockwise to deal with the one on the south side. This leaves you with two targets in the middle. After looting the corpse, head north to inspect Madison's car

ASSAULT IN PROGRESS

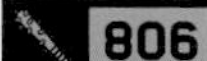 806

ATLAS P. 381

Objective: Loot the chest container by the crashed drone.

Story: Wraiths have taken control of an antenna (a reference to the "Flying Drugs" gig), which they employ to make drones malfunction and fall from the sky.

Strategy: In this scenario you face multiple Wraiths, including one positioned on the elevated walkway around the wind turbine. Though you can quietly take down a few enemies on the periphery, a full-stealth scenario is unlikely. Other options include throwing a grenade to cause a major explosion, engulfing the gas tanks scattered around. Picking your targets off from afar with a sniper rifle also works wonders.

ASSAULT IN PROGRESS

 807

ATLAS P. 381

Objective: Loot the chest container by the crate.

Story: A group of refugees who escaped from a detention center have been caught and neutralized by Militech troops.

Strategy: Approaching from the northwest, quietly eliminate the two guards whose patrol routes isolate them from the others. To stealthily deal with the remaining two, consider causing a distraction with the nearby reflector.

ASSAULT IN PROGRESS

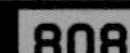 808

ATLAS P. 381

Objective: Loot the chest container by the Wraith car.

Story: Wraiths attacked a Biotechnica convoy. After torturing the crew, they learned of a maintenance team that would soon be sent in secret to work on protein farms in the Badlands.

Strategy: You can sneak up on the lone Wraith on the west side, but the others are gathered in a tight pack. Grenades are the perfect prelude to a firefight here, though you could also make a grand entrance by hitting at least one while driving through at high speed. Accelerate away to lure those that remain into the open – then line 'em up and knock 'em down.

ASSAULT IN PROGRESS

 809

ATLAS P. 381

Objective: Loot the chest container in the enclosed area.

Story: Two Militech veterans refused to leave a hideout on the corporation's territory, and were eliminated as a consequence.

Strategy: Approaching from the rocks to the west of the hostile area, you can try to sneak directly to the enclosed area. If you're feeling bold and time your movements well, you could try to sprint to the chest, open it, and flee. Otherwise, gradually neutralize the guards that pass in front of you until the coast is clear, making sure you quickhack the drone if you can.

HIDDEN GEM

810

ATLAS P. 381

Objective: Loot the body by a shovel in the wind farm, then the shard next to the bodies of the NCPD officers.

Story: Ian Zane was a thug who hid some money in a secret stash after a robbery. Caught by the police, he convinced an officer to go to the stash and split the money.

HIDDEN GEM 811

ATLAS P. 381

Objective: Loot the body next to the car.

Story: Darius Loaf was a trainee journalist at WNS. He was investigating a lead at a farm (encountered during the side job called "The Hunt" – see page 200) and was wounded by a security turret. He fainted while driving back to the city, crashing his car and dying in the process. A Militech drone detected the accident and moved in to investigate.

Strategy: The only challenge here is to neutralize the drone. If you have the required netrunner skills, quickhacking it is the optimal solution.

HIDDEN GEM 812

ATLAS P. 381

Objective: Loot the container inside the bunker.

Story: Two Wraiths, Rita Sweden and Rip Turman, were on the track of a netrunner called B@d. They believed that they had found him hiding in a bunker in the Badlands, but this was a trap.

Strategy: You can access the hostile area from the west, but note that it's littered with explosives. Advance cautiously, destroying or disarming the mines on the way. When you run into a drone, quickhack it if you can, or destroy it otherwise.

HIDDEN GEM 813

ATLAS P. 381

Objective: Loot the body next to the car in the yard.

Story: Dale Robinson was a widower who took his deceased wife back to their former home, in the Badlands. He let himself die next to her so that they could rest in peace together.

HIDDEN GEM 814

ATLAS P. 381

Objective: Loot the body by the van near the sewerage system.

Story: Erik Rhames was a Militech employee dispatched to repair a leak in a pipeline. His request for a security team was denied, leaving him and his assistants with no chance when they were attacked by Wraiths.

HIDDEN GEM 815

ATLAS P. 381

Objective: Loot the body close to the billboard, approaching from the west to remain incognito.

Story: A Militech security force was dispatched to rescue Erik Rhames and his team. The squad was attacked by the same Wraiths who had slaughtered Rhames.

HIDDEN GEM 816

ATLAS P. 381

Objective: Loot the shard inside the shack in the swamp, giving the nearby mines a wide berth.

Story: A former corporate soldier specialized in explosive engineering, who was abandoned by his employer after he retired, was preparing a bombing. He planned to write to Max Jones, a reporter leading an investigation into the outrageous treatment of veterans with PTSD syndrome.

HIDDEN GEM

817

ATLAS P. 381

Objective: Loot the body near the crashed airship.

Story: Mari Vidor was a journalist investigating the death of a pilot working for the DTR corporation. She found evidence suggesting the plane crash causing his death was not due to human error but mechanical failure, which would have forced the company to pay damages to the pilot's family. She was killed before she could publish her story.

HIDDEN GEM

818

ATLAS P. 381

Objective: Loot the body in the bunker at the foot of a broken wind turbine.

Story: A prepper anticipating a cataclysm held a woman by the name of Nicole against her will in his hideout. They both died as she tried to escape.

HIDDEN GEM

819

ATLAS P. 381

Objective: Loot the shards inside the underground shelter in the trailer park.

Story: A prepper retreated to his shelter when the Reunification War broke out in 2069.

HIDDEN GEM

820

ATLAS P. 381

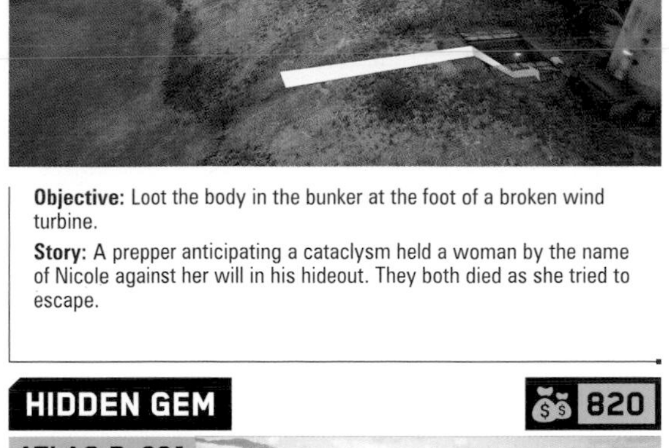

Objective: Loot the bag on the abandoned film set.

Story: When the 24 FPS studio was made insolvent, the entire set of the Hell Lake 3 movie was abandoned in the middle of nowhere.

HIDDEN GEM

821

ATLAS P. 381

Objective: Loot the body in the bunker behind the gas station.

Story: John Lyon was a thug who barely escaped from Militech units after a robbery. He took his wounded partner to a ripperdoc, but the ripperdoc failed to save him – and was subsequently shot by John Lyon.

HIDDEN GEM

822

ATLAS P. 381

Objective: Loot the body inside the trailer at the foot of a wind turbine.

Story: Jack Allen was a ripperdoc who was forced by thugs to operate on a gang member with explosives planted in his belly. Unfortunately for them all, he failed to prevent the explosion.

HIDDEN GEM

823

ATLAS P. 390

Objective: Loot the body near the entrance to the railway tunnel.

Story: JC was a thug trying to catch up with a train with the help of his colleague Little Smoke. He was killed by a train coming from the opposite direction.

HIDDEN GEM 824

ATLAS P. 381

Objective: Loot the backpack at the camping site in the wind farm.

Story: Mason and Joe were two drug addicts testing new products during live streams. They died on air after taking a sample of Glitter sent by a fan.

HIDDEN GEM 825

ATLAS P. 381

Objective: Loot the backpack a short distance to the east of the landfill.

Story: Dwight Blair was an orphan who never got over the fact that a man killed his parents. He decided to get his revenge by murdering the man and recording the whole scene in a braindance for the victim's family to experience his pain and agony.

HIDDEN GEM 826

ATLAS P. 381

Objective: Loot the shard inside the open shipping container in the landfill.

Story: A security breach caused a shipping container meant to be delivered to Phoenix to end up in the Badlands.

HIDDEN GEM 827

ATLAS P. 381

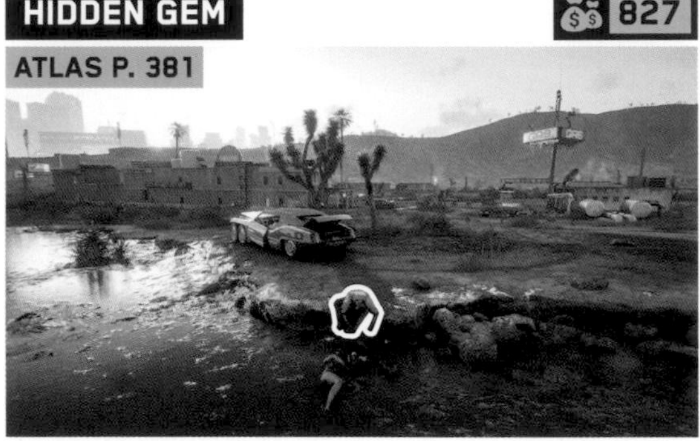

Objective: Loot the body by the river behind the Sunset Motel.

Story: Zachary Rae was a bitter husband who refused to accept that his wife had left him. He tracked her car in the Badlands to exact his revenge.

HIDDEN GEM 828

ATLAS P. 381

Objective: Loot the shard inside the shipping container, in the mine where you fight Nash during MJ-19 (Ghost Town – see page 150), then drive away with the Rayfield Caliburn to add it to your collection.

Story: A man whose parents were murdered when he was a child decided to become a superhero – Murk Man. He died while trying to save Night City from itself.

HIDDEN GEM 829

ATLAS P. 390

Objective: Loot the body in an open refrigerator in the landfill.

Story: Steven Hurt was the host of a myth-buster show. He died while trying to prove that you could survive a large explosion from inside a refrigerator.

HIDDEN GEM 830

ATLAS P. 381

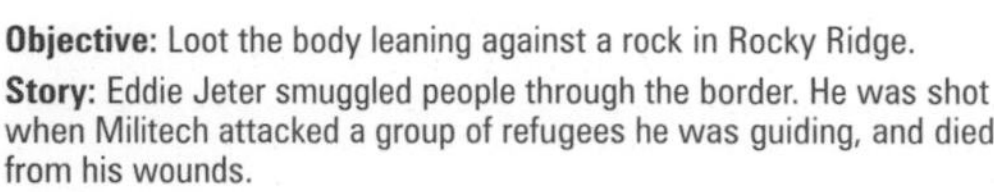

Objective: Loot the body leaning against a rock in Rocky Ridge.

Story: Eddie Jeter smuggled people through the border. He was shot when Militech attacked a group of refugees he was guiding, and died from his wounds.

HIDDEN GEM — 831

ATLAS P. 381

Objective: Loot the body at the site of the massacre.

Story: Militech soldiers were sent to kill a Nomad prisoner and bury him in the desert. The Nomad proved stronger than they expected, and it was them who ended up dead.

HIDDEN GEM — 832

ATLAS P. 381

Objective: Loot the body a few steps away from the Desert Film Set fast travel position, then drive away with the Thorton Colby CX410 Butte to add it to your vehicle collection.

Story: A crew sent by a marketing agency to capture the "rural beauty" of the Badlands was killed by Wraiths during the shooting session.

ASSAULT IN PROGRESS — 833

ATLAS P. 400

Objective: Loot Henry Louis's body.

Story: Henry "Montana" Louis was a specialist in neurovisual implants from the NUSA who agreed to work for Maelstrom. Both Henry and the smuggler helping him to reach Night City were killed by a Militech border patrol.

Strategy: Approaching from the north, hide behind the Militech vehicle and sneak up on the first soldier when he passes nearby. You can then crouch-walk to the guard a short distance to the southwest. Keep moving counterclockwise around the area to quietly take down the remaining enemies.

ASSAULT IN PROGRESS — 834

ATLAS P. 403

Objective: Loot the bag by the power cable.

Story: A Voodoo Boy arrived to "fix" Martha Juste's antenna on her trailer. The device he installed (which plays a part in the "Killing in the Name" side job) caused another antenna used by the Wraiths to malfunction. The Wraiths decided to pay Martha's trailer a visit.

Strategy: Approach from the southwest and quietly neutralize the Wraiths when they are on their own – prioritizing the sniper on the trailer.

ASSAULT IN PROGRESS — 835

ATLAS P. 399

Objective: Loot Martha Liu's body.

Story: Martha Liu was a mercenary who resolved to kill Karubo Bairei (encountered during the "Old Friends" gig) to settle an old feud between them. While attempting to return to Night City to do the deed, she was gunned down by a border patrol.

Strategy: Coming from the north, use the vehicles to conceal your approach. From here, you can sneak up on each soldier in turn, dragging their bodies back behind a vehicle to hide until they're all down. If no enemy is isolated, be patient: it's only a matter of seconds until one of them moves to a different position as part of their patrol route.

ASSAULT IN PROGRESS — 836

ATLAS P. 399

Objective: Loot Robert Conrad's body.

Story: A group of Raffen Shiv recently attacked a Kendachi convoy and stole some of their cyberware. As Kendachi have an arrangement with 6th Street, they asked the gang to retrieve the goods. A Sixer squad led by Robert Conrad set out to retrieve the cyberware, but was defeated by the Raffen Shiv.

Strategy: Approach from the north and gradually neutralize the sentries one after the other, making sure you take their bodies away from the area. Once the coast is clear, feel free to loot Conrad's body even if a couple of enemies are still standing.

SUSPECTED ORGANIZED CRIME ACTIVITY  837

ATLAS P. 403

Objective: Eliminate all enemies and loot the bag on the floor in the surgery room.

Story: Rufus McBride is a ripperdoc running a Wraith clinic in an abandoned motel.

Strategy: We suggest an approach from the east, where cars provide cover and there are no Wraiths posted on vantage points. Observe and tag your enemies, then sneak up on them one by one. If you get detected or simply wish to fight, try to lure them to a defensible position where you can methodically mow them down.

ASSAULT IN PROGRESS  838

ATLAS P. 403

Objective: Loot the bag on the ground by the chopper.

Story: Michael Marcinkowsky was the leader of a Wraith squad smuggling goods across the border with an old chopper. Their most recent sortie ended when they were shot down by Militech.

Strategy: Make your approach from the south and deal with all enemies on the perimeter of the hostile area. Leave the two by the chopper until last.

ASSAULT IN PROGRESS  839

ATLAS P. 403

Objective: Loot the bag.

Story: George Prosky, a Wraith, identified an old drilling platform that could still be used to extract oil.

Strategy: You can sneak up on all the stationary Wraiths with relative ease. Another effective solution is to make use of the gas tanks in the area to engulf your opponents in large explosions.

ASSAULT IN PROGRESS  840

ATLAS P. 402

Objective: Loot the bag on the floor, inside the gas station.

Story: Joe Scalloni, a man who was good with numbers, was employed by Wraiths to arrange occasional transactions with other gangs. When the Wraiths realized that Joe was taking an extra cut from each operation for himself, they decided to eliminate him.

Strategy: The Wraiths outside can be taken down relatively easily as they are spread out; however you also have to pay attention to the sniper on the roof. Use the ladder in the southeast corner of the building to neutralize him first and the rest should be plain sailing.

ASSAULT IN PROGRESS  841

ATLAS P. 403

Objective: Loot the body of the shop owner.

Story: A group of Wraiths needed one of their cars repaired. They tried to force the owner of an auto shop to help them – but he refused outright, as the Wraiths were responsible for the death of his son.

Strategy: Perform silent takedowns on the isolated Wraiths, near the red shipping containers. Use distractions (or explosions) for the remaining foes close to the shop owner's body.

ASSAULT IN PROGRESS 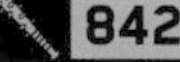 842

ATLAS P. 400

Objective: Loot Steve Harrington's body.

Story: Steve Harrington was a refinery engineer who stole some of the company's oil and sold it to 6th Street. Steve didn't realize he was being followed. The corporation's security forces dispatched both Steve and his Sixer associates.

Strategy: Try to stealthily neutralize as many enemies as you can. You should definitely deal with the one patrolling in the north part of the hostile area, with the containers, and possibly a couple more while no one is looking your way. Once only a few foes are left, either attack them openly, or swiftly loot the body and flee the area.

ASSAULT IN PROGRESS

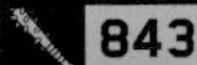 843

ATLAS P. 403

Objective: Loot the backpack on the crates inside the cave.

Story: A group of Wraiths are based in a small cave near the SoCal border. They operate during sandstorms to cover their smuggling operations, and bribe a local border patrol officer, Javier Fonseca, to ensure that their movements are ignored.

Strategy: Facing the cave entrance, crouch-walk alongside the right-hand side of the canyon. Stealthily neutralize all foes except the one immune to grapples – who can either be killed or ignored. Loot the backpack and leave.

HIDDEN GEM

 844

ATLAS P. 398

Objective: Loot Conway's body.

Story: Earl Conway was one of the few survivors of an illegal experiment conducted by Biotechnica (the Nightingale project, as seen during the "Guinea Pigs" gig). Feeling that Biotechnica owed him and his family something, he had been stealing food from the corporation's protein farms. During his most recent trip, he was caught by a drone and killed.

Strategy: The area is guarded by a single drone. You can actually loot the body and leave while the drone is on the other side of the rock.

HIDDEN GEM

 845

ATLAS P. 403

Objective: Loot the body of James Reddington.

Story: James Reddington was one of the two inventors of Glitter, the lucrative narcotic sold by the Tyger Claws. Feeling that his accomplishments were not being met with sufficient acknowledgement or recompense, James offered his services to the Wraiths, who prepared a lab in a heavily guarded trailer in the desert. The Tyger Claws spared no time or expense in reasserting their dominance of the hottest black-market IP in the metropolis.

Strategy: Coming from the southwest, you can sneak past the turrets if you time your moves carefully, but pay attention to the multiple mines deployed on the ground. If you can, quickhack the turrets to make it easier to tread with care.

HIDDEN GEM

 846

ATLAS P. 400

Objective: Loot the bag by the turret in front of the collapsed tunnel.

Story: Sonny Landon was in charge of a project by smugglers to dig a tunnel across the border. Ordered by his boss to keep drilling despite unsafe conditions, he perished when the structure collapsed.

Strategy: You have turrets to deal with here. You can destroy them or employ quickhacks; the choice is yours.

HIDDEN GEM

 847

ATLAS P. 403

Objective: Loot the body on the roof.

Story: A group of Wraiths were sent to shut down a power distributor (thereby enabling the gang to ambush a Kendachi convoy elsewhere under cover of darkness), but were taken by surprise and gunned down by a defense drone.

Strategy: Make your approach from the south, cross the perimeter via the broken fence section, and go around the area counterclockwise. The only real threat here is a drone patrolling near the body you need to loot on the roof. Wait until it moves away before you sneak in to inspect the body, then quickly retrace your steps to avoid a confrontation.

HIDDEN GEM

848

ATLAS P. 403

Objective: Loot Jane's body.

Story: Patrick Witwer used the confusion that reigned prior to imminent war in 2070 to imprison a girl in his basement – later joined by a male abductee. Witwer died when his ageing heart implant failed, condemning his two unwilling guests to a slow death.

Strategy: The building can be entered via a back door, on the southwest side, but be aware that the entire area is booby-trapped, both outside and inside. Avoid, destroy, or disarm the mines, deal with the surveillance camera and the turrets on the roof, then open the locked door. You can do so either with a remote activation via the terminal, by meeting a Technical Ability attribute requirement, or by typing the code (2054) found in the shard on Tony's body. You can then find Jane's body in the basement.

HIDDEN GEM

849

ATLAS P. 402

Objective: Loot the chest container inside the trailer.

Story: Feldheimer was a conspiracy theorist who tried to send messages to the moon. Taking up bandwidth from a real organization, he was given a warning to free up the channel – then dispatched after failing to comply.

HIDDEN GEM

850

ATLAS P. 402

Objective: Loot the body under the dead tree right outside the Biotechnica farm.

Story: Tina Agron was a protein farm worker who sold synthetic meat on the side to various restaurants in Night City. Used to dealing with the previous 6th Street boss, she failed to find an agreement with the new one, Will Gunner.

HIDDEN GEM

851

ATLAS P. 402

Objective: Loot the body next to the truck.

Story: Charlize Fury led an operation to rescue women who were artificially fertilized by Biotechnica. Security forces gave chase and decimated her group.

HIDDEN GEM

852

ATLAS P. 402

Unlock Condition: Complete MJ-21 ("Life During Wartime" – see page 121)

Objective: Loot the shard at the top of the airfield tower; you will need the double jump ability to reach it.

Story: John Wilson was hired to spy on a secret trade between Zetatech and Militech. He was detected by a drone deployed by one of the corporations.

HIDDEN GEM

853

ATLAS P. 403

Objective: Loot the body in the middle of the trailers, close to the solar farm.

Story: Carson Moss found a briefcase full of cash in the desert. He took it to his house, but was tracked by a chip in the briefcase and killed by thugs looking for the money.

HIDDEN GEM

854

ATLAS P. 403

Objective: Loot the chest container in the cave.

Story: Thomas Star was a Militech engineer who was kidnapped by Wraiths. As they forced him to work on a weapon, he secretly built an exoskeleton to fight his captors and escape.

HIDDEN GEM — 855

ATLAS P. 402

Objective: Loot the body by the fence at the protein farm.

Story: Samuel Morton was a Militech employee working on the moon who deserted and joined a criminal organization smuggling people from the moon to Earth. A wanted man, he was found hiding as a protein farm worker near Night City, and refused to die without a fight.

HIDDEN GEM — 856

ATLAS P. 402

Objective: Loot the body inside the crashed shipping container.

Story: Lilian Foray was a Biotechnica employee who was headhunted by Zetatech. Her transport was shot down mid-flight as she was being exfiltrated.

HIDDEN GEM

ATLAS P. 399

Objective: Loot the body inside the crashed car near the solar farm.

Story: Anthony McCormak was a techie determined to show he was the fasted Nomad in the Badlands. Adding considerable horse power to his vehicle, he failed to make the necessary adjustments and died in an accident.

HIDDEN GEM — 858

ATLAS P. 403

Objective: Loot the body by the wrecked van.

Story: Bill Norman tried to sell some unreliable cyberware to the Wraiths – who killed him once they found out.

HIDDEN GEM

ATLAS P. 402

Objective: Loot the body next to the burning car, a few steps from the road, giving the mines scattered in the area a wide berth.

Story: Tyra Barret was a Wraith trying to harvest some explosives from a mine field. She accidentally stepped on a mine and died after a friend failed to rescue her.

HIDDEN GEM — 860

ATLAS P. 402

Objective: Loot the body by the burning tow truck.

Story: Charles Bedella was a car smuggler who triggered the alarm of a vehicle he was attempting to steal. He was caught while trying to rush to the border.

HIDDEN GEM
861

ATLAS P. 402

Objective: Loot the officer's body next to his car, at the edge of the Biotechnica protein farm.

Story: M. Bell, a socal border officer, was paid by Jotaro Shobo to transfer women for his human-trafficking business. Trying to abuse one of these women, he was killed by her.

HIDDEN GEM
862

ATLAS P. 402

Objective: Loot the chest container in the bunker behind the building; you will need to pass a fairly high Body attribute requirement to open the door.

Story: Some corrupt border guards had a stash where they stored all of the merchandise they seized during their working hours. Unfortunately for them, their stash's security wasn't good enough.

HIDDEN GEM
863

ATLAS P. 402

Objective: Loot the body near the southeast edge of the Biotechnica farm complex.

Story: A group of friends met up in the Badlands to play a live action role playing game. They underestimated the dangers of the Badlands and were killed during their session.

HIDDEN GEM
864

ATLAS P. 402

Objective: Loot the body on the chair at the mass-suicide site.

Story: The leader of a cult, the Children of the Ark, convinced a number of devotees to kill themselves in the hope that their souls would be saved in a virtual Ark that would take them to a paradise.

DEATH FROM ABOVE
865

ATLAS P. 403

Objective: Loot the body next to the burning car, then the pod to the west, close to the gas station.

Story: Jackal, an agent tasked to secure the contents of a pod sent from an orbital base, was attacked by a hostile netrunner. He died shortly after receiving the coordinates of the drop site.

HIDDEN GEM
866

ATLAS P. 403

Objective: Loot the body next to the van, under the power line.

Story: Zachary Preston was a thug who smuggled a living cat through the border to deliver it for the birthday of a rich teenager in Night City. He was intercepted by drones before he could make the delivery.

HIDDEN GEM
867

ATLAS P. 403

Objective: Loot the body in the wrecked van, to the south of the solar farm.

Story: Shane Vogel was a clumsy thug who was supposed to buy a cargo of weapons from Tyger Claws. He was duped and given a load of sex toys instead, triggering the fury of his boss.

ASSAULT IN PROGRESS

868

ATLAS P. 384

Objective: Loot Costa's body.

Story: Maria Costa was an NCPD officer who had an ongoing investigation concerning Ladrillo's Dicky Twister club (as seen in the "Sr. Ladrillo's Private Collection" gig). Ladrillo decided to have her killed.

Strategy: Use both sets of stairs to sneak up on the Valentinos at the top. This leaves you with only the ones around the body to finish off.

ASSAULT IN PROGRESS

869

ATLAS P. 388

Objective: Loot the suitcase near the knocked-down vending machine.

Story: Bartek Ochman and his corpo colleagues were determined to celebrate the day's successes even harder than usual, and went to a club in Vista Del Rey. Ochman, under the influence of heavy drugs, killed a prostitute. The Valentinos went after them. Shot in the back, Ochman managed to hide in an underground passage, where he later bled to death.

Strategy: There are two entrances to the underground passage. The one in the southeast is poorly guarded, with a single sentry on your way. Cause distractions to isolate the Valentinos in the tunnel.

ASSAULT IN PROGRESS

870

ATLAS P. 388

Objective: Loot the briefcase on the floor.

Story: Raul Franco, a burrito vendor, was also a gambler. To clear his debts with 6th Street, he agreed to call them when a Valentino by the name of Gustavo Orta (encountered during the "Bring Me the Head of Gustavo Orta" gig) was eating at his place. It didn't take long for the Valentinos to suspect Raul's role in the case.

Strategy: If you enter the hostile area from the footbridge (accessible via the steps across the street), and crouch-walk alongside the wall to your left, it's possible to sneak straight to the location where the briefcase is found, with two Valentinos guarding it. They're both facing away, but other enemies in front of them are standing watch. Distract the latter using the nearby vending machines, then swiftly take down the two sentries on your way, loot the briefcase, and retrace your steps.

ASSAULT IN PROGRESS

871

ATLAS P. 388

Objective: Loot the chest container on the ground, in front of a pile of wooden beams.

Story: Chad McGregor, a foreman at a construction site, laid off Valentino workers and replaced them with illegal immigrants. The Valentinos stormed the site, killing both the workers and Chad.

Strategy: Sneak up on the lone Valentinos on the outside of the perimeter when their patrol routes take them away from their allies, then finish off the ones in the middle of the hostile area.

ASSAULT IN PROGRESS

872

ATLAS P. 388

Objective: Loot the bag on the counter.

Story: The 6th Street gang wanted to convince the citizens of Vista Del Rey that the Valentinos are unreliable guardians. To do so, they raided a popular arcade saloon.

Strategy: Stealth isn't an easy option in such close confines. Powerful weapons, explosions, or contagion quickhacks are all excellent options to dispatch all targets.

SUSPECTED ORGANIZED CRIME ACTIVITY

873

ATLAS P. 388

Objective: Eliminate all enemies and loot the chest container under the desk, inside the trailer.

Story: Valentinos found a vehicle model capable of transporting even more victims in their human-trafficking business, and they've been greasing palms to ensure that their shipments cross the border.

Strategy: Making your approach from either entrance, slowly and methodically sneak up on the Valentinos one by one, dragging them out of the hostile area or behind solid cover. When you reach the middle of the area, combat is hard to avoid. Open hostilities with a powerful explosion to gain a decisive edge.

HIDDEN GEM 874

ATLAS P. 388

Objective: Loot the body inside the shack, which you can reach via a rooftop grate.

Story: Jax Kermith was an illegal braindance creator focusing on nasty experiments and murders. He was himself killed by a secret admirer who gave him a taste of his own medicine.

HIDDEN GEM 875

ATLAS P. 384

Unlock Condition: Complete the "Olive Branch" gig letting the man in the trunk go free.

Objective: Inside the building close to Dicky Twister.

Story: Sergei Karasinsky was a thug who abducted a man called Alexander Pushkin. He wanted to "offer" Pushkin to the Tyger Claws to make up for past mistakes. The delivery didn't go according to plan, though, so Karasinsky was disposed of by the gang.

HIDDEN GEM 876

ATLAS P. 388

Objective: Loot the body on the rooftop, which you can reach using a vending machine and ventilation unit as stepping stones.

Story: George Hall was a thug sent to scare off restaurant employees, but he accidentally ran into corporate drones just before entering the premises, leading to his death.

HIDDEN GEM 877

ATLAS P. 388

Objective: Loot the body on a chair.

Story: Sam Carter was the Sixer who threatened Padre during V's Street Kid origin story. He was killed by the fixer after refusing to apologize and show some respect.

HIDDEN GEM 878

ATLAS P. 388

Objective: Loot the body at the top of the fire escape (reachable with a double jump).

Story: Gustave Berger was having an affair with a married woman. Caught in the act, he was killed by the husband.

HIDDEN GEM 879

ATLAS P. 388

Objective: Loot the body in the electricity substation.

Story: Trevor Estrada was a thug who believed in the plot conspiracies from Garry the prophet (encountered during the "Prophet's Song" side job). After taking unstable drugs, he thought he could turn into a superhero called Lightning Man by connecting to the power network – but got electrocuted doing so.

HIDDEN GEM 880

ATLAS P. 388

Objective: Loot the body between the buildings.

Story: Santiago Diaz was a Valentino snitching for the NCPD. He was caught and killed by fellow gang members who found out about his betrayal.

HIDDEN GEM 881

ATLAS P. 388

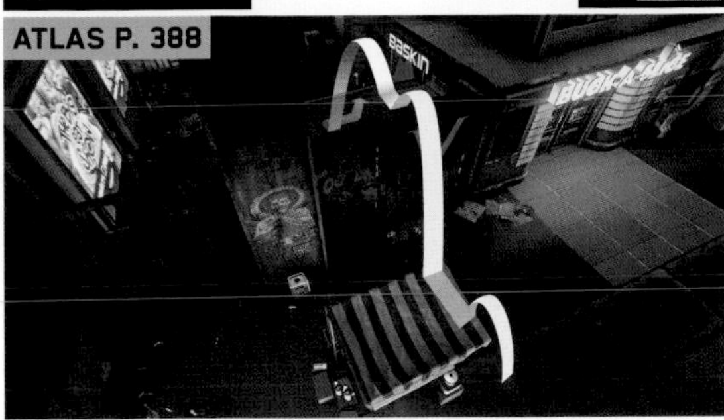

Objective: Loot the body in the enclosed area, which you can reach by jumping from the nearby food stall.

Story: John Doyle was an NCPD officer who drugged a Sixer to make her talk and thought she would forget their encounter. She didn't, and 6th Street eliminated him and his partner as a retaliatory measure.

HIDDEN GEM 882

ATLAS P. 388

Objective: Loot the body between the dumpsters.

Story: Jason Northman was a hitman sent to kill a former solo under witness protection status. Northman underestimated his target and was killed by him.

CHAPEL 883

ATLAS P. 392

Objective: Eliminate all enemies and loot the chest container under the metal canopy.

Story: Valentinos have a deal with locals – make an ex-voto "donation" and they will take care of your request. This chapel is where Valentinos store votive offerings from Heywood.

Strategy: You can neutralize a good number of enemies here by posting yourself on the edge of the hostile area and sneaking up on the sentries that move within range. You can do this on both the west and east sides.

ASSAULT IN PROGRESS 884

ATLAS P. 387

Objective: Loot the chest container in front of the couch.

Story: Valentinos looking for a new car decided to attack Jake Estevez, a mechanic working for 6th Street.

Strategy: By going around the area clockwise, moving closely alongside the wall to your left, you can sneak up on all Valentinos in turn. The man sitting on the couch can also be grappled from behind.

ASSAULT IN PROGRESS 885

ATLAS P. 387

Objective: Loot the bag on the restaurant table.

Story: Valentinos were sent to intimidate Tim Hutchinson, a member of the city council publicly in favor of the eviction of occupants from a residential block on their turf.

Strategy: Coming from the southeast, you can hop over the railing on the west side of the hostile area. From here, observe enemy movements and quietly take down any lone Valentinos you notice. Once the path to the bag is clear, feel free to appropriate its contents and depart.

SMOKING KILLS

886

ATLAS P. 387

Objective: Loot Gabriel Abatangelo's bag.

Story: Gabriel Abatangelo was a politician with moral concerns about the state of corruption in Night City. To get rid of him, a rival put a contract on his head. The sniper who killed him exploited Abatangelo's guilty pleasure: he would always smoke a cigarette on a rooftop after attending a braindance club.

Strategy: Approaching from the south, use the footbridge to get to the ledge where the sniper is positioned. Disarm the laser mines on the way and sneak up on him or neutralize him however you see fit. You can then collect the shard in the bag and read it to reveal a new waypoint, just across the street. Climb up to the designated rooftop, for example, via the vending machines to the southwest of the building, and loot the bag by Abantagelo's body to complete the assignment.

ASSAULT IN PROGRESS

887

ATLAS P. 388

Objective: Loot the container at the foot of the antenna.

Story: The 6th Street gang had suspicions that the Valentinos were preparing something big. They attempted to spy on them by uploading malware to an antenna near the Coyote club.

Strategy: Use the fire escape to the west of the hostile area to climb to the rooftop. From here, proceed cautiously as there are multiple Sixers patrolling, including a sniper on the power unit by the antenna. Sneak up on the sentries on the outer edge of the area when they're on their own, then deal with the sniper, before you finally attend to the man near the antenna.

ASSAULT IN PROGRESS

888

ATLAS P. 387

Objective: Loot the bag by the body.

Story: Sixers decided to shoot a Valentino car for fun, not knowing that Gustavo's wife was inside. She was hit by multiple bullets. Valentinos were sent to murder the culprits in reprisal.

Strategy: You will find gang members fighting when you arrive, making combat unavoidable. Make the most of the many cover positions available and consider tossing a grenade if your foes stand close to each other.

ASSAULT IN PROGRESS

889

ATLAS P. 387

Objective: Loot the chest container by the Militech crate.

Story: Militech has been paid to investigate possible corruption in the Night City government. Javier Alvarado, personal advisor to the mayor, is suspected of working with the Valentinos. His gang contact is a man called Gerardo Estevez. As Alvarado has corporate immunity, Militech was asked to kidnap Estevez instead.

Strategy: Sneak up on the guard in the alleyway, then tag all soldiers in the dead end. You can then neutralize them all with a stealth take down one by one.

ASSAULT IN PROGRESS

890

ATLAS P. 387

Objective: Loot the chest container on the white crates.

Story: A 6th Street unit managed to breach one of the Glen's transmission antennas, enabling them to hijack drones and other corporation tech. Their failure to employ suitable encryption made it possible for the corporations to track them down. A Kang Tao squad was immediately dispatched to eliminate threats.

Strategy: You can enter the perimeter via the entrance to the east of the hostile area. You will run into isolated foes on the way, all ripe for quick and easy takedowns – use the steps on the left and drop down from the elevated platform to deal with the second target. Droids are best disabled with quickhacks, though sneaking past them is also possible. If you wish to avoid fighting all enemies in the area, you can creep to the chest container on the crates, then retrace your steps and leave.

HIDDEN GEM 891

ATLAS P. 392

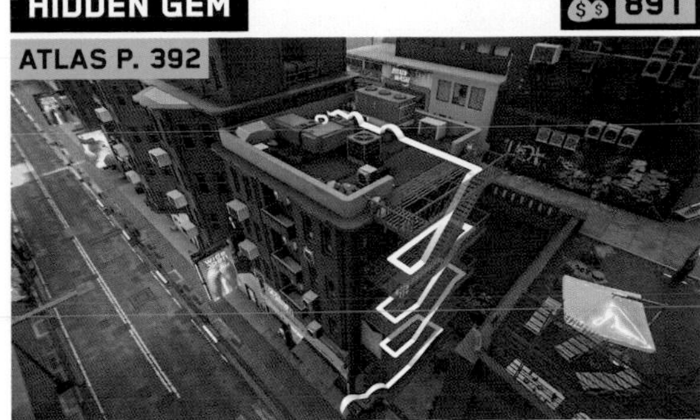

Objective: Loot Max's backpack.

Story: Max was an adept parkour runner who agreed to record a braindance tape while taking unreasonable risks. A failed jump attempt between two buildings led to his demise.

Strategy: Use the crates to reach the fire escape at the south of the building. You will find Max's body on the rooftop.

HIDDEN GEM 892

ATLAS P. 387

Objective: Loot the body under the scaffolding.

Story: Peter Bates was a Zetatech mid-level corpo threatened by an employee he had fired the previous day. Denied assistance by the company's security, he was killed upon leaving the 7th Hell club.

HIDDEN GEM 893

ATLAS P. 387

Objective: Loot the body in the enclosed area.

Story: Eddie McGruff was a thug who took part in a heist but was betrayed by some of his accomplices.

HIDDEN GEM 894

ATLAS P. 387

Objective: Loot the body on the pile of garbage.

Story: David Roy, a district attorney, had a deal with Valentinos. Asking for more money to bury a complicated case, he was killed by the gang.

HIDDEN GEM 895

ATLAS P. 387

Objective: Loot the body between the ventilation units.

Story: John Anderson was a corporate employee who was about to be apprehended by the authorities. Following the instructions of a mysterious caller by the name of ORPH3U5, he died while trying to reach the building's emergency exit via a ledge.

HIDDEN GEM 896

ATLAS P. 387

Objective: Loot the body inside the storage area.

Story: Olena Sorokin was a former KGB agent who left the organization on bad terms. She was caught and killed by KGB agents who tracked her thanks to her illegal weapon business.

HIDDEN GEM 897

ATLAS P. 387

Objective: Loot the body in the truck.

Story: Mike Nelson was a truck driver who suffered from an incompatibility between two leg implants.

HIDDEN GEM

898

ATLAS P. 387

Objective: Loot the body on the rooftop; you can reach it by double-jumping from the top of a vending machine.

Story: Chris Mulligan was a small-time thug who recorded a braindance of himself running away from the Valentinos. Suffering from a cyberware failure, he was caught and killed by the gang members.

HIDDEN GEM

899

ATLAS P. 392

Objective: Loot the body inside the partly open garage.

Story: Felipe Alva was an undercover police officer who infiltrated the Valentinos. When the gang found out about his optics recording implant, he was killed before his superiors could exfiltrate him.

HIDDEN GEM

900

ATLAS P. 392

Objective: Loot the shard on the table inside the garage (opening it requires a high Body level).

Story: A thug carrying powerful explosives accidentally caused the detonation of a touch-sensitive mine.

HIDDEN GEM

901

ATLAS P. 392

Objective: Loot the body in the dead end.

Story: John Dalton was locked away for 15 years by a mysterious man by the name of Evergreen. Released and challenged to discover the truth in five days, he failed and was killed by his former captor.

ASSAULT IN PROGRESS

902

ATLAS P. 386

Objective: Loot the briefcase on the planter by Jude Night's body.

Story: Jude Night was an up-and-coming actor who had just got a lead role after an audition. A jealous rival by the name of Tim Kelly paid some thugs to murder him.

Strategy: First, sneak up on the thugs whose patrol routes isolate them. When only three of them are left, keeping an eye on each other, resort to distractions to create openings.

ASSAULT IN PROGRESS

903

ATLAS P. 386

Objective: Loot the chest container on the ground by Jared Cortez's body.

Story: Jared Cortez was driven mad by extensive drug abuse. People in his neighborhood were so terrified of his behavior and bullying that they paid Valentinos to deal with him.

Strategy: Making your approach on the south side, you can neutralize all Valentinos with ease. Watch their patrol routes and use the vending machines as required to cause distractions.

ASSAULT IN PROGRESS

 904

ATLAS P. 387

Objective: Loot the backpack by Wesley Avedon's body.

Story: Wesley Avedon was an NCPD officer who discovered that a colleague, David Beemer, had a deal with a human trafficker. Rather than blow the whistle, Avedon tried to blackmail Beemer – which cost him his life.

Strategy: Neutralize both sentries on the edge of the area. This leaves you with only two more by the body. Cause a distraction with a nearby radio or similar device to separate the two guards.

LIVING THE BIG LIFE

 905

ATLAS P. 392

Objective: Eliminate all enemies and loot the chest container by the crate, in the main room.

Story: Animals have taken over a garage, turning it into an improvised gym that they use as a cover to prepare and sell the modified lidocaine called Juice that they are so fond of.

Strategy: The hostile area has two entrances. You would be advised to go to both in turn and quietly take out the Animals within range. Deal with the remaining Animals as you see fit; there is ample room for stealth maneuvers.

ASSAULT IN PROGRESS

906

ATLAS P. 387

Objective: Loot the container by the AV.

Story: A Valentino by the name of Jorge Ron agreed to down a Trauma Team AV to steal its medical cargo and distribute it to the local community.

Strategy: To get to the rooftop, climb via the southwest corner of the building. You will find many cover positions on the roof if you prefer stealth over action. Starting from the west side and progressing clockwise can make things easier.

HIDDEN GEM

907

ATLAS P. 382

Objective: Loot the chest container by the crashed vehicle.

Story: Catherina Byrn was a driver in illegal street races. She died after missing a turn and ending up in the bay.

Strategy: Jump over the railing and you will find the crashed vehicle in the water, a short distance to the west of the road.

HIDDEN GEM

 908

ATLAS P. 386

Objective: Loot the body in the enclosed area; you can use the barrels to climb over the fence.

Story: Jacob Miller was a journalist who found out about Callum Black, a corrupt police officer delivering women to Jotaro Shobo. Miller tried to blackmail Black but was killed in the process.

HIDDEN GEM

909

ATLAS P. 386

Objective: Loot the body between the two road lanes.

Story: Kyle Brown was planning to rob a thrift shop with the help of an accomplice, but he was killed by the Animal guarding the premises.

HIDDEN GEM 910

ATLAS P. 386

Objective: Loot the body under the metal structure on the shore.

Story: Leo Wood was a Militech soldier who lost his mind and had to be eliminated by his superiors.

HIDDEN GEM 911

ATLAS P. 391

Objective: Loot the body on the table; drop down from the promenade to get to the restaurant's terrace.

Story: Akira and Yuki Kato were two corpos who fell to a coup. They decided to end their lives (and that of their colleagues) on their own terms rather than fleeing, and opted for suicide by means of food poisoning.

HIDDEN GEM 912

ATLAS P. 392

Objective: Loot the shard on the shelf, which you can reach by jumping from the rooftop of the nearby building.

Story: A thug who stole Militech gear was instructed not to sell it for a while but failed to comply, leading to him being found and killed.

HIDDEN GEM 913

ATLAS P. 387

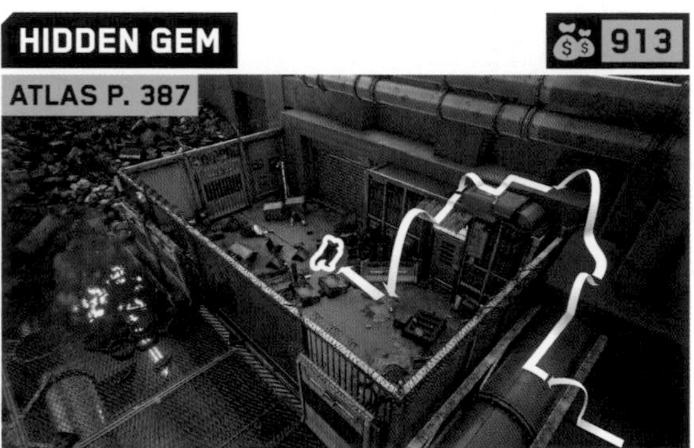

Objective: Loot the body in the enclosed area, which you can reach by jumping from the pipe on the east side; you will need the double jump ability to get out.

Story: Robb Swenson was a football player who injured some Valentinos during a game. Refusing to retire early, he was attacked by gang members who wanted him out of the match.

HIDDEN GEM 914

ATLAS P. 387

Objective: Loot the body in the shack located in the underpass; you can crouch inside via a small opening on the north side.

Story: 8YAGA was an old netrunner abducting children to abuse them. She was traced and eliminated by the brother of one of her victims.

HIDDEN GEM 915

ATLAS P. 387

Objective: Loot the body close to the pillar.

Story: Charlie Wang was a man in a desperate situation calling for Trauma Team. His membership having expired and been seized by authorities, he was left to die.

ASSAULT IN PROGRESS

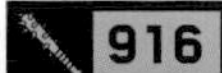
916

ATLAS P. 383

Objective: Loot the chest container on the ground, behind the fuel tank.

Story: Chubby Chip was an employee at the "Empathy" club (encountered during the "A Lack of Empathy" gig). Accused by his boss, Adam Ibrahimovic, from stealing braindance recordings, Chip threatened to report Ibrahimovic to the police. Ibrahimovic then hired a hitman to make sure Chip couldn't talk.

Strategy: Instead of using the front entrance, use the elevated ledge, accessible via stairs on the west side. Sneak up on the sentries on the walkway, then repeat this with the one down below.

ASSAULT IN PROGRESS

917

ATLAS P. 382

Objective: Loot the backpack next to Dario Sanchez's body.

Story: Dario Sanchez was recently released from prison. His friend Claudio Moreno, who took his place among the Valentinos, didn't want to lose his power. He killed Dario, then pretended he was a snitch.

Strategy: Approaching from the west, you have ample room and cover to take down the Valentinos who patrol the south of the hostile area. Launch a surprise attack to dispatch the rest of them swiftly.

ASSAULT IN PROGRESS

918

ATLAS P. 383

Objective: Loot Emilia Morton's body.

Story: Emilia Morton, a former Biotechnica officer, was fired after a disagreement with Joanne Koch (encountered during the "Guinea Pigs" gig). Emilia tried to blackmail Koch – but this only earned her a visit from a hit squad.

Strategy: Hide behind the planter closest to the body. From here, sneak up first on the slightly isolated enemy, then on the two examining the body, and finally the one seated in front of them.

TURN OFF THE TAP

919

ATLAS P. 383

Objective: Loot Sandra Faucet's body, then check the suitcase in her car's trunk.

Story: Sandra Faucet was a corpo who liked to party and to live above her pay grade. When she lost her job, she owed money to Bartolomeo Mordelini. But with her ready cash hidden in her car on the corporation's parking lot, which she no longer had access to, she could not service her debts – and will party no more.

Strategy: Sneak up on the scavengers at the bottom of the steps when the one patrolling near the van looks away. After you loot Sandra's body, head to the parking lot, a short distance to the southwest. It is under heavy surveillance, so proceed cautiously. Run straight to the upper floor via the ramp when the coast is clear. Once upstairs, neutralize the guard patrolling near the top of the ramp. You can then crouch-walk toward the car on the west side of the area, ignoring other hostiles on the way, and neutralize the netrunner in front of the car, for example with a quickhack or a stealth melee attack. If you prefer to eliminate the other foes first, this works too, of course, though you should note the presence of an android, which cannot be grappled.

ASSAULT IN PROGRESS

920

ATLAS P. 383

Objective: Loot Manuel Mendoza's body.

Story: Manuel Mendoza was a journalist leading an investigation into project Nightingale (introduced in the "Guinea Pigs" gig). He was on the verge of securing convincing evidence against Biotechnica, so the corporation had him killed.

Strategy: Use the planters to cover your approach and stealth-kill the thugs within range. Multiple vending machines enable you to create distractions to isolate those that do not move, making a full-stealth resolution possible.

ASSAULT IN PROGRESS

921

ATLAS P. 383

Objective: Loot the suitcase in the shipping container.

Story: Biotechnica troops have been deployed to a parking lot near the corporation's hotel to protect a VIP, Joanne Koch (encountered during the "Guinea Pigs" gig).

Strategy: If you want to avoid a fight, consider sneaking directly to the shipping container (a few steps to the east from the entrance), looting the briefcase, and sprinting back outside. This can be done in a handful of seconds.

HIDDEN GEM

922

ATLAS P. 383

Objective: Loot Greenfield's body on the greenhouse's upper floor.

Story: Jonah Greenfield was a corporate employee working in a greenhouse. He died choking after his company deactivated his cyberware while he was still working in a toxic environment.

HIDDEN GEM

923

ATLAS P. 383

Objective: Loot Mnutchen's body in the storage room behind the fence, which will require a high Body level.

Story: Steve Mnutchen was a drug addict who tried one new product too many.

HIDDEN GEM 924

ATLAS P. 383

Objective: Loot the bodies in the enclosed area, which you can access via the air conditioning units to the southwest.

Story: Alex Anderson and Ellie Grayson were two high-level corpos who settled a dispute over a missing engineer in the most violent way.

HIDDEN GEM

ATLAS P. 383

Objective: Loot Cyber Stallion's body in the garbage disposal dead end gated behind a Body attribute requirement.

Story: Cyber Stallion was a male sex worker who tried to blackmail one of his clients, Richard Flint, and paid with his life.

HIDDEN GEM

ATLAS P. 383

Objective: Loot McBane's body on the roof, near the ventilation shaft.

Story: John McBane attempted to stop terrorists by going through a ventilation system, but things did not end well for him.

HIDDEN GEM — 927

ATLAS P. 382

Objective: Loot the body inside the open crate; hop over the fence via the stack of pallets to enter premises.

Story: Lene Borowitz, a journalist, fell into a trap. Hoping to meet a witness with first-hand information on a serial killer, she was instead greeted by the killer himself.

HIDDEN GEM — 928

ATLAS P. 382

Objective: Loot the body in the storage area; you can either open the door with a Body attribute requirement, or go through the missing fence section on the side.

Story: Aiden Smith and his friend Zane assaulted a man with a briefcase full of money. Willing to celebrate, they called a drug dealer who robbed them and left them dead.

HIDDEN GEM — 929

ATLAS P. 382

Objective: Loot Costigan's body on the rooftop, accessible via the scaffolding and ladder to the south.

Story: Thomas Costigan was a police officer embedded in Night City criminal circles. He was killed after finding out about a snitch in the NCPD.

HIDDEN GEM — 930

ATLAS P. 382

Objective: Loot Ulhrig's body in the underground passage.

Story: Neil Ulhrig was a truck driver and a drug addict. He died from an overdose after trying out Glitter for the first time.

HIDDEN GEM — 931

ATLAS P. 382

Objective: Loot the driver of the submerged truck.

Story: A food delivery man was killed for getting a cheeseburger order wrong.

HIDDEN GEM — 932

ATLAS P. 382

Objective: Loot the container on the balcony.

Story: Larry Fangorn, owner of the Empathy club (visited during the "A Lack of Empathy" gig), was a wealthy man who had a secret stash.

Strategy: To get to the balcony, climb up to it via the crates and scaffolding on the left.

ASSAULT IN PROGRESS

933

ATLAS P. 383

Objective: Loot the suitcase at the rear of the van.

Story: Dum Dum (encountered during "The Pickup" main job) had a connection with an Arasaka warehouse guard. In exchange for payment, the guard let Maelstromers in to steal equipment.

Strategy: Enter the perimeter via the north entrance, and you can avoid most of the enemies in the area. Sneak up on, and neutralize, the couple of sentries you run into, open the suitcase at the rear of the van, then leave.

ASSAULT IN PROGRESS

934

ATLAS P. 383

Objective: Loot the chest container near the foot of the stairs.

Story: Edith Kutaga was a food vendor in one of City Center's busiest metro stations. She would regularly overhear conversations between corpos, and sell information to Dino Dinovic, the fixer. Insufficiently cautious in her choice of communications channels, however, she was eventually traced by Militech, and killed.

Strategy: You can avoid any bloodshed by making your approach from the north stairs. Wait until both patrolling guards move away, hop behind the blue crates at the bottom of the stairs and loot the nearby chest container and leave.

ASSAULT IN PROGRESS

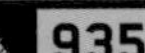
935

ATLAS P. 384

Objective: Loot Case Mod's body.

Story: Case Mod was one of Dino Dinovic's netrunners. Sent on a mission to download footage from a metro station (a reference to the "Serial Suicide" gig), she tried to breach the net via an antenna. She triggered the alarm and was dispatched by security drones.

Strategy: Climb to the rooftop via the planter at the south of the hostile area. Three drones guard the premises, but you can use the many ventilation units to sneak past them – or get rid of them with quickhacks, if you prefer.

ASSAULT IN PROGRESS

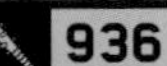
936

ATLAS P. 384

Objective: Loot Jezper's body.

Story: Jezper was a netrunner working for Dino Dinovic. After failing a mission, he tried to lie low in one of the fixer's hideouts, but his Kang Tao pursuers managed to find and kill him.

Strategy: Entering the alleyway from the west, you can sneak up on all soldiers one after the other for a peaceful resolution.

ASSAULT IN PROGRESS

937

ATLAS P. 384

Objective: Loot the drone.

Story: A netrunner called Jezper hacked a corporation transportation drone, which subsequently crashed. A security perimeter was immediately established around the site of the incident.

Strategy: Go up the first ladder and sneak up on the sentry near the top. The second ladder gives you access to the platform where the drone crashed, where you will encounter four more Militech troops. The first two can be neutralized from behind. For the other two, cause a distraction with the reflector in the back to isolate them from each other.

ASSAULT IN PROGRESS 938

ATLAS P. 383

Objective: Loot the bag on the stack of beams.

Story: Larry Carell and his friends were recently hired as interns at Militech. They decided to celebrate by going to the XXX club and getting drunk. After spending more than they could pay and bothering the staff, they were taken outside and beaten to death by the club's bouncers.

Strategy: Approaching from the alleyway to the east, cause a distraction to get rid of the first sentry. Repeat this with the ones in the corner: you have multiple devices available: a forklift, a reflector, and a vending machine.

HIDDEN GEM 939

ATLAS P. 384

Objective: Loot the body on the riverbed.

Story: Carter Smith was the man who, if you chose the corporate background, took V's role at Arasaka's counterintelligence unit. Overwhelmed by pressure and guilt, he committed suicide by jumping from a bridge.

Strategy: The challenge here is to locate the body, which is hidden underwater. You can access it from the nearby docks, then swim back to the ladder to leave the water.

HIDDEN GEM 940

ATLAS P. 387

Objective: Loot Groger's body behind the locked door; you can either open it by meeting a minor Technical Ability attribute requirement, or double-jump over it.

Story: Evan Groger was a technician consuming drugs while on duty. He had a fatal accident just as his position was about to be terminated following a positive drugs test.

HIDDEN GEM 941

ATLAS P. 383

Objective: Loot the body in the grass, under the circular walkway.

Story: A corpo working long hours ordered enhancing drugs to boost his productivity, but was assaulted at the drop spot.

HIDDEN GEM 942

ATLAS P. 383

Unlock Condition: Complete Hidden Gem 922

Objective: Loot the body inside the burning car.

Story: Ian Connell was a corpo under intense pressure who abused narcotics to keep up with the pace. He died from a heart attack.

HIDDEN GEM — 943

ATLAS P. 387

Objective: Loot Reuben's body on the promenade.

Story: Reuben was a thug being chased after a robbery. Following guidance given remotely by a netrunner, he took a wrong turn and was killed seconds later.

HIDDEN GEM — 944

ATLAS P. 384

Objective: Loot Stevens's body inside an open shipping container in the container yard.

Story: Lewis Stevens was tortured by a man sent after him, eventually dying from his wounds.

HIDDEN GEM — 945

ATLAS P. 384

Objective: Loot the netrunner's body in the enclosed area, which you can reach by jumping from the top of a vending machine.

Story: FANCYB34R was a netrunner who got cornered in the middle of an operation. Requiring assistance to shut down some cameras, he called a friend for help but didn't make it because of a computer update that took too long.

HIDDEN GEM — 946

ATLAS P. 383

Objective: Loot Cindy Hogan's body.

Story: Cindy Hogan, a technician in charge of the maintenance of skyscrapers, used her position to steal expensive tech parts and sell them on the black market. While swapping a brand-new air conditioning turbocharger with a used replacement, she caused a short circuit and died on the spot.

Strategy: Go up the steps and hop up onto the roof of a large air conditioning block to find the body.

ATLAS

The pages that follow offer hi-res annotated maps that will help you to explore every last inch of Night City and its surrounding Badlands. Whether you intend to simply take in the sights, or methodically tick off every last activity with the zeal of a true completionist, this chapter has everything you need to plan the many journeys you'll take during Cyberpunk 2077 playthroughs.

AVANTE

MAP LEGEND

This chapter features expanded maps of Night City, with detailed annotations revealing the position of key points of interest in each area.

Whenever there is additional information to accompany an annotation – such as the name of an establishment, or details on the specific whereabouts of a collectible – you will find that such icons are numbered. This will enable you to quickly refer to associated notes at the bottom of each page when required.

Reference numbers are used globally throughout the guide. The very first gig, for instance, is associated to #01. Wherever this activity appears in this book, you will consistently find it represented with that number. Each number is essentially the unique ID of a specific point of interest.

Note that numbers are grouped in logical ranges to further facilitate the identification of corresponding activities or items.

Legend

Base Icon	Point of Interest	Number Range
	GIGS	
	SOS: Merc Needed	01-69
	Thievery	
	Agent Saboteur	
	Search and Recover	
	Gun for Hire	
	Special Delivery	
	FAST TRAVEL	
	Fast Travel Position	101-250
	TAROT CARDS	
	Tarot Card Graffiti	301-320
	DROP POINTS	
	Drop Point	–
	VENDORS	
	Ripperdoc	401-537
	Weapon Shop	
	Melee Weapon Vendor	
	Clothing Vendor	
	Netrunner	

Base Icon	Point of Interest	Number Range
	VENDORS (CONTINUED)	
	Medpoint	401-537
	Food	
	Junk Vendor	
	Fixer	
	VEHICLES	
	Vehicle for purchase	–
	MISCELLANY	
	Apartment	–
	Bar	–
	Joytoy	–
	HUSTLES	
	Assault in Progress	601-946
	Reported Crime	
	Suspected Organized Crime Activity	
	Hidden Gem	
	CYBERPSYCHOS	
	Cyberpsycho Sighting	961-977

INTERACTIVE MAP

This guide comes with a digital extension in the form of an interactive map. By visiting **maps.piggyback.com** and using the unique code included in your copy of the book, you will have access to the premium version of our interactive map, completely free of charge.

At some point in the future, we might need to cease supporting or offering the online interactive map. If and when this happens, then we will try to give as much notice as possible in advance, which could be by email or by a notice published on our website.

DISTRICT MAP

[North Sunrise Oil Fields]
WATSON
[Northside]
[Arasaka Waterfront]
[Kabuki]
[Little China]
WESTBROOK
THE BADLANDS
[North Oak]
[Japantown]
CITY CENTER
[Downtown]
[Corporate Plaza]
[Rocky Ridge]
[Red Peaks]
[Charter Hill]
[Vista del Rey]
HEYWOOD
[Wellsprings]
SANTO DOMINGO
[The Glen]
[Arroyo]
[Coastview]
[Rancho Coronado]
PACIFICA
[West Wind Estate]
[Sierra Sonora]
[Biotechnica Flats]
[Laguna Bend]
[Jackson Plains]
[Rattlesnake Creek]

Night City is divided into six main districts, with the city's surrounding Badlands regarded as an unofficial seventh. Every district features two or more sub-districts, each with its own characteristics, be that in terms of demographics, architecture, or the perils that visitors might face.

Many districts and activities are not immediately available when you begin a new game. During the Prologue, a temporary lockdown means that you are restricted to Watson. You will be free to explore the entirety of Night City after you complete MJ-11 ("Playing For Time" – see page 132).

We would advise those who are eager to explore at the first opportunity to do so with a healthy measure of caution. All districts and sub-districts have a specific difficulty level range, which broadly determines your ability to complete activities in that area. You will likely be at a relatively early stage in your development just after completing the Prologue, leaving you ill-equipped to deal with most challenges and foes in the wider city and its surroundings. If you intend to take a sightseeing trip as soon as you leave Watson, be sure to avoid stirring up trouble on your travels.

If you turn to page 100, you will find a diagram that illustrates the difficulty level range of all map zones. Use this to plan your journeys and avoid difficulty spikes.

FACTION MAP

Wherever you go in the city, you can expect to encounter distinctive factions. These are well-defined groups that have unique characteristics and can often be distinguished by their dress codes, language/dialect, and cyberware.

This map shows the territories of factions that are firmly established in specific locations. Note that certain factions are not represented here. These include Animals (who can be found across the entire city), Wraiths (who are nomadic), and The Mox (who operate almost exclusively from a few key clubs, such as Lizzie's).

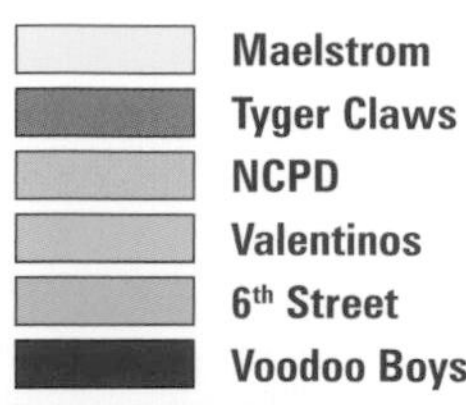

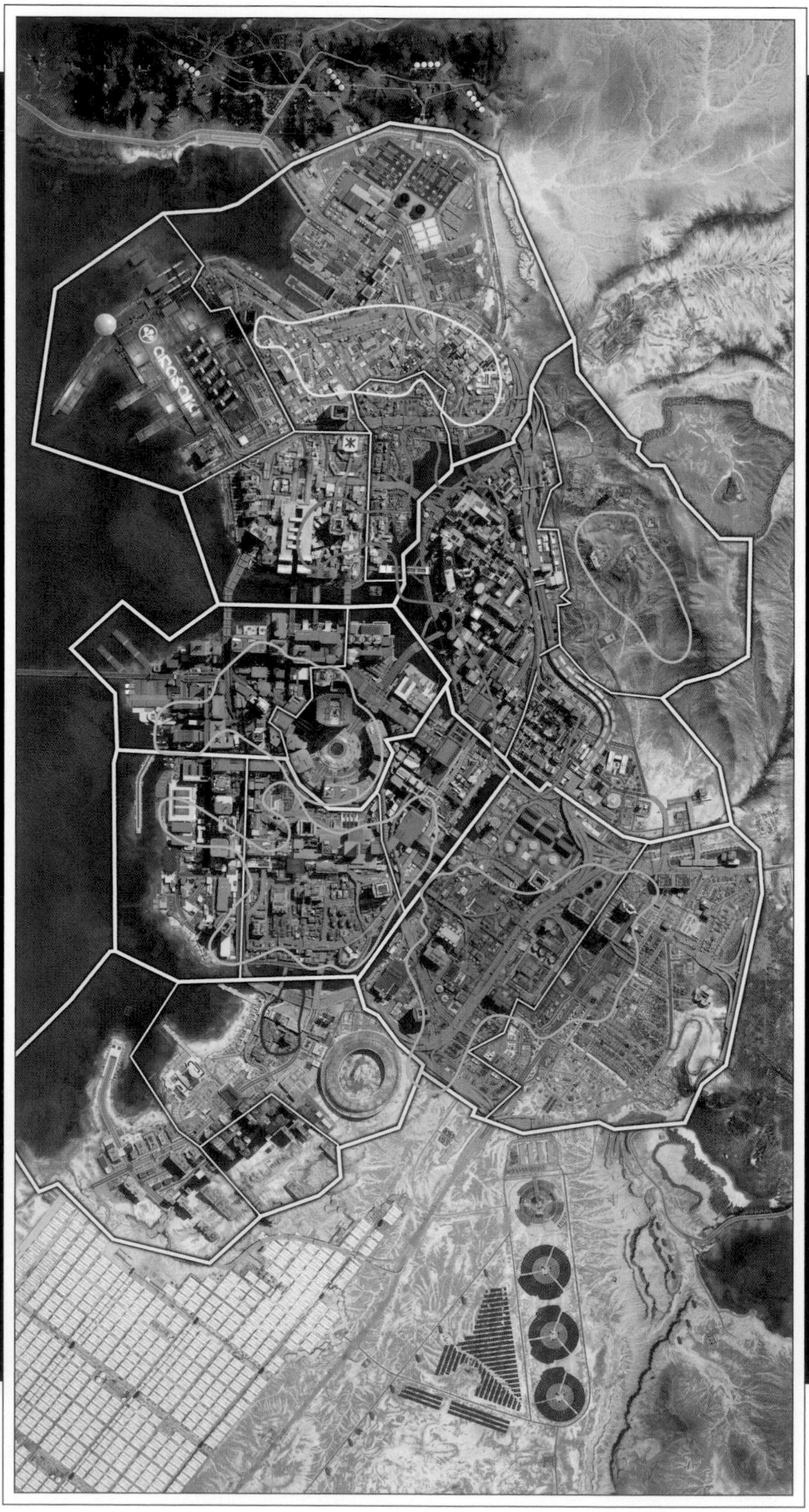

OVERVIEW MAP

In the atlas that begins overleaf, each page features a portion of the world map. The overview below offers a visual index of those map portions. If you are currently exploring a specific region, you can use this to jump immediately to the relevant page.

We have divided the world map in a grid pattern, with each cell corresponding to a map portion. Should you ever happen to be in an area of the game that lies close to the border of a map portion, you will find a page reference in the corresponding margin that will direct you to the page covering the adjacent area.

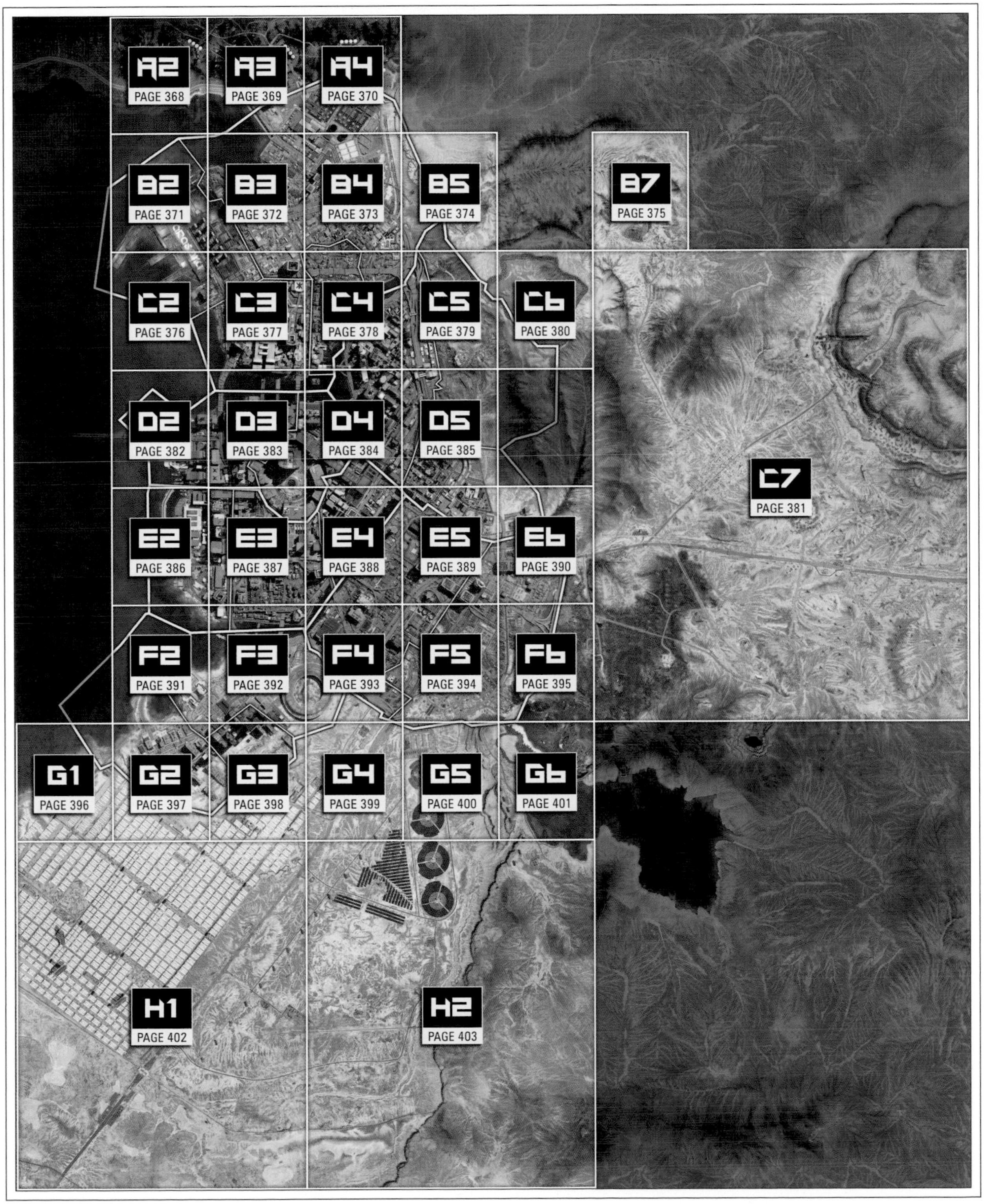

A2 PAGE 368
A3 PAGE 369
A4 PAGE 370
B2 PAGE 371
B3 PAGE 372
B4 PAGE 373
B5 PAGE 374
B7 PAGE 375
C2 PAGE 376
C3 PAGE 377
C4 PAGE 378
C5 PAGE 379
C6 PAGE 380
C7 PAGE 381
D2 PAGE 382
D3 PAGE 383
D4 PAGE 384
D5 PAGE 385
E2 PAGE 386
E3 PAGE 387
E4 PAGE 388
E5 PAGE 389
E6 PAGE 390
F2 PAGE 391
F3 PAGE 392
F4 PAGE 393
F5 PAGE 394
F6 PAGE 395
G1 PAGE 396
G2 PAGE 397
G3 PAGE 398
G4 PAGE 399
G5 PAGE 400
G6 PAGE 401
H1 PAGE 402
H2 PAGE 403

A2

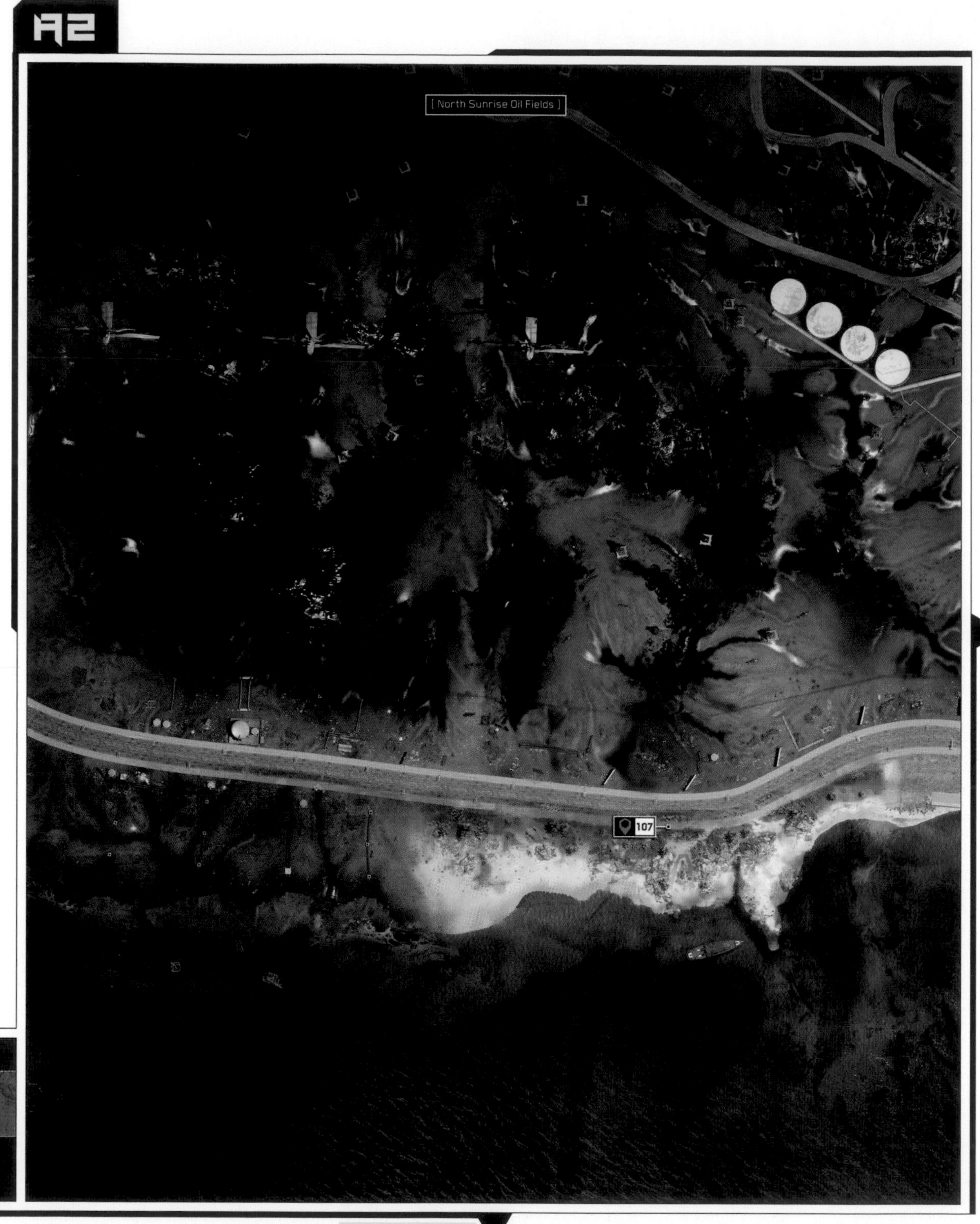

PAGE 369 ■ A3 ■

PAGE 371 ■ B2 ■

107 101 North

A3

PAGE 368 ■ A2 ■

PAGE 370 ■ A4 ■

PAGE 372 ■ B3 ■

105	Oil Fields
305	Tarot Card: The Hanged Man – On a water tower in the oilfields, not far from where a body of significance was discarded
670	Loot the body next to the car; see page 314

[North Sunrise Oil Fields]

[Northside]

657

669

PAGE 369 ■ A3 ■

PAGE 373 ■ B4 ■

657 Loot the shard behind the computer, under a blue sunshade; then investigate the van lying at the bottom of the nearby storage pool; see page 312

669 Loot the body outside the Barely Illegal building; see page 314

B2

PAGE 368 ■ A2 ■

PAGE 372 ■ B3 ■

PAGE 376 ■ C2 ■

194 Arasaka Waterfront North

PAGE 369 ■ A3 ■

PAGE 371 ■ B2 ■

PAGE 373 ■ B4 ■

PAGE 377 ■ C3 ■

15	Gig: Flight of the Cheetah
16	Gig: Dirty Biz
18	Gig: Rite of Passage
21	Gig: Freedom of the Press
22	Gig: Lousy Kleppers
218	Martin St
219	Docks
223	Pershing St
225	Ebunike Docks
465	ParaMED
490	Cassius
500	Colby C125 (see page 426)
533	Iron & Lead
643	Defeat all enemies and loot the designated chest container near the small pagoda structure (see page 310); this hustle's leader will drop the crafting spec required to craft the Buzzsaw weapon
644	Eliminate all Maelstromers and loot the designated chest container at the southeast end of the area (see page 310); this hustle's leader will drop the crafting spec required to craft the Psalm 11:6 iconic weapon
650	Loot Soga's body, then search the suitcase in the container to the west; see page 311
651	Loot the chest container near the van; see page 311
655	Loot the bag by the picnic table; see page 312
658	Loot the suitcase at the rear of the hostile area; see page 312
662	Loot Hax's body in his den; see page 313
664	Loot the body in the dead end, not far from Megabuilding 11; see page 313
665	Loot the body at the top of the spherical tank; see page 313
668	Loot the body at the bottom of the steps; see page 314
964	Cyberpsycho Sighting: Bloody Ritual
965	Cyberpsycho Sighting: Where the Bodies Hit the Floor

NIGHT CITY
PRIMER
COMPLETION ROADMAP
MAIN JOBS
SIDE JOBS
CYBERPSYCHO SIGHTINGS
GIGS
HUSTLES
ATLAS
INVENTORY
REFERENCE & ANALYSIS
EXTRAS
INDEX
MAP LEGEND
DISTRICT MAP
FACTION MAP
OVERVIEW MAP
ATLAS

B4

PAGE 370 ■ A4 ■

PAGE 372 ■ B3 ■
PAGE 374 ■ B5 ■
PAGE 378 ■ C4 ■

12	Gig: Last Login
19	Gig: Scrolls Before Swine
20	Gig: Occupational Hazard
221	Longshore North
222	Offshore St
224	All Foods Plant
487	Bucks' Clinic
495	Quartz EC-L R275 (see page 426)
530	Maelstrom Heat (only available if you complete MJ-08 with a peaceful outcome, see page 120)
646	Eliminate all enemies and loot the bag in the surgery room; see page 310
647	Loot the yellow equipment case near the back of the van; see page 310
648	Loot Alvin's body; see page 310
649	Loot the briefcase in the garage area, then search the chest container next to Kenton's body in the sewers; see page 311
652	Loot the body of the NCPD officer; see page 311
656	Examine the computer under the elevated freeway, then loot the chest container at the foot of the antenna; see page 312
659	Loot the chest container by the far wall; see page 312
660	Loot Drudge's body on the rooftop; see page 312
666	Loot the body atop containers in the storage area; see page 313
667	Read the email on the laptop inside the truck container with a door gated behind a minor Body attribute requirement; see page 314
671	Loot the body next to the crashed AV; see page 314
966	Cyberpsycho Sighting: Six Feet Under

B5

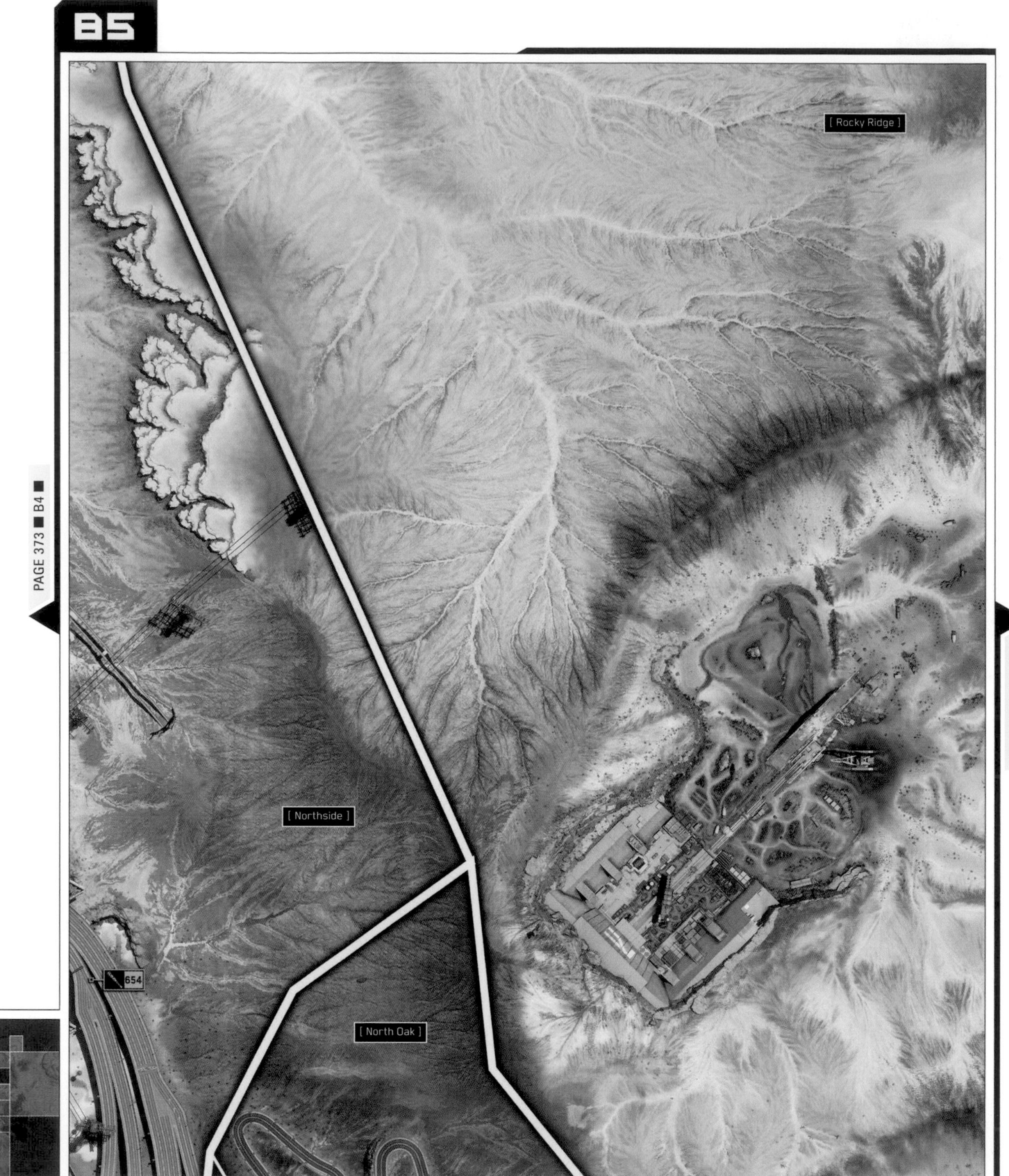

PAGE 373 ■ B4 ■

PAGE 375 ■ B7 ■

PAGE 379 ■ C5 ■

654 Loot the bag close to the second vehicle; see page 311

B7

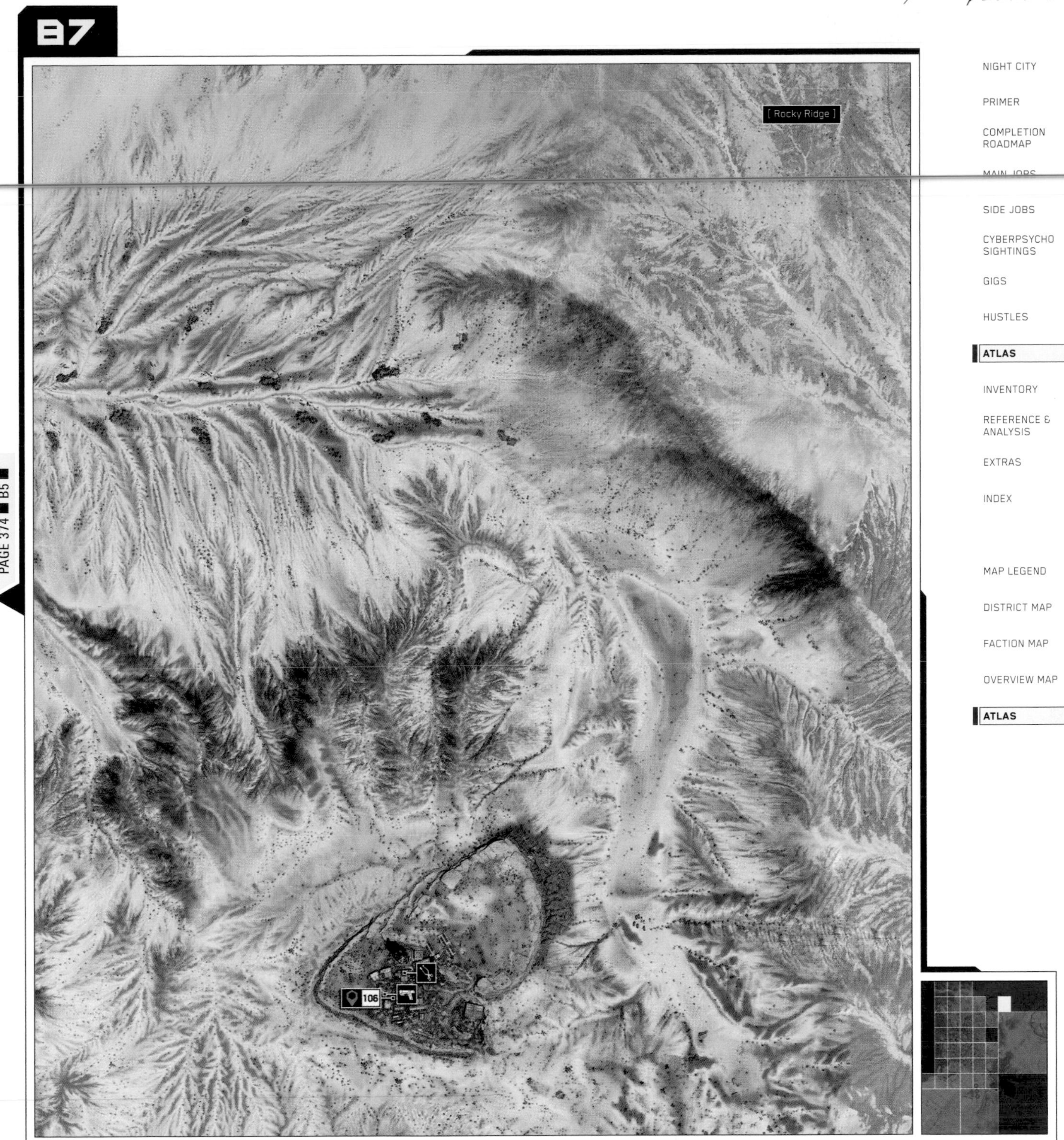

PAGE 374 ■ B5 ■

PAGE 381 ■ C7 ■

106	Nomad Camp

C2

PAGE 371 ■ B2 ■

[Arasaka Waterfront]

[Little China]

PAGE 377 ■ C3 ■

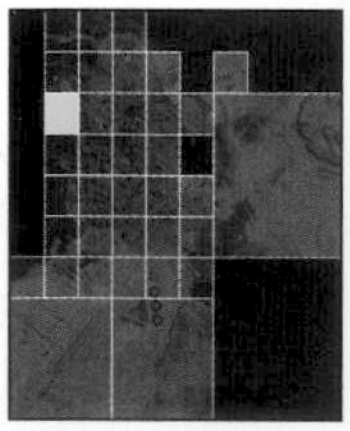

PAGE 382 ■ D2 ■

01	Gig: Playing for Keeps
02	Gig: Catch a Tyger's Toe
03	Gig: Bloodsport
04	Gig: The Heisenberg Principle
17	Gig: Many Ways to Skin a Cat
195	California & Pershing
205	Goldsmith St
206	Drake Ave
207	California & Cartwright
208	Afterlife
209	Bradbury & Buran
210	Clarendon St
211	Megabuilding H10
212	Megabuilding H10: Atrium
213	Riot
214	Metro: Farrier St
216	Metro: Zocalo
217	Metro: Ellison St
226	Metro: Eisenhower St
301	Tarot Card: The Emperor – On a wall next to Konpeki Plaza's main entrance
310	Tarot Card: The Empress – At the bottom of the staircase that leads to the Afterlife's entrance
311	Tarot Card: The World – On the balcony that you can reach via the elevator in the alleyway between Misty's Esoterica and Viktor's clinic
312	Tarot Card: The Chariot – On a wall adjacent to Tom's Diner
313	Tarot Card: The Fool – On the outside wall of V's apartment
314	Tarot Card: The Sun – On the wall by the tunnel
432	Afterlife

C3

PAGE 372 ■ B3 ■

PAGE 376 ■ C2 ■

PAGE 378 ■ C4 ■

[Arasaka Waterfront]

[Northside]

[Little China]

464 17 645 02 211 195 226 619 613 601 620 301 206 207 606 602 205 04 607 618 609 214 604 470 611 532 212 516 03 614 463 209 519 961 608 489 313 311 216 314 210 616 432 01 312 617 208 310 213 217 603 Riot

PAGE 383 ■ D3 ■

463	Yin & Yang Pharmacy
464	Meds Etc.
470	Coach Fred
489	Viktor's Clinic
516	Shion MZ2 (see page 426)
519	Galena G240 (see page 426)
532	2nd Amendment
601	Eliminate all enemies and loot the chest container by the landing pad; see page 302
602	Loot the chest container behind the van; see page 303
603	Search Griffin's body, then loot the bag at the columbarium; see page 303
604	Loot the chest container on the ground outside the shop; see page 303
606	Loot the chest container by the van; see page 303
607	Defeat all enemies and loot the chest container on the bench; see page 304
608	Loot Hunter Hyland's body; see page 304
609	Loot the chest container by the computer; see page 304
611	Loot the bag inside the ripperdoc clinic; see page 304
613	Loot the chest container by the wrecked car, then the one on the seabed; see page 305
614	Loot Shiva's body inside her den; see page 305
616	Loot the body next to the damaged car in the tunnel; see page 305
617	Loot the body in the fenced area; disable the two drones to take no chances; see page 305
618	Loot the body in the alleyway; see page 305
619	Loot the shard inside the shipping container, which is gated behind a Body attribute requirement; see page 306
620	Loot the metal box inside the garage; you will need to meet a Body attribute requirement to open the gate; see page 306
645	Loot Martin Lorenz's body; see page 310
961	Cyberpsycho Sighting: Little China

C4

PAGE 373 ■ B4 ■

PAGE 377 ■ C3 ■

PAGE 379 ■ C5 ■

[Northside]

[Little China]

[Kabuki]

[Japantown]

Lizzie's Bar

Ho-Oh Bar

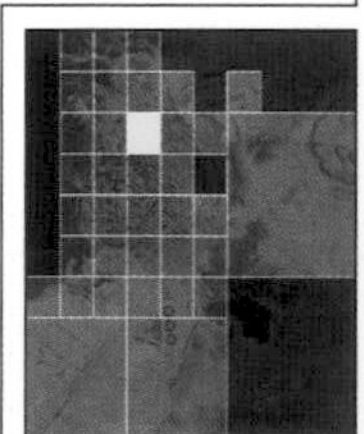

PAGE 384 ■ D4 ■

05	Gig: Welcome to America, Comrade
06	Gig: Troublesome Neighbors
07	Gig: Woman of la Mancha
08	Gig: Shark in the Water
09	Gig: Monster Hunt
10	Gig: Backs Against the Wall
11	Gig: Small Men, Big Evil
13	Gig: Fixer, Merc, Soldier, Spy
14	Gig: Hippocratic Oath
28	Gig: Getting Warmer...
196	Kabuki Market
197	Kennedy North
198	Creek Loop
199	Kabuki: Central
200	Pinewood St South
201	Charter St
202	Sutter St
203	Bellevue Overwalk
204	Allen St South
215	Metro: Med Center
220	East
233	Metro: Monroe St
235	Capitola St
238	Sagan & Diamond
242	Skyline & Salinas
244	Japantown West
307	Tarot Card: The Hierophant – At the beginning of an underground section, a few steps away from where you meet Oda with Takemura during MJ-22
309	Tarot Card: The Magician – On the pillar supporting the elevated highway, facing Lizzie's
412	Blossoming Sakura Clothier
414	Regina Jones
462	Roger Wang (available only after you complete the Shark in the Water gig, see page 265)
476	Yoko
486	Instant Implants
488	Dr. Chrome
531	Straight Shooters
605	Loot the shard by Dirty Fred's body, then the stash; see page 303
610	Loot the bag on the ground; see page 304
612	Loot the backpack on the basketball court; see page 304
615	Loot the body inside the Dime a Duzz shop; see page 305
621	Loot the body in the storage area; see page 306
623	Loot the chest container inside the garage; see page 306
624	Loot the container by the forklift; see page 306
625	Read the message on the computer at the rooftop slums, then loot the police stash; see page 307
626	Loot the bag on the crate between the containers; you can also optionally check the body of Tracy Owens, found inside the shipping container closest to Upmann; see page 307
627	Loot the chest container on the uppermost rooftop; see page 307
628	Loot the container by the garage door; see page 307
629	Loot Keiko's body, on the west side of the footbridge; see page 307

C5

PAGE 374 ■ B5 ■

PAGE 378 ■ C4 ■

PAGE 380 ■ C6 ■

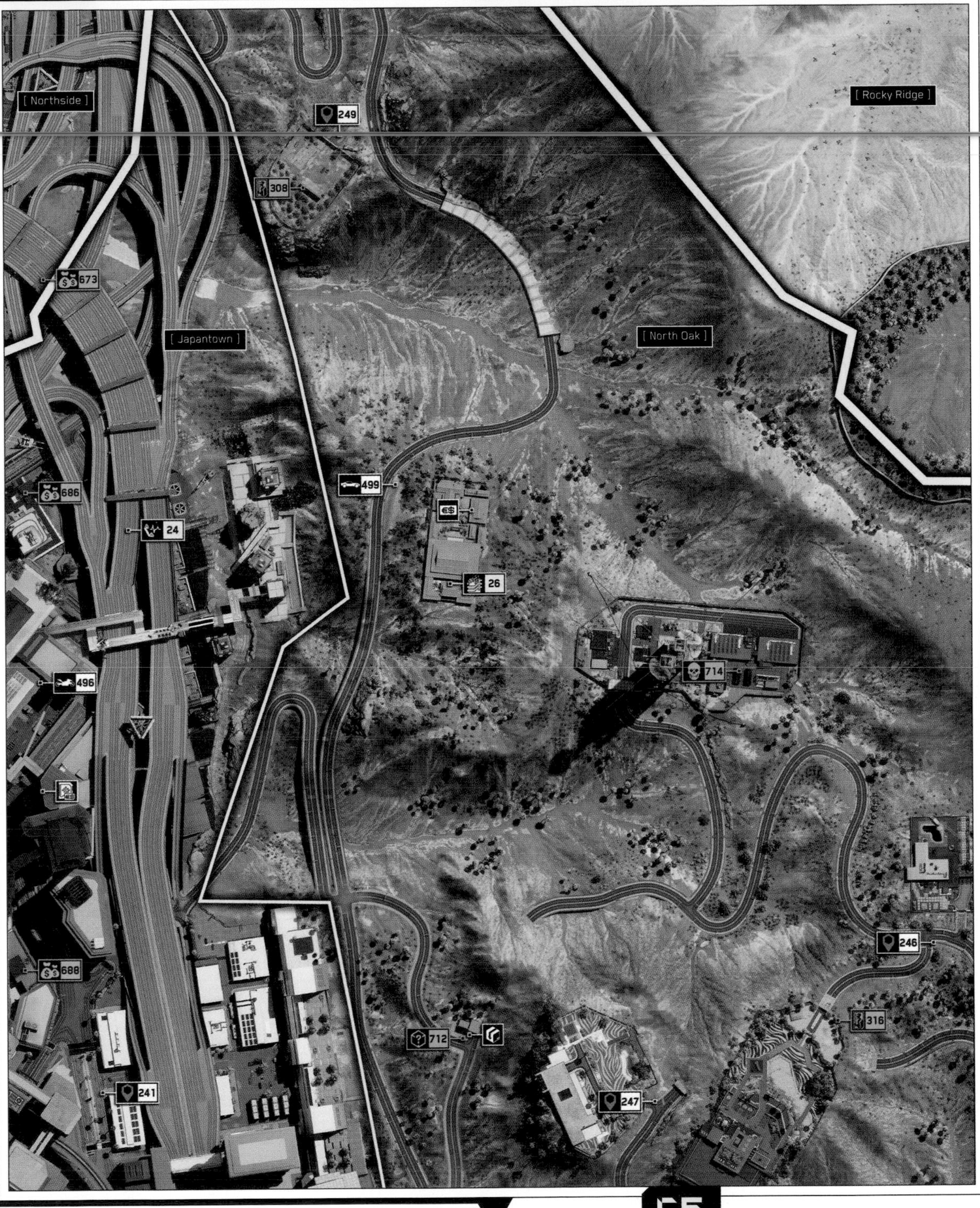

[Northside]
[Rocky Ridge]
[Japantown]
[North Oak]

249 308 673 499 686 24 26 714 496 246 316 688 712 247 241

PAGE 385 ■ D5 ■

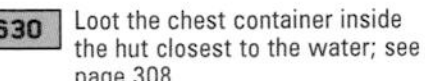

630	Loot the chest container inside the hut closest to the water; see page 308
631	Loot Watcher's body at the very top of the antenna structure; see page 308
632	Loot the body in the shelter under the bridge; see page 308
633	Loot the body on a couch; see page 308
634	Loot the body in a homeless camp under the highway; see page 308
635	Loot the body in a shack on a roof; see page 308
636	Loot the body on the footbridge; see page 308
637	Loot the safe hidden between air conditioning units; see page 309
638	Loot the body at the foot of the scaffolding, then climb up to the suitcase near the top of the structure; see page 309
639	Loot the body in the dumpster behind a food booth on the topmost floor of Kabuki Market, close to the elevator; see page 309
640	Loot the body close to Kabuki Market's drop point; see page 309
641	Loot Philip's body on the bed of the canal; see page 309
642	Loot Oleg Orlov's body on the rooftop; see page 309
653	Loot the bag on the crate close to the Maelstromers; see page 311
661	Loot Izaiah's body after neutralizing the turret; see page 313
663	Loot the body of the Maelstromer on the elevated platform; see page 313
672	Loot the body next to the burning car; see page 314
683	Loot the backpack on the ground near the thugs; see page 316
687	Loot the body on the shore; see page 317
689	Loot the body on the antenna relay above the street; see page 317
696	Loot Oriana's body on the fire escape staircase; see page 318
962	Cyberpsycho Sighting: Demons of War
963	Cyberpsycho Sighting: Help is on the Way

C5

24	Gig: We Have Your Wife
26	Gig: A Shrine Defiled
241	Fourth Wall Studios
246	Arasaka Estate
247	Kerry Eurodyne's Residence
249	Drive-In Theater
308	Tarot Card: The Lovers – Behind the screen of the Silver Pixel Cloud drive-in
316	Tarot Card: The Moon – On the outside wall of Hanako's residence
496	Kusanagi CT-3X (see page 426)
499	Type-66 "Cthulhu" (see page 427)
673	Loot the open shipping container in the underpass; see page 314
686	Loot the body on a landing pad; see page 317
688	Loot the body in the side alley; see page 317
712	Loot Joe's body on the sidewalk, then attend to the computer and container in his stash; see page 321
714	Defeat all enemies and loot the military briefcase in the storage area in the south of the compound (see page 321); this hustle's leader will drop the crafting spec required to craft The Headsman iconic weapon

PAGE 379 ■ C5 ■

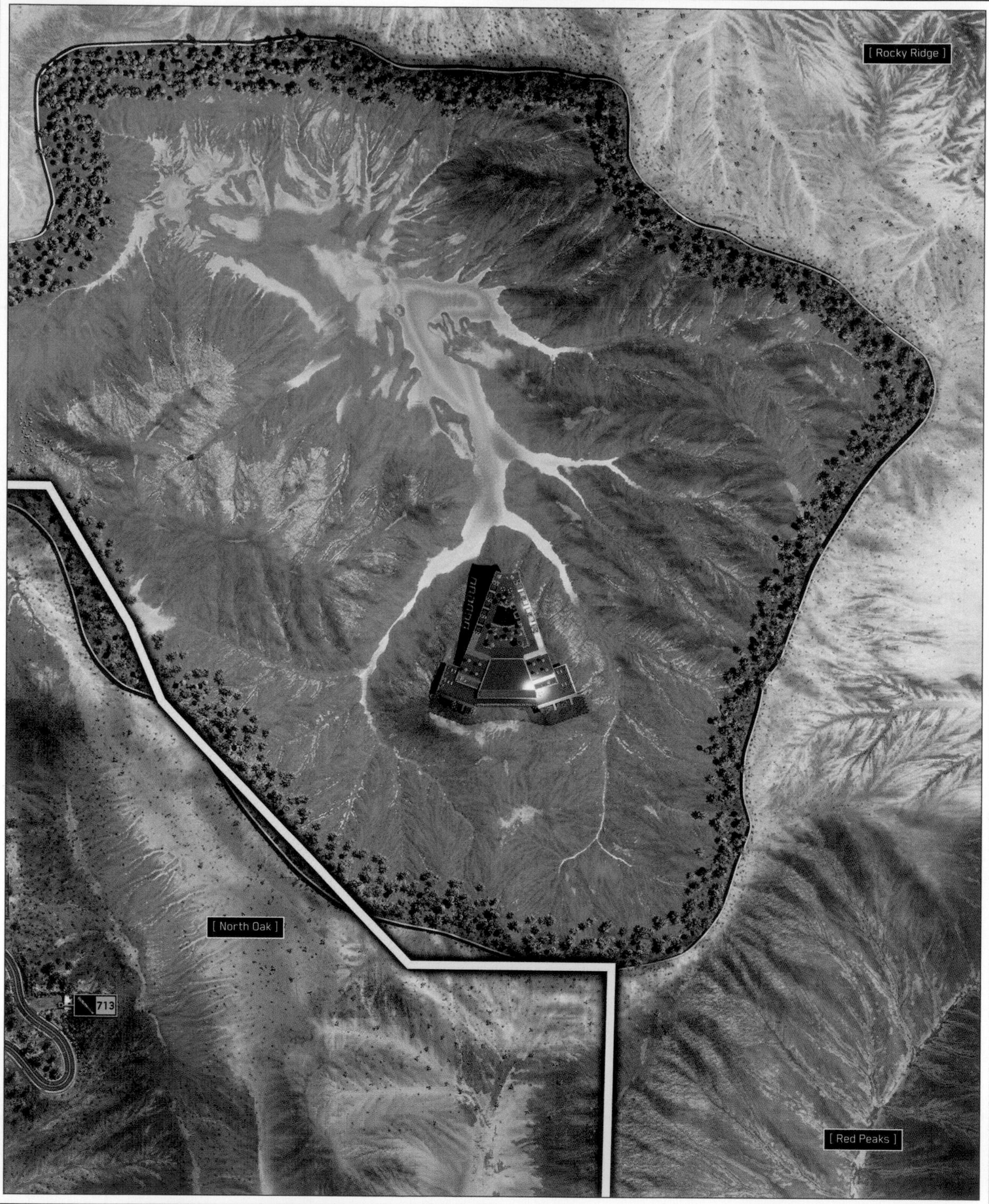

PAGE 381 ■ C7 ■

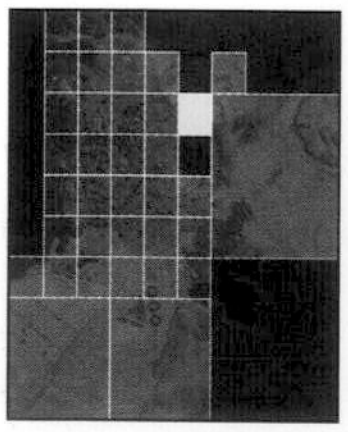

713	Loot Diana's body, near the crashed car; see page 321

44	Gig: Flying Drugs
45	Gig: No Fixers
48	Gig: Dancing on a Minefield
52	Gig: Radar Love
101	Sunset Motel
102	Medeski Fuel Station
103	Mobile Camp
104	Rocky Ridge
114	Old Turbines
115	Wraith Camp
116	Sunshine Motel
117	Big Rock
118	I-9 East
119	Desert Film Set
127	Edgewood Farm
128	Far Ridge
318	Tarot Card: Wheel of Fortune – Under the sign of the Sunset Motel
418	Dakota Smith
505	Colby "Little Mule" (see page 426)
514	Galena "Gecko" (see page 426)
515	Shion "Coyote" (see page 426)
794	Loot Harry's body, then search the chest container; see page 334
795	Loot the chest container by the car; see page 335
796	Loot the chest container at the foot of the tree; see page 335
798	Loot the suitcase by Colleen's body; see page 335
799	Loot the backpack by the tent; see page 335
800	Loot the chest container inside the gas station; see page 335
801	Loot the chest container in the middle of the camp; see page 336
804	Eliminate all enemies and loot the stash; see page 336
805	Loot Madison's body, then search her car; see page 336
806	Loot the chest container by the crashed drone; see page 337
807	Loot the chest container by the crate; see page 337
808	Loot the chest container by the Wraith car; see page 337

C7

PAGE 375 ■ B7 ■

PAGE 395 ■ F6 ■
PAGE 390 ■ E6 ■
PAGE 380 ■ C6 ■

[Rocky Ridge]

[Red Peaks]

Sunset Motel

809	Loot the chest container in the enclosed area; see page 337
810	Loot the body by a shovel in the wind farm, then the shard next to the bodies of the NCPD officers; see page 337
811	Loot the container in the car's trunk; see page 338
812	Loot the container inside the bunker; see page 338
813	Loot the body next to the car in the yard; see page 338
814	Loot the body by the van near the sewerage system; see page 338
815	Loot the body close to the billboard, approaching from the west to remain incognito; see page 338
816	Loot the shard inside the shack in the swamp, giving the nearby mines a wide berth; see page 338
817	Loot the body near the crashed airship; see page 339
818	Loot the body in the bunker at the foot of a broken wind turbine; see page 339
819	Loot the shards inside the underground shelter in the trailer park; see page 339
820	Loot the bag on the abandoned film set; see page 339
821	Loot the body in the bunker behind the gas station; see page 339
822	Loot the body inside the trailer at the foot of a wind turbine; see page 339
824	Loot the backpack at the camping site in the wind farm; see page 340
825	Loot the backpack a short distance to the east of the landfill; see page 340
826	Loot the shard inside the open shipping container in the landfill; see page 340
827	Loot the body by the river behind the Sunset Motel; see page 340
828	Loot the shard inside the shipping container, in the mine where you fight Nash during MJ-19 (Ghost Town – see page 150), then drive away with the Rayfield Caliburn to add it to your collection; see page 340
830	Loot the body leaning against a rock in Rocky Ridge; see page 340
831	Loot the body at the site of the massacre; see page 341
832	Loot the body a few steps away from the Desert Film Set fast travel position, then drive away with the Thorton Colby CX410 Butte to add it to your vehicle collection; see page 341
969	Cyberpsycho Sighting: The Wasteland
970	Cyberpsycho Sighting: Second Chances
971	Cyberpsycho Sighting: House on a Hill

D2

PAGE 376 ■ C2 ■

[Downtown]

929 928 927 136 932 930 137 68 917 511 931 160 907

PAGE 383 ■ D3 ■

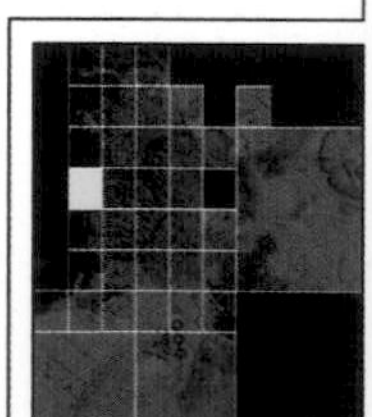

PAGE 386 ■ E2 ■

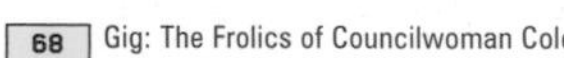

68	Gig: The Frolics of Councilwoman Cole
136	Skyline & Republic
137	Gold Beach Marina
160	Corporation St
511	Caliburn (see page 427)
907	Loot the chest container by the crashed vehicle; see page 353
917	Loot the backpack next to Dario Sanchez's body; see page 355
927	Loot the body inside the open crate; hop over the fence via the stack of pallets to enter the premises; see page 358
928	Loot the body in the storage area; you can either open the door with a Body attribute requirement, or go through the missing fence section on the side; see page 358
929	Loot Costigan's body on the rooftop, accessible via the scaffolding and ladder to the south; see page 358
930	Loot Ulhrig's body in the underground passage; see page 358
931	Loot the driver of the submerged truck; see page 358
932	Loot the chest container on the balcony; see page 358

65	Gig: A Lack of Empathy
66	Gig: Serial Suicide
67	Gig: An Inconvenient Killer
69	Gig: Guinea Pigs
130	Arasaka Tower
132	Metro: Republic Way
133	Metro: Memorial Park
134	Halsey & MLK
135	Berkeley & Bruce Skiv
138	Downtown North
139	Downtown Central
140	Metro: Downtown - Alexander St

D3

PAGE 377 ■ C3 ■

PAGE 382 ■ D2 ■

PAGE 384 ■ D4 ■

PAGE 387 ■ E3 ■

303	Tarot Card: The Tower – In an underground passage at the base of Arasaka Tower
403	Jinguji
413	Dino Dinovic
510	Columbus V340-F Freight (see page 427)
517	Type-66 Avenger (see page 427)
916	Loot the chest container on the ground, behind the fuel tank; see page 355
918	Loot Emilia Morton's body; see page 355
919	Loot Sandra Faucet's body, then check the suitcase in her car's trunk; see page 355
920	Loot Manuel Mendoza's body; see page 355
921	Loot the suitcase in the shipping container; see page 356
922	Loot Greenfield's body on the greenhouse's upper floor; see page 356
923	Loot Mnutchen's body in the storage room behind the fence, which will require a high Body level; see page 356
924	Loot the bodies in the enclosed area, which you can access via the air conditioning units to the southwest; see page 357
925	Loot Cyber Stallion's body in the garbage disposal dead end, gated behind a Body attribute requirement; see page 357
926	Loot McBane's body on the roof, in the ventilation shaft; see page 357
933	Loot the suitcase at the rear of the van; see page 359
934	Loot the chest container near the foot of the stairs; see page 359
938	Loot the bag on the stack of beams; see page 360
941	Loot the body in the grass, under the circular walkway; see page 360
942	Loot the body inside the burning car; see page 360
946	Loot Cindy Hogan's body; see page 361
974	Cyberpsycho Sighting: On Deaf Ears
975	Cyberpsycho Sighting: Phantom of Night City

D4

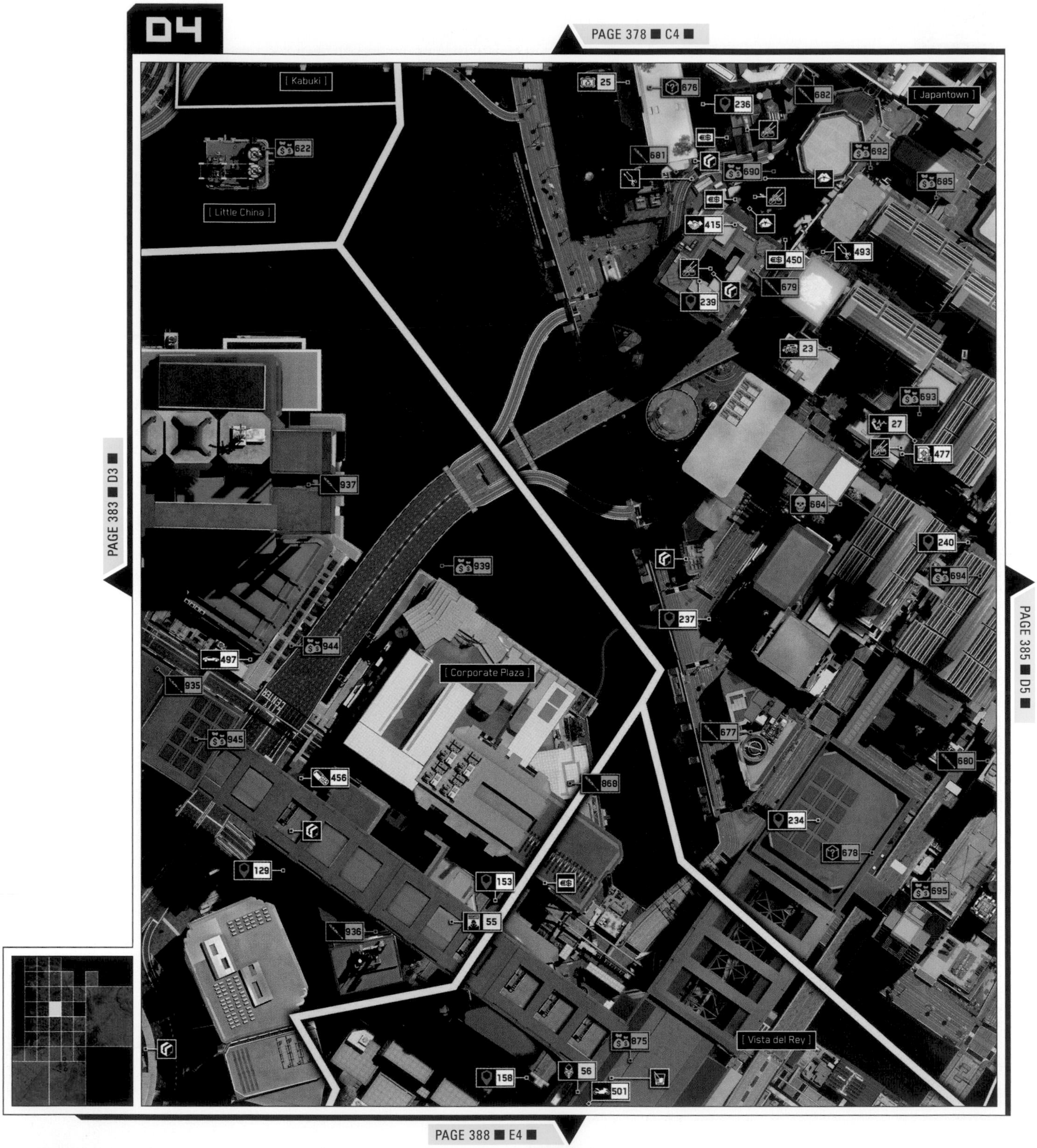

PAGE 378 ■ C4 ■

PAGE 383 ■ D3 ■

PAGE 385 ■ D5 ■

[Kabuki]

[Little China]

[Japantown]

[Corporate Plaza]

[Vista del Rey]

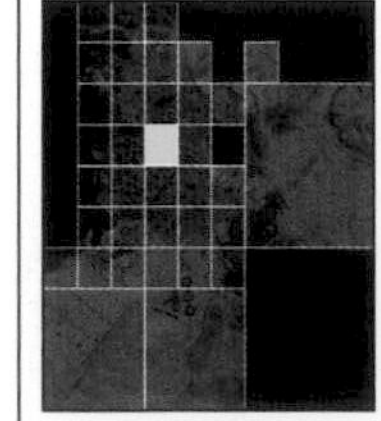

PAGE 388 ■ E4 ■

- **23** Gig: Olive Branch
- **25** Gig: Greed Never Pays
- **27** Gig: Wakako's Favorite
- **55** Gig: Bring Me the Head of Gustavo Orta
- **56** Gig: Sr. Ladrillo's Private Collection
- **129** Ring Road
- **153** Petrel St
- **158** Delamain HQ
- **234** Metro: Japantown South
- **236** Cherry Blossom Market
- **237** Silk Road West
- **239** Megabuilding H8
- **240** Crescent & Broad
- **415** Wakako Okada
- **450** Dealer (the man who sells the XBD during MJ-14, see page 139)
- **456** Old Nature Clinic
- **477** Chang Hoon Nam (available only if you save him during the Wakako's Favorite gig, see page 277)
- **493** Fingers M.D. (available only if you do not harm him during MJ-13, see page 138)
- **497** Outlaw GTS (see page 427)
- **501** Apollo (see page 427)
- **622** Loot the container on the topmost platform; see page 306
- **676** Loot the body in the back alley, then attend to the stash; see page 315
- **677** Loot the bag by Anderson's body; see page 315
- **678** Loot Dante's body, then the chest container in the stash; see page 315
- **679** Loot Max Smith's body; see page 316
- **680** Loot the body in the car's trunk; see page 316
- **681** Loot the bag on the bar counter; see page 316
- **682** Loot the bag near the body of O'Brien; see page 316
- **684** Eliminate all enemies and loot the box on the ground, by the couches (see page 316); this hustle's leader will drop the crafting spec required to craft the Sovereign weapon
- **685** Loot the bag by Matt Maksymowiz's body at the bottom of the shaft; see page 317
- **690** Loot the body inside the shack on the rooftop, above Jig Jig Street's entrance; see page 317
- **692** Loot the body on the walkway, close to the tree; see page 318
- **693** Loot the bag next to the chair; see page 318
- **694** Loot the body in the van, a short walk from the Crescent & Broad fast travel position; see page 318
- **695** Loot the body in the alleyway; see page 318

D5

PAGE 379 ■ C5 ■

PAGE 384 ■ D4 ■

[Japantown]

[North Oak]

[Charter Hill]

675 715 502 250 243 691 248 315 674 711 227 245 699 232 698 29 700 229 491 228

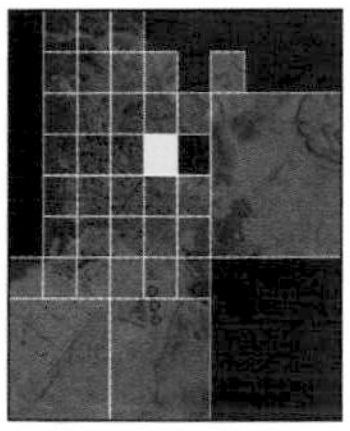

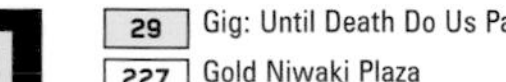

PAGE 389 ■ E5 ■

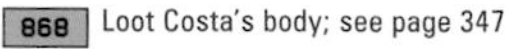

- **868** Loot Costa's body; see page 347
- **875** Inside the building close to Dicky Twister; see page 348
- **935** Loot Case Mod's body; see page 359
- **936** Loot Jesper's body; see page 359
- **937** Loot the drone; see page 359
- **939** Loot the body on the riverbed; see page 360
- **944** Loot Stevens's body inside an open shipping container in the container yard; see page 361
- **945** Loot the netrunner's body in the enclosed area, which you can reach by jumping from the top of a vending machine; see page 361

D5

- **29** Gig: Until Death Do Us Part
- **227** Gold Niwaki Plaza
- **228** Lele Park
- **229** Luxury Apartments
- **232** Metro: Charter Hill
- **243** Redwood Market
- **245** Dark Matter
- **248** Columbarium
- **250** North Oak Sign
- **315** Tarot Card: Temperance – On one of the walls in the North Oak columbarium
- **491** Kraviz's Clinic
- **502** Rayfield Aerondight "Guinevere" (see page 426)
- **674** Loot the suitcase on the ground, next to the van; see page 315
- **675** Loot the bag on the ground, between the two garage ramps; see page 315
- **691** Loot the safe above the gym; see page 318
- **698** Loot the bag lying on an old mattress; see page 319
- **699** Loot the suitcase on the ground; see page 319
- **700** Loot the backpack on the ground; see page 319
- **711** Loot Frank Hover's body, then find his stash; see page 321
- **715** Loot the delivery drone inside the "O" of the North Oak sign; see page 322

E2

PAGE 382 ■ D2 ■

PAGE 387 ■ E3 ■

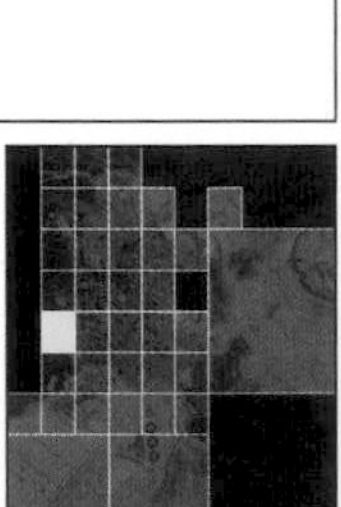

PAGE 391 ■ F2 ■

63	Gig: The Lord Giveth and Taketh Away
64	Gig: Hot Merchandise
161	Cannery Plaza
162	Berkeley & Bay
164	Parque del Mar
165	Palms View Plaza
166	Pumping Station
425	Fresh Food
512	Cortes V5000 Valor (see page 426)
513	Thrax 388 Roosevelt (see page 426)
902	Loot the briefcase on the planter by Jude Night's body; see page 352
903	Loot the chest container on the ground by Jared Cortez's body; see page 352
908	Loot the body in the enclosed area; you can use the barrels to climb over the fence; see page 353
909	Loot the body between the two road lanes; see page 353
910	Loot the body under the metal structure on the shore; see page 354
977	Cyberpsycho Sighting: Letter of the Law

E3

58	Gig: Fifth Column
59	Gig: Psychofan
60	Gig: Eye for an Eye
61	Gig: Going Up or Down?
62	Gig: On a Tight Leash
131	Reconciliation Park
141	Senate & Market
142	Ventura & Skyline
143	Palms View Way
144	El Coyote Cojo
147	Valentino Alley
148	Embers
149	Metro: Glen North
151	Metro: Ebunike
163	Megabuilding H2
167	Metro: Market St
319	Tarot Card: Death – On the side of the building where the Embers restaurant is found
402	Appel de Paris
498	Emperor 620 Ragnar (see page 427)
518	Alvarado V4F 570 Delegate (see page 426)

E3

PAGE 383 ■ D3 ■

PAGE 386 ■ E2 ■

PAGE 388 ■ E4 ■

PAGE 392 ■ F3 ■

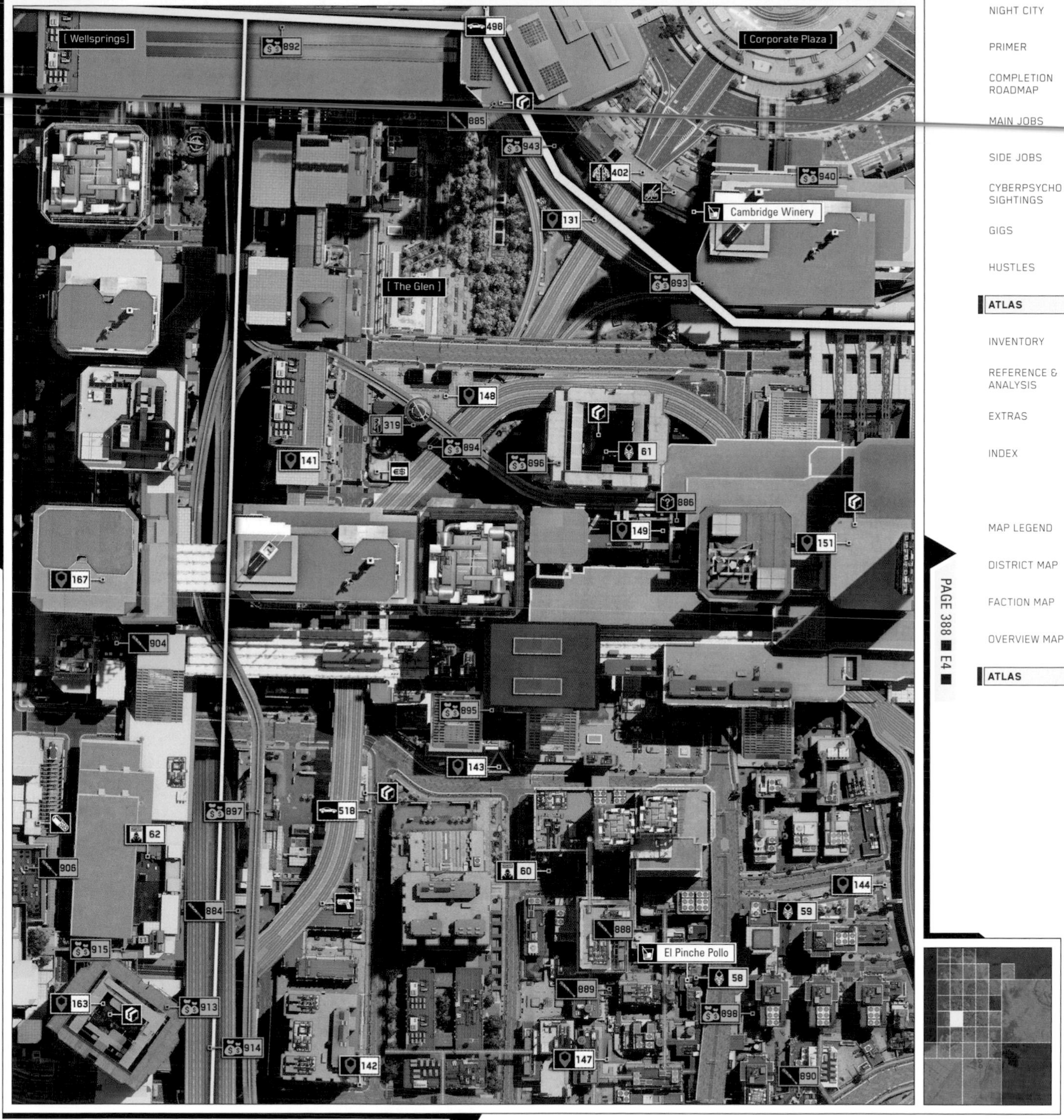

[Wellsprings]

[Corporate Plaza]

Cambridge Winery

[The Glen]

El Pinche Pollo

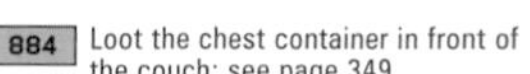

- 884 Loot the chest container in front of the couch; see page 349
- 885 Loot the bag on the restaurant table; see page 349
- 886 Loot Gabriel Abatangelo's bag; see page 350
- 888 Loot the bag by the body; see page 350
- 889 Loot the chest container by the Militech crate; see page 350
- 890 Loot the chest container on the white crates; see page 350
- 892 Loot the body under scaffolding; see page 351
- 893 Loot the body in the enclosed area; see page 351
- 894 Loot the body on the pile of garbage; see page 351
- 895 Loot the body between the ventilation units; see page 351
- 896 Loot the body inside the storage area; see page 351
- 897 Loot the body in the truck; see page 351
- 898 Loot the body on the rooftop; you can reach it by double-jumping from the top of a vending machine; see page 352
- 904 Loot the backpack by Wesley Avedon's body; see page 353
- 906 Loot the container by the AV; see page 353
- 913 Loot the body in the enclosed area, which you can reach by jumping from the pipe on the east side; you will need the double jump ability to get out; see page 354
- 914 Loot the body in the shack located in the underpass; you can crouch inside via a small opening on the north side; see page 354
- 915 Loot the body close to the pillar; see page 354
- 940 Loot Groger's body behind the locked door; you can either open it by meeting a minor Technical Ability attribute requirement, or double-jump over it; see page 360
- 943 Loot Reuben's body on the promenade; see page 361

E4

PAGE 384 ■ D4 ■

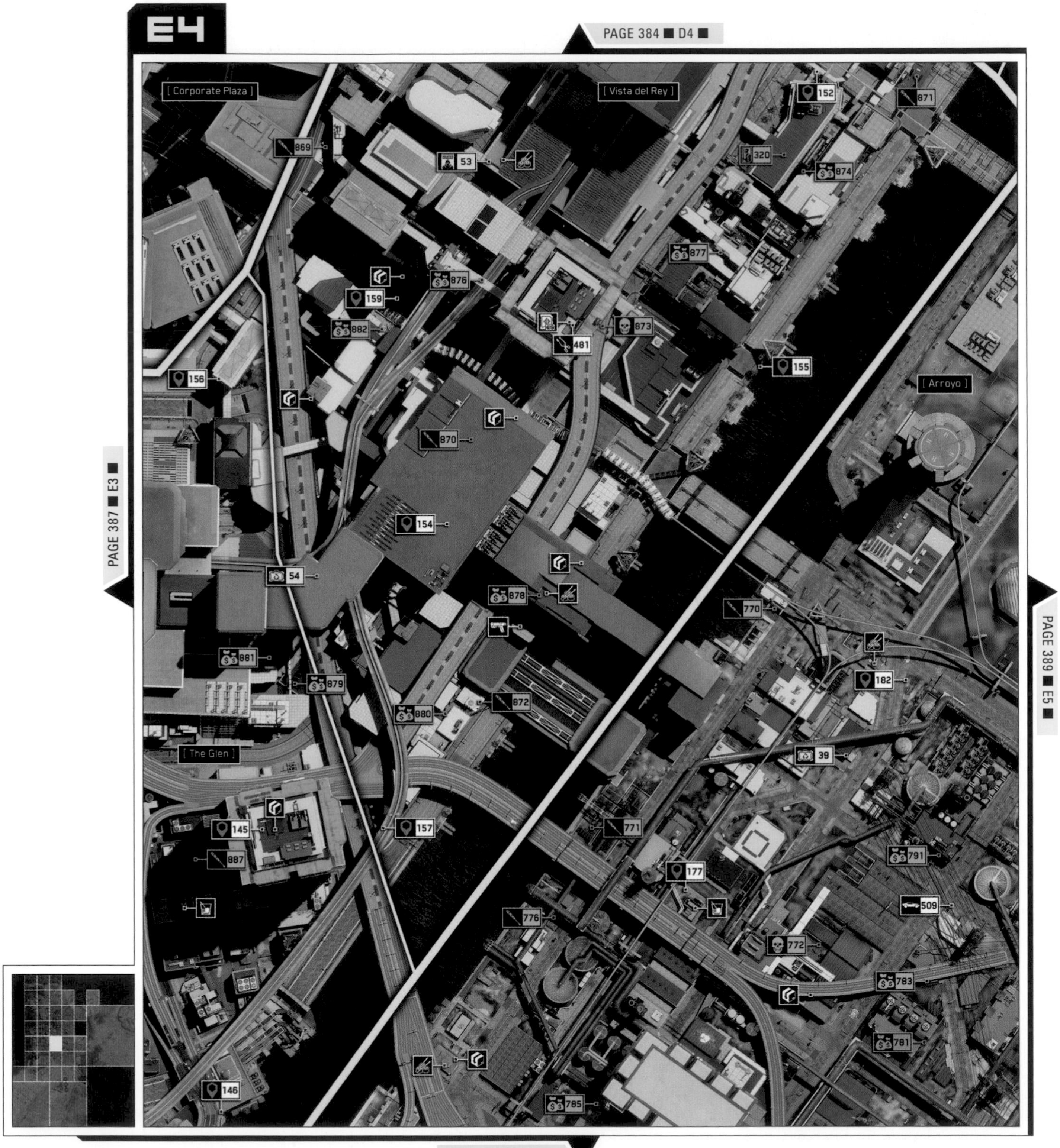

[Corporate Plaza]

[Vista del Rey]

[Arroyo]

[The Glen]

PAGE 387 ■ E3 ■

PAGE 389 ■ E5 ■

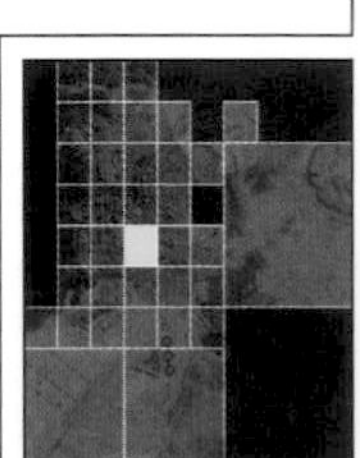

PAGE 393 ■ F4 ■

39	Gig: Serious Side Effects
53	Gig: Old Friends
54	Gig: Jeopardy
145	Megabuilding H3
146	Hanford Overpass
152	Republic & Vine
154	College St
155	Skyline East
156	Congress & Madison
157	Shooting Range
159	Metro: Congress MLK
177	Red Dirt Bar
182	MLK & Brandon
320	Tarot Card: The High Priestess – On the topmost floor of the building where Takemura has his safehouse
481	Ripperdoc (complete HUS873, then wait 24 in-game hours)
509	Mackinaw Larimore (see page 427)
770	Loot Dean's body; see page 331
771	Loot the bag leaning against the crate; see page 331
772	Eliminate all enemies and loot the bag on the crate (see page 331); this hustle's leader will drop the crafting spec required to craft the Comrade's Hammer weapon
776	Loot Jimmy Kreutz's body; see page 332
781	Loot the body on the topmost platform of the scaffolding; see page 333
783	Loot the body on the rooftop, which you can reach by hopping from the nearby street, then the nearby safe hidden under construction equipment; see page 326
785	Loot the body between the shipping containers; see page 333
791	Loot Tom Morris's body at the top of the scaffolding; see page 334
869	Loot the suitcase near the knocked-down vending machine; see page 347
870	Loot the briefcase on the floor; see page 347
871	Loot the chest container on the ground, in front of a pile of wooden beams; see page 347
872	Loot the bag on the counter; see page 347
873	Eliminate all enemies and loot the chest container under the desk, inside the trailer; see page 347
874	Loot the body inside the shack, which you can reach via a rooftop grate; see page 348
876	Loot the body on the rooftop, which you can reach using vending machine and ventilation unit as stepping stones; see page 348
877	Loot the body on a chair; see page 348
878	Loot the body at the top of the fire escape (reachable wit a double jump); see page 348
879	Loot the body in the electricity substation; see page 348
880	Loot the body between the buildings; see page 349
881	Loot the body in the enclosed area, which you can reach by jumping from the nearby food stall; see page 349
882	Loot the body between the dumpsters; see page 349
887	Loot the container at the foot of the antenna; see page 35

E5

PAGE 385 ■ D5 ■

PAGE E4 ■ 388 ■

PAGE 390 ■ E6 ■

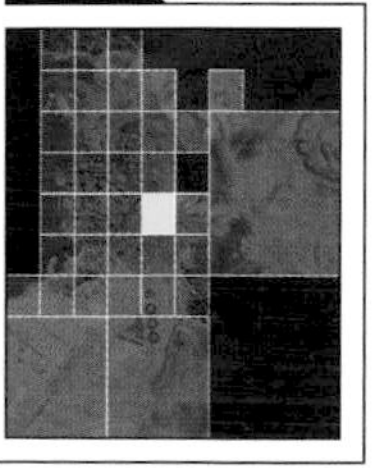

[Charter Hill]
[Arroyo]
[Rancho Coronado]

PAGE 394 ■ F5 ■

30	Gig: Tyger and Vulture
31	Gig: Family Heirloom
33	Gig: Error 404
42	Gig: Hacking the Hacker
175	Republic East
176	Megabuilding H6
193	Metro: Megabuilding H7
230	Longshore South
231	Dynalar
302	Tarot Card: Justice – On the cistern opposite the Electric Corporation power plant
503	Turbo-R 740 (see page 426)
504	MaiMai P126 (see page 426)
697	Loot the backpack on a crate, next to a computer; see page 319
701	Loot Zeitgeist's body, then the stash; see page 319
703	Loot Pushkin's body in the storm drain; see page 320
704	Loot the body on the food vendor's rooftop; see page 320
705	Loot the body on the billboard's metal platform; you can reach it by firing at the ladder to make it drop; see page 320
706	Loot the Militech corporal's body next to the van; see page 320
707	Loot the body in the shipping container; the area can be entered via a missing fence section, either on the east or north side; see page 320
708	Loot the body between the two air conditioning units; see page 320
709	Loot the body near the Trauma Team crate; see page 320
710	Loot the body in the underground control room; see page 321
749	Loot the body of Darius Marks; see page 327
779	Loot the bag on the ground, by the officer's body; see page 332
780	Loot the backpack against the crate, then the body on the nearby rooftop; see page 332
782	Loot the body on the vantage point, which you can reach by climbing up the metal staircase and ladder; see page 333
788	Loot the shard close to the body in the underpass; see page 334

E6

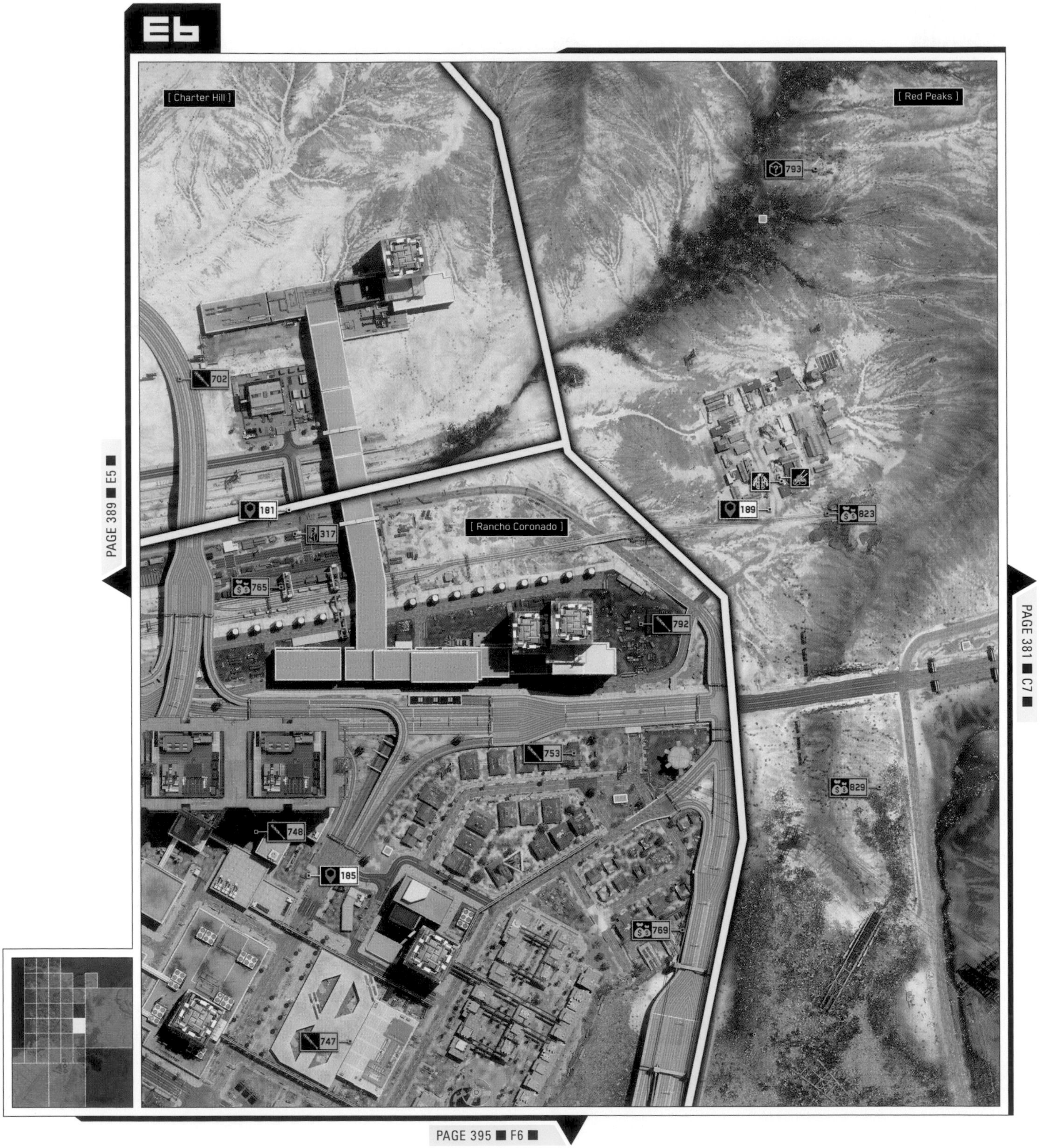

[Charter Hill]

[Red Peaks]

[Rancho Coronado]

793 702 181 317 189 823 765 792 753 829 748 185 769 747

PAGE 389 ■ E5 ■

PAGE 381 ■ C7 ■

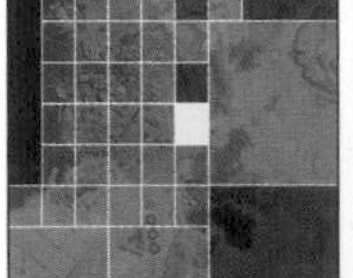

PAGE 395 ■ F6 ■

181	San Amaro St
185	Rancho Coronado North
189	Trailer Park
317	Tarot Card: The Strength – On the side of the small building where you first meet with Panam
702	Loot Takeshi's body; see page 319
747	Loot the bag next to the van; see page 327
748	Loot the briefcase next to the pickup truck; see page 327
753	Loot the backpack on the table in the living room; see page 328
765	Loot the shard inside the shipping container; see page 330
769	Loot the chest in the central alley between the shipping containers; see page 331
792	Loot the chest container outside the warehouse; see page 334
793	Loot the body on the trailer roof, then the body inside the bunker; see page 334
823	Loot the body near the entrance to the railway tunnel; see page 339
829	Loot the body in an open refrigerator in the landfill; see page 340

F2

PAGE 386 ■ E2 ■

PAGE 392 ■ F3 ■

PAGE 397 ■ G2 ■

718	Loot the chest in front of the shipping container; see page 322
726	Loot Oblonsky's body underneath the rollercoaster, in front of the sewer pipes; see page 323
727	Loot the body above the highway's tunnel entrance; see page 324
733	Eliminate all enemies and loot the chest container on the roof at the far end of the amusement park; see page 325
737	Loot the body on the old mattress; see page 325
739	Loot the body on the shore, a few steps from the roller coaster; see page 326
744	Loot the container in the submerged car's trunk; see page 326
911	Loot the body on the table; drop down from the promenade to get to the restaurant's terrace; see page 354
968	Cyberpsycho Sighting: Lex Talionis
976	Cyberpsycho Sighting: Jealous Hearts

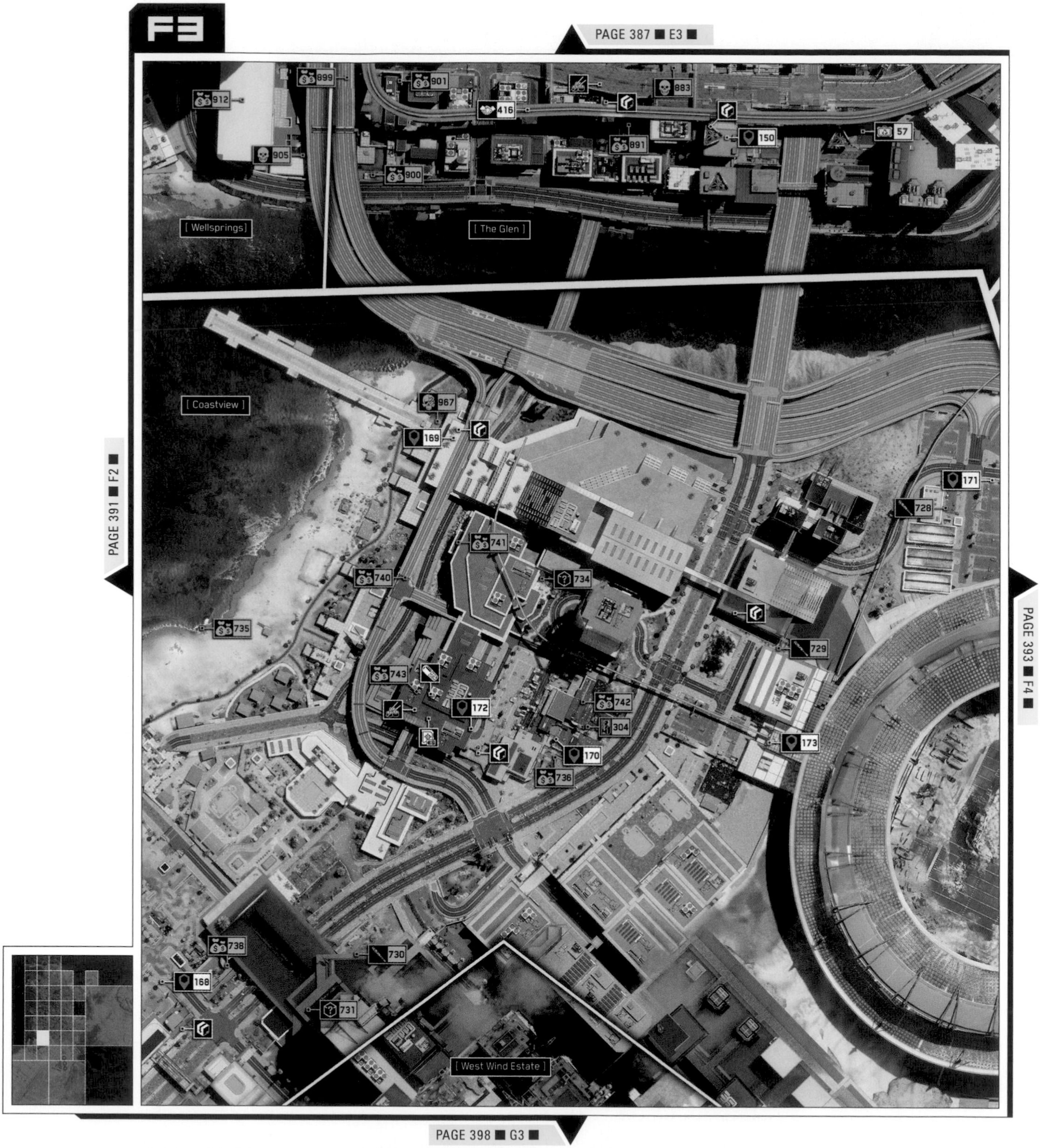

F3

PAGE 387 ■ E3 ■

[Coastview]

PAGE 391 ■ F2 ■

PAGE 393 ■ F4 ■

[West Wind Estate]

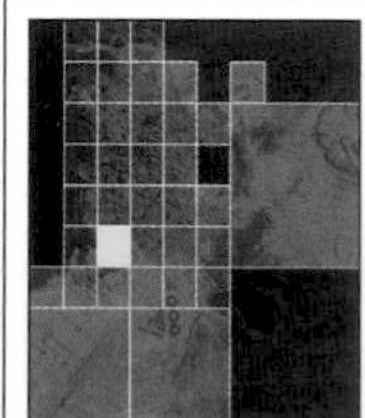

PAGE 398 ■ G3 ■

- **57** Gig: Life's Work
- **150** Metro: Glen South
- **168** Grand Imperial Mall
- **169** Pacifica Pier
- **170** Chapel
- **171** Stadium Parking
- **172** Batty's Hotel
- **173** Metro: Stadium
- **304** Tarot Card: The Hermit – On the side of the chapel that leads into the Voodoo Boys crypt
- **416** Sebastian "Padre" Ibarra
- **728** Loot the chest container by the speakers; see page 324
- **729** Loot the backpack on the ground, near Susan's body; see page 324
- **730** Loot the chest container on the planter, by the radio; see page 324
- **731** Loot Nina's body, then the container in her hideout; see page 324
- **734** Loot Marvin's bag (by his body), then the backpack by the car; see page 325
- **735** Loot the bag by Theo Faron's body; see page 325
- **736** Loot the suitcase by the netrunner chair; see page 325
- **738** Loot the body on the rooftop, which you can reach by hopping from the nearby street, then the nearby safe hidden under construction equipment; see page 326
- **740** Loot the body close to the beach, at the foot of Hotel Merquiss; see page 326
- **741** Loot the body on a Hotel Merquiss terrace; see page 326
- **742** Loot the body on the chapel's roof; see page 326
- **743** Loot the shard on the small table with many bottles; see page 326
- **883** Eliminate all enemies and loot the chest container under the metal canopy; see page 349
- **891** Loot Max's backpack on the rooftop; see page 351
- **899** Loot the body inside the partly opened garage; see page 352
- **900** Loot the shard on the table inside the garage (opening it requires a high Body level); see page 352
- **901** Loot the body in the dead end; see page 352
- **905** Eliminate all enemies and loot the chest container by the crate, in the main room (see page 353); this hustle's leader will drop the crafting spec required to craft the Yinglong weapon

F4

PAGE 388 ■ E4 ■

PAGE 392 ■ F3 ■

PAGE 394 ■ F5 ■

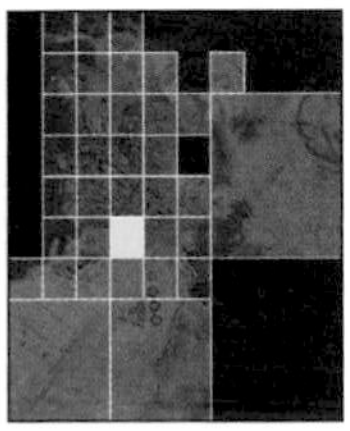

[Arroyo]
[Rancho Coronado]
[Coastview]
[Biotechnica Flats]

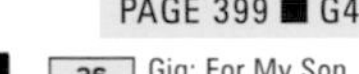
PAGE 399 ■ G4 ■

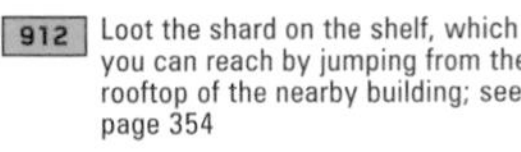

912	Loot the shard on the shelf, which you can reach by jumping from the rooftop of the nearby building; see page 354
967	Cyberpsycho Sighting: A Dance with Death

F4

36	Gig: For My Son
40	Gig: Race to the Top
43	Gig: Severance Package
178	Hargreaves St
179	Megabuilding H4
183	Metro: Wollesen St
186	Rancho Coronado South
469	Melee Weapon Vendor (only available after you complete the "For My Son" gig, see page 282)
508	Supron FS3 (see page 427)
732	Loot the chest container by a dumpster; see page 325
773	Loot Frank Kaufmann's body; see page 331
774	Loot the backpack right next to Thomas's body, then his stash; see page 331
775	Loot Tony Falcetti's body; see page 332
777	Loot the bag in the trunk of the partly buried car; see page 332
778	Loot the body of the Creators' leader; see page 332
786	Loot the body at the rear of the facility adjacent to the Cytech factory; see page 333
787	Loot the body in the basketball hoop; you'll need to jump from the barrels underneath to reach it; see page 333
789	Loot the body in the shipping container storage facility; see page 334
790	Loot the bodies inside the shipping container (whose door is gated behind a minor Technical Ability attribute requirement); see page 334
973	Cyberpsycho Sighting: Too Little, Too Late

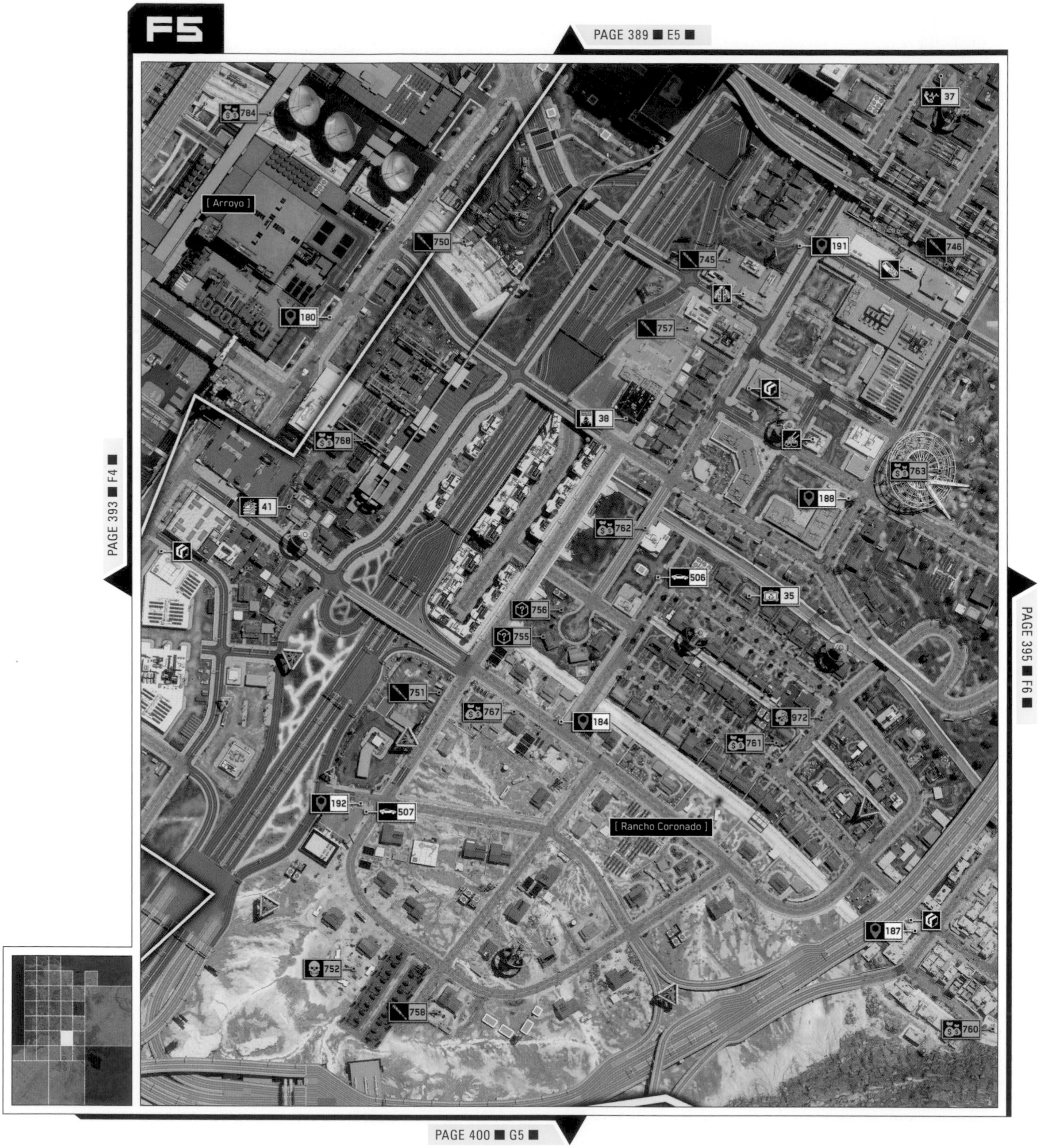

F5

PAGE 389 ■ E5 ■

[Arroyo]

[Rancho Coronado]

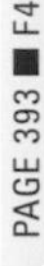
PAGE 393 ■ F4 ■

PAGE 395 ■ F6 ■

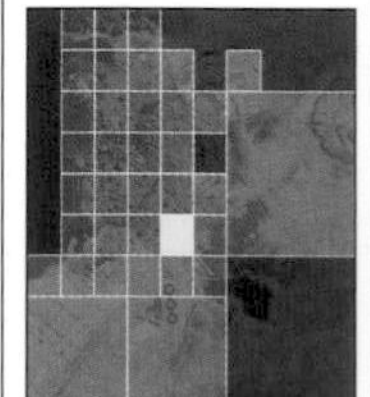

PAGE 400 ■ G5 ■

- **35** Gig: Family Matters
- **37** Gig: Going-away Party
- **38** Gig: The Union Strikes Back
- **41** Gig: Breaking News
- **180** Arasaka Industrial Park
- **184** Almunecar & Jerez
- **187** Rancho Coronado East
- **188** Kendal Park
- **191** Mallagra & Manzanita
- **192** PieZ
- **506** Type-66 640 TS (see page 427)
- **507** Colby CX410 Butte (see page 427)
- **745** Loot the briefcase by the car; see page 327
- **746** Loot the bag on the ground; see page 327
- **750** Loot the bag on the crates; see page 327
- **751** Loot Pablo Silva's body; see page 328
- **752** Eliminate all enemies and loot the bag on the couch (see page 328); this hustle's leader will drop the crafting spec required to craft the Breakthrough weapon
- **755** Loot Robert's body, then plunder the container on the back porch of his nearby house; see page 328
- **756** Read the message on the computer, then loot the bag on the house porch; see page 329
- **757** Loot the bag on the ground, in front of the car; see page 329
- **758** Loot the container by the pool; see page 329
- **760** Loot the body on the rooftop, accessible via the nearby ladder; see page 329
- **761** Loot the body on the house porch; see page 330
- **762** Loot the body in the underpass; see page 330
- **763** Loot the body next to the Ferris wheel cabin; see page 330
- **767** Loot the body close to the police cars; see page 330
- **768** Loot the body inside an open shipping container in the storage facility; you will need to disable the android guarding the entrance; see page 330
- **784** Loot the body in the storm drain; see page 333
- **972** Cyberpsycho Sighting: Discount Doc

Fb

PAGE 390 ■ E6 ■

PAGE 394 ■ F5 ■

PAGE 381 ■ C7 ■

[Red Peaks]

[Rancho Coronado]

PAGE 401 ■ G6 ■

34	Gig: Cuckoo's Nest
49	Gig: Sparring Partner
190	Tama Viewpoint
446	Junk Vendor (can be killed during the "Sparring Partner" gig, in which case he's no longer available)
485	Octavio's Clinic
754	Loot the dealer's body, then his stash; see page 328
759	Eliminate all Wraiths and loot the chest container in the middle of the area; see page 329
764	Loot the body on the balcony; see page 330
766	Loot the shard next to the body, close to the truck; see page 330
797	Loot Darnell's body, then the chest inside the Biotechnica container; see page 335
802	Loot the chest container by the car wreck; see page 336
803	Loot the bag on the ground by the tent; see page 336

G1

PAGE 397 ■ G2 ■

PAGE 402 ■ H1 ■

G2

PAGE 391 ■ F2 ■

PAGE 396 ■ G1 ■

PAGE 398 ■ G3 ■

PAGE 402 ■ H1 ■

32	Gig: Two Wrongs Makes us Right
174	West Wind Apartments
716	Loot Monica Steiner's body; see page 322
717	Eliminate all scavengers and loot the chest container under the metal canopy (see page 322); this hustle's leader will drop the crafting spec required to craft the Moron Labe weapon
719	Loot the bag on the ground; see page 322
720	Loot Fara's body on the rooftop, which you can reach via a ladder to the west; see page 322
721	Loot the suitcase by the two bodies; see page 323
722	Loot Viper's body in the work site inside the fenced enclosure; you can drop down from above to avoid the nearby guards and turret; see page 323
723	Loot Miz's body by the Delamain; see page 323
724	Loot the body on the film set, near the shipping containers; see page 323
725	Loot Smith's body near the crashed car; see page 323

PAGE 392 ■ F3 ■

PAGE 402 ■ H1 ■

844 Loot Conway's body; see page 343

G4

PAGE 393 ■ F4 ■

PAGE 398 ■ G3 ■

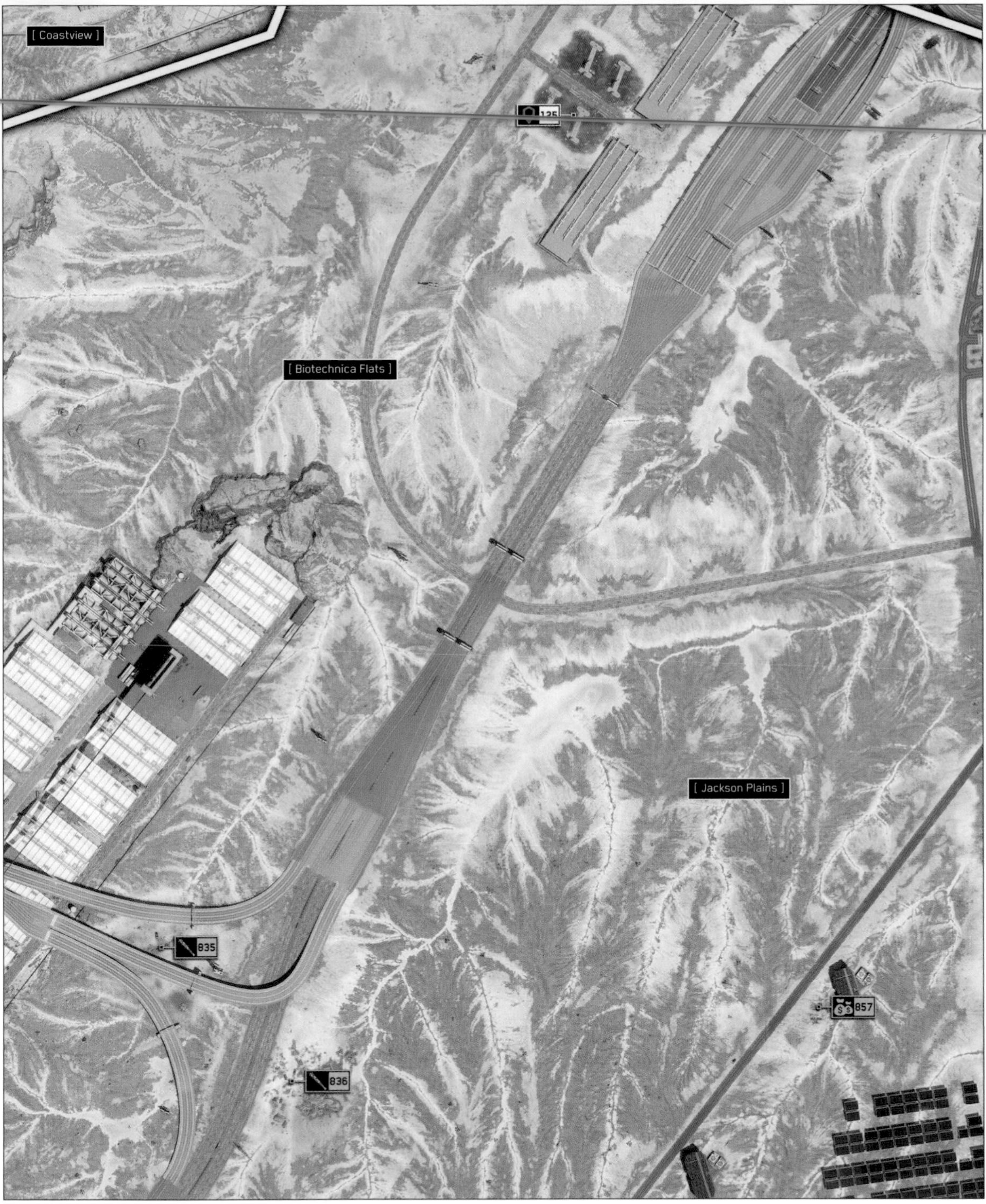

PAGE 400 ■ G5 ■

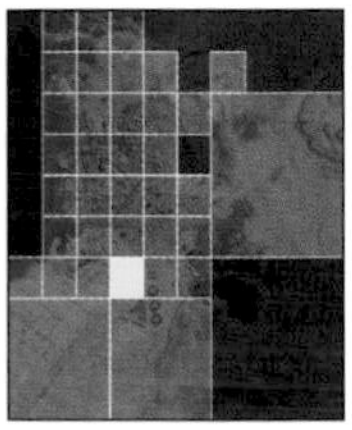

PAGE 403 ■ H2 ■

[Coastview]

[Biotechnica Flats]

[Jackson Plains]

125
835
836
857

125	Abandoned Parking Lot
835	Loot Martha Liu's body; see page 341
836	Loot Robert Conrad's body; see page 341
857	Loot the body inside the crashed car near the solar farm; see page 345

G5

PAGE 394 ■ F5 ■

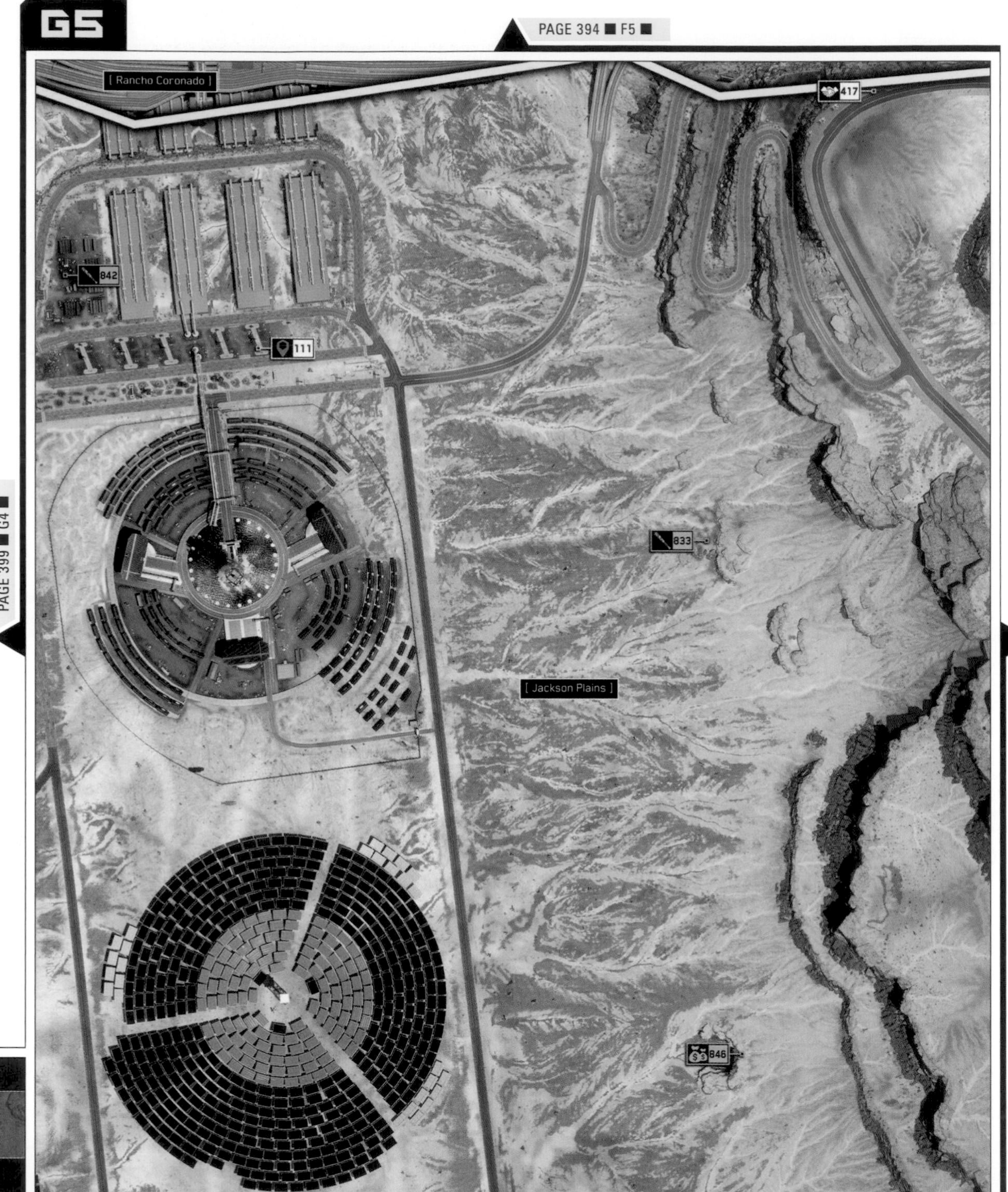

PAGE 399 ■ G4 ■

PAGE 401 ■ G6 ■

PAGE 403 ■ H2 ■

111	Solar Power Station
417	Muamar "El Capitan" Reyes
833	Loot Henry Louis's body; see page 341
842	Loot Steve Harrington's body; see page 342
846	Loot the bag by the turret in front of the collapsed tunnel; see page 343

G6

PAGE 395 ■ F6 ■

PAGE 400 ■ G5 ■

PAGE 403 ■ H2 ■

108 Dam

H1

PAGE 396 ■ G1 ■ PAGE 397 ■ G2 ■ PAGE 398 ■ G3 ■

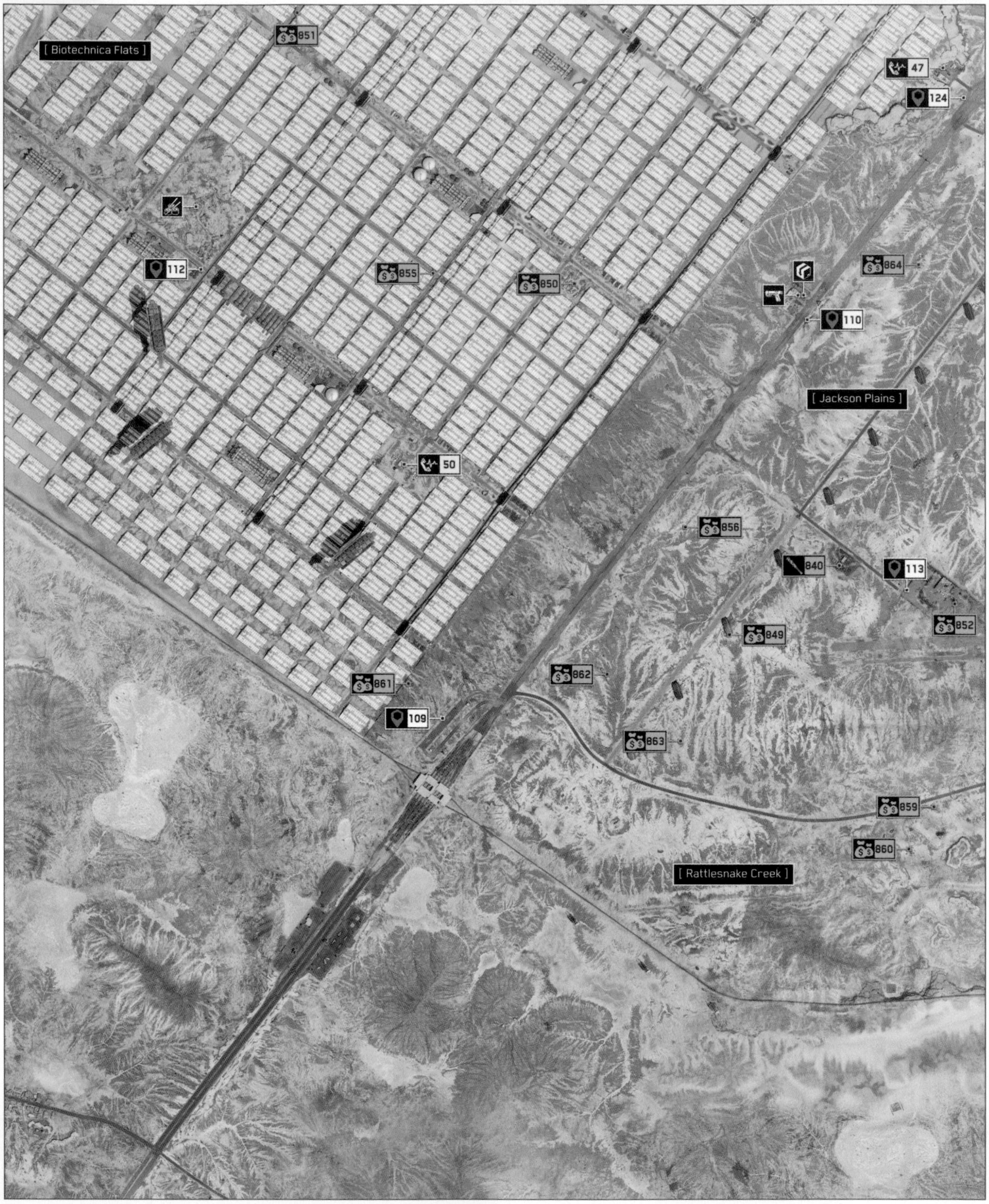

[Biotechnica Flats]

[Jackson Plains]

[Rattlesnake Creek]

PAGE 403 ■ H2 ■

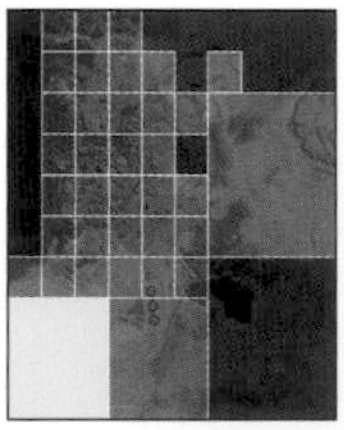

- **47** Gig: Trevor's Last Ride
- **50** Gig: MIA
- **109** Border Checkpoint
- **110** Fuel Station
- **112** Protein Farm
- **113** Regional Airport
- **124** Las Palapas Motel
- **840** Loot the bag on the floor, inside the gas station; see page 342
- **849** Loot the chest container inside the trailer; see page 344
- **850** Loot the body under the dead tree right outside the Biotechnica farm; see page 344
- **851** Loot the body next to the truck; see page 344
- **852** Loot the shard at the top of the airfield tower; you will need the double jump ability to reach it; see page 344
- **855** Loot the body by the fence at the protein farm; see page 345
- **856** Loot the body inside the crashed shipping container; see page 345
- **859** Loot the body next to the burning car, a few steps from the road, giving the mines scattered in the area a wide berth; see page 345
- **860** Loot the body by the burning tow truck; see page 345
- **861** Loot the officer's body next to his car, at the edge of the Biotechnica protein farm; see page 346
- **862** Loot the chest container in the bunker behind the building; you will need to pass a fairly high Body attribute requirement to open the door; see page 346
- **863** Loot the body near the southeast edge of the Biotechnica farm complex; see page 346
- **864** Loot the body on the chair at the mass-suicide site; see page 346

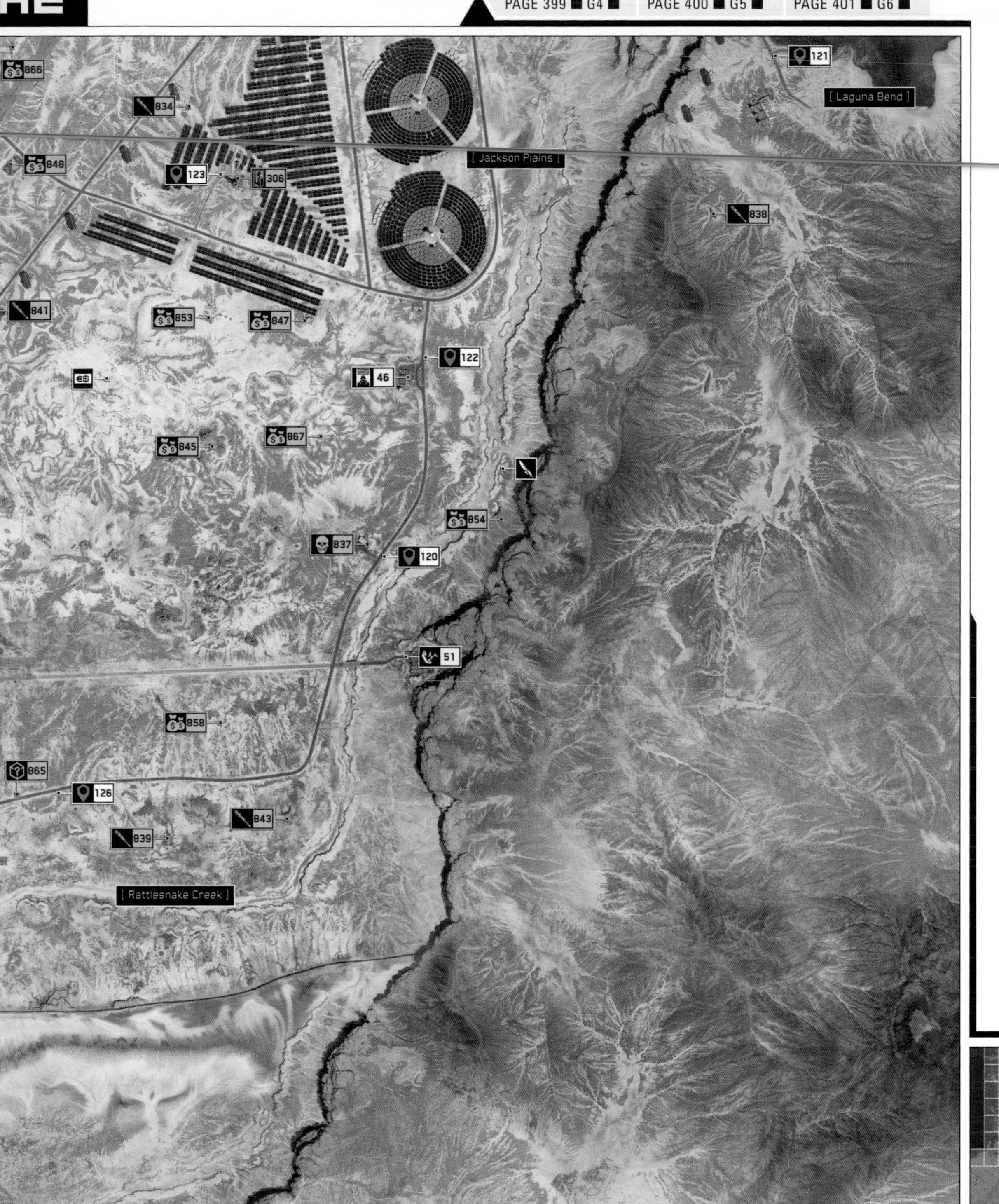

46	Gig: Big Pete's Got Big Problems
51	Gig: Goodbye, Night City
120	Tango Tors Motel
121	Lake Farm
122	Autowerks
123	Solar Arrays
126	Abandoned Fuel Station
306	Tarot Card: The Star – At the base of the antenna tower, in the middle of the solar farm
834	Loot the bag by the power cable; see page 341
837	Eliminate all enemies and loot the bag on the floor in the surgery room; see page 342
838	Loot the bag on the ground by the chopper; see page 342
839	Loot the bag; see page 342
841	Loot the body of the shop owner; see page 342
843	Loot the backpack on the crates inside the cave; see page 343
845	Loot the body of James Reddington; see page 343
847	Loot the body on the roof; see page 343
848	Loot Jane's body; see page 343
853	Loot the body in the middle of the trailers, close to the solar farm; see page 344
854	Loot the chest container in the cave; see page 344
858	Loot the body by the wrecked van; see page 345
865	Loot the body next to the burning car, then the pod to the west, close to the gas station; see page 346
866	Loot the body next to the van, under the power line; see page 346
867	Loot the body in the wrecked van, to the south of the solar farm; see page 346

INVENTORY

Your ability to survive and thrive as you make a name for yourself in Night City is not just a matter of your current level – it's also determined by how well you equip and prepare your character. Stockpiling restorative items, selecting optimal gear, and installing new implants can make a profound difference. With the more involved challenges, a little advance effort can transform a potentially arduous struggle into a relatively straightforward victory.

In this chapter, we reveal the mechanical data for every item that you might encounter. If you have questions about any object that you might find, seek answers over the pages that follow.

RARITY

Rarity is a concept that applies to many items in the game, and offers a general idea of an object's quality.

The rarer an item is, the better you can expect it to be relative to similar items of an inferior rarity. Improvements can take the form of increased stats, additional mod slots, unique effects, and so forth. This chapter details the boons granted to rarer items wherever applicable.

As a general rule of thumb, opportunities to lay claim to rarer equipment increase as you make progress in the adventure, and more specifically as you gain levels. You can also expect rewards of a higher grade when you complete missions such as gigs and NCPD Scanner Hustles – as you will see if you study the accompanying diagrams.

Rarity is not the only consideration that you should employ to evaluate the quality of items, though, as they also have a (hidden) individual level: the higher this is, the better the base parameters should be. As with rarity, you can expect object stats to steadily rise as you gradually ascend through the levels.

Last but not least, you should note the existence of unique weapons of the "Iconic" type. These are one-of-a-kind pieces that typically offer singular features and can only be obtained in a very specific way. When you find one, you receive both the weapon and its crafting specs for its current rarity rank as well as the one above.

Let's imagine, for example, that you defeat Royce (a boss encountered during the Prologue) and loot the Chaos pistol at the Rare rank from his body. You will simultaneously get the handgun's crafting specs for the Rare and Epic ranks. Crafting the Epic model will require you to sacrifice the Rare one which you were using, but will reward you with the crafting spec for the Legendary rank.

Essentially, this system enables you to craft improved versions of each Iconic weapon up to the ultimate, Legendary rank, as long as you have the required components.

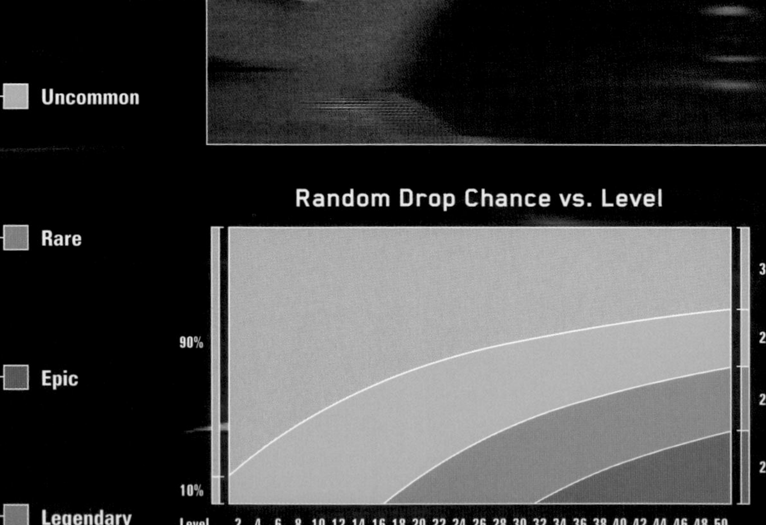

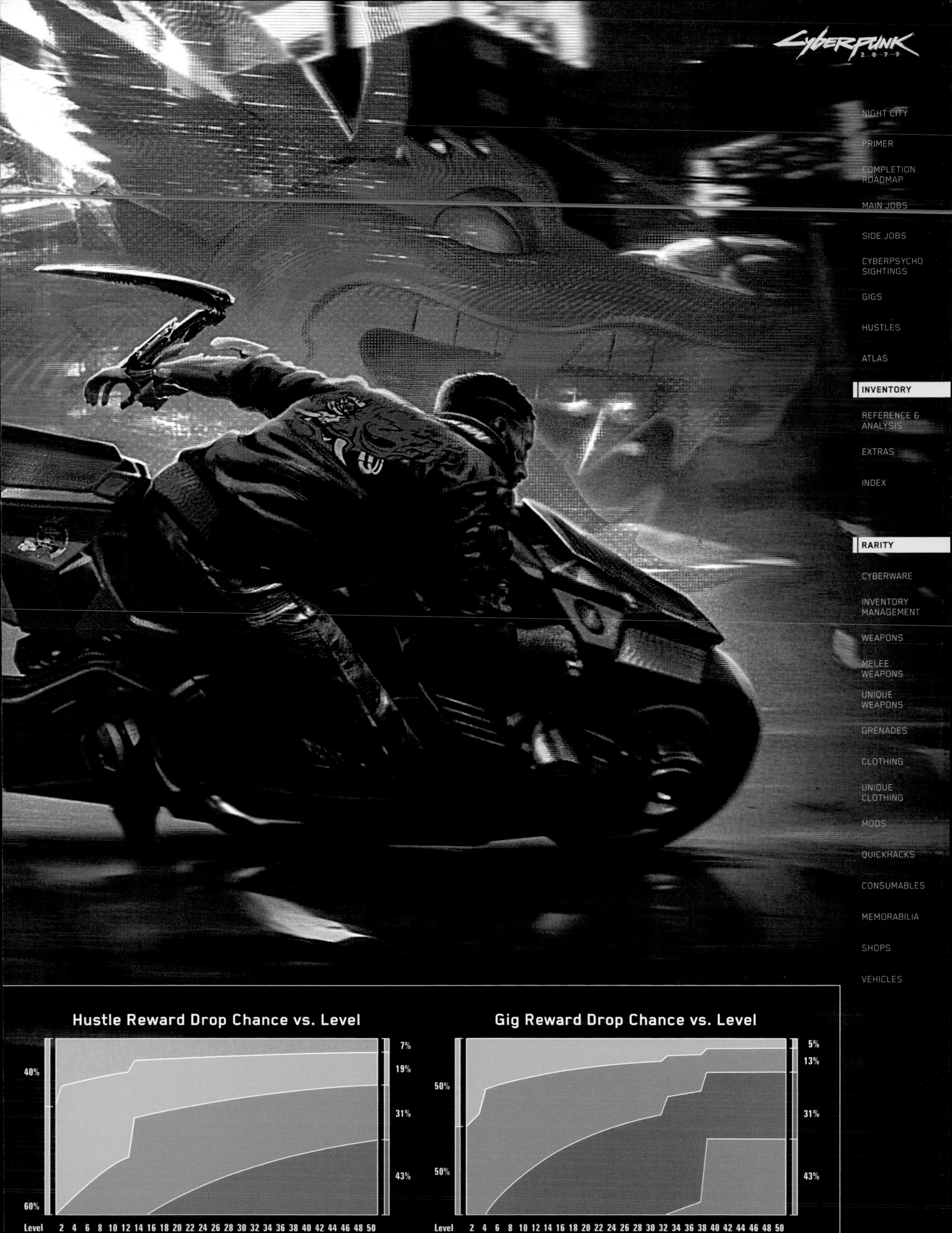
Hustle Reward Drop Chance vs. Level
40%
60%
7%
19%
31%
43%
Level 2 4 6 8 10 12 14 16 18 20 22 24 26 28 30 32 34 36 38 40 42 44 46 48 50
Gig Reward Drop Chance vs. Level
50%
50%
5%
13%
31%
43%
Level 2 4 6 8 10 12 14 16 18 20 22 24 26 28 30 32 34 36 38 40 42 44 46 48 50

CYBERWARE

Cyberware is a collective term that refers to all implants that ripperdocs can install to customize V. The advantages of being equipped with the very best implants you can support and afford cannot be overstated. You should regard cyberware as a priority area for investment whenever you have funds to spare.

The quality of implants is largely determined by their level of rarity. Generally speaking, rarer pieces share the same features as those of inferior rarity, but with superior effects or efficiency. Most implants provide their effects permanently. A few of them, on the other hand, need to be triggered. This applies, for instance, to Optical Camo (turning you invisible) or Sandevistan (slowing down time). You can activate these by pressing L1/LB and R1/RB simultaneously.

CIRCULATORY SYSTEM

Name	Price Per Rarity	Common	Uncommon	Rare	Epic	Legendary
Bioplastic Blood Vessels	2,000 3,000 6,000 10,000 14,000	Health regeneration outside combat +1% per second. Body requirement: 6.	Health regeneration outside combat +2% per second. Body requirement: 8.	Health regeneration outside combat +4% per second. Body requirement: 10.	Health regeneration outside combat +10% per second. Body requirement: 12.	Health regeneration outside combat +50% per second. Body requirement: 14.
Syn-Lungs	1,000 1,500 3,000 5,000 7,000	Stamina regeneration +5%. Body requirement: 8.	Stamina regeneration +10%. Body requirement: 10.	Stamina regeneration +15%. Body requirement: 12.	Stamina regeneration +20%. Body requirement: 14.	Stamina regeneration +25%. Body requirement: 18.
BioConductor	6,000 10,000 14,000	-	-	Cyberware cooldowns -10%. Body requirement: 12.	Cyberware cooldowns -20%. Body requirement: 15.	Cyberware cooldowns -30%. Body requirement: 18.
Second Heart	42,000	-	-	-	-	Revives you if your health is fully depleted, completely restoring the meter. Cooldown of 2 minutes. Body requirement: 16.
Blood Pump	5,000 7,500 15,000 25,000 35,000	Activate to instantly restore 50% health. Cooldown 180 seconds.	Activate to instantly restore 60% health. Cooldown 180 seconds. Body requirement: 8.	Activate to instantly restore 70% health. Cooldown 90 seconds. Body requirement: 10.	Activate to instantly restore 80% health. Cooldown 90 seconds. Body requirement: 13.	Activate to instantly restore 90% health. Cooldown 30 seconds. Body requirement: 16.
BioMonitor	6,000 9,000 18,000 30,000 42,000	Restores 30% health when total drops below 15%. Cooldown 240 seconds.	Restores 40% health when total drops below 15%. Cooldown 240 seconds. Body requirement: 10.	Restores 50% health when total drops below 15%. Cooldown 180 seconds. Body requirement: 12.	Restores 60% health when total drops below 15%. Cooldown 150 seconds. Body requirement: 15.	Restores 100% health when total drops below 15%. Cooldown 120 seconds. Body requirement: 18.
MicroGenerator	1,000 1,500 3,000 5,000 7,000	Releases an EMP blast damaging nearby enemies by a value equal to 20% of their max health when your health drops below 15%.	Releases an EMP blast damaging nearby enemies by a value equal to 30% of their max health when your health drops below 15%. Technical Ability requirement: 8.	Releases an EMP blast damaging nearby enemies by a value equal to 40% of their max health when your health drops below 15%. Technical Ability requirement: 10.	Releases an EMP blast damaging nearby enemies by a value equal to 40% of their max health when your health drops below 15%. Enemies are also shocked. Technical Ability requirement: 12.	Releases an EMP blast damaging nearby enemies by value equal to 50% of their max health when your health drops below 15%. Enemies are also shocked. Technical Ability requirement: 16.
Adrenaline Booster	4,000 6,000 12,000 20,000 28,000	Defeating an enemy restores 10% of stamina.	Defeating an enemy restores 20% of stamina. Body requirement: 8.	Defeating an enemy restores 30% of stamina. Body requirement: 10.	Defeating an enemy restores 40% of stamina. Body requirement: 13.	Defeating an enemy restores 50% of stamina. Body requirement: 18.
Feedback Circuit	9,000 15,000 21,000	-	-	Discharging a fully charged weapon restores 3% of health. Technical Ability requirement: 10.	Discharging a fully charged weapon restores 6% of health. Technical Ability requirement: 12.	Discharging a fully charged weapon restores 10% of health. Technical Ability requirement: 15.
Tyrosine Injector	1,500	-	Increases Breach Protocol mini-game duration by 100%.	-	-	-

FRONTAL CORTEX

Name	Price Per Rarity	Common	Uncommon	Rare	Epic	Legendary
Self-ICE	9,000	-	-	Prevents enemy netrunners from hacking you. Cooldown 45 seconds. Intelligence requirement: 10.	-	-
Limbic System Enhancement	3,000 9,000 21,000	Crit Chance +7%. Intelligence requirement: 6.	-	Crit Chance +15%. Intelligence requirement: 9.	-	Crit Chance +25%. Intelligence requirement: 15.
Visual Cortex Support	3,000 4,500 15,000 21,000	Crit Damage +10%. Intelligence requirement: 6.	Crit Damage +16%. Intelligence requirement: 8.	-	Crit Damage +30%. Intelligence requirement: 12.	Crit Damage +45%. Intelligence requirement: 16.
Ex-Disk	12,000 20,000 28,000	-	-	Max RAM +1. Intelligence requirement: 10.	Max RAM +3. Intelligence requirement: 14.	Max RAM +5. Intelligence requirement: 18.
RAM Upgrade	1,000 1,500 3,000	RAM recovery rate +0.1 per second. Intelligence requirement: 8.	RAM recovery rate +0.2 per second. Intelligence requirement: 10.	RAM recovery rate +0.3 per second. Intelligence requirement: 12.	-	-
Heal-On-Kill	5,000 7,500 25,000 35,000	Defeating an enemy restores 2% health. Intelligence requirement: 8.	Defeating an enemy restores 3% health. Intelligence requirement: 10.	-	Defeating an enemy restores 6% health. Intelligence requirement: 14.	Defeating an enemy restores 10% health. Intelligence requirement: 18.
Memory Boost	4,000 6,000 12,000 20,000	Defeating an enemy restores 1 RAM unit. Intelligence requirement: 7.	Defeating an enemy restores 2 RAM units. Intelligence requirement: 9.	Defeating an enemy restores 3 RAM units. Intelligence requirement: 12.	Defeating an enemy restores 4 RAM units. Intelligence requirement: 15.	-
Camillo RAM Manager	10,000 14,000	-	-	-	Instantly restores 20% of RAM when it drops to 2 units. Cooldown 4 minutes. Intelligence requirement: 12.	Instantly restores 30% of RAM when it drops to 2 units. Cooldown 4 minutes. Intelligence requirement: 16.
Mechatronic Core	3,000 4,500 9,000 15,000 21,000	Damage dealt to Drones, Androids, and Mechs +10%. Intelligence requirement: 8.	Damage dealt to Drones, Androids, and Mechs +20%. Intelligence requirement: 10.	Damage dealt to Drones, Androids, and Mechs +30%. Intelligence requirement: 12.	Damage dealt to Drones, Androids, and Mechs +40%. Intelligence requirement: 14.	Damage dealt to Drones, Androids, and Mechs +50%. Intelligence requirement: 16.

HANDS

Name	Price Per Rarity	Rare	Epic	Legendary
Ballistic Coprocessor	0 15,000 21,000	Greatly increases ricochet potential when using Power weapons.	Bullets ricochet 1 additional time.	Bullets ricochet 2 additional times.
Smart Link	9,000 15,000 21,000	Enables you to use the auto-targeting system in Smart weapons, greatly increasing their efficiency.*	Chance for Smart bullets to home in on the target +10%; Crit Damage +15%.	Chance for Smart bullets to home in on the target +15%; Crit Damage +25%.

* The tattoo you get for free from Cassius Ryder when you complete SJ-07 ("The Gig" – see page 186) has the same effects

ARMS

Name	Price Per Rarity	Rare	Epic	Legendary
Mantis Blades	15,350 25,350 100,350	Two deadly blades useful for melee combat and to lunge at enemies. One mod slot available (edge).	Second mod slot available (rotor).	Third mod slot available (universal).
Monowire	15,450 25,450 100,450	A self-charging wire that can lash multiple enemies simultaneously, with a surprisingly long range for a melee weapon. Attacking discharges the wire, which recharges when equipped but not in use. One mod slot available (wire).	Second mod slot available (battery).	Third mod slot available (universal).
Gorilla Arms	15,250 25,250 100,250	Turns your fists into deadly weapons. Hitting enemies builds a charge that can be released with a strong attack, causing severe damage. One mod slot available (knuckles).	Second mod slot available (battery).	Third mod slot available (universal).
Projectile Launch System	15,450 25,450 100,450	A projectile launcher used to fire missiles over long distances. One mod slot available (missiles).	Second mod slot available (wiring).	Third mod slot available (universal).

OCULAR SYSTEM

Name	Price Per Rarity	Uncommon	Rare	Epic
Kiroshi Optics	0 3,000 5,000	Enables optic zoom. Grants link to bounty system. One mod slot available.	Second mod slot available.	Third mod slot available.

IMMUNE SYSTEM

Name	Price Per Rarity	Common	Uncommon	Rare	Epic	Legendary
Detoxifier	12,000	-	-	Grants full immunity against Poison effects. Body requirement: 10.		-
Metabolic Editor	25,000	-	-	-	Getting poisoned restores 12% health per second instead of dealing damage. Cool requirement: 14.	-
Inductor	20,000	-	-	-	Getting shocked or affected by EMP effects boosts your Armor by 50% instead of dealing damage. Cool requirement: 12.	-
Cataresist	2,000 3,000 10,000 14,000	Increases all resistances by 8%.	Increases all resistances by 13%. Cool requirement: 8.	-	Increases all resistances by 28%. Cool requirement: 23.	Increases all resistances by 35%. Cool requirement: 35.
Shock-n-Awe	1,000 1,500 5,000 7,000	When hit, you have a 2% chance to release an electroshock blast dealing damage to nearby enemies equal to 20% of their max health.	When hit, you have a 4% chance to release an electroshock blast dealing damage to nearby enemies equal to 20% of their max health. Cool requirement: 8.	-	When hit, you have an 8% chance to release an electroshock blast dealing damage to nearby enemies equal to 20% of their max health. Cool requirement: 12.	When hit, you have a 10% chance to release an electroshock blast dealing damage to nearby enemies equal to 20% of their max health. Cool requirement: 15.
Pain Editor	28,000	-	-	-	-	Reduces all incoming damage by 10%. Cool requirement: 16.

NERVOUS SYSTEM

Name	Price Per Rarity	Common	Uncommon	Rare	Epic	Legendary
Kerenzikov (Cooldown 5 seconds)	5,000 7,500 15,000 25,000 35,000	Attacking, aiming or blocking while sliding or dodging triggers a 50% time dilation effect for 1.5 seconds.	Attacking, aiming or blocking while sliding or dodging triggers a 60% time dilation effect for 1.8 seconds.	Attacking, aiming or blocking while sliding or dodging triggers a 65% time dilation effect for 2 seconds. Reflexes requirement: 12.	Attacking, aiming or blocking while sliding or dodging triggers a 80% time dilation effect for 2.5 seconds. Reflexes requirement: 15.	Attacking, aiming or blocking while sliding or dodging triggers a 90% time dilation effect for 3.5 seconds. Reflexes requirement: 18.
Synaptic Accelerator (Cooldown 60 seconds)	5,000 7,500 15,000 25,000 35,000	25% time dilation effect for 2 seconds whenever you are detected by enemies.	30% time dilation effect for 2 seconds whenever you are detected by enemies.	30% time dilation effect for 3 seconds whenever you are detected by enemies. Reflexes requirement: 14.	40% time dilation effect for 3 seconds whenever you are detected by enemies. Reflexes requirement: 16.	50% time dilation effect for 4 seconds whenever you are detected by enemies. Reflexes requirement: 20.
Reflex Tuner	2,500 3,750 7,500 17,500	50% time dilation effect for 2 seconds whenever your health drops below 25%. Cooldown 60 seconds.	60% time dilation effect for 2.5 seconds whenever your health drops below 25%. Cooldown 60 seconds. Reflexes requirement: 8.	70% time dilation effect for 3 seconds whenever your health drops below 25%. Cooldown 50 seconds. Reflexes requirement: 12.	-	80% time dilation effect for 4 seconds whenever your health drops below 25%. Cooldown 40 seconds. Reflexes requirement: 18.
Neofiber	1,000 1,500 3,000 5,000 7,000	Evasion +3%.	Evasion +6%.	Evasion +9%. Reflexes requirement: 12.	Evasion +12%. Reflexes requirement: 15.	Evasion +15%. Reflexes requirement: 18.
Maneuvering System	3,000	-	-	Enables you to perform a dodge while airborne. Reflexes requirement: 14.	-	-
Synaptic Signal Optimizer	6,000 12,000 20,000	-	Duration of Sandevistan and Kerenzikov +0.5 second. Reflexes requirement: 10.	Duration of Sandevistan and Kerenzikov +1 second. Reflexes requirement: 14.	Duration of Sandevistan and Kerenzikov +2 seconds. Reflexes requirement: 18.	-

CYBERDECKS

Name	Quality	RAM	Buffer Size	Slots	Preinstalled Device Hacks	Special Abilities	Required Street Cred	Base Price
Militech Paraline	Common	2	4	2	Distract, Remote Activation, Take Control, Breach Protocol, Steal Data	Short Circuit and Reboot Optics quickhacks already installed.	-	5,000
Arasaka Mk.3	Epic	8	7	5	Distract, Remote Activation, Take Control, Breach Protocol, Steal Data, Overload, Friendly Mode, Assist Mode	Cost of stealth quickhacks is reduced by 1. Combat quickhacks have 30% increased duration. Quickhacking a pinged enemy refreshes Ping duration.	-	25,000
Arasaka Mk.4	Legendary	10	8	6	Distract, Remote Activation, Take Control, Breach Protocol, Steal Data, Overload, Friendly Mode, Assist Mode	Cost of stealth quickhacks is reduced by 2. Combat quickhacks have 40% increased duration. Quickhacking a pinged enemy refreshes Ping duration.	50	35,000
BioDyne Mk.1	Uncommon	6	5	3	Distract , Remote Activation, Take Control, Breach Protocol, Steal Data	-	-	7,500
BioDyne Mk.2	Rare	9	6	4	Distract, Remote Activation, Take Control, Breach Protocol, Steal Data, Overload, Friendly Mode, Assist Mode	Increases RAM recovery rate by 3 units per 60 seconds.	-	15,000
Biotech Σ Mk.1	Uncommon	5	5	3	Distract , Remote Activation, Take Control, Breach Protocol, Steal Data	Increases RAM recovery rate by 6 units per 60 seconds.	-	7,500
Biotech Σ Mk.2	Rare	7	6	4	Distract, Remote Activation, Take Control, Breach Protocol, Steal Data, Overload, Friendly Mode, Assist Mode	Increases RAM recovery rate by 9 units per 60 seconds. Quickhacks deal 10% more damage.	14	15,000
Biotech Σ Mk.3	Epic	10	7	5	Distract, Remote Activation, Take Control, Breach Protocol, Steal Data, Overload, Friendly Mode, Assist Mode	Increases RAM recovery rate by 9 units per 60 seconds. Quickhacks deal 20% more damage.	27	25,000
Fuyutsui Electronics Mk.1	Common	3	5	2	Distract, Remote Activation, Take Control, Steal Data	-	29	5,000
Fuyutsui Tinkerer Mk.3	Legendary	8	7	6	Distract, Remote Activation, Take Control, Breach Protocol, Steal Data, Overload, Friendly Mode, Assist Mode	Increases RAM recovery rate by 9 units per 60 seconds. Quickhack spread distance increased by 40%. Combat quickhacks have 50% increased duration.	37	35,000
NetWatch Netdriver Mk.5	Legendary	11	8	6	Distract, Remote Activation, Take Control, Breach Protocol, Steal Data, Overload, Friendly Mode, Assist Mode	Increases RAM recovery rate by 9 units per 60 seconds. Quickhack spread distance increased by 60%. Combat quickhacks can be uploaded on 3 targets within 6-meter radius. Quickhacks deal 30% more damage.	49	35,000
Raven Microcyber Mk.3	Epic	8	7	5	Distract, Remote Activation, Take Control, Breach Protocol, Steal Data, Overload, Friendly Mode, Assist Mode	Increases RAM recovery rate by 3 units per 60 seconds. Enemy netrunners need 50% more time to hack you. Quickhack spread distance increased by 40%.	49	25,000
Raven Microcyber Mk.4	Legendary	10	8	6	Distract, Remote Activation, Take Control, Breach Protocol, Steal Data, Overload, Friendly Mode, Assist Mode	Increases RAM recovery rate by 6 units per 60 seconds. Enemy netrunners need 100% more time to hack you. Quickhack spread distance increased by 60%.	14	35,000
Seacho Electronics Mk.1	Uncommon	4	5	3	Distract, Remote Activation, Take Control, Steal Data, Overload, Friendly Mode, Assist Mode	Cost of stealth quickhacks is reduced by 1.	-	7,500
Seacho Electronics Mk.2	Rare	6	6	4	Distract, Remote Activation, Take Control, Breach Protocol, Steal Data, Overload, Friendly Mode, Assist Mode	Cost of stealth quickhacks is reduced by 1. Upload time is reduced by 25%.	-	15,000
Stephenson Tech Mk.2	Rare	6	7	4	Distract , Remote Activation, Take Control, Breach Protocol, Steal Data, Overload, Friendly Mode , Assist Mode	Duration of combat quickhacks +30%. All quickhacks have cooldown reduced by 30%.	-	15,000
Stephenson Tech Mk.3	Epic	8	7	5	Distract, Remote Activation, Take Control, Breach Protocol, Steal Data, Overload, Friendly Mode, Assist Mode	Duration of combat quickhacks +40%. All quickhacks have cooldown reduced by 45%.	11	25,000
Stephenson Tech Mk.4	Legendary	10	8	6	Distract, Remote Activation, Take Control, Steal Data, Overload, Friendly Mode, Assist Mode	Duration of combat quickhacks +50%. All quickhacks have cooldown reduced by 45%. Upload time is reduced by 25%.	37	35,000
Tetratronic Mk.1	Uncommon	4	5	3	Distract, Remote Activation, Take Control, Steal Data	Quickhacks deal 10% more damage.	-	7,500
Tetratronic Mk.2	Rare	6	6	4	Distract, Remote Activation, Take Control, Steal Data, Overload, Friendly Mode, Assist Mode	Quickhacks deal 20% more damage. Cost of ultimate quickhacks is reduced by 1.	14	15,000
Tetratronic Mk.3	Epic	8	7	5	Distract, Remote Activation, Take Control, Steal Data, Overload, Friendly Mode, Assist Mode	Quickhacks deal 30% more damage. Cost of ultimate quickhacks is reduced by 2.	37	25,000
Tetratronic Rippler Mk.4	Legendary	10	8	6	Distract, Remote Activation, Take Control, Steal Data, Overload, Friendly Mode, Assist Mode	Ultimate quickhacks can spread once. Cost of ultimate quickhacks is reduced by 3. Upload time is reduced by 75%. All quickhacks have cooldown reduced by 45%.	29	35,000

INTEGUMENTARY SYSTEM

Name	Price Per Rarity	Common	Uncommon	Rare	Epic	Legendary
Subdermal Armor	2,000 3,000 6,000 10,000 14,000	Armor +20.	Armor +50.	Armor +90.	Armor +140.	Armor +200.
Fireproof Coating	12,000	-	-	Grants full immunity against Burn. Body requirement: 12.	-	-
Supra-Dermal Weave	12,000	-	-	Grants full immunity against Bleeding effects. Body requirement: 12.	-	-
Grounding Plating	12,000	-	-	Grants full immunity against Shock effects. Body requirement: 12.	-	-
Optical Camo	15,000 25,000 35,000	-	-	Activate to turn almost invisible for 5 seconds, greatly reducing the likelihood of detection. Cooldown 60 seconds.	Activate to turn almost invisible for 10 seconds, greatly reducing the likelihood of detection. Cooldown 60 seconds.	Activate to turn almost invisible for 15 seconds, greatly reducing the likelihood of detection. Cooldown 60 seconds.
Heat Converter	25,000	-	-	-	Burn effects increase the damage you deal by 10% instead of harming you. Cool requirement: 14.	-

SKELETON

Name	Price Per Rarity	Common	Uncommon	Rare	Epic	Legendary
Microrotors	2,000 3,000 6,000 10,000 14,000	Melee weapon attack speed +5%.	Melee weapon attack speed +10%. Reflexes requirement: 8.	Melee weapon attack speed +15%. Reflexes requirement: 12.	Melee weapon attack speed +20%. Reflexes requirement: 15.	Melee weapon attack speed +25%. Reflexes requirement: 18.
Endoskeleton	4,000 [illegible] 12,000 20,000 28,000	Max health +20%.	Max health +30%. Body requirement: 8.	Max health +40%. Body requirement: 12.	Max health +50%. Body requirement: 15.	Max health +60%. Body requirement: 20.
Bionic Lungs	1,000 1,500 3,000 5,000 7,000	Max stamina +20%.	Max stamina +30%.	Max stamina +40%. Body requirement: 12.	Max stamina +50%. Body requirement: 15.	Max stamina +60%. Body requirement: 18.
Titanium Bones	1,000 1,500 3,000	Carrying capacity +20%.	Carrying capacity +40%.	Carrying capacity +60%. Body requirement: 13.	-	-
Microvibration Generator	7,500 15,000 25,000	-	Melee weapon damage +5%.	Melee weapon damage +10%. Reflexes requirement: 12.	Melee weapon damage +15%. Reflexes requirement: 16.	-
Bionic Joints	6,000 10,000	-	-	Recoil kick after shooting with ranged weapons -12%.	Recoil kick after shooting with ranged weapons -25%. Body requirement: 12.	-
Dense Marrow	3,000 6,000 10,000	-	Melee weapon damage 7% but stamina drain +10%.	Melee weapon damage 15% but stamina drain +10%.	Melee weapon damage 25% but stamina drain +10%. Body requirement: 13.	-

LEGS

Name	Price Per Rarity	Rare	Epic
Reinforced Tendons	45,000	Enables you to perform double jumps.	-
Fortified Ankles	45,000 75,000	Enables you to perform charged jumps.	Enables you to perform hover jumps. Fall damage -15%.
Lynx Paws	85,000	-	You make 50% less noise when moving.

OPERATING SYSTEM

Name	Price Per Rarity	Uncommon	Rare*	Epic**	Legendary***	Legendary (Iconic)***
Zetatech Sandevistan	7,500 15,000 25,000	Activate to dilate time by 25% for 8 seconds. While active, Crit Chance +10%. Cooldown 30 seconds. Reflexes requirement: 6.	Activate to dilate time by 50% for 12 seconds. While active, Crit Chance +15%. Cooldown 30 seconds. Reflexes requirement: 9.	Activate to dilate time by 50% for 16 seconds. While active, Crit Chance +20%. Cooldown 30 seconds. Reflexes requirement: 12.	-	-
Dynalar Sandevistan	7,500 15,000 25,000 35,000	Activate to dilate time by 50% for 8 seconds. While active, damage dealt +5%. Cooldown 30 seconds. Reflexes requirement: 6.	Activate to dilate time by 75% for 12 seconds. While active, damage dealt +10%. Cooldown 30 seconds. Reflexes requirement: 9.	Activate to dilate time by 50% for 16 seconds. While active, damage dealt +15%. Cooldown 15 seconds. Reflexes requirement: 12.	Activate to dilate time by 75% for 16 seconds. While active, damage dealt and Crit Chance +15%. Cooldown 30 seconds. Reflexes requirement: 15.	-
Qiant Sandevistan	35,000 35,000	-	-	-	Activate to dilate time by 75% for 12 seconds. While active, Crit Chance +15% and Damage +15%. Cooldown 15 seconds Reflexes requirement: 15.	Activate to dilate time by 90% for 8 seconds. While active, damage dealt +15%, Crit Chance +10% and Crit Damage +50%. Cooldown 30 seconds. Reflexes requirement: 18.
Militech "Falcon" Sandevistan	35,000	-	-	-	-	Activate to dilate time by 70% for 20 seconds. While active, damage dealt +15%, Crit Chance +20% and Crit Damage +35%. Cooldown 30 seconds. Reflexes requirement: 18.
Moore Tech Berserk	7,500 15,000 25,000	When activated, ranged weapon recoil and sway -10%, melee damage +10% and Armor +5% for 10 seconds. Cooldown 60 seconds. Body requirement: 6.	When activated, ranged weapon recoil and sway -10%, melee damage +15% and Armor +5% for 15 seconds. Max health +10%. Cooldown 60 seconds. Body requirement: 9.	When activated, ranged weapon recoil and sway -10%, melee damage +15% and Armor +10% for 30 seconds. Max health +20%, defeating enemies restores 2% health. Cooldown 60 seconds. Body requirement: 12.	-	-
Biodyne Berserk	7,500 15,000 25,000 35,000	When activated, ranged weapon recoil and sway -15%, melee damage +5% and Armor +5% for 10 seconds. Cooldown 60 seconds. Body requirement: 6.	When activated, ranged weapon recoil and sway -25%, melee damage +5% and Armor +5% for 15 seconds. Ranged attack damage +10%. Cooldown 60 seconds. Body requirement: 9.	When activated, ranged weapon recoil and sway -25%, melee damage +5% and Armor +5% for 30 seconds. Ranged attack damage +15%, defeating enemies restores 3% health. Cooldown 60 seconds. Body requirement: 12.	When activated, ranged weapon recoil and sway -25%, melee damage +5% and Armor +5% for 30 seconds. Ranged attack damage +20%, defeating enemies restores 4% health. Cooldown 60 seconds. Body requirement: 16.	-
Zetatech Berserk	35,000 35,000	-	-	-	When activated, ranged weapon recoil and sway -10%, melee damage +10% and Armor +5% for 10 seconds. Defeating enemies restores 5% health. Cooldown 60 seconds. Body requirement: 16.	When activated, range weapon's recoil and sway -20%, melee damage +20% and Armor +10% for 30 seconds. Defeating enemies restores 5% health. Cooldown 30 seconds. Body requirement: 18.
Militech Berserk	35,000	-	-	-	-	When activated, ranged weapon recoil and sway -15%, melee damage +15% and Armor +10% for 60 seconds. Max health and stamina +40%, defeating enemies restores 5% health. Cooldown 60 seconds. Body requirement: 18.

* Operating Systems of the Rare tier all have one mod slot available ** Operating Systems of the Epic tier all have two mod slots available *** Operating Systems of the Legendary tier all have three mod slots available

INVENTORY MANAGEMENT

Item acquisition and management is a big part of the Cyberpunk 2077 experience, and so the ability to quickly appraise and deal with loot is an important skill – not least because it will reduce the time you spend staring at menus, wracked by indecision.

Until your V has reached max level and is loaded with endgame-level equipment, there's really little reason for sentimentality. It's fine to enjoy the way that a particular firearm barks when you pull the trigger, for example – but if other models that you are encountering have superior bite, it's time to cast it aside without a backward glance. Keeping pace with the difficulty curve and being suitably equipped for the task at hand should always be your priorities.

Collecting loot that you could profitably sell or dismantle can make a significant contribution to your long-term progression, so it pays to travel light. Before any engagement of substance, it's a good idea to ensure that you are only carrying what you actually need. It's never a terrible idea to have "Plan B" tools, but you really don't need to cover every contingency in most missions – especially if you refer to the walkthroughs in this guide to get a sense of the challenges you'll be facing in advance. Any carrying capacity available when you arrive, then, is a potential boost to income when you depart.

That said, you cannot hope to carry everything that you find – and nor should you try. Instead, we suggest that you make use of the pop-up collectible data sheets (as illustrated here) to appraise the relative merits of each item. With a little practice, you'll soon learn how to cherry-pick the most suitable loot and spend less time wrestling with an overstocked inventory.

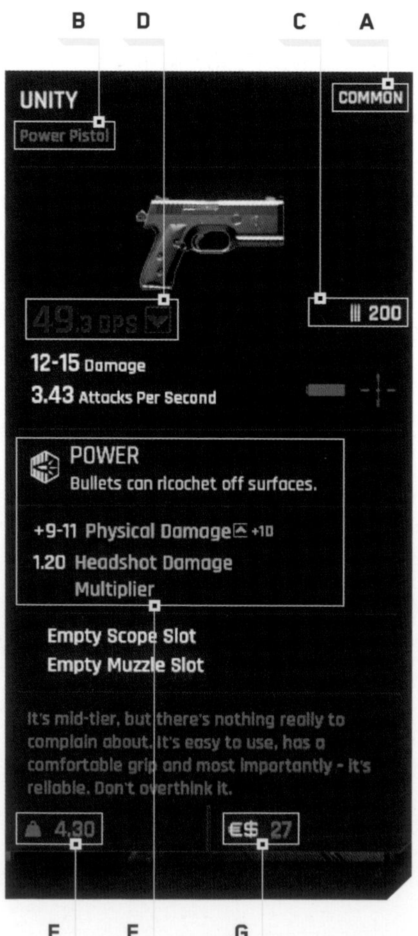

A **Rarity:** The rarity of items is listed in the top-right corner of data sheets. For items of the same level, a higher rarity generally translates into better stats. One fact to consider is that loot dropped by enemies is represented by crosses on your mini-map that employ the universal color code used to classify rarity (see page 404). Whenever you espy the distinctive hues that indicate epic or legendary loot, always take a second to check it out – it could be a stellar drop that will give you an edge for hours to come.

B **Type:** The type of an item is also good information for making snap decisions. If you find an assault rifle when you specialize in stealth and melee combat, for instance, you will know immediately to disregard it unless it carries a high resale or scrappage value.

C **Ammo:** The number displayed here corresponds to your stock of ammunition. Each ranged weapon type is associated to a specific ammo type, as listed in the table on the right-hand page.

D **Core Stat:** The easiest way to assess weapons is the DPS value that appears in large characters on their data sheets. This Damage Per Second stat is a broad estimate of the weapon's potential. There are additional factors to consider, of course, such as how many mod slots a piece has and other special properties – but as a rule of thumb, a weapon with higher DPS (indicated with a green, upward arrow) than your current selection is worth considering. The same principle applies to Armor ratings on clothing.

E **Special Properties:** Many items have a few unique stats or features. Weapons belong to a class (such as Power, Smart, or Tech). Equipment can also improve your chance to inflict critical strikes, or increase your resistance to a specific damage type, or give you access to mod slots for better customization – the list goes on and on. These can be decisive factors. For example, if you're about to fight an enemy who is weak to thermal attacks, choosing a weapon that inflicts thermal damage can make a battle much easier – even if the weapon in question isn't one that excels when compared to your usual loadout.

F **Weight:** The weight of each item is listed in the lower-left corner of its data sheet. You will soon realize that this parameter matters, especially if you have a tendency to hoard. If you go beyond your maximum carrying capacity, as displayed at the top of the Inventory menu, you will endure a severe movement speed penalty, forcing you to engage in potentially time-consuming item management. It's worth noting that the heaviest items are usually weapons, so make these your priority when deciding what you don't need.

G **Price & Dismantling:** The sell price of each item appears in the lower-right corner of the data sheet. If you're looking for ways to raise funds, selling loot (particularly weapons) is a smart bet. Before you make it a habit to regularly offload surplus inventory items to the nearest available buyer or Drop Point, however, keep in mind that there's another way to free up backpack space and make a more indirect profit: dismantling. By holding Ⓐ/Ⓨ while hovering over a item, you can disassemble it – recycling it into crafting components. These materials could potentially be used to build superior equipment if you invest in the Crafting skill tree.

Players who struggle to leave loot behind in role-playing games should note that the Athletics skill and its Perks can greatly increase V's carrying capacity. Another relevant Perk is called Scrapper, in the Crafting tree, which enables you to automatically disassemble all junk items.

WEAPONS

WEAPON TYPES

Each weapon you find in the game belongs to a specific weapon type, which in turn determines the attribute and skill governing your proficiency with that weapon. For optimal results, try to always equip a weapon of a type you are specialized in.

WEAPON TYPES & PROFICIENCY

Name	Related Attribute	Related Skill	Ammo Type
Double-Barrel Shotgun	Body	Annihilation	Shotgun
HMG	Body	Annihilation	HMG
LMG	Body	Annihilation	Rifle
Shotgun	Body	Annihilation	Shotgun
Fists	Body	Street Brawler	-
Blunt Weapons (All)	Body	Street Brawler	-
Gorilla Arms	Body	Street Brawler	-
Monowire	Body	Street Brawler	-
Blades (All)	Reflexes	Blades	-
Mantis Blades	Reflexes	Blades	-
Pistol	Reflexes	Handguns	Pistol
Revolver	Reflexes	Handguns	Pistol
Assault Rifle	Reflexes	Assault	Rifle
Precision Rifle	Reflexes	Assault	Rifle
SMG	Reflexes	Assault	Rifle
Sniper Rifle	Reflexes	Assault	Sniper

WEAPON CLASSES

In addition to their type, ranged weapons also belong to one of three classes that all confer specific properties:

- **Power Weapons** fire projectiles that have a chance (by default, 5%) to ricochet from solid surfaces, which can be used to hit enemies behind cover. Your chance to trigger ricochet, and the number of times that it can occur with each bullet, can be increased by equipping a specific type of hands cyberware, called Ballistic Coprocessor. Additionally, you can use the Trajectory Generator mod to trigger a visual representation of potential ricochet trajectory.
- **Tech Weapons** fire projectiles that are capable of penetrating obstacles such as cover positions and walls. They can also be charged by holding the trigger, resulting in a more powerful attack upon release. Note that your proficiency with Tech weapons can be greatly increased by gaining levels in the Engineering skill and by investing points in the corresponding Perk tree (see pages 431 and 434).
- **Smart Weapons** fire projectiles that can home in on the targeted enemy, though you will need to install the Smart Link hands cyberware to activate this feature. This can prove extremely effective against foes hiding behind cover or employing time-dilation effects such as Sandevistan and Kerenzikov.

Though not considered a class, certain particularly powerful weapons come with a Body attribute requirement. If you wield one of these firearms without satisfying this condition, you will suffer from much greater recoil and a knockback effect every time you press the trigger.

WEAPON SHEETS

The sheets in this section detail key stats for all standard weapons in the game, with most of the parameters covered being entirely self-explanatory.

Two variables, however, require a little more context:

- **The DPS bars** at the bottom of each sheet are visual representations of every weapon's typical progression for all rarity ranks (using the standard color code – see page 404), and are based on the weapon's average DPS in the early game, mid-game, and late game. You should, of course, take these diagrams with a pinch of salt, as they are designed to serve purely as benchmarks: there are many factors, including random damage deviation, damage modifiers, and mods, that can lead to variations. The main purpose of these DPS bars is to enable you to make general comparisons between different models.
- **DPS Variability** corresponds to each weapon's potential damage range. Low-variability weapons (such as Smart-class models) will always have the expected DPS value when you acquire them. High-variability weapons (particularly revolvers and melee weapons), on the other hand, are more unpredictable: every time you find one, their DPS value is randomly picked from a wide spectrum, which can lead to surprises – good or bad. If you're specializing in the mastery of a weapon type with high variability, then, you might need to hunt a little harder to find a model with a stellar DPS value.

REVOLVERS

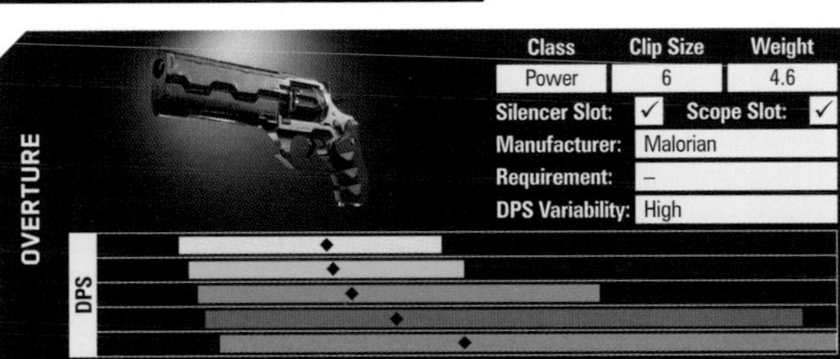

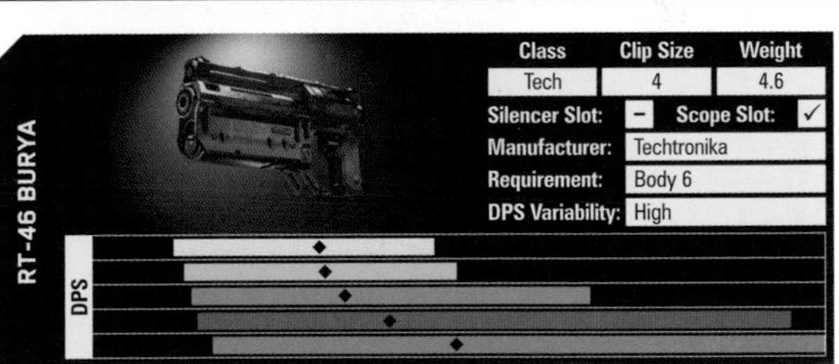

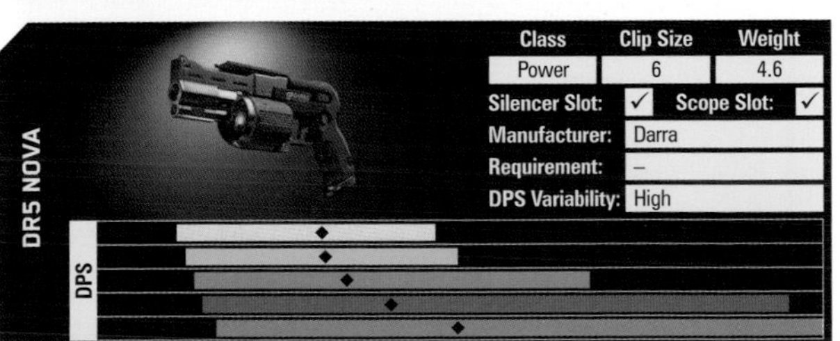

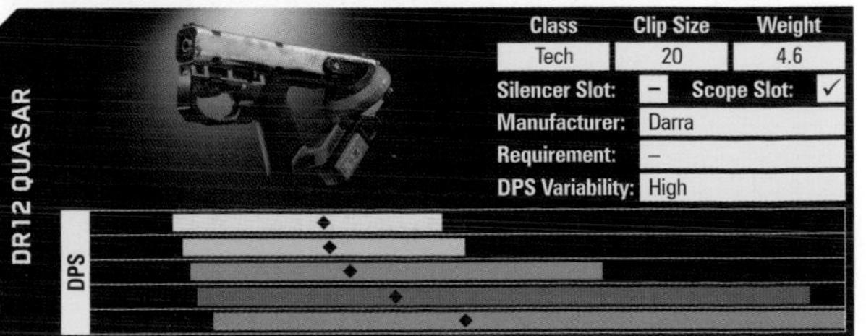

PISTOLS

M-10AF LEXINGTON

Class	Clip Size	Weight
Power	21	4.3

Silencer Slot:	✓
Scope Slot:	✓
Manufacturer:	Militech
Requirement:	–
DPS Variability:	Medium

DPS

SLAUGHT-O-MATIC

Class	Clip Size	Weight
Power	36	4.3

Silencer Slot:	–
Scope Slot:	–
Manufacturer:	Budget Arms
Requirement:	–
DPS Variability:	Medium

DPS

HJKE-11 YUKIMURA

Class	Clip Size	Weight
Smart	30	4.3

Silencer Slot:	–
Scope Slot:	–
Manufacturer:	Arasaka
Requirement:	Smart Link Cyberware
DPS Variability:	Low

DPS

JKE-X2 KENSHIN

Class	Clip Size	Weight
Tech	12	4.3

Silencer Slot:	–
Scope Slot:	✓
Manufacturer:	Arasaka
Requirement:	–
DPS Variability:	Medium

DPS

A-22B CHAO

Class	Clip Size	Weight
Smart	30	4.3

Silencer Slot:	–
Scope Slot:	–
Manufacturer:	Kang Tao
Requirement:	Smart Link Cyberware
DPS Variability:	Low

DPS

NUE*

Class	Clip Size	Weight
Power	10	4.3

Silencer Slot:	✓
Scope Slot:	✓
Manufacturer:	Tsunami
Requirement:	–
DPS Variability:	Medium

DPS

* This weapon also exists in a 2020 version manufactured by Arasaka. The older model, called Tamayura, is technologically a little less advanced, and therefore has slightly inferior stats.

LIBERTY

Class	Clip Size	Weight
Power	12	4.3

Silencer Slot:	✓
Scope Slot:	✓
Manufacturer:	Constitutional Arms
Requirement:	–
DPS Variability:	Medium

DPS

UNITY

Class	Clip Size	Weight
Power	12	4.3

Silencer Slot:	✓
Scope Slot:	✓
Manufacturer:	Constitutional Arms
Requirement:	–
DPS Variability:	Medium

DPS

M-76E OMAHA

Class	Clip Size	Weight
Tech	9	4.3

Silencer Slot:	–
Scope Slot:	✓
Manufacturer:	Militech
Requirement:	–
DPS Variability:	Medium

DPS

ASSAULT RIFLES

D5 COPPERHEAD

Class	Clip Size	Weight
Power	30	7.2

Silencer Slot:	✓
Scope Slot:	✓
Manufacturer:	Nokota
Requirement:	–
DPS Variability:	Medium

DPS

D5 SIDEWINDER

Class	Clip Size	Weight
Smart	30	7.2

Silencer Slot:	–
Scope Slot:	✓
Manufacturer:	Nokota
Requirement:	Smart Link Cyberware
DPS Variability:	None

DPS

HJSH-18 MASAMUNE*

Class	Clip Size	Weight
Power	30	7.2

Silencer Slot:	✓
Scope Slot:	✓
Manufacturer:	Arasaka
Requirement:	–
DPS Variability:	Medium

DPS

M251S AJAX

Class	Clip Size	Weight
Power	30	7.2

Silencer Slot:	✓
Scope Slot:	✓
Manufacturer:	Militech
Requirement:	–
DPS Variability:	Medium

DPS

* This weapon also exists in a 2020 version manufactured by Arasaka. The older model, called Nowaki, is technologically a little less advanced, and therefore has slightly inferior stats.

PRECISION RIFLES

M-179 ACHILLES

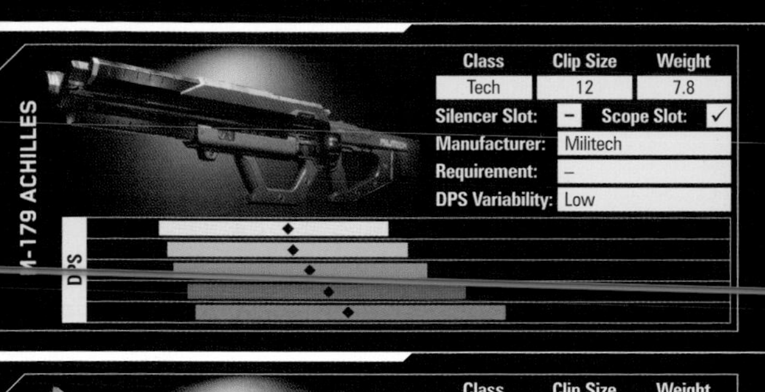

Class	Clip Size	Weight
Tech	12	7.8

Silencer Slot:	–
Scope Slot:	✓
Manufacturer:	Militech
Requirement:	–
DPS Variability:	Low

DPS

SOR-22

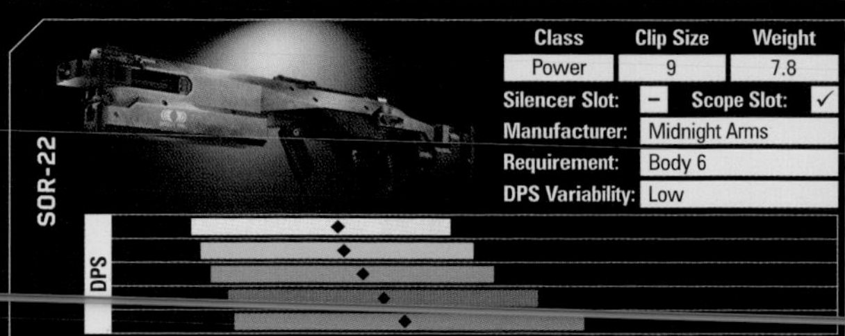

Class	Clip Size	Weight
Power	9	7.8

Silencer Slot:	–
Scope Slot:	✓
Manufacturer:	Midnight Arms
Requirement:	Body 6
DPS Variability:	Low

DPS

SNIPER RIFLES

NEKOMATA

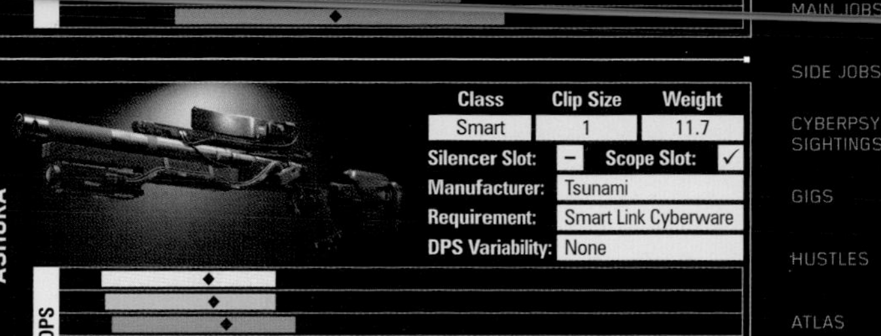

Class	Clip Size	Weight
Tech	4	11.7

Silencer Slot:	–
Scope Slot:	✓
Manufacturer:	Tsunami
Requirement:	–
DPS Variability:	None

DPS

ASHURA

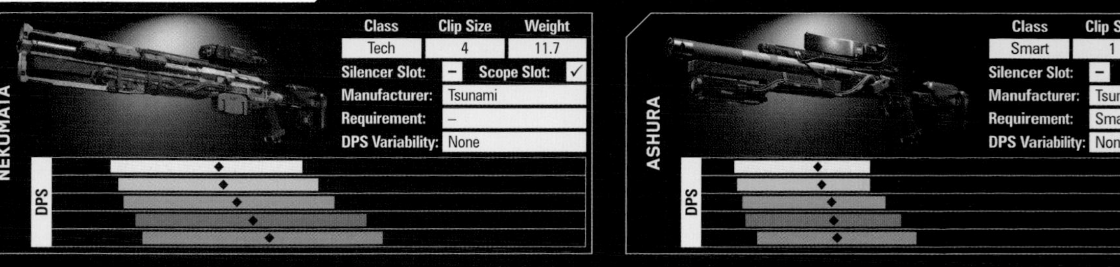

Class	Clip Size	Weight
Smart	1	11.7

Silencer Slot:	–
Scope Slot:	✓
Manufacturer:	Tsunami
Requirement:	Smart Link Cyberware
DPS Variability:	None

DPS

SPT32 GRAD

Class	Clip Size	Weight
Power	4	11.7

Silencer Slot:	–
Scope Slot:	✓
Manufacturer:	Techtronika
Requirement:	–
DPS Variability:	None

DPS

SHOTGUNS

M2038 TACTICIAN

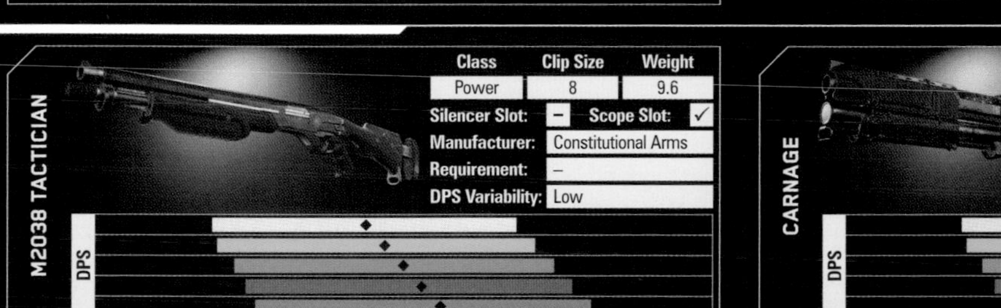

Class	Clip Size	Weight
Power	8	9.6

Silencer Slot:	–
Scope Slot:	✓
Manufacturer:	Constitutional Arms
Requirement:	–
DPS Variability:	Low

DPS

CARNAGE

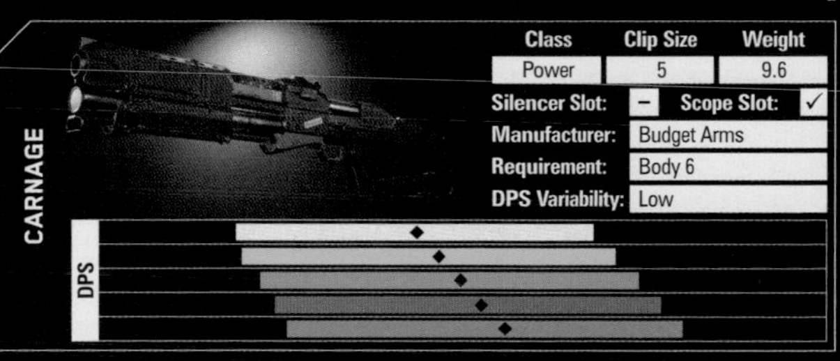

Class	Clip Size	Weight
Power	5	9.6

Silencer Slot:	–
Scope Slot:	✓
Manufacturer:	Budget Arms
Requirement:	Body 6
DPS Variability:	Low

DPS

CRUSHER

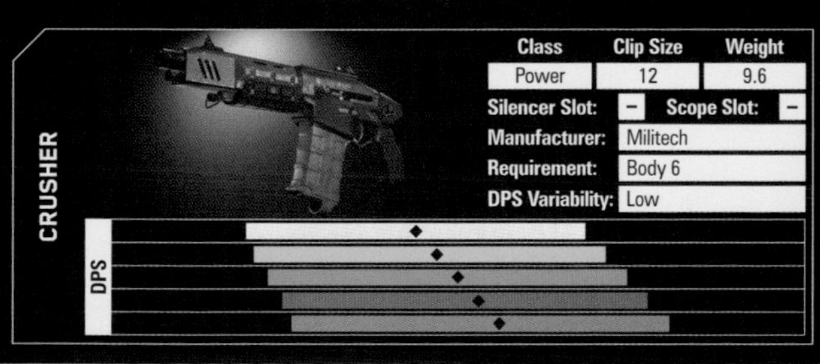

Class	Clip Size	Weight
Power	12	9.6

Silencer Slot:	–
Scope Slot:	–
Manufacturer:	Militech
Requirement:	Body 6
DPS Variability:	Low

DPS

L-69 ZHUO

Class	Clip Size	Weight
Smart	4	9.6

Silencer Slot:	–
Scope Slot:	–
Manufacturer:	Kang Tao
Requirement:	Smart Link Cyberware
DPS Variability:	Low

DPS

DOUBLE-BARREL SHOTGUNS

DB-2 SATARA

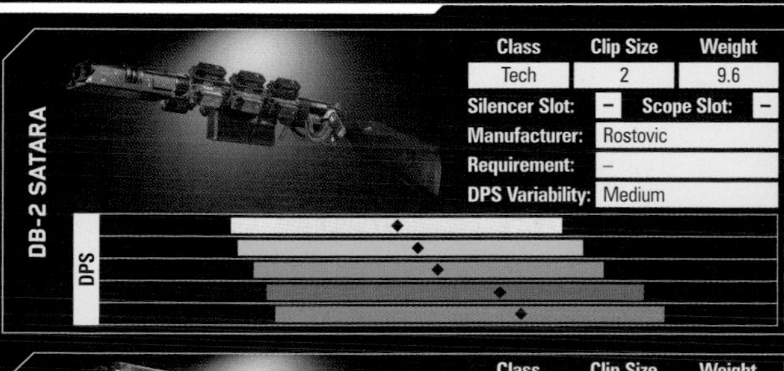

Class	Clip Size	Weight
Tech	2	9.6

Silencer Slot:	–
Scope Slot:	–
Manufacturer:	Rostovic
Requirement:	–
DPS Variability:	Medium

DPS

DB-4 IGLA

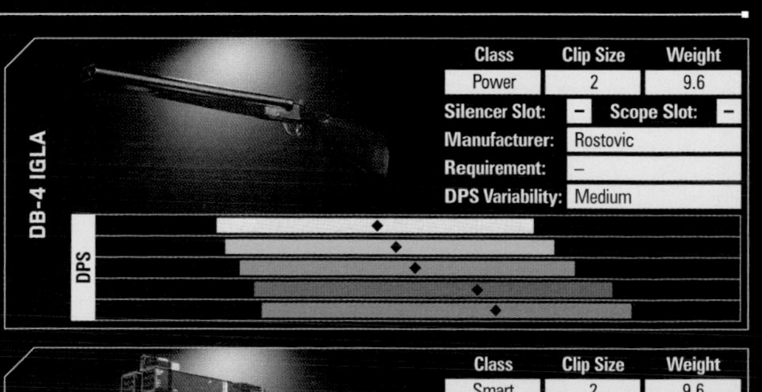

Class	Clip Size	Weight
Power	2	9.6

Silencer Slot:	–
Scope Slot:	–
Manufacturer:	Rostovic
Requirement:	–
DPS Variability:	Medium

DPS

DB-2 TESTERA

Class	Clip Size	Weight
Power	2	9.6

Silencer Slot:	–
Scope Slot:	–
Manufacturer:	Rostovic
Requirement:	–
DPS Variability:	Medium

DPS

DB-4 PALICA

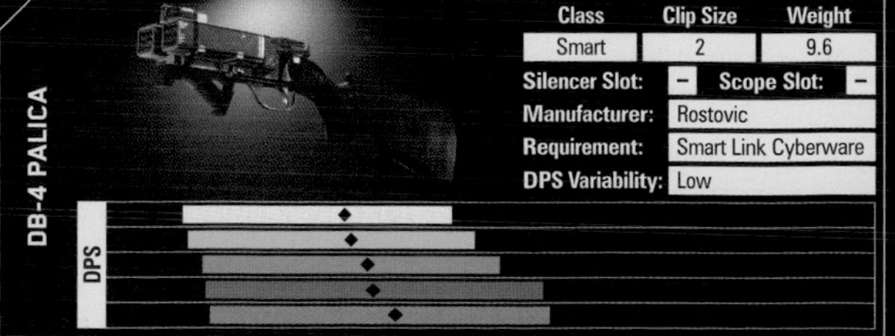

Class	Clip Size	Weight
Smart	2	9.6

Silencer Slot:	–
Scope Slot:	–
Manufacturer:	Rostovic
Requirement:	Smart Link Cyberware
DPS Variability:	Low

DPS

SMGS

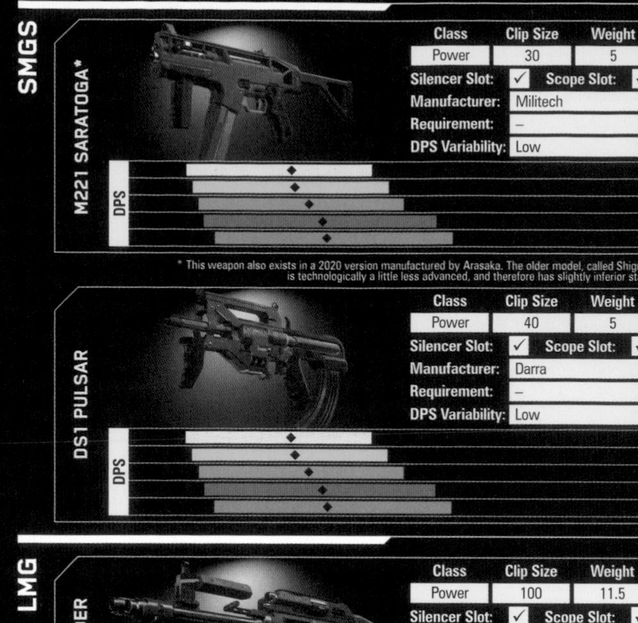

M221 SARATOGA*

Class	Clip Size	Weight
Power	30	5

Silencer Slot:	✓
Scope Slot:	✓
Manufacturer:	Militech
Requirement:	–
DPS Variability:	Low

DPS

* This weapon also exists in a 2020 version manufactured by Arasaka. The older model, called Shigura, is technologically a little less advanced, and therefore has slightly inferior stats.

TKI-20 SHINGEN

Class	Clip Size	Weight
Smart	30	5

Silencer Slot:	–
Scope Slot:	–
Manufacturer:	Arasaka
Requirement:	Smart Link Cyberware
DPS Variability:	None

DPS

DS1 PULSAR

Class	Clip Size	Weight
Power	40	5

Silencer Slot:	✓
Scope Slot:	✓
Manufacturer:	Darra
Requirement:	–
DPS Variability:	Low

DPS

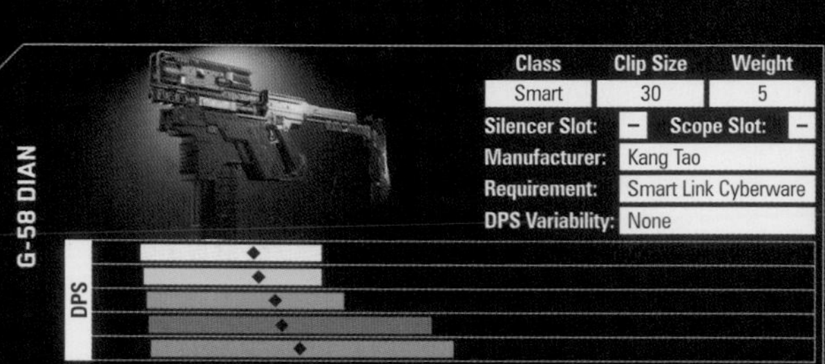

G-58 DIAN

Class	Clip Size	Weight
Smart	30	5

Silencer Slot:	–
Scope Slot:	–
Manufacturer:	Kang Tao
Requirement:	Smart Link Cyberware
DPS Variability:	None

DPS

LMG

M2067 DEFENDER

Class	Clip Size	Weight
Power	100	11.5

Silencer Slot:	✓
Scope Slot:	✓
Manufacturer:	Constitutional Arms
Requirement:	Body 6
DPS Variability:	Low

DPS

康陶 Kang Tao

智 能 电 子 解 决 方 案

MELEE WEAPONS

BLADES

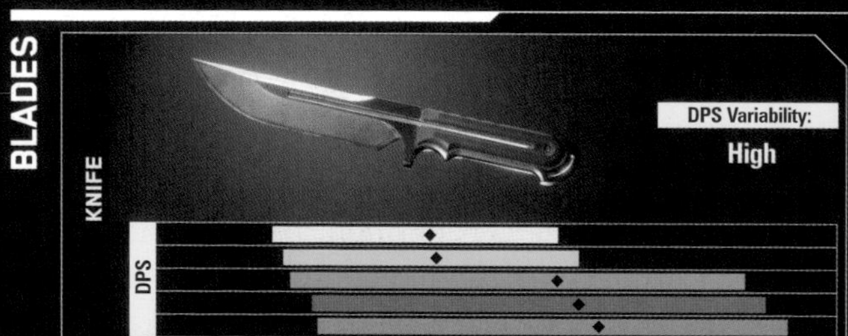

KNIFE

DPS Variability: **High**

DPS

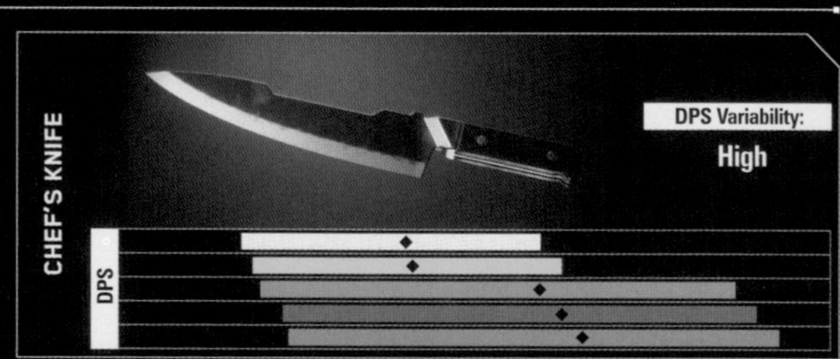

CHEF'S KNIFE

DPS Variability: **High**

DPS

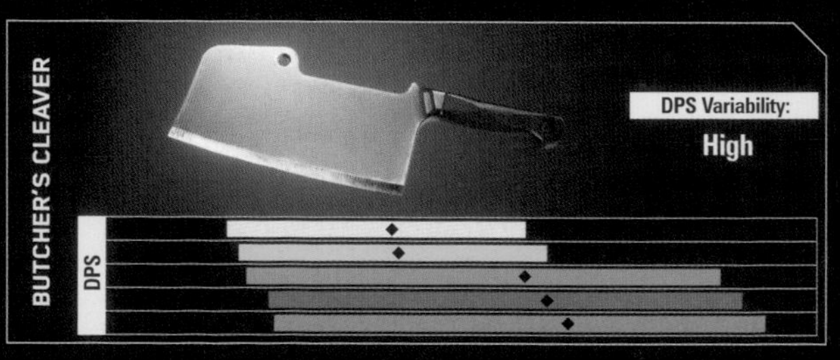

BUTCHER'S CLEAVER

DPS Variability: **High**

DPS

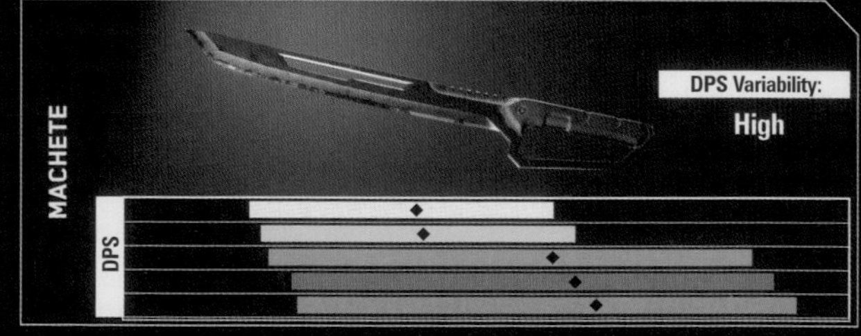

MACHETE

DPS Variability: **High**

DPS

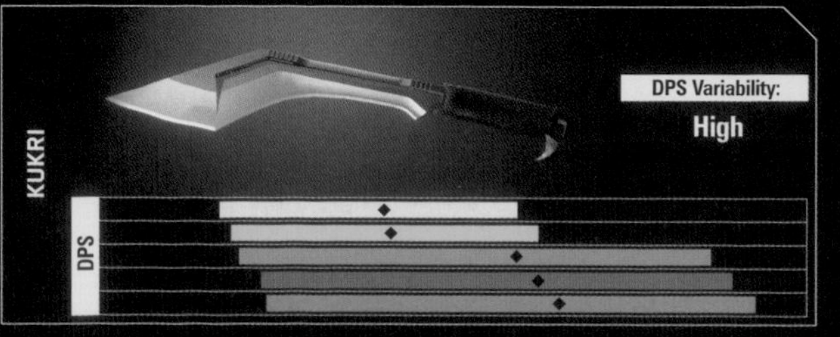

KUKRI

DPS Variability: **High**

DPS

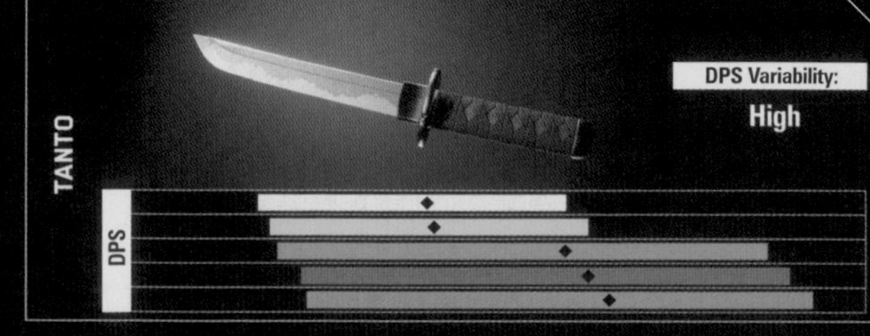

TANTO

DPS Variability: **High**

DPS

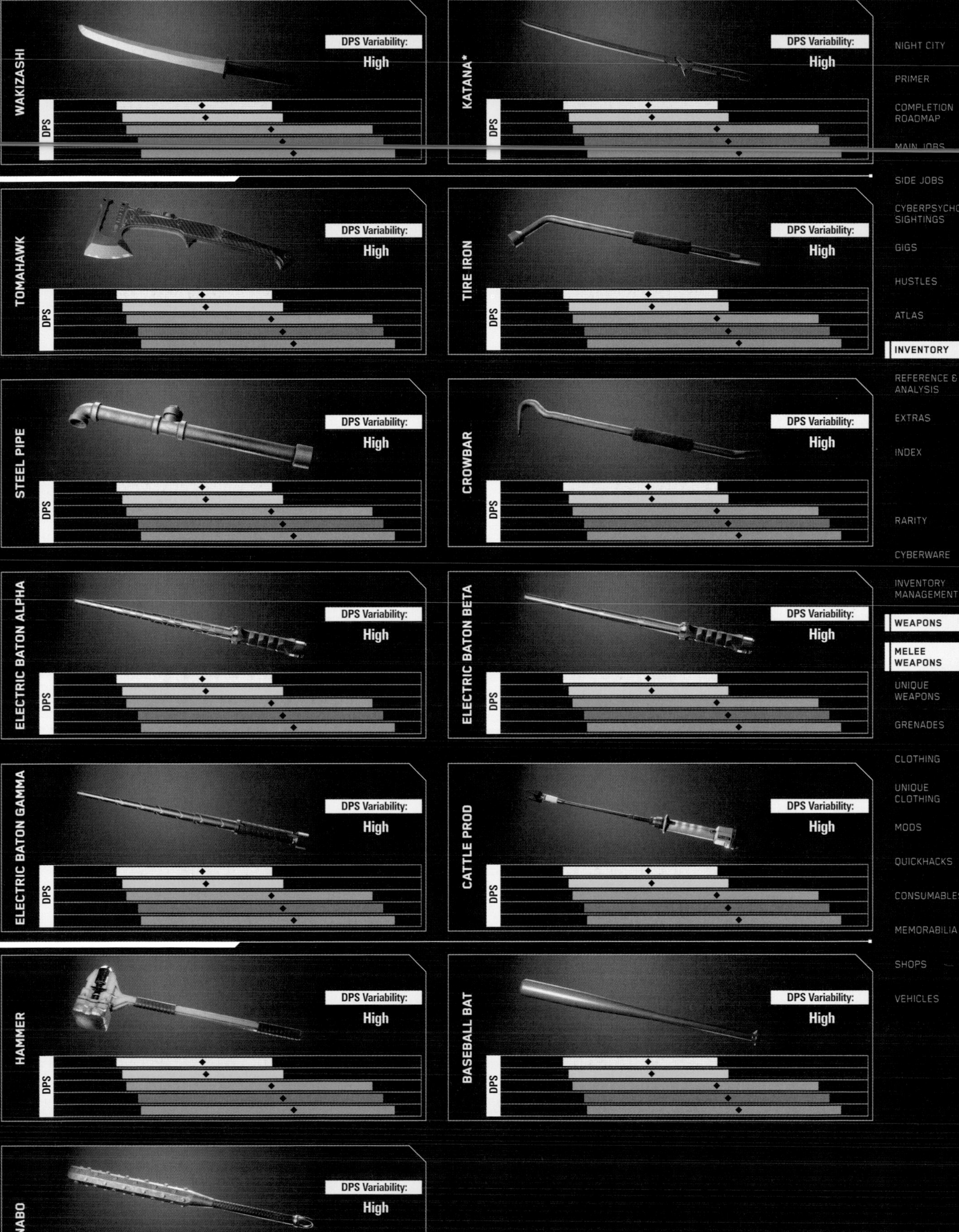

* Katanas also exist in a 2020 version manufactured by Arasaka. These older models have the same name but slightly inferior stats.

UNIQUE WEAPONS

If you can ensure that you are in the right place at the right time, Cyberpunk 2077 has a surprising number of unique weapons with unusual characteristics to find.

Before you continue, a few notes on the information that you can find in each column:

- **Availability:** How, when, and where the weapon can be acquired. These conditions are often quite specific.
- **Single Chance:** You only have one opportunity to obtain many of these weapons. If you miss them, they will be unavailable for the rest of your playthrough.
- **Base Weapon & Special Properties:** All unique weapons are actually variations of a base model with a custom appearance and, in most cases, special properties that make them stand out.

UNIQUE WEAPONS OVERVIEW

Name	Availability	Single Chance	Base Weapon	Special Properties
Amnesty	Earned by completing Cassidy's bottle-shooting challenge at the Nomad party during MJ-31 ("We Gotta Live Together" – see page 174). Cassidy is found in the camp's southeast corner.	✔	Overture	Improved handling and firepower.
Apparition	Can be looted from Frank's body after SJ-51 ("War Pigs" – see page 234).	✔	JKE-X2 Kenshin	Increases Critical Chance, fire rate, reload speed and damage when your health is very low. Charged shots deal double damage.
Archangel	Given by Kerry during SJ-42 ("Off the Leash" – see page 224).	✔	Overture	Reduced recoil. Deals electrical damage with a chance to stun targets.
Ba Xing Chong	Can be crafted if you have the Edgerunner Artisan Perk (Crafting tree) and loot the spec from Adam Smasher's vault (the shipping container unlocked by Grayson's key during SJ-35 – see page 216) after you enter the elevator taking you to Embers during MJ-26 ("Nocturne Op55N1" – see page 164).	✔	L-69 Zhuo	Fires explosive rounds and rips enemies to shreds.
Breakthrough	Can be crafted if you have the Edgerunner Artisan Perk (Crafting tree) and loot the spec from the leader in hustle 752 (Suspected Organized Crime Activity in Rancho Coronado – see page 328).	✔	Nekomata	Fires piercing projectiles that can ricochet.
Buzzsaw	Can be crafted if you have the Edgerunner Artisan Perk (Crafting tree) and loot the spec from the leader in hustle 643 (Suspected Organized Crime Activity in Northside – see page 310).	✔	DS1 Pulsar	Fires piercing projectiles.
Chaos	Can be obtained during MJ-08 ("The Pickup" – see page 120) by looting Royce after neutralizing him in the deal sequence, or during the boss fight.	✔	JKE-X2 Kenshin	Crit Chance, damage type and status effect application are randomized every time you reload.
Cocktail Stick	Can be found in the make-up room of the Clouds club, upstairs, during MJ-12 ("Automatic Love" – see page 134).	✔	Katana	High base damage.
Comrade's Hammer	Can be crafted if you have the Edgerunner Artisan Perk (Crafting tree) and loot the spec from the leader in hustle 772 (Suspected Organized Crime Activity in Arroyo – see page 331).	✔	RT-46 Burya	Deals high thermal damage, but has low clip size and long reload times.
Cottonmouth	Can be collected in Fingers' bedroom during MJ-13 ("The Space In Between" – see page 138).	✔	Electric Baton Gamma	Deals electrical and chemical damage. Small chance to apply Poison and/or Shock.
Crash	Given to you by River atop the water tower during SJ-21 ("Following the River" – see page 202).	✔	Overture	Charging for a brief time while aiming enables full auto mode. Decreases recoil, bullet spread and fire rate.
Divided We Stand	Reward for winning the shooting contest during SJ-58 ("Stadium Love"). Can also be looted from the sixers if you neutralize them (page 238).	✔	D5 Sidewinder	Can target up to five enemies simultaneously. Deals chemical damage with a chance to apply Poison.
Doom Doom	Can be obtained during SJ-38 ("Second Conflict" – see page 220) by looting Dum Dum in the Totentantz club; note that this is only possible if you took steps to ensure that Dum Dum survived the events of MJ-08.	✔	DR5 Nova	Fires four rounds per shot, with increased damage, rate of fire and chance to dismember at the cost of increased recoil and bullet spread.
Dying Night	Reward for winning the shooting contest during SJ-11 ("Shoot to Thrill" – see page 190).	✔	m-10AF Lexington	Headshot damage increased by 50%; significantly reduced reload time
Fenrir	Can be collected from a table near the monk you need to rescue during SJ-06 ("Losing My Religion" – see page 186).	✔	M221 Saratoga	Deals thermal damage with increased chance to apply Burn. Reduced bullet spread and increased bullet impact, at the cost of high recoil.
Genjiroh (源二郎)	Can be found behind a closed door on the way to the second sniper during MJ-24 ("Play it Safe" – see page 158). The door in question is located on your right when you walk out of the elevator, just before you reach the long ladder on floor 21. It's gated behind a Technical Ability attribute requirement, but you can alternatively open it via the nearby terminal (the code is 2906).	✔	HJKE-11 Yukimura	Fires four rounds per shot. Increases ammo clip size, projectile speed and can target up to six targets simultaneously. Bullets deal additional electrical damage with an increased chance to apply Shock.
Gold-Plated Baseball Bat	Available in the pool at Denny's villa, after the argument, during SJ-38 ("Second Conflict" – see page 220).	✔	Baseball Bat	High chance to apply Bleeding, low chance to stun targets.
Jinchu-maru (尽忠丸)	Dropped by Oda during MJ-24 ("Play it Safe" – see page 158).	✔	Katana	Crit Chance increased to 100% while Kerenzikov is active. Final combo attack damage doubled as standard, but quadrupled if the target has more health than you.
Kongou (金剛)	Can be found on the nightstand next to Yorinobu's bed in his penthouse during MJ-10 ("The Heist" – see page 128).	✔	Liberty	Ricochet effect functions without supporting cyberware. Lower recoil and increased fire rate, but reduced clip size.
La Chingona Dorada	After you complete SJ-10 (Heroes – see page 189), you can find the La Chingona Dorada pistol on the table where all the offerings were displayed.	✖	Nue	Reduced reload time and extra mod slot. Higher chance to apply Burn and to stun the target.

UNIQUE WEAPONS OVERVIEW (CONTINUED)

Name	Availability	Single Chance	Base Weapon	Special Properties
Lizzie	Can be found in the basement of Lizzie's after MJ-13 ("The Space in Between" – see page 138).	✖	Omaha	Fires an extra round per shot. Further increases the number of rounds fired when fully charged.
Malorian Arms 3516	Obtained from Grayson during SJ-35 ("Chippin' In" – see page 216).	✔	Unique handgun	Johnny Silverhand's weapon.
Moron Labe	Can be crafted if you have the Edgerunner Artisan Perk (Crafting tree) and loot the spec from the leader in hustle 717 (Suspected Organized Crime Activity in West Wind Estate – see page 322).	✔	M251s Ajax	High dismembering probability and fire rate.
Mox	Given by Judy if you share a romantic relationship with her, or after MJ-12 ("Automatic Love" – see page 134) if she decides to leave Night City.	✔	Carnage	Low reload speed but reduced spread while aiming.
O'Five	Can be collected during SJ-01 ("Beat on the Brat: Champion of Arroyo" – see page 181) after neutralizing Buck.	✔	SPT32 Grad	Shoots explosive projectiles.
Overwatch	Reward for saving Saul during SJ-45 ("Riders on the Storm" – see page 228).	✔	SPT32 Grad	Increased reload speed, custom silencer.
Ozob's Nose	Reward for completing SJ-16 (Send in the Clowns – see page 194).	✔	Frag Grenade	High damage.
Plan B	Can be looted from Dex's body in the scrapyard after MJ-11 ("Playing for Time" – see page 132).	✖	Liberty	Bullets have a high chance to apply Bleeding. Each shot costs a Eurodollar instead of a bullet.
Prejudice	Can be picked up behind the bar in the Afterlife at the beginning of MJ-29 ("For Whom the Bell Tolls" – see page 172).	✔	HJSH-18 Masamune	Piercing projectiles.
Pride	Can be collected close to where Adam Smasher kills a character of note during MJ-30 ("Knockin' on Heaven's Door" – see page 172).	✔	Liberty	Increased Crit Chance and headshot damage. Small chance to apply Stun.
Problem Solver	Dropped by the large enemy guarding the Wraith camp's front entrance in SJ-45 ("Riders on the Storm" – see page 228).	✔	M221 Saratoga	Increased ammo clip size and fire rate.
Prototype Shingen: Mark V	Can be found in shipping container 667, in the warehouse's loading bay, during MJ-23 ("Gimme Danger" – see page 156). The container is booby-trapped, so make sure you disarm the laser mine inside.	✔	TKI-20 Shingen	Fires explosive rounds. The modified automated targeting system guides bullets to up to three targets while aiming.
Psalm 11:6	Can be crafted if you have the Edgerunner Artisan Perk (Crafting tree) and loot the spec from the leader in hustle 644 (Suspected Organized Crime Activity in Northside – see page 310).	✔	D5 Copperhead	High thermal damage with a chance to apply Burn.
Satori (覚)	After T-Bug opens the penthouse's balcony door during MJ-10 ("The Heist" – see page 128), climb up the stairs leading to the AV landing pad: the weapon is inside the vehicle.	✔	Katana	Reduced base damage but very high Crit Damage multiplier.
Scalpel	Reward for completing SJ-08 ("Big in Japan" – see page 187).	✔	Knife	Deals electrical damage. While Sandevistan cyberware is active, increases Crit Chance by 50% and blows apply Bleeding.
Second Opinion	Can be picked up in Maiko's office (adjacent to Woodman's) during MJ-12 ("Automatic Love" – see page 134).	✔	Nue	Shoots one additional projectile per shot and deals electrical damage, with a chance to apply Shock.
Sir John Phallustiff*	Offered by Stout after your one-night stand with her ("Venus in Furs"). It is obtained by completing the following steps: call Stout before you head to the All Foods warehouse during MJ-08 ("The Pickup" – see page 120), then accept her credchip and use it to buy the Flathead without cracking the chip or warning Royce. A few days later, Stout will message you and offer to meet at the No-Tell Motel; attend, and the weapon can be found as a collectible in the room after your liaison.	✔	Electric Baton Gamma	High damage.
Skippy	Found on the ground at the beginning of SJ-63 ("Machine Gun" – see page 242).	✔	TKI-20 Shingen	Scales to your level and makes amusing comments.
Sovereign	Can be crafted if you have the Edgerunner Artisan Perk (Crafting tree) and loot the spec from the leader in hustle 684 (Suspected Organized Crime Activity in Japantown – see page 316).	✔	DB-4 Igla	Shoots two rounds at a time, with reduced reload time and spread
Stinger	Reward for completing SJ-53 ("I'll Fly Away" – see page 235).	✔	Knife	Deals additional chemical damage with a moderate chance to apply Poison.
The Caretaker's CyberSpade	Leaning against a tree near the conference table during MJ-30 ("Knockin' on Heaven's Door" – see page 172).	✔	Two-Handed Hammer	High damage.
The Headsman	Can be crafted if you have the Edgerunner Artisan Perk (Crafting tree) and loot the spec from the leader in hustle 714 (Suspected Organized Crime Activity in North Oak – see page 321).	✔	M2038 Tactician	Increased number of pellets shot, reduced reload time, chance to apply Bleeding
Tinker Bell	Found under the tree closest to Peter Pan's house on the Edgewood farm during SJ-20 ("The Hunt" – see page 200).	✔	Electric Baton Gamma	Reduced damage, but strong attacks have a chance to stun the target.
Tsumetogi (爪とぎ)	Can be looted from the room where the meeting with Maiko and the Tyger Claw bosses takes place during SJ-30 ("Pisces" – see page 211).	✔	Katana	Deals electrical damage with a chance to apply Shock. Also increases electrical resistance.
Widow Maker	Can be looted from Nash after defeating him during MJ-19 ("Ghost Town" – see page 149).	✔	M-179 Achilles	Fires two projectiles per shot and deals chemical damage, with an increased chance to apply Poison. Charged shots deal more damage.
Yinglong	Can be crafted if you have the Edgerunner Artisan Perk (Crafting tree) and loot the spec from the leader in hustle 905 (Suspected Organized Crime Activity in Wellsprings – see page 353).	✔	G-58 Dian	Deals high electrical damage.

* This weapon is unavailable in region-specific game versions that censor sexual content.

GRENADES

Grenades can play a vital role in battles due to their sheer versatility: they can be employed to hit multiple targets at once, inflict high DPS on an individual target with a precision throw, and can offer immediate tactical solutions if you need to flush adversaries from cover, or deter onrushing melee-focused assailants.

To use grenades, you first need to assign them to your gadget slot in the Inventory, then press R1/RB to throw them.

The table to the right offers an indication of total damage you can expect to deal with grenades in the early game (lv. 3), mid-game (lv. 25), and late game (lv. 50). These are only points of reference, though: a multitude of factors can alter the damage you deal, including the level of your enemies and various Perks governed by the Technical Ability attribute.

Note that there are three types of grenades:

- **Standard grenades** land where you throw them.
- **Sticky grenades** can stick to targets or surfaces.
- **Homing grenades** will automatically home in on the closest target.

GRENADES OVERVIEW

Category	Name	Type	Rarity	Special Property	Damage Lv. 3	Damage Lv. 25	Damage Lv. 50
Frag	**F-GX Frag Grenade**	Standard	Common	-	144-176	777-950	5,088-6,219
	F-GX Frag Grenade	Sticky	Uncommon				
	F-GX Frag Grenade	Homing	Rare				
Flash	**X-22 Flashbang Grenade**	Standard	Common	Applies Blind status effect for 3 seconds; does not deal damage	-		
	X-22 Flashbang Grenade	Homing	Rare				
EMP	**EMP Grenade**	Standard	Common	Deals electrical damage over time	~68 every 5 seconds	~388 every 5 seconds	~2,692 every 5 seconds
	EMP Grenade	Sticky	Uncommon				
	EMP Grenade	Homing	Rare				
Biohazard	**MOLODETS BioHaz Grenade**	Standard	Common	Applies Poison status effect	~68 every 5 seconds	~388 every 5 seconds	~2,692 every 5 seconds
	MOLODETS BioHaz Grenade	Homing	Rare				
Incendiary	**CHAR Incendiary Grenade**	Standard	Uncommon	Applies Burn status effect	~55 every 4 seconds	~311 every 4 seconds	~2,153 every 4 seconds
	CHAR Incendiary Grenade	Sticky	Rare				
	CHAR Incendiary Grenade	Homing	Epic				
Recon	**Recon Grenade**	Standard	Uncommon	Scans its surroundings and highlights detected enemies	-		
	Recon Grenade	Sticky	Uncommon				
Laser	**GASH Antipersonnel Grenade**	Standard	Epic	Deals physical damage over time	55-67	296-362	1,938-2,369
Legendary	**Ozob's Nose**	Standard	Legendary	Deals massive damage	144-176	777-950	5,088-6,219

CLOTHING

Just like weapons, clothes have levels, ranging from 1 to 500 – the higher they are on that scale, the better their parameters will be. They are also governed by the rarity system, which determines how many mod slots they offer.

Two items for the same body part and of the same level and rarity will always have identical data sheets, minor variations or randomization factors notwithstanding. This makes it easier to customize V's appearance to suit your sartorial preferences without a constant need to compromise in terms of stats.

CLOTHING OVERVIEW

Body Part		Armor (Common)			Armor (Uncommon)			Armor (Rare)				Armor (Epic)				Armor (Legendary)			
		Item Level			Item Level			Item Level			Max Mod Slots	Item Level			Max Mod Slots	Item Level			Max Mod Slots
	Examples	30	250	500	30	250	500	30	250	500		30	250	500		30	250	500	
Head	**Balaclava**	5.4	30.9	59.9	5.4	30.9	59.9	5.4	30.9	59.9	1	5.4	30.9	59.9	2	5.4	30.9	59.9	3
	Cap																		
	Hat																		
	Helmet																		
	Scarf																		
Face	**Glasses**	5.4	30.9	59.9	5.4	30.9	59.9	5.4	30.9	59.9	1	5.4	30.9	59.9	2	5.4	30.9	59.9	3
	Mask																		
	Techpiece																		
	Visor																		
Outer Torso	**Coat**	13.8	100.9	199.8	13.8	100.9	199.8	13.8	100.9	199.8	1	13.8	100.9	199.8	2	13.8	100.9	199.8	3
	Dress																		
	Formal Jacket																		
	Jacket																		
	Jumpsuit																		
	Loose Shirt																		
	Vest																		
Inner Torso	**Formal Shirt**	13.8	100.9	199.8	13.8	100.9	199.8	13.8	100.9	199.8	1	13.8	100.9	199.8	2	13.8	100.9	199.8	3
	Shirt																		
	T-Shirt																		
	Tank-top																		
	Tight Jumpsuit																		
	Undershirt																		
Legs	**Formal Pants**	7.8	50.9	99.9	7.8	50.9	99.9	7.8	50.9	99.9	1	7.8	50.9	99.9	2	7.8	50.9	99.9	3
	Pants																		
	Shorts																		
	Skirt																		
Feet	**Boots**	7.8	50.9	99.9	7.8	50.9	99.9	7.8	50.9	99.9	1	7.8	50.9	99.9	2	7.8	50.9	99.9	3
	Casual Shoes																		
	Formal Shoes																		

UNIQUE CLOTHING

The table below details unique pieces of clothing that can only be acquired via the conditions stated in the "Availability" column; they cannot be bought, or looted from enemies. Some of them can be missed, and the ones that pertain to Johnny Silverhand are tied to unlocking a Trophy/Achievement. If you want to collect them all, be sure to read the table carefully.

UNIQUE CLOTHING OVERVIEW

Name	Availability
Johnny's Shirt	Obtained automatically at the end of SJ-34 ("Parasite" – see page 215)
Johnny's Aviators	Obtained automatically during SJ-35 ("Chippin' In" – see page 216)
Johnny's Pants	Can be found in a pink suitcase in the bedroom during the Psychofan gig (see page 294)
Johnny's Shoes	Can be found in the locker with the bootleg during the Family Heirloom gig (see page 279)
Aldecaldos Rally Bolero Jacket	Obtained automatically during MJ-31 ("We Gotta Live Together" – see page 174)
Retrothrusters	Picked up from behind the Afterlife's bar during MJ-29 ("For Whom The Bell Tolls" – see page 172)
Neoprene Diving Suit	Obtained automatically during SJ-31("Pyramid Song" – see page 212)
Fake SAMEREI Jacket	Obtained during SJ-67 ("Small Man, Big Mouth" – see page 245)
Arasaka Spacesuit	Obtained automatically during the "Path of Glory" Epilogue (**spoiler warning** – see page 457)

MODS

Mods are objects you can use to customize equipment featuring at least one mod slot. You can assign and swap mods from the Inventory menu.

As with other gear, there are different mod tiers: the rarer a mod is, the better the quality of the effect it confers.

MOD OVERVIEW

Name	Type	Rarity	Effect	Weight
Crunch	Ranged Mod	Random	Damage +5 (with an additional +1 per mod rarity rank).	0.1
Penetrator	Ranged Mod	Random	Crit Chance +2% (with an additional +1% per mod rarity rank).	0.1
Pacifier	Ranged Mod	Random	Crit Chance +6% (with an additional +2% per mod rarity rank).	0.1
Combat Amplifier	Ranged Mod	Rare	Chance to apply status ailment +5% (Bleeding, Burn, Poison, Shock – in accordance with attack type).	0.1
Countermass	Ranged Mod	Epic	Nullifies vertical recoil while aiming.	0.1
Pulverize	Ranged Mod	Uncommon	+5% to damage inflicted to enemy limbs	0.1
Weaken	Ranged Mod	Rare	Hitting enemies reduces their accuracy by 10% for 10 seconds.	0.1
Autoloader	Ranged Mod	Rare	Reload times after fully emptying an ammo clip are reduced.	0.1
Pax	Ranged Mod	Uncommon	Bullets become non-lethal.	0.1
Phantom	Ranged Mod	Rare	Rate of fire +5%.	0.4
Neon Arrow	Ranged Mod	Rare	Reload time -5%.	0.4
Vendetta	Ranged Mod	Rare	Headshot damage +20%.	0.4
OS-1 GimletEye	Short Scope	Common	Zoom level increased by 0.2; swapping in and out of aim stance takes 0.05 of a second longer.	0.3
Hyakume	Short Scope	Common	Zoom level increased by 0.5; swapping in and out of aim stance takes 0.05 of a second longer.	0.3
Add-Vantage	Short Scope	Common	Zoom level increased by 0.2; swapping in and out of aim stance takes 0.05 of a second longer.	0.3
CQO Mk.72 Kanone MINI	Short Scope	Common	Zoom level increased by 0.4; swapping in and out of aim stance takes 0.05 of a second longer.	0.3
Type 2067	Short Scope	Common	Zoom level increased by 0.4; swapping in and out of aim stance takes 0.05 of a second longer.	0.3
Mk.2x Grandstand	Long Scope	Common	Zoom level increased by 0.5; swapping in and out of aim stance takes 0.1 of a second longer.	0.3
E255 Percipient	Long Scope	Common	Zoom level increased by 1.1; swapping in and out of aim stance takes 0.1 of a second longer.	0.3
Mk. 8 ClearVue	Long Scope	Common	Zoom level increased by 0.9; swapping in and out of aim stance takes 0.1 of a second longer.	0.3
SO-21 Saika	Long Scope	Common	Zoom level increased by 0.9; swapping in and out of aim stance takes 0.1 of a second longer.	0.3
HPO Mk.77 Kanone MAX	Sniper Scope	Common	Zoom level increased by 3; swapping in and out of aim stance takes 0.2 of a second longer.	0.3
E305 Prospecta	Sniper Scope	Common	Zoom level increased by 3; swapping in and out of aim stance takes 0.2 of a second longer.	0.3
Silencer	Muzzle	Common	Damage in active combat -30%; damage dealt by sneak attacks x2.	0.3
XC-10 Strix	Muzzle	Uncommon	Damage in active combat -30%; damage dealt by sneak attacks x2.5; Crit Chance +10%.	0.3
XC-10 Cetus	Muzzle	Uncommon	Damage in active combat -25%; damage dealt by sneak attacks x2.5; Crit Chance +5%.	0.3
XC-10 Alecto	Muzzle	Rare	Damage in active combat -15%; damage dealt by sneak attacks x2.5.	0.3
Scourge	Melee Mod	Rare	Crit Damage +10%.	0.4
White-Knuckled	Melee Mod	Rare	Crit Damage +7%.	0.4
Cold Shoulder	Melee Mod	Rare	Damage +7.	0.4
Kunai	Melee Mod	Rare	Attack speed +0.3 per second.	0.4
Armadillo	Clothing Mod	Random	Armor +2 to +150 depending on mod level, with an additional +20% per mod rarity rank.	0.3
Resist!	Clothing Mod	Random	Damage taken from status ailments -5%, with an additional -3% per mod rarity rank.	0.3
Fortuna	Clothing Mod	Legendary	Crit Chance +15%.	0.3
Bully	Clothing Mod	Legendary	Crit Damage +30%.	0.3
Backpacker	Clothing Mod	Random	Carry Capacity +5, with an additional +2 per mod rarity rank.	0.3
Footloose	Clothing Mod	Random	Evasion +20%, with an additional +10% per mod rarity rank.	0.3
Showtime	Clothing Mod	Random	Damage dealt to moderate- and high-threat enemies +5%, with an additional +1.5% per mod rarity rank.	0.3

MOD OVERVIEW (CONTINUED)

Name	Type	Rarity	Effect	Weight
Osmosis	Clothing Mod	Random	Oxygen +5, with an additional +1.5 per mod rarity rank (base oxygen = 100).	0.3
Plume	Clothing Mod	Random	Fall damage -5%, with an additional -3% per mod rarity rank.	0.3
Zero Drag	Clothing Mod	Random	Movement speed +0.1, with an additional +0.03 per mod rarity rank.	0.3
Tenacity	Clothing Mod	Random	Stamina cost of melee attacks -5%, with an additional -1% per mod rarity rank.	0.3
Vanguard	Clothing Mod	Random	Block Effort Reduction +5%, with an additional +3% per mod rarity rank.	0.3
Boom-Breaker	Clothing Mod	Random	Damage taken from explosions -5%, with an additional -3% per mod rarity rank.	0.3
Coolit	Clothing Mod	Legendary	Immunity to Burn status effect.	0.3
Antivenom	Clothing Mod	Epic	Immunity to Poison status effect.	0.3
Panacea	Clothing Mod	Legendary	Immunity to Poison and Shock status effects.	0.3
Superinsulator	Clothing Mod	Epic	Immunity to Shock status effect.	0.3
Soft-Sole	Clothing Mod	Epic	You make no noise when landing.	0.3
Cut-It-Out	Clothing Mod	Epic	Immunity to Bleeding status effect.	0.3
Predator	Clothing Mod	Legendary	Damage dealt to low- and high-threat enemies +25%.	0.3
Deadeye	Clothing Mod	Legendary	Crit Chance +15%, Crit Damage +30%.	0.3
Blade – Physical Damage	Mantis Blades Edge	Rare	Changes type of damage dealt to physical.	0
Blade – Thermal Damage	Mantis Blades Edge	Rare	Changes type of damage dealt to thermal.	0
Blade – Chemical Damage	Mantis Blades Edge	Rare	Changes type of damage dealt to chemical.	0
Blade – Electrical Damage	Mantis Blades Edge	Rare	Changes type of damage dealt to electrical.	0
Slow Rotor	Mantis Blades Rotor	Epic	Attack speed +20%.	0
Fast Rotor	Mantis Blades Rotor	Epic	Attack speed +40%.	0
Haming-8 Rotor	Mantis Blades Rotor	Legendary	Attack speed +25%.	0
Knuckles – Physical Damage	Gorilla Arms Knuckles	Rare	Changes type of damage dealt to physical.	0
Knuckles – Thermal Damage	Gorilla Arms Knuckles	Rare	Changes type of damage dealt to thermal.	0
Knuckles – Chemical Damage	Gorilla Arms Knuckles	Rare	Changes type of damage dealt to chemical.	0
Knuckles – Electrical Damage	Gorilla Arms Knuckles	Rare	Changes type of damage dealt to electrical.	0
Animals Knuckles	Gorilla Arms Knuckles	Legendary	Changes type of damage dealt to physical. Punching enemies applies Bleeding status effect.	0
Battery, Low-Capacity	Gorilla Arms Battery	Epic	Damage with Gorilla Arms +10%.	0
Battery, Medium-Capacity	Gorilla Arms Battery	Epic	Damage with Gorilla Arms +25%.	0
Battery, High-Capacity	Gorilla Arms Battery	Epic	Damage with Gorilla Arms +50%.	0
Black-Market Battery	Gorilla Arms Battery	Legendary	Damage with Gorilla Arms +100%.	0
Rin3U Battery	Gorilla Arms Battery	Legendary	Damage with Gorilla Arms +10%; restores 100% stamina upon killing an enemy.	0
Monowire – Physical Damage	Monowire Cable	Rare	Changes type of damage dealt to physical.	0
Monowire – Thermal Damage	Monowire Cable	Rare	Changes type of damage dealt to thermal.	0
Monowire – Chemical Damage	Monowire Cable	Rare	Changes type of damage dealt to chemical.	0
Monowire – Electrical Damage	Monowire Cable	Rare	Changes type of damage dealt to electrical.	0
Monowire Battery, Low-Capacity	Monowire Battery	Epic	Damage with Monowire +10%.	0
Monowire Battery, Medium-Capacity	Monowire Battery	Epic	Damage with Monowire +25%.	0
Monowire Battery, High-Capacity	Monowire Battery	Epic	Damage with Monowire +50%.	0
Explosive Round	Projectile Launcher Round	Rare	Normal shots explode on impact and deal physical damage. Charged shots increase damage, explosion range and dismembering chance.	0.4
Electrical Round	Projectile Launcher Round	Rare	Normal shots explode on impact and deal electrical damage. Charged shots increase explosion range and stun targets.	0.4
Thermal Round	Projectile Launcher Round	Rare	Normal shots explode on impact and deal thermal damage with a 20% chance to apply Burn. Charged shots increase damage, explosion range, and chance to apply Burn to 50%.	0.4
Chemical Round	Projectile Launcher Round	Rare	Normal shots explode on impact and deal chemical damage with a 20% chance to apply Poison. Charged shots increase damage, explosion range, and chance to apply Poison to 50%.	0.4
Tranquilizer Rounds	Projectile Launcher Round	Rare	Normal shots can render a single target unconscious. Charged shots have a larger area of effect.	0.4
Neoplastic Plating	Projectile Launcher Wiring	Rare	Crit Chance +10%.	0.4
Metal Plating	Projectile Launcher Wiring	Rare	All resistances +10%.	0.4
Titanium Plating	Projectile Launcher Wiring	Epic	Armor +7%.	0.4
Sensory Amplifier	Universal Cyberarm Fragment	Rare	Crit Chance +10%.	0
Sensory Amplifier	Universal Cyberarm Fragment	Rare	Crit Damage +30%.	0
Sensory Amplifier	Universal Cyberarm Fragment	Rare	Health +15%.	0
Sensory Amplifier	Universal Cyberarm Fragment	Rare	Armor +5%.	0
Sandevistan: Overclocked Processor	Sandevistan Fragment	Random	Sandevistan duration +0.5 second, with an additional +0.2 per mod rarity rank.	0.2
Sandevistan: Prototype Chip	Sandevistan Fragment	Rare	Crit Chance while Sandevistan is active +5%.	0.2
Sandevistan: Neurotransmitters	Sandevistan Fragment	Rare	Crit Damage while Sandevistan is active +15%.	0.2
Sandevistan: Heatsink	Sandevistan Fragment	Random	Sandevistan cooldown -2 seconds, with an additional -0.5 per mod's rarity rank.	0.2
Sandevistan: Micro-Amplifier	Sandevistan Fragment	Legendary	Activating Sandevistan clears status effects (Burn, Poison, Bleeding and Shock).	0.2
Sandevistan: Tyger Paw	Sandevistan Fragment	Epic	Defeating enemies while Sandevistan is active restores 15% stamina.	0.2
Sandevistan: Rabid Bull	Sandevistan Fragment	Epic	Defeating enemies while Sandevistan is active restores 5% health.	0.2
Sandevistan: Arasaka Software	Sandevistan Fragment	Legendary	While Sandevistan is active, enemies take 70% longer to detect you.	0.2
Extended Berserk	Berserk Fragment	Random	Berserk duration +1 second, with an additional +1 per mod rarity rank.	0.2

MOD OVERVIEW (CONTINUED)

Name	Type	Rarity	Effect	Weight
Chained Berserk	Berserk Fragment	Random	Berserk cooldown -5 seconds, with an additional -0.5 per mod rarity rank.	0.2
Armored Berserk	Berserk Fragment	Random	Bonus to armor and resistance +5% while Berserk is active, with an additional +1% per mod rarity rank.	0.2
Bruising Berserk	Berserk Fragment	Random	Bonus to melee damage +10% while Berserk, with an additional +3% per mod rarity rank.	0.2
Focused Berserk	Berserk Fragment	Random	Bonus to sway and recoil reduction +10% while Berserk is active, with an additional +5% per mod rarity rank.	0.2
Invigorating Berserk	Berserk Fragment	Random	Health regeneration +10% while Berserk is active, with an additional +3% per mod rarity rank.	0.2
Devastating Berserk	Berserk Fragment	Rare	Crit Chance while Berserk is active +15%.	0.2
Sharpened Berserk	Berserk Fragment	Rare	Crit Damage while Berserk is active +25%.	0.2
Beast Mode	Berserk Fragment	Legendary	While Berserk is active: bonus to armor and resistance +15%, health regeneration +15%, melee damage +100%.	0.2
Target Analysis	Kiroshi Optics Fragment	Rare	All weapons become non-lethal. Headshots do not deal additional damage. Smart weapons primarily target limbs.	0.4
Explosive Analysis	Kiroshi Optics Fragment	Uncommon	Grenade trajectory and area of effect are visible.	0.4
Threat Detector	Kiroshi Optics Fragment	Rare	Enemies that detect you are automatically highlighted.	0.4
Trajectory Analysis	Kiroshi Optics Fragment	Legendary	Bonus damage from headshots +50%.	0.4
Weakspot Detection	Kiroshi Optics Fragment	Uncommon	Crit Chance +5%.	0.4
Trajectory Generator	Kiroshi Optics Fragment	Uncommon	Ricochet trajectory is visible when aiming. Requires the Ballistic Coprocessor hands cyberware.	0.4

QUICKHACKS

Quickhacks are the programs that you can install on your cyberdeck and then cast on your enemies. The beating heart of pure netrunner builds, but also hugely useful in other character setups, quickhacks can be divided into four distinct categories:

- **Stealth Quickhacks** are used in infiltration scenarios to elude or escape the attention of enemies.
- **Combat Quickhacks** are the bread and butter of netrunners once enemies are aware of your presence. You can cast them to deal damage.
- **Control Quickhacks** are also useful in combat situations, as they can greatly impede opponents. They can prove particularly decisive against bosses and mini-bosses when deployed to disable cyberware they rely on.
- **Ultimate Quickhacks** are the most powerful programs, but also the most costly in terms of RAM and upload time. Used correctly, they can potentially eliminate targets instantly.

The table overleaf lists all quickhacks available in the game with all relevant details. The following notes will help you to make sense of the contents of each column:

- **Rarity & Effect:** Quickhacks come in assorted degrees of rarity, just like other items. The rarer a program, the better its effects. One critical factor to take note of is that most of these effects are cumulative: a quickhack of the Epic rank, for instance, will usually enjoy all of the effects that the Uncommon and Rare versions have, in addition to those introduced by the Epic rank itself.
- **Parameters:** All values provided in the table correspond to base parameters. These can vary in the field in accordance with the level difference between you and your target, the Perks you have unlocked, and so forth.
    - **RAM Cost:** How many points of memory are required to cast the quickhack.
    - **Upload Time:** How long it takes, in seconds, for the program to be uploaded to the target.
    - **Duration:** How long the quickhack affects the target.
    - **Cooldown:** How long you have to wait after using a program before you can cast it again.
    - **Price:** The quickhack's default price.

QUICKHACK OVERVIEW

Category	Quickhack	Rarity	Effect	RAM Cost	Upload Time	Duration	Cooldown	Price
Stealth	Sonic Shock	Uncommon	Deafens the target, reducing their ability to detect you.	3	2	30	10	300
		Rare	Isolates the target from the local network, preventing them from communicating with their allies.	4	2	30	10	600
		Epic	Excludes the target from the perception range of their squad, causing them to be ignored.	5	2	30	10	1,000
		Legendary	Passive while equipped: enemies under the effects of any quickhack are cut off from the local network.	6	2	30	10	1,400
	Request Backup	Uncommon	Calls in squad members that are not in combat mode, all gathering in the same spot.	4	2	10	10	60
		Epic	Also works against enemies in combat mode.	6	2	10	10	200
	Whistle	Uncommon	The affected target will enter a heightened state of alertness and move to your current position.	2	2	10	10	300
		Rare	The target will no longer be in a state of alertness when moving to your current position.	2	2	10	10	300
		Epic	Can be executed on enemies engaged in combat.	4	2	10	10	1,000
	Memory Wipe	Rare	Causes the target to exit combat mode and forget about your presence.	4	2	8	120	600
		Epic	Affects the target's entire squad.	5	2	8	120	1,000
	Ping	Uncommon	Reveals enemies and devices connected to the local network.	1	1	20	0	60
		Legendary	Highlighted targets can be scanned and quickhacked through solid obstacles.	1	1	20	0	280
Combat	Short Circuit	Uncommon	Deals damage to the target. Very effective against mechanical enemies and targets with weak spots.	3	3	-	10	60
		Rare	Applies an EMP effect for a few seconds.	4	3	3	10	600
		Epic	Deals extra damage to enemies below a high threat level.	5	3	3	10	1,000
		Legendary	Passive while equipped: Crit Hits with any weapon apply this quickhack's uncommon effect.	6	3	3	10	1,400
	Synapse Burnout	Rare	Deals damage that scales higher based on how much health the target is missing. Less efficient against mechanical enemies.	6	3	-	10	600
		Epic	If a target is defeated by this quickhack, they burst into flames, causing nearby enemies to pani.	7	3	2	10	1,000
		Legendary	Passive while equipped: defeating an enemy with any quickhack causes nearby enemies to panic.	8	3	2	10	1,400
	Overheat	Uncommon	Applies Burn to the target, dealing damage over time. Less effective against mechanical enemies.	3	3	4	10	300
		Rare	Affected targets are temporarily unable to take any action.	4	3	4	10	600
		Epic	Burn from Overheat lasts significantly longer.	5	3	8	10	1,000
		Legendary	Affected targets are unable to use cyberware abilities.	6	3	8	10	1,400
	Contagion	Uncommon	Applies Poison to the target. Spreads to nearby targets. Effective against closely grouped enemies.	4	1	2	10	300
		Rare	Poison lasts significantly longer.	5	1	6	10	600
		Epic	Each subsequent target receives more damage from Contagion.	6	1	6	10	1,000
		Legendary	Passive while equipped: quickhacks with spread capability can reach additional targets.	9	1	6	10	1,400
Control	Cyberware Malfunction	Uncommon	Disables the target's cyberware, potentially affecting their movement or resistances. Very effective against fast-moving targets and netrunners.	4	5	30	0	300
		Rare	Spreads to the nearest target within a set radius.	5	5	30	0	600
		Epic	Causes a random implant to explode once the effect's duration expires.	6	5	30	0	1,000
	Cripple Movement	Uncommon	Prevents the target from moving from their current position.	4	5	8	0	300
		Rare	Spreads to the nearest target within a set radius.	5	5	8	0	600
		Epic	Affected enemies are also unable to attack.	6	5	8	0	1,000
		Legendary	Passive while equipped: enemies under the effect of any quickhack cannot sprint.	7	5	8	0	1,400
	Weapon Glitch	Uncommon	Causes the target's weapon to malfunction, reducing its accuracy and disabling Smart tracking and obstacle penetration.	4	5	30	0	60
		Rare	Spreads to the nearest target within a radius.	5	5	30	0	600
		Epic	Causes the target's weapon to explode, causing damage.	6	5	30	0	1,000
		Legendary	Passive while equipped: enables the Weapons Jammer daemon during Breach Protocol.	7	6	50	0	1,400
	Reboot Optics	Uncommon	Resets an enemy's optical cyberware, rendering them temporarily blind.	4	5	16	10	300
		Rare	Spreads to the nearest target within a set radius.	5	5	16	10	600
		Epic	Greatly increases the effect's duration.	6	5	32	10	1,000
		Legendary	Enables the Optics Jammer daemon during Breach Protocol.	7	5	32	10	1,400
Ultimate	Suicide	Epic	Forces a target to commit suicide.	11	8	-	120	1,000
		Legendary	Passive while equipped: causing an enemy to panic reduces the RAM cost of your next Ultimate quickhack.	14	8	-	120	1,400
	Detonate Grenade	Epic	Forces a target to trigger a carried grenade. The type of explosion and its effects are based on the target's grenade type.	11	8	-	120	1,000
		Legendary	Passive while equipped: defeating an enemy with any explosion reduces the RAM cost of the next Ultimate quickhack.	14	8	-	120	1,400
	System Reset	Epic	Cripples a target's nervous system, causing them to lose consciousness. The affected target will not make any noise when passing out.	10	8	-	120	1,000
		Legendary	Passive while equipped: defeating an enemy reduces the RAM cost of the next quickhack.	13	8	-	120	1,400
	Cyberpsychosis	Epic	Causes the target to attack enemies and allies indiscriminately. If no other allies are nearby, the target will commit suicide.	12	8	60	120	1,000
		Legendary	Passive while equipped: enemies under the effect of any quickhack will no longer try to avoid friendly fire.	15	8	60	120	1,400

CONSUMABLES

Consumables are single-use items that can serve a variety of purposes, and can be used via the Inventory (hold ⊗/Ⓐ).

Don't forget to assign an emergency consumable to the dedicated Quick Access slot in your Inventory: this will enable you to activate it with a single press of ✪, which can be the difference between life and death in more challenging encounters.

CONSUMABLES OVERVIEW

Category		Name	Quality	Effect	Duration	Price
Category	Inhalers	MaxDoc Mk.1	Uncommon	Instantly restores 40% health.	Instant	9
	Inhalers	MaxDoc Mk.2	Rare	Instantly restores 60% health.	Instant	18
	Inhalers	MaxDoc Mk.3	Epic	Instantly restores 80% health.	Instant	30
	Injectors	Bounce Back Mk.1	Common	Instantly restores 15% health and 3% regen per second.	30 seconds	6
	Injectors	Bounce Back Mk.2	Uncommon	Instantly restores 20% health and 4% regen per second.	30 seconds	9
	Injectors	Bounce Back Mk.3	Rare	Instantly restores 25% health and 6% regen per second.	30 seconds	18
	Boosters	Health Booster	Rare	Increases max health by 20%.	30 minutes	2,250
	Boosters	Stamina Booster	Uncommon	Increases max stamina by 50%.	30 minutes	1,125
	Boosters	RAM Jolt	Uncommon	Increases max RAM by 2.	30 minutes	1,125
	Boosters	Capacity Booster	Uncommon	Increases max carry capacity by 50%.	30 minutes	1,125
	Boosters	Oxy Booster	Common	Enables underwater breathing.	30 minutes	750
	Shards	Perk Shard	Epic	Grants 1 Perk Point.	Instant	500
	Shards	Skill Shard: Handguns	Epic	Grants 500 XP to Handguns skill.	Instant	500
	Shards	Skill Shard: Assault	Epic	Grants 500 XP to Assault skill.	Instant	500
	Shards	Skill Shard: Blades	Epic	Grants 500 XP to Blades skill.	Instant	500
	Shards	Skill Shard: Street Brawler	Epic	Grants 500 XP to Street Brawler skill.	Instant	500
	Shards	Skill Shard: Athletics	Epic	Grants 500 XP to Athletics skill.	Instant	500
	Shards	Skill Shard: Annihilation	Epic	Grants 500 XP to Annihilation skill.	Instant	500
	Shards	Skill Shard: Quickhacking	Epic	Grants 500 XP to Quickhacking skill.	Instant	500
	Shards	Skill Shard: Breach Protocol	Epic	Grants 500 XP to Breach Protocol skill.	Instant	500
	Shards	Skill Shard: Stealth	Epic	Grants 500 XP to Stealth skill.	Instant	500
	Shards	Skill Shard: Cold Blood	Epic	Grants 500 XP to Cold Blood skill.	Instant	500
	Shards	Skill Shard: Engineering	Epic	Grants 500 XP to Engineering skill.	Instant	500
	Shards	Skill Shard: Crafting	Epic	Grants 500 XP to Crafting skill.	Instant	500
	Shards	Tabula e-Rasa	Legendary	Allows you to redistribute your Perk Points	Instant	100,000
	Edibles	Food	Common	Increases max health by 5%. Regenerates 0.5% health every second outside combat.	450 seconds	5
	Edibles	Drinks	Common	Increases max stamina by 10%. Increases stamina regeneration rate by 50%.	450 seconds	10
	Edibles	Alcohol	Common	Reduces movement speed by 10% and weapon spread by 50%. Stacks three times.	30 seconds	30

MEMORABILIA

As you complete important jobs, you will gradually unlock items of memorabilia that will appear in your apartment to commemorate past deeds. The accompanying table lists these items and explains how to obtain them.

MEMORABILIA OVERVIEW

Item	Availability
Car model on the desk	Complete MJ-01 ("The Nomad" – see page 113)
Arasaka clock on the desk	Complete MJ-02 ("The Street Kid" – see page 114)
Night City diorama on the desk	Complete MJ-03 ("The Corpo-Rat" – see page 115)
Pin-up poster	Complete SJ-10 ("Heroes" – see page 189)
Lizzy Wizzy poster	Complete SJ-13 ("Violence" – see page 192)
Peralez poster	Complete SJ-19 ("Dream On" – see page 198)
Augmented reality game box	Complete SJ-21 ("Following the River" – see page 202)
Box with diving suit	Complete SJ-31 ("Pyramid Song" – see page 212)
Record player and vinyl discs	Complete SJ-34 ("Parasite" – see page 215)
Kerry poster	Complete SJ-43 ("Boat Drinks" – see page 224)
Dreamcatcher near the bed	Complete SJ-44 ("Fool on the Hill" – see page 225)
Monk altar	Complete SJ-48 ("Imagine" – see page 231) and the following three jobs in that quest line
Aldecaldo jacket	Complete SJ-50 ("Queen of the Highway" – see page 233)
Scorpion figure	Complete SJ-53 ("I'll Fly Away" – see page 235)
Brancesi painting	Complete SJ-57 ("Space Oddity" – see page 238)
Skippy	Complete SJ-63 ("Machine Gun" – see page 242) and choose not to return Skippy to Regina
Legendary weapons	Legendary weapons that you store in your apartment's stash will appear on the wall

SHOPS

Night City is home to a large number of shops. The selection of goods for sale is not fixed, so it's impossible to offer a definitive list of what you will find whenever you visit a vendor. However, the system that determines shop inventories can be broadly explained as follows: low-value or basic items tend to be available most of the time, while rarer and/or more valuable items appear at random.

To avoid overwhelming you with information, the table in this section reveals a selection of the best items that can be found at each shop (using the usual color-coding system to convey their rarity – see page 404), along with any Street Cred requirements they are gated behind. If you meet the specified conditions but do not see an object listed here, it means you need to refresh the random selection. You can achieve this by visiting the same vendor again after 48 in-game hours or, alternatively, make another visit after first traveling to a very distant part of the Night City map.

Prices are dynamic and can fluctuate in accordance with various factors, including each vendor's category and your overall progression. Note that it's possible to earn discounts from certain shops when you meet specific requirements:

- **Charles Bucks**, the ripperdoc who owns Bucks' Clinic in Kabuki, can be persuaded to give you a discount on his wares. To achieve this, check the laptop on the desk in the basement during the "Last Login" gig (see page 268) or SJ-15 ("Full Disclosure" – see page 194), and read the email proving that Charles has a deal with the scavengers. Once you have completed this step, head upstairs and confront him. Charles will offer to buy your silence with a discount.
- **Roger Wang**, the man who runs the Medpoint in northeast Kabuki, can give you a discount if you ask for one after you handle his little debt problem by completing the "Shark in the Water" gig (see page 265).
- **Chang Hoon Nam** will give you a discount on his netrunner gear after you rescue him during the "Wakako's Favorite" gig (see page 277).
- **Darrell** will give you a discount if you save his life during SJ-47 ("A Day In The Life" – see page 230).
- **Zane Jagger**, the owner of Downtown's Jinguji clothing shop, will offer you a special discount after you complete SJ-64 ("Bullets" – see page 243).
- Last but not least, as you gain Street Cred levels, you will receive messages from the various fixers in Night City that inform you that you are entitled to discounts in the shops in their districts.

BEST ITEMS PER SHOP

Category				Item 1		Item 2		Item 3		Item 4		Item 5	
		Name	District	Name	Street Cred	Name	Street Cred	Name	Street Cred	Name	Street Cred	Name	Street Cred
Clothing Vendors		Clothing Vendor	Badlands	Coolit	17	Spec: Blue menpō with protective padding	-	Spec: Padded Denki Hachi hybrid-weave bra	-	Spec: Upgraded farmer hat with gauge	-	Spec: Powder Pink light polyamide blazer	-
Clothing Vendors		Appel de Paris	Corpo Plaza	Antivenom	17	Spec: Composite Geisha combat shirt	-	Spec: Deadly Lagoon armored syn-silk pozer-jacket	-	Spec: Uniware Brass office pants with membrane support	-	Spec: Multilayered Kasen exo-jacks with anti-shrapnel lining	-
Clothing Vendors		Jinguji	Downtown	Panacea	17	Spec: Durable Emerald Speed polyamide beanie	-	Spec: Aoi Tora enhanced BD wreath	-	Spec: Chic Pink Dragon skirt with fiberglass sequins	-	Enhanced Daemon Hunter tongues	-
Clothing Vendors		Clothing Vendor	Wellsprings	Spec: Mírame reinforced-composite cowboy hat	-	Spec: Sun Spark thermoset chemglass infovisor	-	Spec: Daemon Hunter resistance-coated tank top	-	Spec: SilveRock bulletproof-laminate biker vest	-	Spec: Gold Fury neotac bulletproof pants	-
Clothing Vendors		Clothing Vendor	Coastview	Antivenom	17	Soft-Sole	17	Cut-It-Out	17	Spec: Laminated security hardhat with headset	-	Spec: Stylish Ten70 Daemon Hunter coat	-
Clothing Vendors		Clothing Vendor	Arroyo	Coolit	17	Antivenom	17	Spec: Blue Brick reinforced hotpants	-	Spec: GREEN GRAFFITI athletic shoes with protective coating	-	Spec: Milky Gold trench coat with bulletproof triweave	-
Clothing Vendors		Clothing Vendor	Rancho Coronado	Coolit	17	Antivenom	17	Spec: GREEN GRAFFITI athletic shoes with protective coating	-	Spec: Blue Brick reinforced hotpants	-	Spec: Trilayer steel ocuset	-
Clothing Vendors		Clothing Vendor	Kabuki	Superinsulator	17	Soft-Sole	17	Cut-It-Out	17	Spec: Ten70 Bada55 polycarbonate bandana	-	Spec: Classic aramid-weave denim shorts	-
Clothing Vendors		Clothing Vendor	Little China	Coolit	17	Soft-Sole	17	Deadeye	17	Spec: Stylish turquoise sport glasses	-	Spec: Denki-shin thermoset hybrid crystaljock bomber	-
Clothing Vendors		Clothing Vendor	Northside	Spec: PSYCHO flexiweave long-sleeve	-	Spec: GLITTER laceless sturdy-stitched steel-toes	-	Spec: Darra Polytehcnic tactical balaclava	-	Spec: Mox gas mask with custom protective layer	-	Spec: Green Viper double-nanoweave pencil dress	-
Clothing Vendors		Clothing Vendor	Charter Hill	Deadeye	17	Predator	17	Soft-Sole	17	Spec: Trilayer steel ocuset	-	Spec: Milky Gold trench coat with bulletproof triweave	-
Clothing Vendors		Blossoming Sakura Clothier	Japantown	Antivenom	17	Superinsulator	17	Predator	17	Spec: That good old red, white and blue.	-	Spec: Abendstern polycarbonate dress wedges	-
Clothing Vendors		Karim's Vinyls	Japantown	Samurai 2020 Tour T-shirt	-	SAMURAI sturdy-stitched cargo pants	-	Second Conflict flight jacket	-	Vintage SAMURAI strongweave T-shirt	-	Stylish polarized aviators	-
Weapon Shops		Gun Vendor	Badlands	D5 Copperhead	-	m-10AF Lexington	43	CHAR Incendiary Grenade	-	Spec: M2038 Tactician	-	Spec: Crusher	-
Weapon Shops		Gun Vendor	Badlands	Liberty	-	D5 Sidewinder	-	A-22B Chao	43	Spec: Nekomata	-	Spec: D5 Copperhead	-
Weapon Shops		Gun Vendor	Downtown	M-179e Achilles	-	L-69 Zhuo	-	TKI-20 Shingen	50	Spec: Palica	-	Spec: D5 Sidewinder	-
Weapon Shops		Gun Vendor	The Glenn	DB-2 Testera	-	Ashura	47	Spec: Overture	-	Ranged Mod: Countermass	-	Spec: SPT32 Grad	-
Weapon Shops		Gun Vendor	Vista Del Rey	HJSH-18 Masamune	47	DB-2 Testera	-	Spec: A-22B Chao	-	Spec: DB-2 Testera	-	Spec: A-22B Chao	-
Weapon Shops		Gun Vendor	Wellsprings	SPT32 Grad	-	JKE-X2 Kenshin	49	Carnage Spec:	-	JKE-X2 Kenshin Spec:	-	Carnege Spec	-
Weapon Shops		Gun Vendor	West Wind Estate	DB-4 Palica	-	M2038 Tactician	37	Spec: DR12 Quasar	-	Spec: M2038 Tactician	-	DB-2 Satara Spec	-
Weapon Shops		Gun Vendor	Arroyo	Overture	-	SPT32 Grad	43	RT-46 Burya Spec:	-	Spec: Nue	-	Spec: Unity	-
Weapon Shops		Gun Vendor	Rancho Coronado	Crusher	-	Nue	39	Spec: Nekomata	-	Spec: m-10AF Lexington	-	Spec: M-76e Omaha	-
Weapon Shops		Straight Shooters	Kabuki	Katana	14	DB-2 Satara	-	Hammer	-	Spec: D5 Copperhead	-	Spec: Nekomata	-
Weapon Shops		2nd Amendment	Little China	Baseball Bat	11	Unity	-	Ranged Weapon Mod: Weaken	-	Spec: Knife	-	Spec: m-10AF Lexington	-

BEST ITEMS PER SHOP (CONTINUED)

Category	Name	District	Item 1 Name	Item 1 Street Cred	Item 2 Name	Item 2 Street Cred	Item 3 Name	Item 3 Street Cred	Item 4 Name	Item 4 Street Cred	Item 5 Name	Item 5 Street Cred
Weapon Shops	Iron & Lead	Northside	Knife	-	DS1 Pulsar	-	Nekomata	17	Spec: X-22 Flashbang Grenade	-	Ranged Mod: Combat Amplifier	-
	Gun Vendor	Japantown	M-76e Omaha	-	Carnage	27	Machete	27	Spec: DR-12 Quasar	-	Ranged Mod: Weaken	-
	Straight Shooters	Kabuki	DR5 Nova	-	Defender	14	Ranged Mod: Countermass	-	Spec: Nekomata	-	Spec: D5 Copperhead	-
Medpoints	All Medpoints	All	Bounce Back Mk.3	-	MaxDoc Mk.3	-	Spec: Bounce Back Mk.3	-	Spec: MaxDoc Mk.3	-	-	-
	Meds Vendor	Badlands	Health Booster	-	Oxy Booster	-	-	-	-	-	-	-
	Old Nature Clinic	Corpo Plaza	Health Booster	-	-	-	-	-	-	-	-	-
	Meds Vendor	Downtown	Capacity Booster	-	Oxy Booster	-	Stamina Booster	-	-	-	-	-
	Meds Vendor	Wellsprings	Stamina Booster	-	Capacity Booster	-	-	-	-	-	-	-
	Meds Vendor	Coastview	Health Booster	-	Oxy Booster	-	-	-	-	-	-	-
	Meds Vendor	Arroyo	Health Booster	-	Stamina Booster	-	RAM Jolt	-	-	-	-	-
	Meds Vendor	Rancho Coronado	Stamina Booster	-	Capacity Booster	-	-	-	-	-	-	-
	Roger Wang	Kabuki	Health Booster	-	Stamina Booster	-	-	-	-	-	-	-
	Yin & Yang Pharmacy	Little China	Health Booster	-	Stamina Booster	-	RAM Jolt	-	Capacity Booster	-	-	-
	Meds Etc.	Northside	Health Booster	-	RAM Jolt	-	-	-	-	-	-	-
	ParaMED	Northside	Health Booster	-	-	-	-	-	-	-	-	-
	Meds Vendor	Japantown	Health Booster	-	Stamina Booster	-	RAM Jolt	-	Capacity Booster	-	Oxy Booster	-
Netrunners	Netrunner	Vista Del Rey	Legendary Quickhack Components	-	Eoic Quickhack Components	-	Wide range of quickhacks	-	Wide range of quickhacks	-	-	-
	Netrunner	Coastview	Legendary Quickhack Components	-	Eoic Quickhack Components	-	Wide range of quickhacks	-	Wide range of quickhacks	-	-	-
	Yoko	Japantown	Rare Quickhack Components	-	Uncommon Quickhack Components	-	Wide range of quickhacks	-	-	-	-	-
	Netrunner	Japantown	Rare Quickhack Components	-	Uncommon Quickhack Components	-	Wide range of quickhacks	-	-	-	-	-
	Chang Hoon Nam	Japantown	Rare Quickhack Components	-	Uncommon Quickhack Components	-	Wide range of quickhacks	-	-	-	-	-
Ripperdocs	Ripperdoc	Badlands	BioMonitor	43	Blood Pump	-	BioConductor	43	Adrenaline Booster	-	Bioplastic Blood Vessels	-
	Ripperdoc	Downtown	QianT "Warp Dancer" Sandevistan Mk.5	50	Bioplastic Blood Vessels	-	Arasaka Mk.4	50	Shock-n-Awe	50	Inductor	-
	Ripperdoc	Wellsprings	Militech \"Falcon\" Sandevistan Mk.5	49	Kiroshi Optics Mk.2	14	Second Heart	49	Syn-Lungs	-	Feedback Circuit	-
	Ripperdoc	West Wind Estate	Fuyutsui Tinkerer Mk.3	37	Stephenson Tech Mk.4	37	Camillo RAM Manager	37	Ex-Disk	-	Visual Cortex Support	-
	Ripperdoc	Arroyo	Zetatech Berserk Mk.4	43	Kerenzikov	43	Neofiber	-	Synaptic Signal Optimizer	-	Reflex Tuner	-
	Octavio's Clinic	Rancho Coronado	MicroGenerator	-	BioMonitor	-	Blood Pump	-	Ballistic Coprocessor	20	Bioconductor	-
	Instant Implants	Kabuki	Microrotors	14	Ballistic Coprocessor	-	Lynx Paws	-	Dense Marrow	-	Synaptic Signal Optimizer	-
	Bucks' Clinic	Kabuki	Feedback Circuit	-	Adrenaline Booster	14	BioConductor	-	BioMonitor	-	Tetratronic Mk.2	14
	Dr. Chrome	Kabuki	Zetatech Berserk Mk.5	14	Subdermal Armor	-	Raven Microcyber Mk.4	14	Heat Converter	-	Fireproof Coating	-
	Viktor's Clinic	Little China	Dynalar Sandevistan Mk.4	11	Smart Link	11	Kiroshi Optics Mk.3	-	Ballistic Coprocessor	-	Stephenson Tech Mk.3	11
	Cassius	Northside	Heal-On-Kill	-	Mechatronic Core	17	Camillo RAM Manager	-	Self - ICE	-	Limbic System Enhancement	-
	Kraviz's Clinic	Charter Hill	Militech Berserk Mk.5	29	Tetratronic Rippler Mk.4	29	Endoskeleton	-	Bionic Lungs	29	Microrotors	-
	Ripperdoc	Japantown	BioDyne Berserk Mk.4	27	Synaptic Accelerator	-	Limbic System Enhancement	27	Reflex Tuner	27	Biotech Σ Mk.3	27
	Fingers M.D.	Japantown	Pain Editor	-	QianT Sandevistan Mk.4	27	CataResist	27	Inductor	-	Fortified Ankles	-

VEHICLES

As you explore Night City and take jobs, you will gradually unlock opportunities to acquire new vehicles – usually by purchasing them from fixers. Others will be offered to you as rewards for completing missions. You can find a complete overview in the sheets overleaf, along with useful information and stats.

When you own multiple vehicles, you can change the currently active model – that is, the vehicle that will appear when you call for one – by holding ⭘.

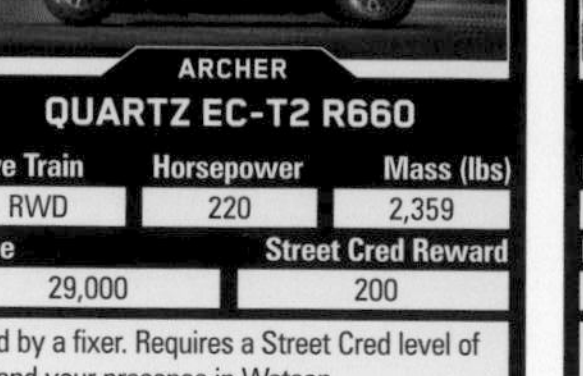

ARCHER — QUARTZ EC-T2 R660

Drive Train	Horsepower	Mass (lbs)
RWD	220	2,359

Price	Street Cred Reward
29,000	200

Sold by a fixer. Requires a Street Cred level of 12 and your presence in Watson.

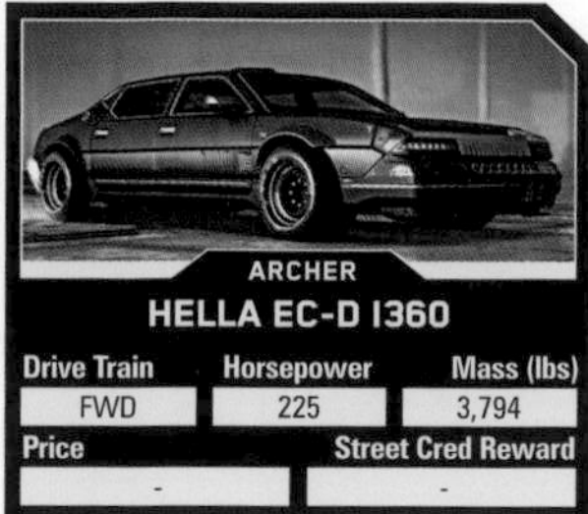

ARCHER — HELLA EC-D I360

Drive Train	Horsepower	Mass (lbs)
FWD	225	3,794

Price	Street Cred Reward
-	-

V's starting car.

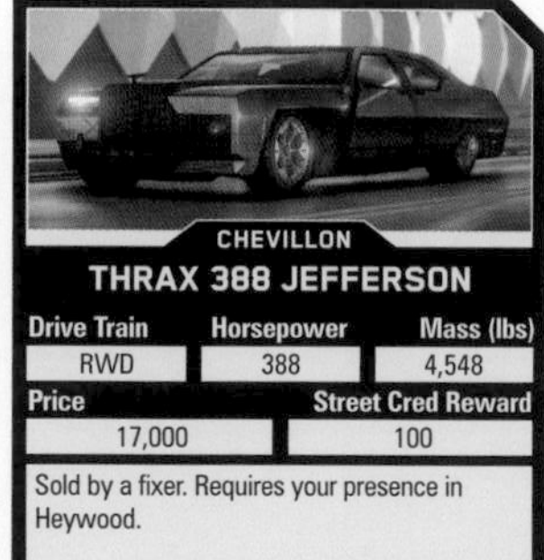

CHEVILLON — THRAX 388 JEFFERSON

Drive Train	Horsepower	Mass (lbs)
RWD	388	4,548

Price	Street Cred Reward
17,000	100

Sold by a fixer. Requires your presence in Heywood.

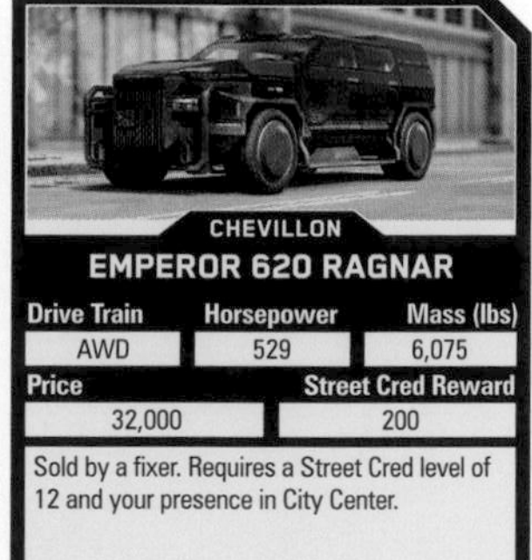

CHEVILLON — EMPEROR 620 RAGNAR

Drive Train	Horsepower	Mass (lbs)
AWD	529	6,075

Price	Street Cred Reward
32,000	200

Sold by a fixer. Requires a Street Cred level of 12 and your presence in City Center.

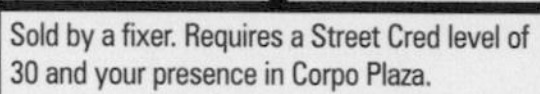

HERRERA — OUTLAW GTS

Drive Train	Horsepower	Mass (lbs)
AWD	755	3,999

Price	Street Cred Reward
62,000	500

Sold by a fixer. Requires a Street Cred level of 30 and your presence in Corpo Plaza.

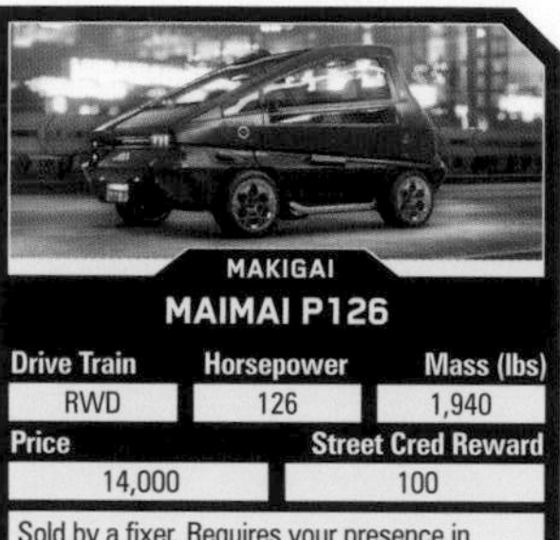

MAKIGAI — MAIMAI P126

Drive Train	Horsepower	Mass (lbs)
RWD	126	1,940

Price	Street Cred Reward
14,000	100

Sold by a fixer. Requires your presence in Westbrook.

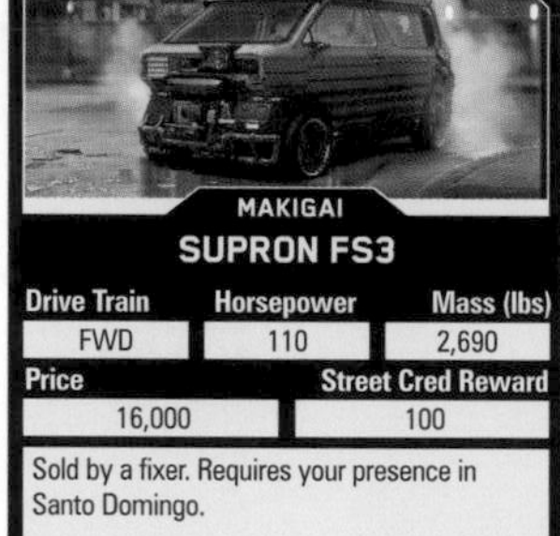

MAKIGAI — SUPRON FS3

Drive Train	Horsepower	Mass (lbs)
FWD	110	2,690

Price	Street Cred Reward
16,000	100

Sold by a fixer. Requires your presence in Santo Domingo.

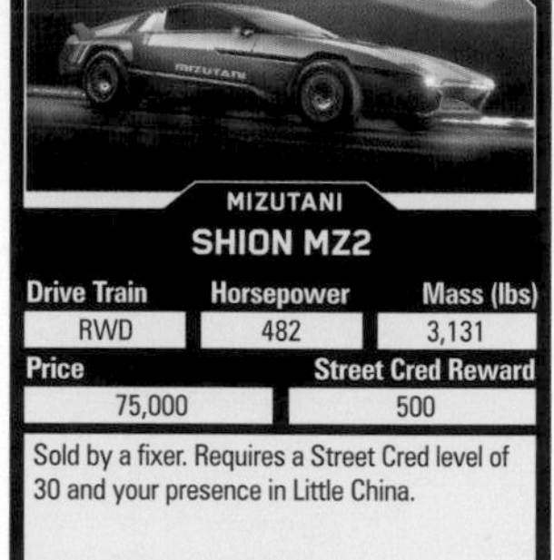

MIZUTANI — SHION MZ2

Drive Train	Horsepower	Mass (lbs)
RWD	482	3,131

Price	Street Cred Reward
75,000	500

Sold by a fixer. Requires a Street Cred level of 30 and your presence in Little China.

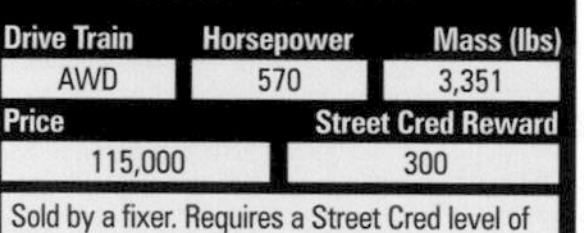

MIZUTANI — SHION "COYOTE"

Drive Train	Horsepower	Mass (lbs)
AWD	570	3,351

Price	Street Cred Reward
115,000	300

Sold by a fixer. Requires a Street Cred level of 20 and your presence in the Badlands.

MIZUTANI — SHION "COYOTE"

Drive Train	Horsepower	Mass (lbs)
AWD	570	3,351

Price	Street Cred Reward
-	-

Reward for completing SJ-50 ("Queen of the Highway", see page 233).

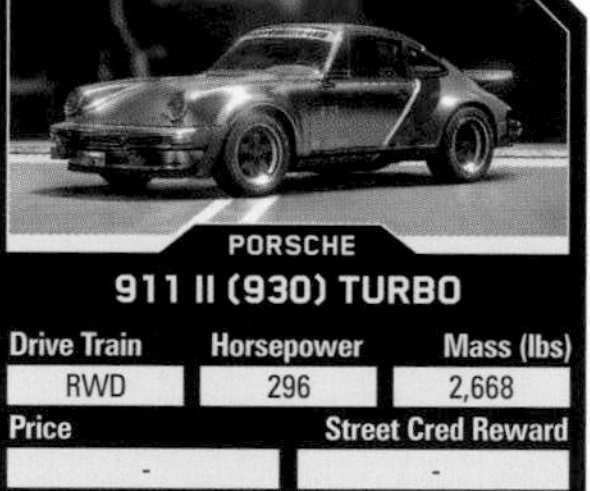

PORSCHE — 911 II (930) TURBO

Drive Train	Horsepower	Mass (lbs)
RWD	296	2,668

Price	Street Cred Reward
-	-

Reward during SJ-35 ("Chippin' In", see page 216) if you retrieve the key from Grayson and open the shipping container.

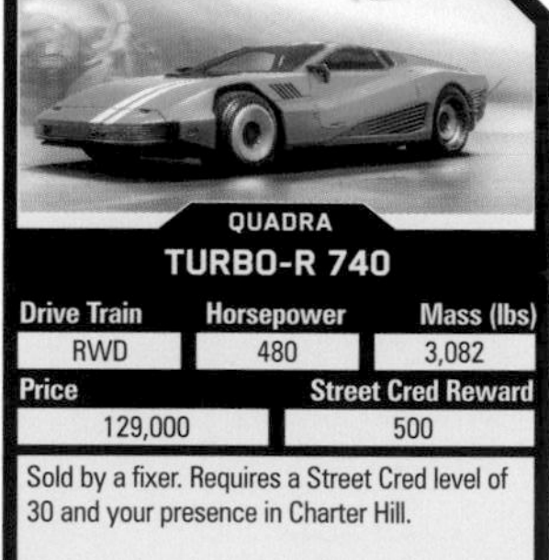

QUADRA — TURBO-R 740

Drive Train	Horsepower	Mass (lbs)
RWD	480	3,082

Price	Street Cred Reward
129,000	500

Sold by a fixer. Requires a Street Cred level of 30 and your presence in Charter Hill.

QUADRA — TURBO-R V-TECH

Drive Train	Horsepower	Mass (lbs)
RWD	740	3,131

Price	Street Cred Reward
-	-

Reward for completing "Sex on Wheels" (see page 293).

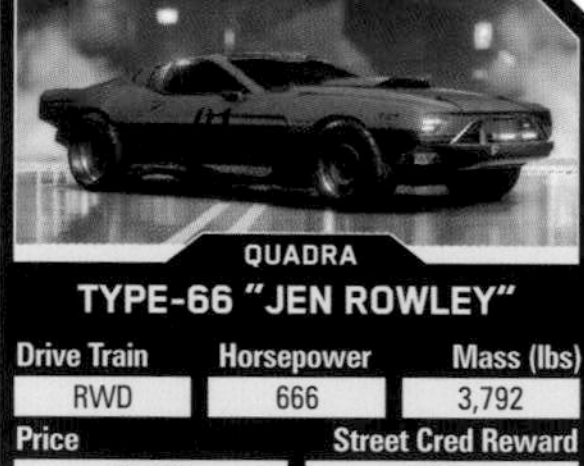

QUADRA — TYPE-66 "JEN ROWLEY"

Drive Train	Horsepower	Mass (lbs)
RWD	666	3,792

Price	Street Cred Reward
58,000	300

Sold by a fixer. Requires a Street Cred level of 20 and your presence in Santo Domingo.

QUADRA — TYPE-66 "CTHULHU"

Drive Train	Horsepower	Mass (lbs)
RWD	666	3,792

Price	Street Cred Reward
76,000	300

Reward for sparing Sampson during SJ-09 ("The Beast in Me", see page 189). If you let Sampson die instead, you can buy this vehicle in Watson.

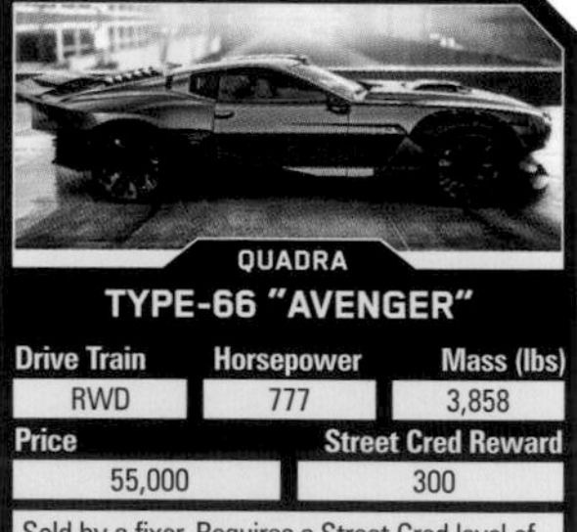

QUADRA — TYPE-66 "AVENGER"

Drive Train	Horsepower	Mass (lbs)
RWD	777	3,858

Price	Street Cred Reward
55,000	300

Sold by a fixer. Requires a Street Cred level of 20 and your presence in City Center.

QUADRA — TYPE-66 "JAVELINA"

Drive Train	Horsepower	Mass (lbs)
AWD	1,000	4,057

Price	Street Cred Reward
73,000	500

Sold by a fixer. Requires a Street Cred level of 30 and your presence in the Badlands.

RAYFIELD — AERONDIGHT "GUINEVERE"

Drive Train	Horsepower	Mass (lbs)
RWD	950	4,052

Price	Street Cred Reward
225,000	5,000

Sold by a fixer. Requires a Street Cred level of 50 and your presence in North Oaks.

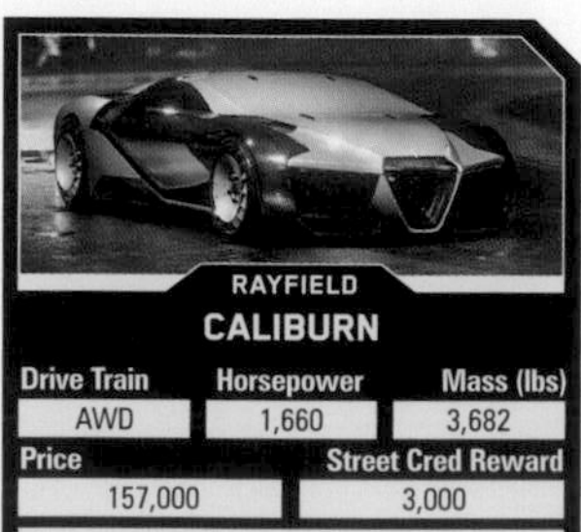

RAYFIELD — CALIBURN

Drive Train	Horsepower	Mass (lbs)
AWD	1,660	3,682

Price	Street Cred Reward
157,000	3,000

Sold by a fixer. Requires a Street Cred level of 40 and your presence Downtown.

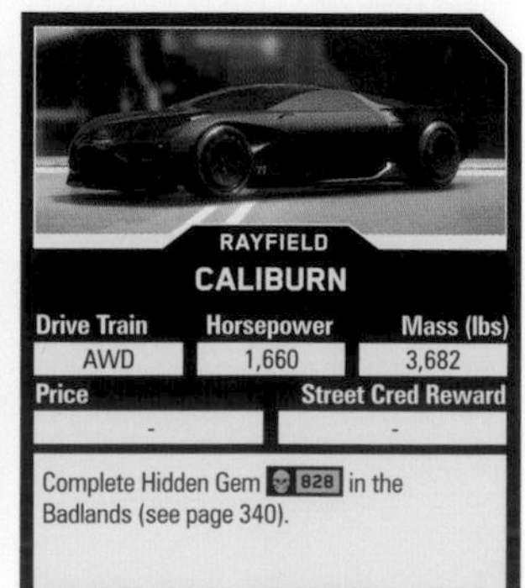

RAYFIELD — CALIBURN

Drive Train	Horsepower	Mass (lbs)
AWD	1,660	3,682

Price	Street Cred Reward
-	-

Complete Hidden Gem 828 in the Badlands (see page 340).

THORTON
COLBY C125

Drive Train	Horsepower	Mass (lbs)
FWD	182	3,311

Price	Street Cred Reward
39,000	300

Sold by a fixer. Requires a Street Cred level of 20 and your presence in Watson.

THORTON
COLBY CX410 BUTTE

Drive Train	Horsepower	Mass (lbs)
AWD	235	3,571

Price	Street Cred Reward
43,000	200

Sold by a fixer. Requires a Street Cred level of 12 and your presence in Santo Domingo.

THORTON
COLBY CX410 BUTTE

Drive Train	Horsepower	Mass (lbs)
AWD	235	3,571

Price	Street Cred Reward
-	-

Complete Hidden Gem 832 in the Badlands (see page 341).

THORTON
COLBY "LITTLE MULE"

Drive Train	Horsepower	Mass (lbs)
AWD	369	3,726

Price	Street Cred Reward
49,000	200

Sold by a fixer. Requires a Street Cred level of 12 and your presence in the Badlands.

THORTON
GALENA G240

Drive Train	Horsepower	Mass (lbs)
FWD	86	2,255

Price	Street Cred Reward
13,000	100

Sold by a fixer. Requires your presence in Watson.

THORTON
GALENA "RATTLER"

Drive Train	Horsepower	Mass (lbs)
AWD	294	2,601

Price	Street Cred Reward
-	-

Reward for completing SJ-52 ("These Boots Are Made For Walkin'", see page 235) – exclusive to a Nomad V.

THORTON
GALENA "GECKO"

Drive Train	Horsepower	Mass (lbs)
AWD	365	3,175

Price	Street Cred Reward
21,000	100

Sold by a fixer. Requires your presence in the Badlands.

THORTON
MACKINAW MTL1

Drive Train	Horsepower	Mass (lbs)
RWD	420	5,454

Price	Street Cred Reward
128,000	500

Sold by a fixer. Requires a Street Cred level of 30 and your presence in the Santo Domingo.

THORTON
MACKINAW "BEAST"

Drive Train	Horsepower	Mass (lbs)
AWD	560	4,894

Price	Street Cred Reward
-	-

Complete SJ-09 ("The Beast in Me", see page 189) by going after Sampson.

VILLEFORT
ALVARADO V4F 570 DELEGATE

Drive Train	Horsepower	Mass (lbs)
RWD	407	5,004

Price	Street Cred Reward
62,000	300

Sold by a fixer. Requires a Street Cred level of 20 and your presence in Heywood.

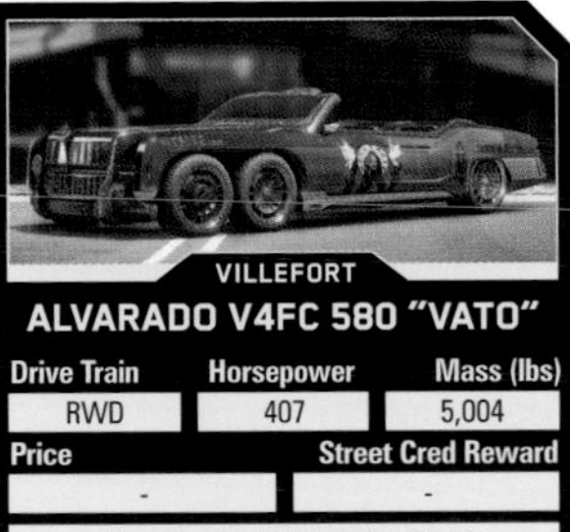

VILLEFORT
ALVARADO V4FC 580 "VATO"

Drive Train	Horsepower	Mass (lbs)
RWD	407	5,004

Price	Street Cred Reward
-	-

Reward for defeating César during SJ-01 ("Beat on the Brat", see page 181).

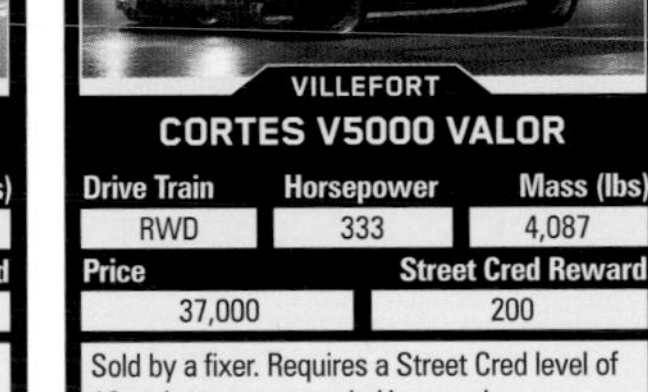

VILLEFORT
CORTES V5000 VALOR

Drive Train	Horsepower	Mass (lbs)
RWD	333	4,087

Price	Street Cred Reward
37,000	200

Sold by a fixer. Requires a Street Cred level of 12 and your presence in Heywood.

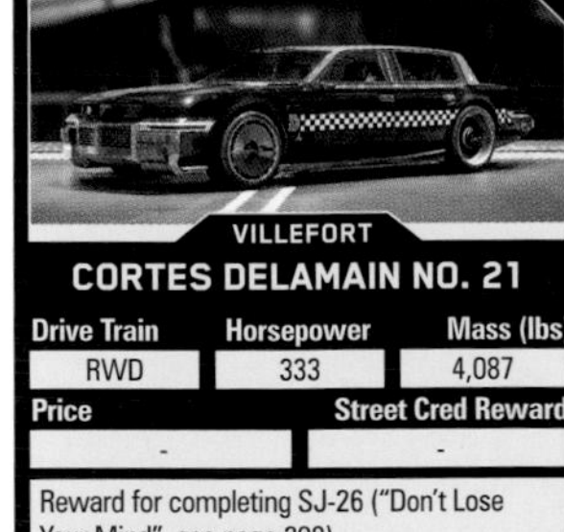

VILLEFORT
CORTES DELAMAIN NO. 21

Drive Train	Horsepower	Mass (lbs)
RWD	333	4,087

Price	Street Cred Reward
-	-

Reward for completing SJ-26 ("Don't Lose Your Mind", see page 208).

VILLEFORT
COLUMBUS V340-F FREIGHT

Drive Train	Horsepower	Mass (lbs)
RWD	210	4,453

Price	Street Cred Reward
19,000	100

Sold by a fixer. Requires your presence in City Center.

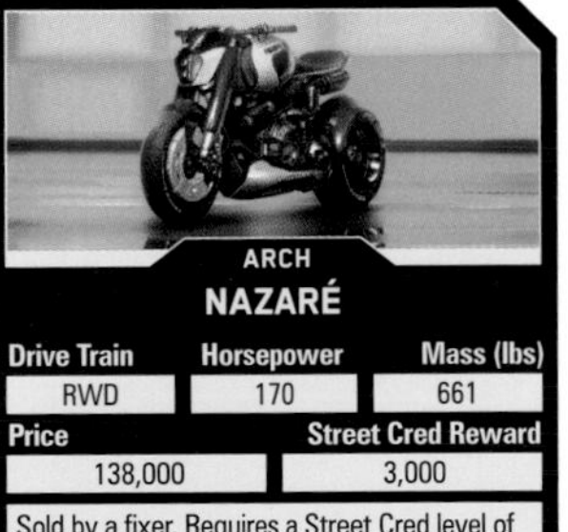

ARCH
NAZARÉ

Drive Train	Horsepower	Mass (lbs)
RWD	170	661

Price	Street Cred Reward
138,000	3,000

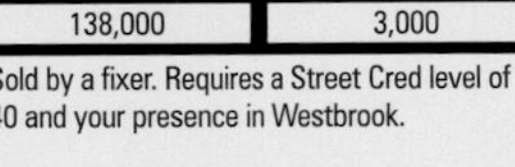

Sold by a fixer. Requires a Street Cred level of 40 and your presence in Westbrook.

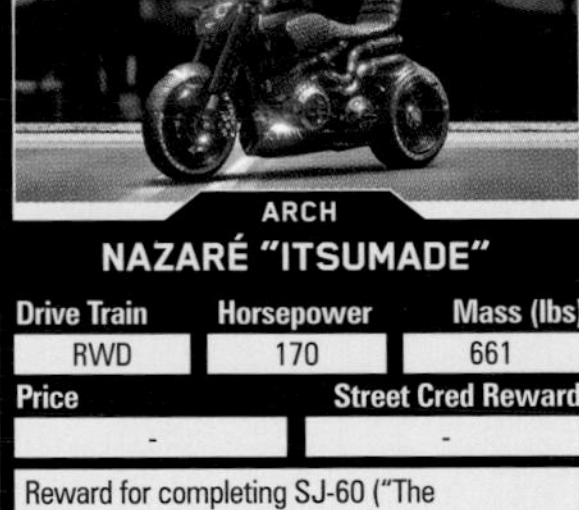

ARCH
NAZARÉ "ITSUMADE"

Drive Train	Horsepower	Mass (lbs)
RWD	170	661

Price	Street Cred Reward
-	-

Reward for completing SJ-60 ("The Highwayman", see page 240).

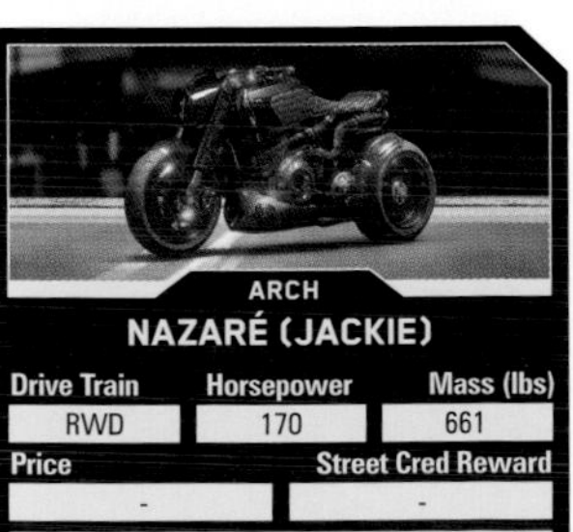

ARCH
NAZARÉ (JACKIE)

Drive Train	Horsepower	Mass (lbs)
RWD	170	661

Price	Street Cred Reward
-	-

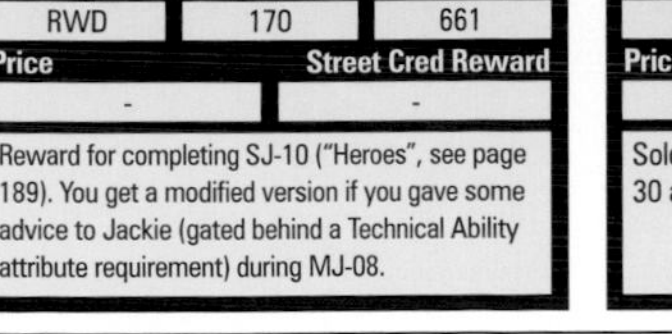

Reward for completing SJ-10 ("Heroes", see page 189). You get a modified version if you gave some advice to Jackie (gated behind a Technical Ability attribute requirement) during MJ-08.

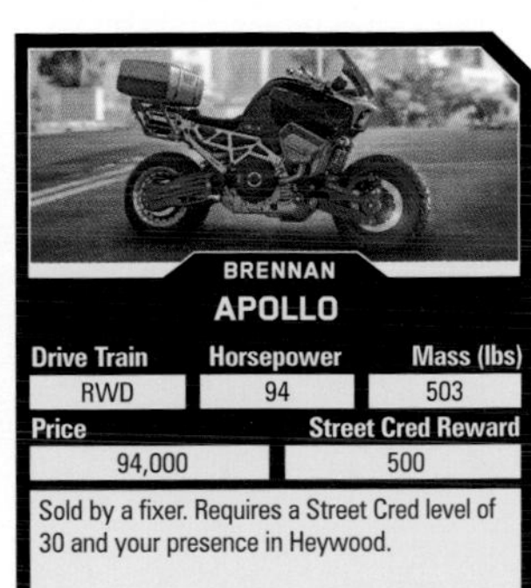

BRENNAN
APOLLO

Drive Train	Horsepower	Mass (lbs)
RWD	94	503

Price	Street Cred Reward
94,000	500

Sold by a fixer. Requires a Street Cred level of 30 and your presence in Heywood.

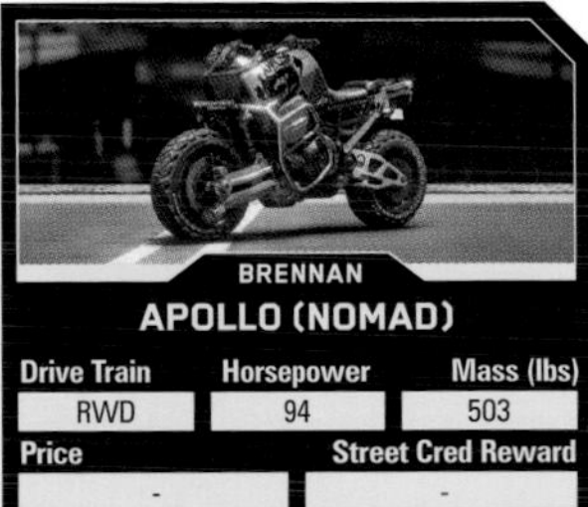

BRENNAN
APOLLO (NOMAD)

Drive Train	Horsepower	Mass (lbs)
RWD	94	503

Price	Street Cred Reward
-	-

Reward for completing MJ-21 ("Life During Wartime", see page 152).

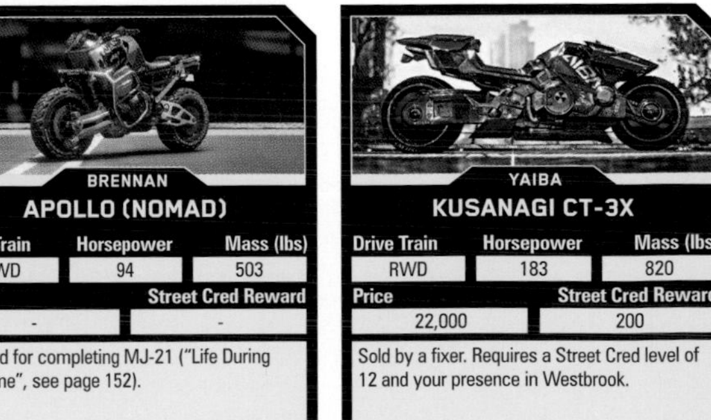

YAIBA
KUSANAGI CT-3X

Drive Train	Horsepower	Mass (lbs)
RWD	183	820

Price	Street Cred Reward
22,000	200

Sold by a fixer. Requires a Street Cred level of 12 and your presence in Westbrook.

REFERENCE & ANALYSIS

Cyberpunk 2077 features many multilayered, interdependent systems that govern the prowess of your character and the opponents that you will face. If you aspire to achieve true mastery of all options at your disposal, this chapter has much to teach you.

CHARACTER PROGRESSION

There are many systems that determine V's progression and relative proficiency.

XP & Street Cred Levels

As you complete activities and take down enemies (particularly those with bounties on their head), you gradually obtain experience points (XP) and Street Cred points. You level up every time you hit specific milestones.

As a general rule of thumb, levels – both V's level and those of enemies – offer a reliable indication of the challenge you will face in open conflict. Any foe a few levels above you will likely represent a significant threat. The greater the difference in their favor, the higher the difficulty they might pose – and vice versa. When enemies are marked with a skull icon, it means that the level difference is so significant that they will be profoundly dangerous if engaged. Attempts to take such opponents out with grapple-based stealth attacks are inadvisable: they will invariably shrug you off and raise the alarm.

Points Required To Level Up

XP and Street Cred Level Milestones

Level	Points Required To Level Up	Cumulative Points Required	Level	Points Required To Level Up	Cumulative Points Required
1	0	0	26	2,606	42,052
2	1,000	1,000	27	2,712	44,764
3	1,041	2,041	28	2,823	47,587
4	1,083	3,124	29	2,938	50,525
5	1,127	4,251	30	3,057	53,582
6	1,173	5,424	31	3,182	56,764
7	1,221	6,645	32	3,311	60,076
8	1,271	7,916	33	3,446	63,522
9	1,322	9,238	34	3,587	67,109
10	1,376	10,614	35	3,733	70,841
11	1,432	12,046	36	3,885	74,726
12	1,491	13,537	37	4,043	78,769
13	1,551	15,088	38	4,207	82,976
14	1,614	16,702	39	4,379	87,355
15	1,680	18,383	40	4,557	91,912
16	1,749	20,131	41	4,743	96,655
17	1,820	21,951	42	4,936	101,591
18	1,894	23,845	43	5,137	106,727
19	1,971	25,816	44	5,346	112,073
20	2,051	27,867	45	5,564	117,637
21	2,135	30,002	46	5,790	123,427
22	2,222	32,223	47	6,026	129,453
23	2,312	34,535	48	6,271	135,724
24	2,406	36,942	49	6,527	142,251
25	2,504	39,446	50	6,792	149,043

ATTRIBUTES

There are five main attributes in the game. Each of these grants passive bonuses (permanent boons that strengthen your character), and determines how well you perform with a related subset of skills.

You start the adventure with 22 attribute points: a mandatory minimum of three in each of the five attributes, and seven that you may allocate freely (within a maximum of three per attribute) during the character creation process.

You will thereafter receive one attribute point (to assign to any of your attributes) every time you level up. With your maximum level capped at level 50, this means that you can potentially acquire and invest a maximum of 49 extra attribute points.

As you cannot hope to max out all attributes (there simply are not enough points), your choices are therefore of great significance. Attributes are the cornerstone of character progression, and the areas in which you spend your hard-earned points determine how your version of V will evolve.

ATTRIBUTE OVERVIEW

Attribute	Effect
Body	Directly affects your health and stamina
	Makes you capable of controlling certain powerful weapons (for instance, the SPT32 Grad and the M2067 Defender) without experiencing adverse effects such as recoil
	Influences the damage you deal with your fists, Gorilla Arms, and all melee weapons
	Enables you to meet physical attribute requirements, for example to force-open doors, intimidate individuals during conversations, or forcibly remove people from their vehicles
	Slightly improves your movement speed when carrying a body
Reflexes	Determines your movement speed, attack speed, and evasion (your chance to avoid enemy ranged attacks)
	Affects your Crit Hit chance
	Influences your proficiency with rifles, SMGs, handguns, and blades
	Increases the damage you deal with Mantis Blades
Technical Ability	Directly affects your Armor total
	Enables you to meet tech-oriented attribute requirements, for example to open locked doors or shutters, or select unique dialogue options related to technical topics
Intelligence	Directly affects your quickhacking proficiency, which can be used in both stealth scenarios and during combat, but also enables you to unlock new paths (by remotely activating doors, for example)
	Improves your cyberdeck's RAM (memory capacity)
	Enables you to meet related attribute requirements, for example to unlock door terminals, access encrypted computers, or select unique dialogue options
Cool	Directly affects your Crit Hit damage, damage resistances, Monowire damage, and how rapidly enemies might detect you in stealth scenarios
	Determines how long you can grapple enemies before they escape – and therefore how far you can drag them to avoid being seen or heard when you neutralize them
	Increases the damage you deal when you shoot with silenced weapons from outside combat

SKILLS

Cyberpunk 2077 features 12 different skills, all closely connected to an attribute. Both the Engineering and Crafting skills, for example, are governed by the Technical Ability attribute.

All skills within an attribute subset are capped by the attribute in question. If your Reflexes stat is at three, for instance, you can only hope to develop the skills governed by Reflexes up to rank three. Both attributes and skills have a hard cap at level 20.

You "skill up" by performing actions related to each skill, as detailed in the table below. Before you study these, there are two qualifiers that you should bear in mind:

- The skill XP figures provided here are base values. The values you actually earn in the game increase with the target's level.
- Quickhacking the same target multiple times leads to diminishing returns.

POINT-GENERATING ACTIONS TO SKILL UP

Skill	Action	Skill XP
Annihilation	Damaging enemies with shotguns, LMGs, and HMGs; awarded when the target is neutralized	Varies with damage dealt
Assault	Damaging enemies with rifles and SMGs; awarded after the target is neutralized	Varies with damage dealt
Athletics	Performing actions gated behind a Body attribute requirement	100
	Performing actions with a cumulated cost of 500 stamina points or more	25
Blades	Damaging enemies with katanas, knives, one-handed blades, and Mantis Blades; awarded after the target is neutralized	Varies with damage dealt
Breach Protocol	Quickhacking devices	75
	Performing actions gated behind an Intelligence attribute requirement	100
Cold Blood	Performing finishing moves on enemies	100
	Defeating enemies while Cold Blood is active	Varies with damage taken
Crafting	Crafting items; upgrading items	Varies with item crafted
	Disassembling items	5
Engineering	Performing actions gated behind a Technical Ability attribute requirement	100
	Damaging enemies with grenades; awarded after the target is neutralized	Varies with damage dealt
	Damaging enemies with wall-piercing shots; awarded after the target is neutralized	Varies with damage dealt
Handguns	Damaging enemies with pistols and revolvers; awarded after the target is neutralized	Varies with damage dealt
Quickhacking	Quickhacking enemies	75
Stealth	Damaging enemies with sneak attacks; awarded after the target is neutralized	Varies with damage dealt
	Performing a takedown (lethal or nonlethal)	100
	Concealing neutralized adversaries in hiding places	100
	Performing a takedown and dumping the body in a hiding place simultaneously	200
Street Brawler	Damaging enemies with fists, blunt weapons, Gorilla Arms, and Monowire; awarded after the target is neutralized	Varies with damage dealt
	Damaging enemies with the Superhero Landing while Berserk is active	Varies with damage dealt

SKILL LEVEL MILESTONES

Level	Skill XP Required To Level Up	Cumulative XP Required	Level	Skill XP Required To Level Up	Cumulative XP Required	Level	Skill XP Required To Level Up	Cumulative XP Required
1	0	0	8	15,197	56,544	15	43,947	267,050
2	2,000	2,000	9	18,228	74,772	16	49,852	316,902
3	3,710	5,710	10	21,561	96,334	17	56,348	373,251
4	5,592	11,302	11	25,228	121,563	18	63,494	436,745
5	7,661	18,964	12	29,261	150,824	19	71,354	508,099
6	9,938	28,903	13	33,698	184,523	20	80,000	588,099
7	12,443	41,346	14	38,579	223,102			

Every time you skill up, you obtain a unique reward. The final reward for each skill (unlocked when you max it out by reaching skill level 20) is referred to as a "trait." These are unique Perks that can be improved for as long as you can afford them, enabling you to continue developing your V with Perk points after you have purchased all standard Perks of interest to you.

SKILL UP REWARDS

Skill Level	Handguns	Assault	Blades	Athletics	Annihilation	Street Brawler
1	-	-	-	-	-	-
2	Aiming speed +20%	Aiming speed +20%	Attack speed +10%	Carry capacity +20	Aiming speed +20%	Block effort* -10%
3	Perk Point	Perk Point	Perk Point	Perk Point	Perk Point	Perk Point
4	Recoil -10%	Recoil -10%	Stamina Costs -10%	Max stamina +5%	Recoil -10%	Attack speed +5%
5	Spread -25%	Spread -25%	DPS +2%	Stamina regen +10%	Spread -25%	Stamina costs -10%
6	Perk Point	Perk Point	Critical damage +10%	Carry capacity +40	Perk Point	Perk Point
7	Critical chance +5%	Critical chance +5%	Critical chance +5%	Perk Point	Critical chance +5%	Critical damage +10%
8	Recoil -10%	Recoil -10%	Perk Point	Perk Point	Recoil -10%	DPS +2%
9	Perk Point	Perk Point	Perk Point	Max health +5%	Perk Point	Perk Point
10	Perk Point	Perk Point	Perk Point	Perk Point	Perk Point	Perk Point
11	Critical damage +15%	Critical damage +15%	Attack speed +10%	Perk Point	Critical damage +15%	Critical chance +5%
12	Perk Point	Perk Point	Stamina costs -10%	Max health +5%	Perk Point	Perk Point
13	Recoil -10%	Recoil -10%	Attack speed +10%	Carry capacity +100	Recoil -10%	Block effort* -10%
14	Recoil -15%	Recoil -15%	Perk Point	Armor +3%	Recoil -15%	Attack speed +10%
15	Perk Point	Perk Point	Block effort* -25%	Health regen out of combat +10%	Perk Point	Perk Point
16	Spread -25%	Spread -25%	Perk Point	Perk Point	Spread -25%	Max stamina +5%
17	Spread -10%	Spread -10%	Perk Point	Max health +5%	Spread -10%	Max health +5%
18	Perk Point	Perk Point	Max stamina +5%	Armor +3%	Perk Point	Perk Point
19	Recoil -15%	Recoil -15%	DPS +3%	Perk Point	Recoil -15%	Max stamina +5%
20	Trait	Trait	Trait	Trait	Trait	Trait

Skill Level	Breach Protocol	Quickhacking	Stealth	Cold Blood	Engineering	Crafting
1	-	-	-	-	-	-
2	Perk Point	Perk Point	Evasion +3%	Critical chance +10%	Perk Point	Perk Point
3	Minigame time +5%	Quickhack duration +5%	Perk Point	Armor +3%	Armor +3%	Crafting costs -5%
4	Data mining materials +10%	Perk Point	Visibility -10%	Perk Point	Tech weapon charge time -5%	Crafting costs -5%
5	Minigame time +5%	Max RAM +1	Perk Point	Perk Point	Tech weapon DPS +5%	Perk Point
6	Perk Point	Quickhack cooldowns -5%	Health regeneration out of combat +10%	Max health +10%	Perk Point	Uncommon crafting specs unlocked
7	Minigame time +5%	Quickhack duration +5%	Perk Point	Max stamina +10%	Armor +3%	Chance to get some materials back after crafting +5%
8	Max RAM +1	Quickhack cooldowns -5%	Movement speed +3%	All resistances +5%	Perk Point	Perk Point
9	Data mining materials +10%	Perk Point	DPS +3%	Perk Point	Tech weapon Critical chance +5%	Rare crafting specs unlocked
10	Perk Point	Max RAM +1	Perk Point	Perk Point	Perk Point	Perk Point
11	Minigame time +5%	Perk Point	DPS +2%	Perk Point	Armor +3%	Crafting Costs -5%
12	Data mining materials +10%	Quickhack cooldowns -5%	Evasion +3%	All resistances +5%	All resistances +5%	Chance to get some materials back after crafting +5%
13	Max RAM +1	Quickhack duration +5%	Perk Point	Perk Point	Tech weapon Critical chance +5%	Epic crafting specs unlocked
14	Perk Point	Perk Point	Movement speed +2%	Critical damage +5%	Perk Point	Perk Point
15	Minigame time +5%	Max RAM +1	Visibility -10%	Critical chance +10%	Tech weapon Critical damage +15%	Chance to get some materials back after upgrading +5%
16	Perk Point	Quickhack cooldowns -5%	Evasion +4%	Movement Speed +3%	Armor +4%	Upgrade costs -15%
17	Data mining materials +10%	Quickhack duration +5%	Perk Point	Perk Point	Perk Point	Perk Point
18	Perk Point	Quickhack cooldowns -5%	Perk Point	Armor +7%	Perk Point	Iconic crafting specs unlocked
19	Minigame buffer +1	Perk Point	Visibility -10%	Critical damage +5%	Tech weapon charge time -10%	Upgrade costs -15%
20	Trait	Trait	Trait	Trait	Trait	Trait

* Block Effort refers to the stamina cost of blocking enemy melee attacks.

PERKS

Each skill in the game gives you access to a number of Perks. Perks are unique bonuses that enable you to specialize your character in specific fields, such as stealth or weapon proficiency. You can obtain Perk Points in three ways:

- Every time you level up, you get a Perk Point to spend.
- You also occasionally obtain Perk Points by skilling up.
- Finally, you receive a Perk Point for every Perk Shard that you find. These consumables can be obtained in NCPD Scanner Hustles (primarily the Hidden Gem type). You can locate these collectibles by referring to the Atlas chapter (see page 362).

The tables in this section list all Perks in the game, and feature the following information:

- **Tiers:** How many times a Perk can be upgraded. For instance, the Invincible Perk in the Athletics tree, which increases your maximum health by 10%, can be upgraded three times for a total boost of 30%. Each tier requires a Perk point to be unlocked.
- **Description:** Notes on the benefits provided by the Perk.
- **Attribute Requirement:** Each Perk tree features a handful of Perks that are available by default. Further Perks in each tree only become available after you have invested sufficient points in the corresponding attribute.

ATHLETICS PERKS

Icon	Name	Tiers	Description	Attribute Requirement
	Regeneration	1	Health slowly regenerates during combat.	-
	Pack Mule	1	Increases carrying capacity by 60.	-
	Invincible	3	Increases max health by 10%/20%/30%.	5 Body
	True Grit	3	Increases max stamina by 10%/20%/30%.	5 Body
	Epimorphosis	3	Health regenerates up to 70%/80%/100% of maximum outside combat.	7 Body
	Soft On Your Feet	3	Reduces fall damage by 5%/10%/20%.	7 Body
	Steel and Chrome	2	Increases melee damage by 10%/20%.	9 Body
	Gladiator	2	Reduces stamina cost while blocking by 20%/40%.	9 Body
	Divided Attention	1	Enables you to reload weapons while sprinting, sliding and vaulting.	11 Body
	Multitasker	1	Enables you to shoot while sprinting, sliding and vaulting.	11 Body
	Like a Butterfly	1	Dodging does not drain stamina.	11 Body
	Transporter	1	Enables you to shoot handguns and sprint while carrying a body.	12 Body
	Stronger Together	1	Increases damage you deal while carrying a body.	12 Body
	Cardio Cure	1	Health regenerates 25% faster when moving.	12 Body
	Human Shield	1	Increases Armor by 20% when grappling an enemy.	14 Body

ATHLETICS PERKS (CONTINUED)

Icon	Name	Tiers	Description	Attribute Requirement
	Marathoner	1	Sprinting does not drain stamina.	14 Body
	Dog of War	2	Increases health regeneration in combat by 15%/30%.	16 Body
	Wolverine	2	Health regeneration activates 50%/90% faster during combat.	16 Body
	Steel Shell	1	Increases Armor by 10%.	18 Body
	The Rock	1	Enemies cannot knock you down.	20 Body
	Indestructible	1	Reduces all incoming damage by 10%.	20 Body

ANNIHILATION PERKS

Icon	Name	Tiers	Description	Attribute Requirement
	Hail of Bullets	3	Shotguns and LMGs deal 3%/6%/10% more damage.	-
	Pump It, Louder!	2	Reduces recoil of shotguns and LMGs by 10%/20%.	5 Body
	In Your Face	2	Reduces reload time of shotguns and LMGs by 20%/40%.	5 Body
	Bloodrush	2	Increases movement speed in combat while carrying an LMG or shotgun by 5%/10%.	7 Body
	Dead Center	2	Increases damage to torsos by 10%/20%.	7 Body
	Bulldozer	1	Increases Crit Chance with shotguns and LMGs by 10%.	9 Body
	Mongoose	1	Increases Evasion by 25% while reloading shotguns and LMGs.	9 Body
	Momentum Shift	3	Defeating an enemy grants a 10%/15%/20% movement speed boost for 10 seconds.	11 Body
	Massacre	3	Increases Crit Damage with shotguns and LMGs by 15/30%/45%.	11 Body
	Skeet Shooter	1	Deal 15% more damage to moving targets.	12 Body
	Heavy Lead	1	Shotguns and LMGs knock back enemies with greater force.	12 Body
	Unstoppable	1	Dismembering an enemy increases rate of fire by 10% for 8 seconds. Stacks up to 3 times.	14 Body
	Manic	1	When entering combat, movement speed increases by 20% for 10 seconds.	14 Body
	Speed Demon	1	You deal more damage the faster you're moving.	16 Body
	Burn Baby Burn	1	Doubles the duration of the Burn status effect.	16 Body
	Hit The Deck	2	Increases damage to staggered and knocked-down enemies by 10%/20%.	18 Body
	Poppin' Off	2	Shotguns and LMGs have a 25%/50% higher chance of dismembering enemies.	18 Body
	Biathlete	1	Weapon spread does not increase while moving.	20 Body

STREET BRAWLER PERKS

Icon	Name	Tiers	Description*	Attribute Requirement
	Flurry	3	Increases damage from combo attacks with Blunt weapons by 30%/40%/50%.	-
	Crushing Blows	3	Increases damage from strong attacks with Blunt weapons by 30%/40%/50%.	-
	Juggernaut	2	Increases Armor while blocking by 15%/30%.	4 Body
	Dazed	2	Attacks with Blunt weapons have a 15%/30% chance to stun the target.	4 Body
	Rush	2	Successful attacks with Blunt weapons recover 3%/5% health over two seconds.	6 Body
	Efficient Blows	2	Reduces the stamina cost of all attacks with Blunt weapons by 25%/50%.	6 Body
	Opportune Strike	1	Increases damage with Blunt weapons against stunned enemies by 50%.	8 Body
	Human Fortress	1	Reduces the stamina cost of blocking attacks by 50% while using a Blunt weapon.	8 Body
	Reinvigorate	3	Defeating an enemy by performing a strong attack with a Blunt weapon restores 10%/20%/30% stamina.	10 Body
	Payback	3	Increases damage with Blunt weapons by 1%/2%/3% for every 1% of missing health.	10 Body
	Breathing Space	2	Increases stamina regen while blocking with Blunt weapons by 50%/100%.	12 Body
	Relentless	2	Successful attacks with Blunt weapons against stunned enemies restore 20%/30% stamina.	12 Body
	Frenzy	1	Defeating an opponent increases damage with Blunt weapons by 100% for 10 seconds.	15 Body
	Thrash	1	Strong attacks with Blunt weapons reduce target Armor by 30% for 10 seconds.	15 Body
	Unshakable	3	Successful attacks with Blunt weapons against stunned enemies restore 5%/10%/15% health and 5%/10%/15% stamina. Can trigger once every five seconds.	18 Body
	Biding Time	3	Blocking attacks with a Blunt weapon restores 5%/10%/15% health. Can trigger once every five seconds.	18 Body

* The term "Blunt weapons" when used in the context of Street Brawler Perks also refers to V's fists, Gorilla Arms and Monowire.

ASSAULT PERKS

Icon	Name	Tiers	Description	Attribute Requirement
	Bulletjock	3	Increases damage with rifles and SMGs by 3%/6%/10%.	-
	Eagle Eye	3	Speeds up rifle and SMG aiming by 10%/25%/50%.	-
	Covering Killshot	2	Increases Crit Chance with rifles and SMGs by 10%/20% when firing from behind cover.	5 Reflexes
	Too Close for Comfort	2	Quick melee attacks with rifles and SMGs deal 50%/100% more damage.	5 Reflexes
	Bullseye	1	Increases rifle and SMG damage while aiming by 10%.	7 Reflexes
	Executioner	1	Deal 25% more rifle and SMG damage to enemies when their health is above 50%.	7 Reflexes
	Shoot, Reload, Repeat	2	Defeating an enemy with a rifle or SMG increases reload speed by 20%/40% for 5 seconds.	9 Reflexes
	Duck Hunter	2	Increases rifle and SMG damage to moving enemies by 10%/20%.	9 Reflexes

ASSAULT PERKS (CONTINUED)

Icon	Name	Tiers	Description	Attribute Requirement
	Nerves of Steel	2	Increases headshot damage with sniper rifles and precision rifles by 20%/30%.	11 Reflexes
	Feel the Flow	2	Reduces reload time for full-auto rifles and SMGs by 10%/20%.	11 Reflexes
	Trench Warfare	2	Increases rifle and SMG damage by 5%/10% when firing from behind cover.	12 Reflexes
	Hunter's Hands	2	Reduces recoil with rifles and SMGs by 20%/40% when firing from behind cover.	12 Reflexes
	Skull Skipper	1	Each headshot with rifles and SMGs reduces their recoil by 5% for 10 seconds. Stacks up to five times.	14 Reflexes
	Named Bullets	1	Increases Crit Damage from rifles and SMGs by 35%.	14 Reflexes
	Bunker	1	Increases Armor and resistances by 15% when shooting with rifles and SMGs from behind cover.	16 Reflexes
	Recoil Wrangler	1	Reduces rifle and SMG recoil by 10%.	16 Reflexes
	In Perspective	1	Bullets fired from rifles and SMGs ricochet an additional two times.	18 Reflexes
	Long Shot	1	Rifle and SMG damage increases the farther you are located from enemies.	18 Reflexes
	Savage Stoic	1	Increases rifle and SMG damage by 35% when standing still.	20 Reflexes

HANDGUNS PERKS

Icon	Name	Tiers	Description	Attribute Requirement
	Gunslinger	3	Reduces reload time for pistols and revolvers by 10%/15/25%.	-
	High Noon	3	Increases Crit Chance with pistols and revolvers by 4%/8%/12%.	-
	Rio Bravo	3	Increases headshot damage multiplier with pistols and revolvers by 10%/20%/30%.	5 Reflexes
	Desperado	3	Increases damage with pistols and revolvers by 3%/6%/10%.	5 Reflexes
	On The Fly	2	Reduces draw/holster time for pistols and revolvers by 25%/50%.	7 Reflexes
	Long Shot Drop Pop	2	Increases damage to enemies over five meters away by 15%/25%.	7 Reflexes
	Steady Hand	1	Reduces recoil from pistols and revolvers by 30%.	9 Reflexes
	O.K. Corral	1	Deal 50% more damage with pistols and revolvers to enemies whose health is below 25%.	9 Reflexes
	Vanishing Point	1	Evasion increases by 25% for six seconds after performing a dodge with a pistol or revolver equipped.	9 Reflexes
	A Fistful of Eurodollars	2	Increases Crit Damage from pistols and revolvers by 10%/20%.	11 Reflexes
	From Head to Toe	2	Increases damage to limbs with pistols and revolvers by 7%/15%.	11 Reflexes
	Grand Finale	1	The last round in a pistol or revolver clip deals double damage.	12 Reflexes
	Acrobat	1	You can now dodge while aiming a pistol or revolver.	12 Reflexes

HANDGUNS PERKS (CONTINUED)

Icon	Name	Tiers	Description	Attribute Requirement
	Attritional Fire	1	Firing consecutive shots with a pistol or revolver at the same target increases damage by 10%.	14 Reflexes
	Wild West	1	Removes the damage penalty from pistols and revolvers when shooting from a distance.	14 Reflexes
	Snowball Effect	1	After defeating an enemy, fire rate for revolvers increases by 5% for six seconds. Stacks up to five times.	16 Reflexes
	Westworld	1	Increases Crit Chance for pistols and revolvers by 10% if fully modded.	16 Reflexes
	Lead Sponge	1	Enables you to shoot with pistols and revolvers while dodging.	18 Reflexes
	Brainpower	1	After a successful headshot with a pistol or revolver, Crit Chance increases by 25% for five seconds.	20 Reflexes

BLADES PERKS

Icon	Name	Tiers	Description	Attribute Requirement
	Roaring Waters	3	Strong attacks with blades deal 30%/40%/50% more damage.	-
	Sting Like a Bee	3	Increases attack speed with blades by 10%/20%/30%.	-
	Crimson Dance	2	Combo attacks with blades have a 15%/30% chance to apply Bleeding.	4 Reflexes
	Slow and Steady	2	Armor is increased by 15%/30% while moving.	4 Reflexes
	Offensive Defense	2	Block attacks with blades deal 200% more damage	6 Reflexes
	Flight of the Sparrow	2	Reduces the stamina cost of all attacks with blades by 30%/50%.	6 Reflexes
	Stuck Pig	3	Increases Bleeding duration by 1/2/3 second(s).	8 Reflexes
	Shifting Sands	3	Dodging recovers 15%/20%/25% stamina. Can trigger once every two seconds.	8 Reflexes
	Blessed Blade	1	Increases Crit Chance with blades by 20%.	10 Reflexes
	Unbroken Spirit	1	Successful deflections with blades restore 25% health and stamina.	10 Reflexes
	Bloodlust	2	While wielding a blade, recovers 7%/10% health when applying Bleeding to an enemy or hitting an enemy affected by Bleeding.	12 Reflexes
	Float like a Butterfly	2	Dodging increases damage dealt with blades by 25%/50% for five seconds.	12 Reflexes
	Judge, Jury, and Executioner	3	Damage with blades is increased by 50%/75%/100% against targets with max health.	15 Reflexes
	Fiery Blast	3	Increases damage with blades by 1% for every 1%/2%/3% of health the enemy is missing.	15 Reflexes
	Deathbolt	1	While wielding a blade, defeating an enemy restores 20% health and increases movement speed by 30% for five seconds.	18 Reflexes
	Crimson Tide	1	Bleeding applied with blades can stack three times.	18 Reflexes

CRAFTING PERKS

Icon	Name	Tiers	Description	Attribute Requirement
	Mechanic	1	Gain more components when disassembling.	-
	True Craftsman	1	Enables you to craft Rare items.	5 Technical Ability
	Scrapper	1	Junk items are automatically disassembled.	5 Technical Ability
	Workshop	3	Disassembling items grants a 5%/10%/15% chance to gain a free component of the same quality as the disassembled item.	7 Technical Ability
	Innovation	2	Effects from crafted consumables last 25%/50% longer.	9 Technical Ability
	Sapper	2	Crafted grenades deal 10%/20% more damage.	9 Technical Ability
	Field Technician	2	Crafted weapons deal 2.5%/5% more damage.	11 Technical Ability
	200% Efficiency	2	Crafted clothes gain 2.5%/5% more armor.	11 Technical Ability
	Ex Nihilo	1	Grants a 20% chance to craft an item for free.	12 Technical Ability
	Efficient Upgrades	1	Grants a 10% chance to upgrade an item for free.	12 Technical Ability
	Grease Monkey	1	Enables you to craft Epic items.	12 Technical Ability
	Cost Optimization	2	Reduces the component cost of crafting items by 15%/30%.	14 Technical Ability
	Let There Be Light!	2	Reduces the component cost of upgrading items by 10%/20%.	14 Technical Ability
	Waste Not Want Not	1	When disassembling an item, you get attached mods back.	16 Technical Ability
	Tune-up	1	Enables you to upgrade lower-quality components into higher-quality ones.	16 Technical Ability
	Edgerunner Artisan	1	Enables you to craft Legendary items.	18 Technical Ability
	Cutting Edge	1	Crafted Legendary weapons automatically get one stat improved by 5%.	20 Technical Ability

ENGINEERING PERKS

Icon	Name	Tiers	Description	Attribute Requirement
	Mech Looter	3	When looting robots, drones and mechs, there is a 25%/50%/75% chance of looting a weapon mod or attachment.	-
	Blast Shielding	3	Reduces damage taken from explosions by 10%/20%/30%.	-
	Can't Touch This	1	Grants immunity to all effects from your own grenades.	5 Technical Ability
	Grenadier	1	The explosion radius of grenades is visible.	5 Technical Ability
	Shrapnel	1	All grenade types deal 20 damage in addition to their normal effects.	7 Technical Ability
	Bladerunner	2	Increases damage to robots, drones and mechs by 20%/40%.	9 Technical Ability

ENGINEERING PERKS (CONTINUED)

Icon	Name	Tiers	Description	Attribute Requirement
	Lock and Load	2	Increases Smart weapon reload speed by 5%/10%.	9 Technical Ability
	Up to 11	2	Allows you to charge Tech weapons up to 75%/100% capacity.	9 Technical Ability
	Bigger Booms	5	Grenades deal 5%/10%/15%/20%/ 25% more damage.	11 Technical Ability
	Tesla	3	Increases the charge multiplier for Tech weapons by 15%/35%/55%.	12 Technical Ability
	Lightning Bolt	3	Increases Crit Chance with Tech weapons by 3%/6%/10%.	12 Technical Ability
	Gun Whisperer	1	Fully charged Tech weapons do not shoot automatically.	14 Technical Ability
	Übercharge	1	Fully charged Tech weapons deal 50% more damage.	14 Technical Ability
	Insulation	1	Grants immunity to Shock.	14 Technical Ability
	Fuck All Walls	1	Tech weapons discharge 50% faster.	16 Technical Ability
	Play the Angles	1	Ricochets deal an additional 50% damage.	16 Technical Ability
	Lickety Split	2	Tech weapon reload time is reduced by 15%/30%.	18 Technical Ability
	Jackpot	1	Grenades can now deal Crit Hits.	20 Technical Ability
	Superconductor	1	Tech weapons ignore Armor.	20 Technical Ability

BREACH PROTOCOL PERKS

Icon	Name	Tiers	Description	Attribute Requirement
	Big Sleep	2	Unlocks the Big Sleep daemon during Breach Protocol, which disables all cameras in a network for 3/6 minutes.	-
	Mass Vulnerability	2	Unlocks the Mass Vulnerability daemon during Breach Protocol, which reduces physical resistance for all enemies in the network by 30% for 3/6 minutes.	-
	Almost In!	2	Increases the breach time for Breach Protocol by 20%/40%.	5 Intelligence
	Advanced Datamine	2	Upgrades the Datamine daemon, increasing the quantity of Eurodollars acquired from access points by 50%/100%.	5 Intelligence
	Extended Network Interface	1	Automatically highlights nearby access points.	7 Intelligence
	Mass Vulnerability: Resistances	1	Upgrades the Mass Vulnerability daemon, reducing all resistances for enemies in the network by 30%.	7 Intelligence
	Datamine Mastermind	2	Upgrades the Datamine daemon, increasing the quantity of components acquired from access points by 50%/100%.	9 Intelligence
	Turret Shutdown	2	Unlocks the Turret Shutdown daemon during Breach Protocol, which disables security turrets in the network for 3/6 minutes.	9 Intelligence
	Total Recall	1	The ICEpick daemon reduces all quickhack costs by an additional RAM unit.	11 Intelligence
	Datamine Virtuoso	2	Upgrades the Datamine daemon, increasing the chance to acquire a quickhack from access points by 50%/100%.	12 Intelligence

BREACH PROTOCOL PERKS (CONTINUED)

Icon	Name	Tiers	Description	Attribute Requirement
	Turret Tamer	2	Unlocks the Turret Tamer daemon during Breach Protocol, which sets the status of every turret in the network to friendly for 3/6 minutes.	12 Intelligence
	Efficiency	2	Uploading three or more daemons in the same Breach Protocol increases cyberdeck RAM recovery by 3/6 units per minute. Lasts five minutes.	14 Intelligence
	Cloud Cache	2	Completing Breach Protocol restores RAM units by 1/2 time(s) the number of daemons uploaded.	14 Intelligence
	Totaler Recall	1	The ICEpick daemon reduces all quickhack costs by an additional RAM unit.	16 Intelligence
	Mass Vulnerability: Quickhacks	1	Upgrades the Mass Vulnerability daemon, causing enemies in the network to also take 30% more damage from quickhacks.	16 Intelligence
	Head Start	1	Automatically uploads the first daemon in the list at the start of every Breach Protocol.	18 Intelligence
	Hackathon	1	Uploading three or more daemons in the same Breach Protocol shortens quickhack cooldowns by 33% for five minutes.	18 Intelligence
	Compression	1	Reduces the length of the sequences required to upload daemons by one. Cannot be reduced below two.	20 Intelligence
	Buffer Optimization	1	Increases the duration of daemon effects by 100%.	20 Intelligence

QUICKHACKING PERKS

Icon	Name	Tiers	Description	Attribute Requirement
	Bloodware	3	Quickhacks deal 10%/20%/30% more damage.	-
	Biosynergy	3	Enables RAM recovery during combat (at a rate of 4/8/12 units per minute).	-
	Forget-me-not	1	Eliminating a target affected by a quickhack instantly recovers one RAM unit.	5 Intelligence
	I Spy	1	Reveals an enemy netrunner when they're attempting to hack you.	5 Intelligence
	Hackers Manual	1	Unlocks crafting specs for Uncommon quickhacks	5 Intelligence
	Daisy Chain	3	Eliminating a target affected by a quickhack reduces the cooldown for all other active quickhacks by 10%/35%/50%.	7 Intelligence
	Weak Link	3	Reduces the required cyberdeck RAM for quickhacks used on devices by 1/2/3 unit(s).	7 Intelligence
	Signal Support	2	Increases quickhack duration by 25%/50%.	9 Intelligence
	Subliminal Message	2	Quickhacks deal 50%/100% more damage to unaware targets.	11 Intelligence
	Mnemonic	1	Reduces the cost of quickhacks used against an enemy already affected by a quickhack by two RAM units.	12 Intelligence
	Diffusion	1	Quickhack spread distance is doubled.	12 Intelligence
	School of Hard Hacks	1	Unlocks crafting specs for Rare quickhacks	12 Intelligence

QUICKHACKING PERKS (CONTINUED)

Icon	Name	Tiers	Description	Attribute Requirement
	Plague	3	Quickhacks that spread can jump to 1/2/3 additional target(s).	14 Intelligence
	Hacker Overlord	1	Unlocks crafting specs for Epic quickhacks	16 Intelligence
	Critical Error	1	Quickhacks can now deal Crit Hits based on your Crit Chance and Crit Damage stats.	16 Intelligence
	Anamnesis	3	Available cyberdeck RAM cannot drop below 2/3/4 units.	18 Intelligence
	Optimization	1	Reduces the cost of quickhacks by one RAM unit.	20 Intelligence
	Bartmoss' Legacy	1	Unlocks crafting specs for Legendary quickhacks	20 Intelligence

COLD BLOOD PERKS

Icon	Name	Tiers	Description	Attribute Requirement
	Cold Blood	3	After defeating an enemy, gain Cold Blood for 10 seconds and increase movement speed by 2%. Stacks up to 1/2/3 time(s).	-
	Will to Survive	2	Increases all resistances by 2.5%/5% per stack of Cold Blood.	5 Cool
	Icy Veins	2	Reduces weapon recoil by 2.5%/5% per stack of Cold Blood.	5 Cool
	Critical Condition	2	Increases duration of Cold Blood by 5/10 seconds.	7 Cool
	Frosty Synapses	2	Reduces quickhack cooldowns by 3%/6% per stack of Cold Blood.	7 Cool
	Defensive Clotting	2	Increases Armor by 1%/2% per stack of Cold Blood.	9 Cool
	Rapid Bloodflow	2	Increases health regeneration in and out of combat by 50%/100% per stack of Cold Blood.	9 Cool
	Coldest Blood	1	Increases max stack amount for Cold Blood by one.	11 Cool
	Frozen Precision	1	Increases headshot damage by 50%.	11 Cool
	Predator	2	Increases attack speed by 1%/3% per stack of Cold Blood.	12 Cool
	Blood Brawl	2	When Cold Blood is active, increases damage with melee weapons by 5%/10%.	12 Cool
	Quick Transfer	2	Reduces quickhack upload time by 1%/2% per stack of Cold Blood.	12 Cool
	Bloodswell	1	When your health reaches 45%, a max stack of Cold Blood is automatically activated.	14 Cool
	Cold and Calculating	1	Landing a Crit Hit has 25% chance of applying a stack of Cold Blood.	14 Cool
	Coolagulant	1	Stacks of Cold Blood are removed one by one, not all at once.	16 Cool
	Unbreakable	1	Increases max stack amount for Cold Blood by one.	16 Cool
	Pain Is an Illusion	1	When Cold Blood is active, reduces damage taken by 5%.	18 Cool
	Immunity	1	When Cold Blood is active, you are immune to Bleeding, Poison, Burn and Shock.	20 Cool

STEALTH PERKS

Icon	Name	Tiers	Description	Attribute Requirement
	Silent and Deadly	1	Increases damage dealt by silenced weapons by 25% while sneaking.	-
	Crouching Tiger	1	Increases movement speed while sneaking by 20%.	-
	Hidden Dragon	1	Enables you to perform non-lethal aerial takedowns on unaware targets.	5 Cool
	Dagger Dealer	1	Enables you to throw knives. Hold L2/LT to aim and press R2/RT to throw.	5 Cool
	Strike From The Shadows	1	Increases your Crit Chance by 15% while sneaking.	7 Cool
	Assassin	1	Deal 15% more damage to human enemies.	7 Cool
	Leg Up	1	Movement speed after a successful takedown is increased by 30% for 10 seconds.	7 Cool
	Sniper	2	Increases damage from headshots fired while not in active combat by 30%/50%.	9 Cool
	Cutthroat	2	Thrown knives deal 30%/60% more damage.	9 Cool
	Clean Work	1	You can pick up an enemy's body immediately after performing a takedown by holding R3/RS.	11 Cool
	Stunning Blows	1	Quick melee attacks with ranged weapons stagger enemies, giving you an opportunity to grapple them.	11 Cool
	Aggressive Antitoxins	1	Grants immunity to Poison	11 Cool
	Ghost	2	Detection time is increased by 20%/40%.	12 Cool
	From The Shadows	2	Upon entering combat, Crit Chance increases by 25%/50% for seven seconds.	12 Cool
	Commando	1	You cannot be detected underwater.	14 Cool
	Rattlesnake	1	Enemies affected by Poison are slowed.	14 Cool
	Venomous Fangs	1	All knives apply Poison.	14 Cool
	Hasty Retreat	1	Boosts movement speed by 50% for five seconds when detected by an enemy.	16 Cool
	Silent Finisher	1	Enemies with less than 15% health are defeated instantly when attacked with a knife. Does not work on enemies several levels above your own.	16 Cool
	Restorative Shadows	1	While in stealth, increases health regeneration by 25%.	16 Cool
	Neurotoxin	1	Damage from Poison is doubled.	18 Cool
	Cheat Death	1	When your health drops below 50%, all incoming damage is reduced by 50% for 10 seconds. Cannot occur more than once per minute.	18 Cool
	Hasten the Inevitable	1	Deal 20% more damage to enemies affected by Poison.	18 Cool
	Ninjutsu	1	Crouch attacks from stealth with melee weapons deal 100% more damage and guarantee a Crit Hit.	20 Cool

TRAITS

Traits are the final Perks unlocked in each skill tree. They each become available when you max out the related attribute and skill.

Though they essentially work like any other Perks, Traits have one defining feature: they have no hard cap, and can be upgraded for as long as you have Perk Points to invest. If you have a late-game character build where there are no other Perks of interest to you, you can invest all further Perk Points in a desirable Trait to enhance its efficiency.

TRAIT OVERVIEW

Icon	Skill	Trait	Base Effect	Additional Tier Bonus	Requirement
	Athletics	**Hard Motherfucker**	When entering combat, Armor and resistances increase by 10% for 10 seconds.	+1% per Perk Point	20 Body 20 Athletics
	Annihilation	**Bloodbath**	Dismembering enemies reduces weapon recoil by 50% for six seconds.	+1% per Perk Point	20 Body 20 Annihilation
	Street Brawler	**Guerrilla**	Increases Crit Damage by 60% for 10 seconds after entering combat.	+2% per Perk Point	20 Body 20 Street Brawler
	Assault	**Punisher**	After defeating an enemy with a rifle or SMG, weapon sway is nullified and weapon spread does not increase for 10 seconds.	+0.2 seconds per Perk Point	20 Reflexes 20 Assault
	Handguns	**The Good, the Bad, and the Ugly**	After a successful Crit Hit with a pistol or revolver, damage and Armor increase by 30% for five seconds.	+1% per Perk Point	20 Reflexes 20 Handguns
	Blades	**Dragon Strike**	Increases Crit Damage with blades by 25%.	+1% more damage per Perk Point	20 Reflexes 20 Blades
	Crafting	**Crazy Science**	Increases the sale price of crafted items by 10%.	+1% per Perk Point	20 Technical Ability 20 Crafting
	Engineering	**Revamp**	Increases damage from Tech weapons by 25%. Charge damage is increased by 10%.	Charge damage +1% per Perk Point	20 Technical Ability 20 Engineering
	Breach Protocol	**Transmigration**	Increases breach time of Breach Protocol by 50%.	+5% per Perk Point	20 Intelligence 20 Breach Protocol
	Quickhacking	**Master RAM Liberator**	Increases RAM recovery rate by 50%.	+1% per Perk Point	20 Intelligence 20 Quickhacking
	Stealth	**Toxicology**	Increases the duration of Poison effects applied to enemies by five seconds.	+0.2 second per Perk Point	20 Cool 20 Stealth
	Cold Blood	**Merciless**	When Cold Blood is active, increases Crit Chance by 10% and Crit Damage by 25%.	+1% Crit Chance and +3% Crit Damage per Perk Point	20 Cool 20 Cold Blood

BUILDS

There are no predefined jobs or classes in Cyberpunk 2077, but this doesn't mean that you cannot specialize your character in specific fields. How you choose to spend your hard-earned resources, particularly attribute points, is a process of creating your own unique class – with a focus on the proficiencies that best suit your desired playstyle.

The accompanying table offers an overview of the areas in which you might want your version of V to specialize. You can use this to identify which attributes might be appropriate for your character build.

CHARACTER BUILD PLANNER

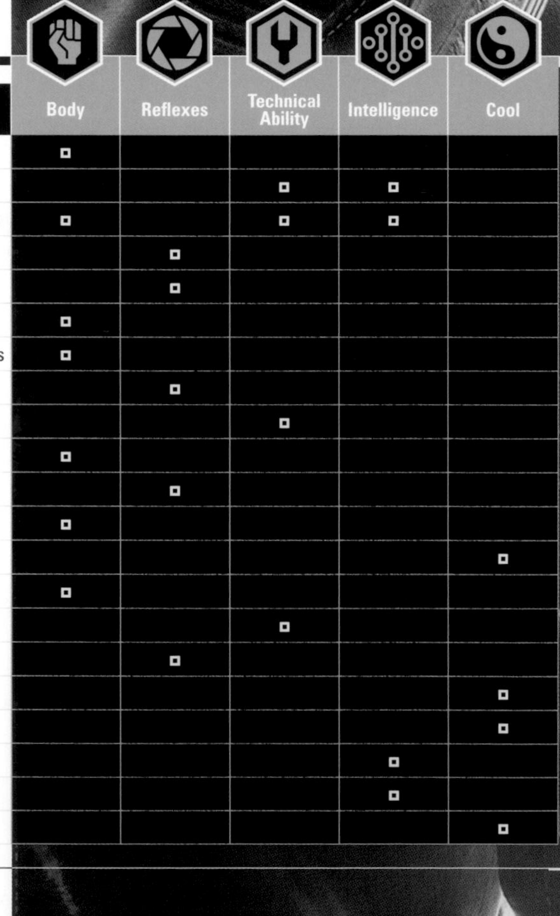

Category	Area of Specialization	Body	Reflexes	Technical Ability	Intelligence	Cool
Inventory	Carry capacity	□				
	Crafting and upgrading			□	□	
Exploration and Alternative Solutions	Exploration actions gated behind attribute requirements and remote activations	□		□	□	
	Movement speed, agility		□			
Combat: Offensive Abilities	Movement speed, agility, reaction time		□			
	Max health & health regeneration	□				
	Combat proficiency: bare knuckles, blunt weapons, shotguns, and machine guns	□				
	Combat proficiency: rifles, SMGs, handguns, and blades		□			
	Combat proficiency: grenades, Tech weapons			□		
	Stamina	□				
	Crit Chance		□			
	Crit Damage	□				
	Cold Blood					□
Combat: Defensive Abilities	Damage Resistance	□				
	Armor			□		
	Evasion		□			
	Cold Blood					□
Stealth Situations	Stealth proficiency					□
	Breach Protocol mini-game proficiency				□	
	Quickhacks, max RAM, RAM regeneration				□	
	Grapple proficiency					□

You begin the adventure with three points automatically allocated per attribute. You then have seven points to assign during the character creation process, and 49 that can be gradually acquired *en route* to reaching level 50. This means that there are 56 potential points to spend in total. You need 17 points to elevate any attribute to level 20 – and so you can, at best, hope to max out three attributes.

In the section that follows, we offer ideas for prospective character builds based on the assumption that you opt for extreme specialization, with three attributes developed to level 20 in each instance. These are mere suggestions to inform your own creative process, but each one should also help you to enjoy some of the more distinct playstyles. In Cyberpunk 2077, there is no such thing as a perfect build: every advance in one aspect of your character's development represents a sacrifice elsewhere.

SOLO

Priority Attributes: Body, Reflexes, Cool.

The principle here is simple: you develop all combat-related abilities to their fullest.

Build's Key Features

- High speed, mobility, and reaction times
- Solid defensive capabilities through a combination of high health, Evasion, and damage resistance
- Proficiency with all weapon types
- Excellent stamina for melee combat
- Strong Crit Damage and Crit Chance contribute to increasing your damage output
- Cold Blood makes you stronger during battles
- Good carry capacity enables you to keep a varied arsenal to hand at all times
- You can pass Body skillchecks, both to force-open doors and to intimidate susceptible characters

Key Perk Trees

- Athletics
- Cold Blood
- The trees corresponding to your favorite weapon type (for instance, Annihilation for shotguns)

Complementary Gear

- Powerful weapons and mods
- Clothing with strong Armor
- Combat-enhancing cyberware
- Sandevistan operating system and Kerenzikov nervous system

STEALTH NETRUNNER

Priority Attributes: Cool, Intelligence, Body

The idea with this build is to combine physical stealth skills with netrunner capabilities, enabling you to avoid detection in the vast majority of scenarios.

Build's Key Features

- Mastery of all stealth moves: thrown knives, increased movement speed, increased damage, improved detection time, Poison, sneak attacks, et al.
- You can keep enemies under control for a long time when grappling them, enabling you to make takedowns on *your* terms – even if that means dragging them to exactly where you intend to hide them
- Full netrunner abilities offer a complete suite of techniques for sneaking past, debilitating, and harming enemies
- Breach Protocol enables you to trigger powerful effects against targets in the network and reduce the RAM cost of your own quickhacks
- Access to blunt weapons and shotguns for emergency situations
- You can pass all Body skillchecks and remotely activate certain doors and shutters to open new passages.

Key Perk Trees

- Stealth
- Breach Protocol
- Quickhacking
- Athletics
- Annihilation
- Street Brawling

Complementary Gear

- Cyberdeck with high RAM, buffer size, and numerous quickhack slots
- Nervous system equipped with a Synaptic Accelerator to slow down time when you are about to be detected
- Knives for takedowns outside of melee range
- Full range of quickhacks that you can swap on the fly to adapt to each situation
- At least two powerful weapons when you are detected and things go awry: a blunt melee weapon and a shotgun

TECHIE

Priority Attributes: Technical Ability, Body, Reflexes

The goal with this build is to become a master crafter, giving you access to the best gear and gadgets in the game.

Build's Key Features

- Top-level Crafting expertise will enable you to create and upgrade the best items, particularly weapons
- High carry capacity to ensure a fair selection of your most useful creations can be available in your inventory
- Strong affinity against mechanical enemies
- Grenade virtuoso, giving you excellent crowd-control potential, with crafting enabling you to replenish your stocks on the fly
- Mastery of Tech weapons, allowing you to pierce through armor and shoot enemies through solid obstacles
- Decent defensive capabilities through high damage resistance and Armor, and virtually endless access to consumables via crafting
- Proficiency with shotguns and machine guns will help you to turn the tide when your back is against the wall
- You can pass a large number of skillchecks to avoid all kinds of hostile situations

Key Perk Trees:

- Crafting
- Engineering
- Athletics
- Annihilation

Complementary Gear

- Obtain as many crafting specs as you can
- Specialize in Tech weapons
- Maintain a large and varied supply of grenades
- At least one top-of-the-shelf shotgun or machine gun for "Plan B" situations
- Be constantly on the lookout for components, particularly the rarer ones

COMBAT NETRUNNER

Priority Attributes: Intelligence, Body, Technical Ability

The objective with this build is to use a perfect blend of conventional combat and netrunner tactics.

Build's Key Features

- Access to the full netrunner arsenal (though with a clear focus on quickhacking) enables you to wreak havoc among hostiles in all sorts of ways
- Mastery of shotguns, machine guns, grenades, and Tech weapons means that you have powerful tools to deal with all kinds of enemies and predicaments
- Superior health, health regeneration, and Armor give you great survivability
- You can pass skillchecks in the three main categories, giving you great flexibility in the way you might approach a given scenario during storyline objectives
- Excellent carry capacity makes it possible to carry a varied arsenal, or collect more loot for later resale.

Key Perk Trees

- Quickhacking
- Athletics
- Annihilation
- Engineering

Complementary Gear

- Full range of quickhacks of the combat and ultimate varieties
- Sandevistan operating system to increase your damage output on demand, or an advanced cyberdeck if you prefer focusing on quickhacks
- Powerful shotguns and machine guns
- A large stock of grenades to open hostilities with a bang and control crowds
- Clothing with high Armor to enhance your survivability

STEALTH SOLO

Priority Attributes: Reflexes, Intelligence, Cool

This build turns you into a cyber-ninja, giving you the best stealth abilities and complementing them with mastery of whisper-quiet blade weapons.

Build's Key Features

- Expertise in all stealth areas: aerial takedowns, thrown knives, Poison, sneak attacks, increased movement speed, damage, detection time, and more.
- Complementary stealth skills via netrunner tricks (shutting down surveillance cameras, setting turrets to Friendly Mode, and so forth)
- Access to quickhacks of the stealth type to lure, deafen, blind, or wipe the memory of sentries
- Breach Protocol triggers powerful effects against targets in the network while reducing the cost of quickhacks
- Further bonuses to movement speed, attack speed, melee damage, and quickhack upload time through Cold Blood
- Mastery of powerful blades, which prevent enemies from raising the alarm if you kill them instantly with a sneak attack

Key Perk Trees

- Stealth
- Cold Blood
- Breach Protocol
- Quickhacking
- Blades

Complementary Gear

- Legs cyberware that improves navigation and traversal possibilities – double jumps or charged jumps are particularly helpful here, enabling you to sneak up on enemies even when they are stationed on elevated vantage points
- Mantis Blades
- Operating System with high RAM, buffer size, and numerous quickhack slots
- Nervous system equipped with a Synaptic Accelerator to slow down time when you are about to be detected
- Knives to throw
- Full range of quickhacks of the stealth and control types
- A truly *kickass* blade

CRAFTING

To craft an item via the main menu, you need both an item's crafting specs and the required ingredients, which are known as components. You can study details of a crafted item before you commit to the process, giving you a chance to evaluate it beforehand.

As with so many other objects in the game world, components are graded by rarity. Lesser-found materials beget superior crafting results – or, more plainly, rare items require rare materials.

Crafting is a blanket term that actually refers to two distinct categories:

- **Crafting gear** refers to the creation of equipment: weapons, clothing, mods, and so forth. All of the specs in this category require standard components, and all crafting activities involving them, including the unlocking of high-rarity specs, are governed by the Technical Ability attribute and the Crafting skill.
- **Crafting quickhacks** refers specifically to the creation of quickhacks. Specs in this category require quickhack components. To unlock these specs, you will need to invest points in your Intelligence attribute and the Quickhacking skill.

The grade of a created item is improved by your Crafting or Quickhacking skill, with a bonus of 0.2 per level. For example, if your Crafting skill is currently at 10, the level of the equipment you craft will be improved by 2 (10 x 0.2), enabling you to create pieces ahead of the general progression curve.

SOURCING COMPONENTS

Standard components can be obtained in different ways while exploring, but most commonly by looting defeated enemies or rifling through item stashes. As a rule of thumb, generic item caches found in the open world tend to yield low-rarity materials, while stashes found during missions and activities are more likely to feature high-end components.

You can also accumulate standard materials by disassembling equipment in your inventory. To recycle items, select an object and hold Ⓐ/Ⓨ to convert them into components; this is, of course, a one-way process. You can get advance notice on which materials will be added to your stocks in the window on the left of the Backpack screen. If you see "81 (+3)," for example, this means that you already have 81 materials of that kind, and that dismantling the selected item will add three to your total.

Quickhack components are most commonly gathered by datamining, in other words by successfully completing the Breach Protocol mini-game every time you jack in physically to an access point. The odds of obtaining such materials can be improved by investing points in the Datamine Mastermind Perk.

PERKS

Spending attribute points on Technical Ability and investing Perk points in the Crafting skill is essential if you plan on excelling at crafting equipment. While many of the Perks are extremely beneficial, some are downright indispensable if you intend to make the most of the system.

- By default, you can only craft common and uncommon items. Successive rarity tiers are unlocked after you acquire specific Perks.

CRAFTING REQUIREMENT

Rarity Tier	Perk Required
Rare	True Craftsman
Epic	Grease Monkey
Legendary	Edgerunner Artisan

- A number of Crafting Perks improve individual aspects of the items you create – such as increasing the active duration of consumables, or imbuing equipment with superior stats or effects.
- Last but not least, some Perks (Mechanic, Scrapper, Workshop, and Waste Not Want Not) make you more proficient at disassembling.

Adept netrunners might prefer to invest attribute points in Intelligence and Perk points in the related skills. Of particular interest, four Perks under the Quickhacking skill give you access to rarer quickhack crafting specs: Hacker's Manual, School of Hard Hacks, Hacker Overlord, and Bartmoss' Legacy. Additionally, several Perks in the Breach Protocol can make the process of datamining access points much, much more lucrative.

UPGRADING

Upgrading is the process of increasing an item's level, raising its stats in the process. You can upgrade any weapon or piece of clothing in your inventory.

The principle here is that you take an existing item (for example, a firearm), and you improve it by consuming components. The process can be repeated multiple times, on the proviso that you can afford the necessary materials, enabling you to regularly enhance items that you have an affinity for.

CRAFTING SPECS

Crafting specs provide you with a list of components required to craft an item, and these Crafting specs must be stored in your inventory for you to create the object in question. The tables in this section document all crafting specs and information pertinent to their acquisition – both standard specs (for gear) and quickhack specs (for quickhacks). Should the development team significantly alter this system after release of the game, we will endeavor to provide online updates to these tables in our digital extension to the guide, which you can access by visiting **maps.piggyback.com.**

You should note that crafting specs sold in shops appear at random. This means that there is no guarantee you will find them for sale when you visit any given vendor. If you want to try your luck again after a fruitless shopping trip, you can refresh a store's inventory by visiting it again after two in-game days, or by traveling to the far reaches of Night City.

STANDARD CRAFTING SPECS OVERVIEW

Category	Crafting Specs	Availability
Grenades	X-22 Flashbang Grenade Regular	Random drops and weapon shops: Badlands, Japantown, Downtown
Grenades	X-22 Flashbang Grenade Homing	Random drops and weapon shops: Badlands, Japantown, Downtown
Grenades	F-GX Frag Grenade Regular	From the start
Grenades	F-GX Frag Grenade Sticky	Random drops and weapon shops: Badlands, Japantown, Rancho Coronado
Grenades	F-GX Frag Grenade Homing	Random drops and weapon shops: Northside, Little China and The Glenn
Grenades	Ozob's Nose	Reward for completing SJ-16 ("Send in the Clowns" – see page 194)
Consumables	Bounce Back Mk.1	From the start
Consumables	Bounce Back Mk.2	Medpoints once your Street Cred level reaches 14
Consumables	Bounce Back Mk.2	Medpoints once your Street Cred level reaches 27
Consumables	MaxDoc Mk.1	From the start
Consumables	MaxDoc Mk. 2	Medpoints once your Street Cred level reaches 14
Consumables	MaxDoc Mk.3	Medpoints once your Street Cred level reaches 27
Weapon Mods*	Ranged Mod: Crunch	Weapon shops: Badlands, Little China, Kabuki, Vista Del Rey, Arroyo, Rancho Coronado, West Wind Estate
Weapon Mods*	Ranged Mod: Penetrator	Weapon shops: Badlands, Kabuki, Wellsprings, Japantown, Rancho Coronado, West Wind Estate
Weapon Mods*	Ranged Mod: Pacifier	Weapon shops: Badlands, Kabuki, Downtown, Wellsprings, Vista Del Rey, Arroyo, Rancho Coronado
Weapon Mods*	Ranged Mod: External Bleeding	Weapon shops: Northside, Little China, Japantown, Downtown, Wellsprings, The Glenn, Vista Del Rey, West Wind Estate
Clothing Mods*	Armadillo	Clothing shops: Northside, Little China, Japantown
Clothing Mods*	Resist!	Clothing shops: Northside, Little China, Japantown
Clothing Mods*	Fortuna	Clothing shops: Downtown, Heywood
Clothing Mods*	Bully	Clothing shops: Downtown, Heywood
Clothing Mods*	Backpacker	Clothing shops: Northside, Little China, Japantown
Clothing Mods*	Coolit	Clothing shops: Downtown, Heywood
Clothing Mods*	Antivenom	Clothing shops: West Wind Estate, Rancho Coronado, Badlands
Clothing Mods*	Panacea	Clothing shops: Downtown, Heywood
Clothing Mods*	Superinsulator	Clothing shops: West Wind Estate, Rancho Coronado, Badlands
Clothing Mods*	Soft-Sole	Clothing shops: West Wind Estate, Rancho Coronado, Badlands
Clothing Mods*	Cut-It-Out	Clothing shops: West Wind Estate, Rancho Coronado, Badlands
Clothing Mods*	Predator	Clothing shops: Downtown, Heywood
Clothing Mods*	Deadeye	Clothing shops: Downtown, Heywood
Mantis Blades Mods	Blade – Physical Damage	Ripperdoc: Badlands
Mantis Blades Mods	Blade – Thermal Damage	Ripperdoc: Northside
Mantis Blades Mods	Blade – Chemical Damage	Ripperdoc and random loot in Kabuki
Mantis Blades Mods	Blade – Electrical Damage	Ripperdoc: Japantown
Mantis Blades Mods	Slow Rotor	Ripperdoc: Japantown
Mantis Blades Mods	Fast Rotor	Ripperdoc: Kabuki
Monowire Mods	Monowire – Physical Damage	Ripperdoc: West Wind Estate
Monowire Mods	Monowire – Thermal Damage	Ripperdoc: Charter Hill
Monowire Mods	Monowire – Chemical Damage	Ripperdoc: Kabuki
Monowire Mods	Monowire – Electrical Damage	Ripperdoc: Badlands
Monowire Mods	Monowire Battery, Low Capacity	Ripperdoc: Japantown
Monowire Mods	Monowire Battery, Medium Capacity	Ripperdoc: Wellsprings
Monowire Mods	Monowire Battery, High Capacity	Ripperdoc: West Wind Estate
Projectile Launcher Mods	Explosive Round	Ripperdoc: Japantown
Projectile Launcher Mods	Electrical Round	Ripperdoc: Rancho Coronado
Projectile Launcher Mods	Thermal Round	Ripperdoc: Badlands
Projectile Launcher Mods	Chemical Round	Ripperdoc: Kabuki
Projectile Launcher Mods	Neoplastic Plating	Ripperdoc: Kabuki
Projectile Launcher Mods	Metal Plating	Ripperdoc: Northside
Projectile Launcher Mods	Titanium Plating	Ripperdoc: Wellsprings
Arms Cyberware Mods	Sensory Amplifier (Crit Chance)	Ripperdoc: Arroyo
Arms Cyberware Mods	Sensory Amplifier (Crit Damage)	Ripperdoc: Little China
Arms Cyberware Mods	Sensory Amplifier (Max Health)	Ripperdoc: Charter Hill
Arms Cyberware Mods	Sensory Amplifier (Armor)	Ripperdoc: Wellsprings

Category	Crafting Specs	Availability
Gorilla Arms Mods	Knuckles – Physical Damage	Ripperdoc: Northside
Gorilla Arms Mods	Knuckles – Thermal Damage	Ripperdoc: Arroyo
Gorilla Arms Mods	Knuckles – Chemical Damage	Ripperdoc: Rancho Coronado
Gorilla Arms Mods	Knuckles – Electrical Damage	Ripperdoc: Downtown
Gorilla Arms Mods	Battery, Low Capacity	Ripperdoc: Japantown
Gorilla Arms Mods	Battery, Medium Capacity	Ripperdoc: Kabuki
Gorilla Arms Mods	Battery, High Capacity	Ripperdoc: Charter Hill
Kiroshi Optics Mods	Target Analysis	Ripperdoc: Kabuki
Kiroshi Optics Mods	Explosives Analysis	Ripperdoc: Little China
Kiroshi Optics Mods	Threat Detector	Ripperdoc: Downtown
Kiroshi Optics Mods	Trajectory Analysis	Ripperdoc: Little China
Berserk Mods	Beast Mode	"Instant Implants" ripperdoc clinic in Kabuki
Sandevistan Mods	Sandevistan: Overclocked Processor	Ripperdocs: Northside, Japantown
Sandevistan Mods	Sandevistan: Prototype Chip	Ripperdocs: Charter Hill, Arroyo
Sandevistan Mods	Sandevistan: Neurotransmitters	Ripperdocs: Charter Hill, Arroyo
Sandevistan Mods	Sandevistan: Heatsink	Ripperdocs: Northside, Japantown
Sandevistan Mods	Sandevistan: Tyger Paw	Ripperdocs: Coastview, Rancho Coronado
Sandevistan Mods	Sandevistan: Rabid Bull	Ripperdocs: Coastview, Rancho Coronado
Sandevistan Mods	Sandevistan: Arasaka Software	Ripperdocs: Downtown, Wellsprings
Component Upgrades	Uncommon Components	Unlocked by Tune-up Perk (Crafting skill)
Component Upgrades	Rare Components	
Component Upgrades	Epic Components	
Component Upgrades	Legendary Components	
Default Weapons	m-10AF Lexington	Always available
Default Weapons	DR5 Nova	
Default Weapons	D5 Copperhead	
Default Weapons	DB-4 Igla	
Default Weapons	Overture	
Default Weapons	G-58 Dian	
Default Weapons	M-76e Omaha	
Default Weapons	M251s Ajax	
Default Weapons	DS1 Pulsar	
Default Weapons	m-10AF Lexington	
Default Weapons	Unity	
Default Weapons	DR5 Nova	
Acquired Weapons	All weapons	Random loot
Acquired Weapons	All weapons	
Acquired Weapons	All weapons	
Acquired Weapons	All weapons	
Uncommon Clothing	Darra polytechnic tactical balaclava	Clothing shops: Northside, Japantown
Uncommon Clothing	Durable LIME SPEED modular helmet	Clothing shops: Little China, Charter Hill
Uncommon Clothing	Mox gas mask with custom protective layer	Clothing shops: Northside
Uncommon Clothing	Arasaka tactical techgogs	Clothing shops: Kabuki, Japantown
Uncommon Clothing	5hi3ld Superb combatweave aramid breastplate	Clothing shops: Kabuki
Uncommon Clothing	Green Viper double-nanoweave pencil dress	Clothing shops: Northside
Uncommon Clothing	Hebi Tsukai cashmere-nanofiber shirt	Clothing shops: Westbrook Japan Town
Uncommon Clothing	Red Leopard button-up with composite insert	Clothing shops: Kabuki, Charter Hill
Uncommon Clothing	Spotted flexi-membrane bustier	Clothing shops: Little China

STANDARD CRAFTING SPECS OVERVIEW (CONTINUED)

Category	Crafting Specs	Availability
Uncommon Clothing	Golden Mean aramid-stitch formal skirt	Clothing shops: Little China, Charter Hill
	Durable Smiley HARD loose-fits	Clothing shops: Northside, Japantown
	Sunny Ammo synthetic high-tops	Clothing shops: Kabuki
	Reinforced biker boots	Clothing shops: Little China, Charter Hill
Rare Clothing	Ten70 Bada55 polycarbonate bandana	Clothing shops: Kabuki
	Upgraded farmer hat with gauge	Clothing shops: Badlands, Arroyo
	Stylish turquoise sport glasses	Clothing shops: Little China, Rancho Coronado, Coastview
	Trilayer steel ocuset	Clothing shops: Charter Hill, Arroyo
	PSYCHO flexiweave long-sleeve	Clothing shops: Northside, Coastview
	That good old red, white and blue	Clothing shops: Japantown, Arroyo, Rancho Coronado
	Denki-shin thermoset hybrid crystaljock bomber	Clothing shops: Little China
	Powder Pink light polyamide blazer	Clothing shops: Badlands, Rancho Coronado
	Milky Gold trench coat with bulletproof triweave	Clothing shops: Charter Hill. Arroyo
	Classic aramid-weave denim shorts	Clothing shops: Badlands, Kabuki
	Bái Lóng formal pants with reinforced neo-silk	Clothing shops: Coastview, Rancho Coronado
	Abendstern polycarbonate dress shoes	Clothing shops: Badlands, Japantown
	GLITTER laceless sturdy-stitched steel-toes	Clothing shops: Coastview, Northside
Epic Clothing	Stylish leather flat cap with light armor layer	Clothing shops: Rancho Coronado
	Laminated security hardhat with headset	Clothing shops: Coastview
	GRAFFITI thermoset synweave hijab/ GRAFFITI thermoset syn-weave keffiyeh	Clothing shops: Corpo Plaza
	Blue menpō with protective padding	Clothing shops: Badlands
	Gold Punk Aviators	Clothing shops: Downtown, Corpo Plaza
	Paris Blue office shirt and vest with reinforced seams	Clothing shops: Downtown
	Padded Denki Hachi hybrid-weave bra	Clothing shops: Badlands
	Stylish Ten70 Daemon Hunter coat	Clothing shops: Coastview
	Cyan multiresist evening jacket	Clothing shops: Downtown
	Blue Brick reinforced hotpants	Clothing shops: Wellsprings, Arroyo
	Geisha flexi-weave cargo pants	Clothing shops: Corpo Plaza
	GREEN GRAFFITI athletic shoes with protective coating	Clothing shops: Wellsprings, Arroyo
	Midday Glow polycarbonate formal pumps/Midday Glow polycarbonate dress shoes	Clothing shops: Rancho Coronado
Legendary Clothing	Mírame reinforced-composite cowboy hat	Clothing shops: Wellsprings
	Durable Emerald Speed polyamide beanie	Clothing shops: Downtown
	Aoi Tora enhanced BD wreath	Clothing shops: Downtown
	Sun Spark thermoset chemglass infovisor	Clothing shops: Wellsprings
	Daemon Hunter resistance-coated tank top	Clothing shops: Wellsprings
	Composite Geisha combat shirt	Clothing shops: Corpo Plaza

Category	Crafting Specs	Availability
Legendary Clothing	SilveRock bulletproof-laminate biker vest	Clothing shops: Wellsprings
	Deadly Lagoon armored syn-silk pozer-jacket	Clothing shops: Corpo Plaza
	Uniware Brass office pants with membrane support	Clothing shops: Corpo Plaza
	Chic Pink Dragon skirt with fiberglass sequins	Clothing shops: Downtown
	Gold Fury neotac bulletproof pants	Clothing shops: Wellsprings
	Multilayered Kasen exo-jacks with anti-shrapnel lining	Clothing shops: Corpo Plaza
	Enhanced Daemon Hunter tongues	Clothing shops: Downtown
Character Progression: Uncommon	D5 Copperhead	Reward for reaching level 6 in the Crafting skill
	DB-2 Satara	
	Electric Baton Alpha	
	Nue	
	Cotton motorcycle cap with protective inset	
	Lightweight tungsten-steel BD wreath	
	Inner Flame flame-resistant rockerjack	
	Simple Biker Turtleneck	
	Sturdy synfiber pleated pants	
	Classic evening pumps with polycarbonate support	
Character Progression: Rare	DR5 Nova	Reward for reaching level 9 in the Crafting skill
	DS1 Pulsar	
	Knife	
	SPT32 Grad	
	Steel microplated kabuto	
	Titanium-reinforced gas mask	
	Polycarbonate western fringe vest	
	Stylish Atomic Blast composite bustier	
	Venom Dye duolayer riding pants	
	Robust Spunky Monkey kicks	
Character Progression: Epic	Baseball Bat	Reward for reaching level 13 in the Crafting skill
	HJKE-11 Yukimura	
	M2038 Tactician	
	SOR-22	
	Boss Mafioso trilby with protective inner lining	
	Yamori tungsten-steel biker techgogs	
	AQUA Universe luxe aramid-weave shirt	
	Ultralight TESTED ON ANIMALS polyamide tank top	
	Hēisè trilayer formal skirt	
	Pixel Neige snow boots with canvas duolayer	
Character Progression: Legendary	Carnage	Reward for reaching level 18 in the Crafting skill
	DR12 Quasar	
	Katana	
	Nekomata	
	Sandy Boa shock-absorbent headband	
	Synleather plastic goggles	

STANDARD CRAFTING SPECS OVERVIEW (CONTINUED)

Category	Crafting Specs	Availability
Character Progression: Legendary	Lightning Rider reinforced racing suit	Reward for reaching level 18 in the Crafting skill
Character Progression: Legendary	Red Alert anti-surge netrunning suit	
Character Progression: Legendary	Composite Ko Jag silk-threaded hotpants	
Character Progression: Legendary	Crystal Lily evening pumps with extra-durable soles/Crystal Lily evening shoes with extra-durable soles	
Iconic Weapons**	Sovereign	Dropped by the leader in hustle 684 (Suspected Organized Crime Activity in Japantown – see page 316)
Iconic Weapons**	Buzzsaw	Dropped by the leader in hustle 643 (Suspected Organized Crime Activity in Northside – see page 310)
Iconic Weapons**	Breakthrough	Dropped by the leader in hustle 752 (Suspected Organized Crime Activity in Rancho Coronado – see page 328)
Iconic Weapons**	Comrade's Hammer	Dropped by the leader in hustle 772 (Suspected Organized Crime Activity in Arroyo – see page 331)
Iconic Weapons**	Psalm 11:6	Dropped by the leader in hustle 644 (Suspected Organized Crime Activity in Northside – see page 310)
Iconic Weapons**	Moron Labe	Dropped by the leader in hustle 717 (Suspected Organized Crime Activity in West Wind Estate – see page 322)
Iconic Weapons**	Ba Xing Chong	Can be found in Adam Smasher's vault (the shipping container unlocked by Grayson's key during SJ-35 – see page 216) after you enter the elevator taking you to Embers during MJ-26 ("Nocturne Op55N1" – see page 164).
Iconic Weapons**	Yinglong	Dropped by the leader in hustle 805 (Suspected Organized Crime Activity in Wellsprings – see page 353)
Iconic Weapons**	The Headsman	Dropped by the leader in hustle 714 (Suspected Organized Crime Activity in North Oak – see page 321)
Iconic Weapons**	Chaos	Can be obtained during MJ-08 ("The Pickup" – see page 120) by looting Royce after neutralizing him in the deal sequence, or during the boss fight.
Iconic Weapons**	Doom Doom	Can be obtained during SJ-38 ("Second Conflict" – see page 220) by looting Dum Dum in the Totentantz club; note that this is only possible if you took steps to ensure that Dum Dum survived the events of MJ-08.
Iconic Weapons**	Sir John Phallustiff	Offered by Stout after your one-night stand with her ("Venus in Furs"). See page 417.
Iconic Weapons**	Kongou	Can be found on the nightstand next to Yorinobu's bed in his penthouse during MJ-10 ("The Heist" – see page 128).
Iconic Weapons**	O'Five	Can be collected during SJ-01 ("Beat on the Brat: Champion of Arroyo" – see page 181) after neutralizing Buck.
Iconic Weapons**	Satori	After T-Bug opens the penthouse's balcony door during MJ-10 ("The Heist" – see page 128), climb up the stairs leading to the AV landing pad: the weapon is inside the vehicle.
Iconic Weapons**	Fenrir	Can be collected from a table near the monk you need to rescue during SJ-06 ("Losing My Religion" – see page 186).
Iconic Weapons**	Crash	Given to you by River atop the water tower during SJ-21 ("Following the River" – see page 202).
Iconic Weapons**	La Chingona Dorada	After you complete SJ-10 ("Heroes" – see page 189), you can find the La Chingona Dorada pistol on the table where all the offerings were displayed.
Iconic Weapons**	Scalpel	Reward for completing SJ-08 ("Big in Japan" – see page 187).
Iconic Weapons**	Plan B	Can be looted from Dex's body in the scrapyard after MJ-11 ("Playing for Time" – see page 132).
Iconic Weapons**	Apparition	Can be looted from Frank's body after SJ-51 ("War Pigs" – see page 234).
Iconic Weapons**	Cottonmouth	Can be collected in Fingers' bedroom during MJ-13 ("The Space In Between" – see page 138).
Iconic Weapons**	Overwatch	Reward for saving Saul during SJ-45 ("Riders on the Storm" – see page 228).
Iconic Weapons**	Problem Solver	Dropped by the large enemy guarding the Wraith camp's front entrance in SJ-45 ("Riders on the Storm" – see page 228).
Iconic Weapons**	Tinker Bell	Found under the tree closest to Peter Pan's house on the Edgewood farm during SJ-20 ("The Hunt" – see page 200).
Iconic Weapons**	Cocktail Stick	Can be found in the make-up room of the Clouds club, upstairs, during MJ-12 ("Automatic Love" – see page 134).
Iconic Weapons**	Mox	Given by Judy if you share a romantic relationship with her, or after MJ-12 ("Automatic Love" – see page 134) if she decides to leave Night City.
Iconic Weapons**	Second Opinion	Can be picked up in Maiko's office (adjacent to Woodman's) during MJ-12 ("Automatic Love" – see page 134).
Iconic Weapons**	Widow Maker	Can be looted from Nash after defeating him during MJ-19 ("Ghost Town" – see page 149).
Iconic Weapons**	Gold-Plated Baseball Bat	Available in the pool at Denny's villa, after the argument, during SJ-38 ("Second Conflict" – see page 220).
Iconic Weapons**	Lizzie	Can be found in the basement of Lizzie's after MJ-13 ("The Space in Between" – see page 138).
Iconic Weapons**	Dying Night	Reward for winning the shooting contest during SJ-11 ("Shoot to Thrill" – see page 190).
Iconic Weapons**	Tinker Bell	Found under the tree closest to Peter Pan's house on the Edgewood farm during SJ-20 ("The Hunt" – see page 200).

Category	Crafting Specs	Availability
Iconic Weapons**	Amnesty	Earned by completing Cassidy's bottle-shooting challenge at the Nomad party during MJ-31 ("We Gotta Live Together" – see page 174).
Iconic Weapons**	Archangel	Given by Kerry during SJ-42 ("Off the Leash" – see page 224).
Iconic Weapons**	Genjiroh	Can be found behind a closed door on the way to the second sniper during MJ-24 ("Play it Safe"). See page 417.
Iconic Weapons**	Jinchu-maru	Dropped by Oda during MJ-24 ("Play it Safe" – see page 158).
Iconic Weapons**	Tsumetogi	Can be looted from the room where the meeting with Maiko and the Tyger Claw bosses takes place during SJ-30 ("Pisces" – see page 211).
Iconic Weapons**	Divided We Stand	Reward for winning the shooting contest during SJ-58 ("Stadium Love"). Can also be looted from the sixers if you neutralize them (page 238).

QUICKHACK CRAFTING SPECS OVERVIEW

Crafting Specs	Perk Required	Quickhack Required
Contagion		-
Cripple Movement		-
Cyberware Malfunction		-
Overheat		-
Ping		-
Reboot Optics	Hacker's Manual	-
Request Backup		-
Short Circuit		-
Sonic Shock		-
Weapon Glitch		-
Whistle		-
Contagion		Uncommon Contagion
Cripple Movement		Uncommon Cripple Movement
Cyberware Malfunction		Uncommon Cyberware Malfunction
Memory Wipe		-
Overheat		Uncommon Overheat
Ping	School of Hard Hacks	Uncommon Ping
Reboot Optics		Uncommon Reboot Optics
Short Circuit		Uncommon Short Circuit
Sonic Shock		Uncommon Sonic Shock
Synapse Burnout		-
Weapon Glitch		Uncommon Weapon Glitch
Whistle		Uncommon Whistle
Contagion		Rare Contagion
Cripple Movement		Rare Cripple Movement
Cyberpsychosis		-
Cyberware Malfunction		Rare Cyberware Malfunction
Detonate Grenade		-
Memory Wipe		Rare Memory Wipe
Overheat		Rare Overheat
Ping		Rare Ping
Reboot Optics	Hacker Overlord	Rare Reboot Optics
Request Backup		Uncommon Request Backup
Short Circuit		Rare Short Circuit
Sonic Shock		Rare Sonic Shock
Suicide		-
Synapse Burnout		Rare Synapse Burnout
System Reset		-
Weapon Glitch		Rare Weapon Glitch
Whistle		Rare Whistle
Contagion		Epic Contagion
Cripple Movement		Epic Cripple Movement
Cyberpsychosis		Epic Cyberpsychosis
Detonate Grenade		Epic Detonate Grenade
Overheat		Epic Overheat
Ping		Uncommon Ping
Reboot Optics	Bartmoss' Legacy	Epic Reboot Optics
Short Circuit		Epic Short Circuit
Sonic Shock		Epic Sonic Shock
Suicide		Epic Suicide
Synapse Burnout		Epic Synapse Burnout
System Reset		Epic System Reset
Weapon Glitch		Epic Weapon Glitch

* Crafting specs for weapon mods and clothing mods can also be obtained as random loot from chest containers and suitcases.

** Iconic weapons are each found at a specific rarity rank. To craft a superior version, you will need to consume the weapon at its current rank.

HACKING

We've already discussed the general principles behind the concept of hacking in our Primer chapter – see page 80 if you need a refresher. In this section, we take a more in-depth look into how the system works. In case you're confused, let us begin with a terminology clarification: "quickhacks" are the programs you install on your cyberdeck and can then cast on enemies; "daemons" refer to the malware you upload when you successfully complete sequences in the Breach Protocol mini-game.

BREACH PROTOCOL MINI-GAME

The Breach Protocol mini-game enables you to hack each network you encounter. While standard quickhacks usually work on single targets, the Breach Protocol quickhack has the unique benefit of affecting all targets in the network.

Physical Breach: When you connect physically to a device such as an access point or a computer, a successful hack rewards you primarily with datamining resources: money on a regular basis, but also, potentially, hacking-specific crafting components and even quickhacks.

Remote Breach: When you initiate Breach Protocol remotely – casting it on an enemy, for example – the mini-game features multiple objectives in accordance with the daemons that you have unlocked in the Breach Protocol Perk tree. Every sequence you successfully add to your buffer will yield its own reward.

Let's imagine, for instance, that you have three daemons requiring the following sequences:

55 - 1C - E9 ▶ **ICEpick** (reduces all quickhack RAM costs by 1)

1C - E9 - 1C ▶ **Mass Vulnerability** (reduces the physical resistance for all enemies in the network by 30% for 3 minutes

E9 - 1C - 55 ▶ **Turret Shutdown** (disables all security turrets in the network for 3 minutes)

You could complete all three simultaneously (and, therefore, enjoy the benefits of the associated programs) by selecting the following sequence in the matrix:

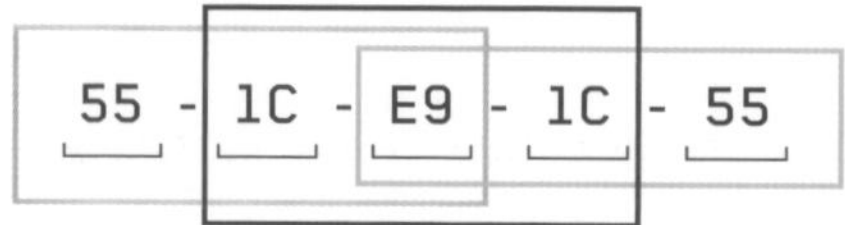

You can improve your chances of success in various ways:

- By extending the breach time (the amount of time you have to complete each puzzle).
- By increasing the buffer size (how many characters you can select).
- By reducing the length of the daemon data sequence (how many characters are required to complete a sequence).

This can be achieved primarily by purchasing Perks under the Breach Protocol skill, by gaining levels in that same skill, and by equipping advanced cyberdecks (see page 408). Maxing out the Breach Protocol skill and Perk tree is highly recommended for a netrunner, making it possible to trigger powerful, multilayered effects every time you complete the mini-game.

The Quickhacking skill tree is also one that deserves your attention if you intend to become a full-fledged netrunner, enabling you to cast potent quickhacks at a high frequency against individual targets thanks to improved RAM and memory regeneration – our next topic.

RAM

The quickhacks you can cast on remote targets are the ones that you equipped in your cyberdeck's slots. In very simple terms: equip a quickhack and you can then cast it. Each cyberdeck has a predefined number of slots: the more available, the greater flexibility this gives you in the midst of the action.

You can find the complete list of cyberdecks and quickhacks in the Inventory chapter (refer to pages 408 and 422 respectively).

One ever-present consideration with quickhacks is the limited resource they consume when you cast them: RAM. Each quickhack has a base cost that can be reduced by, for instance, successfully uploading the ICEpick daemon during a Breach Protocol sequence, or by unlocking specific Perks. Costs also scale (up or down) based on the level difference between you and your target.

If you're seeking to improve your ability to bend the world to your will with quickhacks, there are two parameters that you should look to improve whenever possible:

- **Max RAM:** You can increase the size of your RAM meter via character progression and by equipping superior cyberware. The larger your meter, the more quickhacks you can cast successively.
- **RAM Regeneration:** You can also improve the rate at which your RAM meter replenishes over time. With a high restore speed, your gauge can fill fast enough that you will rarely run out of memory. By default, you regenerate RAM only outside combat (after a five-second delay), at a rate of 18 RAM units per minute.

The tables on the right-hand page detail how you can optimize your max RAM and enhance the recovery rate.

METHODS TO EXTEND MAX RAM

Category	Source	Max RAM
Character progression	Intelligence: 20 attribute points	+7
Character progression	Quickhacking skill: level 5	+1
Character progression	Quickhacking skill: level 10	+1
Character progression	Quickhacking skill: level 20	+1
Character progression	Breach Protocol skill: level 8	+1
Character progression	Breach Protocol skill: level 13	+1
Cyberware	Ex-Disk (Rare quality)	+1
Cyberware	Ex-Disk (Epic quality)	+3
Cyberware	Ex-Disk (Legendary quality)	+5
Cyberware	Militech Paraline	+2
Cyberware	Arasaka Mk.3	+8
Cyberware	Arasaka Mk.4	+10
Cyberware	BioDyne Mk.1	+6
Cyberware	BioDyne Mk.2	+9
Cyberware	Biotech Σ Mk.1	+5
Cyberware	Biotech Σ Mk.2	+7
Cyberware	Biotech Σ Mk.3	+10
Cyberware	Fuyutsui Electronics Mk.1	+3
Cyberware	Fuyutsui Tinkerer Mk.3	+8
Cyberware	NetWatch Netdriver Mk.5	+11
Cyberware	Raven Microcyber Mk.3	+8
Cyberware	Raven Microcyber Mk.4	+10
Cyberware	Seacho Electronics Mk.1	+4
Cyberware	Seacho Electronics Mk.2	+6
Cyberware	Stephenson Tech Mk.2	+6
Cyberware	Stephenson Tech Mk.3	+8
Cyberware	Stephenson Tech Mk.4	+10
Cyberware	Tetratronic Mk.1	+4
Cyberware	Tetratronic Mk.2	+6
Cyberware	Tetratronic Mk.3	+8
Cyberware	Tetratronic Rippler Mk.4	+10
Consumables	RAM Jolt	+2

METHODS TO INCREASE RAM REGENERATION

Category	Source	Regeneration Rate
Character progression	Biosynergy (Quickhacking Perk)	Enables RAM to recover during combat. Tier 1: +4 RAM units per minute. Tier 2: +8 RAM units per minute. Tier 3: +12 RAM units per minute.
Character progression	Master Ram Liberator (Quickhacking Trait)	Increases RAM recovery rate by 50%. Each further Perk Point spent in the Trait adds another +1%.
Cyberware	Common RAM Upgrade (Frontal Cortex)	+4 RAM units per minute
Cyberware	Uncommon RAM Upgrade (Frontal Cortex)	+8 RAM units per minute
Cyberware	Rare RAM Upgrade (Frontal Cortex)	+12 RAM units per minute
Cyberware	BioDyne Mk.2 (Cyberdeck)	+4 RAM units per minute
Cyberware	Biotech Σ Mk.1 (Cyberdeck)	+8 RAM units per minute
Cyberware	Biotech Σ Mk.2 (Cyberdeck)	+12 RAM units per minute
Cyberware	Biotech Σ Mk.3 (Cyberdeck)	+12 RAM units per minute
Cyberware	Raven Microcyber Mk.3 (Cyberdeck)	+4 RAM units per minute
Cyberware	Raven Microcyber Mk.4 (Cyberdeck)	+8 RAM units per minute
Cyberware	Fuyutsui Tinkerer Mk.3	+12 RAM units per minute
Cyberware	NetWatch Netdriver Mk.5	+12 RAM units per minute

HACKING DEVICES

Even if your V does not specialize in netrunning, hacking is still a staple ability – even if you only use it to create simple distractions. The tables in this section list the types of quickhack that can potentially be cast on devices.

All distractions (such as erratic device behavior or glitching screens) can serve to lure nearby guards to that position.

DEVICE QUICKHACK OVERVIEW

Quickhack	Description	Examples of Devices
Distract	Causes a device to malfunction, drawing the attention of nearby guards	Appliance, Arcade Machine, Billboard, Computer, Disposal Device, Electric Light, Forklift, Fusebox, Generator, Holo Table, Industrial Shutters, Intercom, Jukebox, Pachinko Machine, Radio, Reflector, Screens, Security Alarm/Gate, Smoke Machine, Sound System, Speaker, Surveillance Camera, Terminal, Turret, TV, Vehicle, Vending Machine
Remote Activation	Enables you to activate a device remotely – for example, to open a door or to turn a surveillance camera on or off. Advanced netrunners can use this to hack locking mechanisms that normally require a pincode, such as door terminals	Display Glass, Door, Electric Light, Elevator Terminal, Explosives, Industrial Shutters, Road Block, Surveillance Camera, Switch, Terminal, Turret
Take Control	Enables you to operate devices such as surveillance cameras and turrets; you can use this to tag enemies within range of the device and, in the case of turrets, to open fire	Surveillance Camera, Turret
Friendly Mode	Swaps the device's target recognition system and detects/targets your enemies instead of you	Explosives, Security Gate, Surveillance Camera, Turret
Assist Mode	Turrets forced into Assist Mode will attack targets that you have tagged as a priority	Turret
Steal Data	Used contextually during missions that require you to retrieve data from a specific computer	Computer, Laptop, Terminal
Overload	Causes a device to short-circuit or explode, potentially harming nearby targets	Bench Press Machine, Explosives, Fusebox, Generator, Netrunner Chair, Reflector, Smoke Machine, Speaker, Surveillance Camera

ENEMIES

ARCHETYPES

Enemies you face in Cyberpunk 2077 belong to preset AI archetypes defined by their equipment, abilities, and behavior. Each archetype is divided into tiers. The higher an enemy is within this classification, the more dangerous they will be. As a general rule, certain aspects of an individual's appearance can reflect the tier they belong to. Trench coats, heavy clothes, armor, or helmets, for example, might typically indicate a greater threat.

The table below lists all the main archetypes you will encounter in the game, providing essential details on what you should expect from them. This includes their use of cyberware (see page 406) and special abilities (see next section), which you would do well to familiarize yourself with.

ARCHETYPE OVERVIEW

Archetype	Favored Weapon Types	Abilities	Examples of Names
Ranged Tier 1-3	Assault Rifle SMG Handgun	Can use cover Can restore health Can shoot while moving Can sprint Can use Tech or Smart weapons Can throw grenades Can have Masking Ink, which may deflect Smart weapon projectiles	Beat Cop, Crow, Devil, Fanatic, Gangoon, Goon, Guard, Gunner, Gunslinger, Hunter, Infantry Scout, Inquisidor, Inspector, Malfini, Marauder, Nomad, Ogre, Racketeer, Ranger, Rapid, Raptor, Rat, Recon Support, Recruit, Sanguinario, Soldier, Support Unit, Tiger
Melee Tier 1-3	One-handed melee weapon Fists	Rush toward you Can restore health Can have Masking Ink, which may deflect Smart weapon projectiles	Beat Cop, Bouncer, Cockroach, Ghost, Goon, Guard, Hunter, Mauler, MaxTac Raider, Mutt, Outlaw, Ranger, Ravager, Recruit, Scout, Soldier, Thug
Fast Melee Tier 2	Katana One-handed blade	Rush toward you Can restore health Can break your blocking stance Can parry your attacks Can have Sandevistan Possible faction abilities: static camo and charged jump	Adept, Agent, Guererro, Jackal, Sergeant, Spirit, Zealot
Fast Melee Tier 3	Katana Mantis Blades	All Tier 2 abilities Can have Kerenzikov Possible faction ability: optical camo	Fiend, Hyena, Kunoichi, Ninja, Revenant
Heavy Melee Tier 2	Gorilla Arms Two-handed hammer	Can restore health Can break your blocking stance Can parry your attacks Possible faction ability: charged jump	Bodyguard, Cur, Maton, Undertaker
Heavy Melee Tier 3	Gorilla Arms Two-handed hammer	All Tier 2 abilities Can have Subdermal Armor Can have a Berserk operating system	Claw, Juggernaut, Thickskull, Toro
Shotgun Tier 2	Shotgun	Can shoot while moving Can use Tech or Smart weapons	Blitzer, Brutalizer, Hound, Macho, Maniac, MaxTac Enforcer, Ranger, Rapid, Sentry, Sergeant, Shade, Snakecharmer, Specialist, Timador
Shotgun Tier 3	Shotgun	All Tier 2 abilities Can have a Berserk operating system	Blitzer, Elite Rapid, Jackhammer, MaxTac Officer, Operative, Patrol, Punisher, Sicario, Spec Ops Soldier, Specter, Terminator
Fast Gunner Tier 2	SMG Dual Pistols	Can use cover Can shoot while moving Can sprint Can use Tech or Smart weapons Can throw grenades Can have Sandevistan Possible faction ability: charged jump	Assault, Dragon, Ghoul, Operator, Sergeant,
Fast Gunner Tier 3	SMG Dual Pistols	All Tier 2 abilities Can have Kerenzikov Possible faction ability: optical camo	Executor

ARCHETYPE OVERVIEW (CONTINUED)

Archetype	Favored Weapon Types	Abilities	Examples of Names
Heavy Gunner Tier 2	Light Machine Gun	Can shoot while moving Can use Tech or Smart weapons	Armored Enforcer, Crusader, Tactical Officer, Vulture
Heavy Gunner Tier 3	Heavy Machine Gun	All Tier 2 abilities Can have a Berserk operating system	Goliath, Heavy Gunner, Juggernaut
Netrunner Tier 2	Combat Quickhacks Pistol Revolver	Will cast quickhacks whenever they have you in their line of sight Can use cover (especially while uploading quickhacks) Can shoot while moving Can sprint Can use Tech or Smart weapons Can throw grenades Possible faction ability: static camo	Apostle, Jonin, Netrunner, Spider
Netrunner Tier 3	Combat Quickhacks Pistol Revolver	All Tier 2 abilities Possible faction abilities: optical camo and Sandevistan	Manbo
Sniper Tier 2	Sniper Rifle Precision Rifle	Will fire powerful charged sniper shots whenever possible Can shoot while moving Can sprint Can use Tech or Smart weapons Can throw grenades Can have Sandevistan Possible faction ability: static camo	Sniper
Sniper Tier 3	Sniper Rifle Precision Rifle	All Tier 2 abilities Possible faction abilities: optical camo and Sandevistan	Francotirador, Sniper
Android	Rifles Machine Guns	Can cause shock bursts Can charge shots Immune to grapples	-

FACTION BEHAVIORS

Enemies are influenced by one of five combat temperaments – from reckless foes who like to take risks and move in close, taking cover only when there is no room for them to attack, to cautious enemies who prefer to stay behind cover and will not give chase if you flee. This table shows the standard temperament of each faction in the game.

FACTION BEHAVIOR OVERVIEW

Faction	Reckless	Aggressive	Balanced	Defensive	Cautious
6th Street			✔		
Aldecaldos				✔	
Animals	✔				
Arasaka			✔		
Generic				✔	
Kang Tao					✔
Maelstrom	✔				
Mercs			✔		
Militech				✔	
NCPD & MaxTac			✔		
Scavengers		✔			
Security					✔
Trauma			✔		
The Mox		✔			
Tyger Claws		✔			
Valentinos			✔		
Voodoo Boys				✔	
Wraiths		✔			

BOUNTIES & ENEMY DATA SHEETS

Many enemies that you will encounter on your travels will have a bounty on their head for other misdeeds, and are actively wanted by the NCPD. Whenever you neutralize such individuals, you earn the payment listed in the data sheet that appears when you scan them. As a rule, you can expect each bounty to grant you: XP, Street Cred, and money.

This makes bounty-hunting a very efficient way to develop your character. As you complete objectives (jobs, gigs, NCPD Scanner Hustles, and random hostile situations in the streets of Night City), you can gradually accrue significant financial rewards.

Enemy data sheets also give you vital information on the target you're currently scanning:

- Affiliation shows the faction the individual belongs to.
- Rarity indicates how tough the target is within their archetype (in ascending order: Weak, Normal, Rare, Elite, Boss).
- The bottom field reveals when a combatant is weak or resistant to a specific damage type, along with the corresponding damage modifier. This is vital intel: exploiting weaknesses and avoiding resistances can make a massive difference when you fight tougher enemies.

DAMAGE TYPES

All potential combatants in the game (including V) have varying degrees of resistance and susceptibility to the four key damage types: Physical, Thermal, Chemical, and Electrical.

Weaknesses and resistances are both measured on a scale from 0 to 100%. A value of 0 corresponds to no added effect: the damage taken is normal. Any value above 0 will lead to increased damage sustained in the case of a weakness, or reduced damage if a target is resistant.

The relationship that each foe you encounter has with the core damage types can vary greatly, and is scaled in accordance with your progression in the adventure, so there is no way to offer a reliable catalogue of values for every potential adversary you might face. However, certain factions have defining strengths and weaknesses that you might commonly expect to encounter when you face them – as revealed in the following table.

DAMAGE TYPE AFFINITIES PER FACTION

Faction	Can Deal	Strengths/Weaknesses			
		Thermal	Chemical	Electrical	Hacking
6th Street	-	Normal	Weak	Normal	Very Weak
Aldecaldos	Thermal	Normal	Weak	Normal	Weak
Animals	-	Weak	Strong	Weak	Weak
Arasaka	Electrical	Normal	Normal	Normal	Normal*
Kang Tao	Electrical	Normal	Normal	Very Strong	Very Strong
Maelstrom	Electrical	Normal	Strong	Weak	Normal*
Militech	-	Strong	Normal	Normal	Normal
NCPD & MaxTac	-	Weak	Weak	Weak	Normal*
Scavengers	Chemical	Very Weak	Strong	Weak	Very Weak*
The Mox	-	Normal	Weak	Normal	Normal
Tyger Claws	Electrical	Weak	Strong	Strong	Normal*
Valentinos	Thermal	Strong	Normal	Weak	Weak*
Voodoo Boys	-	Weak	Strong	Strong	Very Strong
Wraiths	Chemical	Weak	Very Strong	Normal	Weak

* Netrunners' resistance to hacking is one rank higher than that of other members of their faction

STATUS EFFECTS

The accompanying table lists all status effects that V can inflict or (in most instances) endure, as well as measures that will confer resistance, or even immunity, to such attacks.

STATUS EFFECT OVERVIEW

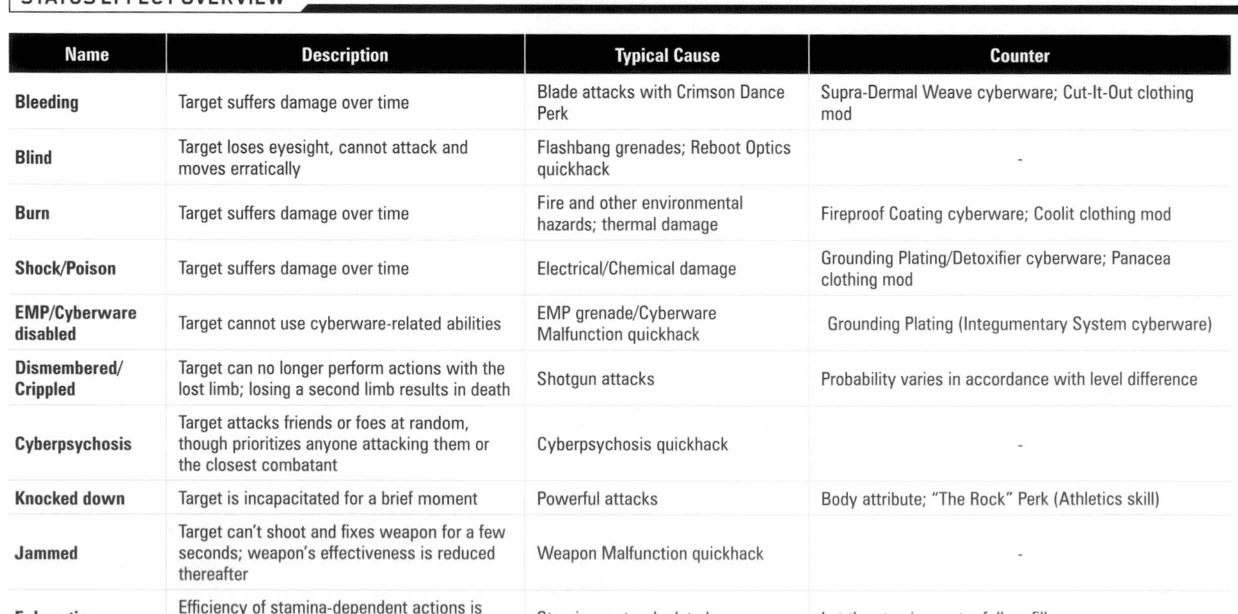

Name	Description	Typical Cause	Counter
Bleeding	Target suffers damage over time	Blade attacks with Crimson Dance Perk	Supra-Dermal Weave cyberware; Cut-It-Out clothing mod
Blind	Target loses eyesight, cannot attack and moves erratically	Flashbang grenades; Reboot Optics quickhack	-
Burn	Target suffers damage over time	Fire and other environmental hazards; thermal damage	Fireproof Coating cyberware; Coolit clothing mod
Shock/Poison	Target suffers damage over time	Electrical/Chemical damage	Grounding Plating/Detoxifier cyberware; Panacea clothing mod
EMP/Cyberware disabled	Target cannot use cyberware-related abilities	EMP grenade/Cyberware Malfunction quickhack	Grounding Plating (Integumentary System cyberware)
Dismembered/ Crippled	Target can no longer perform actions with the lost limb; losing a second limb results in death	Shotgun attacks	Probability varies in accordance with level difference
Cyberpsychosis	Target attacks friends or foes at random, though prioritizes anyone attacking them or the closest combatant	Cyberpsychosis quickhack	-
Knocked down	Target is incapacitated for a brief moment	Powerful attacks	Body attribute; "The Rock" Perk (Athletics skill)
Jammed	Target can't shoot and fixes weapon for a few seconds; weapon's effectiveness is reduced thereafter	Weapon Malfunction quickhack	-
Exhaustion	Efficiency of stamina-dependent actions is reduced	Stamina meter depleted	Let the stamina meter fully refill

DAMAGE MODIFIERS

Attacks can deal different amounts of damage whenever modifiers are active.

WEAPON MODIFIERS

Damage modifiers are most commonly granted by weapons, primarily in the form of bonuses to one or more damage types. An example would be a pistol that deals X base damage, but also offers an extra kick via supplementary electrical damage.

Any weapon can also feature additional modifiers, though this is more common with weapons of Rare quality or higher. As a rule, Rare weapons can have one additional modifier, while Epic weapons can have two and Legendary weapons three.

The pool of certain possible modifiers depends on the weapon's class:

- **Power firearms:** Crit Chance, Crit Damage, headshot damage, ricochet damage.
- **Tech firearms:** Crit Chance, Crit Damage, headshot damage, charge time, charge multiplier.
- **Smart firearms:** Crit Chance, Crit Damage, headshot damage.
- **Melee weapons:** Crit Chance, Crit Damage, attack speed, stamina cost reduction.

Crit Damage and Crit Chance are more important than you may imagine. Every time you launch an attack, there's a probability that you will perform it exceptionally well, leading to bonus damage (100% base). Crit Chance determines the probability that a critical will occur; Crit Damage determines the exact modifier applied. V has default values for these stats, but they can be improved by multiple methods, chiefly cyberware and equipment.

The tables below reveal damage modifiers that are specific to certain types of attacks.

FIREARM MODIFIERS

Weapon Type	Multiplier
Pistol	Headshot: x1.2
Revolver	Headshot: x2.5
Precision Rifle	Headshot: x1.5
Tech Precision Rifle	Charged Shot: x1.05
Sniper Rifle	Headshot: x4
Shotgun	Headshot: x1
SMG & LMG	Headshot: x0.85
Assault Rifle	Headshot: x0.85

MELEE COMBAT MODIFIERS

Attack Type	Blunt Weapons	Knife	Other Blades
Strong attack	200%	200%	200%
Throw attack	-	400%	-
Block attack	50%	50%	50%
Other attacks (fast attack, combo attack, et al.)	100%	100%	100%

EXPLOITING DAMAGE TYPES

In addition to standard physical damage, there are three elemental damage types: thermal, chemical, and electrical. All combatants (V included) have potential resistances and vulnerabilities to these damage types.

To find out how a foe might respond to different types of damage, all you have to do is scan them. The bottom part of their data sheet will reveal their strengths and weakness. If you discover, for example, that an opponent has a 30% susceptibility to thermal, then your attacks using that element will deal that approximate amount of bonus damage. Exploiting weaknesses and avoiding resistances is key to optimizing your damage output and overall combat efficiency.

The most common method to deal damage of a specific type is via weapons. When you check the data sheet of any given weapon, you can find out what damage type(s) it deals. It often pays to try to keep a varied selection of equipment in your Inventory, with at least one weapon offering each damage type: doing so will enable you to adapt immediately to inflict maximum harm on each opponent you face when required.

DEFENSIVE MODIFIERS

The gear you equip can provide all sorts of defensive modifiers. The following table lists the stats that can be improved in this manner, with examples of item categories providing the effects in question.

DEFENSIVE MODIFIER OVERVIEW

Stat	Description	Example of Stat Source
Armor	Reduces damage taken from physical attacks and Bleeding status effect.	Every clothing item
Thermal/ Chemical/ Electrical Resistance	Reduces damage taken from thermal/chemical/electrical attacks and Burn/Poison/ Shock status effects.	"CataResist" cyberware (immune system)
Damage Over Time Reduction	Reduces damage taken from all status effects.	"Resist!" clothing mod
Fall Damage Reduction	Reduces damage taken while landing from a significant height (20 meters or higher).	"Plume" clothing mod
Explosion Damage Reduction	Reduces damage taken from explosions (grenades, laser mines, et al.).	"Boom-Breaker" clothing mod
Overall Damage Reduction	Reduces damage from all sources.	"Pain Editor" cyberware (immune system)
Bleeding Immunity	Grants invulnerability against Bleeding status effect.	"Supra-Dermal Weave" cyberware (integumentary system)
Burn Immunity	Grants invulnerability against Burn status effect.	"Fireproof Coating" cyberware (immune system)
Poison Immunity	Grants invulnerability against Poison status effect.	"Detoxifier" cyberware (integumentary system)
Shock Immunity	Grants invulnerability against Shock status effect.	"Grounding Plating" cyberware (integumentary system)
Knockdown Immunity	Prevents you from being knocked down.	"The Rock" Perk (Athletics skill)

HUMANOIDS VS. MECHS

Whether your current target is humanoid or mechanical has practical implications regarding their behavior and reactions to damage types. The accompanying table offers an overview of the most common considerations.

HUMANOIDS VS. MECHS: OVERVIEW

Category	Mechanical	Humanoid
Distinctive Features	Cannot use cover Cannot cast quickhacks Immune to headshots Immune to takedowns	Can use cover Netrunners can cast quickhacks Can have powerful cyberware such as Kerenzikov and Sandevistan
Resistances	Thermal Damage Chemical Damage	Varies per individual, faction, and archetype
Weaknesses	Electrical Damage Cyberpsychosis Quickhack	Headshots Takedowns Other weaknesses vary per individual, faction, and archetype

STEALTH

We offer a detailed introduction to stealth mechanics in our Primer chapter, on page 79. Here, we provide a few additional (and a little more technical) facts about the system.

- The line of sight of enemies is a combination of two geometrical figures: a long frontal detection cylinder, and short peripheral view of approximately 120 degrees (see accompanying diagram).

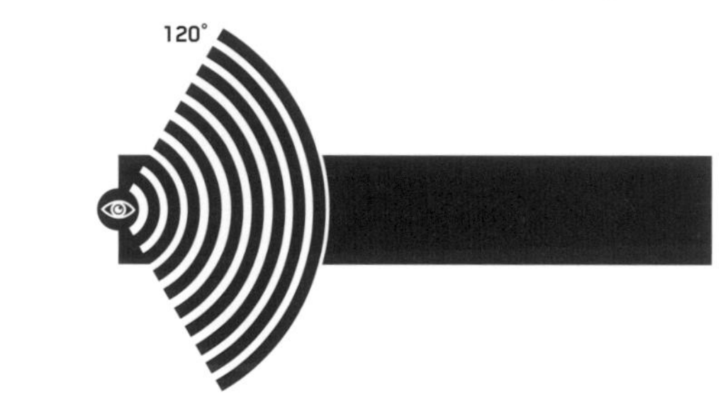

- Detection speed varies in accordance with the distance between you and the threat: the closer you are to the sensorial perception source (be it a guard or a device such as a surveillance camera), the faster the detection meter will fill. In practical terms, this means that you can afford to be a little less careful when you are relatively distant, even briefly staying in an upright position or sprinting in short bursts. Conversely, you need to be extremely cautious at close range, where standing up for even a fraction of a second might be sufficient to fill a detection gauge almost instantly.
- How long you can keep an enemy in a chokehold depends on your Cool level: the higher this attribute is, the longer you can grapple your opponents – which makes it possible to drag them for longer distances, and affords you the luxury of being a little more tactical with your takedowns.
- As a general rule, enemies react to you and alter their routine only if their detection meters fill completely. As long as the meter is only partially full, they will stick to their standard patrol route or designated post, even if you should let yourself be seen or heard for a brief moment. With practice, you will soon acquire an intuitive understanding of when you can expect to get away with slipping between two cover positions, or making a dash to get through a door.
- Actions generating sounds that can alert foes to your presence include the following: walking, sprinting, attacking, explosions, and landing from heights. By default, the only movement type that does not make noise is crouch-walking. Crouching also reduces your visibility, making it slightly less likely for enemies to notice you in the open if their field of vision is at least partially occluded.
- There are three primary methods to neutralize enemies while remaining stealthy: silent takedowns (after grappling a target that you have approached from behind), silent weapons, on the proviso they incapacitate the target in one shot (firearms equipped with a silencer, blades, or thrown knives), and lethal quickhacks such as System Reset.
- If a guard finds the body of one of his colleagues that you have casually left in your wake, all enemies in the area will enter a permanent state of increased vigilance. This is shown on your mini-map by a rippling circle effect that appears around the dot of each applicable foe. In this scenario, the alarm has not been raised and your opponents are still unaware of your position. However, they will more watchful, abandon patrol routes, and move around more erratically, making their behavior far more unpredictable. This is why it is generally important to hide anyone that you incapacitate: once you drop a body in a crate, refrigerator, or any other suitable hiding place, it is effectively removed from the map and will lead to no future repercussions.
- Note that enemies will also adopt an increased state of vigilance if you enter open conflict but manage to escape. After looking for you at your last known position for a while, they will eventually end the search – but will remain wary.

NETRUNNER STEALTH TACTICS

Netrunners can specialize in stealth tactics where they use quickhacks to clear their path with artful diversions. You should already be familiar with the many ways to confuse or debilitate enemies during infiltration sequences, but there are two advanced techniques that you might have overlooked.

Remote Activation

The Remote Activation quickhack can occasionally be used to override skillchecks that a netrunner might not otherwise pass. This only applies to mechanical devices – such as locked doors, shutters, or gates, which normally require a high Body or Technical Ability level.

Surveillance Cameras

It is understandable that you might automatically regard surveillance cameras as hostile objects – but for an adept netrunner, every one of these represents an ally of sorts.

When you cast the Take Control quickhack on a surveillance camera, it becomes a powerful tool. Once your point of view switches to its visual feed, it's almost as if you have warped to the position in question: you can again scan your environment, tag potential adversaries that you have yet to detect, and – best of all – perform additional quickhacks. Each surveillance camera you run into, then, becomes a potential extension of yourself. You could, for example, engineer a scenario in which you hack a camera to gain access to another nearby camera, which might in turn enable you to neutralize or lure away an awkwardly placed enemy.

If you develop your character as a netrunner, with many points invested in the Intelligence attribute, you should always regard surveillance cameras – whether active (red beams) or inactive (green beams) – as potential opportunities. These toys might belong to someone else, but they're yours to play with.

STAMINA

When you perform physically demanding actions, a stamina meter appears at the top of the screen. Each successive applicable action depletes the bar; it will regenerate once you cease such activities. If the bar is fully depleted, you become exhausted, which negatively affects stamina-dependent actions, reducing dodge range, jump height, sprint speed, and melee attack speed. You will need to let the meter refill completely to end the exhausted status.

The tables in this section reveal the base cost of all moves that consume stamina, and how you might reduce stamina expenditure.

STAMINA COSTS: MOVEMENT

Action	Cost
Sprint	2,5 per second
Slide	5 per second
Jump	5
Double Jump	5+5
Charge Jump	5
Hover Jump	5
Fast Swimming/Swimming Underwater	7,5 per second
Dodge	10
Air Dodge	15

STAMINA COSTS: MELEE ATTACKS

		Blunt weapons						
Attack Type	**Description**	**Fists**	**Electric Baton**	**One-handed Blunt**	**Two-handed Blunt**	**Two-handed Hammer**	**Gorilla Arms**	**Monowire**
Fast/Combo attack	Press R2/RT	10	10	10	10	15	10	10
Final combo attack	Final attack in a continuous sequence	10	10	10	10	25	10	10
Strong attack	Hold then release R2/RT	25	25	25	25	25	25	15
Jump attack	Attack while jumping	10	10	10	10	15	10	10
Crouch/slide attack	Attack while crouching	10	10	10	10	15	10	10
Sprint attack	Attack while sprinting	10	10	10	10	-	10	10
Block attack	Attack while blocking	10	10	10	10	20	10	10
Deflect attack	Block just before an incoming attack connects	0	0	0	0	0	0	0
Safe attack	Attack while your weapon is lowered	-	10	10	10	20	-	-
Equip attack	Unsheathe a katana by holding R2/RT	-	-	-	-	-	-	-
Throw attack	While holding L2/LT press R2/RT	-	-	-	-	-	-	-
Quick melee attack	With weapon drawn, press R3/R	-	-	-	-	-	-	-
Block effort	Number of consecutive blocks that can be performed before your entire stamina meter is drained	8	4	3	5	5	10	10

		Blades				
Attack Type	**Description**	**Katana**	**One-handed Blade**	**Knife**	**Mantis Blades**	**Firearms**
Fast/Combo attack	Press R2/RT	10	10	10	7	-
Final combo attack	Final attack in a continuous sequence	10	10	10	10	-
Strong attack	Hold then release R2/RT	25	25	25	25	-
Jump attack	Attack while jumping	10	10	10	10	-
Crouch/slide attack	Attack while crouching	10	10	10	10	-
Sprint attack	Attack while sprinting	20	10	10	10	-
Block attack	Attack while blocking	10	10	10	10	-
Deflect attack	Block just before an incoming attack connects	0	0	0	0	-
Safe attack	Attack while your weapon is lowered	10	10	10	-	-
Equip attack	Unsheathe a katana by holding R2/RT	10	-	-	-	-
Throw attack	While holding L2/LT, press R2/RT	-	-	2	-	-
Quick melee attack	With weapon drawn, press R3/R	-	-	-	-	15
Block effort	Number of consecutive blocks that can be performed before your entire stamina meter is drained	4	3	0.5	7	-

METHODS TO REDUCE THE STAMINA COSTS OF MELEE ATTACKS

Category	Method	Cost Reduction
Character progression	Blades skill up reward (level 4)	10%
	Blades skill up reward (level 12)	20%
	Street Brawler skill up reward (level 5)	10%
	Flight of the Sparrow Perk (Blades skill tree)	30/50% for blades
	Efficient Blows Perk (Street Brawler skill tree)	25/50% for blunt weapons
Items	Melee weapons of Rare quality or higher	Potential linear reduction that caps at 50% at the weapon's max level
	Tenacity clothing mod	5%, then +1% per mod rarity rank

METHODS TO REDUCE THE STAMINA COSTS OF MOVEMENT

Category	Method	Cost Reduction
Character progression	Marathoner Perk (Athletics skill tree)	100% (sprinting no longer consumes stamina)
	Like a Butterfly Perk (Athletics skill tree)	100% (dodging no longer consumes stamina)

METHODS TO IMPROVE BLOCK EFFORT

Category	Method	Cost Reduction
Character progression	Blades skill up reward (level 15)	20%
	Street Brawler skill up reward (level 2)	10%
	Street Brawler skill up reward (level 13)	20%
	Gladiator Perk (Athletics skill tree)	20/40%
	Human Fortress Perk (Street Brawler skill tree)	50%
Items	Vanguard clothing mod	5%, then +3% per mod's rarity rank

ECONOMY PRINCIPLES

There are many ways to earn and spend cash in Night City. The following overview lists the most common methods you will encounter.

Sources of Income

- Completing jobs, gigs, and NCPD Scanner Hustles.
- Completing the Breach Protocol mini-game on physical access points to datamine resources – a particularly lucrative method for netrunner builds
- Picking up Eurodollars as random loot from bodies, stashes, or as physical collectibles.
- Selling items from your inventory to vendors.
- Incapacitating enemies that have a bounty on their head.

Spending Methods

- Buying items from vendors, cyberware from ripperdocs, or vehicles from fixers
- Choosing dialogue options that involve a monetary payment to facilitate progress

Vendor Rules

- The higher the position of an item in the rarity tier system, the more expensive it is.
- Most vendors have high-quality items gated by minimum Street Cred requirements.
- Items sold by vendors scale to your current level.
- Vendor stocks regenerate after 48 in-game hours, or when you move far away.
- Vendors can offer discounts on their wares (see page 424).

PHOTO MODE

To enter this special mode, press both sticks simultaneously. As soon as you enter Photo Mode, all action is frozen and you are free to move the camera as you please. You also have access to a vast number of settings – including depth of field adjustments, contrast tweaks, special effects, and even stickers, among dozens of other possibilities. Available contextual options are detailed on your screen.

Essentially, Photo Mode is a screenshot-capturing tool with powerful editing functions. If you have an artistic eye, this can be a fantastic way to create pictures of breathtaking vistas, dramatic combat scenes, and slices of Night City life.

TROPHIES & ACHIEVEMENTS

Cyberpunk 2077's collection of Trophies and Achievements acknowledge your efforts in reaching key story and gameplay milestones.

MAIN STORY ACCOLADES

Icon	Name	Trophy	G	Unlock Condition
	The Fool	Bronze	15	Complete one backstory from the possible three: Streetkid, Nomad, Corpo – see page 113.
	The Lovers	Bronze	15	Complete MJ-05 ("The Rescue" – see page 116).
	The Hermit	Bronze	15	Complete MJ-18 ("Transmission" – see page 148).
	The Wheel of Fortune	Bronze	15	Complete MJ-21 ("Life During Wartime" – see page 152).
	The High Priestess	Bronze	15	Complete MJ-25 ("Search and Destroy" – see page 162).
	The World	Gold	90	Complete Cyberpunk 2077's main storyline with any ending (see page 166).
	The Devil	Silver	30	Complete the "Where Is My Mind" Epilogue (**SPOILER WARNING:** see page 457).
	The Star	Silver	30	Complete the "All Along the Watchtower" Epilogue (**SPOILER WARNING:** see page 457).
	The Sun	Silver	30	Complete the "Path of Glory" Epilogue (**SPOILER WARNING:** see page 457).
	Temperance	Silver	30	Complete the "New Dawn Fades" Epilogue (**SPOILER WARNING:** see page 457).

OPTIONAL ACTIVITY ACCOLADES

Icon	Name	Trophy	G	Unlock Condition
	To Protect and Serve	Bronze	15	Complete SJ-21 ("Following the River" – see page 202).
	To Bad Decisions!	Bronze	15	Complete SJ-43 ("Boat Drinks" – see page 224).
	Judy vs Night City	Bronze	15	Complete SJ-31 ("Pyramid Song" – see page 212).
	Life of the Road	Bronze	15	Complete SJ-50 ("Queen of the Highway" – see page 233).
	Bushido and Chill	Bronze	15	Complete SJ-36 ("Blistering Love" – see page 218).
	Never Fade Away	Silver	30	Collect all items in the Johnny Silverhand set. There are four clothing pieces: Johnny's Aviators, Johnny's Shirt, Johnny's Pants, and Johnny's Shoes. You can find details on how to obtain them on page 419.
	The Wandering Fool	Silver	30	Complete SJ-44 ("Fool on the Hill" – see page 225).
	I Am The Law	Bronze	20	Complete all gigs that feature cyberpsychos: "Backs Against the Wall" (see page 267), "Occupational Hazard" (see page 267), "Going Up or Down?" (see page 295), "Family Matters" (see page 282).
	It's Elementary	Silver	30	Complete all gigs and NCPD Scanner Hustles* in Watson.
	Greetings from Pacifica!	Silver	30	Complete all gigs and NCPD Scanner Hustles* in Pacifica.
	The Wasteland	Silver	30	Complete all gigs and NCPD Scanner Hustles* in the Badlands.
	Little Tokyo	Silver	30	Complete all gigs and NCPD Scanner Hustles* in Westbrook.
	Mean Streets	Silver	30	Complete all gigs and NCPD Scanner Hustles* in Heywood.
	The Jungle	Silver	30	Complete all gigs and NCPD Scanner Hustles* in Santo Domingo.
	City Lights	Silver	30	Complete all gigs and NCPD Scanner Hustles* in City Center.
	Autojock	Silver	30	Buy all vehicles sold by fixers. You will need to reach Street Cred level 50 to unlock them all – see page 426 for details.

* Excluding Hidden Gems

EXPLORATION & SPECIAL FEAT ACCOLADES

Icon	Name	Trophy	G	Unlock Condition
	Gun Fu	Bronze	15	Using a handgun, take out three enemies at melee range (no more than a five meter radius) within 3.5 seconds.
	Christmas Tree Attack	Bronze	15	Complete a Breach Protocol hacking mini-game with at least three daemons successfully uploaded. Practice regularly on access points, devices, and enemies, and this should pose little problem (see page 445 for tips). Note that gaining levels in the Breach Protocol skill can make this challenge much easier.
	Right Back At Ya	Bronze	15	Kill an enemy while they are attempting to throw a grenade.
	Ten out of Ten	Bronze	15	Max out any skill by reaching level 20.
	Full Body Conversion	Bronze	15	Install implants in every available cyberware slot.
	Gunslinger	Bronze	15	Shoot a grenade thrown by an enemy with a revolver. Activating Sandevistan (see page 409) can greatly facilitate this maneuver.
	Two Heads, One Bullet	Bronze	15	Kill two enemies with a single sniper rifle shot. The Nekomata can be a weapon of choice here, as its Tech class means that it has piercing properties.
	Rough Landing	Bronze	15	Neutralize two enemies simultaneously with a Superhero Landing. This can be achieved after activating Berserk, which requires that you equip one of the following four operating systems: Moore Tech Berserk, Biodyne Berserk, Zetatech Berserk, or Militech Berserk (see page 409). After jumping you can fall at high speed, landing with sufficient force to create a powerful shockwave that damages nearby enemies. Note that you can preemptively weaken your targets if required.
	Stanislavski's Method	Bronze	15	Select 10 dialogue lines exclusive to your given background (Streetkid, Nomad, or Corpo).
	Master Crafter	Bronze	15	Craft three Legendary items. This requires the Edgerunner Artisan Perk in the Crafting tree (see page 434).
	Daemon In The Shell	Bronze	15	Kill or incapacitate three enemies with a single Detonate Grenade quickhack. This can be achieved by first casting the Request Backup quickhack on a guard located in an area with at least two allies nearby. Once they're all closely grouped, initiate the Detonate Grenade quickhack to engulf all five targets in the explosion.
	The Quick and the Dead	Bronze	15	Defeat 50 enemies while with an active time-dilation effect. Time dilation can be triggered at will with a Sandevistan operating system (see page 409).
	Must Be Rats	Bronze	15	Distract 30 enemies without engaging them. This simply requires you to cast the quickhack and be on your way.
	Legend of The Afterlife	Silver	30	Reach Street Cred level 50. This will happen eventually if you complete many jobs, gigs, and NCPD Scanner Hustles.
	V for Vendetta	Bronze	15	Equip a Second Heart (circulatory system cyberware that requires a Body attribute of at least 16 – see page 406), allow an enemy to kill you, then eliminate them after your resurrection.
	True Soldier	Silver	30	Kill or incapacitate 300 enemies using ranged weapons.
	True Warrior	Silver	30	Kill or incapacitate 100 enemies using melee weapons.
	Frequent Flyer	Bronze	20	Find all fast travel locations (see page 362)
	Breathtaking	Platinum	-	*PS4 & PS5 Only:* Obtain all other Trophies.

EXTRAS

This chapter covers highly sensitive topics such as different game endings and how to reach them, romance possibilities, and Easter eggs. If you're looking for an excuse to make another playthrough, you'll find plenty of inspiration here.

WARNING: It should go without saying that this chapter is filled with **MAJOR SPOILERS**, so we urge you to avoid even browsing through it until you have completed the main storyline *at least once*.

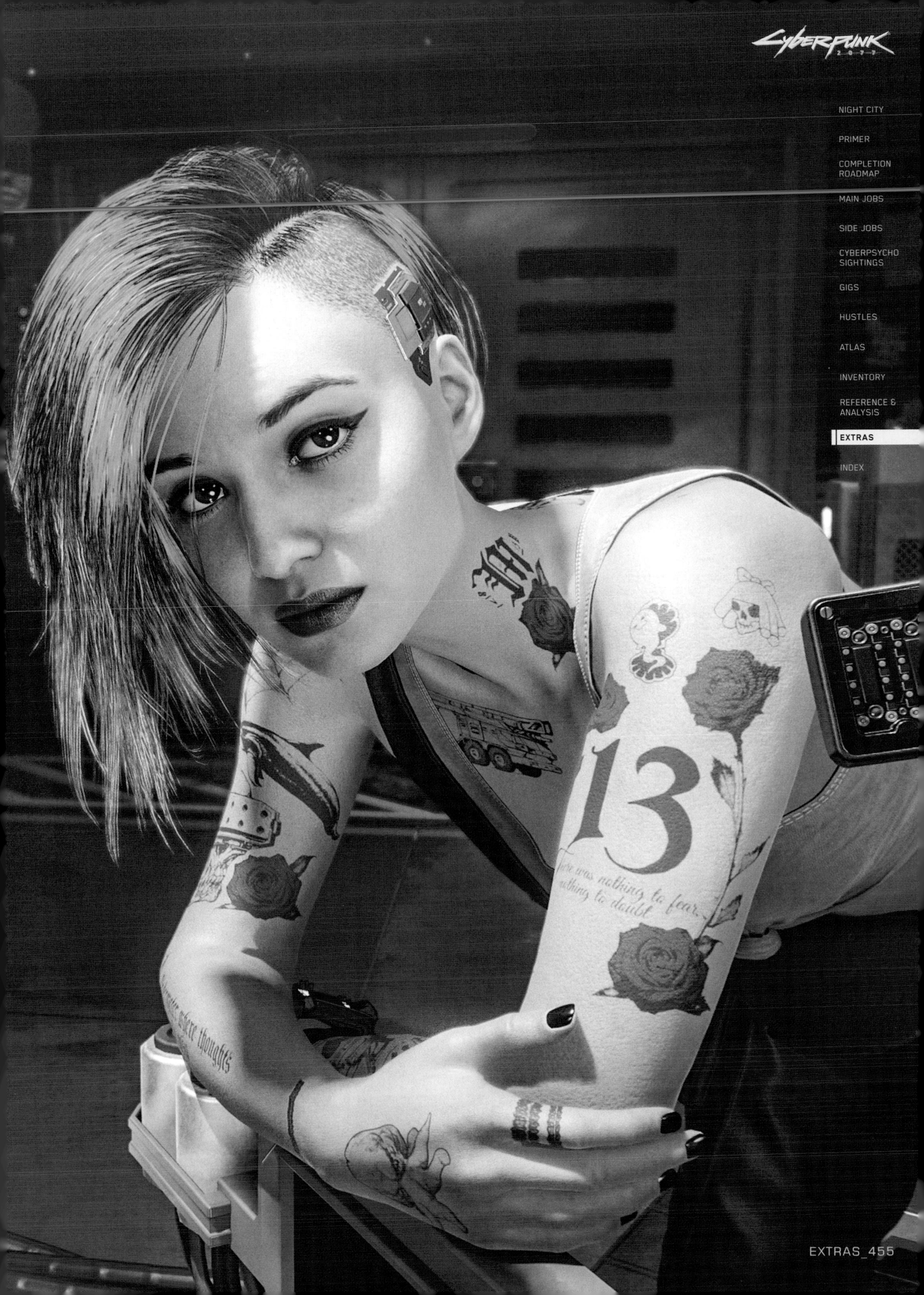
There was nothing to fear,
nothing to doubt

REQUIREMENTS

There are four potential romantic partners in Cyberpunk 2077: Panam, Judy, Kerry, and River. To ensure that your interest is reciprocated, you will need to meet specific requirements and make a handful of key decisions – as detailed below.

PANAM

- Panam will only have a relationship with a V who has a **male** body type.
- Flirt with Panam at the end of SJ-45 ("Riders on the Storm" – see page 228).
- Do *not* disclose Panam's plan to Saul at the beginning of SJ-49 ("With a Little Help from my Friends" – see page 232).
- Do *not* imply that you're helping Panam for the money during your conversation with her at the junction (also during SJ-49).
- After familiarizing yourself with the Basilisk controls during SJ-50 ("Queen of the Highway" – see page 233), accept Panam's offer to push the neural synchronization ("Oh yeah. Let's go").

JUDY

- Judy will only have a relationship with a V whose voice tone and body type are set to **feminine**.
- Either refuse to go along with Maiko's plan during SJ-30 ("Pisces" – see page 211), or turn down her payment.
- Accept the SJ-31 mission ("Pyramid Song" – see page 212) and agree to Judy's invitations: first to dive with her, and then to spend the night in the bungalow.
- Kiss her when given the opportunity in the bathroom.
- The next morning, join her on the pier outside and tell her your night together was "the beginning of something amazing."

KERRY

- Kerry will only have a relationship with a V whose voice tone and body type are set to **masculine**.
- Once the yacht is in the middle of the bay during SJ-43 ("Boat Drinks" – see page 224), kiss Kerry when he asks for your help inside the yacht.
- After the scene on the beach, make sure you select the dialogue line confirming your interest in Kerry.

RIVER

- River will only have a relationship with a V with a **female** body type.
- Save Randy during SJ-20 ("The Hunt" – see page 200).
- Select dialogue lines that indicate your interest in River during the final conversation in the SJ-20 side job.
- During SJ-21 ("Following the River" – see page 202), kiss River in both instances where the opportunity is presented to you.
- Confirm your interest the next morning when he asks you where this is going ("I feel good around you").

EPILOGUE SCENES

Romantic partners may play a part in the game's Epilogue in accordance with certain choices you make. The possibilities are as follows:

- **"Nocturne Op55N1" (MJ-26):** During the scene that takes place on the balcony with Misty after your brief visit to Viktor's clinic, you are given an opportunity to call your romantic interest, should you have one. Doing so will cause the character in question to make an appearance during the Epilogue. If you don't, or decide not to have them involved, you will be on your own in the corresponding scene.
- **"Where is My Mind?" (Epilogue):** You are allowed to contact your love interest during this scene. You will also receive a call from that same character during the credits.
- **"All Along the Watchtower" (Epilogue):** If you are with Panam or Judy, they will join you as you leave Night City. River and Kerry, on the other hand, will not follow you. You will receive a call from your romantic partner during the credits.
- **"Path of Glory" (Epilogue):** You will have a conversation with your love interest at your penthouse. He or she will also give you a call during the credits.
- **"New Dawn Fades" (Epilogue):** Your romantic partner will not appear during this Epilogue, but they will call you during the credits.

ENDINGS

The game ending you will experience is largely determined during the scene that occurs on the balcony with Misty after your brief visit to Viktor's clinic in the "Nocturne Op55N1" main job (MJ-26, see page 164).

By default, you will have a single possibility: relying on Hanako to help you, which leads to a corporation-oriented finale. There are, however, conditions you can fulfill to unlock additional outcomes. These are all summarized in the accompanying flowchart.

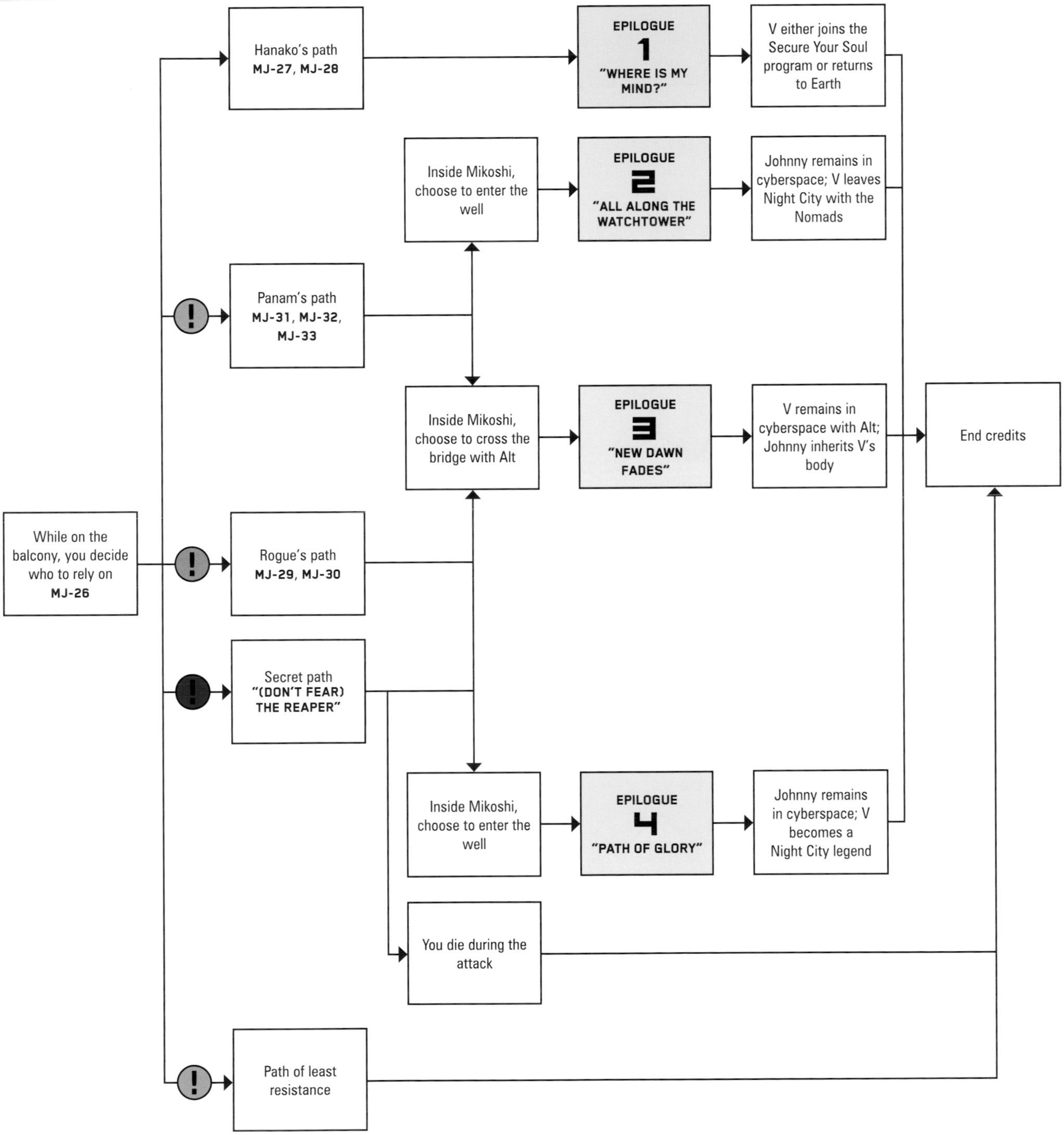

While on the balcony, you decide who to rely on **MJ-26**

Hanako's path **MJ-27, MJ-28**

Panam's path **MJ-31, MJ-32, MJ-33**

Rogue's path **MJ-29, MJ-30**

Secret path **"(DON'T FEAR) THE REAPER"**

Path of least resistance

Inside Mikoshi, choose to enter the well

Inside Mikoshi, choose to cross the bridge with Alt

Inside Mikoshi, choose to enter the well

You die during the attack

EPILOGUE 1 "WHERE IS MY MIND?"

EPILOGUE 2 "ALL ALONG THE WATCHTOWER"

EPILOGUE 3 "NEW DAWN FADES"

EPILOGUE 4 "PATH OF GLORY"

V either joins the Secure Your Soul program or returns to Earth

Johnny remains in cyberspace; V leaves Night City with the Nomads

V remains in cyberspace with Alt; Johnny inherits V's body

Johnny remains in cyberspace; V becomes a Night City legend

End credits

(!) Only available if you completed SJ-50 ("Queen of the Highway" – see page 233)

(!) Only available if you completed SJ-36 ("Blistering Love" – see page 218)

(!) Only available under very specific conditions: see "The Secret Ending"

(!) Only available if you reconsider your choice while on the balcony after selecting one of the three primary choices, then look at either your hand holding the pills or your gun and choose to commit suicide by crushing the pills

THE SECRET ENDING

You can trigger a hidden finale during MJ-26 ("Nocturne Op55N1" – see page 164). This can be achieved during the scene where you reflect on how to proceed while on the balcony once Misty leaves you to your thoughts.

As detailed in the flowchart on the previous page, you have access to up to four options during the conversation with Johnny – as long as you have completed the requisite side jobs, of course.

You can, however, unlock a fifth secret option. To accomplish this, all you have to do is to remain quiet. If you do not select any of the options on your screen and wait for a few minutes, Johnny will eventually interpret your silence as a sign that you do not want to endanger the lives of your friends. He will then offer you an alternative solution. In the words of Johnny, it's "a wild suicide run"; V describes it as "going out with a bang." Read the following notes if you want to know more:

- This has nothing to do with the "path of least resistance" option, despite the mention of suicide. Instead, you will attempt to raid Arasaka Tower solo in what can only be described as one of the tougher challenges in the game.
- We would recommend that you do not attempt this scenario unless you are perfectly familiar with all systems, own elite-level equipment, and have a maxed-out character build that you are wholeheartedly comfortable with in all potential combat situations.
- If you are killed, you will not be able to try again from your last checkpoint. Yes, you read this correctly: you have only one shot at this secret ending. Fail, and the credits will roll.
- From a gameplay perspective, this path will require you to make your way through Arasaka Tower's main entrance, then find an elevator and carve a path to Mikoshi through the Netrunners Operations area. As these locations appear in other finales, it's advisable to complete these at least once to familiarize yourself with the layout before you commit to a secret ending attempt.
- The only challenge – and what a challenge it is – will be to survive the many high-tier enemies determined to stop you. To optimize your preparations, we suggest you take the time to study our Inventory and Reference & Analysis chapters (see pages 404 and 428 respectively), and then employ every last trick that you learn to conquer one of the hardest optional missions in the game.

MISTY'S PREMONITIONS

Misty's side job (SJ-44, "Fool on the Hill" – see page 225) challenges you to find and scan 20 pieces of graffiti representing major arcanum tarot cards. Each card has a symbolic meaning which is closely tied to both the location where you can find it *and* corresponding plot developments – as revealed in the accompanying table.

Card	Meaning	Location
The Fool	The protagonist	On the outside wall of V's apartment.
The Chariot	Determination, path	On a wall adjacent to Tom's Diner, where you begin the main adventure after the Prologue.
The Magician	Capabilities, resources	On the pillar supporting the elevated highway, facing Lizzie's, the club where you have to prove your worth during the Prologue.
The Empress	Fruitfulness, communication	Near the entrance to the Afterlife, where you find the connections required for your adventure to progress on more than one occasion.
The Emperor	Structure, authority	At the entrance to Konpeki Plaza, where your conflict against corporations begins.
The Hierophant	Tradition, alliance	Near the spot where you meet with Takemura after the Prologue – a man of tradition who will become an essential ally.
The High Priestess	Silence, mystery	On the topmost floor of the building with Takemura's safehouse, where you first encounter a very silent Hanako.
The Hermit	Enlightenment, treason	Near the den of the Voodoo Boys, a gang seeking edification in cyberspace – but who swiftly betray you at the end of your foray into the Grand Imperial Mall.
Strength	Courage	On the side of the small building where you first meet Panam – one of your bravest potential allies.
Wheel of Fortune	Change, luck	Under the sign of the Sunset motel, where chance has you end up multiple times during your dealings with Panam and the Nomads.
Justice	Honesty, equity	On the cistern opposite the Electric Corporation power plant, which you explore with Judy – one of the most forthright characters in the story.

THE SECRET TAROT CARDS

Two hidden tarot cards can be found in the adventure's closing scenes.

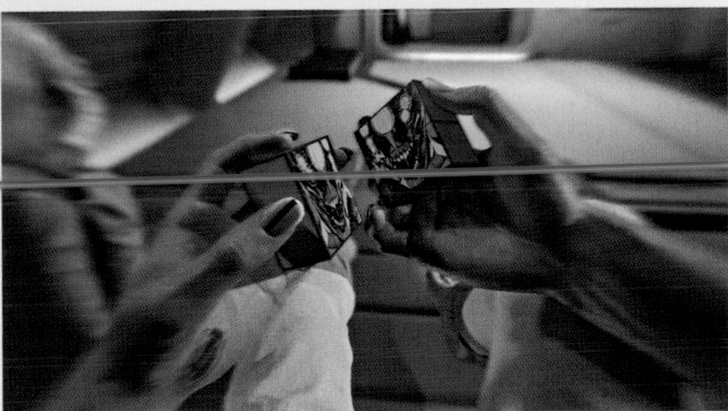

The Devil: Inside the Rubik's Cube, during the "Where Is My Mind?" Epilogue.

Judgment: Inside Mikoshi, in the arena where you fight Smasher during any of the other three finales. It's found on one of the retractable servers.

Card	Meaning	Location
The Lovers	Love, attraction	Behind the screen of the Silver Pixel Cloud drive-in, where Johnny and Rogue get a chance to revive their long-dormant love affair.
The Tower	Adversity, distress	In an underground passage at the base of Arasaka Tower, where both V and Johnny have faced great dangers.
The Hanged Man	Sacrifice, wisdom	On a water tower in the oilfields, not far from where Johnny's body was discarded.
Death	Mortality, transition	Near the Embers restaurant, where the final leg of V's journey begins.
The Moon	Deception, illusion	On the outside wall of the residence where, in the corporate-focused finale, you rescue Hanako – the embodiment of manipulative behavior and hidden agendas.
The World	Voyage, fulfillment	On the balcony near Misty's Esoterica and Viktor's clinic – where important decisions are made and V's destiny is sealed.
The Sun	Power, success	At the foot of the building where V's apartment is located in the "Path To Glory" Epilogue, in which V has become a living legend.
The Star	Hope, optimism	At the base of the antenna tower, in the middle of the solar farm, where you leave Night City for good on a quest for freedom if you complete the adventure with the help of the Nomads.
Temperance	Moderation, balance	On one of the walls in the North Oak columbarium, which Johnny visits in the New Dawn Fades Epilogue.

When you complete this quest, Misty shares a number of premonitions by explaining to you the meaning of certain critical tarot cards. In retrospect, there are two lines in particular that eventually prove especially relevant to the game's possible Epilogues and the critical choices you have to make:

"All the tarot can tell me is that you will reach the World by one of four paths. (...) The final leg of the journey goes through the Sun, the Star, Temperance, or the Devil."

Though it might have seemed cryptic when you heard it for the first time, this comment by Misty clearly alludes to the adventure's four possible game endings, as discussed earlier in this chapter.

What you may find interesting, however, is that Misty refers to two additional, hidden tarot cards:

"Hm... You're still missing two arcana – Judgement and The Devil."

These are actually available in the game (see "The Secret Tarot Cards") and can be seen as a representation of the core choice you have to make in the Epilogue.

Regarding the first hidden card, Judgment, Misty makes the following comment:

"One possible future. Of redemption, transition, awakening. The angel with the trumpet symbolizes the end of an era – and a call to rebirth, to a new beginning."

Remember: this is the card available inside Mikoshi – in other words in any of the Epilogues where you choose not to rely on Arasaka, but instead on your friends or yourself alone. During all of these finales you have a major decision to make, where either V or Johnny will have a chance of redemption.

As for The Devil, Misty has the following to say:

"That's the card of primal, dormant desires, but also the will to survive. It also represents a false world – the trap these desires lay for you."

This alludes to the path you take if you choose to ask for Hanako Arasaka's help – the corpo path. You and Johnny have been fighting against corporations throughout the story, so siding with them at the last minute is indicative of a desperate need to survive. By going down this path, you spare your own hide and doom Johnny, yet you are still given no more than six months to live – or an eternity ensnared as an engram inside Mikoshi. Hanako, meanwhile, has used you to prevail over her brother and bring the corporation back under her father's control. The "false world," then, is the one where Arasaka holds all the cards that truly matter.

EASTER EGGS

The Cyberpunk 2077 development team has clearly had a lot of fun while hiding a wide variety of Easter eggs across Night City. You will find a selection of some of the more interesting examples in this section, with screenshots to help you to find them for yourself if you wish.

Development Team Pictures: There is a secret room in the Kabuki Market, on the northwest side of Kabuki Roundabout, where you can see pictures of members of the Cyberpunk 2077 development team on a TV. The room can be unlocked with a code found on the message from the CD Projekt team included with each copy of the game – 605185. You can access this area after completing MJ-05 ("The Rescue").

!: During MJ-10 ("The Heist"), make a small detour to the bar when you arrive at Konpeki Plaza. On arrival, take a close look at the Japanese gentleman having a conversation. This is a cameo by legendary game creator Hideo Kojima, a self-professed fan of CD Projekt Red's *Witcher* titles.

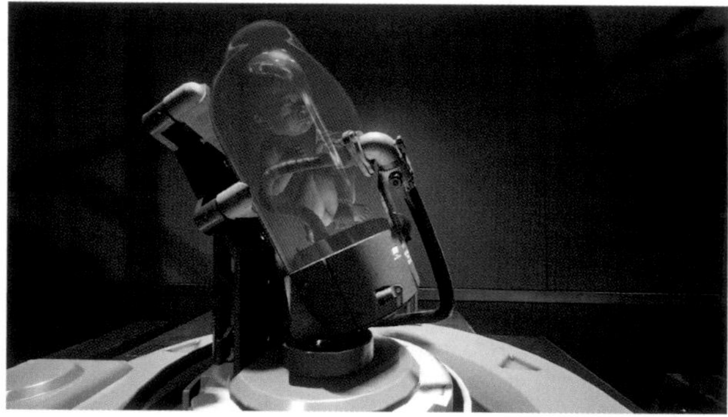

BB Pod: While you visit the NCPD lab's evidence room during SJ-20 ("The Hunt" – see page 202), note that presence of a BB pod. This is a reference to Hideo Kojima's *Death Stranding*.

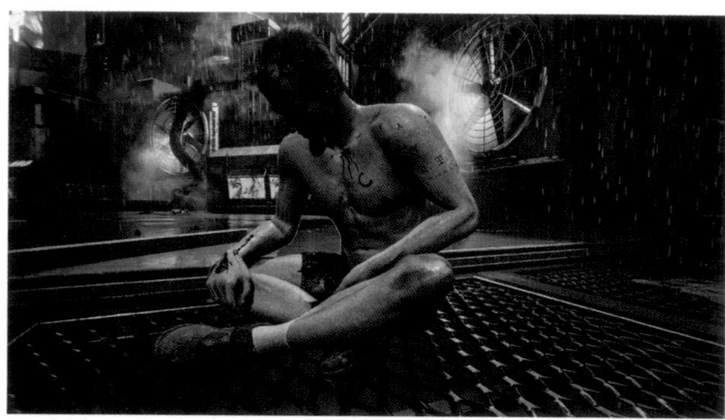

"I've seen things you people wouldn't believe": All fans of *Blade Runner* should make a pilgrimage to the rooftop of Vista del Rey's abandoned "Advocet Hotel." Open the front door, use the elevator to reach the rooftop terrace and, once outside, follow the walkway until you reach this character holding a white pigeon in his hands – a reverential nod to the film's famous denouement.

"Let me tell you about my mother": During the "Where is My Mind" Epilogue, you are invited to take part in a Voight-Kampff test. This is another tip of the hat to *Blade Runner*, where the test is employed to evoke and detect physical manifestations of emotional responses that might enable investigators to identify "replicants" – manufactured androids who are virtually indistinguishable from humans.

Ozob Bozo: The SJ-16 job ("Send in the Clowns" – see page 194) is given to you by a character who has a grenade for a nose. This individual, Ozob, is inspired by a character from a Brazilian tabletop RPG podcast.

Three Billboards: If you played V's Nomad origin story, you may have noticed this trio of billboards, close to the farm where you first meet Jackie – a reference to the movie *Three Billboards Outside Ebbing, Missouri*.

"Get over here!": When you complete SJ-53 ("I'll Fly Away" – see page 235), Mitch gives you a Scorpion figurine as memorabilia, which you can display on the coffee table in V's apartment. This figure is supposed to resemble Mitch's friend – but, in a playful bending of the fourth wall, actually looks like the *Mortal Kombat* character of the same name.

Smuggler's Cache: These floating barrels are a self-deprecating joke by the CD Projekt Red team. If you took the time to collect every last smuggler's cache in *The Witcher 3*, especially those off the coast of Skellige, you'll know *exactly* how to react.

Seashells: Your apartment, accessible after you complete MJ-05 ("The Rescue") at the beginning of the game, features a toilet. Look closely, and you will notice a small detail that will appear utterly incongruous to many players. This is a reference to the movie *Demolition Man*, in which seashells are used in place of toilet paper in matters of personal hygiene.

Dewdrop Inn: The name of this hotel (visited during the "Serious Side Effects" gig – see page 284) is a reference to a Tori Amos song called *Muhammed My Friend*, in which the following lyrics can be heard: "do drop in at the dew drop inn."

Columbarium Residents: There are a number of unexpected guests in the North Oak columbarium, including (but not limited to) Conrad B. Hart (the protagonist of the video game classic *Flashback*), Logan 5 (the protagonist of the movie *Logan's Run*), and Syd Mead (the concept artist known for his designs for science-fiction films such as *Blade Runner* and *Aliens*). They even have epitaphs that pay homage to their accomplishments!

NORTH OAK COLUMBARIUM

You will almost certainly have visited the North Oak columbarium more than once during your travels through Night City, and we'll wager that many of you might have spotted a few of the Easter eggs placed there by the developers (see previous page). What you might not have noticed, however, is that many in-game characters will also reside at the columbarium once specific conditions have been met. You will find all of these listed in the accompanying table.

Name	Appearance Conditions	Page
V	Trigger the "New Dawn Fades" Epilogue	457
Robert John "Silverhand" Linder	From the start	-
Alt Cunningham	From the start	-
Arthur Jenkins	Complete MJ-03 ("The Corpo-Rat")	115
Dum Dum	Dum Dum dies during either MJ-08 ("The Pickup") or SJ-38 ("Second Conflict")	120 or 220
Simon "Royce" Randal	Royce dies during either MJ-08 ("The Pickup") or SJ-38 ("Second Conflict")	120 or 220
Brick	You do not rescue Brick during MJ-08 ("The Pickup")	120
Rogue Amendiares	Rogue dies during MJ-28 ("Totalimmortal")	168
Crispin Weyland	Weyland dies during MJ-28 ("Totalimmortal")	168
Andrew Weyland	From the start	-
Evelyn Parker	Complete SJ-27 ("Both Sides, Now")	209
Maiko Maeda	Maiko dies during SJ-30 ("Pisces")	211
Hiromi Sato	Hiromi dies during SJ-30 ("Pisces")	211
Jackie Welles	Complete SJ-10 ("Heroes")	189
Finn "Fingers" Gerstatt	Complete MJ-13 ("The Space in Between")	138
Oswald "Woodman" Forrest	Woodman dies during MJ-13 ("The Space in Between") or SJ-28 ("Ex-Factor")	138 or 209
Lucius Rhyne	Complete MJ-10 ("The Heist")	128
Antonio Peralez	From the start	-
Caroline Jablonsky	From the start	-
Bill Jablonsky	Bill dies during SJ-22 ("Sinnerman")	203
Joshua Stephenson	Complete SJ-23 ("They Won't Go When I Go")	204
River Ward	River dies during SJ-20 ("The Hunt")	200
Randy Kutcher	If River dies during SJ-20 ("The Hunt") or you pick the wrong farm during that same mission	200
Dean Russell (Claire's husband)	From the start	-
Peter Sampson	Sampson dies during SJ-09 ("The Beast in Me")	188
Ofelia "Patricia" Sirawian	Patricia dies during SJ-38 ("Second Conflict")	220
Jeremiah Grayson	Grayson dies during SJ-35 ("Chippin' In")	216
Ruby Barrett	Ruby dies during SJ-35 ("Chippin' In")	216
Andrew	Unlocked during SJ-12 ("Happy Together")	191

Name	Appearance Conditions	Page
Ozob Bozo	Punch Ozob's nose when you fight him during SJ-01 ("Beat on the Brat"), or if he dies during SJ-16 ("Send in the Clowns")	181 or 194
Jessie Johnson	Jessie dies during SJ-04 ("Burning Desire")	184
Darrell Zhou	Darrell dies during SJ-47 ("A Day in the Life")	230
Kirk Sawyer	Complete SJ-67 ("Small Man, Big Mouth")	245
Frank Nostra	Frank dies during SJ-51 ("War Pigs")	234
Buck Arnold	Buck dies during SJ-01 ("Beat on the Brat")	181
The Rhino	Rhino dies during the "For My Son" gig	182
Leonard Swedenborg-Riviera	Choose to disable Swedenborg during SJ-59 ("Killing in the Name")	239
Geralt "Garry the Prophet" Winkler	Complete SJ-05 ("The Prophet's Song")	184
Aoi "Blue Moon" Tsuki	Blue Moon dies during SJ-62 ("Every Breath You Take")	242
Akai "Red Menace" Kyōi	Red Menace dies during SJ-62 ("Every Breath You Take")	242
Griselda "Green Cloud" Martinez	Complete SJ-62 ("Every Breath You Take") by arresting the correct target	242
Brendan	Complete SJ-17 ("Coin Operated Boy")	195
Vic Vega	Kill him during the "The Union Strikes Back" gig	283
Big Pete	Kill him during the "Big Pete's Got Big Problems" gig	288
Anna Hamill	Kill her during the "Woman of la Mancha" gig	265
Logan Garcia	Kill him during the "For My Son" gig	282
Joanne Koch	Kill her during the "Guinea Pigs" gig	299
Karubo Bairei	Kill him during the "Old Friends" gig	290
Rebeca Price	Kill her during the "Hot Merchandise" gig	296
Jae-hyun	Kill him during the "Small Man, Big Evil" gig	267
Taki "Furaido Chikin" Kenmochi	Kill him during the "Troublesome Neighbors" gig	264
Blake Croyle	Kill him during the "Shark in the Water" gig	265
Tucker Albach	Kill him during the "Eye For an Eye" gig	294
Jotaro Shobo	Kill him during the "Monster Hunt" gig	266
Beatrice "8ug8ear" Ellen Trieste	Fail to cool down her body before disconnecting her during the "Getting Warmer..." gig	277
Jose Luise	Kill him during the "On a Tight Leash" gig	295
Gustavo Orta	Kill him during the "Bring Me the Head of Gustavo Orta" gig	291
Jack Mausser	Kill him during the "An Inconvenient Killer" gig	298

QUEST-RELATED WEBSITE LISTINGS

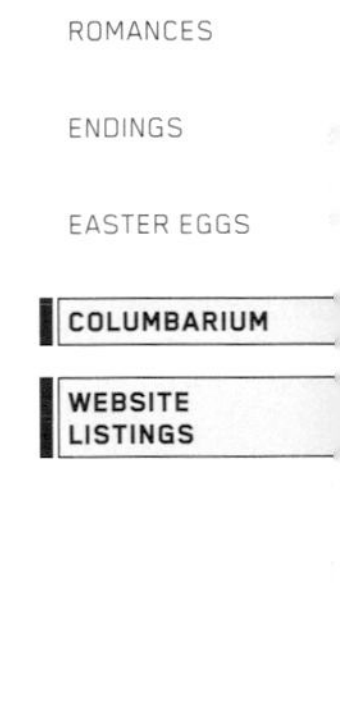

Night City's net is home to a large number of websites that you can visit from any computer. The following table lists all of the sites that are linked to jobs or gigs. Consulting them can offer additional background information on the assignments in question – and, as you will know by now, is sometimes required to proceed. If you've missed any of them, use the links provided here to visit the pages.

Website	Website Address	Related Quest(s)	Page
Drugs Are Bad	NETdir://ncity.drugsarebad.pub	SJ-20	201
Pleasures of NC	NETdir://ncity.pleasures.pub	MJ-13	138
Pleasures of NC (underground)	NETdir://forbiddenpleasures.web	MJ-13	138
The Ho-Oh	NETdir://ncity.hooh.pub	Gig: "Monster Hunt"	266
NC Inquirer	NETdir://ncinquirer.web	Gig: "Freedom of the Press"	274
Samurai	NETdir://samurai.web	MJ-11	132
NC Guide	NETdir://ncity.guide.pub	SJ-18	148
NCPD	NETdir://ncity.ncpd.law	SJ-18	148
Smuggler's Cache	NETdir://smugglerscache.web	SJ-32	214
The Shuttle Dock	NETdir://shuttledock.web	Gig: "Dirty Biz"	271
Holtt	NETdir://ncity.holtt.pub	Gig: "Error 404"	280
Wake Up, sheeple!	NETdir://timetowakeup.web	SJ-59	239
Holt's Campaign Site	NETdir://ncity.holt.pub	SJ-18, SJ-19	196, 198
Peralez's Campaign Site	NETdir://ncity.peralez.pub	SJ-18, SJ-19	196, 198
Konpeki Plaza	NETdir://konpekiplaza.corp	MJ-10	128
Fingers MD	NETdir://fingersmd.web	MJ-13	138
Revere Courier Service	NETdir://ncity.reverecourier.pub	Gig: "Many Ways to Skin a Cat"	272
Kendachi	NETdir://kendachi.corp	Gigs: "Race to the Top," "Breaking News"	284, 285
Cytech	NETdir://cytech.corp	Gig: "Severance Package"	286
Bryce Stone	NETdir://brycestone.corp	Gig: "Dirty Biz"	271
Denya Jinja Shrine	NETdir://ncity.shrine.pub	Gig: "A Shrine Defiled"	276
Center for Psychiatric Health	NETdir://ncity.behhealth.pub	Gig: "Cuckoo's Nest"	281
Dicky Twister	NETdir://ncity.dickytwister.pub	Gig: "Sr. Ladrillo's Private Collection"	292
Night City Landfill	NETdir://ncity.junkyard.pub	Gig: "Sparring Partner"	289

NIGHT CITY UNCENSORED

Within minutes of encountering the streets of Night City, you become aware of the ad campaigns and company and product logos that surround you: contemporary brands for fast food, soft drinks, music bands, clubs, braindance recordings, with messaging in all forms, from a fly-poster on a random bar door to the holographic Towers of Light that dominate the Night City skyline.

This section offers a visual tour of Night City's unrestrained hospitality and leisure industries through a selection of images from poster and TV campaigns, along with associated branding. You may already have realized that by the year 2077, values and customs have changed significantly. Many former taboos, such as gratuitous sex and objectification, have become established norms through the proliferation of 21st-century consumerism.

Everything in Night City is for sale, and you can seemingly cut a deal on anything with anyone. Body parts can be replaced; synthetic food is lab mass-produced; fantasies can be bought and climaxes triggered in all kinds of ways; memories can be recorded and sold to others. Anything and everything is available – assuming your pockets are deep enough.

The gallery that unfolds over the following pages is a vertical slice of this advertising culture, of what makes Night City both fascinating and shocking, and it will give you a taste of how extreme the world of Cyberpunk 2077 can be – a world where the quest for satisfaction knows virtually no limits. Enjoy the gallery!

BRAINDANCES

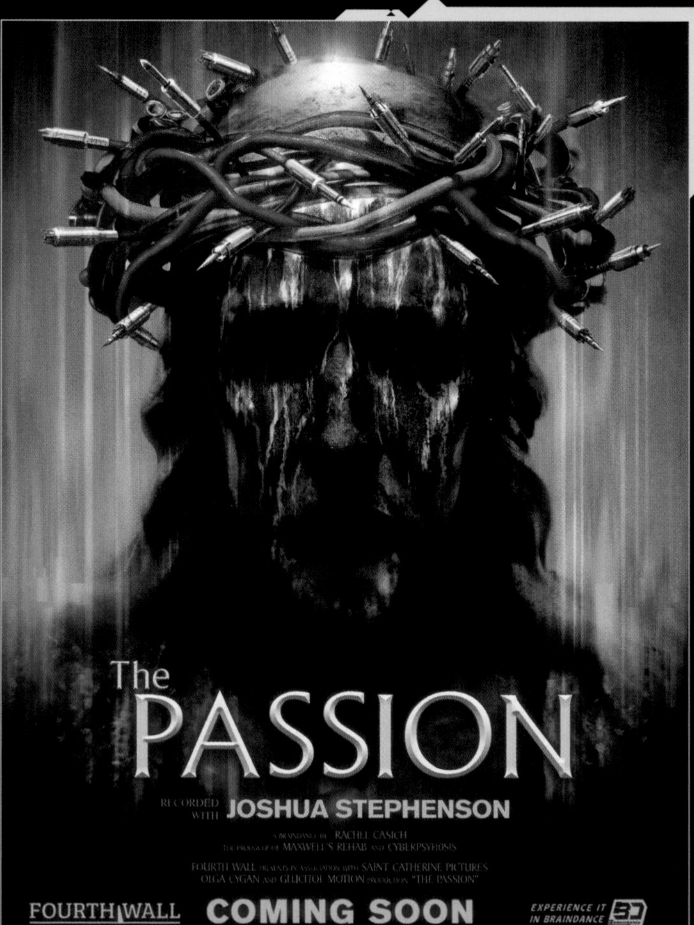

The Passion – You are privy to the creative process behind this braindance through two side jobs (see pages 203 and 204) where V plays an active part in the process, either positive, disruptive or, alternatively, walks away at any time.

Fourth Wall, the studio behind this braindance, began development when market research identified an audience curious to experience what Jesus might have felt during his final hours. A major hurdle was identified early in pre-production: to ensure the highest fidelity possible, the "actor" playing the role would need to die by crucifixion.

Joshua was Fourth Wall's solution: a convict sentenced to death and converted to Christianity. Joshua was happy to agree, believing this to be a sign from God – redemption through contrition and donating his fee to the families of his victims.

In a modern miracle of an *entirely* different tenor to anything you might read in a holy book, Fourth Wall's investment in expert legal advice (and significant bribes) persuaded the Night City authorities to sanction Joshua's highly unorthodox execution.

3 Mouths 1 Desire – A pornographic braindance offering two related yet distinct alternatives: one where the user is gratified by three mouths, and a second in which they, as the owner of the mouths, enact a rather more selfless version of the same scenario.

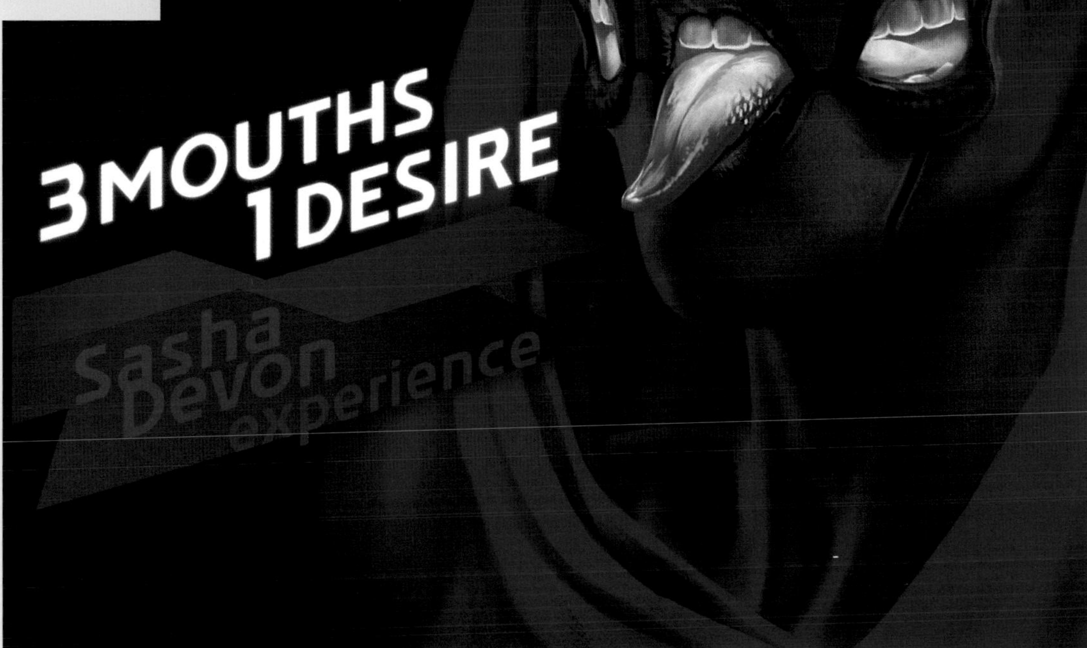

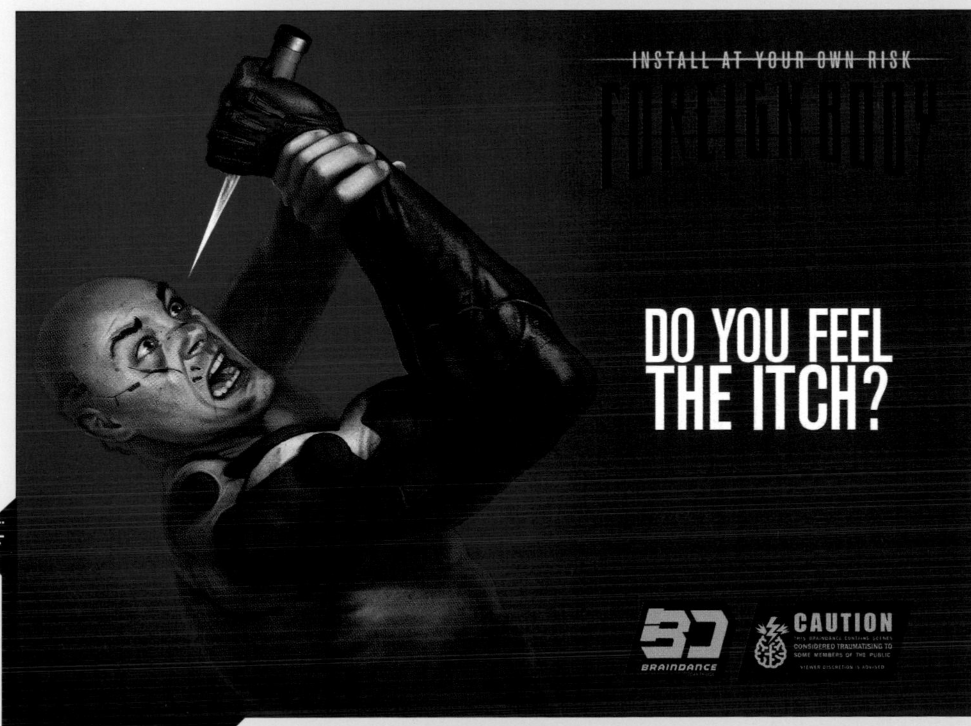

Foreign Body – In this braindance thriller, a cyberware arm attacks its host. The experience plays upon a topical fear of errant implants.

Wet Dream – A braindance in which you either partake in the dream or play a more passive role as the dreamer.

Bottoms Up – An erotic braindance with a title that leaves little room for interpretation. Voted Best Braindance at the 2077 Kampala Porn Festival.

UNLIMITED STREAMING, ACTION
LUSTY ROSE

Blast Dance – A streaming solution offering subscribers unlimited access to its catalogue of braindances.

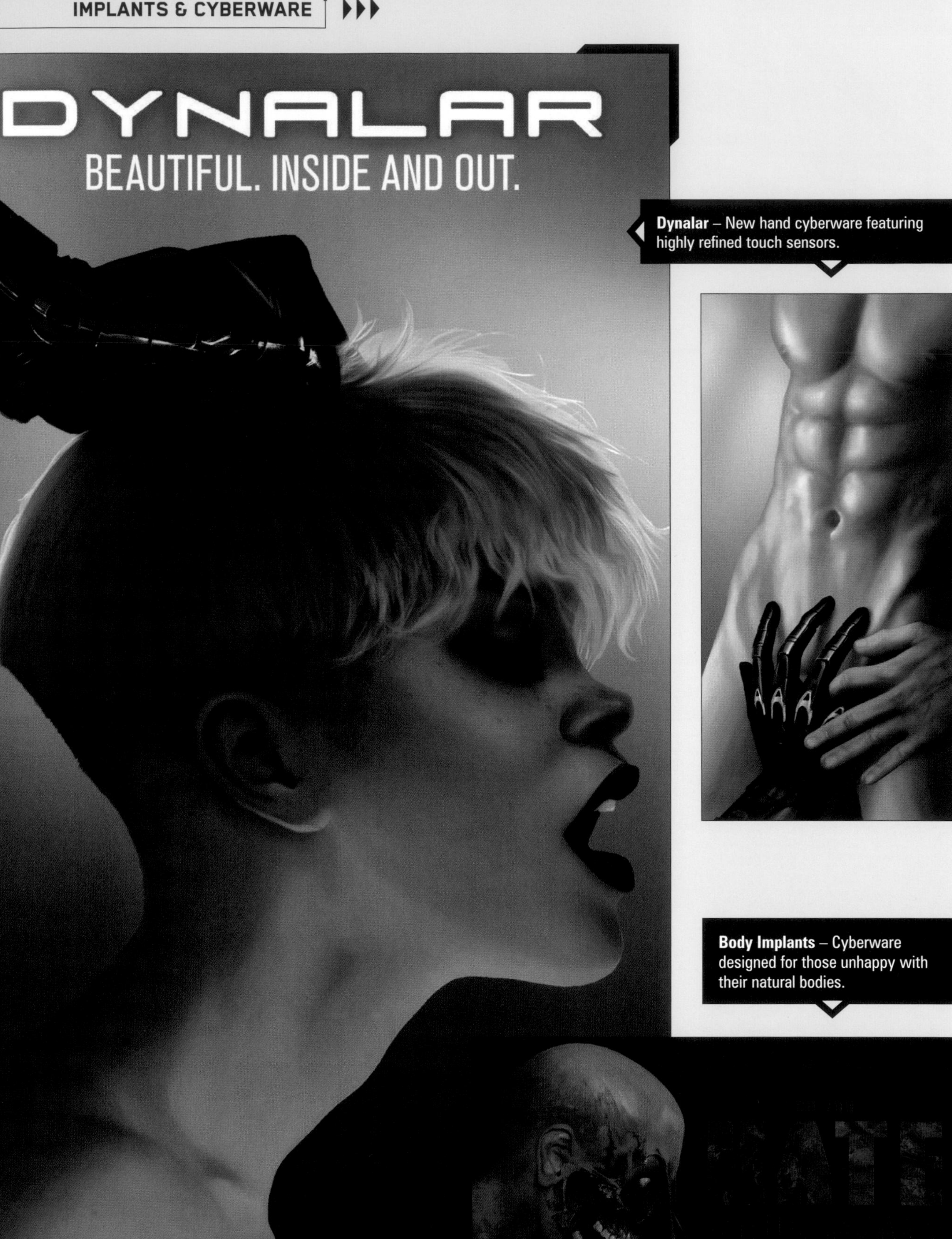

Dynalar – New hand cyberware featuring highly refined touch sensors.

Body Implants – Cyberware designed for those unhappy with their natural bodies.

"It happens
in a blink of an eye."

BEN "LIGHTNING" MICHURIN
VETERAN FIGHTER PILOT

Kiroshi Opticals – Kiroshi have signed a sponsorship deal with the Us Cracks girl band to use all three band members in their advertising campaigns.

"Look where eyes
can't see."

SU-WEI DAVENPORT
EXPLORER, SPELEOLOGIST

KIROSHI
OPTICALS

MoorE Technologies – Many people replace some choice organs or body parts with cyberware, usually to gain a competitive edge in their professional field. Only the wealthiest can afford full-body conversions, whereby most of the body is replaced with superior manufactured parts.

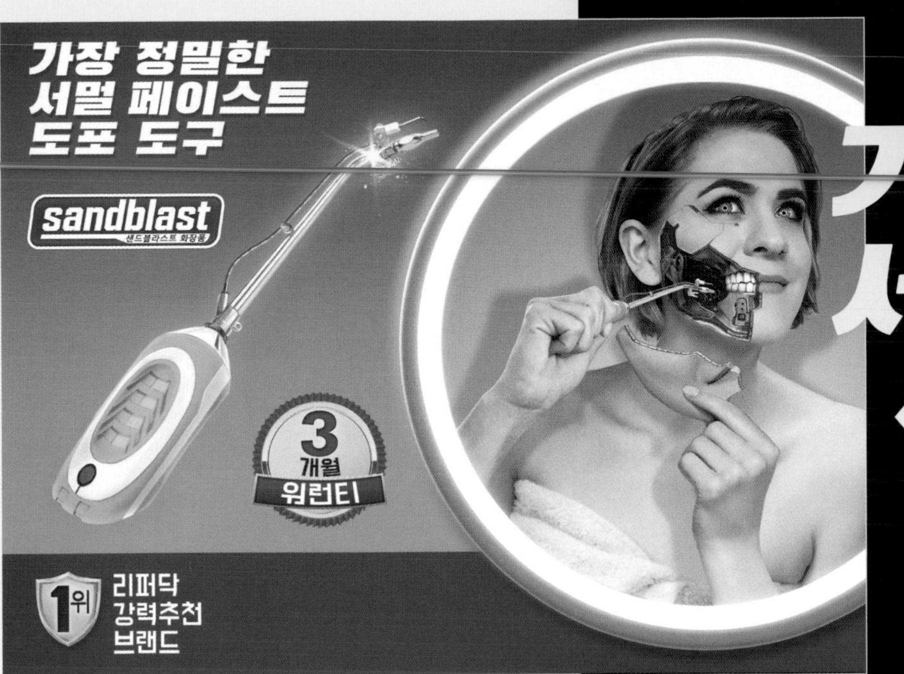

Sandblast – Best known for its toothpaste and cosmetics brands, Sandblast recently launched a new range: devices enabling the cleansing and maintenance of cyberware.

Midnight Lady Accessories – A cyberware provider specializing in breast implants suitable for almost every occasion.

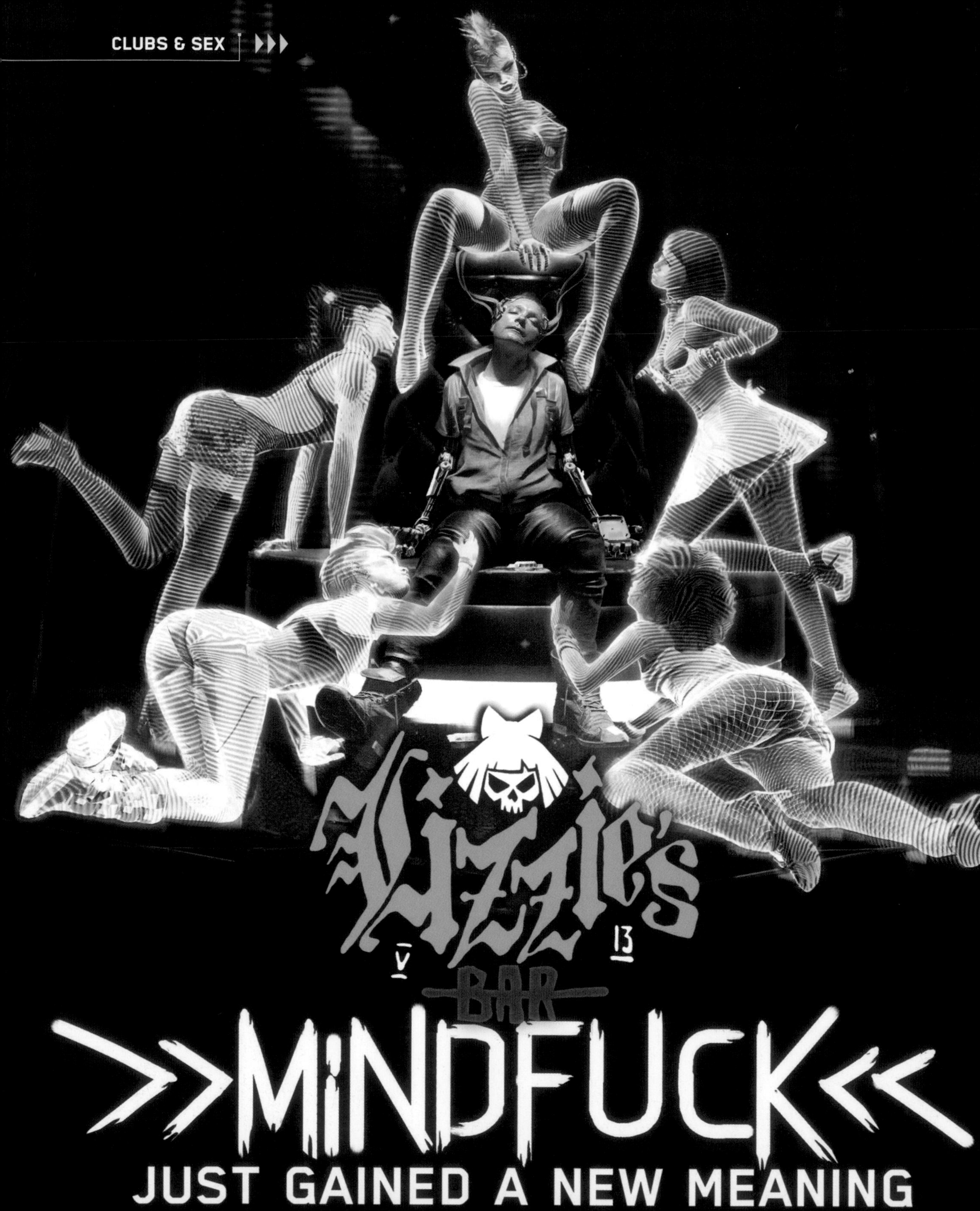

Kennedy and Sutter
Watson, Night City

Lizzie's – This Mox-owned braindance club frequently hosts regulars Judy Alvarez and Evelyn Parker. You visit here during the prologue while preparing for the Konpeki Plaza heist.

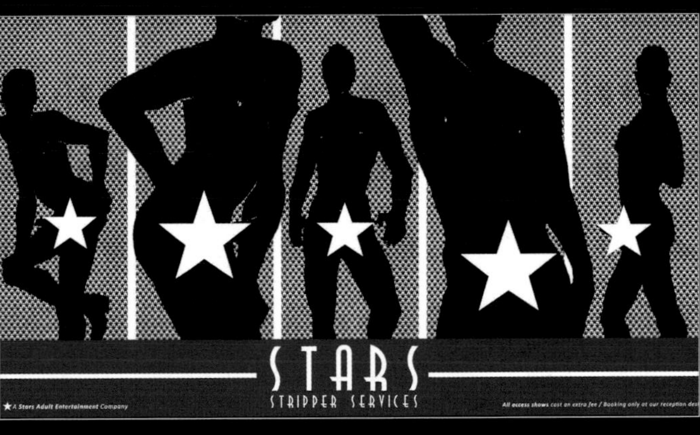

Jig Jig Street – A maze of alleyways teeming with outlets selling joytoys, aphrodisiacs, and all manner of specialist items. Jig Jig Street is also Night City's most popular red-light district, and home to a wide variety of clubs.

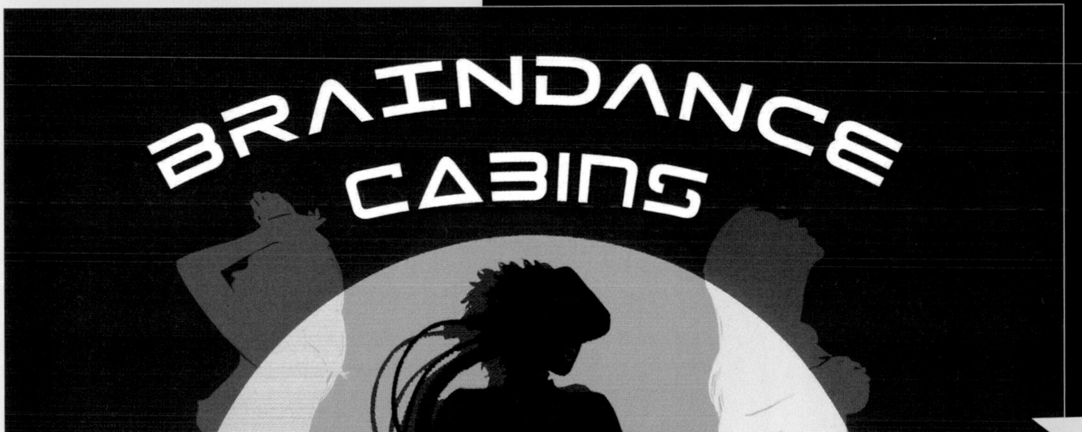

BRAINDANCE
CABINS
100%
INTIMATE
DISCLAIMER: ANY SIDE-EFFECTS YOU TAKE UPON THE USES OF THIS SERVICE IS STRICTLY AT YOUR OWN RISK

Strip clubs – Night City's diversity and laidback approach to the sex industry is reflected in its many strip clubs, with establishments catering to every conceivable taste.

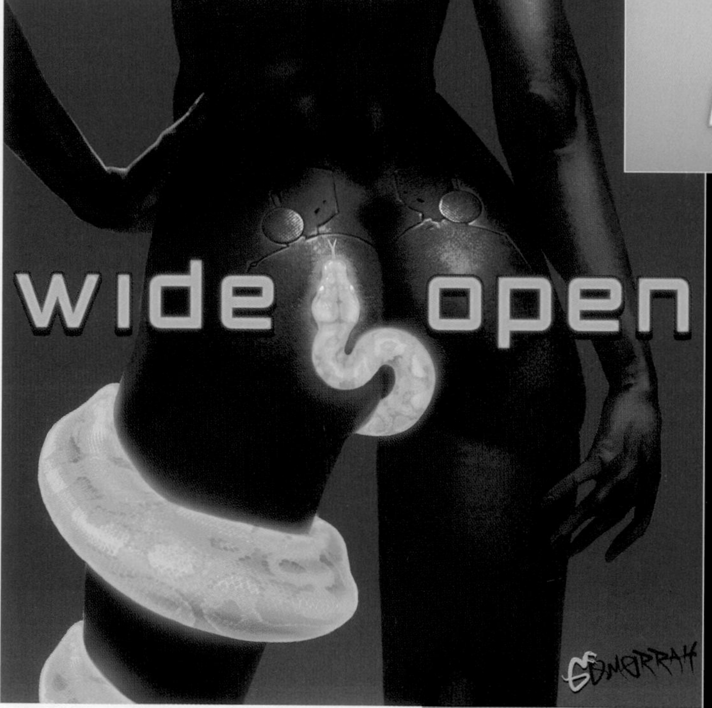

Mr. Stud

All night. **Every Night.**

UPGRADE NOW:

V3.0 FREE!

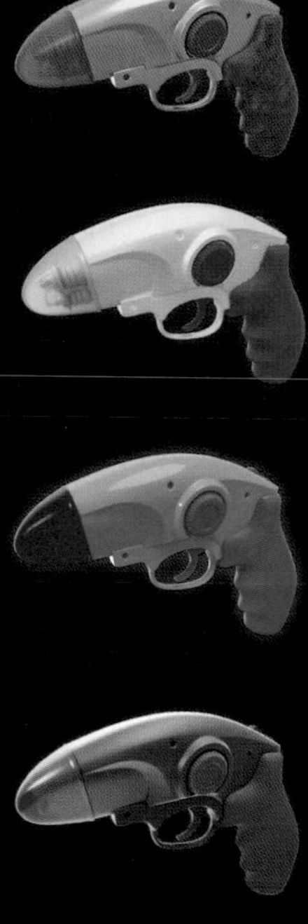

Joytoys – Self-stimulation is no taboo in the Cyberpunk 2077 world. There are countless companies that specialize in the production and distribution of devices and accessories designed to facilitate and intensify every imaginable form of personal pleasure.

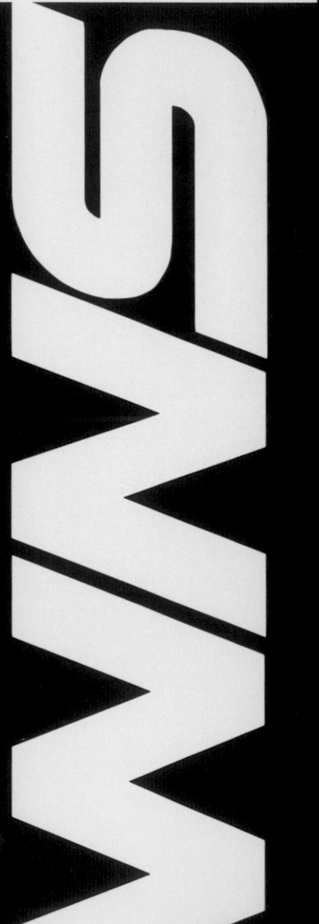

Electronic Murderer: A Feast for the Eyes – In this installment of the celebrated Electronic Murder franchise, a young girl falls victim to a sinister netrunner. He hacks her old eye implants and forces her to witness vile murders that only she can see. Unable to convince others that these horrific crimes have in fact taken place, the protagonist gradually loses her mind.

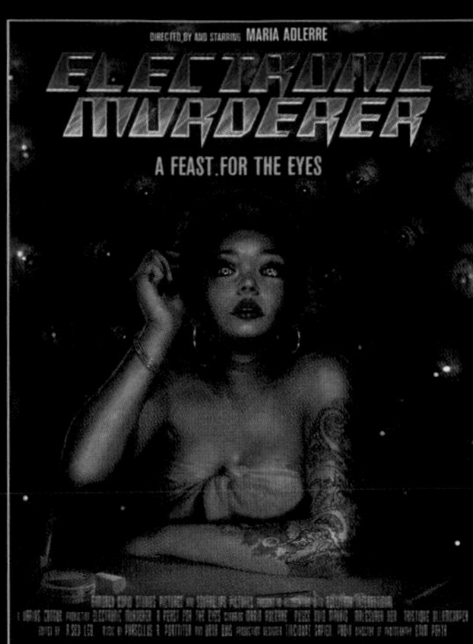

Brides of Satan – A highly-acclaimed movie celebrated for its fusion of the horror and hardcore pornography genres. The scene is a portal to hell within a convent run by compliant nuns.

Brides of Satan won many awards for its faithful special effects.

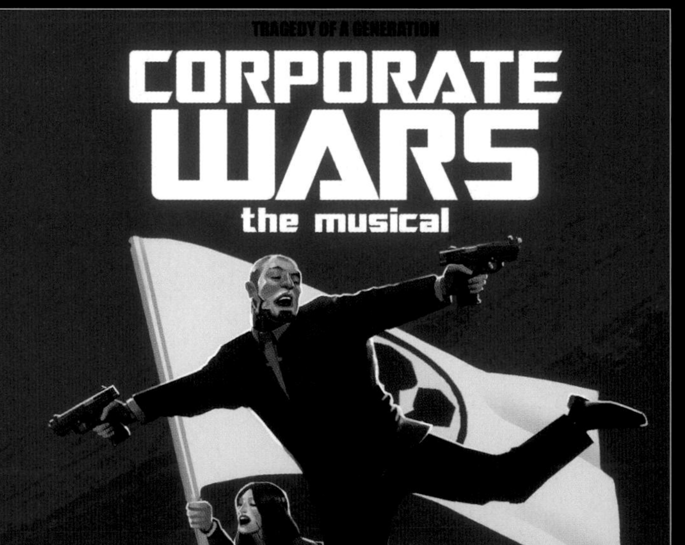

Fixer – This film tells the story of a young boy taken under the wing of a professional fixer, and it follows his journey as he learns the tricks of the trade.

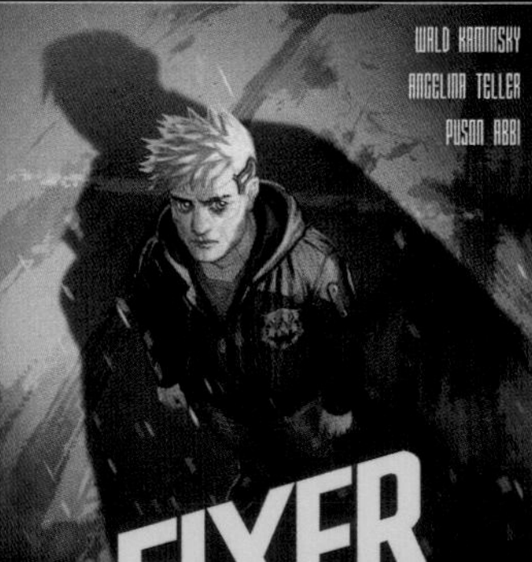

In Vitro Homicide – This action movie explores the notion of immortality by portraying a process of perpetual cloning.

Switchblade 2 – The sequel to a hugely successful action movie starring a powerful female protagonist. Released almost a decade later, the follow-up is widely regarded as a major disappointment having failed to recapture what had made the original such a success.

Watson Whore – This reality TV show explores the life of a man desperate for attention, and his readiness to go to any lengths to achieve fame and fortune. The show's slogan is: "He'll do anything to scratch every itch…"

From Samurai to Us Cracks and Kerry Eurodyne to the Cartesian Duelists, and from small radios to brand-new boomboxes, music is *everywhere* in Night City.

Us Cracks – アス・クラックス (Us Cracks) is a popular Japanese girl band who pack major arenas with their screaming fans – and now they've set their sights on America. The band was formed when the media conglomerate MSM put out a global call for three candidates with the perfect blend of charisma, talent, and stage presence in order to compete against the increasingly more successful AIs making music. It just so happens that the three winners were young, American-born Japanese girls. Us Cracks are trendsetters in the Lazrpop genre, and are famous for their bombastic performances and charming, kawaii interactions with fans.

MEET THE BAND!

パープルフォース (Purple Force): Sensible and decisive – a natural-born leader. Her passions include expensive tea and meditation. She's always the peacekeeper when the other girls get into a fight. After all, purple is a mix between red and blue! Favorite color: purple. Blood type: O. What does she like most about America? Hamburgers! They're delish! (￣ω￣)

ブルームーン (Blue Moon): The poet of the band – always lost in thought. And the most adorable of the three! In her free time she writes poems and munches on dorayaki. Favorite color: blue. Blood type: A. What does she like most about America? Feeders! They're super-duper kawaii! (^___^)

DISCOGRAPHY

- Chainsaw Lollipop – 2074
- メタル・バニ (Metaru Bani) – 2075
- 私のユニコーン (Watashi no Yunikon) – 2075
- MissU1790 – 2076
- ポンポン・シット (Ponpon Shit) – 2077

レッドメネース (Red Menace): A combative girl with fire flowing through her veins! She collects katanas and computer games. It's best not to get in her way unless you want your ass kicked! Favorite color: red. Blood type: B. What does she like most about America? Rockerboys! Duh! Total studs! (¬‿¬)

妄想 アイドル

EURODYNE

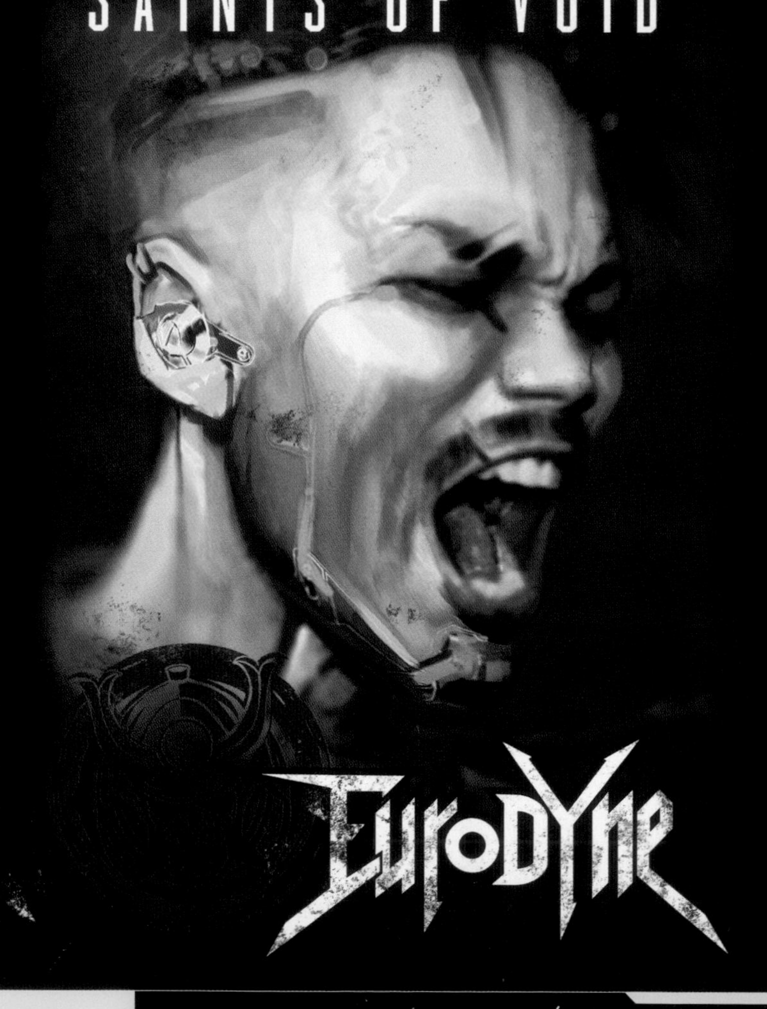

Kerry Eurodyne – Rockerboy. Star. Charismatic guitarist and vocalist. A legend. Kerry Eurodyne is this era's undisputed king of REAL rock. Adored by his fans, praised by his critics, respected by his rivals. For years he's been riding a wave of popularity, resulting in instantly sold-out concerts and record-breaking plays of his songs.

His career started in the underground punk band Samurai, until, he says, "One day I just decided to grow up," beginning his journey to true fame. Kerry went solo. The rest is history, filled with explosive sounds, unforgettable lyrics, Richter-scale-breaking stadium concerts, and countless hits.

Kerry Eurodyne's career soared under the wings of MSM. From the moment he signed, thus began the Golden Age of Kerry Eurodyne – month after month of topping the charts with hit singles like "Holdin' On" or "Scream and Whisper," perfectly choreographed, spectacular concert tours (how could anyone forget the "chrome" zeppelins in Memphis?!) and unprecedented artistic heights reached. The rockerboy lives in his beloved Night City and is currently working on his latest album, brought to you soon by MSM.

From his debut album, "False Terrorist" to the mystical "Aether," the hit "Spiral Distortion" and the surprisingly conceptual "Persuasion of the Undecided," all the way to the controversial "Second Conflict" – Kerry Eurodyne's music is a masterpiece of rock, with uncompromising lyrics, sounds, and ideas that bring everyone together, no matter their ideological or spiritual creed – a one-size-fits-all.

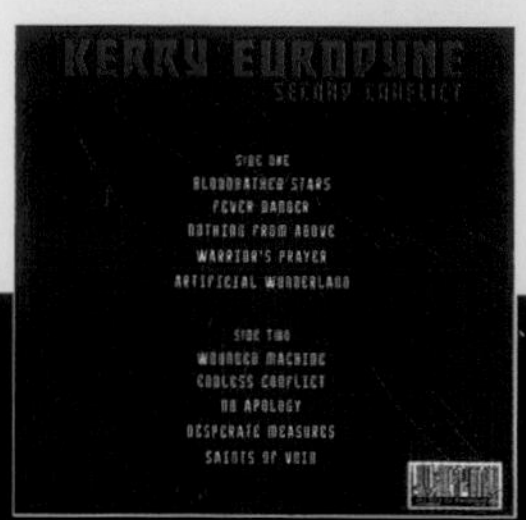

JUNE
15TH
22:00
IRVING
PLAZA

SECOND CONFLICT

EURODYNE

CRITIC REVIEWS

Kerry Eurodyne is one of the last crazy prophets of rock. His songs are savage, his lyrics provocative. In an era where everything has become a copy of a copy of a copy, Eurodyne remains one-of-a-kind.

Ted Hunst

This isn't music for teeny-boppers. Eurodyne makes music for people whose veins flow with real rock 'n' roll.

Moira S. Ritz

"Persuasion of the Undecided" is a masterpiece. Period. Every time I listen to that album, I uncover new layers of meaning. It could even be the pinnacle of Kerry Eurodyne's artistic achievement. It's a story – painted in brutal brushstrokes and chrome noise – of a country that has faded out of existence before our own eyes. It's about freedom, whose taste evaporates from our lips like a distant memory. It's about a man who gives up his old life to pursue his ideals, only to discover they were all lies.

Antimusic Magazine

An album about hopelessness? A lullaby for those on the verge of suicide? Or maybe a subtle joke about a rockerboy too edgy for his time? The problem with a clear-cut interpretation of "Aether" is paradoxically also the record's greatest strength – until now, fans on the Net have been debating what kind of story this album is telling. An artist couldn't dream of anything more. Hats off, Eurodyne, you'll always be our Prince of the Aether.

Hannah Icona

"Second Conflict" is clearly inspired by events from the rockerboy's life, like every record ever made. But here the references to the corporate wars and the brief, tumultuous friendship with Johnny Silverhand is Eurodyne at his most confessional – his nightmares and failed dreams laid bare for all of us. Hit play and indulge yourself in a cathartic, macabre listening experience of a lifetime.

Duane Foss

SAMURAI

Johnny Silverhand & Samurai – When Silverhand formed Samurai, he did so as a fully fledged artist. He knew what he wanted, and as the group's charismatic leader, he knew how to impose his vision on the rest of the band. The roles in the group were clearly divided.

Johnny and Kerry Eurodyne were the inspired provocateurs, the continually conflicted soul of the band.

Meanwhile, Henry (bass) lived in his own world, even in those rare instances when he wasn't high out of his mind. He may never have known how good he was. Rumor had it Silverhand was sleeping with Henry to keep him in the band. Silverhand was also rumored to be sleeping with Kerry to boost the latter's morale. The truth is, Johnny was sleeping with everyone, though his heart wasn't always in it. Soon after Samurai's breakup, Henry suffered a literal shock in an accident, after which he began behaving even more strangely than usual. And then, almost as if he'd been ready and waiting to jump at the chance, he hit rock bottom.

Nancy (keyboards) was the sole reasonable, normal person in the group – she came to a gig, played to the best of her ability, then wen home. Only thing was, her toxic, aggressive husband was at home, too. He ended up tightening his grip on her so much that she lef the band. Soon after, he tried to turn the screv some more, but something in Nancy snapped She finally remembered her murky gang past, and her husband had more than enough to think about as he fell eighty floors. After seven months spent in jail, Nancy returned to Samurai, but it wasn't the same. In the end, she left again, this time for good, and started a new media career as Bes Isis for N54 News.

Denny, drummer and high-functioning neurotic plagued by thousands of real and imagined obsessions, was only truly herself on stage. Off stage, she spent most of her time trying to prove to herself she wasn't as mad as everybody seemed to think. That's likely why she took up with Henry – compared to him, Denny was normal indeed.

If it hadn't been for Silverhand's legendary hatred of managers, Samurai could have achieved much greater success. Instead, they always remained a punk alternative, icons of cool and uncompromising rebellion. One day, you can't get into one of their gigs; the next you could walk right by a whacked-out Silverhand throwing up into the river. And that's what Johnny would call true freedom, before barfing on your shoes. Silverhand's death was what truly launched Samurai into the realm of legend – and out of reality.

Cyberpunk 2077
SAMURAI
CHIPPIN' IN
SAMURAI
BLISTERING LOVE
WE'RE ALL
MAY 15TH
PARIS
BATACL
JUNE 10TH
LONDON
KOKO
JULY 3RD
BERLIN
CASSIOPEIA
AUG 15TH
CRACOW
ALCHEMIA
PUPPETS
SI ER
HAND
IN THIS WORLD

LIZZY WIZZY

"We are who we pretend to be. I've pretended to be everything – that's why I've found the truth." – **Lizzy Wizzy** is an artist par excellence. Her work includes movie appearances, award-winning albums and concerts, as well as (for lack of a better term) conceptual or performance art. Her latest artistic obsession features the medium of braindance. In recent interviews Lizzy has brought up questions about the border between documentary and reality, and how the latter is shaped.

BIOGRAPHY

The turning point in Lizzy's career came in 2071, when she unveiled herself in her true cybemodified form – an erotic re-imagining of Snow White. At the end of her concert, Lizzy ate a synthetic apple laced with specially prepared poison that induced cardiac arrest. For a full minute, the LED screens showed a close-up of the flat line on her electrocardiogram while her body lay motionless on the stage. The concert was put on hold for five and a half hours while a team of ripperdocs swapped out her biological organs for the latest generation of MoorE Technologies implants.

After being revived, Lizzy sang "Re-start, Re-heart, Repeat," which sat at the top of the world charts for the next full year. "I always felt like my mission was to cross the ultimate frontier," she said later in an interview on N54 News, "That frontier is death."

Lizzy's anarcho-terrorist "performances" are inspired by the artist's frequent stylistic transformations. She had been fond of giving away used clothes to friends before simply leaving them out on the street for people. She wanted to do the same with implants, though it turned out that top-tier cyberware was linked to its user and couldn't simply be "given away."

Lizzy Wizzy is best known for waging war against implant homogenization by mounting an armed assault against a BioDyne Systems factory, during which Lizzy and a group of mercenaries took control of the building and stole approximately 1,200 different implants that were then given out during an impromptu concert. The heist was broadcast live – an insurance for Lizzy. She knew no corporate soldier or police officer would dare to kill or harm her on live TV.

In the years following, the media argued that the heist was arranged beforehand with BioDyne and that Lizzy paid for the implants and the renovation of the factory. That theory is seemingly supported by the fact that BioDyne never pressed charges against Lizzy Wizzy. Lizzy still denies these allegations, claiming that Biodyne co-opted her heist as free advertising.

Cartesian Duelists – Acclaimed rockerboy Slavoj McAllister, lead singer and guitarist of the Cartesian Duelists band, has ruffled feathers yet again following his most recent performance at nightclub Totentanz. While a rock concert brawl is no big news in itself, several unofficial sources allege it was McAllister who instigated the violent outbreak after hurling a tear gas canister at paparazzi in the crowd.

Before the booze-fueled melee got heated, the Cartesian Duelists premiered new songs "Cybernetic Soul," "Mind Is Freedom," and "Cognito Ergo Sum," which, as usual, have critics divided. Lyrically, the new singles touch on issues such as the internal struggle of body and mind, the limitations of our senses, and the search for absolute truths. Some critics consider the new material pseudointellectual drivel – others praise the band's fresh, innovative spin on the genre.

Beyond the brawl, even McAllister's headlines are making headlines. When asked in an interview with N54 News what the cryptic title of the track "Cogito Ergo Sum" meant, the rockerboy replied he "Ain't revved by questions from gonkbrained frauds... What are you?"

Despite (or perhaps thanks to?) the numerous controversies ever swirling around the Cartesian Duelists frontman, his popularity continues to swell. The band's new album is slated for release soon, and if you believe the chatter on the Net, it will be entitled "War of Truths."

Most of the food consumed in Night City is synthetic and produced in factories by corporations that compete in on-going product launches; it's the *brand* that really matters, not the contents of the packaging. Fully synthetic and entirely non-organic foods have become a compelling option for Night City consumers.

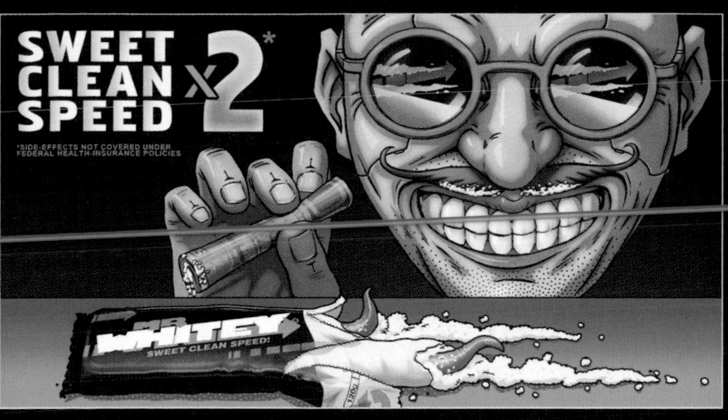

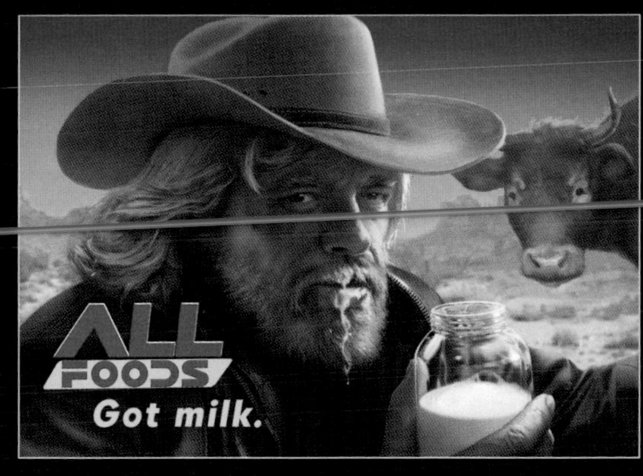

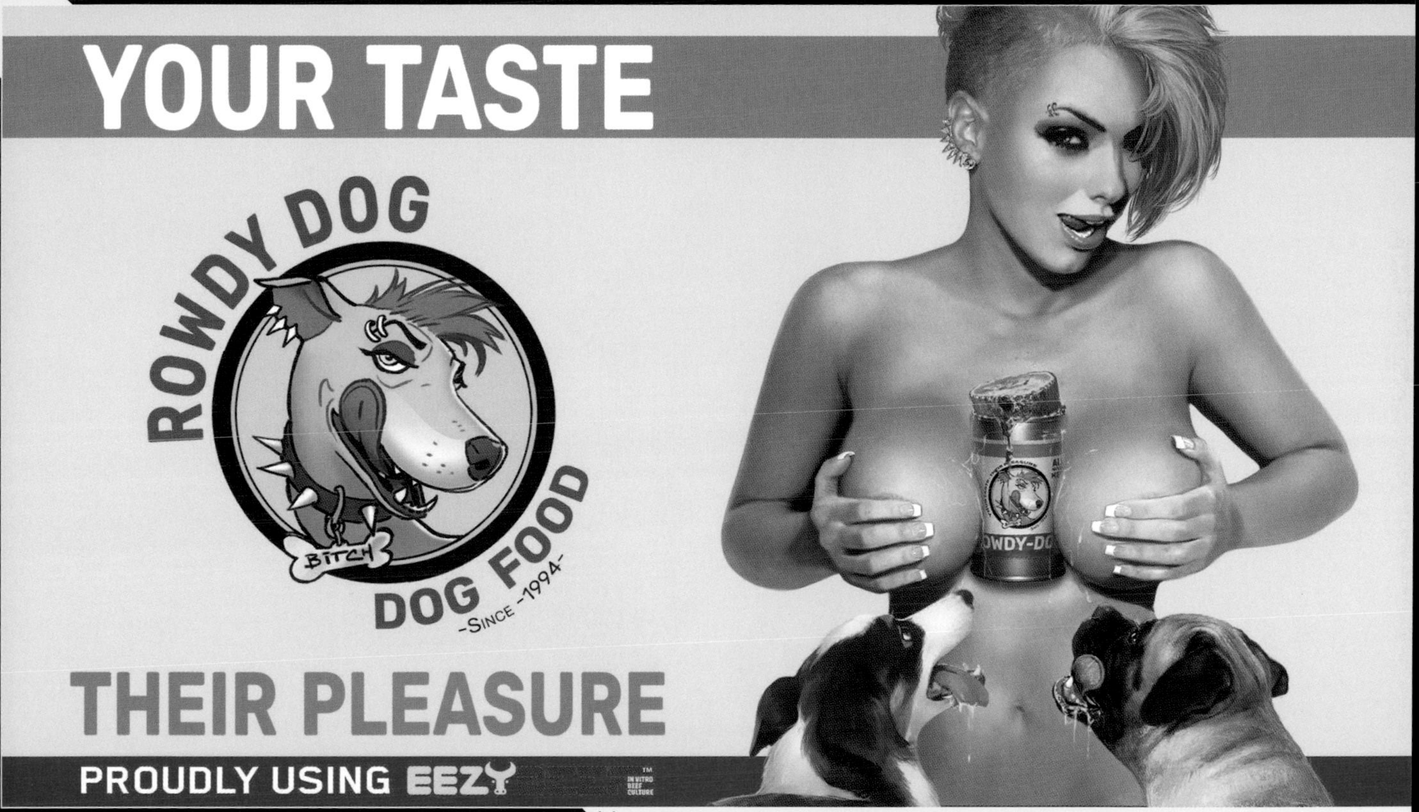

YOUR TASTE

ROWDY DOG

BITCH

DOG FOOD

-SINCE -1994-

THEIR PLEASURE

PROUDLY USING EEZY™ IN VITRO BEEF CULTURE

ALL FOODS

MIX IT UP

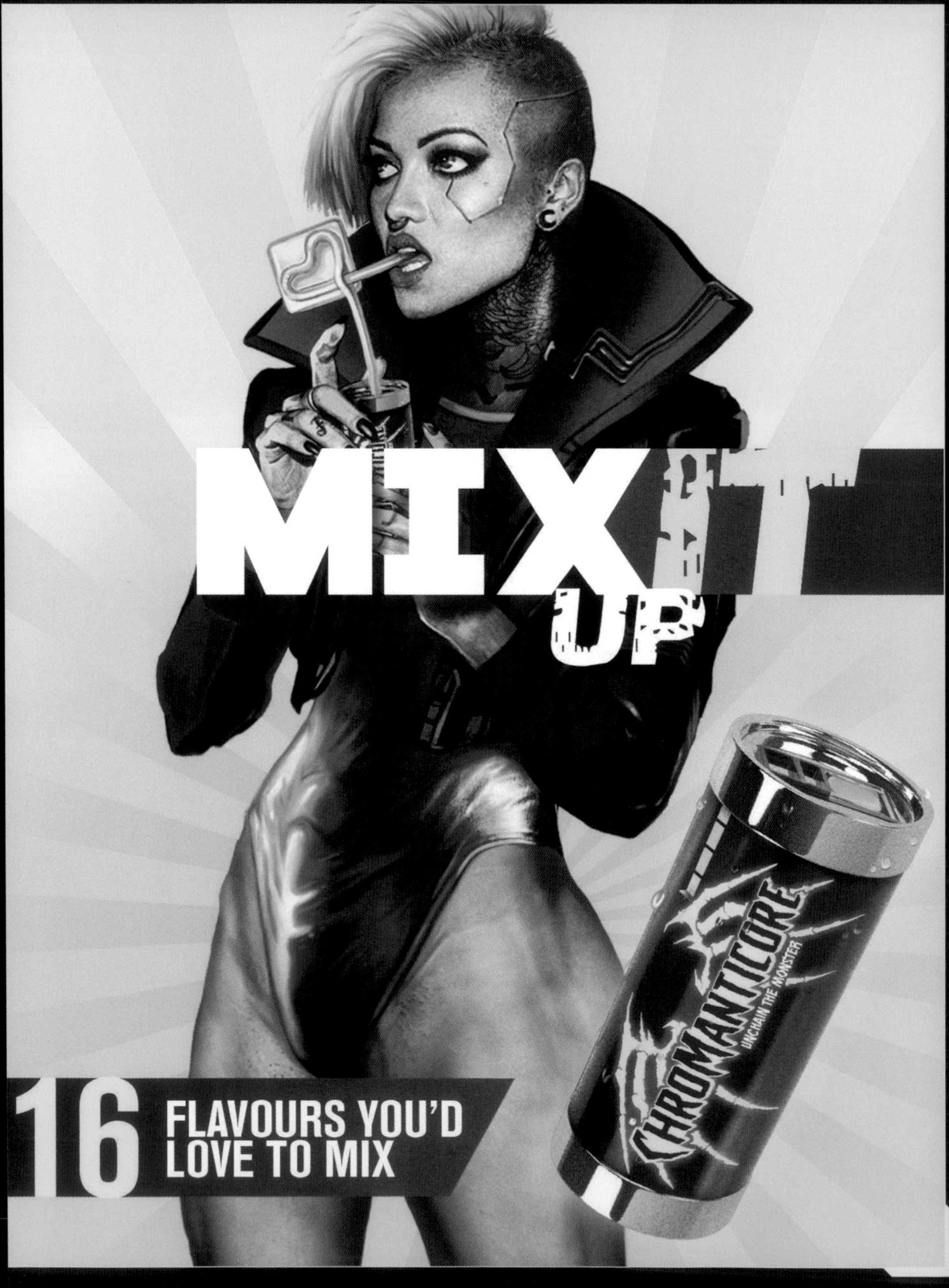

CHROMANTICORE
UNCHAIN THE MONSTER

16 FLAVOURS YOU'D LOVE TO MIX

ALL FOODS
Vinegar+Chilli
Wasabi+Ginger
OMNIFLAVE™
Salsa+Agave
SPECIAL EDITION

Set Sail
For Flavor!
ONLY 1E$
CALIENTE

BROSEPH
BREWING CO.
est.2042
Boston, Massachusetts
HEALTH WARNING
Drinking alcohol during pregnancy may adversely affect the development of your fetus.

ALL FOODS
COMPREHENSIVE
FEEDING SERVICE
FOR YOUR FAMILY

CHROMANTICORE

FEEL FREE
CIRRUS COLA

CIRRUS COLA
FEEL FREE

JINGUJI'S NEW COLLECTION

This upcoming spring, don't forget to aim higher with the Jinguji Spring-Summer 2077 Collection. Whether you value essence over flair, flair over essence, or both in harmonious balance, Jinguji will guide you on the path to find yourself.

- **Graphite Gem:** The immortal aesthetic of neomilitaristic chic. This graphite-black, knee-length pencil dress with asymmetrical cuts brings out the steely edge of a born leader, while simultaneously accenting the subtle elegance of your subdermal enhancements. It pairs effortlessly with the Arasaka JKE-X2 Kenshin pistol.

- **Military Vintage:** Masculine distinction with an accent of vintage couture. This short, ivory blazer featuring an oblique front cut will set you apart from the crowd at both corporate HQ and the most exclusive yacht galas. The delicate geometric design and distinguished epaulets craft a bold mix of modernity and tradition.

- **Paradise Red:** Sometimes nature knows best. Turn heads this spring with a unisex, studded-leather jacket fashioned from pure organic sources. Embrace the perfection of nature's greatest showstoppers – birds of paradise. Each feather lining the collar has been hand-selected from specimens cultivated and grown for their unmatched beauty.

- **Golden Python:** For those who want to coil around the city and squeeze out every last drop. These custom-tailored pants crafted from in-vitro ball python skins are ideal for an evening promenade around an art or dining district. These reflective scales will glimmer in the envious eyes following you all over town.

- **Harmony Forest:** Tunic? Dress? Frock? However you wish to catalog your wardrobe, this unisex piece will find its place in your 2077 rotation. The wavy patterning evokes the rustic grains of fired wood – sure to add that additional personal touch to your spring garden strolls. True to its raw, agrestal essence, the fabrics used contain no synthetic additives.

OK, so what do you need?

EJI

REAL MAN'S SMELL
kh
KT HENRY

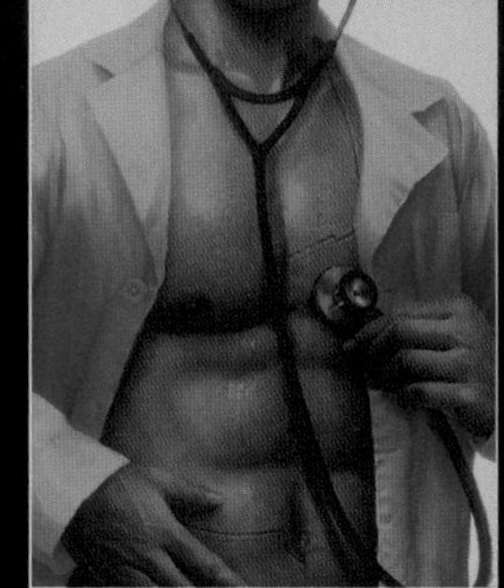

Giovanni Brizzi
FABBRICAZIONE DI ALTA OROLOGERIA
AVVIATA MMXXIV VENEZIA

NEW EMPIRE
FOCUS ON WINNING THIS FALL

TAMPONIZER
Feel confident when you need it the most
TESTED ON ANIMALS

ZEIG DICH

sudo

AVANTE
SI PARLA MODA
NEW LOOK / GOLDEN ROME

Corporations in 2077 are global financial conglomerates at the heart of practically every aspect of life. They control the factories that produce the goods that Night citizens need and consume daily: energy, food, furniture, implants, vehicles, you name it.

The most powerful – from Arasaka to Militech and Kang Tao – are essentially at war with their competitors. It therefore comes as no surprise that the manufacturing of firearms is a principal business for these multinationals. Almost every weapon in Night City is corporation-issued. In a world as violent as Cyberpunk 2077, rivalry between corporations permeates every aspect of their activities, and this is also reflected in their advertising.

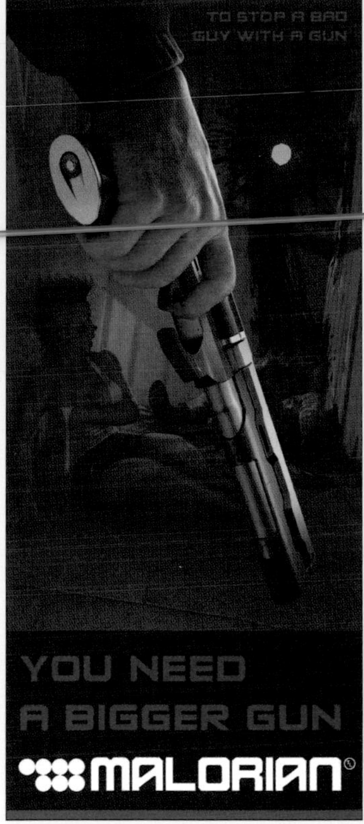

COMBAT CABS 

A common sight in Night City, combat cabs are heavily armed vehicles that transport Night City citizens to their destination whilst ensuring protection from a variety of attacks. These are primarily used by wealthier people travelling to unsafe districts.

V and Jackie take a Delamain combat cab during the prologue's Konpeki Plaza heist, when they get to test the vehicle's infamous combat mode during their escape.

If you are looking for specific information, this alphabetical listing is just what you need.
To avoid potential spoilers, note that critical page references are written in **red**.

The Complete Official Guide to Cyberpunk 2077 is a Piggyback Interactive Limited production.

PIGGYBACK

Publishers: Louie Beatty, Vincent Pargney
Project Leads: Simone Dorn, Matthias Loges, Carsten Ostermann
Editorial Director: Mathieu Daujam
Editor: James Price
Finance Director: Anskje Pargney
Logistics: Angela Kosik
Sales & Marketing: Debra Kempker
Art Directors: Jeanette Killmann & Martin C. Schneider (Glorienschein)
Designers: Christian Runkel
IT and Filehandling: Markus Bösebeck

ENGLISH VERSION

Sub-Editing: Maura Sutton

FRENCH VERSION

Editors: Claude-Olivier Eliçabe, Mathieu Daujam

GERMAN VERSION

Editor: Klaus-Dieter Hartwig
Sub-Editing: Barbara Bode

ITALIAN VERSION

Localization Managers: Emanuele Scichilone, Marco Auletta (Keywords Studios Italy)
Translation and Review: Filippo Facchetti, Luca Priami

POLISH VERSION

Localization Manager: Piotr Januszka (QLOC S.A.)
Translation and Review: Dominika Chodkowska-Czerwińska, Marcin Kosakowski, Aleksandra Lazić, Paweł Oleszczuk, Mateusz Sajna (QLOC S.A.)

SPANISH VERSION

Localization Managers: Emanuele Scichilone, Jesús J. Lloret, Miguel Cachafeiro Iglesias (Keywords Studios Spain)
Linguists: José M. Gallardo, Beatriz Tirado, Juan Ramón Acedo, Marco Fernández

Preprint Ulrich Banse, Tino Bordusa, Niels Dreppenstedt, Astrid Feyerabend, Lea Hartgen, Nicole Hannowsky, Ilse Hüttner, Margarita de Lemos, Anke Mattke, Ralf Müller-Hensmann, Stefan Reiter, Arwed Scibba, Rabea Tilch, Anke Wedemeier, Torsten Wedemeier, Lisa-Marie Zschätzsch (AlsterWerk)

IMPORTANT:

The publisher of this book, Piggyback Interactive Limited, has made every effort to determine that the information contained in this book is accurate. However, the publisher makes no express warranty as to the accuracy, effectiveness, or completeness of the material in this book. The publisher excludes liability for all damages that may result from using the information in this book to the maximum extent permissible under applicable law, but this does not affect your statutory rights.

Piggyback cannot provide information regarding gameplay, hints and strategies, or problems with hardware or software. Questions relating to the foregoing should be directed to the support numbers provided by the game and device manufacturers in their documentation. Some gameplay techniques may require precise timing and may require repeated attempts before the desired result is achieved.

CD PROJEKT RED

Business Development: Jan Rosner
Project Manager: Magdalena Darda-Ledzion
Associate Project Manager: Michał Malenta
Production Team: Przemysław Wójcik, Paweł Błasiak, Olek Lebiedowicz, Aleksandra Adamska, Alicja Kseń, Alicja Wolak, Grzegorz Olszewski, Jan Strzyżewski, Marcin Jefimow, Monika Janowska, Olga Cyganiak-Rembiś, Slava Lukyanenka, Urszula Kominek
Characters: Paweł Mielniczuk, Ben Andrews, Lea Leonowicz, Bill Daly, Wojciech Michalski, Łukasz Poduch, Marek Brzeziński, Marta Dettlaff, Martha Jackowiak, Waldemar Kamiński, Yee-Ling Chung
DevOps: Jakub Kutrzuba, Marcin Kulikowski
Encounter Design: Michał Dobrowolski
Environment: Lucjan Więcek, Alexander Dudar, Alicja Użarowska, Bogna Gawrońska, Danel Valaisis, Joseph Noel, Marcin Tomalak, Marta Leydy, Marthe Jonkers, Masahiro Sawada, Siarhei Hlushakou, Ward Lindhout, Yamandu Orce
Gameplay Design: Artur Sobczyk, Benjamin Le Moullec, Denis Asensio, Maximien Mabru, Patryk Fiutowski
In-Game Ads: Katarzyna Redesiuk
IT: Marcin Korzycki, Mateusz Zalewski, Wojciech Bodzento
Level Design: Tid Cooney, Matthew Bradley, Andrzej Giełzak, Kendal Husband, Manuel Mendiluce, Max Pears, Miles Tost, Natalia Tiurina, Sebastian McBride
Localization: Mikołaj Szwed, Ainara Echaniz, Alexander Radkevich, Jared Dye, Anna Sierhej
Mission Design: Ian Rooke, Jacek Matuszewski, Michał Pałka, Michał Walek
Open World: Bartosz Ochman, Przemysław Sawicki, Arnold Haponik, Jakub Ostapiuk, Jan Lipczyński, Kacper Tyc, Maciej Duda, Maciej Maksymowicz, Maciej Nakonieczny, Michał Marcinkowski, Piotr Golus, Szymon Dzięgiel
Programming: Séamus Epp
QA: Łukasz Babiel, Artur Zaręba, Jakub Ogiela, Juliia Mahdii, Julia Włastowska, Katarzyna Gołąbek, Maciej Kucharczyk, Mariusz Kubów, Mateusz Sykuła, Matylda Knapek, Mirosław Łękowski-Dawid, Paweł Kucal, Szymon Skowron, Tomasz Madziar, Tomasz Żwirski, Wiktoria Paciorek, Witold Popławski, Wojciech Mincewicz
Quest Design: Mateusz Tomaszkiewicz, Paweł Sasko, Błażej Augustynek, Danisz Markiewicz, Despoina Anetaki, Dominika Kuczyńska, Eero Varendi, Joanna Radomska, Katarzyna Władyka, Konrad Chlasta, Mateusz Albrewczyński, Moritz Lehr, Oleksiy Chapay, Patrick Mills, Philipp Weber, Rafał Jankowski, Sarah Gruemmer, Stoyan Stoyanov
RPG Design: Andrzej Zawadzki, Christopher Schulte
Story: Marcin Blacha, Tomasz Marchewka, Paweł Ciemniewski
Technical Design: Łukasz Szczepankowski
UI/UX: Mateusz Kanik, Robert Bielecki, Daria Grzybowska, Karolina Kłos
Marketing: Christine Farmer, Przemysław Juszczyk, Bartłomiej Kubik, Łukasz Ludkowski, Wojciech Sokołowski, Martyna Śpiechowicz, Jacek Szaroszyk, Joanna Wieliczko, Maciej Zoń
Community Team: Marcin Momot, Sebastian Siejka
PR: Radosław Grabowski
Communication: Ryan Bowd, Marcin Łukaszewski, Robert Malinowski
Special Thanks: Adam Badowski and the entire Cyberpunk 2077 Team!

Published in 2020 by Piggyback Interactive Limited, under licence from CD Projekt S.A. ul. Jagiellońska 74, 03-301 Warsaw, Poland.

Printed in the United States of America.
978-1-911015-76-5
978-1-911015-77-2

For residents of Australia only:
This product comes with guarantees that cannot be excluded under the Australian Consumer Law. You are entitled to a replacement or refund for a major failure and for compensation for any other reasonably foreseeable loss or damage. You are also entitled to have the goods repaired or replaced if the goods fail to be of acceptable quality and the failure does not amount to a major failure.

This product comes with a 1-year warranty from date of purchase. Defects in the product must have appeared within 1 year from date of purchase in order to claim the warranty.

All warranty claims must be facilitated back through the retailer of purchase, in accordance with the retailer's returns policies and procedures. Any costs incurred as a result of returning the product to the retailer of purchase are the full responsibility of the consumer.